THE AMBIVALENT FORCE

Perspectives on the Police

THIRD EDITION

Abraham S. Blumberg

Director, Administration of Justice
Professor of Sociology and Law
University of Missouri, Kansas City

Elaine Niederhoffer

Editor, *Public Productivity Review*
National Center for Public Productivity
John Jay College of Criminal Justice,
City University of New York

HOLT, RINEHART AND WINSTON

New York Chicago San Francisco Philadelphia
Montreal Toronto London Sydney
Tokyo Mexico City Rio de Janeiro Madrid

Library of Congress Cataloging in Publication Data
Main entry under title:

The Ambivalent force.

Second ed. compiled by Arthur Niederhoffer,
Abraham S. Blumberg. c1976.
Includes bibliographies.
1. Police—United States—Addresses, essays, lectures.
I. Blumberg, Abraham S. II. Niederhoffer, Elaine.
HV8138.A595 1985 363.2'0973 84-19132

ISBN 0-03-062044-X

Address correspondence to:
383 Madison Avenue
New York, N.Y. 10017

Printed in the United States of America
Published simultaneously in Canada
5 6 7 8 016 9 8 7 6 5 4 3 2 1

CBS COLLEGE PUBLISHING
Holt, Rinehart and Winston
The Dryden Press
Saunders College Publishing

If law is not made more than a policeman's nightstick, American society will be destroyed.

Justice Arthur Goldberg

This book is dedicated in loving and grateful memory

to ARTHUR NIEDERHOFFER.

Whose multifaceted career in sociology and criminology
As police officer, professor, author, and researcher
Has enlarged and sharpened our "perspectives on the police."

PREFACE

This is a major revision of *The Ambivalent Force* designed to reflect the substantive changes in the police world which have occurred since the edition was published in 1976. In this third edition, more than three-fourths of the articles consist of entirely new or substantially revised material; eleven of the readings are original essays written specifically for this book. Several older works have been retained because they possess a timeless pertinence and validity and have become classics in the field. That the editors' introductions to each section needed so little revision can be attributed, in part, to the in-depth perception of the late Arthur Niederhoffer.

The unrelenting forces of social change have placed the police at the center stage of history. Widespread disruption of existing social arrangements is an inevitable feature of the historical agenda in the years ahead. We may be sure that it will be the police who will be at the storm center of each episode of crisis or catastrophe that is bound to occur with grim regularity. And it is obvious that too much of the thinking about the police tends to polarize around the simplistic approaches of the flattering police buff or the excoriating critic.

In the inner cities of America, on the campus, at demonstrations, or wherever social protest is most threatening, the spotlight is on the police. Society is asking the police not only to protect it, but also to preserve it. The people turn to them as saviors and demand an end to lawlessness and violence. In spite of this ostensible acceptance, there is still distrust and resentment.

If these readings on the police may be said to be bound by an overarching theme, it is the stress on the uncertainties, ambiguities, and ambivalences inherent in the police role in our society in the past and the present—all of which will probably persist in the future. The police remain from all the evidence a beleaguered, estranged group, drawn in upon themselves as a protective reaction against a society which they feel not only does not understand them, but also may scorn them. For us, this underscores the relevancy and the percipience of the title for this book—*The Ambivalent Force*.

We wish to acknowledge the support and cooperation of our many friends, contributors, and colleagues. In particular, we express our gratitude to Eileen Sherman of the University of Missouri, Kansas City, and to Ruth Stark, project editor at Holt, Rinehart and Winston, whose organizational skills and production expertise helped us bring this revised edition to fruition.

A. S. B.
E. N.

CONTENTS

SECTION 5

SECTION 6

SECTION 7

SECTION 8

SECTION 9

SECTION 10

SECTION 11

SECTION 12

INTRODUCTION

We have sought as a realistic goal to bring together the variegated approaches of the academic behavioral scientist, the journalist, the psychiatrist, the lawyer, the policeman, the historian, and the administrator in their assessments of some major features of the police occupation and role.

Among some of the key areas for discussion in this revised edition are: the problems and issues attendant upon the role of women in policing, a new section on the use of deadly force, the dramatic changes in police power and responsibility wrought by the Burger Court, a major section on the impact of the police occupational role on the police family, the significance of unions and unionization, an overview of the problem of police stress, and an original essay which will lay to rest the myths and misperceptions regarding the efficacy of punishment as a means of achieving deterrence of crime. The problems raised by the concept of deterrence are of central importance for the police and policing. This is so because the police constitute the preeminent cultural symbol and institutional instrument of social control in the enforcement of the deterrent efficacy of the criminal law.

In Section 1, "The Social, Historical, and Comparative Setting," we have attempted to fill what seems to be a void in all serious discussions of the social context in which the police function. Strikingly delineated are amazing historical similarities in the relative permanence and continuity of the problems of the police as they confront the violent and disruptive episodes of every epoch. Further, it is revealing to learn in terms of a cross-cultural perspective that British policing now faces many of the same problems and dilemmas as does the United States, when confronted by the turmoil produced by inner-city racial tensions, ethnic and class conflict exacerbated by the national economic distress of long-term high rates of unemployment. Under those conditions, the traditional British system of reliance on community support for policing by consent gives way to a paramilitary police response.

Following the agonizing reappraisals of our society and its institutions occasioned by the aftermath of Vietnam and Watergate, many of our most cherished hopes and beliefs were demolished. It is in this spirit that Section 2, "Police Role and Career," examines some of the truths, as well as the myths and masks of the police role, utilizing racial, ethnic, and class variables as the focus of analysis. The readings in this section depict the impact of race, class, ethnicity, gender, occupational speciality, and the rather special socialization process on the police role.

Section 3, "Police Organization and Control," deals with the organizational and institutional constraints of the police system with careful attention to the bureaucratic qualities that determine the life-styles, career lines, and policy decisions of police organizations. It will be readily apparent from this group of readings that the police share many of the dilemmas and unresolved conflicts of professionalization common to other occupations. In this revised edition, however, we have introduced an important element of police organization which is seldom discussed in the literature: an analysis of the paramilitary constraints on police professionalism and police systems of internal discipline.

The police world view is explored in Section 4, "Police Values and Culture," and the sources of the carefully nurtured values, including loyalty, authoritarianism, and defensiveness, are surveyed. Of interest is the fact that other professional groups (such as medical students, bankers, and politicians) undergo rather similar estrangement as they become more experienced and sophisticated in their work situation. In addition, we have included a summary article dealing with the theme of police corruption, a constant issue which has more recently surfaced as a major cause for concern in many communities.

Section 5, "Police Discretion," opens up one of the gray arenas of police work. The art of being a police officer involves a prudent exercise of virtually unlimited and uncontrolled discretion in the performance of duty. The selections present some of the social, organizational, psychological, and ideological variables that operate in this unstructured field. Supreme Court decisions can barely penetrate this area, which is shrouded by a blue curtain of secrecy. We believe the new material introduced in this section does much to clarify old problems and develops new tools and insights for understanding police discretion.

The next section, "Police and Society," emphasizes the most sensitive aspect of modern police work-relations with the ghetto and other urban communities. The sad fact emerges that the great bulk of police time is devoted to service for people in trouble, but the level of hostility toward police is as great as ever. A new dimension in this section stresses that component of policing which relates to the political structure of our society and has some important things to say about the consequences of police behavior and tactics for the other sectors of our social order. Coupled with that material are some terse, but powerful comments with regard to terrorism which has emerged as a more serious problem in Europe but has its counterpart in today's urban America.

In Section 7, "Police and the Legal System," a sense of the range of legal issues that touch upon the police is described. Of special interest for police in the future is the ongoing discussion of the emerging reappraisal and reshaping of judicial doctrines with regard to the exclusionary rule and "search and seizure." These are thorny problems that will certainly be with us for a long time to come, despite the seemingly more favorable disposition of the United States Supreme Court towards the police and the judgments that they make in the field. We have attempted to present materials that would apprise police practitioners and theorists of some of the possible directions in which the legal system appears to be moving and the manner in which these trends affect police practice. In addition we have incorporated current material with respect to the civil liabilities of police in connection with lawsuits brought against the police and the rights of police officers vis-à-vis their employers and the public whom they serve.

Section 8, "Critiques of the Police," comprises a sober and balanced view of the police by serious and responsible individuals who find much that they would like to see changed in our police institutions. Many of the controversies over the police are seen in a new perspective connected with broader ideological positions ranging along the political continuum. However, on the whole, our emphasis is on maintaining a sense of balance and avoiding doctrinaire positions that are not supported by data or experience.

Section 9, "The Use of Deadly Force," presents us with a fascinating array of ideas and with one of the most exciting and promising areas of policy research in connection with the police. In addition to a review of the emerging literature, some important questions as to the role of race and the use of deadly force are explored in terms of the data that have been developed.

Section 10, "Police Stress," examines the multidimensional factors that produce stress in the police occupation. Explored are the correlates of stress and their impact not only on job performance, but also on the police family.

Section 11, "The Police Family," brings us into the dynamics of family relationships of police personnel and the manner in which the police family's stability is so dependent on the adaptations that the spouses and children must make in coping with the psychological, social, and physical hazards of police work. Noteworthy in this regard is the compelling experience of the college professor turned policeman whose family life undergoes a dramatic transformation as a consequence.

It is our feeling that the final section, "The Future of Law Enforcement," constitutes an important statement embodying perceptions of the directions of law enforcement in the crucial decades to follow. The material ranges from attempts to look at the future of policing to that of police education and the future of police unionism. As a consequence, the views presented are, we hope, national and diverse in their scope rather than parochial. Finally, it is important to remember that much of the research and writing about the police was done prior to the time when women began to play a significant role in the police profession. As consequence, many of the references to police officers are expressed in a masculine context.

1

THE SOCIAL, HISTORICAL, AND COMPARATIVE SETTING

For all its seeming variety, law enforcement remains a slowly evolving creature of the past, rather than a new institution born in recent decades and fashioned by the exigencies of the present. Our objective in this section is to place the past and the present of law enforcement in a historical context. The concern with law enforcement problems depicted in the Magna Carta could be translated into the headlines of today. Between the lines of the law can be found the same problems and complaints about the police: abuse of power, false arrest, oppression, apathy, and ignorance of and contempt for the law. For example, the Magna Carta of June 15, 1215, is replete with restrictions upon the police of those days, the sheriffs, bailiffs, and constables. It is a fair and reasonable assumption that since the following chapters were part of that epochal document, they were meant to correct abuses that were widespread.

> 28. No constable or other bailiff of ours shall take anyone's grain or other chattels without immediately paying for them in money. . . .
>
> 29. No constable shall require any knight to give money in place of his ward of a castle. . . .
>
> 30. No sheriff or bailiff of ours or anyone else shall take horses or wagons of any free man for carrying purposes except on the permission of that free man. . . .
>
> 38. No bailiff for the future shall place any one to his law on his simple affirmation without credible witnesses brought for this purpose.

And the remedies of that ancient time were no different from those proposed today: recruit better police officers, stiffen the penalties for malfeasance, create a civilian review board as an external control upon the police. King John agreed that

> 45. We will not make justiciars, constables, sheriffs, or bailiffs except of such as know the law of the realm and are well inclined to observe it.

The barons opposing King John wanted more than mere promises and forced the king to consent to the supervision of a civilian review board of twenty-five barons with power to enforce compliance with the law. In fact, four of those barons acted as ombudsmen empowered to make preliminary investigations and complaints about transgressions by the King's police.

> 61. . . . if we or our justiciar, or our bailiffs, or any of our servants shall have done wrong in any way toward any one, or shall have transgressed any of the articles of peace or security: and the wrong shall have been

shown to four barons of the aforesaid twenty-five barons, let those four barons come to us or to our justiciar, if we are out of the kingdom, lay before us the transgression, and let them ask that we cause that transgression to be corrected without delay.

In that century another important rule for police officers was promulgated in the Statute of Westminster, 3 Edward 1 (1275), to the effect that any sheriff who took a reward for doing his duty was committing the crime of extortion. He would be fined twice the amount he received and punished at the king's pleasure.

By the middle of the fourteenth century the situation had changed because of the spread of armed violence and rioting. The demand for law and order became paramount, and as a result the power of the police was increased. The counterpart of the "stop-and-frisk" law—the Statute of Northampton, 2 Edward 3 (1328)—gave the sheriffs legal power to arrest those who rode about armed by night or day. It became the duty of the sheriffs to arrest those who participated in assemblies or riots that disturbed the peace.

The beginning of the fifteenth century brought an intensification of the campaign for law and order. The Riot Act of 1411 not only made it mandatory for justices of the peace and sheriffs to arrest rioters, but also if they failed to do so, they were fined 100 pounds to be paid to the king. With the riots came looting, and the response was the Forcible Entry Act of 1429 directing justices and sheriffs to arrest anyone taking part in insurrections, riots, routs, and assemblies in disturbance of the peace. There was also a reminder for the sheriffs, under pain of prison and fine, to arrest those "malefactors" who "make forcible entries."

Behind the pages of history a powerful undercurrent of crime, violence, and public disorder was the force that directly and indirectly produced law and law enforcement. In general, an increase in disorder resulted in an increase in police power. A limit to this grant of power has been the traditional suspicion of the police in England and the United States. Sometimes the near-unanimous praise of Scotland Yard causes us to forget that this vaunted police force was born under a cloud, and only after seven years of political maneuvering by its sponsor, Robert Peel, was it able to overcome powerful resistance. The very word "police" aroused in the British people the repugnance and fear of a sinister spy system, and the idea of creating a large central police force was strongly opposed in the early decades of the nineteenth century by "men of good-will in all classes who genuinely believed, with the example of France before them, that police of any kind were synonymous with tyranny and the destruction of liberty." Because of that distrust, the Metropolitan Police Force was disarmed. Only the naïve believe that "bobbies" never carry weapons because England has always been so law-abiding.

The lesson of history teaches us that for almost seven centuries the problems of law enforcement have been:

1. Abuse of power
2. Corruption
3. The quality of personnel and recruitment of suitable candidates
4. Deployment of personnel
5. Police relations with the public
6. Fear of violence and crime
7. The role of women in crime
8. The role of police in quelling riots and civil disturbances
9. The question of control of the police
10. The optimal size of the police force
11. Police training
12. The problems raised in connection with the granting of pardons and amnesties
13. The question of effectiveness of law enforcement vis-à-vis offenders who were politically and economically powerful
14. The problem of overcriminalization

Each of the foregoing remains a current issue. Even such a seemingly novel approach to police performance as granting additional compensation for more effective crime control had been employed in the medieval period in Europe.

The general duties of the police, their methods of patrol, the submission of law enforcement to judicial control, and the early involvement of police organizations in politics are all matters that have persisted and survived all the intervening political and social cataclysms. Indeed, it would seem that police institutions possess qualities that resist the impact of historical and social change. While the police are often seen as parochial, the reality is that the police culture transcends international boundaries and intergenerational differences.

The probability is that a police officer of one hundred years ago, or one from a nation remote in distance and culture, could with a very short period of orientation take his post in any one of our major urban centers and do a fairly acceptable job. The implications of this statement may generate a good deal of resistance. But it is important that police officers reflect on the historical issues and perspectives that have indelibly stamped their profession. They will then realize that their problems, roles, and duties are transhistorical in that they deal with fundamentals of society and of human survival.

The Police and the Social System: Reflections and Prospects

Abraham S. Blumberg

There are trades in which it is impossible for a man to be virtuous.

SOCRATES

Because the application of the law depends to a large degree on the definition reached by the patrolman, he, in effect, makes the law; it is his decision that establishes the boundary between legal and illegal.

ARTHUR NIEDERHOFFER
Behind the Shield

POLICE RECRUITMENT: MULTIDIMENSIONAL ROLES AND FUNCTIONS

Any systematic examination of the workings of the criminal justice system must begin with the police, who have become the most critical and perhaps even the most powerful subsystem in the enforcement and adjudication structure. Most of us do not fully comprehend the implications of the awesome power that the police possess in exercising their discretion to arrest.[1]

This article was revised for this edition from the original article written with the late Arthur Niederhoffer.

In a simple situation involving a defendant of modest means, arrest may cause a loss of job, a period of detention, the indignities of being fingerprinted and photographed, immeasurable psychological pain, at least several court appearances, and the expenditure of hundreds, even thousands of dollars for bail bond[2] and a lawyer.[3] Arrest can be a powerful weapon—indeed, a form of summary punishment. The crux of the matter is that the police perform more important judicial functions in many cases than do judges;[4] and that critical variable is the source of the anxiety, resentment, confrontation, and violence that invariably occur between the police and other groups in our society.

The police—with limited formal training and minimal qualification requirements—are granted more latitude and discretion in dealing with the lives and welfare of people than any other professional group. In 1966 there were more than 400,000 police officers in the United States with a median level of 12.4 years of formal education. According to the research staff of the International Association of Chiefs of Police, the minimum training requirements for various occupations in the different American states, in terms of hours, in 1966 were 11,000 for physicians, 5,000 for embalmers, 4,000 for barbers, 1,200 for beauticians—but less than 200 for police officers.[5]

Approximately a decade later, in 1975, the International Association of Chiefs of Police reported that out of approximately 500,000 police officers in the nation, 54,838 were enrolled in college programs.[6] By 1981 there were 718,000 police officers in more than 40,000 departments who, as of 1980, earned an average minimum salary of $15,159 per annum up to an average maximum of $20,566 per annum in larger cities.[7] For the fiscal year 1979 the sum of $13,981,000 was expended by local, state, and federal governments for police protection. This expenditure represents more than half the total amount spent on the entire criminal justice system (see Figure 1). By 1984 the total amount spent on the criminal justice system had increased by approximately ten percent—and the police continued to receive more than half the total budget.

The college-trained man or woman who entered and remained in a police career continued to be an anomaly, except in the case of superiors who were career officials in the larger departments. As of 1984 the equivalent of high school training remained the educational requirement in most local police organizations, although in a few situations junior college credentials were required for entry or promotion to a superior rank. Police fraternal organizations and unions continued to resist the introduction of college training as a prerequisite for police work, although in terms of salary, fringe benefits, and career opportunities the police occupation has begun to equal and even exceed that of many service occupations requiring a baccalaureate degree.

Police recruitment continued to draw its candidates largely from the ranks of manual and service workers in the working class, and from the children of the lower-middle classes. Examination standards and investigation of candidates virtually preclude the recruitment of underclass, black, and Hispanic applicants. Indeed, almost universally the process is calculated to bring into the police force men and women of average intelligence, socially as well as politically moderate and cautious, generally concerned with economic security, who usually shun the "off beat" and unconventional, and who have internalized middle-class norms of conformity and the importance of "appearances."[8] As in the case of medicine and law, the police occupation recruits the sons and daughters of job incumbents by way of generational succession. In some urban departments there are still large contingents of Irish officers, many of whose relatives are also in police work.[9] However, other ethnic groups such as blacks and Italian-Americans have begun to occupy posts of administrative pre-eminence. Affirmative action programs have introduced blacks and Hispanics into many departments where they were previously unknown even as token members. Most blacks, however, continue to shun police work although for many it has furnished a remarkable ladder of mobility.

Constituting the traditional screening and recruitment process are the civil service written examinations, oral interviews, physical agility tests, and character and background investigations. Whatever objectives they are intended to achieve, these procedures primarily result in the recruitment of police candidates who possess world views, values, and temperament compatible with police discipline and authority, and who share existing police perspectives emphasizing order, stability, and resistance to change. The net effect of the physical agility tests has been the virtual exclusion of many potential Mexican-American and Oriental candidates.[10] This is not to say that the police recruit's profile resembles a stereotypical set of social-psychological characteristics, or that police agency testing instruments have the net effect of sorting out candidates so that each recruit appears to have been stamped out by a cookie press. On the contrary, people who enter the police occupation represent a diverse array of "normal" personalities, somewhat above average in intelligence, and quite obviously superior to most of their contemporaries in terms of physical condition and agility. In psychological terms they are *less* neurotic than samples of other occupational groupings.[11]

Despite relative increases in the ratings of occupational prestige scales, the police self-image remains unfavorable. The North-Hatt Scale of Occupational Prestige employs a list of 90 occupations; when administered to a national sample in 1947, the occupational prestige of police ranked 55th. By 1963, when the scale was again administered, the occupational prestige of the police had risen to 47th place—just below newspaper columnist and welfare worker for a city government, and just above reporter for a daily newspaper and radio announcer.[12] The rise of the occupational status of the police should not be underestimated in view of the fact that during a period of only 16 years it had moved up eight positions in the prestige ladder, a gain equaled only by chemists and lawyers, and exceeded only by nuclear physicists and labor leaders.[13] It is perhaps ironic that although the police themselves tend to view their own prestige in mostly negative or, at best, uncertain terms, police recruitment continues to emphasize the qualities and characteristics that assure no dramatic changes in their occupational prestige patterns in the near future, despite considerable improvements in salaries and work-

FIGURE 1 Expenditures for Criminal Justice Activities, by Type of Activity and Level of Government, United States, fiscal year 1979.

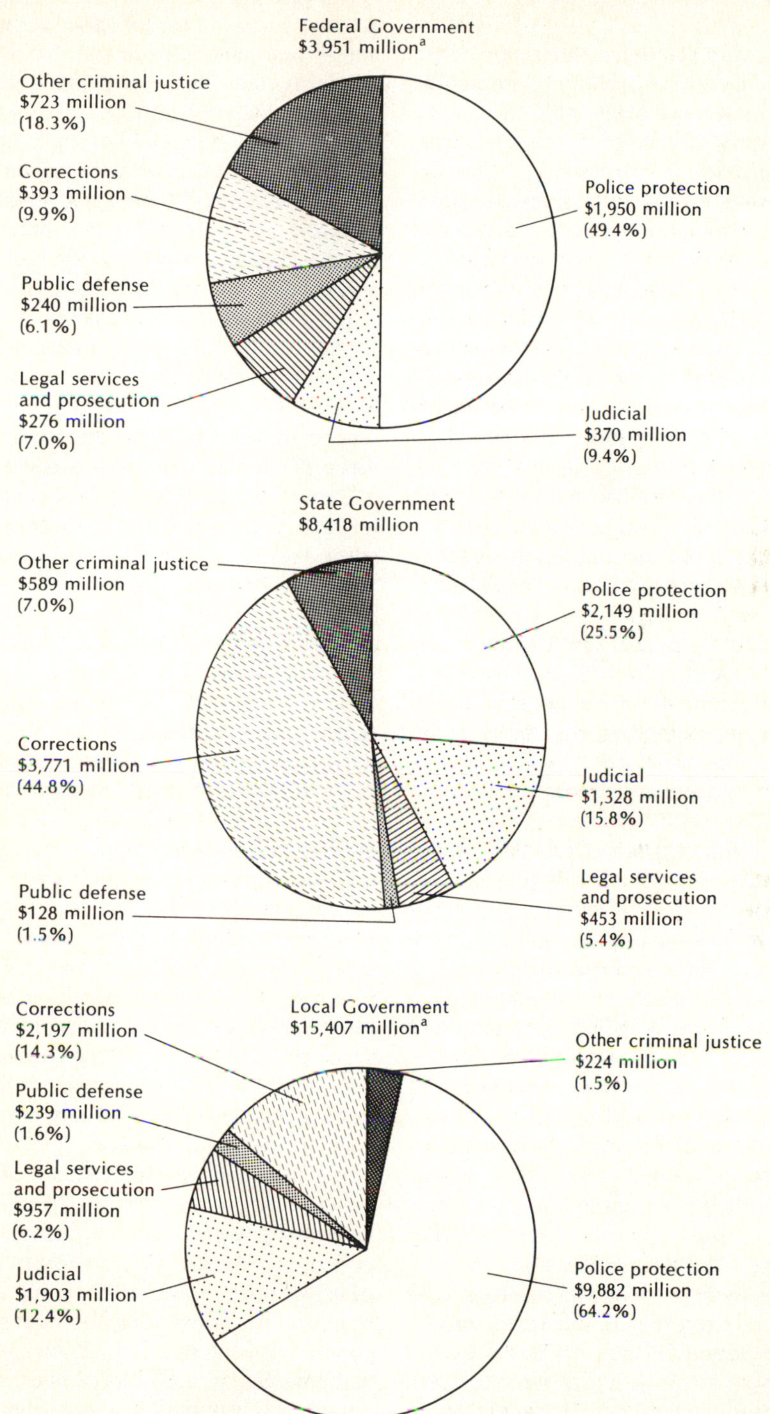

[a] Because of rounding, detail does not add to total.

SOURCE: Figure provided to SOURCEBOOK staff by the U.S. Department of Justice, Bureau of Justice Statistics.

ing conditions that make the police career more attractive than ever.

In the period of severe economic depression of the 1930s, almost all civil servants, including the police, were an envied group because of the certainty of a pay check. In reviewing the history of the police during that period, however, one is impressed with the singular fact that they were feared by all classes as violent, lawless, brutal, and corrupt. It is not a coincidence that public contempt for the police during the 1920s and 1930s was coupled with a lack of meaningful judicial and legislative restraint that was only gradually imposed in the decades following the end of World War II, where a sequence of landmark United States Supreme Court decisions created restraint on police organizations, free-wheeling work styles, and repressive administrative procedures.[14]

During the 1960s, the police became the lightning rod against which all social grievances were directed.[15] The major riots and civil disorders during that decade in urban areas such as Detroit, Newark, Los Angeles, Chicago, Atlanta, Tampa, and Cincinnati served to polarize attitudes toward the police. On the one hand, the middle classes took a more benign view of the police as the thin blue line saving America from revolution and anarchy; at the other extreme, for the urban poor, the police are those who arrest you.[16]

To speak of *the police* as a unified entity is a misnomer; policing is a multidimensional institution, consisting of widely disparate sets of job skills, functions, organizations, jurisdictions, levels of expertise, prestige, and rewards. Modern technology imposes a set of demands on police organizations and personnel to acquire a variety of skills and expertise including operation of sophisticated electronic equipment such as radar, computers, instruments for the analysis of evidence, and listening devices; a knowledge of chemistry; and the ability to pilot helicopters and airplanes with their intricate electronic and propulsion equipment.[17] Related to those skills are the competencies that must be acquired as an interpreter of law, a first-aid medic, social worker, marriage counselor, athlete, race relations expert, auto-repair mechanic, photographer, youth adviser, and a good deal more.[18]

Further, these divergent occupational roles are to be found in an array of departments and organizations ranging from a five-person village force to forces and agencies that resemble an army such as the New York City police force, 30,000 strong, or at the federal level, the FBI with its staff of about 7,800 agents in 59 field offices.

Not only the size of the force, but also the level of government examined (federal, state, or municipal) makes important differences in recruitment criteria and standards, the quality of personnel, the profile of its administrative hierarchy, its style of policing, its order of priorities in enforcement, and the resources available to it. In connection with resources one can safely make the blanket statement that federal police agencies as a rule are the best funded, but it does not follow that they will necessarily be the best managed or most effective for any particular task.

The concept of *the police* is usually employed in connection with the highly visible field man or woman who is engaged in street patrol, enforcement, peace keeping, traffic control, and a multitude of emergency service activities that are performed routinely, and services identical at municipal and village levels.

Crime investigation and crime control were not historically part of the police function in society, or a special responsibility of urban police departments. In 19th-century America, the role of the constabulary was more that of watchman; it was only on rare occasions that an outrageous crime would involve the police in investigative work. Even in those instances, however, their function was regulating and maintaining public order—peace keeping rather than crime detection. Railroads, mining companies, and other large industrial enterprises maintained their own private police forces such as the Pinkerton Agency to patrol their property. Large-scale immigration, which created proliferating urban centers inhabited by ever-growing numbers of poor persons, changed the functions of the police. The solution to the problems of more visible urban crime involved the emergence of military-style police forces to control what was perceived by those in power as an unruly, unacculturated mass of new urban poor Americans. However, while crime-control activities became a larger part of their activities and focus of concern, the police remained in large measure a general service institution.[19]

The so-called "crime function" of the police may in reality only constitute 10 to 20 percent of their total time on a given work day.[20] Many calls to the average police unit involve requests for information or health services, people who are in some way incapacitated or in trouble, complaints about noisy parties, the misconduct of juveniles, help in connection with a medical emergency, a swarm of bees, a missing child or parent, a lost domestic animal, horse, or cow, landlord–tenant disputes, and family conflicts involving the need for protection.[21] A pipe bursting in one's kitchen can result in a call to the police about the "emergency" rather than to a plumber.

In the series of shootings and murders of young people, primarily women, that occurred during 1976–1977 in New York City, the police received almost 7,000 phone calls about the crimes, only one of which actually focused on the man arrested as the deranged "Son of Sam" killer. More than 200 officers had been assigned to the case, yet it was the routine check of a parking ticket that led to the apprehension of the assailant. Despite the commitment of extraordinary numbers of staff and resources, more than a year elapsed from the first attack until a suspect was arrested, underscoring the formidable time- and resource-consuming difficulties the police encounter in solving major crimes in an impersonal urban environment unless they have the cooperation and support of the public they serve.[22] "The bulk of police business, measured in terms of contacts with citizens takes place *before* invoking the criminal justice system . . . makes use of the system for *purposes* other than prosecution . . . or occurs in its entirety *outside* the system. . . ."[23]

In addition to the law enforcement, order maintenance, and service functions, the police serve as an important social barometer in any social system. That is to say that the police are a reagent that signals not only the existence of a social issue, but its dimensions.

Politically, the police constitute a social lightning rod. Protests of all kinds, directed at any of the varied institutional subsystems of American society, invariably become confrontations with the police before they clash with the intended target of their grievances. In the process, the anger and the fury of a protest movement are diverted, diluted, and sometimes even extinguished. The initial quotient of hostility is redirected at the police, who become the barrier that must be surmounted and subdued before the movement can address itself to the programs and priorities of its original agenda. It is in this role that the police serve their most important function in society—that of acting as a buffer in insulating and protecting existing political and social structures.[24]

On the other hand, it is naïve to think of the police as simply a conservative force maintaining strict control in furtherance of the status quo. They perform a further, more subtle role in acting to keep a society within structural confines that tend to be somewhat narrower than its stated ideological commitments. Thus the police are the vehicle for testing the limits, boundaries, and permissibility of social tolerance. In this vein, the limits of social tolerance with respect to such issues as sexual mores, civil liberties, obscenity, political expression, and related matters are subjected to scrutiny and testing.

Another important police function symbolic in character is the police role in class relations. To the vast middle class of America, the police represent sober reassurance that their tenuous status, security, and hard-won possessions will not be wrested from them. The middle classes welcome the police rushing into the breach wherever the turbulence of the have-nots precipitates disorder or threatens existing arrangements. However, it is the lower-middle class and the police who have the greatest symbolic attraction and affection for one another. Both groups tend to perceive themselves as "in-betweens," being pressured from the top by onerous taxes levied by an inept, impersonal government and from below by the heretofore disprivileged ethnics—newcomers who jostle them in the sensitive areas of schools, housing, and jobs. To the lower classes the police are a symbol of repression and control of their lives. Gambling, prostitution, and illegal drug and liquor distribution in lower-class areas are well-known in their most minute details to the inhabitants, but are often overlooked by or unknown to the police. The lower-class person concludes that police presence is not to deter crime or to protect, but to supervise and control the activities of the lower-class slum dweller.[25]

Regardless of the physical attributes, interpersonal skills, and the level of intellectual achievement that are viewed as prime requisites of adequate police performance, debates about what the police role should be will continue indefinitely. Overlooked is the fact that for the foreseeable future the police will continue to perform their major tasks of law enforcement—the settling of what are essentially civil disputes and peace keeping—and the multiplicity of service tasks almost simultaneously. Even if government budgets were to make possible the appointment of paramedical and social-work specialists to render aid in disasters or to intervene in family conflicts, such limiting of the police role would not be altogether salutary for the police. If, through job specialization, the police focus of activity were to be limited to law enforcement and peace keeping, the police would seldom be able to perform community service in disasters and emergencies, opportunities that serve to (1) stress the positive, helping attributes of the present police functions, and (2) establish rapport between the police and the public. Unless police are part of the social fabric of a community, they will be perceived as an alien force, and unless they are clearly visible in their roles of helping people in trouble, they will be seen as a mercenary army of enforcers. A cloistered, almost invisible group of law enforcers would be viewed as "outsiders" and would receive precious little cooperation in connection with the gathering of evidence or from witnesses to a crime.

In most instances police have only rudimentary, and often distorted knowledge about what they will find when responding to a call in the field. Stereotyped radio descriptions such as "B and E" (breaking and/or entering), "family trouble," "somebody screaming," "a theft report," "a man down" (person lying in a public place, cause unknown), "outside ringer" (burglar alarm ringing), or "the boys" (any trouble with juveniles), are some of the raw data that are the daily features of police life. But often they are not an accurate reflection of the situational reality. It is the citizen informant or complainant, biased though those reports may be, *that is crucial to policing.*[26]

Most crimes are not readily susceptible to detection, and as previously indicated, the police must rely on informants and complainants.[27] Except in those instances where police observe violations on their own, as in the case of traffic infractions, by infiltrating a narcotics distribution system, or by employing an informant, they detect very little crime without the help of citizen complainants. Police process more victim-complainants than criminals. Most police action is "reactive" in that it is citizen initiated, rather than "proactive" wherein it is police-initiated as in the case of a "field interrogation" or the "stop-and-frisk" of a "suspicious" person.[28]

THE PROBLEMATIC CHARACTER OF POLICE "CRIME CONTROL"

Criminologists with an interest in history are quick to recognize that ours is not the best of times nor the worst of times in comparison to other epochs in producing criminals, assorted villains, social deviants, and grim deeds of violence, murder, terrorism, and genocide. While the technology available for inflicting harm upon others has undergone a radical maximization, it is probably safer to walk the streets of an American city today than it was those of medieval Italy or the Manhattan of one hundred years ago.[29]

We owe an everlasting intellectual debt to Emile Durkheim for his insightful notion that crime is an inevitable feature of social structure—that "crime is normal because a society exempt from it is utterly impossible."[30] In contemplating the meaning and pervasiveness of crime and deviance in the human situation, his classic formulation provides us with a timeless perspective that transcends the recurring hysteria epitomized in the catch-all political slogans of "crime in the streets" and "law and order." It is abundantly clear that Durkheim's analysis has been confirmed, *inter alia*, by compelling historical evidence. It should, therefore, not surprise us that most (if not all) of us have violated legal norms on more than one occasion without being labeled or officially adjudicated as delinquents and criminals.[31]

No matter which version of the official crime statistics one accepts, it is quite evident that very few of us are brought to book—i.e., apprehended, processed in the official enforcement and court machinery, and adjudged as criminals and delinquents. A society that committed the energy, resources, and personnel necessary to root out and punish all "wrongdoers" would create enough mass paranoia, violent conflict, and savage repression so as to become a charnel house and pass into oblivion. On the other hand, every society tends to produce its quotient of crime and deviance along with an apparatus to sort out those malefactors deemed most suitable for processing—usually those persons and kinds of behavior readily vulnerable to a successful labeling and adjudication process.[32] We have been told that "the quality of a nation's civilization can be largely measured by the methods it uses in the enforcement of its criminal law."[33] If that is the case, then the system of criminal justice in this nation is symptomatic of the crisis facing America today. Our law enforcement and court bureaucracies are organized and geared largely to detecting, sorting out, and adjudicating the kinds of crimes and delinquencies most often and most visibly committed by the lower class and the socially marginal strata. The selection of suitable candidates for adjudication process is not some version of a roulette game but has fairly well-defined limits that traditionally have been imposed by the stratification system. The clients of our enforcement, court, prison, parole, and other rehabilitation systems are drawn largely from the lower classes.[34] This situation produces serious consequences for the police and other components of the criminal justice system and for those who are unfortunate enough to be caught up in it.

In large measure the police role meets with failure in that except for offenses such as homicide, rape, kidnapping, and certain assaults where the offender is known, often the major law enforcement activity of police in our cities is to control disruptive and/or troublesome individuals and groups. In essence, law enforcement becomes peace keeping and order maintenance among a marginal working class–underclass clientele who are generally arrested for either of the two leading causes, public intoxication or "disorderly conduct."

One of the most obviously negative consequences of our system is that police organizations tend to concentrate on the public order and commonplace offenses that constitute the bulk of crimes duly reported in the *Uniform Crime Reports of the FBI* in any given year. Not unlike any other bureaucracy, police organizations are anxious about their productivity and the budgetary allocations directly related to it. Scarce resources must be carefully husbanded to get "the biggest bang for the buck." As a consequence, such highly visible commonplace offenses as drunkenness, prostitution, drug-related offenses, gambling, disorderly conduct, and the like serve as the requisite statistical data bolstering law-enforcement budgets.

Actual crime and crime rates appear not to have much relation to the number or deployment of police personnel. Police do not control or prevent crime.[35] Even the investigative operations of detectives are largely concerned with the clerical and office tasks of preparing extensive reports on crime and arrests. The activities of detectives usually do not in and of themselves generate many arrests. Studies conducted by the New York City Rand Institute concluded that such arrests for property crimes were in large measure random events not related to the skills or time expended by the detective force. Further, arrests for crimes of violence such as murder, rape, and assault were in large measure a consequence of data furnished by victims, and not attributable to any special investigative expertise or techniques that the detective force furnished. In short, very little time or effort is expended in developing new leads or in pursuing new suspects. Insofar as detective work tends to rely on data furnished by others it is a reactive activity rather than proactive.[36]

It is important to note one further datum with respect to the problematic character of the police as agents of crime control or crime prevention. In April 1982, the federal agency known as the Law Enforcement Assistance Administration (LEAA) was terminated after nearly 14 years of existence. Between 1969 and 1980 the agency expended $7.7 billion to local governments to upgrade the training and equipment of local police, courts, and corrections agencies. The bulk of the funding was spent on the police. Nevertheless, the national crime rates are higher now than when LEAA came into being.

The universal dilemma of any police officer is best conceptualized in what has been termed the "justice proposition": "Anger occurs in a man when his rewards are less than proportional to his investments."[37] The working police officer experiences frustration, tension, disappointment, and ultimately alienation because he or she perceives that the higher the degree of emotional investment in work, the less satisfaction is accrued because of the rejections experienced as a consequence of official behavior on the part of other elements in crime control and law enforcement systems. In time, the officer's only defense against continuing disappointment in the role is to resent the judges, prosecutors, lawyers, and correctional officials who, it is concluded, are negating the officer's effectiveness and the integrity of role. The result? The police officer develops a defensive strategy of low emotional investment in his or her work role in order to attenuate the anger, resentment, and frustration that comes with the meager rewards and satisfactions achieved.

In order for a working police officer to maintain a healthy equilibrium with respect to his or her occupation, the person must gain a realistic perspective of the nature of this function and role in the system of criminal justice as an ongoing process. Much of the tension in a police officer's life is due to the fact that a democratic society attempts to systematize two distinctive models of justice, the *due process model* and the *crime-control model*, which are often at odds with one another in terms of day-to-day operations and long-range goals. In essence, the police are cast in an impossible role that assigns them the "no-win" task of controlling a crime problem rooted in historical and social inequities that are well beyond management by police resources. Simultaneously, intense organizational pressures demanding high levels of police productivity result in an administrative operating bias in favor of the "crime-control" model rather than the "due process" model.

However, an examination of the due process and crime control models reveals that the police officer is expected to perform effectively in terms of *both* models, thereby producing an unusual degree of strain and confusion in the work situation.

Due Process Model

The due process model,[38] formulated by Herbert L. Packer, consists of the following 12 elements and is prescribed in ideal terms as the official model for police behavior.

1. The legal system exists as an obstacle course in order to protect the rights of the accused persons. At the outset, therefore, such legal questions as jurisdiction, venue, statute of limitations, double jeopardy,

and criminal responsibility must be examined and satisfied before an adjudication can be made.

2. Fact-finding and enforcement agents such as the police are seen as possessing a bias in their perceptions of a given case.

3. The criminal enforcement process is understood to be an adversary one in every phase of fact finding and guilt determination. In short, the enforcement process may be characterized as a struggle that focuses on the combative elements, and emphasizes that truth emerges through the conflict produced by adversariness.

4. The emphasis is on quality controls. Each case is seen as a challenge in terms of producing a subjective product described as justice, and every case must be treated in terms of meeting minimum standards with respect to probable cause for arrest, notification of rights and of charges, a proper hearing, appropriate safeguards including the assistance of counsel, constitutional privileges and immunities, a fair and speedy trial, absence of coercion, and rights to appeal.

5. Notions of efficiency as measured by the quantity of cases disposed of as an end in itself are rejected. Instead, efficiency is measured in terms of quality to the degree that a particular case has met due process requirements.

6. The primacy of the individual is central. Human beings are seen as rational creatures willing to give up a modicum of freedom to the state and abiding by social rules promulgated for the common good in order to achieve personal safety, security in the home, on the street, and in connection with possessions.

7. Although individuals are willing to surrender some degree of personal action for the greater good of all (for example, by giving the state police power), the due process model requires that there be precise limitations placed on the powers of officialdom and others who govern them.

8. Power is an instrument that is potentially subject to abuse no matter how well-intended the possessors and wielders of power may be.

9. Efficiency for efficiency's sake can be a form of tyranny in that it becomes a ritualized worship of the timetable, the clock, the quota, and the great appeal of high output of product in return for relatively low input in terms of resources. Efficiency for efficiency's sake is ultimately destructive of the human values of personal liberty, safety, and security.

10. The presumption of innocence attaches to an individual regardless of what the factual or legal case may be at the outset. An individual may be guilty of some deed, in fact, but, nevertheless, in legal terms, he or she must be considered "innocent."

11. Every accused person is considered equal; regardless of condition or station in life, the accused must receive all the quality inputs of the due process model. No distinctions can be drawn because of an individual's race, sex, or social class. The only inquiry that can be made to draw distinctions is that which involves an individual's ultimate criminal responsibility due to immaturity or mental condition.

12. The due process model recognizes that there are serious limitations to the ultimate effectiveness of the use of the criminal sanction in attempting to regulate human behavior. Much human behavior is better regulated by other social agencies such as the family, peer groups, and professional colleagues.

Crime-Control Model

The crime-control model is the actual "work style" many enforcement organizations implement as most efficient and productive in day-to-day operations. It includes 12 elements.

1. Repression of all criminal conduct is seen by the police and other enforcement personnel as of paramount value in society.

2. The failure to apprehend and convict wrongdoers is seen as leading to disorder and chaos in society. In terms of the crime-control model, enforcement agents tend to see all human beings as essentially destructive. Without the police and other keepers of the peace, humanity would descend to levels of savagery. The maintenance of public order and the safety of individual persons and property would be impossible without police measures to safeguard social stability.

3. The law-abiding individual is seen as a victim of predatory criminals who have received more concern than their innocent victims.

4. Only an efficient enforcement process that focuses ultimate responsibility upon those who disrupt society can guarantee the freedom and safety of all.

5. As a consequence, the primary attention of our limited resources must be allocated to screening suspects, assessing culpability and guilt, and securing appropriate dispositions.

6. The high level of crime and other forms of antisocial behavior present in modern mass society can only be suppressed by the maximum utilization of the criminal process.

7. In keeping with this concept, special stress must be placed on a high apprehension and conviction rate

in order to deter potential offenders and to neutralize and incapacitate actual offenders.

8. Toward this end, speedy, unceremonious routines must be employed to move each case from pre-arrest investigation and arrest to post-arrest investigation, preparation for trial, trial or entry of plea, and conviction, through disposition. Due process quality controls not only hamper police and other enforcement agents, but also release many offenders to commit further social harm. Certainty of apprehension and punishment are the only efficacious measures available to control crime and similar antisocial behavior.

9. In order to implement this objective, assembly-line techniques of efficiency, uniformity, and speed must be the performance ideal of the crime-control model and its accompanying structure.

10. There must be an early determination of guilt once a "suspect" becomes a "defendant."

11. As a practical matter, once a suspect becomes the focus of an investigation and moves toward becoming a defendant, police perceptions of this fact must inevitably produce a presumption of guilt. If not, most working police officers would see their investigative efforts, intended to assist formal agencies affix guilt, as meaningless gestures. More important for the police is that in the crime-control model, "factual" guilt is all that is necessary; the idea that an individual must be "legally" guilty as well under our system of law is rejected as absurd.

12. Finally, the emphasis must be on the early stages of administrative fact finding. Both the police and prosecution are seen as crucial, otherwise the case will collapse at later stages after valuable resources have been expended in its prosecution.

POLICE CONCEPTIONS OF THEIR ROLE

Many of the dilemmas the police face occur as a result of the attempt to create an intellectual synthesis and a practical fusion of elements of both the due process and crime-control models of the criminal process. The impact of attempting to do so is greatest upon the police because they are the most visible actors in initiating the criminal process. Because of their visibility and because of misconceptions of their role in the criminal process, they often bear the brunt of the criticism from the public, from those in political power, and from other elements in the enforcement system. The basic contradiction may be expressed in the form of two conflicting conceptions of the police role: one, what the police mistakenly believe to be their function; and the other, what is justified in terms of the structural realities. The police officer's conception of his or her role vis-à-vis other groups is depicted in Figure 2.

It should be noted from the illustration that police officers conceive of themselves as the fulcrum of the entire criminal justice system. It is because of this mistaken belief and their inability to assign an appropriate degree of significance in terms of power to other segments of the criminal process that tension, resentment, and ultimate disappointment are produced. It is one of the ironies of police work that although the powerful weapon of police discretion may initiate a prosecution, other actors and agencies may alter and reformulate a routine arrest, thereby imposing their authority and reality on the matter. What appears to police officers to be their responsibility is now transformed into the focus of responsibility and task performance of other groups who will want to impose their perceptions and policies on the case at hand. In summary, the police have little control over other official agencies, organizational behavior, or the consequences of their official policies.

Depicted below is a second, more realistic conceptualization of the police role vis-à-vis the criminal justice system. (See Figure 3.)

From the foregoing a more accurate assessment of the police role in the criminal justice system would be that of *only one of a variety of criminal justice agencies* that ultimately focus upon the accused person in

FIGURE 2 Police Officer's Conception of His or Her Role

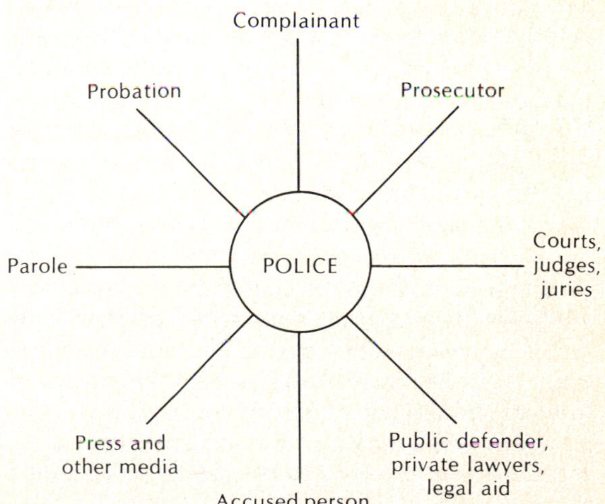

FIGURE 3 Police Role vis-à-vis the Criminal Justice System

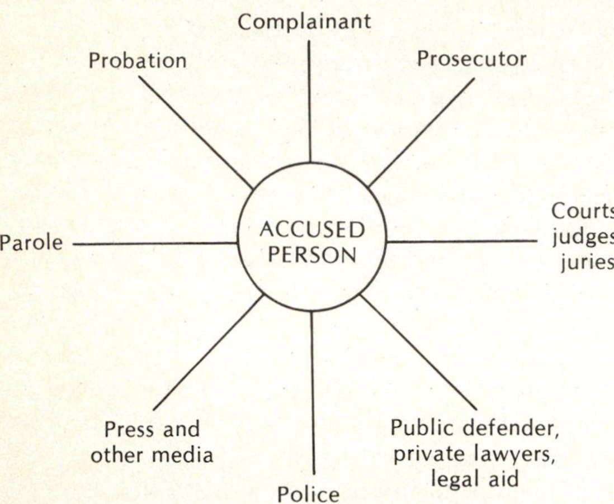

weighing such matters as the propriety of the arrest, the decision to prosecute, bail setting, determination of guilt or innocence, sentencing, probation, and parole supervision.

The police officer's sense of frustration is ultimately intensified by the fact that he or she is held to a due process standard by agencies that review the officer's work, whereas the crime-control model is the one used by immediate superiors reacting to the cross-pressures of production norms and political demands. These cross-pressures lead to the mistaken self-perception that the officer is not only that, but simultaneously a judge, a jury, a prosecutor, as well as a probation and parole officer. The officer's tacit assumption is that he or she has the burden of all of these in the crime-control system. It is this unfortunate bias grounded in an erroneous conception of reality that places the police officer in an untenable position. Although unable to control the input in the work situation, he or she is nevertheless held responsible for any of the negative features of the end product of the criminal process. The officer thereby becomes a suitable target of displayed hostility on the part of the public because of their chronic dissatisfaction with ever-increasing crime rates, which are often attributed to defects in policing and law enforcement.

The fundamental myth of our system of criminal justice is the assertion that ours is the "accusatorial" as opposed to the "inquisitorial" system. We point with pride to our rejection of methods of coercion, be they savage or subtle, in securing convictions. Instead, the burden is said to belong to the state to procure independent evidence to establish an individual's guilt. What the rules envision is a combative procedural system wherein prosecution and defense—who are admittedly possessed of unequal resources—will clash, and after the dust has settled, the data that determine guilt or innocence will emerge.

Unfortunately this model of criminal justice does not exist, in fact. At each stage of the screening process a tacit but erroneous assumption is made. It is assumed that the accused ultimately will have a "day in court," that oversights, mistakes of judgment, and capricious behavior of enforcement officials will be reviewed carefully by the next higher authority. All the screening agencies in the system of criminal justice move a case along toward a trial that seldom occurs for ultimate resolution of the issues involved.[39] In most communities, only about 6 percent of criminal cases at the felony level ever go to trial; the rest are bargain-plea cases. The conviction rate in these few trials may range from 70 percent to 90 percent.

THE NATURE AND IMPACT OF POLICE CULTURE

Police, who have already been socialized and shaped in the larger society, are required to become part of a new world when they enter the environment of a police bureaucracy. For the most part, entering recruits are not attracted to police work by a desire for an authoritarian role, or to act out deep-seated power needs under the guise of policing. Candidates generally are attracted by more mundane, "here and now" considerations such as salary, job security, vacations, and fringe benefits including liberal pensions. Black police recruits are enticed by the fact that police work as a civil service situation is relatively free of discrimination, at least at entry level, in the absence of better opportunities in other sectors of employment.[40] However, it is the police bureaucracy that shapes, molds, and resocializes an otherwise intellectually, emotionally, and physically above-average group of recruits into a police culture and value system: "Police authoritarianism does not come into the force along with the recruits, but rather is inculcated in the men through strenuous socialization. It is the police system, not the personality of the candidate, that is the more powerful determinant of behavior and ideology."[41]

In approaching the question of the origins and nature of what has come to be somewhat pejoratively termed "police culture," most researchers have engaged in the art of "savage discovery." The phrase "savage discovery" has been employed in the context of reprimanding social science researchers who study the poor, the ill, the jobless, all the distressed and disinherited who are redefined to make it possible for us to view the *victims* of a social problem as the *causative agents* of that problem. In a similar fashion some researchers have examined the police as some sort of exotic, esoteric occupational tribe. They have tended "to conduct or interpret the research that shows how these people think in different forms, act in different patterns, cling to different values, seek different goals, and learn different truths. Which is to say that they are strangers, barbarians, savages."[42] In reviewing the basic features of police culture and values as they have emerged in the social science literature, it would be advisable to consider the degree to which other occupations share a number of the characteristics researchers have attributed to the police.

A recital of the properties of police culture should serve to help us better understand the pivotal feature of the police occupation—*police discretion*.[43]

Kinship and Solidarity. The qualities of kinship and solidarity refer to a characteristic common to many occupations and professions. It is the unique sense of identity that one develops as part of a group of colleagues in a work situation—the commonality of interests, problems, concerns, and even life styles. In the case of the police and the military, however, it is said that it is the sense of danger that promotes group solidarity.[44]

Common Hazards and Dangers. Although many other industrial, mining, and service occupations entail far greater risk of injury, long-term illness, or death, one cannot minimize the many risks to which police are exposed even in the course of routine "service" tasks. These include not only the physical risks involved in police intervention in family disputes, for example, but also their exposure to the assorted forms of brutality that angry, disturbed individuals inflict on each other, and the related wide range of violence that affects the lives of marginal working-class poor.[45] But the kind of ever-present danger most crucial to understanding police behavior is what Arthur Niederhoffer describes as "the hostility and fear that almost palpably press against a policeman in lower-class areas, and aggravate his impulse to 'get tough.' "[46]

Another police researcher and commentator writes:

> Danger is a part of a fair number of occupations, but only among a few does it occupy a significant part of the occupational "line" or public ideology. Being a policeman is one of these occupations. The police possess what might be called a "threat–danger–hero" notion of their everyday lives. The structure of rewards within police departments is very conducive to this ideology. Violent or dramatic public action—whether solving or preventing a crime, shooting a man, or aggressively patrolling traffic—is a source of promotion to the detective bureau, a way to "get out of the bag." In fact, much of police work is boring or involves frustrating, contentious hassles with citizens. The dangerous activities represent considerably less than 10 percent of police patrol time, and less than 1 percent of citizen initiated complaints concern violent or dramatic crime (rape, murder, assault). The highly unpredictable, but potentially possible, dangerous scene is always a part of police patrol.[47]

Another facet of hazards and danger peculiar to the police is the almost universal requirement that police personnel carry firearms at all times on-and-off-duty. In off-duty situations improper or inappropriate use of firearms can often result in tragic accidents, or unlawful behavior on the part of police who may then seek to "cover" the violent incident with an arrest.[48] On the other hand, it is important to remember that many police officers retire after a long career without once firing their service revolver in an enforcement encounter. In reality, actual violence occurs in probably less than 2 or 3 percent of police–civilian encounters.[49]

Depicted in Figure 4 are the actual contexts in which the FBI reports 1,143 police were killed during the period 1970–1979.

Respect for Power and Authority. Police work brings its practitioners near the seats of power almost routinely. Police have a keen awareness of their role as protectors and defenders of the "establishment." They fully understand the interplay of economic forces and political power. All major social and political events are interpreted in terms of power relations—"Who did what for whom—and how much did he get for it?" Individual police may not always identify with power holders, but they cannot help admiring those who use power resourcefully and shrewdly. In many organizational environments, including that of the police, informal systems of patronage develop. Rewards, privileges, and immunities that are granted or withheld are

FIGURE 4 Law Enforcement Officers Killed

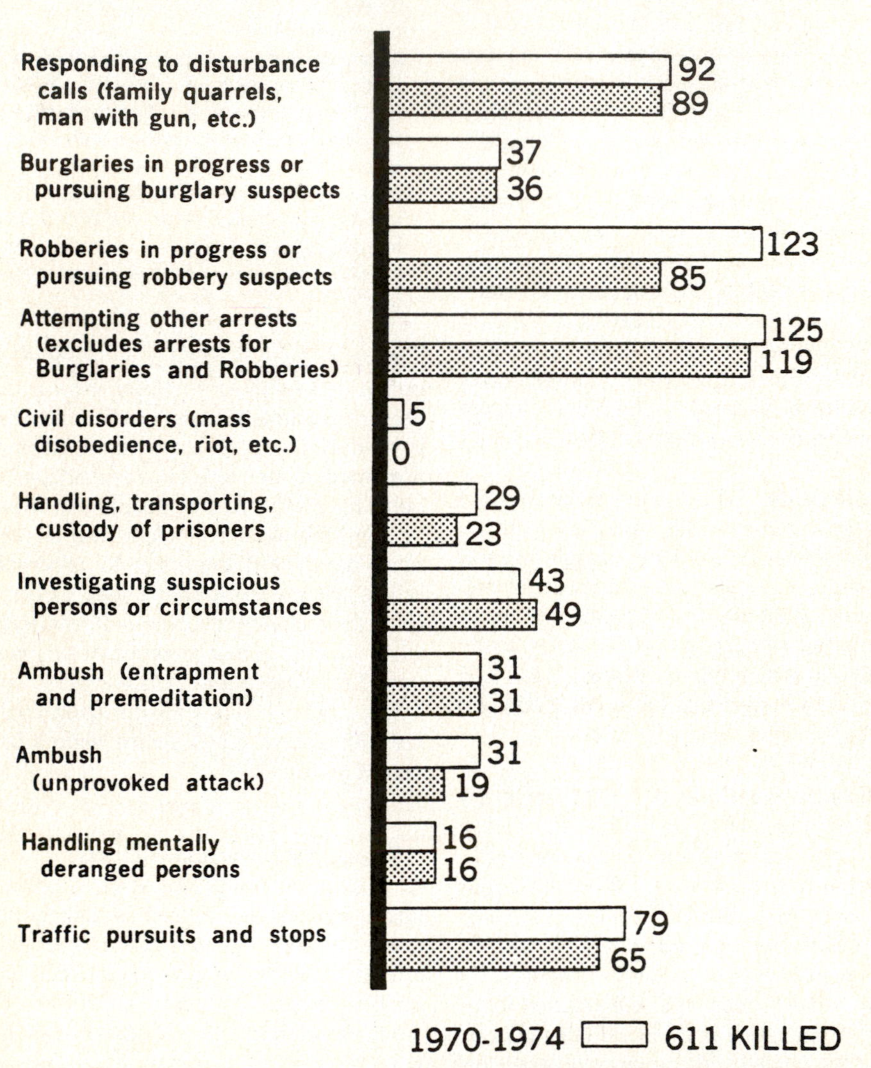

SOURCE: Federal Bureau of Investigations, *Uniform Crime Reports*—1980. Washington, D.C., p. 310.

a function of the amount of "clout" or "muscle" one can command.

In some police departments there is a "Rabbi" system that functions to effect economic and political exchanges within the organization. An individual officer's sponsor, protector, or patron is known as his or her "Rabbi." Job assignments, promotions, special work detail opportunities or job visibility, and protection within the police hierarchy are some of the services that may be rendered by an influential Rabbi. The Rabbi system is critical to internal police politics and many informal personnel decisions in urban police departments. Often the arrangements or agreements made by police officials to perform some service or favor, or to execute an obligation is referred to legalistically as a "contract." It connotes an act that one is honor-bound to perform. In the police world when one refers to a "contract" to be executed, one's individual honor and reputation for integrity are bound up with the certainty of performance. But how different are the police in these matters than what one may observe in any other setting such as an academic department, a corporate executive suite, a political club, or a family, a hospital, or a law firm?

Secrecy. A hallmark of bureaucracy, secrecy takes on a special meaning and purpose for the police. Much police work involves tailoring and reformulation of laws, departmental procedures, and officially prescribed conduct to meet the stresses, contingencies, and exigencies of the field situation. The myriad acts of omission and commission, apart from outright corruption, that can subject the individual police officer to sanctions ranging from mild reproof to dismissal and indictment are the taboo subject matter covered by police secrecy. This is the equivalent of a blue-coat "code of omerta," a blanket of silence that must be maintained among the police "brotherhood" in the face of official inquiry or review to shield one's colleagues. For example, officers may cover up a fellow officer's brutal acts, petty thefts, extortionate behavior, abuses of police power, and related illegalities.[50] Secrecy provides the glue that binds police solidarity and shields the "blue brotherhood" against assaults of the press, external review, or internal police superiors.

Secrecy constitutes loyalty to the group and represents the essence of police solidarity and cohesiveness against an environment that is perceived to be hostile.[51] "Blowing the whistle," "finking," and "squealing" are breaches of the code of silence and secrecy that represent the most heinous offense in the police world. "The one overriding rule among the police seems to be: never squeal on a brother officer no matter what he does. . . . This rule is also typically observed by police commanders, taking the form: protect an officer from outsiders, including the courts, no matter what he has done."[52] Official secrets and harsh sanctions imposed for "whistle blowing" are not peculiar to police bureaucracies, however. In at least three major instances at the federal level, officials respectively employed in bureaucracies at the Pentagon, the Public Health Service, and the Food and Drug Administration went public with information indicating that the taxpayers' interests were being violated, and summarily lost their jobs. In the first instance, an employee "blew the whistle" on a $2-billion cost overrun in a Lockheed cargo plane; in another case, the employee complained that the Public Health Service was lax in setting safety standards for factory workers exposed to dangerous chemicals; and in a third instance, the FDA dismissed a virologist who warned that the swine flu vaccine was worthless and could be dangerous. The expert proved to be correct, but was fired anyway.[53]

Loyalty. The sense of identity, belonging, and cohesion that is precipitated by the sense of danger and isolation in the police world is also present in the military, and even in the most prestigious of professions, medicine. However, organizational and group loyalty among the police is best expressed as follows:

> *Brotherhood.* It means a fraternity of legally frustrated men with clean-cut hair, large coffee-ridden stomachs and impaired social lives who show up in embarrassing numbers to give blood to their wounded and race to 10-13's (assist officers) with their 38's loosened and the adrenalin shifting extra blood to the stomach and other vital organs, making them breathe faster. Men who stand at massive cop funerals in stricken lines and socialize with each other and look at clocks that have 13, 14, 15, etc., written over the normal hours; men who are linked always to each other by $700 walkie-talkies and their Bad-News car radio; men who feel despite societies for ethnic cops, "We are all blue." The department is the family; the precinct is "the House."[54]

A Sense of Minority-Group Status. The police, prosecution, and criminal courts represent a closed community manifesting a defensive attitude toward "outsider" and "critics." However, it is the police who are the most visible persons on the firing line; therefore they tend to polarize all others into those who are "with us" and those who are "against us." Efforts to maintain organizational equilibrium and personal stability amid bureaucratic production, "efficiency" requirements, and stresses from without and within produce a high level of tension and anxiety. Many police officers feel as if they are caught in a double bind—that they will be criticized no matter what they do.

The police officer in the ghetto is a symbol not only of law, but also of the entire system of law enforcement and criminal justice. As such, he or she becomes the tangible target for grievances against the shortcomings of the system—assembly-line justice in teeming lower courts; wide disparities in sentences; antiquated correctional facilities; the basic inequities imposed by the system on the poor (to whom, for example, the option of bail means only jail). The police officer in the ghetto is the object of increasingly bitter social debate over law enforcement.

Further, there is a recurring theme among police officers to the effect that they do not get the support, understanding, and fair treatment they expect from the people they serve. They complain rather bitterly of their role as "pawns" in a political game, and as convenient targets of the mass media, politicians, the courts, and judges as a way of explaining their own shortcomings in connection with increasing crime rates or related social problems.[55]

Political Conservatism. Police conservatism is a function of an occupational socialization that stresses order, discipline, and respect for authority. There is a sense in the literature that the police mood is one of deep pessimism about the future prospects of civilization, which they see as in decline because of the erosion of "law and order." Political conservatism of police is a product of the fusion of their pessimism and a concurrent moralism about the depravity of others, the theme of several police novels.[56]

Cynicism. Cynicism is obviously not unique to the police. It is generously shared with such professions as medicine, law, academia, and politics, and is found in a variety of occupational settings. In the police world it takes on a special import because of the power of the police, whose decisions may be the result of viewing the world through the lens of cynicism. Varying with the stage of a police officer's career, it first develops during the initial stages of academy training,[57] and reaches its greatest degree of intensity between the seventh and tenth year of service. Thereafter it begins to decline, and reaches a rather benign level in the years just preceding retirement. Cynicism is rationalized as knowing the real world and "what the score is."[58] In essence, the cynic sees the world in terms of dualisms such as good–evil, citizens–savages, friends–enemies. At its root, the cynical perspective is pejorative and has a contempt for a substantial portion of the human race. However, over time, many police officers develop a "tragic sense" and come to recognize that there is a complex "interweaving of chance, free will, and necessity; accident, self-control, and inevitable factors outside the control of the individual each had substantial influence on his or her life."[59] Yet in spite of the cynicism there is an unquestioning belief in and loyalty to country, flag, family, and religion; an unswerving conviction that police do an exemplary job in combating crime, but are hamstrung by judges, courts, and corrections officials; an assumption that the trouble with America is lack of respect for the law, police, and constituted authority; and an associated doctrine that the cause of crime and related social problems is widespread permissiveness.

Suspiciousness. Police manuals virtually indoctrinate each new recruit to value suspiciousness as a positive, functional attitude. Police are exhorted to be suspicious of people who appear to be in places where "they do not belong," cars that do not look "right," people who appear "evasive," people who "loiter," hitchhikers, unescorted women in public places, etc. On the whole, a working milieu is established in which all the world becomes a predatory, dangerous habitat in which the worst is likely to happen.[60] However, this Hobbesian view is shared by those in other occupations such as bankers, lawyers, and accountants. But suspiciousness is not the exclusive methodological tool of the police in appraising the world. It is the sociologist who elaborates suspiciousness to a form of consciousness that is central to the discipline of sociology. One of the leading introductory works in the field describes the sociological perspective in terms of "seeing through" games, "looking behind" facades, "being up on all the tricks," the "debunking motif"—in short, the sociologist practicing the "art of mistrust" in explaining the social world. Further, "it [sociology] may even presuppose a measure of suspicion about the way in which human events are officially interpreted by the authorities. . . ."[61]

Social Isolation. The police occupation imposes a set of constraints on the usual network of social relationships most of us take for granted. For the policeman or policewoman it often involves a set of awkward and potentially uncomfortable or embarrassing situations. Since an officer's total life is colored by his or her occupation, police find that in most instances their circle of friends are other police and their families. This is not a consequence of lack of personal affability or congeniality, but instead is due to the perceptions of others who make the possibility of social interaction more difficult than it might be otherwise.[62] Further, there is ample evidence that the police occupation introduces stresses and problems into an officer's marital relationship and family life that are not present in most other occupations.[63] The nature of the police occupation furnishes opportunities for extramarital sexual encounters, and often these are the source of marital conflict and dissolutions. Erratic work hours and changing shifts introduce elements of contingency, inconvenience, and tension to the non-police spouse. The presence of the service revolver in the home can pose a hazard for younger children in a police family. The patterns of consumption of the amount and quality of consumer goods, clothing, automobiles, and vacations are observed and noted by neighbors as to whether any and all purchases are consistent with an officer's income. The police family, in a sense, lives in a goldfish bowl.

Regardless of what a number of now-dated studies may show, it is my experience in contact with a variety of police departments that the "new breed" of police recruit is more prepared to reach beyond the narrow police circle in establishing a friendship network than were predecessors, and that the "social isolation" of police is somewhat exaggerated.

Pressure To Produce. There is in police departments an emphasis on "activity," "batting averages," "quotas," and "collars" as yardsticks to measure the worth of performance for purposes of promotion or assignment to less onerous duties. The refrain that one hears from many officers is, "You've got to keep yourself covered. No one is going to back you; if you make a mistake it's *your ass* that gets burned." And mistakes are made in the frantic and often feverish milieu in which policework is performed.

Pressure to set statistical records as justification of police budgets has been overwhelming. This may be seen especially in narcotics cases where police objectivity becomes problematic. Drug-related cases in the criminal courts of the larger cities constitute an important part of the caseload and are an interesting example of police craftsmanship in establishing probable cause. The phrase "probable cause" is an elusive concept, and does not have a rigorous, exacting definition. It is more than a mere suspicion, but is certainly less than guilt established beyond a reasonable doubt.

The establishment of probable cause as a basis for arrest or for a warrant is said to exist when there is a reasonable belief that embodies an appreciable measure of certainty that a crime has been committed and that the accused person is the violator.

Pressure to produce is an endemic source of tension in the work life of many occupations in diverse industrial, service, and professional settings. It is not peculiar to the police culture. However, in the police world it becomes critical in explaining total police behavior. The police occupation is unique in that in no other organization does the field person exercise greater *actual* authority and independence than more senior police officers in the hierarchy of administrative powerholders.[64] Their high visibility, extraordinary authority within their organizational setting, and the element of danger capped by overriding pressures to produce are said to crystallize the "working personality" of the police. This conceptualization is probably simplistic in that it tends to obscure the multifaceted subtleties and wide differences in performance of any occupational role.

One legal authority has stated five basic facts about police behavior and policy he thought to be "astonishing": (1) Much of it is illegal or of doubtful legality; (2) it is lower-echelon officers who "make" much police policy in the field; (3) much of this conduct is kept secret; (4) police policy is often based on guesswork and not on systematic studies or investigations by qualified specialists; and (5) much police policy is exempt from the kind of limited judicial review deemed necessary for other administrative agencies.[65] Formal legal rules of arrest, charge, and prosecution are quite meaningless, for they do not reflect the underlying reality of what it is that police departments and offices of prosecution actually do. The internal stresses and organizational environments contribute more to the nature and quality of police performance than do formal rules and legal etiquette.[66]

During the course of the past two decades, the United States Supreme Court has been tortuously attempting to balance the scales of rights and equities of the privileges and immunities of accused persons, and the concomitant personal and community needs to feel physically secure. Almost uniformly the Court has chosen, especially in close, difficult situations, to come down in favor of police action that involves the procurement of nontestimonial evidence of crime.[67] However, there is more involved than agonizing Court deliberations over liberty versus security. Police power and authority are derived from law. So much residual power has been granted to the police in achieving their formal statutory responsibilities that *they have carved out a large, amorphous, de facto area of informal power and authority*—and the courts have sustained this control. Thus, searches incidental to a lawful arrest, stopping and questioning of "suspicious persons," the use of informants, infiltration of organizations perceived to be "radical" in terms of police culture, monitoring of telephone conversations under specific circumstances, and seizure of evidence—which may include body fluids—have been recognized by the courts as acceptable police activities. Furthermore, the police have been granted exceptional legal powers, far greater than those permitted other occupational segments of society. In the performance of police duty, an officer may use firearms, run traffic lights, commandeer vehicles, clear streets of civilians, and under specific circumstances enter premises without warrants.

When coupled with the pessimism, resentment, cynicism, and bureaucratic insulation that shape the police world view, these powers—granted by law and judicial authority—convince many police officers that they are not merely servants of the law, but are in fact masters of it. From this base, some police officers develop the rather peculiar philosophy that they can in good conscience exploit the legal mantle of their authority for their own purposes.

It is from this background that we are more easily able to understand police innovation in attempting to evade the legalistic strictures imposed by appellate courts in the attempt to regulate police field conduct.[68] This is especially apparent in areas such as search and seizure and "stop-and-frisk." Understanding this feature of police culture teaches us that institutional restraints such as the United States Supreme Court can never be more than partially successful. Experienced patrol officers and detectives, especially in those instances where they sense they enjoy community and political support, are incredibly resourceful in perfecting strategies of evasion and seemingly nominal compliance with appellate court requirements. Most of the law enforcement personnel who fall into these patterns are the hardworking, competent backbone of police organizations, and are neither vicious nor corrupt. Their immersion in police bureaucracy and its accompanying police culture, however, lead them to fervently believe that their methods are not really evasions or violations

FIGURE 5 Pressures on Police: Proximate and Remote

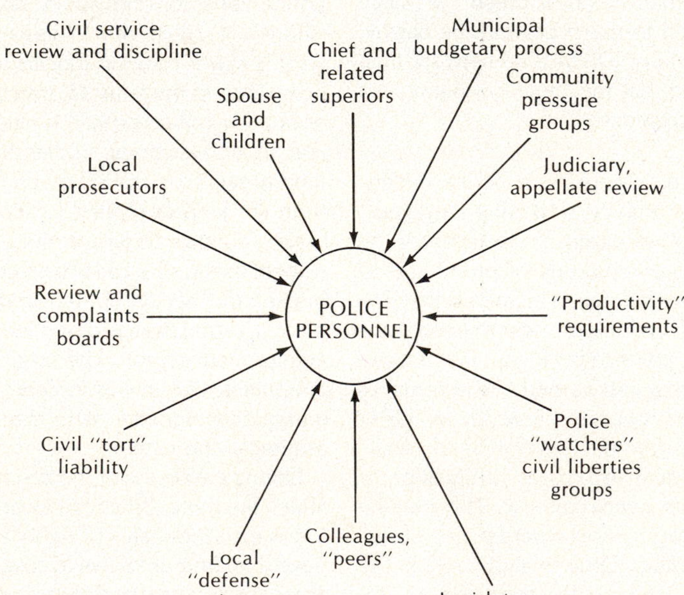

but are instead their own intelligent, resourceful adaptations in furtherance of police goals of achieving law, order, and justice in a threatened democratic society.[69]

THE POLICE AS A MILITANT PROLETARIAT

It is difficult to conceive of the emerging "class consciousness" of the police as evidenced by their growing politicization and drift toward organization into police unions. Simultaneously, police management and police career professionals emphasize a thrust toward professionalism. The ironic dualism of police unions and professionalization are actually two prongs derived from a single set of world views. Police are keenly aware of their position in the stratification system—of their role as protectors and defenders of the "establishment"—but at the same time they experience a sense of occupational, economic, and political marginality. In large departments police are alienated from their work, and from their administrative superiors. They feel they are "ciphers," "numbers"; they distrust their own organization. They believe they are subjected to corruption, poor treatment, and venality. If they treat others as objects, it is because they feel they are being treated as objects by their organization. Police tend to see all rules and structures as facades, and all interaction in society as a series of exchanges in which even the simplest act of humanity is based upon some anticipated prearranged *quid pro quo*. This is the essence of the police "contract." Since the world is a jungle, it must be ordered in some predictable fashion; the "contract" structures otherwise amorphous relationships to achieve concrete goals as benefits.[70]

The symbols of the material world pervade police consciousness, and much of the economic thought of industrial enterprise dominates their daily talk—"How's business?" "How are things at the shop?" "Are you making a living?" Their sensitivity to power and its uses has converted them into active lobbyists not simply for collective bargaining rights and its concomitant wages, hours, fringe benefits, and working condition "packages," but also in the courts and political arena. Police are quite sophisticated in being able to galvanize their political muscle and sense of public relations to ward off meaningful external review, to negotiate favorable work contracts, to reward "friends" and punish political "enemies" at the ballot box, and to undermine the traditional autocratic role of the chief.

The primary impact of police unionization has been to compel police management to focus greater attention on the need to improve personnel practices. As workers, police have become almost as militant as any industrial wage worker. Because of their strategic function in municipalities they have been able to engage in "job actions," slow downs, and "blue flu" sickouts with remarkable effectiveness. By disrupting essential municipal services they have succeeded in establishing police unions as powerful new forces in many cities. The sources of police power, at least as new municipal labor unions, are (1) the police capacity to make powerful political alliances; (2) "law and order" slogans that are employed to polarize all opposition to them as simply "anti-police"; (3) public fear of crime and the willingness of municipalities, with strong federal assistance, to allocate higher budgetary priorities to the police; and (4) a culture that creates a high degree of solidarity and cohesion not found in similar work groups.[71] As a "proletarianized" police seek to create strong unions to protect themselves against the arbitrariness of police and municipal managements, and to achieve new goals in terms of "bread and butter" wage and working conditions issues, they are also paradoxically and vigorously pursuing "professionalization." It is not suggested that professionalism and unionization are inconsistent or mutually exclusive goals. Professional groups such as social workers, nurses, and college professors have unions. However, when one examines the essential requisites of professionalism, it is evident that at the present level of police training, it is self-defeating and almost delusory to think that any group can achieve professional status by simply proclaiming it, or by fiat.[72] At this time a fairly typical police department would require a person to be a high school graduate and to attend a police academy for twelve to sixteen weeks, with varying refresher and special courses during a career.

Richard Harris's study of the police academy reluctantly concludes, "The police academy seems to institutionalize role distance by reinforcing and sanctioning the recruit's belief that his training and image in the academy are irrelevant to police work."[73] Yet, two of the most important predictor variables as to the caliber of a recruit's future job performance are an officer's training scores on written examinations at the police academy and his or her ratings while on probationary status.[74]

Apart from any other factors, the one significant formal barrier to police professionalization is the fact that currently not one municipal department requires a college degree at the entry-level position of patrol officer. Although police salaries are more and more linked to collective bargaining growing out of police unionism, any continued upward pressure of wage rewards for police work will be a function of more rigorous higher education requirements.[75] In the process of the drift toward professionalization of many occupations as the key to resolving economic problems of wages and working conditions, and the social-psychological problems of marginality, boredom, and lack of job satisfaction, the essential ingredients that make up a profession have been ignored. Parenthetically, many of the police complaints about job routinization, boredom, and lack of autonomy also afflict the ancient professions of law, medicine, the military, the clergy, and academic life.

THE PROBLEMS OF POLICE PROFESSIONALIZATION

Given all the unanswered questions and thorny problems, it is amazing that the police in America can agree that there is one universal solution—professionalization. It has become a mystique of police philosophy, a Holy Grail. So much has been written on the positive contributions of professionalization that a totally unrealistic view of the matter has prevailed.[76] In view of some of the negative implications present in the public thrust toward professionalization, the concept requires critical re-examination in order to achieve a more balanced perspective.

In the major police departments, control of the system has continued within the orbit of a self-defined, self-perpetuating group. In many departments in the eastern United States, police have been called the "Irish Mafia"; in others they represent a particular political force in a given city. Generally we can say, as we can of the governments of developed nations, that with continued power has come a reliance on tradition and a conservative ideology that resist any change as a threat to continued power. Concomitant with this resistance has been a general upgrading of the police occupation, mainly as the result of two important trends, one internal and the other external. The former is the move toward professionalization that has come about through technological sophistication, specialization, and the formation of elite cadres whose well-educated members have pushed for recognition as professionals. The latter is the growing importance in America of the police as a domestic army whose purpose is to control demonstrations, riots, and disorders, and to monitor the activities of dissidents of every stripe. Out of this unique responsibility a greater recognition of and a higher status for the police system has developed. Nevertheless the movement toward professionalism has been a mixed blessing.

Professionalism and professionalization create a struggle for power and polarize a police force into two warring camps—the pros (professionals) and cons (conservatives). Whenever there is conflict at the top, it filters down; the people in the lower ranks are caught in a no-man's land and are the ultimate victims of such intraorganizational conflict. In essence, the internal struggle is characterized by an entrenched administrative oligarchy on the defensive against an innovative younger group seeking to capture the old regimes. The younger members often use the jargon, style, and ideological slogans of professionalism to accomplish their objectives. However, it remains to be seen, as they assume power and leadership, whether their professionalism is one of substance or merely a careerist, politically motivated veneer.

Professionalism, by its stress on formal education, creates divisions and enmities among members of a police force in other ways. Many police officers, especially the oldtimers, are upset by the thought of returning to school. They resent the favoritism toward college graduates; they fear the competition of the educated; and they respond with cynicism or aggression because of their own frustration. On a more subtle level, the academic influence creates malcontents. The latent effect of professionalism is that many are forced into academic environments far from the police orbit; here they become socialized into norms and ideologies wholly different and inconsistent with purely local concerns and narrow bureaucratic commitments. Professionalism and its concomitant colleagueship breed a cosmopolitanism destructive of authoritarian structures. The educated person is often a disenchanted person.

Professionalism creates turmoil in that it cannot be grafted onto a traditional department. It requires radical changes in policy, techniques, and social relations; old customs and values are threatened. The men and women become uneasy, and as the process speeds up, they become disgruntled. Morale suffers.

Professionalism creates alienation. Necessarily exposed to the academic viewpoint, professionals lose their narrow organizational loyalty and become "cosmopolitans." Seeking the larger perspective, professionals sometimes tend to violate fundamental postulates of "tried-and-true" police tradition.

Professionalism creates many dilemmas for the police in the modern world. Professionalism increases the police demand for efficiency and objective standards in police work. In practice, this means that the professional police force is tougher and more impersonal than the nonprofessional can be in dealing with minority groups, youth, the urban poor, and political dissenters.

Professionalism intensifies the demand for self-policing and autonomy. Despite this, the experience of our large cities proves that "civilianization," community control, and external reviews may be forthcoming, regardless of what the police perceive as a threat to their integrity and professionalization.

Professionalism needs constant renewal by the recruitment of college-educated individuals. However, the competition for a limited number of job slots may unfortunately pit ethnic groups, as well as male and female candidates, against each other. And all of these candidates can assert a legitimate claim for consideration.

Professionalism is the assertion that there is no political interference in police affairs. Professionalism, on the other hand, does stimulate police interference in political affairs. A major example was the advertising and voting campaigns of the Patrolmen's Benevolent Association speaking as the representative of the New York City Police Department opposing the suggested Civilian Review Board in 1966.

Professionalism can be achieved or maintained only as long as the police are held in high esteem by the public. Therefore, there is a tendency to cover up or falsify reports and statistics of crime in order to maintain that prestige. Every bureaucracy is ultimately a self-serving instrument supportive of its own world views and the decisions it has already made or is about to make; the police are no exception.[77]

Police departments, like other large bureaucracies, have accepted the claims of psychological testing and psychiatric examination and screening. In one sense this is an improvement; it tends to replace the polygraph examination as a method of attracting and selecting candidates. The one important criticism of these selection methods is that police departments are searching desperately for the unique qualities that might predict the ideal, superior police officer who will have a trouble-free, simon-pure career. The major fallacy in this search is that a police force is most effective when it is composed of men and women who are different from one another in temperament, intellect, life-style, ideology, motivating personality, fund of knowledge, skills, and expertise; in other words, it needs the college person, the ghetto resident, and the soft-spoken intellectual, as well as the hard-nosed, rough-and-ready daredevil who enthusiastically welcomes dangerous assignments.

Increasingly, modern policing requires a variety of personality types to fit different organizational roles, intellectual requisites, and role responses. Ultimately, more highly selective requirements will be needed to attract even more sophisticated candidates. Contrary to the conventional wisdom of some police observers, a good deal of police work is not as monotonous, routine, or boring as depicted. Unlike many of their industrial and corporate counterparts, the police are *not* like Balzac's bureaucrats "who find themselves sooner or later in the condition of a wheel screwed onto a machine." The greatest psychological police hazard is that the nature of the police career leaves the officer prey to cynicism and a Hobbesian view of the world. The majority of their occupational experiences are concerned with people in trouble, in conflict, or in violation of law. The main source of difficulty is in the teeming inner city, where police middle-class sensibilities are shocked by what is considered an alien, obscene, inferior way of life. Here people are seen at their most reprehensible and vulnerable moments. The officer feels that the police are the only experts holding this skewed segment of hard data. All arguments that are made stressing human decency and perfectibility are rejected.

Toward the department itself a strange ambivalence exists. In the back rooms of police precincts there are no more virulent critics of the police establishment than the police themselves. Although often an unwitting victim of a demanding bureaucracy, the officer develops fierce loyalties to the system and unites with other police against all outsiders critical of police activities. As retirement approaches, a process of gradual disengagement takes place, in which the officer makes tentative efforts at re-establishment in a social and emotional stance more compatible with civilian roles and world views.

There is at present a growing anxiety and a trend toward self-examination within the criminal justice system involving a number of unanswered, perhaps unanswerable, questions such as: What is (or should be) the role of justice in America today? What is justice? How can the police improve their public image? What direction will police–minority group relations take? Are restraint or the application of massive force proper strategies to use against confrontation demonstrations? Within the police system what can or should be done about the increasing antagonism between white and black members of the force? Is there a conflict of loyalty for the black police officer in situations involving black demonstrators? Is professionalization really an effective solution to the problems of the police? Is there a contradiction in policy when a department that wants to recruit college graduates is forced to seek minority-group candidates with little formal education? What should be the policy toward the introduction of civilians into police work? Can the police maintain what they believe to be proper standards of efficiency in law enforcement and still abide by the limitations imposed by Supreme Court decisions? What guidelines should be established over the gray area of police discretion? What is the proper relationship between the police and other institutions of criminal justice? Should the police be law enforcers or peace keepers?

POLICE ISSUES FOR THE 1980S

Regardless of the responses we might formulate to the foregoing queries, there are a number of other issues and emerging phenomena that will be critical in the decade ahead.

Police unionization and an intensified orientation toward an industrial labor–management model of police organization appear to be an accomplished fact. The impact of this trend is yet to be felt as a pervasive problem in undermining the traditional paramilitary police discipline. Job actions, strikes, and slowdowns may become more common forms of rank-and-file protest to achieve the usual trade union goals of wage benefits, job security, grievance and due process procedures, protection against layoffs, and the like. The wide import of police unionization is still to be felt within police organizations and the communities they serve.

The role of policewomen remains a difficult one for many departments. The unease and resentment of male colleagues and their wives will continue to create a climate of ambiguity for female recruits. Further, on-the-job performance of policewomen remains to be evaluated since the evidence of performance remains fragmentary and incomplete.

Local police appear to be losing much control to federal and state agencies. Although there is considerable revulsion toward the notion of a national police force, there is an unmistakable drift in that direction, especially in terms of financial dependence and control of data systems.

A high rate of unemployment that will last into the 1990s poses a serious threat to society. Because many of the jobs in America's basic industries no longer exist or continue to be exported by multinational corporations, chronic unemployment is bound to have a disastrous effect on our society.[78] When significant unemployment is linked with enduring racial hostilities, decaying cities, industrial stagnation, ever-greater disparities of wealth and privilege, and class inequities, the result may be a desperate willingness to experiment with the extremist politics of the authoritarian ideologies of the right or left. In the past the police have been employed to control picket lines in cases of labor disputes and to contain serious civil disturbances that were a product of labor protests, strikes, lockouts, and demonstrations by unemployed persons. As a consequence of austerity budgets and other severe economic dislocations, the police will be called upon with greater regularity to furnish the "shock troops" to defuse the inevitable protests and disorders arising out of frustration and economic distress.

Municipal austerity will impose demands for greater productivity on the part of all civil servants, including the police. How will pressures for increased productivity affect police discretion? What shape will these pressures take? And how will they be applied?

As more personnel possess college credentials and graduate degrees, police responses to their critics and defenses against their political superiors will become increasingly sophisticated. This aspect of police development will be interesting to watch, especially as the police develop men and women whose credentials, talents, and stature are the equivalent of those civil servants in some federal executive departments and the judiciary. It is of value to note that the British police system recruited its commissioners for more than a century largely from the military, until they developed their own intellectual elite and professional leaders from within.

The police will continue to be one of the major critics of the criminal justice system, since they are the major source of input to that system.

The intrusion of the police into the privacy of citizens for the goal of their protection and that of the community will be sharply defended as not being very different from what is already being done by a variety of social scientists.

Some of the major problems of the 1950s, such as gang delinquency, and the civil disorders of the 1960s will return as major police problems.

A more sympathetic Supreme Court may deflect the police from a service-oriented or legalistic role, back to an older, cruder style of policing, although it will probably be difficult to turn the clock back.

The implications of the Kansas City patrol experiment appear to challenge traditional beliefs as to the effectiveness of routine police patrol.[79] The experiment demonstrated that police radio patrol-cars are not the positive deterrent to crime that prevailing theory had claimed them to be. There will be much further research of this kind to confirm or disconfirm the Kansas City findings, which appeared to fly in the face of all police theory regarding the positive utility of radio-car patrol.

Of major concern to police organizations is the future direction of the FBI. Critics and advocates alike are concerned with the future of the FBI because of its extraordinary influence and residual prestige, despite Watergate and other misadventures of the agency. If the FBI continues to employ an army of domestic paid informants to spy on Americans who have not contemplated, nor committed any crimes, but may simply have espoused views unpopular with FBI functionaries, then the agency could take us down the road to the totalitarian police state.

In spite of the incredible volume of published data about the police, there remain many problems with regard to the validity of the data, especially relating to personality, social class, police culture, etc.

The foregoing issues skim only the surface. Every day brings new dilemmas; policy reverses from week to week. Under conditions of attack from without and anxiety and confusion within, the police are at the point of desperation. More than anything else law enforcement requires a restatement and clarification of its mission.

However, a police professionalism oriented toward technical expertise and proficiency, with an overlay of the argot of the academic world but without any real internalization of the traditional humanistic values of the ancient professions, is dangerous for police practitioners and the society they are intended to serve and protect. To date the police appear more interested in power than in the conventional norms and values of a profession. They applaud and vigorously seek the autonomy of the professional but are rather superficial and perfunctory in developing the kind of systematic knowledge base, academic involvement and research orientation, colleagueship, service ideal, critical self-analysis, and nonbureaucratic controls that are hallmarks of professionalism.

However, the latent consequences of sending young police officers into the academic world portend radical change in the traditional values of the police and ultimately in their impact on society.[80] The irony is that what may have been an employment of the vehicle of professionalism to achieve and hold power could instead produce a disenchanted group of dissidents who displace their politically motivated superiors and work for real change in the police system instead of superficial adjustment.

Even if any of the assorted political, social, or military catastrophes that have been predicted should fail to occur, the police and their organizations are sure to be at the center of every storm in the decades ahead. The traditional route of "professionalization" alone will not be enough, either for the police or society, to assure a nonmilitary, nonpolitical police force oriented toward goals of due process, without which no society that calls itself a democracy can survive. There are at least six steps that every police officer and police organization must implement in the decade ahead to insure a truly professional force committed to due process while at the same time enjoying the perquisites and status that other professional groups in society possess. These are: (1) "embourgeoisement"; (2) debureaucratization; (3) cosmopolitanization; (4) academization; (5) service ideal; and (6) role redefinition.

Many a police officer at the time of recruitment is already possessed of well-defined perspectives characterized by simplistic views of the world. Tending to see society through the lens of limited experience, meager education, and in terms of their knowledge of people who are much like themselves, recruits have very little real knowledge or experience of contrasting life-styles. If anything, they are likely to revere authority and mistrust the new, strange, different, intellectual, or "arty." Their tolerance, if any, for sexual misconduct, atheism, extreme styles in clothing or hair, or "liberal" political views is rather low. Their handling of aggression by "directing it outwards"[81] is said to be one of the reasons they are attracted to a police career.

Yet if only part of what has been reported in the behavioral science literature is true about the attributes of the working class,[82] from which most police officers are recruited, there is an urgent need to "middle class-ify" the force. There is no intention here to extol the alleged virtues of the middle class, for there is much in middle-class culture and its relentless pursuit of material acquisition, long-term hedonism, and insensitivity to human suffering that are not worthy of emulation. Indeed, my purpose is to extract only the rational, growth aspect of middle-class life, especially those involving intellectuality, emotional restraint, tolerance, planning, and the development of skills, and apply them to the police role. In summary, that is what is proposed by the process of *embourgeoisement.*

Debureaucratization is admittedly a more difficult project—rather like growing roses without thorns. Eliminating the negative, socially destructive features of bureaucracy while retaining its productive features would require the services of a divinely endowed virtuoso. For police organizations the most negative aspect of their bureaucratic structure is the protection afforded the inept, the incompetent, the mediocre, or the pathological individual. Bureaucracy tends to compromise the service ideal—the client is too often a secondary consideration; bureaucracies make demands on the service of the organization at the expense of service to the community. The very secrecy of bureaucracy and its admonition to "cover yourself" defeat the professional goals sought by police and other aspiring professionals.

For too long the police as an occupational group have been out of the mainstream of society. This is due to more than the fact that the individual police officers find comfort in mutual support. The police simply have not been part of the other institutional communities; rather they have been a beleaguered group, functioning in an almost self-segregated enclave that tends to nourish the often resentful style characteristic of other marginal groups in society. The process of *cosmopolitanization* is one that is inevitably tied to that of *academization*; the process of planting the police occupation in a firm academic base similar to library science, nursing, or social work. Criminal justice courses are the mere beginning—an opening wedge into the academic community. Once established, there is much in the liberal arts to absorb and enjoy. Without both the social and intellectual experience of academia, there is no possibility of the police developing a base in which to nourish, develop, and transmit any sort of professional body of theory, knowledge, or technical skills.

The *service ideal* is nothing more than dedication to the needs of one's clients or constituency. Whenever there is a conflict between personal goals and that of client's interests, it is the client who must prevail. Too often bureaucracy defeats the needs of the client because it conceives of its own purposes as being paramount. Development of a service ideal is especially difficult since lip-service is given to it while much of the time the client's needs are ignored.

It will perhaps be somewhat easier in the short run to effect *role redefinition* than any of the other processes. Much police work is of the social work, caretaker, counseling type. Thus, the police function must be reviewed and at least narrowed to the kind of activities that would make the occupation more reasonable in its scope. At present, these varied activities have reduced the law enforcement–crime control functions of the police to less than 20 percent of their total working time. By the same token, to organize police crime-control activities in order to largely deal with those offenses engaged in by the marginal working classes and the underclass constitutes a mockery of their function and betrays the essence of policing. The police should not continue to serve in their historical role as "zoo-keepers" of the "dangerous classes." A more sophisticated, professionalized police could pay more attention to "upperworld" crimes that constitute the sort of problem that some government academic consultants would prefer to ignore since they enjoy warm economic and personal relationships with the persons who are corporate directors and university trustees. Limited police resources should not be diverted and expended on skid row, the problems of the mentally ill, the addicted, the alcoholic, and the emotionally disturbed individuals and their families. Appropriate funding should be made available to genuinely service those problems; not have it excised by stealth from police budgets.

Admittedly, the police have no choice; they have been thrust into the role of caretakers of every malaise of the underside of society, its neglect, and its failures. When one is responsible for "everything," one is also vulnerable for the inevitable mistakes in carrying out the impossible. That is the heart of the police officer's lot. It is well to remember the most important aspect of the police that is seldom spelled out in the police literature—governments may come and go, but the police remain, regardless of the character or composition of political systems.

REFERENCES

1. Abraham S. Goldstein, "The State and the Accused: Balance of Advantage in Criminal Procedure," *Yale Law Journal* 69 (June 1960), pp. 1148–1199; Donald Black, *The Manners and Customs of the Police*. New York: Academic Press, 1980.

2. See Ronald Goldfarb, *Ransom* (New York: Harper & Row, 1965), for an excellent analysis of the manner in which an archaic bail system tends to corrupt and often defeat the pursuit of justice; and Edward J. Shaughnessy, *Bail and Preventive Detention in New York* (Washington, D.C.: University Press of America, 1982).

3. Abraham S. Blumberg, "The Practice of Law As Confidence Game," *Law and Society Review* (June 1967), pp. 15–39; Alan M. Dershowitz, *The Best Defense*. New York: Random House, 1982.

4. Norval Morris, "Politics and Pragmatism in Crime Control," *Federal Probation*, XXXII (June 1968), 9–16; Arthur I. Stinchcombe, "Institutions of Privacy in the Determination of Police Administrative Practice," *American Journal of Sociology*, LXIX (September 1963), 150–160.

5. Seymour M. Lipset, "Why Cops Hate Liberals—and Vice Versa," *Atlantic Monthly* (March 1969), p. 83.

6. *Law Enforcement and Criminal Justice: Education Directory* 1975–1976, Gaithersburg, MD.: International Association of Chiefs of Police, 1975.

7. *Statistical Abstract of the United States, 1982–1983*, Washington, D.C.: U.S. Bureau of the Census, pp. 185 and 303.

8. Arthur Niederhoffer, *Behind the Shield*. Garden City, N.Y.: Doubleday, 1967, pp. 33–40; and John H. McNamara, "Uncertainties in Police Work: The Relevance of Police Recruits' Background and Training," in David J. Bordua, Ed., *The Police: Six Sociological Essays*. New York: Wiley, 1967, pp. 191–195.

9. James Q. Wilson, "Generational and Ethnic Differences among Career Police Officers," *American Journal of Sociology*, LXIX (March 1964), 522–528.

10. Alan E. Bent, *The Politics of Law Enforcement*. Lexington, Mass.: Heath, 1974, pp. 15–16.

11. C. Abraham Fenster, Carl F. Wiedeman, and Bernard Locke, "Police Personality: Social Science Folklore and Psychological Measurement," in B. D. Sales, Ed., *Psychology in the Legal Process*. New York: S. P. Books Division of Spectrum Publications, 1978, pp. 89–109.

12. McNamara, *op. cit.*, p. 167.

13. Robert M. Fogelson, *Big City Police*. Cambridge, Mass.: Harvard University Press, 1977, p. 236.

14. David Fellman, *The Defendant's Rights Today*. Madison, Wis.: University of Wisconsin Press, 1976, pp. 25–42.

15. *Report of the National Advisory Commission on Civil Disorders*, New York, 1968. Washington, D.C.: U.S. Government Printing Office.

16. Michael Harrington, *The Other America*. New York: Penguin Books, 1964, p. 16.

17. Niederhoffer, *op. cit.*, p. 17.

18. Ramsey Clark, *Crime in America*. New York: Simon and Schuster, 1971, p. 139.

19. Lloyd L. Weinreb, *Denial of Justice*. New York: Free Press, 1977, pp. 13–43.

20. See, for example, James Q. Wilson, *Varieties of Police Behavior*. New York: Atheneum, 1971, pp. 18–19.

21. Elaine Cumming, Ian M. Cumming, and Laura Edell, "Policeman as Philosopher, Guide and Friend," *Social Problems*, 12 (Winter 1965), 276–286, especially p. 279. (This reading is included in this book; see Section 6, the first reading.)

22. Andrew Hacker, "Safety Last," *New York Review of Books*, September 15, 1977, pp. 3–8.

23. Herman Goldstein, *Policing a Free Society*. Cambridge, Mass.: Ballinger, 1977, pp. 32–33.

24. See William Turner, *The Police Establishment* (New York: G. P. Putnam's Sons, 1968), *passim*; and Richard Quinney, *Critique of Legal Order* (Boston: Little, Brown, 1974), pp. 95–135.

25. Paul Chevigny in *Police Power* (New York: Pantheon, 1969) documents a good deal of the criticism of police in a major city.

26. Donald G. Black, "Production of Crime Rates," *American Sociological Review*, XXXV (August 1970), 733–748.

27. William A. Westley, *Violence and the Police*, Cambridge, Mass.: MIT Press, 1970, pp. 40–42; Jonathan Rubinstein, *City Police*, New York: Farrar, Straus and Giroux, 1973, pp. 174–217; Albert J. Reiss, Jr., *The Police and the Public*, New Haven: Yale University Press, 1971, pp. 13–15, 19–21, 83–84; and Jerome H. Skolnick, *Justice without Trial*, New York: Wiley, 1966, pp. 112–138.

28. Donald J. Black and Albert J. Reiss, Jr., "Police Control of Juveniles," *American Sociological Review*, XXXV (February 1970), 63–87.

29. See William M. Bowsky, "The Medieval Com-

mune and Internal Violence: Police Power and Public Safety in Siena, 1287–1355," *American Historical Review*, 73, 1 (October 1967), 1–17; Herbert Asbury, *The Gangs of New York* (New York: Knopf, 1928); James McCague, *The Second Rebellion: The Story of the New York City Draft Riots of 1863* (New York: Dial Press, 1968); Joseph Boskin, *Urban Racial Violence in the Twentieth Century*. (Beverly Hills, Ca.: Glencoe Press, 1969); and Joel Samaha, *Law and Order in Historical Perspective* (New York: Academic Press, 1974).

30. Emile Durkheim, *The Rules of Sociological Method*. New York: Free Press, 1964, p. 67.

31. James S. Wallerstein and Clement J. Wyle, "Our Law-Abiding Lawbreakers," *Probation*, 25, March–April, 1947, 107–112; Austin L. Porterfield, *Youth in Trouble*. Fort Worth, Tex.: Leo Potishman Foundation, 1946; F. Ivan Nye, *Family Relationships and Delinquent Behavior*. New York: Wiley, 1958.

32. Kai T. Erikson, *Wayward Puritans*. New York: Wiley, 1966; Howard S. Becker, *Outsiders: Studies in the Sociology of Deviance*. New York: Free Press, 1963.

33. Walter V. Schaefer, "Federalism and State Criminal Procedure," *Harvard Law Review*, LXX (November 1956), 26.

34. L. P. Tiffany, D. M. McIntyre, and D. L. Rotenberg, *Detection of Crime*. Boston: Little, Brown, 1967; and Donald J. Newman, *Conviction*. Boston: Little, Brown, 1966.

35. Chevigny, *op cit.*; and James Q. Wilson, "Do The Police Prevent Crime?" *New York Times Magazine*, October 6, 1974, p. 8. See also James Q. Wilson, "Dilemmas of Police Administration," *Public Administration Review*, XXVIII (September–October 1968), 407–417.

36. Thomas A. Reppetto, "The Uneasy Milieu of the Detective," in Arthur Niederhoffer and Abraham S. Blumberg, Eds., *The Ambivalent Force* (New York: Holt, Rinehart and Winston, 1976, pp. 130–136); Richard V. Ericson, *Making Crime: A Study of Detective Work* (Toronto: Butterworths, 1981); William B. Sanders, *Detective Work* (New York: Free Press, 1977); Peter Manning, *The Narcs' Game* (Cambridge, Ma.: MIT Press, 1980).

37. George E. Homans, *Social Behavior: Its Elementary Forms*. New York: Free Press, 1961.

38. Herbert L. Packer, *The Limits of the Criminal Sanction*. Stanford, Ca.: Stanford University Press, 1968.

39. Abraham S. Blumberg, *Criminal Justice* (New York: Franklin Watts, 1979); Jerome H. Skolnick, *Justice without Trial* (New York: Wiley, 1975); Arthur Rosett and Donald R. Cressey, *Justice by Consent* (New York: Lippincott, 1976).

40. Nicholas Alex, *Black in Blue*. New York: Appleton-Century-Crofts, 1969.

41. Arthur Niederhoffer, *Behind the Shield*. Garden City, N.Y.: Doubleday, 1967, p . 151. See also David H. Bayley and Harold Mendelsohn, *Minorities and the Police* (New York: Free Press, 1969).

42. William Ryan, *Blaming the Victim*, rev. ed. New York: Vintage Books, 1976, p. 10.

43. Wayne R. LaFave, *Arrest: The Decision to Take Suspect into Custody* (Boston: Little, Brown, 1965); and James Q. Wilson, *Varieties of Police Behavior* (New York: Atheneum, 1976).

44. Morris Janowitz, *The Professional Soldier*. New York: Free Press, 1964, p. 175.

45. George L. Kirkham, "From Professor to Patrolman," *Journal of Police Science and Administration*, II, June 1974, 127–137; and Studs Terkel, *Working*. New York: Avon Books, 1974, pp. 739–748.

46. Niederhoffer, *op. cit.*, p. 131.

47. Peter Manning, "The Researcher: An Alien in the Police World," in Niederhoffer and Blumberg, *op. cit.*, p. 120.

48. Chevigny, *op. cit.*, pp. 242–247; and Joseph Wambaugh, *The Choir Boys*. New York: Dell, 1976.

49. Richard E. Sykes, James C. Fox, and John P. Clark, "A Socio-Legal Theory of Police Discretion," in Niederhoffer and Blumberg, *op. cit.*, p. 181.

50. William Ker Muir, Jr., *Police: Streetcorner Politicians*. Chicago: University of Chicago Press, 1977, pp. 71–72, 77–79.

51. William A. Westley, *Violence and the Police*. Cambridge, Mass.: MIT Press, 1970, p. 111.

52. Rodney Stark, *Police Riots* (Belmont, Ca.: Wadsworth, 1972, p. 181.

53. Helen Dudar, "The Price of Blowing the Whistle," *New York Times Magazine*, October 30, 1977, pp. 41–54.

54. Julie Baumgold, "Cop Couples: Till Death Do Them Part," *New York*, June 19, 1972, pp. 31–36.

55. Nicholas Alex, *New York Cops Talk Back: A Study of a Beleaguered Minority*. New York: Wiley, 1976.

56. Joseph Wambaugh, *The Blue Knight*. Boston: G. K. Hall, 1973; and Joseph Wambaugh, *The New Centurions*. Boston: Little, Brown, 1971.

57. Richard N. Harris, *The Police Academy: An Inside View*. New York: Wiley, 1973, p. 18.

58. Niederhoffer, *op. cit.*, p. 232.

59. Muir, *op. cit.*, pp. 178–179.

60. Rubinstein, *op cit.*, pp. 218–226.

61. Peter Berger, *Invitation to Sociology*. Garden City: Doubleday, 1963, pp. 25–53.

62. Michael Banton, *The Policeman in the Community*. New York: Basic Books, 1964, p. 198.

63. Arthur Niederhoffer and Elaine Niederhoffer, *The Police Family: From Station House to Ranch House*. Lexington, Mass.: Heath, 1978.

64. LaFave, *op. cit.*, pp. 83–89, 114–124. See also Egon Bittner, *The Function of Police in Modern Society*, Washington, D.C.: National Institute of Mental Health, 1970.

65. Kenneth Culp Davis, "An Approach to Legal Control of the Police," *Texas Law Review*, LII, 1974, pp. 703–725.

66. See Arthur Niederhoffer, *Behind the Shield, op. cit.*; Jerome H. Skolnick, *op. cit.*; Albert J. Reiss, Jr., *op. cit.*; Paul Chevigny, *Cops and Rebels* (New York: Pantheon Books, 1972); James Q. Wilson, *Varieties of Police Behavior* (New York: Atheneum, 1971); Jonathan Rubinstein, *op. cit.*; Thomas A. Reppetto, *The Blue Parade* (New York: Free Press, 1978); Donald Black, *op. cit.*; Michael K. Brown, *Working the Street* (New York: Russell Sage Foundation, 1981).

67. Ruth G. Weintraub and Harriet Pollack, "The New Supreme Court and the Police," in Arthur Niederhoffer and Abraham S. Blumberg, *op. cit.*, pp. 257–268.

68. See, for example, L. P. Tiffany, et al., *op. cit.*

69. See Peter K. Manning, *Police Work: The Social Organization of Policing* (Cambridge, Mass.: MIT Press, 1977).

70. Arthur Niederhoffer and Abraham S. Blumberg, Eds., *The Ambivalent Force: Perspectives on the Police*, 2nd ed., New York: Holt, Rinehart and Winston, 1976.

71. Charles E. Silberman, *Criminal Violence, Criminal Justice*. New York: Random House, 1978, pp. 199–252.

72. Harold L. Wilensky, "The Professionalization of Everyone?" *American Journal of Sociology*, LXX (September 1964), 137–158.

73. Richard N. Harris, *op. cit.*, p. 38.

74. Bernard Cohen and Jan M. Chaikin, *Police Background, Characteristics and Performance*. New York: The Rand Corporation, 1972.

75. David Lewin and John H. Keith, "Managerial Responses to Perceived Labor Shortages: The Case of the Police," *Criminology*, XIV (May 1976), 65–87.

76. Howard M. Vollmer and Donald J. Mills, Eds. *Professionalization*. Englewood Cliffs, N.J.: Prentice-Hall, 1966.

77. James C. Thompson, Jr., "How Could Vietnam Happen?" *Atlantic Monthly*, April 1968, pp. 47–53.

78. Barry Bluestone and Bennett Harrison, *The Deindustrialization of America*. New York: Basic Books, 1982.

79. G. L. Kelling, T. Pate, C. Dieckman, and C. E. Brown, *The Kansas City Preventive Patrol Experiment*. Washington, D.C.: Police Foundation, 1974.

80. See Harris, *op. cit.*, for a critical view of police academy training.

81. Albert K. Cohen and Harold M. Hodges, "Lower-Blue-Collar-Class Characteristics," *Social Problems*, X (Spring 1963), 303–334.

82. Seymour M. Lipset, *Political Man*. Garden City, N.Y.: Doubleday, 1960, pp. 97–130.

The Triumph of Reform: Police Professionalism 1920–1965

David R. Johnson

Police departments changed dramatically between 1920 and 1965. The nineteenth century police had emphasized a flexible approach to law enforcement as a way of dealing with the diversity and conflicts of urban society. This approach had allowed local politicians to dictate police policies, department organization, and personnel selection. After 1920, new reformers campaigned successfully to alter the philosophy, organization, and personnel of police departments across the nation. An emphasis on uniform standards replaced the previous reliance on flexibility. Uniform enforcement policies drastically reduced the role politicians formerly had in police affairs because the new em-

SOURCE: Reprinted by permission of the publisher, Forum Press, Inc., from David Johnson, *American Law Enforcement: A History*, copyright © 1981, by The Forum Press, Inc., Arlington Heights, Illinois.

phasis undermined the politician's role as mediator between behavior and the law. Changes in departmental organization also diminished political meddling. Reformers replaced the old, decentralized precincts with highly centralized bureaucracies. Ward politicians therefore had less influence over the administrative decisions which affected their communities. At the same time, centralization increased the power and importance of police chiefs. Finally, the reformers were able to increase the quality of policemen by imposing more rigorous educational and physical standards, and by introducing more effective training. The combined changes in the philosophy, organization, and personnel of the police created a new approach to law enforcement which was significantly different from the nineteenth century's approach.

All of these changes were the consequences of a single idea: the desire to make policing a profession. There was, and is, considerable debate over whether policing can ever be a profession, but the reformers responsible for transforming the police after 1920 had no doubts. They thought that policing *ought* to be a profession, and set out to make it one. In order to achieve that goal, the reformers sought one thing above all else: autonomy. Freedom from outside interference in departmental affairs was absolutely vital. Protected by this freedom, police officials would have the ability to correct many of the defects in their organizations and personnel which prevented the public from regarding policing as a profession.

The new reform campaign owed a great deal to three separate developments: 1) the influence of European achievements on law enforcement; 2) changes in society and politics in American cities after 1920; and 3) the emergence of a new kind of police reform movement. Each development made fundamental contributions to the emergence of a professional police in the twentieth century. In fact, professionalization would have been impossible without them and the quest for police autonomy would have failed.

EUROPEAN ACHIEVEMENT: CRIMINALISTICS

Europeans pioneered in the application of scientific methods to police work. Their progress in this area was due to the special characteristics of continental police administration and to the impact of science on late nineteenth century life. With few exceptions, the national government in each European country controlled the police departments of every large city. Policemen served their central, not their local, governments, and had far greater powers to interfere in the lives of ordinary people than was the case in England or America. Department officials belonged to the national civil service, and therefore had no political allegiances within the cities which would interfere with their duties. Furthermore, these officials did not obtain their jobs after years of service as patrolmen. They were university graduates who usually had training as army officers or lawyers before they became police officials. As professional civil servants who had broad theoretical knowledge about law enforcement, these men were committed to efficient, effective policing.

As university graduates, these officials had been exposed to a wide variety of advances in science. By the middle of the nineteenth century sciences such as biology, zoology, and geology had captured the attention of most informed Europeans. Major theories, such as Charles Darwin's ideas about natural selection, undermined the dominant explanations about the nature and progress of mankind. Whatever one thought of the new theories, there was no denying that science and scientists suddenly enjoyed tremendous prestige. Their work caused a major change in the way people thought. European police officials joined in the general enthusiasm for the scientific method. They read widely in many areas, such as anthropology, biology, and chemistry, for solutions to practical problems in law enforcement. In effect, these officials became amateur scientists seeking to advance knowledge within their particular profession.

Among the practical problems facing police officials at the time, none were more important than the investigation and prosecution of crime and criminals. Both problems had become critical because there were almost no guidelines for identifying suspects, assembling evidence at a crime scene, and presenting cases in court. Criminals often escaped detection or punishment through police ineptitude. The two most important men who worked on these problems were Alphonse Bertillon and Hans Gross. During the 1880s these two men founded the modern police science of criminalistics.

Bertillon (1853–1914) became the more widely known of these two amateur police scientists. He was born to a middle-class French family whose father, a doctor, dabbled with statistics and anthropology. These subjects influenced Bertillon's own intellectual development and gave him some preparation for his first job in the Paris Prefecture of Police. Shortly thereafter promotion to records clerk marked the beginning of a brilliant career.

His new job required Bertillon to record the descriptions of all prisoners being held by the Paris Police. It did not take long for him to develop a contempt for the chaotic system in use at the time. His familiarity with the ideas and methods of anthropology made him aware of the appalling state of the basic information in these files. Uniform standards for describing and identifying criminals simply did not exist.

Bertillon remedied this situation. In 1878 he began devoting much of his time to developing a more systematic descriptive method. His goal was to identify individual, repeat offenders so that the judicial system could deal with this class of criminals more effectively. After years of work, Bertillon finally made his first positive identification of a recidivist in 1883. Further research perfected his methods, and in 1885 he published *Identification Anthropométrique (Anthropometric Identification)*, a landmark in the development of criminalistics. For the first time in the history of law enforcement, the police had the ability to identify individual criminals by means of their physical characteristics.

The Bertillon System had four components: precise physical measurements; precise notations on the location of distinguishing features like scars; a photograph; and, later, fingerprints. In an effort to simplify the system, Bertillon eventually devised eleven key physical measurements grouped into three general categories (the entire body; the head; the appendages). He also invented several standardized instruments to promote uniform recording procedures. Although pictures of offenders had been in use for some time, Bertillon standardized the types of photographs (full front; full profile). During the 1890s he incorporated fingerprints into his system because they represented one more piece of physical evidence.

By 1900 the Bertillon System had become the standard method for classifying criminal records in Europe and America. But Bertillon's contribution to criminalistics did not rest solely upon his famous system. He also had a number of important ideas for improving the collection and analysis of evidence. Among other things, Bertillon introduced the use of photography to preserve a crime scene; he developed a means for preserving footprints; and he advocated handwriting analysis as a crucial tool in investigations. These ideas were important steps in the development of police laboratories where the physical evidence of a crime could be subjected to scientific analysis.

While Bertillon concentrated on the problem of identifying criminals, Hans Gross devoted most of his time to the difficulties of gathering and interpreting evidence. Gross (1847–1915) was the son of an Austrian army administration officer. After completing his formal education, and earning a Doctor of Jurisprudence degree in 1870, Gross became an examining justice, a court official responsible for the detection of crime.

As a court prosecutor, Gross soon learned about the inadequacies of ordinary patrolmen and detectives as state witnesses in criminal trials. He discovered that their only resources in solving cases were individual shrewdness and practical experience, a combination of skills not every officer possessed. Furthermore, policemen had no systematic methods for dealing with physical evidence. In fact, they frequently overlooked important clues or failed to appreciate their significance. During the 1870s Gross searched for solutions to these problems, reading widely to familiarize himself with the latest scientific theories and methods of his era.

Gross published the results of his studies in 1883, in *Handbuch für Untersuchungsrichter als System der Kriminalistik (Manual for the Examining Magistrate: A System of Criminalistics)*. This seminal work was based on two assumptions: 1) the police should become familiar with the psychology of criminal behavior; and 2) the police should adopt any technical and scientific procedures which might be useful in analyzing a crime scene and its evidence. The second assumption became the basis of modern criminalistics. Every chapter dealt with a major issue in a systematic fashion. Gross wrote in considerable detail about the proper qualifications for police investigators, and he provided the first explanation of the appropriate techniques for analyzing a crime scene. Other chapters described the kinds of special equipment an investigator needed and discussed the role of experts in criminal cases. Gross also wrote about the importance of bloodstains and other physical evidence. His book was so thorough that it remains significant after nearly a century.

Having placed crime detection on a scientific basis, Gross next helped make criminalistics a respected subject for advanced study. Between 1898 and 1914 several European universities established professorships in scientific crime detection. Gross held several of these appointments before returning to his hometown to accept a professorship at the Universsity of Graz in 1905. Later, in 1912, he opened one of the first Criminalistic Institutes, an idea which spread quickly to other universities in Lausanne, Rome, Bucharest, and Vienna. Gross and other pioneers in criminalistics trained dozens of students in his new field, and as these graduates took positions in law enforcement they spread the doctrine of scientific police work. Their expertise and availability made it possible for many European cities to establish police laboratories prior to 1914. Thanks to the efforts of men like Bertillon and Gross, European police were thoroughly committed to scientific approaches to their work by World War I.

EUROPEAN ACHIEVEMENTS: FINGERPRINTING

Bertillon based his famous system on the assumption that every individual's physical features are unique. Anthropological studies at the time supported this assumption, but unfortunately they were wrong. In 1904 federal prison officials at Leavenworth discovered two convicts who had precisely the same measurements. This discovery undermined the Bertillon System and created the need for a more accurate identification method. Although it had not yet been widely accepted, the solution to this problem had already been developed. Dactyloscopy, the technique of collecting, classifying, and identifying fingerprints, was destined to become yet another major contribution Europeans made to the emergence of police science.

Amateur scientists were once again in the forefront of criminalistic innovations. Dr. Henry Faulds and Sir William J. Herschel pioneered the study of fingerprints. Faulds was an English Presbyterian minister who worked as a missionary in Japan; Herschel spent his career as a British civil servant in India. Neither man had any training in law enforcement. They developed their interest in fingerprints through highly specialized circumstances related to their work, and neither knew of the other's research for many years.

Faulds (1843–1930) began collecting fingerprints as a hobby during the 1870s. In 1879 the Japanese police asked Faulds to try his luck at identifying a burglar from some fingerprints he had left. Shortly afterward, Faulds did so. He then exceeded that feat by developing a method for lifting latent prints and using the evidence he collected to identify yet another thief. Convinced that he now had developed a scientific means for crime detection, Faulds published an article about his research in the prestigious journal *Nature* in 1880. He thereby became the first person to recognize the use of fingerprints for identifying individuals in criminal cases.

Independently of Faulds and at the same time, William Herschel (1843–1917) arrived at similar conclusions from a different perspective. Herschel had a practical problem to solve in his work as magistrate: he needed a way to prevent fraud in settling native claims against the British government. He accomplished this by using an Asian superstition that manual contact with a business contract created a taboo against its violation. Claimants were required to acknowledge payments by affixing their partial, inked prints to legal papers. In 1877 he proposed that the British record the prints of all Indian prisoners as a way to discourage recidivism. The prison officials rejected his idea, and Herschel retired in 1879 without pursuing the matter further.

Except for a bitter fight between Herschel and Faulds over which man had "discovered" fingerprints, nothing significant occurred in the use of this new idea until 1888. Then Sir Francis Galton, one of England's most renowned scientists, received an invitation to lecture about the Bertillon System at a leading scientific institute. In preparing for his speech, Galton investigated fingerprints as an alternative method of identification. What he found intrigued him. Galton obtained Herschel's collection of prints and used it to prove two critical ideas which the amateur scientists had only asserted. First, Galton determined that an individual's prints do not change over his lifetime. Second, he demonstrated that each individual's prints are unique. Galton then made his last important contribution by devising the first system for classifying prints. This system appeared in his classic book, *Fingerprints*, published in 1892. As a result of Galton's work, Scotland Yard in 1894 adopted a modified version of the Bertillon System which included prints.

After some further refinements, European police quickly accepted fingerprints as an important tool. Elsewhere, progress was much slower. Argentina, in 1896, actually became the first nation to adopt fingerprints as the official means for identifying criminals. This achievement was due to Juan Vucetich, an Austrian immigrant who developed his own classification system independently of other researchers. The American police lagged behind, although an important breakthrough occurred in 1904 at the St. Louis World's Fair, where Scotland Yard detective John Ferrier demonstrated fingerprinting to an interested group of police officials. The St. Louis police promptly established the first fingerprint bureau in the United States. But the prevailing philosophy of policing, which sacrificed professionalism to politics, hindered progress. Too few policemen had a commitment to improving their work by scientific means.

European advances in criminalistics had created a credible basis for connecting law enforcement to science by 1914. This was a major contribution to the development of police professionalism. European police officials rapidly adopted criminalistics because the traditions of centralized administration and responsible civil service gave them the authority and ability to do so. American police reformers would eventually capitalize on these achievements too. Once they acquired power, these reformers would increase the prestige of policing by incorporating scientific precision, impartiality, and decisiveness into crime detection. The American public would learn to respect lawmen who successfully used this European heritage. But improvement in the image and performance of the police awaited other developments within the United States.

SOCIETY AND POLITICS IN AMERICAN CITIES

Urban America underwent extraordinary changes between 1920 and 1965, which affected the ways Americans lived, worked, and thought. While none of these developments involved the police directly, they reshaped the society which law enforcement served. After 1920 a new social and economic environment would encourage the police to adopt a different approach to their work.

The American economy shifted its emphasis during the 1920s. Prior to World War I businessmen had developed the nation's natural resources, transformed agriculture, built a national transportation system, and created the world's most productive iron and steel industry. After 1920, businessmen turned to the production of consumer goods. Factories which made consumer products needed large land areas to accommodate their assembly lines and sought space on the edges of cities. Workers followed the factories into suburbia. The central cities therefore lost thousands of jobs and residents.

Cities also lost many of their inhabitants because of suburbanization. By the mid-1960s nearly 70 percent of all Americans would be living in metropolitan areas. Within those areas, the most rapid growth occurred in the suburbs. The American dream of homeownership was fulfilled primarily by buying a house in a new subdivision outside the central city. By 1970 suburbanites outnumbered city residents.

As the upper classes moved to the suburbs, they left behind people who were increasingly unlike them. Dramatic changes in immigration, and new trends in population movements within America, produced a very different type of inner-city resident. After Congress severely restricted European immigration beginning in 1921, thousands of Spanish-speaking immigrants from Mexico, Puerto Rico, and Cuba streamed into the United States. Like the Europeans before them, most of these people settled in cities, in neighborhoods close to the downtowns.

Black Americans joined the cityward migration. Job opportunities attracted them to cities, beginning in World War I. Thousands, and then millions of blacks left rural areas in search of better wages, working conditions, and living standards. Northern factories hired large numbers of them, while others found employment in hotels, restaurants, nightclubs, and other booming service industries. By the mid-1960s black Americans had essentially relocated themselves. Nearly 75 percent of them lived in cities. Like the Spanish-speaking immigrants, blacks concentrated in the inner-city neighborhoods.

These new city residents shared four things in common: they were nonwhite, unskilled, poor, and powerless. Mexicans, Puerto Ricans, Cubans, and blacks would be subjected to enormous discrimination. Their ability to improve themselves would be restricted because whites would systematically exclude them from high paying jobs, good schools, and decent housing. Economic changes reinforced social discrimination. These newcomers had arrived in cities at a time of decreasing demand for unskilled labor. American industry now needed well-trained, highly skilled workers, and nonwhites (with some exceptions) did not have those qualifications. Poverty had driven these people to seek opportunities in the cities, but for many of them poverty would remain a way of life. And until the 1960s blacks and Spanish-speaking Americans would be almost powerless to help themselves. Whites dominated urban politics and paid little attention to the needs of the new inner-city residents.

Urban politics had to adjust to two basic developments after 1920. First, the organization of politics altered. Secondly, voters' expectations and attitudes changed. Both changes resulted from the ways urban society and economics evolved after World War I. Politicians did not become less important, nor did they necessarily become less powerful, but they did have to modify their behavior to deal with new situations and ideas.

Metropolitan fragmentation was one important trend which affected the organization of politics after 1920. Suburbanites increasingly incorporated as separate political units. In the long run, this fragmentation meant an enormous duplication of services and a decline in per capita tax revenues in the central cities. Politicians therefore found it nearly impossible to organize effective solutions to problems shared by all the communities within a metropolitan area.

The use of experts also affected politics. During the Progressive era many Americans became convinced that cities could improve their services by employing people specifically trained to perform certain tasks. After 1920, cities across the nation began hiring thousands of experts who complicated the lives of politicians in two ways. First, the use of experts deprived politicians of valuable patronage. Secondly, municipal departments run by experts were harder to control. Experts regarded politicians as ignorant meddlers who should be resisted whenever possible.

Changes in voter expectations and attitudes, which also affected politics, reflected the increasing importance of middle-class values which stressed efficiency, honesty, and economy as the basis of sound government. Until the 1920s urban politics had been notorious for being so totally opposite to these values. Corruption, inefficiency, and excessive costs certainly did not disappear from local government. But compared to the nineteenth century, these problems became less common. Political organizations and officeholders had to make serious efforts to implement the standards which the largest voting block in the cities demanded.

The predominance of middle-class values and the deconcentration of political power in a transformed metropolis contributed substantially to the emergence of a new model for law enforcement. Expertise, honesty, and efficiency were the basis for professionalism. These ideals had shaped the development of many professions prior to World War I, and the progressives had laid the groundwork for applying these standards to police work. After 1920 the concept of professionalism could be used as the framework for police reform because middle-class Americans understood its advantages and supported its application to law enforcement. Urban politicians no longer had the ability or the desire to block this development. Reformers would now acquire the independence to reshape police departments according to their own desires.

POLICE REFORM, 1920–39: INITIAL DEVELOPMENTS

Police professionalism did not immediately become the dominant model in law enforcement. Professionalism would triumph only after nearly three decades of struggle. In these initial years, progress came in two forms: 1) efforts to redefine the police mission and 2) changes forced upon departments by the Great Depression.

The effort to redefine the police mission concentrated on a single idea: crime fighting. It did not matter that the police had a long and important historical role in community relations work or that they spent a great deal of their time with mundane affairs. What mattered was the public's *image* of the police. The average citizen who knew nothing about routine police work did know about crime. Crime concerned and frequently frightened him. In order to change their image the police realized they needed to emphasize the dramatic aspects of their work. They set out to do exactly that.

During the 1930s J. Edgar Hoover, as director of the Federal Bureau of Investigation, did a great deal to advance the crime-fighter image. A variety of gangs and individuals were making spectacular names as bank robbers and desperadoes. Hoover, in a stroke of genius, labeled these people "public enemies" and ordered his agents to hunt them down. Within a few years the FBI violently ended the careers of John Dillinger, Baby Face Nelson, Pretty Boy Floyd, and Ma Barker. The nationwide pursuit of these criminals, followed by their demise in an orgy of bloodletting, captivated the public. Hoover used this campaign as a means to make the FBI the most important law enforcement agency in America. But his efforts reinforced the growing image of all policemen as crime fighters. . . .

The police also sought scientific support for their image. Fingerprinting had been making slow progress since its initial appearance before World War I. The International Association of Chiefs of Police lobbied unsuccessfully for years to establish a national bureau which would collect and analyze prints. Progress had been somewhat better in the states. By 1921 five states had established identification bureaus. Then in 1924 Congress finally authorized such a bureau within the Justice Department. Following this victory, the IACP, with Hoover's help, increased its efforts to establish a nationwide system of fingerprint agencies. By 1931 almost half the states had done so. During the thirties Hoover began offering the FBI's services in identifying prints and in training local officers in the use of this kind of evidence. The United States had finally accepted fingerprints as the basis for criminal identification.

Science and technology bolstered the police crime-fighting image in other ways as well. The St. Valentine's Day Massacre prompted a group of Chicago businessmen to establish the nation's first crime detection laboratory at Northwestern University in 1929. Three years later the FBI founded its laboratory, setting an example which encouraged several state and local governments to follow suit. After ignoring criminalistics for so long, the American police were moving rapidly to match and exceed European progress in this area. Radios and automobiles introduced policemen to the wonders of technology. The first radio patrol car appeared in Detroit in 1929. During the thirties police departments across the country largely abolished foot patrols, put their men in cars, and coordinated their activities through radio communications.

Police officials rapidly became devoted to scientific and technological innovations because these developments had the greatest immediate potential to transform the policeman's image. Criminalistics helped overcome the notion that the average cop was a dumb brute who beat confessions out of prisoners. Scientific investigations required intelligence and skill, not brute force. Patrol cars and radios made the police more mobile and more able to respond rapidly to calls for help. Gone (supposedly) were the patrolmen who slept on their beats and who were never around when needed. Technology had made the police more effective and efficient. Reality did not always match the new image, but a public long accustomed to the old-fashioned, corrupt, incompetent cop was impressed by the change and delighted with the idea of a scientific crime fighter.

The Great Depression also made important contributions to the growth of reform. Financial problems overcame political opposition to a major reform objective: greater departmental centralization. During the 1930s the number of precinct stations in most cities declined significantly. Police chiefs, inspired by the example of European administrators, seized this opportunity to increase their power. They switched more men to patrol car duty and proliferated the use of specialized squads which operated from central headquarters. More patrolmen came under the direct orders of headquarters personnel who used the radio network to monitor their activities more closely. Membership in specialized squads also enhanced supervisory controls, since these men now answered directly to a superior officer rather than to a ward politician.

Hard times also made more qualified police recruits available. For the first time in history, police work became attractive to men from the middle class who had better educations than the average, old-style patrolman. The presence of these recruits enabled administrators to find men who could understand the importance of criminalistics and who would make good commanders. In addition, police chiefs now had the excuse they needed to raise intelligence and educational standards for applicants. Men who were less-well-trained now found it more difficult to obtain positions, or, if they were already on a department's roster, they found it harder to win promotions. The Depression therefore contributed to an upgrading in the overall quality of police personnel.

POLICE REFORM 1939–65: THE NEW PROFESSIONALS

By the end of the 1930s, the police had made considerable progress toward establishing their claim to professional status. One last obstacle remained: the absence of an effective national leadership which could achieve autonomy from politics. The initial period of reform prepared the way for the emergence of men who would assume leadership roles after 1939. Most of these men rose through the ranks of local departments to become police chiefs. Some came from the FBI, where professionalism had received an early and enthusiastic boost from Hoover. All had one thing in common: they had chosen a career in law enforcement at a time of widespread experimentation in policing. They therefore experienced at firsthand the impact of the crime-fighting image, scientific detection, and technology on the public's attitude toward the police.

Orlando W. Wilson and William H. Parker became the two most prominent spokesmen for the new professionalism. Wilson learned police reform while a patrolman under August Vollmer at Berkeley in 1921. As police chief in Wichita, Kansas, beginning in 1928,

Wilson transformed the police force. He sought more qualified, better educated recruits. At the same time, Wilson began a program to upgrade their training. His national reputation began to develop when he convinced the Kansas League of Municipalities to create a statewide police training school in 1931, and appoint him the school's director. Prominent reformers from around the country lectured to policemen-students about the latest innovations in their work.

Technology fascinated Wilson; he became a leading, if controversial, expert in its use. During his term as Wichita's police chief he attracted widespread attention by conducting the first systematic study of patrol cars. He decided that single-man squad cars were both feasible and necessary because they fulfilled the requirements of professionalism. He argued that single-man cars were efficient, effective, and economical—three key ideas in the professional model emerging in the 1930s. Brushing aside patrolmen's complaints about their personal safety when they had no partner to depend upon, Wilson claimed that the public received better service with single-man cars. This idea aroused considerable interest. The ensuing debate, which continued for the next four decades, placed Wilson at the center of an important controversy which enhanced his growing reputation.

By 1939, Wilson had achieved national prominence, but he had also irritated too many Wichita politicians for the last time. His political support gone, Wilson resigned as a police chief and accepted a professorship in police administration at the University of California at Berkeley. College training for policemen was a relatively new idea in the United States. The first complete police curriculum was offered at San Jose State College only in 1931. Congress helped popularize this notion by authorizing funds for vocational training in law enforcement in 1936. By the end of the decade several thousand officers were attending classes, but the outbreak of war halted this promising beginning. Wilson, though, was now in a position to become one of the pioneers in college programs for policemen. After World War II ended, he founded the first professional School of Criminology. As dean of this school, Wilson became an extremely influential reformer. The essence of his ideas summarized the basic ingredients of the new professionalism: 1) complete independence from politics; 2) a highly centralized command structure; 3) a college-educated rank and file; 4) the application of the most modern technology available to police work; and 5) absolute obedience and minimum discretion at the level of patrolmen. Wilson's students spread his doctrine across the nation. More than one hundred graduates of his school eventually achieved important positions in local law enforcement and implemented his ideas.

In 1960, Wilson carried the reform banner to Chicago, a city notorious for its boss system and its resistance to police professionalism. Typically, Wilson demanded complete freedom from political interference as a condition for accepting the offer to become chief of police. Ward heelers howled, but Mayor Richard Daley agreed. For the next seven years Daley consistently supported Wilson in any controversies which arose. Operating with the protection of Chicago's most powerful politician, Wilson proceeded to implement reform. He began by reorganizing the department's administrative structure. Precincts were consolidated into new units called districts. Wilson then insisted on a precise chain of command to control his men. Superior officers and their orders had to be obeyed, or individuals faced a variety of disciplinary actions. At police headquarters, Wilson reduced the staff and sent many officers back to the field. He restricted the number of people who reported directly to him by creating a small number of assistant-to-the-chief positions. Each assistant handled a particular administrative area, leaving Wilson free to deal with general policy and further reforms. Technological change became a hallmark of his administration. Wilson introduced the latest communications equipment. Experiments with this technology enabled him to distribute the department's personnel more efficiently. Eventually, the police could respond to a call for aid within five minutes. Wilson retired in 1967, generally praised by grateful Chicagoans who were convinced that he had professionalized their police.

William H. Parker's fame rested on his career as chief of police in Los Angeles. Although he was not a protegé of Vollmer, many of Parker's career experiences paralleled Wilson's. Parker began as a patrolman in Los Angeles in 1927. He demonstrated an early commitment to professionalism by earning a law degree and by becoming a member of the California bar in 1930. An adept politician, Parker used his legal training to advance his career. By 1934 he was the department's trial prosecutor and an assistant to the chief. After serving in the army during World War II, Parker gained invaluable administrative experience by participating in the reorganization of the police in several German cities from 1945 to 1947. Home again, he graduated from Northwestern University's Traffic Management School. Returning to the Los Angeles Police Department (L.A.P.D.), he became an inspector of the traffic division. Parker underscored his commitment to professionalism in 1949 when he became a deputy chief in charge of prosecuting dishonest cops.

Parker became police chief in 1950 when a scandal forced the mayor to find someone with credentials in the new professionalism. Unlike Wilson, Parker assumed office without securing immediate freedom from political interference. He had to fight to achieve department autonomy. An uproar over charges of police brutality gave him the opportunity he sought in 1951. Parker conducted an intensive investigation which resulted in the dismissal or punishment of over forty officers. Shortly afterward Parker turned over some evidence of vice-squad corruption to prosecutors before a scandal erupted. Both incidents demonstrated to the public that he could handle internal problems without interference. Thereafter Parker had all the political independence he needed. In fact, he became a formidable political figure who used his power to advance reform and to undermine criticism of his department.

Firmly in power, Parker launched a campaign to transform the L.A.P.D. His greatest success, so typical of the new professionalism, came in administrative reorganization. The command structure was simplified. Then Parker combined several headquarters divisions into a single Bureau of Administration which provided general services (planning, internal investigations, etc.) to more specialized bureaus. Parker was especially fond of planning, another mark of the new professionalism. He used planning as a major propaganda weapon in his campaign to increase public respect and admiration for the police. Planners had instructions to implement middle-class values as the basis for further reforms. They worked hard to increase police efficiency and to reduce costs. Every savings, every new indicator of efficiency, became the subject of press releases in Parker's continuous public relations campaign.

Efficiency came in several forms. Parker aggressively sought ways to get every possible policeman on the streets. He freed some 200 men for patrol duty by forcing the county sheriff to assume his responsibilities for guarding prisoners. After another battle, the California Highway Patrol took over traffic control duties on the freeways criss-crossing Los Angeles. That freed more men for other work. Parker also adopted one-man patrol cars, a move which allowed him to enhance police visibility by increasing the number of cars on the streets. On a more mundane level, changes in booking procedures and traffic control also reduced costs and made more effective use of personnel.

Parker also made rigorous personnel selection and training a major characteristic of the L.A.P.D. Less than ten percent of the applicants who passed the required civil service exam actually were accepted as recruits. Higher standards of physical fitness, intelligence, and scholastic attainments weeded out many men. Others failed the psychiatric examinations which Parker now required as part of the screening process. Once accepted, recruits attended a thirteen-week academy where a rigorous physical program, rigid discipline, and intensive study in basic skills and criminal law caused many more to drop out. Those who survived soon learned that they had to maintain their high performance levels on the job. Parker thus molded an image of a tough, competent, polite, and effective officer by controlling recruitment. During the 1950s this image made the L.A.P.D. the model for reform across the nation. By the time of his death in 1966 Parker had become one of the most prominent reformers of his generation.

The 1950s marked a turning point in the history of professionalism. Following major scandals, reformers came to power across the nation. Politicians had real choices between the traditional and new models of policing because a number of professional police reformers were available for the first time. With an enraged middle class threatening their livelihoods, the politicians began opting for reform. Robert V. Murray became police chief of Washington, D.C. in 1951; Wyman W. Vernon assumed the helm in Oakland, California, in 1956; James Slavin arrived in Denver in 1962; and Edmund L. McNamara took over Boston's police in the early sixties. Many other cities also acquired chiefs dedicated to the new model of policing. By 1965 the gospel of professionalism had triumphed.

SUGGESTED READINGS

The history of twentieth century law enforcement is just beginning to attract the attention of American scholars. Samuel Walker, *A Critical History of Police Reform: The Emergence of Professionalism* (Lexington:

Lexington Books, 1977) and Robert M. Fogelson, *Big City Police* (Cambridge: Harvard University Press, 1977) approach police reform from somewhat different perspectives, but both are excellent studies for students to consult for further elaboration of the themes of professionalism. William J. Bopp assesses Wilson's career in *"O. W.": O. W. Wilson and the Search for a Police Profession* (Port Washington: Kennikat Press, 1977). Joseph G. Woods, "The Progressives and the Police: Urban Reform and the Professionalization of the Los Angeles Police" (unpublished Ph.D. thesis, University of California, L.A., 1973) is the only full-length biography of a modern police department. Woods deals extensively with William Parker's career in his closing chapters. European scholars have done most of the work on the history of criminalistics and its pioneers. Henry T. F. Rhodes, *Alphonse Bertillon* (London: G. G. Harrap, 1956), Douglas G. Browne and Alan Brock, *Fingerprints: Fifty Years of Scientific Crime Detection* (London: G. G. Harrap, 1953), and George W. Wilton, *Fingerprints: History, Law and Romance* (London: W. Hodge and Company, 1938) are all useful works in English. Shorter introductions to criminalistics can be found in articles on Bertillon, Gross, and fingerprinting in two edited books: Hermann Mannheim, Ed., *Pioneers in Criminology* (2nd ed.; Montclair, N.J.: Patterson Smith, 1972), and Philip J. Stead, *Pioneers in Policing* (Montclair, N.J.: Patterson Smith, 1977).

"To Serve and Protect": Learning from Police History

Mark H. Moore and George L. Kelling

Over the last three decades, American police departments have pursued a strategy of policing that narrowed their goals to "crime fighting," relied heavily on cars and radios to create a sense of police omnipresence, and found its justification in politically neutral professional competence. The traditional tasks of the constable—maintaining public order, regulating economic activity, and providing emergency services—have been deemphasized, and those of the professional "crime fighter" have increased. Joe Friday's polite but frosty professionalism ("Just the facts, Ma'am") is a perfect expression of the modern image.

In many ways, this strategy has been remarkably successful. Thirty years ago, the idea that the police could arrive at a crime scene anywhere in a large city in less than five minutes would have been idle dreaming, yet we now have that capability. Similarly, the idea that the police would have moved out from under the shadow of political influence and flagrant abuses of individual rights would also have seemed unrealistic, yet most people now think of the police as much more honest and professional than in the past. In fact, in many ways the current strategy of policing is the apotheosis of a reform spirit that has guided police executives for over eighty years.

It is ironic, then, that precisely at the moment of its greatest triumph, the limits of this strategy have also become apparent. The concrete experience of citizens exposed to this strategy of policing is different from what the reformers had imagined. Officers stare suspiciously at the community from automobiles, careen through city streets with sirens wailing, and arrive at a "crime scene" to comfort the victim of an offense that occurred twenty minutes earlier. They reject citizen requests for simple assistance so that they can get back "in service"—that is, back to the business of staring at the community from their cars. No wonder so many citizens find the police unresponsive. Officers treat problems which citizens take seriously—unsafe parks, loud neighbors—as unimportant. And when a group of citizens wants to talk about current police policies and procedures, they are met by a "community relations specialist" or, at best, a precinct patrol commander, neither of whom can respond to their problems without calling headquarters.

This situation would not be so bad if the police were succeeding in their crime-fighting role. But the fact of the matter is that they are not. Crime rates continue to

SOURCE: Reprinted with permission of the author from: *The Public Interest*, No. 70 (Winter 1983), pp. 49–65.

increase, and the chance that a violent crime among strangers will be solved to the satisfaction of the police (let alone the prosecutors and the courts) is still less than 20 percent. The reason for this poor performance, research now tells us, is that the police get less help than they need from victims and witnesses in the community.

How has this peculiar situation come about? How is it that the one public body that promises "to serve and protect" today seems incapable of doing either satisfactorily? And how might police procedures be reformed to allow officers to control crime effectively *and* give citizens the kind of service they need to feel safe and comfortable in their communities? A useful way to begin answering these questions is to review the history of American policing and note some of the paths abandoned along the way. While much of this history is well known to some, what is less well understood is how the pursuit of a professionalized, politically neutral police force—narrowly focused on "serious crime" and relying on new technologies—eventually weakened the bonds between private citizens and the police, and shifted the burdens of enforcement to a public agency that could not succeed by itself.

PRIVATE AND PUBLIC POLICING

It is easy to forget that publicly-supported police agencies were only recently created in the United States. Throughout the colonial period and up until the mid-nineteenth century, everyday policing was performed by night watchmen who also lit lamps, reported fires, managed runaway animals, and stood ready to help in family emergencies. Their role as "crime fighters" was restricted to raising a general alarm whenever they saw criminal misconduct—an event that must have been rare, given the small number of watchmen and the haphazard methods of patrol. Apprehension of the fleeing felons then depended on vigorous pursuit by private citizens. The investigation of past criminal offenses also depended on private initiative. When sufficient evidence was gathered, a victim could enlist the aid of a constable to regain his property or make an arrest, but the constable would ordinarily rely on the victim to locate the suspect.[1]

By the 1840s, this informal arrangement became insufficient to deal with the increasing lawlessness of American cities, so city governments began experimenting with new forms of policing. The most important model for these changes was England, which was also debating about and experimenting with new forms of policing. The old English system, which had served as the model for the American, also placed heavy reliance on private individuals for crime prevention, apprehension, and investigation; beyond that, there was only a loose network of publicly supported watchmen, constables, and courts. Publicly supported policing was, however, supplemented by commercial "thief catching" firms, the "Bow Street Runners" being the most famous. These firms depended on informants and undercover operations, as well as more traditional investigative techniques. While these methods seemed to give commercial firms a competitive advantage in solving crime, the potential for corruption and abuses was quite high. (Some of their success seems to have depended on arranging for the crimes to occur in the first place!)[2]

Despite the traditional authority of the constables, and the vitality and ingenuity of private commercial policing, the English forces of public order tottered before the social challenges of the 1830s. As in the United States, the problem lay in the growing cities, where authorities not only had to cope with street crime, but also with riots, demonstrations, and increasing assaults on public decency (i.e., drunkenness and "juvenile delinquency"). And the street lights still had to be lit.

Much as the American "crime wave" and riots of the 1960s led to the creation of federal commissions and independent research centers to study the prevention of crime, the English social disturbances of the early-nineteenth century led to a fundamental reevaluation of policing. Jeremy Bentham and Patrick Colquhoun proposed a form of "preventative policing" and drafted legislation mandating the regular supervision of known criminals, people in "dangerous" occupations (e.g., minstrels), and even specific ethnic groups (e.g., Jews).[3] The English also looked across the Channel at the "continental model" of policing based on informants and covert surveillance rather than overt patrols.[4]

In the end, neither "detective policing," as suggested by the Bow Street Runners and the French, nor "preventative policing," as conceived by Colquhoun, was adopted as a strategy for English policing in the mid-1800s. Instead, Parliament chose a model of policing based on the success of the Thames River Police. Originally established as an experiment funded privately by insurance companies to reduce property losses, the Thames River Police were so successful that they became the first police organization in England to be financed entirely by public revenues. Publicly-supported policing was then mandated throughout England in 1829 by the Metropolitan Police Act, and the Metropolitan Police began patrolling the streets of London shortly thereafter.[5]

The British approach to policing consolidated older traditions. The strategy was still based on overt, reactive patrol, and the patrol force, armed only with concealed truncheons, was trained to be civil in confronting citizens. The only major changes were that the patrol force became larger, trained, and were deployed more carefully, and were organized in chains of command that would allow operations in large units as well as small. Investigation was still privately supported, and no use of informants or covert police was explicitly sanctioned to gather prior information about crimes.

The transformation of British policing in the early-nineteenth century had a tremendous impact on American thinking and practice. New York City established a municipal police force based on the British model in 1845, followed quickly by Boston and Philadelphia; by 1855, cities as far west as Milwaukee had police departments. As in England, these departments consisted of overt, reactive patrol forces capable of operating in large or small units. And because the forces were accessible to citizens at all hours, they retained their constabulary functions, providing emergency service as well as controlling crime and maintaining public order.

The establishment of publicly-supported police departments patrolling city streets was clearly a major event shaping the institutional development of police departments. Indeed, current strategies of policing are the direct descendants of these innovations. As important as these events were, however, the innovations of the mid-1800s were a less decisive resolution of basic issues in the design of police strategies than is often supposed.

The reforms did not mean, for example, that the responsibility for crime control had passed irrevocably from private to public hands. Private police forces, in the form of railroad police, "Pinkertons," and private detectives, played a major role in controlling crime and disorder well into the twentieth century. And though these private police forces were less prominent through the 1960s, they are now reappearing in the form of commercial security guards and volunteer citizen block-watches. (And the police remain dependent, as they always have been, on the willingness of citizens to alert them to crime and aid them in the identification, apprehension, and conviction of suspects.)

Nor did the American reforms of the mid-1800s focus the attention of the police exclusively on crime, demonstrations, and riots. The scope of police responsibilities remained very broad: They were responsible for discouraging lesser forms of public disorder (e.g., drunkenness, vandalism, obscenities, harassment, lewdness), for regulating economic activity (e.g., enforcing traffic laws, coping with unlicensed peddlers, inspecting facilities), and for handling everyday medical and social emergencies (e.g., traffic accidents, fires, lost children).

Similarly, although the adopted strategy seemed to emphasize overt, reactive patrols, other strategies did not entirely disappear. By the late 1800s, most metropolitan police departments had developed detective as well as patrol divisions. These units not only conducted investigations of past crimes at public expense (a major change from the earliest traditions), but also began using informants and covert methods that allowed them to prevent future crimes, as well as solve past ones.[6] And while no explicit authorization was given for "preventative policing" as it existed on the Continent, the police were able to use their authority to enforce public order and regulate commerce to accomplish the same purpose.

Perhaps the most significant question left unresolved by the innovations of the 1850s, however, was the basis of the new institution's legitimacy. What gave the new police force the right to interfere in private matters? Were they to be considered agents of the state, allies of current political figures, neutral instruments of the law, or specialized as professionals? In England, the police were able to draw on the traditional authority of the crown and explicit parliamentary authorization, and even so the legitimacy of the police was suspect. (Upper class people reportedly whipped the police as they passed in carriages, and the press commented favorably whenever a policeman was killed in a crowd.)[7] In the United States, the police had even less on which to rely. Local political support would always be fickle in a democratically-spirited country ever skeptical of authority and claims to "expertise," so it should come as no surprise that the new police forces would be suspect and considered potentially dangerous.

FROM CONSTABLE TO CRIME FIGHTER

The tension between the need to maintain order in a growing country and the inherent distrust of authority profoundly shaped the development of the American police between 1870 to 1970. The first phase began immediately when the new municipal police forces became allied with local politicians. In the words of Robert Fogelson, police departments in the 1800s became "adjuncts to the political machine," and a major source of jobs and upward mobility for newly-arrived immigrants.[8] Their duties ran from maintaining public order, economic regulation, and crime and riot control, to providing lodging and soup kitchens for vagrants. Of course, since their legitimacy rested on local political support, rather than an abstract notion of full and impartial enforcement of the laws, their enforcement efforts were far from even-handed. By accommodating differences among ethnic neighborhoods and the purposes of local politicians, the police were more a central cog than a mere adjunct of the big city machines.

By the end of the 1800s the police became a favorite target of reformers in the Progressive movement, who despised both the established power of the political machines and the "disorder" that characterized those parts of the cities where police had stopped enforcing vice laws. Ending the "corruption" of the police became a central feature of the Progressive program, as was the transfer of social welfare functions from the police to the new social work professionals. The Progressive conception of the police was one radically different from the practices which had developed over the previous century, and consisted of several significant departures: The police were to become a highly disciplined, paramilitary organization independent of local political parties; to ensure that independence, the force would be organized along functional rather than geographic lines; personnel procedures would be strictly meritocratic rather than political; and police duties would be limited to the strict enforcement of existing laws.

The first wave of reform did not succeed completely, mainly due to Prohibition. Popular opposition to the liquor control laws was so widespread that "equal enforcement of the laws" was out of the question, and "corruption" reappeared to accommodate the unwillingness of responsible citizens to comply with the laws. This experience taught a significant new lesson to the reformers: Not all laws command equal respect, so only those laws that are widely supported should be enforced. (Later, this idea was expanded to cover so-called "victimless" crimes.)

This "lesson," whatever its flaws and whatever its unforeseen consequences, laid the basis for the next phase of American policing, in which the police became primarily concerned with serious crime: murder, assault, robbery, rape, burglary, and theft. "Victimless" crimes, disorderliness, economic regulation, and social services became less important after the 1930s because, it was argued, police activity in these aroused citizen opposition, encouraged unequal enforcement, and spawned corruption. The clean, bureaucratic model of policing put forward by the reformers could be sustained only if the scope of police responsibility was narrowed to "crime fighting."

Several other developments reinforced the notion of police officer as "crime fighter." One was the improvement of communication and transportation technologies. With cars, telephones, and radios, all of which became widely available to the police in the 1940s and 1950s, it seemed that an omnipresent patrol force could be created.[9] Moreover, the new technology complemented the objective of creating centralized, tightly disciplined police organizations. The second influence was the development of the *Uniform Crime Reports* which publish rates of homicide, rape, robbery, aggravated assault, burglary, larceny, and motor vehicle theft for every city in the country. These data inevitably became important indicators of police performance, and encouraged police administrators to focus on these crimes as the most important targets of police work.

The net result of these recent developments—cars, radios, and statistics—has been a new reform strategy that resembles the old in its commitment to equal enforcement of the laws and its emphasis on a disciplined police bureaucracy, but differs in that it focuses narrowly on property crimes and violent crimes rather than the enforcement of all laws—especially those regarding public order and economic regulation. To a great extent, the professionalized "crime fighting" strategy of policing that emerged after World War II is the current dominant police strategy. Its explicit goal is the control of crime, not maintaining public order or providing constabulary services. It depends on even-handed, non-intrusive enforcement of the laws, but only those laws with widespread public support. Its basic mode of operation includes motorized patrol, rapid responses to calls for service, and retrospective investigation of offenses, not high-profile foot patrol or "preventative policing."

THE CONSEQUENCES OF REFORM

By now, the goal of "professionalizing" police forces—of making them conform to the reform strategy—has become an orthodoxy. Police executives, experts on policing, the police themselves, even mayors and legal philosophers, are all eager to trade constables and cops on the beat for professional crime fighters—to transform their "street corner politicians" into Joe Fridays and then into SWAT teams. The irony is that this orthodoxy has become powerful in shaping police aspirations and practices at about the same time that embarrassing weaknesses are beginning to appear.

It is now clear, for example, that there is a limit to the deployment of police resources (squad cars, rapid-response police teams, investigators) beyond which the rate of violent crime is very insensitive. The most recent research convincingly establishes three points. First, neither crime nor fear of crime are importantly affected by major changes in the number of officers patrolling in marked cars.[10] Apparently, within broad ranges, neither criminals nor citizens can tell whether an area is heavily or superficially patrolled when the patrolling is done in cars. Second, rapid responses to calls for service do not dramatically increase the apprehension of criminals.[11] The reason is that citizens do not call the police until long after a crime has been completed, and the attacker has fled the scene. Given these delays, even instantaneous police responses would do little good. Third, police investigators are unable to solve crimes without major assistance from victims and witnesses.[12] Indeed, unless they can identify the offender, chances are overwhelming that the crime will not be solved. On the other hand, if citizens can identify the offender, it is difficult to see what modern detectives add to what the local constables used to do. And, at any rate, the capacity of the police to solve crimes—particularly those involving violence among strangers—remains shockingly low. Fewer than 20 percent of robberies are solved, and an even smaller fraction of burglaries.[13] All this suggests that the orthodox police strategy provides neither general deterrence, nor successful apprehension of individual offenders.

Besides running up against limits to professionalized crime fighting, it is now clear that contemporary police strategies ignore a large number of tasks which the police have traditionally performed. There are no streetlamps to light anymore, but there are a large number of constabulary functions—maintaining order in public places (parks, buses, subway platforms), resolving marital disputes, disciplining non-criminal but harmful juvenile behavior, preventing public drug and alcohol use—which no other public organizations have taken up since they were abandoned by the police. These jobs simply are not done, and what is worse, they have come to be seen as illegitimate functions of *any* public body or private citizen. The role of modern legal philosophy is very important here, for it has been most responsible for making many of these once implicitly-sanctioned practices explicitly illegal for the police, and without that implicit support individual private citizens have become unwilling to take matters into their own hands.

The bitter irony of this development is that it is probably these constabulary functions, properly performed, that make people feel safer in their neighborhoods than a drop in the "crime rate" as measured in the *Uniform Crime Reports*. Seeing a cop on the beat, allowing one's children to play unsupervised in the park, not being offered drugs on the street, taking the bus or subway late at night without being approached by vagrants—all these things probably make citizens feel safer than a drop in average police response time from five to three minutes. The sort of infringements on public order we are describing are often "unlawful," but they are not serious crime. As a result, the police neglect these offenses and escape the charge of discriminatory enforcement. Yet such offenses may matter more to citizen security than relatively rare "crime" as the police now define it.

Perhaps the most significant and least obvious limitation of the current police orthodoxy is the loss of a political base for police organizations. This is obscure largely because the current orthodoxy claims an opposite virtue: Once freed from corrupting political influence, the police become legitimate, neutral instruments of the law. Yet the weakness of politically neutral police departments was evident in the mid-1960s when local police confronted the peaceful civil rights movement, large-scale student demonstrations, inner-city riots, and political terrorist groups. These activities challenged orthodox police strategy—since none is ordinary "crime"—and the police simply could not respond effectively. Zealously pursuing ordinary street crime, they were accused of exacerbating rather than controlling riots. Dealing with terrorism required proactive policing, and the police found themselves without local political allies in conducting these operations. The strategy of professionalized crime fighting simply could not deal effectively with the political attack on city governance in the 1960s; and rather than fundamentally rethink their strategy, local forces made lame gestures toward improving "police-community relations"—a phrase that only highlights the false distinction at the heart of modern policing.

There is a common element in each of these areas of weakness: an insufficient link between the aspirations and interests of local communities, and the operations of the police. In professionalizing crime fighting, the "volunteers," citizens on whom so much used to depend, have been removed from the fight. The effect has not been increased security, but impotence in apprehending offenders, widespread fear triggered by disorder, and a sense that things must really be bad if police departments with all their capabilities cannot seem to cope with the problem.

REFORMING THE REFORMS

If there is anything to be learned from the relatively short history of the American police it is that, whatever the real benefits of professionalization (e.g., reduced corruption, due process, serious police training), the reforms have ignored, even attacked, some features that once made the police powerful institutions in maintaining a sense of community security. Of course, it would be hopelessly romantic to think that modern police could immediately reclaim an intimate relationship with well defined communities in today's cities, or resume their broad social functions. And, indeed, there is much in the modern conception and operations of police departments that is worth preserving.

But still, within bounds, it may now be possible for imaginative police executives and those who supervise their operations to make changes that could reclaim some of the old virtues while sacrificing little of value in the modern reforms. We offer ideas in four distinct areas: police dealings with private self-defense efforts; scope of police responsibility; police deployment; and the organizational structure of the force. In each case, the proposals are designed to link the police more surely to the communities in which they now operate.

Private and Public Enforcement. Private citizens inevitably play an important role in controlling crime. By limiting their exposure to risk, investing in locks and guns, banding together to patrol their own streets, or financing a private security force, private citizens affect the overall level of crime, and the distribution of the benefits and burdens of policing. Police strategists should encourage those private mobilizations, provide guidance and technical assistance, and position the police as back-ups to private efforts.

To a degree, of course, police forces now do this. They pass out police whistles, urge people to mark their property so that it can be more easily identified when stolen, help to organize block watches, and set up emergency call systems tied to rapid responses to calls to service. Yet, apart from responding to calls for service, one has the feeling that the police do not really take such activities seriously; and when the private efforts become powerful, the police often attack them as a danger to liberty (though their greater concern might well be the economic security that comes from monopolizing crime-control efforts).

Nowhere is this ambivalence more obvious than in the general response to the growth of the Guardian Angels, a private paramilitary group that began in New York City and spread across the country. Many consider the Guardian Angels a useful auxiliary patrol force that reminds private citizens of their public responsibilities, and dignifies the young men and women who join; opponents (often including the police) see the Angels as vigilantes threatening the rights of citizens with undisciplined enforcement. Neither view is quite appropriate. Those who welcome the Angels as a novelty forget that private policing was the only form of policing for centuries, and that the creation of a public police force was conceived as a great reform.

Those who think of the Angels as dangerous vigilantes forget the value of private crime-control efforts, and the crucial difference between vigilantes and responsible citizens playing their traditional role in crime control. The Guardian Angels limit their functions to deterrence and, occasionally, apprehension; they neither judge guilt nor mete out punishment. And the Angels do not take offense or intervene easily; they respond only to serious crimes that they observe. In so doing, they assume nothing more than the rights and responsibilities of good democratic citizens. It is somewhat ironic that the appearance of several thousand Guardian Angels attracts such great public interest and worry, when the emergence of a *commercial* private security force numbering in the millions has attracted almost no notice at all.

In sum, the Guardian Angels serve as a reminder that, while private policing entails some risks, it remains a useful part of over-all crime-control efforts. Each increase in public policing may be offset by some reduction in private policing, and it is not uncommon for citizens to refuse involvement, saying, "Let the police do it, they get paid for it." But if the public is made to understand that public policing *complements* private efforts, private individuals will take more public responsibility. They will call the police when they see offenses, agree to act as witnesses, and even intervene themselves precisely because public police are available to support them. To the extent possible, the local police must encourage, rather than resist, these private efforts.

The Scope of Police Responsibility. If the police are going to ask for more help from their communities, it seems likely that they will have to produce more of what communities want. As we have seen, police agencies have narrowed their purpose to combatting serious crime. This narrowing is applauded by a general citizenry that thinks "serious crime" is what it fears, by legal philosophers who think the enduring social interest in non-intrusive and fair policing can best be served by focusing attention on a few serious and visible crimes, by professional police administrators who want to allocate scarce resources to the most urgent areas, and by the police themselves who prefer the imagery of "combatting bad guys" to the more complex, mundane tasks. This is a strategic error. The error comes not in emphasizing the importance of controlling violent crime—no one looking at U.S. crime statistics could possibly propose not taking violent crime seriously—but rather in imagining that effective control can be gained simply by complaining about court decisions that "handcuff" the police. More effective control of violent crime depends on an increased willingness on the part of communities to help the police identify and prosecute offenders, but the police miss many opportunities to establish closer relationships with the community, relationships that would encourage such assistance.

Take, for example, the current police response to victims of violent crime. When a violent crime occurs, the police dispatch a patrol car. The officer takes a statement from the victim and identifies witnesses; occasionally an arrest is made at the scene. The officer disappears, and the case is turned over to a detective who may, or may not, interview the victim. The offender is taken to court and often released on bail. The terrified victim may well be intimidated by the offender, yet when he or she calls the police, the call is given a low priority. Neither the arresting officer nor the detective is likely to hear of, or allay, the victim's fear. Surely there is more that can be done by the police to reassure victims: They could be given a name and number of another to call, and the police might even arrange to visit periodically, in unusual cases, or to stake out the home of the victim. Note that the *police* should do this, not some social work agency. Police involvement is important, not only because they have a plausible capacity to protect, but also because they can simultaneously earn credit with the community and strengthen their case against the offender.

In a similar vein, the police could take more seriously their responsibilities to maintain public order. If, as an accumulating body of evidence suggests, it is public disorder and incivility—not violent crime—that increases fear, and if the police wish to reassure citizens, they must maintain public order—in parks, on busy street corners, at bus stops—as well as fight crime. Similarly, commercial regulation such as traffic and parking control, which is now performed mechanically, should be explicitly organized to support local commerce. Finally, police departments should *welcome* their role in providing emergency services—coping with traffic accidents, fires, health emergencies, domestic disputes, etc. Officers will inevitably perform these services, so they might as well incorporate them in their mission, perform them well, and get credit for them. After all, it is an important and popular function which the police typically do well.

DEPLOYMENT AND ORGANIZATION

Deployment. Current police deployment strategy is based heavily on overt, reactive patrol: About 60 percent of the resources of most police departments are committed to patrol, and most of that to uniformed officers riding the streets in clearly marked cars. In addition, most police departments devote 10 percent of the resources to a detective unit engaged in retrospective investigations of criminal offenses. The rest of the resources are devoted to other tasks such as vice squads, juvenile units, narcotics division, and so on.[14]

This strategy is consistent with a focus on serious crime and a strong interest in evenhanded, non-intrusive policing. The capacity of patrol to thwart crimes through general deterrence, and their capacity to respond quickly to calls for service, are assumed to control crime; when deterrence fails and the police force arrives too late to catch the offender, the detectives take over to solve the crime. The enforcement effort is even-handed because patrol surveillance is general, and because anyone, for the price of a phone call, can claim services. And modern policing is non-intrusive in that intensive investigation begins only after a crime has been committed and focuses narrowly on the solution of that crime. Thus, the decision made in the mid-1800s to make public policing a patrol and detective activity, rather than a system of preventive policing, carries on until today: the police skim the surface of social life.

Given the success of this deployment in protecting important social values, it is not surprising that it has been widely utilized. Still, this deployment has internal contradictions as a crime-fighting strategy, to say nothing of the limitations as a device to draw the community into a closer relationship with the police. One basic contradiction has already been noted: In the vast, anonymous cities of today, this deployment apparently fails to deter crime or apprehend offenders. A second difficulty is that once an overt patrol force is made available to citizens at the price of a phone call, officers will be involved in much more than crime fighting. The commitment to "accessibility" then conspires to defeat the narrow focus on crime fighting: We end up with police forces that invite more citizens' requests than can be handled, then frustrate them by failing to take some calls seriously, and finally fail to control crime.

It is now time for police executives to reconsider their deployment strategies. The enormous investment in telephones, radios, and cars that now allow the police to respond to crime calls in under five minutes (often with more than one car) has bought little crime control, no greater sense of security, and has prevented the police from taking order maintenance and service functions seriously. To the extent that victim services, order maintenance, and a general community presence are valuable not only in themselves, but also as devices for strengthening crime control and building the police as a popular community institution, it is crucial that police executives get some of their officers out of cars and away from dispatchers at least some of the time. Some recent evidence suggests that foot patrol *does* promote a sense of security, and also reduces calls for service. Apparently cops on the beat can deal effectively with many citizen complaints.[15]

For "crime fighting," other tactics may be appropriate and effective. Special decoys or stake-outs targeted at muggers and robbers may be more effective in controlling such offenses than random patrol. Similarly, if current evidence about the large number of offenses committed by a small number of offenders turns out to be correct, it may make sense for the police to develop intelligence systems for "street crimes" similar to those used in combatting organized crime and narcotics traffic. It is even possible that expanded use of informants would be possible. Obviously these methods are more intrusive and proactive than the current deployment, but they may be tolerable if they prove to be effective, and if they enjoy the support of local communities.

Departmental Organization. Most police departments are currently organized along functional lines: There is a patrol division, a narcotics bureau, a youth division and so on. This structure is consistent with many reform ambitions: it allows for convenient reallocation of resources across the city to respond to changing circumstances; it promotes the development of specialized expertise; and, most importantly, it strengthens the control police chiefs have over their subordinates. The alternative scheme is to organize along geographic lines, giving area commanders responsibility for all police operations within a given geographic area. This geographic organization would also make the police department policy-making and operations more accessible to citizens in the community because the area commander would have both the interest and the capacity to respond to local requests.

Geographic organization was the traditional form attacked by the reformers because precinct-level politicians had become too powerful and had bent the police to their corrupt purposes. It was preferable, the reformers thought, to organize in a way that moved power towards the chief (and those who influenced him) rather than leave it in the hands of precinct captains vulnerable to local political machines. The functional organization served these purposes; but there was a price to be paid. Local community groups such as PTA's, merchants' associations, block associations, churches, and individual citizens frightened by crimes—all no longer organized in political machines—now have no one to turn to in the local precinct. There is the precinct commander, but his direct authority typically extends only to the patrol division, and he feels more responsible to those "downtown" than to the citizens of the community. There may also be a "community relations officer," but his authority usually extends nowhere. It is no wonder, then, that citizens who have interests and problems different from those of the city as a whole feel abandoned by the police. If police executives wish to cultivate stronger political support from local neighborhoods, they should consider a more geographic division of responsibilities, shifting more power to local precinct commanders, or even to lower levels in the department such as lieutenants or sergeants who could serve as leaders for "team policing" units. Again, the point is that the police must become more visible and active in neighborhood affairs.

A POST-DRAGNET ERA?

Police strategies do not exist in a vacuum. They are shaped by important legal, political, and attitudinal factors, as well as by local resources and capabilities, all factors which now sustain the modern conception of policing. So there may be little leeway for modern police executives. But the modern conception of policing *is* in serious trouble, and a review of the nature of that trouble against the background of the American history of policing gives a clear direction to police forces that wish to improve their performance as crime fighters *and* public servants.

The two fundamental features of a new police strategy must be these: that the role of private citizens in the control of crime and maintenance of public order be established and encouraged, not derided and thwarted, and that the police become more active, accessible participants in community affairs. The police will have to do little to encourage citizens to participate in community policing, for Americans are well practiced at undertaking private, voluntary efforts; all they need to know is that the police force welcomes and supports such activity. Being more visible and accessible is slightly more difficult, but hiring more "community relations" specialists is surely *not* the answer. Instead, the police must get out of their cars, and spend more time in public spaces such as parks and plazas, confronting and assisting citizens with their private troubles. This is mundane, prosaic work but it probably beats driving around in cars waiting for a radio call. Citizens would surely feel safer and, perhaps, might even be safer.

REFERENCES

1. See T. A. Critchley, *A History of Police in England and Wales*, (London: Constable and Company, Ltd., 1967).

2. Critchley, pp. 19–20; Sir Leon Radzinowicz, *A History of English Law*, Vol. 2, (London: Stevens and Sons Ltd., 1956), p. 289.

3. Radzinowicz, Vol. 2, pp. 271–273.

4. Radzinowicz, Vol. 3 (1956), p. 539.

5. Critchley, p. 51.

6. David R. Johnson, *Policing the Urban Underworld*, (Philadelphia: Temple University Press, 1979).

7. Critchley, p. 54.

8. Robert Fogelson, *Big City Police*, (Cambridge, MA: Harvard University Press, 1977), Chapter 1.

9. O. W. Wilson and Roy Clinton McLaren, *Police Administration*, Third Edition, (New York: McGraw-Hill, 1983).

10. G. L. Kelling, T. Pate, C. Dieckman and C. E. Brown, *The Kansas City Preventive Patrol Experiment*, (Washington, D.C.: Police Foundation, 1974); J. F. Schnelle, et al. "Patrol Evaluation Research: A Multiple-Baseline Analysis of Saturation Police Patrolling During Day and Night Hours," *Journal of Applied Behavior Analysis* (1976) 10, no. 1.

11. William Bieck, *Response Time Analysis*, (Kansas City Police Department).

12. Peter W. Greenwood, Jan M. Chaiken, Joan Petersilia, *The Criminal Investigation Process*, (Lexington, MA: D.C. Heath and Company, 1977).

13. *Uniform Crime Reports for the United States, 1980*, (Washington, D.C.: U.S. Department of Justice, 1981), p. 180.

14. *Survey of Police Operational and Administrative Practices—1981* (Washington, D.C.: Police Executive Research Forum and Police Foundation), pp. 22–24.

15. *Newark Foot Patrol Experiment*, (Washington, D.C.: Police Foundation, 1981); Robert C. Trojanowicz, "An Evaluation Report: The Flint Neighborhood Foot Patrol," unpublished; Dato Steenhuis, paper presented at American Society of Criminology Annual Meeting, November 5, 1982, Toronto, Canada.

The Police and Ethnic Minorities: A British Policing Dilemma

David W. Pope

In this paper it is my intention to look very briefly at the police–coloured ethnic minority relationship which developed during the later 1970s, to concentrate upon the more dramatic events that marked the opening of the '80s, and to draw from these a number of observations which reflect the problems now facing British police forces in policing an unequal, and multi-racial, society. I would add that these ideas are personal ones which in no way reflect an official police (or Police Staff College) view of the events and occurrences of the last decade.

It is pertinent to point out that there is still comparatively little coloured settlement in Scotland, Northern Ireland and Wales (except for Cardiff, a port where a coloured presence has been visible for some considerable time and in which police–community relations have been remarkably free of strife). Thus my overwhelming interest lies in English forces and, above all, with those force areas in which is found the bulk of New Commonwealth residence.

As will become obvious to readers, it is people of Asian and West Indian descent who mostly constitute the coloured ethnic minority with whom this paper deals. Of a total population in England now numbering some 54,000,000, it has been estimated that about 4.1% (2,200,000) were, in mid-1980, of New Commonwealth and Pakistani origin. A further estimate saw this figure rising by the end of the century to 6.7% (3,300,000) at which the coloured population will stabilize.

THE LEGACY OF THE '70S

Whilst numbers themselves create problems, much more important has been the concentration of immigrants and their dependents in the decaying area of inner cities. Restrictions of space make me very largely take for granted that, in the leading of their day-to-day lives, coloured residents of the United Kingdom do experience some degree of prejudice and discrimination in education, housing and employment; largely taken-for-granted, too, is:

a. The existence of an immigration policy which appears to give more emphasis to excluding further coloured immigration than to attempting to redress the grievances and deprivations of those already settled here

and

b. A policy for the inner cities which has fluctuated in its vigour and lacked focus in its direction.

The latter has meant that the difficulties posed to inner-city residents have only been overcome to a limited degree by somewhat piecemeal attempts at urban rejuvenation; the former has created more mistrust of government intentions and weakened faith in British democratic ideals.

If we briefly examine, at this stage, a specific inner city area—the London Borough of Lambeth (one of 13 inner city boroughs in London)—then we are able to appreciate far more vividly the kind of social conditions which have been allowed to develop in our large towns and cities and the considerable stress under which many people—especially, perhaps, sections of our coloured minorities—lead their day-to-day lives. The authority for this brief examination of Lambeth is a vital document to which I will later make more specific reference—the Scarman Report.

Lambeth is a well established area of mixed residential, commercial and industrial activity. Residential settlement predominates with large estates of local authority provided housing. Since the First World War economic decline has been evident and the borough has more recently suffered from planning blight—boarded up sites and decaying property provide ". . . a daily reminder of the vagaries of policy, the dangers of indecision, and the depressing effects of physical decay and economic decline."

Despite local authority and governmental aid, the housing situation is critical. Approximately 20% of households in the borough are homeless (37% for blacks); there is a shortfall of 20,000 dwellings com-

This article was written expressly for inclusion in this edition.

pared to the number of households requiring a separate home, 10% of households are overcrowded: over 12,000 dwellings are defined as unfit and a further 8,250 lack one or more basic amenity. In total some 20% of total housing stock is sub-standard and a further 12% in need of major renovation.

To this must be added the social effects of recession—a declining population, a movement away of the professional and skilled in the 25–60 years age grouping, a high turnover of populations and substantial unemployment. Young and old are disproportionately represented as are the number of children in local authority care, the mentally and physically handicapped, low income households and one-parent families. It is little wonder that the local Area Health Board has one of the highest revenue expenditures, per capita, in the whole of England.

In that part of Lambeth settled by coloured ethnic minorities, Scarman adds other dimensions to the problem: the lack of leisure and recreational facilities, the need to improve the quality of the educational service within schools, the especial difficulty for West Indian families of not having the support of an extended network of kin and losing the mother as a focal point of home life when she is forced to seek work. The Report forcefully makes the sombre observations:

> . . . it would be surprising if they [young black people] did not feel a sense of frustration and deprivation. And living much of their lives on the streets, they are brought into contact with the police who appear to them as the visible symbols of the authority of a society which has failed to bring them its benefits or do them justice.

For the police, such factors served to complicate the policing task and were recognised as so doing in many statements by senior police officers. The 1974 Report by Her Majesty's Chief Inspector of Constabulary, for example, emphasised the police concern for the deprived areas of the urban areas, the need to work hard at the task of improving community relations, and categorically stated the view "that until coloured people are treated as equal in our society, and feel themselves to be equal—until colour is genuinely no more than a physical distinction, and not one on which judgments of worth and ability are made—race relations will remain an important matter for the police."

The increasing public attention given to policing in the 1970s and the specially sensitive relationships with the residents of certain inner-city areas, aggravated as they were by an ailing economy and a more fractious society, led to police and police organisations becoming the focus of substantial critical appraisal; the major concerns appeared to be:

1. The nature of policing and its impact upon the policed.
2. The lack of accountability, more so at local level, of Chief Constables for their policies and practices.
3. The inadequacy of a complaints system which was seen to lack an independent element in the investigating of police malpractice.

Internally there is little doubt that police forces themselves were facing disruptive changes and that adapting to them was difficult; there was a revolution in communications, rapid developments in police science and technology, the application of command and control systems, amalgamations and the use of new patrol procedures. In the latter part of the decade there was also the shock of corruption and brutality charges against members of some constabularies which occupied—and to a lesser extent persists in occupying—media attention; corruption in the Metropolitan Police was such that its Commissioner, Sir Robert Mark, was forced to direct his energies to restoring higher standards of personal and professional integrity during his term of office.

Externally there was the task of dealing with coloured communities sharing a common concern for what they perceived as a law enforcement agency which, like white society itself, was prejudiced and discriminating, which abused its powers and aligned itself with the Establishment in preserving the status quo. West Indians were very loud in their complaints of police harassment. Asians felt police were ignoring their demands for service and unsympathetic to the racially inspired attacks perpetrated on their members.

EVENTS AND ISSUES OF THE '80S

The new decade opened, then, to an already lively debate about policing and a flurry of official activity in the form of the continuing deliberations of the Royal Commission on Criminal Procedure and the Home Affairs Committee into issues like police powers, race relations and immigration, and public order. The latter led, in April 1980, to a Green Paper in which was raised the critical problem of how to preserve ". . . the rights, on the one hand, of those who wish to demonstrate and, on the other, of the rest of the public." At this time, one must remember, a feature of police action was the frequent banning of marches, a move which appeared to please neither the coloured minority with genuine grievances to air, nor those of political extremes who wished to make capital of the situation.

The real drama, however, began with the disturbances in Bristol arising from a police raid on a cafe situated in a predominantly West Indian area of settlement. Rioting led to 49 injuries to police officers (22 of which were categorized "serious") and damage to 21 police vehicles; vandalism, arson and looting produced considerable destruction to the environment and the intensity of the rioting itself was of an order which made the police temporarily withdraw. The Deputy Chief Constable was reported as saying that he took this decision ". . . in the interest of the safety of police officers . . . until we had sufficient manpower."

In addition, 1981 saw the publication of the White Paper on "British Nationality Law" which outlined proposed legislation. Of it Ushar Prashar, Director of the Runnymede Trust, said ". . . an abyssmal document. . . . It fails to deal with any of the central issues of nationality and citizenship and instead has become an opportunity for further restriction of non-white immigration to Britain."

One must also bear in mind that unfortunate relationships develop for any police force which has to involve itself in activities such as passport and illegal immigration raids. In the period with which we are concerned those were a constant source of friction between police and some immigrants. One might also add that the conduct of discussion about nationality law was found offensive by many—it often seemed insensitive to immigrants and British born blacks by being carried on as if they were non-persons. Police relations with the black community "were at the breaking point."

The increasing sensitivity of the coloured ethnic minority to its disadvantaged position was made overwhelmingly evident in the emotional reaction to the fire in a house in Deptford (London) which led to the death of 13 young blacks. In condemning what was felt to be police inactivity at the time, and indifference over a long period of racial attacks, many black people of all ages engaged in persistent, vociferous and highly emotional protest, including a march soon afterwards when some 6,000 people protested against ". . . police handling of the investigation, at racist attacks, at the biased and sparse media coverage of the fire, and the lack of official response following the incident." Incidentally, the march produced an estimated 100,000 pounds of damage and stolen property together with much vandalizing of police equipment.

One might not be surprised, given a climate of the kind described, that disturbances broke out at Brixton (London) which appeared to trigger off a series of riots countrywide. Most severely hit, other than Brixton itself, was the Moss Side district of Manchester and the Toxteth district of Merseyside. Rioting was so severe in the latter that C.S. gas was used for the first time in mainland Britain. The Chief Constable, Kenneth Oxford, was reported as saying, "I have no doubt at all that this is not a racial issue. It is exclusively a crowd of black hooligans intent on making life unbearable and indulging in criminal activities."

Whether the Chief Constable was correct or not, an enquiry that had been set up into the Brixton Riots under Lord Scarman took evidence from numerous people and groups from whom the cause of the incidents ranged from the more specific, like police harassment of young blacks, to the more general, such as the so-called "copy-cat" theory which accused the media of presenting behaviour models to young people simply by their coverage of the actual events.

An appealing typology of the reactions to the riots is provided by Colin Vick in his use of Conservative, Liberal and Radical categories of Responses. The Conservative Response is focused upon the breakdown in law, order and authority; order and control must be reasserted which means, in policing terms, an emphasis upon "positive" policing, the control of crime and the proper processing of criminal offenders. The Liberal Response sees the riots more as a product of social malfunctioning, including a dilution of the quality of the police–community relationship; remedial action must stem from the evaluation of the problem and the creating of the right kind of policies and strategies—police have to work much harder at winning public support. The Radical Response perceives much more fundamental schisms in society that are deeply rooted and structural; society and the police need "thorough democratization and police themselves are a cause of disaffection."

If we look specifically at police reactions to the riots then their public utterances fall almost wholly into the Conservative category. They were linked to statements about the failure of our social institutions, particularly the family and the school, to instill obedience and respect in the young, and alongside them went demands for the better equipping and training of police officers for public order duties and keeping the Queen's Peace. However, these views solidly embraced the belief in community relations and the tradition of policing by consent—the Liberal Ideology, one suspects, also plays a part in police thinking but the times were not propitious for it to surface.

One notable exception has to be made in the case of the then Chief Constable of Devon and Cornwall, John Alderson. He did not endear himself to his colleagues in refusing to train his men in the use of C.S. gas and plastic bullets, nor by his view that "there has to be a better way than blind repression" as a means of dealing with violence. His accusation against fellow Chief Officers of preparing to tool up for war on the public and of misunderstanding the causes of the riots stemmed from a long held conviction that it was in the community that police had to win public support; his own philosophy was firmly of the liberal order and went as far as advocating a statutory duty for police to liaise with their local communities.

The Radical Response, predictably, was not to be seen in policing circles but was more than adequately reflected in all those who had been persistent critics of police performance and now used the Summer Riots as an ideal means of justifying their apprehensions of the inner-city tensions and for gaining media attention. Continuing sporadic disturbances, especially in Toxteth, kept the critical spotlight firmly fixed on the police, on calls for local consultation and greater responsibility.

In an atmosphere of considerable interest and speculation, the Scarman Report was published in November of 1981 and immediately those elements in it which appeared, however tenuously, to justify the stance they had taken, were seized upon by the various parties to the debate. Most satisfactory from a police perspective was Scarman's insistence that "Nothing can excuse the unlawful behaviour of the rioters" and his rejection of the thesis that oppressive policing of black youth was the primary cause of the disorders. In the context of Brixton itself, he found that police did not over-react, did not delay action, though he accepted that there had come about a significant loss of confidence by sections of the community in them and that much of the rioting was directed against police personnel.

Lord Scarman saw the real problem rooted in "a complex political, economic and social situation which is not special to Brixton" but which embraces prejudice and discrimination, acute deprivation and feelings of anxiety and insecurity. With regard to the West Indians, he also emphasized particular and detrimental changes which had taken place in their family life and singled out working mothers and the absence of fathers from the home as contributing toward the lack of discipline amongst West Indian youth. Yet all these factors amount, in Scarman's view, not to causes of the riots but to "conditions which create a predisposition toward racial violence."

One might briefly and usefully speculate at this stage on the kind of dilemma created for police forces when the fundamental causes of social unrest affecting their relationships with sections of the community lie very largely, if not wholly, outside their control. It was these broader and more fundamental matters which, earlier in the year, had led the Chairwoman of the Merseyside Police Authority, Lady Margaret Simey, to make the provocative remark that the people of Toxteth "ought to riot"—it was not an opinion which endeared her to her police force, but it did reflect the sincere opinion held by a local councillor that the conditions under which certain members of our country live are abhorrent and should not be tolerated in a civilized society.

However, Lord Scarman indicated the paths police should follow and, for the sake of simplicity, I shall type them as those "within" (not requiring the co-operation of outside agencies) and those "without" (where co-operation is an essential ingredient):

A. *"WITHIN"*

1. *RECRUITMENT*
   i. Ways should be studied of identifying racial prejudice in potential recruits and incorporating them into selection procedures.

2. *TRAINING*

   Basic Constable Training

   i. Basic training should be lengthened to 6 months.

   ii. More should be done to include in that training knowledge of coloured ethnic minority cultures and attitudes.

   iii. The handling of public disorder should receive greater attention.

Supervisory and Managerial Training

iv. More management training should be given to sergeants and inspectors.

v. Compulsory training for all ranks in community relations up to, and including, superintendent.

vi. Developing, in conjunction with the Home Office, common standards and programmes for handling public disorder, and training in the management of the latter for all ranks up to and including the level of Assistant Chief Constable/Commander.

3. *DISCIPLINE*
The Police Discipline Code should include a specific offense to cover racially prejudiced or discriminatory behaviour, the penalty for such should be instant dismissal.

4. *EQUIPMENT*
Water cannon, plastic bullets, C.S. gas and other protective equipment should be held in reserve by forces but not used unless authority is given by the Chief Constable and only when loss of life is feared.

B. *"WITHOUT"*

1. *OPERATIONAL PRACTICES AND PHILOSOPHY*
In consultation with Police Authorities and local community leaders, Chief Constables should reexamine their methods of policing inner-city areas.

2. *LIAISON*
   i. Co-operation between Police Authorities and Chief Constables to establish consultative arrangements should be compulsory (N.B. Whilst this was coming about Scarman recommended that existing powers should be used to set up such arrangements).

   ii. In London a statutory provision should be made for consultation at Borough or Police District level with the possibility of something like an Advisory Branch for the force as a whole.

THE POLICE RESPONSE

Police reactions to these recommendations were fairly predictable; a general rejection by police representative bodies was made of the suggested disciplinary offence, the Association of Chief Police Officers expressed its disapproval of statutory liaison committees—but all welcomed the report and overwhelmingly endorsed the remarks Scarman had made about training. The dilemma that Scarman saw was unanimously supported, "The essence of the policing problem is as simple to state as it was and remains difficult to resolve—how to cope with a rising level of crime and particularly street robbery (in the colloquial phrase, mugging) while retaining the confidence of all sections of the community, especially the ethnic minority groups."

Before we turn to the police response to Scarman of a more practical nature, it is worth considering three reports that, in their different ways, were helping to confuse and compound the tensions of the police–minority relationships:

1. A Home Office Research Study gave no ground for optimism when it held that one could still see in this country, "continuing discrimination against minorities on a large scale, particularly minorities perceived as coloured."
2. The coloured minority, especially Asian, fear of racial attacks was apparently vindicated by the release of a Home Office Report in November in which it stated that black people were 50 to 60 times more likely to be victims of racially motivated incidents than whites. Its recommendations seemed generally acceptable to police.
3. Coloured confidence in obtaining redress of their many grievances was weakened by a report of the Commission for Racial Equality, the major official body working in this sphere: It was accused of incompetence and inadequacy as a law enforcement body, some saw its report as anti-black, and many felt it provided a cover for what were basically the faults of government.

In total one might argue that, at national level, the Summer riots of 1981 and the Scarman Report heightened the consciousness of the government to the deprivations of the inner city, to the need for consistency in policies, and to the essentially co-operative and corporate nature of any remedial action it might take. The complexity of the problems are such that no social agency in isolation can cope; the multi-causal characteristic of matters like crime, unemployment and inadequate housing, demand that statutory and voluntary bodies work together and integrate their endeavours.

One might even more vigorously argue police awareness of the part all social institutions have to play in preventing crime and public disorder since their cry, as individuals and as members of forces and professional organizations, has been that they (the police) are a refuse bin for the problems other social agencies cannot deal with and are offered precious little real help in dealing with them. The internal debate that has taken place both pre- and post-Scarman in the Service appears, and this is a very personal opinion, to have produced a rationale for community relations which is of the following order:

> Society decides what is unlawful behaviour and it is its members who commit criminal acts. At the formal level society has created a criminal justice system of which the police are a very important part; even here, however, the public has to play its part if law breaking and law breakers are to be effectively dealt with.
>
> Additionally, informal mechanisms exist to create and maintain order and control in society, such as the church, the family and the school, in which the role of individuals, communities and organizations is crucial in developing predispositions toward socially responsible conduct—the bedrock upon which the formal system is erected.
>
> Given the complex nature of social order and control, therefore, society cannot abdicate its own duties and responsibilities in the move to create a more law abiding way of living, it cannot hand over to police the sole burden of maintaining public tranquility.
>
> It thus follows that the police–community relationship, especially as a panacea for the ills of the inner city, requires the wholehearted support of the public; the police alone cannot fight crime (and the statistics for arrests and convictions bear adequate testimony to that fact) nor should they attempt to do so.

In the brief post-Scarman period available to us for study, one notices, at national level, the usual danger of too much rhetoric and too little action. Yet the sphere of policing has been quite lively—training is under close examination and has already included, in the Met., more specific instruction in human awareness skills; a "Model Police Liaison Committee" has been at work in Lambeth since 1982; the Home Office has issued guidance to forces for the monitoring of racial attacks and racial tension; the Police Staff College has inaugurated short courses on managing the problems of racially sensitive areas and recently run a most successful exercise on the policing of inner cities, a marked feature of which was the liaising with statutory and voluntary bodies.

Individual forces have continued to develop established practices and to initiate new procedures, and there has been a marked effort to return men to the beat. The recent salary awards have made policing a more attractive occupation and this, together with the unfortunate phenomenon of unemployment, has brought most forces up to establishment. Thus at this moment the problem is not the quantity and quality of manpower but rather more the training demands of large numbers of probationers who are now in the training schools or in-force training.

Yet, and here I return to a dilemma earlier mentioned of policing an unequal and inequitable society, economic pundits see little immediate potential for growth in our economy and this immediately and inevitably means lack of funds for the attack on inner-city problems; such monies spent to date have yielded disproportionately small returns. Critics of government policy see, in recent months, little real help being provided where it is most needed; financial constraints are such that local authority spending has been under severe restraint, welfare services have been cut back and environmental decay continues. The vulnerable, amongst whom coloured ethnic minorities feature substantially, remain in the declining city confines.

THE PROSPECT FOR THE FUTURE

The point to be made is that the most optimistic police officers cannot expect to see any marked improvement, certainly in the immediate future, in those aspects of life which constitute many of Scarman's "predisposing" factors to urban rioting and violence: education, housing, welfare and leisure facilities, and—above all—employment. In time this is likely to mean that ethnic minority members will not view the police any differently and that Scarman's recommendations to improve coloured ethnic recruitment will bear little fruit even if vigorously pursued by forces.

Whether the police–ethnic minority relationship will be helped by the abolition of the "Sus" law (which allows police to arrest anyone suspected of intending to commit a crime) is a matter for conjecture since the Criminal Attempts Act which replaced it is too recent an innovation for an informed judgment to be made. But the new standardised police procedure for dealing with racial attacks introduced by Scotland Yard is a promising step toward promoting greater harmony; an integral part of it is regular visiting by local police officers to all victims of racial incidents to make sure that they are on the road to recovery. (It may not wipe out the memory of the Met.'s release of figures showing coloured minority involvement in "mugging offences" a few months earlier, however.) The cry for greater police accountability will certainly continue.

Let me narrow the focus of my attention and move on to what I consider to be an organisational dilemma of some magnitude if the major thrust of policing the eighties is to lie in the field of improving the quality and quantity of the police-community relations effort—the status of uniformed patrol work and of community relations itself. In so doing I am not ignoring the coloured minority–police relationship: rather I am using it to highlight a broader and more fundamental occupational malfunction which has serious implications for the spirit in which policemen actually deal with the public and in which law enforcement is executed.

Uniformed patrol work—taking to heart the sentiments expressed by recruiting literature, senior officers, working parties, royal commissions, police historians, and even many laymen—is at the heart of all successful police–community relations. It is here a police officer wins or loses public support by his day-to-day contact with them, it is here that the reputation of the Service is forged. The post-Scarman climate has, if anything, even more emphatically emphasised this kind of rhetoric.

Accepting that this is so, and using the phrase coined to describe it—"The Beat Ideology"—one finds that police organisational practices not only fail to endorse the vital nature of the beat patrol officer but produce a view amongst a large number of those at the "sharp end" that they have failed in their policing careers. This comes about in a number of ways:

1. The depicting in the media of the more exciting and glamourous aspects of police work—especially criminal investigation. This was compounded until comparatively recently by recruiting literature which emphasised specialist activities within the police.
2. The necessary use of the uniformed branch as a training vehicle. It thus becomes a basic process from which officers move elsewhere, particularly for "promotion."
3. The existence of specialist branches which look to the uniformed pool for the brighter officer and, by their very existence, deskill uniformed work.
4. The filling of all vacancies, even if temporary ones, from the uniformed branch.
5. The system of discipline in specialist branches which punishes officers by "returning" them to uniformed duty.
6. The system of appraisal used by senior officers which clearly indicates to men that they should move away from beat patrol work to broaden their experience and so be better candidates for promotion.

This dilemma is not a newly perceived one by any means. Such forms of growth are not all gain. They have two great disadvantages. They are apt to absorb the more experienced, intelligent and far-seeing members of the service. This inevitably reduces the relative standard of the remainder and is likely to have an adverse effect upon their morale. Secondly, once isolated in this way, the resources of manpower and equipment tend to be "frozen" in the sense that they cannot be used for anything else.

The youthfulness and inexperience of beat officers was a feature of policing upon which Lord Scarman forcefully commented but he was also perceptive enough to locate a further dimension of the problem when he expressed the wish to see more status accorded to Home Beat officers. These are individuals, variously called Resident Beat or Neighbourhood Constables, who are given a particular beat area to patrol, who are kept—as far as is organizationally possible—upon that patch, and whose job is to make contact with their community at every opportunity.

In giving a priority to community relations activities, evidence suggests that the view of those who are so deployed is that colleagues see them as "Hobby Bobbies," "Chocolate Bobbies" or "Immunity Constables," as not doing proper police work and reflecting an approach to crime that is "soft." Officers working in the inner cities have spoken to me of the frustration they feel in responding to strategies which appear to carry the message that certain crimes in certain situations must be ignored in pursuit of the general peacekeeping function. To them a section of the community is being indulged, they are engaged in a form of positive discrimination beneficial to the criminally disposed.

Police organizations, therefore, have much to do to convince men on the ground that policies and strategies will work and that the return will be an enhanced ability by the police to combat crime; equally, if not more importantly so, they have to create the climate which gives status to uniformed patrol and community relations activities. Crucial to both of these is the proper communication of senior management thinking to patrol officers and the greater involvement of them in the making of operational decisions.

The paradox, of course, is that these things most need to be done in those areas where young officers tend to have the most disillusioning experience of the police role and to respond, quite understandably, in a law enforcement and reactive style of policing. There are lessons to be learnt in this respect by all forces in how best to train officers for beat work, how to introduce them to the foot patrol system and how to prevent cynicism developing from their dealings with human frailties. Numerous officers comment on how beat work is demand led, unstructured, and not conducive to following a task through, especially of a community relations nature; the response must be to manage beat patrol and give meaning and cohesion to beat duties.

Whether we speak of job enrichment, job enlargement or enhanced job status, police forces cannot ignore the fact that the early promotions to senior positions which have prominently figured over relatively recent years have restricted promotion prospects of those joining the Service. Yet those recruits are very well qualified and probably of a standard that has not been seen in such numbers for a very long time; high unemployment and good salaries have allowed forces to pick and choose from a glut of applicants, to have the luxury of waiting lists.

If uniformed duty is not capable of being made more attractive and rewarding, then what is happening at the moment might prove to be more a curse than a blessing to police organizations; alert and capable young men and women will become frustrated, feel let down, and wonder where the satisfactions have disappeared which were extolled in recruit literature and advertising campaigns. On the other hand, should changes come about to revitalise and reinvigorate the foot patrol function, then the Service has made an excellent investment in capable young people who will wish to remain in public contact functions.

These views, opinions and interpretations, personal though they may be, are shared by growing numbers of police officers in British forces and by many who comment from other occupations and other perspectives on police performance. The fundamental causes of the policing dilemma may not be directly under police control; yet the healthy move toward more effective consultation with social agencies and communities, together with a police service somewhat less reticent to put its own problems before the public, should at least help those who address those causes to arrive at more effective policies and to better gauge the import of their decisions upon law and order and law enforcement.

From the point of view of the overseas observer it might well appear that British police forces are responding to the pressure of factors such as the rise in violent crime, economic recession, unemployment and racial tension, by moving along lines that will ultimately produce a para-military law enforcement system not unlike, for example, that of America. There is ample evidence for those who adopt this outlook to substantiate their interpretation in rigourous and persuasive terms.

The election of the Tory Party to office in May 1979 was looked upon as heralding a law and order movement by a government concerned by what it perceived as a nation requiring direction and discipline. The Conservative Government promised that more resources would be spent upon the fight against crime and nowhere was this made more apparent than in the substantial increase in police pay and in the growth of police establishments at a time when severe restraints and fierce cutbacks were being applied elsewhere.

In the wake of the Summer Riots and the Scarman Report of 1981, to which Government and police had brought arguments and explanations of a law and order nature, monies were found to allow police forces to adequately gear themselves for public order situations; the anti-riot gun, rubber bullets and plastic baton rounds, C.S. gas and water cannon, now became part of the standard police armoury. All officers were trained in riot control techniques and specialist units were set up which could rapidly respond to local needs and to external requests for mutual support. Further, a variety of legislation was held to extend police powers to the detriment of the individual and of justice.

To these wider apprehensions and censures of government and police can also be added the lack of progress in creating a completely independent system of investigating complaints against police, the failure to make racially prejudiced behaviour a disciplinary offence (as Scarman had suggested) and the refusal to provide police–community consultative committees with more than advisory powers. The return of a Tory government in the general election of June 1983, with a vastly increased overall majority (from 44 seats to 145), was argued to portend further moves in a law and order direction amongst which was expected to be new public order legislation.

More especially in the context of ethnic minorities, there is still the backcloth of a British Nationality Act which causes them a deeply felt resentment, a persistent and pernicious exercise of prejudice and discrimination in society at large and a disproportionate featuring of their numbers in unemployment statistics. The attempts by government to combat the evils of inner city deprivation are not having a marked impact although a number of initiatives are going ahead both with public and private fundings.

Sporadic disturbances have continued to take place in which bricks and petrol bombs have been thrown at police, shops and premises looted, and injuries and damage caused to police personnel and police equipment respectively. Charges of harassment and police brutality regularly arise, as does the old cry of police indifference to racial attacks. Recruitment of ethnic minorities to the police service, despite intense efforts, has been very poor—nor does it show very many signs of improving.

The public standing of police has not been helped by a number of incidents in police dealings with the public. More serious, however, was the so-called "Hernandez Affair" when a member of the Civilian Academic staff at the Metropolitan Police Cadet School at Hendon released essays written by students which were overly racist in nature. National publicity caused substantial embarrassment over this issue particularly as it followed closely upon the heels of a Home Office research report conducted in Leeds which states that "no detailed and consistent goals" could be identified in police training in race relations.

Nevertheless to see only what has been described as the "adversarial nature" of the debate about British policing is very dangerous and misses what can be seen as even more substantial evidence of government and police as determined to continue the tradition of policing by consent and to increase both the accountability of the police service and its consultation with the community. In the light of developments in 1983 these issues are worth developing.

As a preamble it is necessary to be aware that the "law and order" thrust that some have perceived in the Conservative government has had considerable public support. Nevertheless the reaction of the House of Commons to the proposal to re-introduce capital punishment was hardly the reflection of a constitutional body led by a retribution seeking government—despite the support of the Prime Minister and the Home Secretary for hanging for certain offences. Even the clause which would have allowed the hanging of anyone convicted of killing a police officer was rejected by a majority of 81.

More specifically, in regard to the police, the Home Office circular on local consultation arrangements between the community and the police which begat the pilot scheme in Lambeth, has now had time to be digested by Chief Officers and to stimulate the setting up of consultative committees across all forces. The Lambeth experience suggests already that they can be very successful not only in contributing toward the reduction of crime but also in widening the accountability at local level of local authority officials and their departments.

Thus the Lambeth police have found that residents quickly perceived the potential of consultation as a means to ask searching questions about the provision of services other than policing—such as education, employment, welfare and housing. This had the further benefit, as police perceive it, of diverting public attention to the real causes of the majority of policing problems and of once again underlining the fact that the inner city environment requires a co-operative and systematic endeavour by all parties if conditions are to be improved.

Another important development has been the commencement of Lay Visitors Pilot Schemes which the Home Office is monitoring and upon which it has issued guidelines to all forces. Such schemes allow periodic visits to police stations by an independent panel of citizens; they prepare a report upon their findings for consideration by the Lay Visitors Board—which includes police representatives. The purpose is to increase public confidence in the police by more open access to station premises.

In addition, emphasis was placed upon more community and race relations training and upon the need to equip officers with a "fundamental corpus of knowledge—a survival kit." All forms of continuation training were given the highest priority—as was the need for such training to develop practical policing skills. Probationer officers would not patrol alone until they had received 7 months of the 2 year probationer training programme and would remain under constant supervision and instruction until graduation as a fully-fledged constable. All of these developments take place, of course, alongside a massive effort to return men to the beat and to involve the community in the battle against crime. The most recent police strategy in the latter sphere is to organise Neighbourhood Watch schemes;

the American experience of these has been drawn upon substantially, as indeed has American experience of all aspects of policing ethnic minorities and of police–community relations.

The Chief Inspector of Constabulary's Report for 1982 showed, yet again, that crime had increased by some 10% and that the detection rate had fallen. Violence against police had increased with 6 police deaths recorded compared with 2 in 1981. The message of the police having to rely on public good will was repeated and it was said, "It may be a difficult task to break down barriers which may have grown up over many years, but we rightly expect police officers to attempt it and we have already seen that it can be successful."

Sir Kenneth Newman, as Commissioner of the Metropolitan Police, frankly admits in his report on the policing of the Metropolis that the demands are too great for his force to handle—"I cannot pretend that the force has the capacity to respond with equal competence and promptness to all the demands on it." His declared strategy, both on appointment and at each public pronouncement, is that increasing crime is a matter for police and public; this has already led him to take steps to devolve responsibility to more local levels, to deploy more men in gauging public demands, and to encourage the whole process of consultation.

It is interesting to note that the Commissioner's "Report" saw the charge made again that a dedicated campaign existed to denigrate police endeavours, that many of those who supported such a move were not at all representative of the people, and that those same critics would not be satisfied irrespective of the steps police take to put their own house in order. In other words, perhaps, we might say that there is a dimension to the policing of the inner city which demands actions from other than the police if political opportunists are not to feed richly upon the deprivations of urban life and are not to succeed in making the police a scapegoat for all Society's ills.

My final point is that the answer to the policing dilemma, if such there be, is that policing has to be construed in a much wider way and government has to help in drawing together those agencies and institutions which, in harness, are the only ones who can devise the policies and muster the resources which will make for a healthier urban environment. Fortunately, there are promising signs that government has recognised its responsibilities and that such a movement is already under way.

The accumulation of research in recent years has shown what a complex matter crime is and that the increasing of police establishments is no panacea for a rising crime rate. In particular, government thinking is moving toward a more sophisticated approach to crime prevention in which central and local government has to be supportive of police initiatives and respond constructively to those aspects of social life which can make a breeding ground of crime.

Critics of police have been busy reconstructing police history in their efforts to "correct" the image of the police service in public regard. The opinions that the post-Scarman developments endorse remain, nevertheless, those which see a British society very reluctant indeed to tread the path to a para-military form of policing. Instead the desire is to preserve the principle of policing by consent which is a cornerstone of the liberal-democratic tradition.

POLICE ROLE AND CAREER

This section illustrates the central theme of this book, which focuses on the ambivalence of the police and, parenthetically, the concomitant conflict on the part of academics, scholars, and researchers who are equally confused and inconsistent in assessing the police role in society. If the police are not sure whether their principal function is to prevent crime or serve the public, the researchers are no more consistent in their conclusions. At one extreme is a group of experts who declare that the police personality is authoritarian or unduly suspicious so that the officer perceives clientele as potential "symbolic assailants." On the other hand, research would appear to underscore findings that stress the essential mental health and altruism of police personnel.

In truth, the ambivalence of the police is built into the very structure of law enforcement by the variety of duties imposed upon police practitioners by the law, custom, and ethical requirements of the society they live in. To illustrate, the police officer may be the enforcer with a gun shooting to kill, or a savior who risks his or her own life willingly in the hope of saving someone who needs help. The officer knows that in every important incident his or her action will draw vituperation as well as applause.

Legal codes, departmental regulations, and municipal ordinances governing police conduct generally can be arranged into five categories:

1. Protection of life and property
2. Preservation of the peace
3. Detection of crime and arrest of offenders
4. Enforcement of laws
5. Crime prevention

As an officer moves through each of these levels during the course of a working tour, the conflicting demands imposed by these distinct roles create the anxiety, conflict, and frustration that characterize the ambivalence of the police in today's world. Few other occupations create as much stress, nor do they have as much potential for serious repercussions. Indeed, behavioral scientists tell us that laboratory experiments embodying such conflicts, demands, and stresses often produce symptoms of neurosis and other dysfunctions in their subjects. Police officers face these hazards without the cushioning of malpractice insurance to rescue them when matters go awry.

Police systems and organizations spontaneously generate special purpose units such as tactical patrol forces, crime prevention units, vice squads, and police–community relations units; each of these generates an empire and a power base within a department. In the competition for aggrandizement and for a larger share of the always-limited resources, the entire agency often becomes a battleground where there is a shifting balance of power. This situation is the structural and systemic equivalent to personal social-psychological ambivalence. Each reinforces the other. The net effect is that a police officer's personal uncertainties and role conflicts are symbiotically compounded by the organizational dilemmas.

Perhaps it is the dynamic nature of the subject matter, or the ephemeral style of the police environment, that causes confusion for academic researchers so that they too are uncertain as to the appropriateness of their concepts, data, findings, and conclusions with respect to the police. The difficulties inherent in police research are further exacerbated by the turbulent character of the modern academic environment in terms of distribution of grant money, promotions, and the political implications of one's findings. Finally, there is always the hidden agenda of ideological considerations.

Explanations of Police Behavior: A Critical Review and Analysis

John F. Galliher

PROLOGUE FOR THE 1980S

It was more than a decade ago when I wrote this review of research on police behavior. In the intervening years, of course, much more of the same type of research has been conducted, but sadly the same shortcomings of such studies that I noticed approximately ten years ago are still evident. A recent edition of the *Annals* (November 1980) devoted to the police, for example, shows the same tendency toward a microscopic focus on detail that existed a decade ago. Across all of the articles in the issue, there is no discussion of concepts or theories that could further our understanding of police behavior. Every article focusing on police behavior offers a different ad hoc piecemeal explanation. And one article even claims that my review of explanations of police behavior, which relies instead on a social structural interpretation, can be discredited because it is 1) "radical," 2) reduces "functions of the police in the United States to nothing more than acts of capitalist oppression," and 3) is a "denial of the legitimacy of the entire police function" (Klockars, 1980:42). Readers can judge for themselves if this is true. In any event, such allergic reactions to social structural analysis help explain the lack of theoretical advances toward more parsimonious explanation in the study of the police and law enforcement.

SOURCE: *The Sociological Quarterly* 12 (Summer 1971), pp. 308–318.

In recent years many social scientists have attempted to explain why police behave the way they do in performing their duties. What follows is a review of some dominant themes running through the myriad of articles and books which have appeared on this subject in the last few years. This survey does not purport to offer an exhaustive coverage of all relevant literature but is intentionally selective to highlight some observable patterns. After this review, some observations will be made regarding the theoretical and empirical weaknesses in this research, and an analysis of some reasons for these deficiencies will be discussed. Finally, some suggestions will be made for profitable new directions for future research on police behavior.

PSYCHOLOGICAL PERSPECTIVE

Several sociologists have focused upon the personality of the individual police officer as important in determining how he performs his role. Skolnick (1966:42–70) suggests that policemen have a "working personality" by which he means a set of cognitive tendencies which influence their work. By virtue of enforcing the law, the police become very supportive of the status quo. Skolnick argues that to believe in their task and appear consistent to themselves, police become extremely politically conservative. Moreover, because of their job, police officers are highly sensitive to signs of danger.

> A young man may suggest the threat of violence to the policeman by his manner of walking or "strutting," the insolence in the demeanor being registered by the policeman as a possible preamble to later attack (Skolnick, 1966:46).

This helps explain police willingness to act against some citizens which might otherwise be interpreted merely as harassment.

Niederhoffer (1967:103–151, especially 118–119) speculates that police officers are transformed into authoritarian personalities by virtue of the police role. He (Niederhoffer, 1967:90–102) also suggests that they develop a cynicism toward the public which is a consequence of performing their job. Because their job throws them into contact with so many dishonest people, officers begin to see everyone as corrupt. Niederhoffer (1967:95) quotes a detective as follows: "I am convinced that we are turning into a nation of thieves. I have sadly concluded that nine out of ten persons are dishonest."

McNamara (1967:211–212) administered F scales to police recruits and found an increase in authoritarianism before and after recruit police training and a further increase after one year on the job. Police with two years of experience were found to be even more authoritarian than any of the other groups. This supports the notion that police apparently become more authoritarian as a result of their experience as police officers. McNamara (1967:212) suggests that this increased authoritarianism is likely to lead to disagreement with the courts' emphasis upon individual rights.

It should be noted that the significance of McNamara's research is somewhat blunted by Bayley and Mendelsohn's (1969:17–18) finding that police are, in fact, *less* authoritarian than other citizens. Also, Niederhoffer (1967:150) observes that in McNamara's research the mean score on the F scale was slightly less than that found by the developers of the instrument when testing civilians of a similar social class. Moreover, even if police are made more authoritarian by their occupational role, this says nothing about the structural determinants of this influence. Why is it that the environment is structured to give officers experiences that increase their authoritarianism?

DEMANDS OF THE IMMEDIATE SITUATION

Recently a number of articles have emphasized the great amount of discretion police are free to use in deciding to make an arrest. It has been found that police rely heavily on the characteristics of the immediate situation in making these decisions.

For example, Bittner (1967) found that police on skid row make their decision to arrest an individual mainly on the basis of the perceived risk of the person creating a disorder rather than on the basis of degree of guilt. Black (1970) and Black and Reiss (1970) found that a major component in this decision to arrest is the preference of the complainant. Some studies have also found that the deference displayed by the suspect has a bearing on the use of discretion by the officer (Westley, 1953; Piliavin and Briar, 1964). Regarding the choice of a disposition, Piliavin and Briar (1964:210) suggest that, "in the opinion of juvenile patrolmen themselves the demeanor of apprehended juveniles was a major determinant of their decisions for 50–60 percent of the juvenile cases they processed."

However, police use of discretion as well as suspects' behavior are not random occurrences. All occur within a social structural context. Unfortunately, some sociologists are mainly concerned with the demands of the immediate situation and neglect the broader social structure within which this interaction occurs. A relevant question in this connection, which is seldom asked is, why does it seem that black Americans more frequently than other citizens are loath to show respect for the police?

ROLE CONFLICT

Some studies of police behavior locate explanations in a social psychological, role conflict model. The basic idea is that officers perceive conflicting expectations from others regarding how they should carry out their job. Skolnick (1966:1–22) discusses the policeman's "dilemma" of enforcing the law while at the same time maintaining order. The police believe they are expected to do both, but order maintenance may at times require the officer to work outside the law ignoring a suspect's constitutional rights. Wilson (1963:199) suggests that this conflict between achieving order or catching a suspect is especially intense when a "crusade" is launched by a department to solve an important case. The rules of law require respect for civil liberties but during times of crisis, police feel compelled to forget this and to consider only the efficiency of means in catching the criminal.

Wilson (1963:198–199) observes another source of conflicting expectations. In a heterogeneous society one part of the public may want different kinds of enforcement from the police than do other parts. For example, urban liberals and blacks feel differently about police use of force than other citizens.

Preiss and Ehrlich (1966:94–121) also report on police officers' perceptions of conflicting expectations of the various audience groups in which they are involved. One example of this role conflict which they report is discrepancies perceived between officers' wives' views and their supervisors' views regarding the appropriate limitations in the demands of their job (Preiss and Ehrlich, 1966:99–101). That is, officers perceive their wives as believing the obligations to the job should end after eight hours, while their supervisors see their obligations as continuing 24 hours a day.

The implication in all of this literature is that because of these role conflicts officers may be forced to make certain compromises, accommodations, and choices. Unfortunately, no theoretical models are offered to help predict the specific choices made. Perhaps this is true because of insufficient attention to structural bases of the role conflict.

SUBCULTURAL APPROACH

Other studies have sought to explain police behavior by using what is essentially a subcultural approach. The argument is that police officers are a unique group. Somewhat like delinquent boys, they are subjected to special strains and make collective rather than individual adjustments to these problems.

In an early police study, Westley (1953) found evidence of a police subculture as reflected in a code justifying the use of violence to coerce respect.

> The most significant finding is that at least 37 percent of the men believed that it was legitimate to use violence to coerce respect. This suggests that policemen use the resource of violence to persuade their audience (the public) to respect their occupational status. In terms of the policeman's definition of the situation, the individual who lacks respect for the police, the "wise guy" who talks back, or any individual who acts or talks in a disrespectful way, deserves brutality (Westley, 1953:39).

Westley also found that this code forbids police from informing against fellow officers. Typically, officers indicated that they would adhere to this rule of secrecy which functions to protect the police against attacks from the community (Westley, 1956).

> However, policemen cannot and do not employ sanctions against their colleagues for using violence, and individual men who personally condemn the use of violence and avoid it whenever possible refuse openly to condemn acts of violence by other men on the force (Westley, 1953:40).[1]

More recent research by Stoddard (1968), Savitz (1970), and Reiss (1968) supports the notion of a code of secrecy.

Skolnick (1966:53–58) suggests that the dangerousness of the police mission as well as the requirement that officers use authority against civilians contributes to solidarity. The reasoning is that the more hostility the police receive from the public the more isolated they become and consequently the more dependent they become upon each other.[2]

Although these studies have used socio-cultural variables in their analyses of police behavior, they have erred in defining the environment of the police as a given, as constant across all communities. One problem with such an approach is that it is impossible to use it to explain variations in police attitudes and behavior found in different communities. If we can observe differences in law enforcement practices in various communities, then it seems reasonable to expect differences in the nature of the subculture and related structural strains.

DEPARTMENTAL CHARACTERISTICS APPROACH

The problem of explaining differences in policing styles has received some attention from those focusing on departmental characteristics as independent determinants of police behavior and attitudes. The argument is that police behavior is a result of the particular situation found in each department.[3]

[1] Westley's internal footnotes have been omitted.

[2] A similar point is made in Fogelson (1968) and Westley (1956:254–255).

[3] I am indebted to Patrick Donovan for suggesting this type of explanation.

Wilson (1968a:9–30) compares the handling of juveniles in an efficient, highly-trained professional department and in a nonprofessional department. He found that the former was much more likely to process juvenile law violators officially than the latter. The nonprofessional department relied much more heavily on informal alternatives such as issuing warnings.

In *Varieties of Police Behavior*, Wilson (1968b) isolates three types of law enforcement style displayed by various departments. One style of law enforcement emphasizes service to the community, another strict enforcement of all laws, and one is mainly oriented to maintenance of order. Most important for this discussion is that Wilson pictures police departments as having some independence, as not being directly controlled by the community. One reflection of this independence is that it is not always possible to predict the style of law enforcement given the characteristics of the community (Wilson, 1968b:227–277).

Gardiner (1969:72) explains much of the difference in traffic law enforcement in two communities by the differences in the desires of the chiefs of the two departments. One problem with this type of analysis is that it implicitly assumes that the recruitment of chiefs into a department is random or at least not significantly affected by the social structure.

Neither Gardiner nor Wilson claim that the law enforcement style is completely independent of the community, but they are, nonetheless, unable to develop a conceptual model to handle these social structural relationships.

SOCIO-CULTURAL APPROACH

A few attempts have been made to describe how societies or communities seem to determine the characteristics of local police.

In comparing European police with those in the United States, Berkley (1969) found the latter much more prone to violence. This he claims is a direct reflection of American values.

> If the American police are prone to use violent and repressive tactics, American society offers them the means and the climate to do so. No other democratic nation compares to the United States in the acceptance and even glorification of violence as a way to solve problems (Berkley, 1969:197).

Banton (1964:86–126) explains many of the differences he found in comparing British and American police officers by virtue of the greater social integration in Great Britain. Since Britain is a more homogeneous society with citizens holding more consistent values, it is predictable that British police would be exposed to less violence. This allows the police to operate differently. There is less reason to smother all internal strains within a department and less reason for solidarity (Banton, 1964:118–119).

Stinchcombe (1963) compares urban and rural differences in the structural conditions which affect policing. In cities, large numbers of people are concentrated into relatively small amounts of public space. This makes police control of public places more economical. Moreover, it is in the cities that informal controls are weakest and where patrol is most necessary. Therefore, Stinchcombe says this makes sense of the fact that police in the cities can and do frequently act on their own initiative in making arrests. In rural areas it is both less economical and less necessary to patrol public places and, therefore, the rural police initiate fewer of their arrests and rely more on citizen complaints to attract their attention to a problem (Stinchcombe, 1963:152).

Although the approaches in this section take greater account of social structural influences than any of those preceding, on the whole they still offer an incomplete conceptual framework. *The fundamental problem in all the social science explanations of police behavior is that they take no systematic account of the influence of class conflict on law enforcement.*

CONCEPTUAL MODELS AND EMPIRICAL EVIDENCE

We have just seen that if the psychological characteristics of officers are studied, the implication is that this is important in understanding police behavior. By studying the demands of the immediate situation which officers face or their role conflicts, it is also sometimes assumed that we can better understand their method of operation. Others point to a police subculture or the department leadership to explain officers' behavior. Only those studies that emphasize the social structural environment of policing have the potential of directing attention to social class as a determinant of law enforcement style. All others, of necessity, would miss the importance of class conflict since they direct attention away from the social structure toward a low-level description of the action in immediate law enforcement situations.

Much of police behavior seems most easily explained if one considers that whenever there is a conflict of interests between the dominant classes in a society and less powerful groups, the police protect the interests of the former and regulate the behavior of the latter. If the police role attracts authoritarian individuals and increases their authoritarianism once on the job, perhaps this happens because of the demands made upon the police to suppress economic and racial minorities. Such tasks are most attractive to the authoritarian personality and undoubtedly any of the officer's initial doubts about such activities are lessened by an increasingly authoritarian orientation. The literature indicating that police are free to use discretion in making arrests also shows that this discretion is used to the disadvantage of minority groups (Skolnick, 1966:85; Goldman, 1963; Wald, 1967:139–151; Wilson, 1968a). Wilson's (1963:198–199) observations regarding the differing demands of blacks and urban liberals compared to other citizens as a source of role conflict for the police can be interpreted in class conflict terms. Officers can be seen as experiencing role conflict in part because of different and conflicting demands from various social classes in the community. There is some evidence that police subcultures develop in a department both to legitimize and keep secret suppression of economic and racial minorities (Reiss, 1968; Westley, 1970). Department leadership and methods of operation can be interpreted as a response to the demands of powerful interest groups (Walker, 1968; especially 13–14). Simple descriptions of police personalities or specific situations faced by the police take no account of class interests and class conflict.

Mills (1943) observes that concern with specific situations among social scientists leads to such a low level of abstraction that the data can't be brought together within a theoretical framework. Moreover, he contends that this low level of abstraction does not permit an examination of the normative structures and how they are related to the distribution of power. This is exactly what seems to have happened in studies of the police. Social scientists have been busy collecting disparate "facts" about policing and have either been unable or unwilling to develop related conceptual frameworks which take account of the social structure, including a consideration of social class. Newman (1966:181–182) claims that sociological treatment of the criminal justice system including the police is lacking in a theoretical framework and, as a consequence, is empirically naive. This reflects Merton's (1968:139–155) well-known argument that without an integrated theoretical framework even intelligent fact-gathering is impossible.

An important test of any conceptual model is the degree to which it is congruent with and clarifies the bulk of relevant empirical data. Kitsuse and Cicourel (1963:136–137) maintain that since official rates of deviant behavior are compiled by specific organizations, these rates reflect organizational methods of operation. Using this reasoning, one readily available pool of information regarding police behavior is arrest data.

It is well established that in most areas of the United States the majority of those people arrested are poor and/or black. As indicated earlier, some observers of arrest practices who emphasize that police can exercise great discretion show that in those cases where this discretion can be most easily exercised, the bulk of those arrested are poor and black (Skolnick, 1966:85; Goldman, 1963; Wald, 1967:139–151; Wilson, 1968a). There is also an awareness of other discriminatory treatment given to economic and racial minorities by the police such as verbal and physical harassment (Reiss, 1968; Schwartz, 1967:446–447).

Curiously, these patterns found in arrest practices and other police treatment of minorities haven't influenced the theoretical models used in explaining police behavior. If they were used, social class and class conflict would necessarily be incorporated into explanations of police behavior. Cook (1967:120) observes that "there is no recognition that the processes of law enforcement serve the interests of dominant groups in the society and either ignore or oppose the interests of those in lower social strata." Perhaps the reason for this is that social scientists have been misusing arrest data. They have been using it as a basis upon which to generate theories of criminal behavior and have been neglecting its uses as a reflection of police behavior.

Here and there some cursory recognition of class does appear. Quite early in *Behind the Shield*, Niederhoffer (1967) introduces the notion of class and its effects on law enforcement. He quotes Joseph Lohman, the late Dean of the School of Criminology of the University of California at Berkeley, who was himself a police officer at one time. "The police function [is] to support and enforce the interests of the dominant political, social, and economic interests of the town, and only incidentally to enforce the law" (Niederhoffer, 1967:12). But if Niederhoffer mentions class quickly, he drops it even more quickly in favor of "the principle of equilibrium" meaning that police are mainly concerned with protecting themselves from all criticism from whatever source (Niederhoffer, 1967:13–15).

Wilson (1963:213) suggests in passing that a professional police force which applies the law equally to all citizens is impossible in a highly stratified community. Elsewhere in the same paper he says:

> Property owners, for example, may want maximum protection of their property and of their privacy; slum dwellers, however, may not like the amount of police activity necessary to attain the property owners' ends. Negroes and urban liberals may unite in seeking to end "police brutality"; lower-middle-class homeowners whose neighborhoods are "threatened" with Negro invasion may want the police to deal harshly with Negroes or to look the other way while the homeowners themselves deal harshly with them (Wilson, 1963:198–199).

Even though class is introduced, Wilson either cannot or will not follow through with any analysis. All he can bring himself to say is that this presents the police with an inconsistency.

In his Ph.D. dissertation, which was only recently published in full, Westley (1970) shows that police indicated they respond differently to different social classes. One policeman is quoted as saying that "in the better districts the purpose is to make friends out of the people and get them to like you. If you react rough to them, naturally they will hate you" (Westley, 1970:98). On the other hand, it seems just as obvious to the police that they can only elicit respect and obedience from slum dwellers by resorting to force (Westley, 1970:99). Westley (1970:96–99) suggests that part of the difference in the police perception of the affluent and poor is due to the differences in their political power—police are afraid to brutalize the wealthy because of their political influence. Moreover, the poor are seen as more disposed to law violation and conflict with the police because of their great economic need. Just as it appears that Westley is on the verge of a thorough structural analysis of police behavior, he tells the reader that police attitudes and behavior have subcultural roots, and surprisingly, he ignores the effects of class conflict upon this subculture.

[*Editors' Note:* A review of police studies that have been preeminent in the past ten years underscores Galliher's assertion that most researchers on the police tend to ignore the variable of class conflict in their analyses of police culture and police organization. See for example: Jonathan Rubinstein, *City Police* (1973); Herman Goldstein *Policing a Free Society* (1977); Robert M. Fogelson, *Big City Police* (1977); William Ker Muir, Jr., *Police: Street Corner Politicians* (1977); James Q. Wilson, *The Investigators* (1978); Donald J. Black, *The Manners and Customs of the Police* (1980); Michael K. Brown, *Working the Street* (1981); and Susan Ehrlich Martin, *Breaking and Entering* (1982).]

DIRTY WORK AT HOME AND ABROAD

The fact that social scientists have not recognized the nature of police work is perhaps in some ways similar to the German citizens' unfamiliarity with the operation of the S.S. Hughes (1962) describes the apparent ignorance of Germans regarding the systematic extermination of the Jews. He contends that the S.S. was used by the German people to solve their Jewish problem. Most Germans felt that a Jewish problem did exist, but once the S.S. was created it not only took care of the problem but allowed most German citizens to remain uninvolved in the solution. Since the S.S. was sworn to secrecy, German citizens could claim ignorance of what this group was doing. One of Hughes' major assumptions is that the public doesn't accurately perceive the morally outrageous nature of dirty work and that this obfuscation is indeed a function of dirty work.

Some immediate similarities appear between the S.S. role in wartime Germany and the police role in the United States. Many Americans would doubtlessly agree that we have a "Negro problem." The police, like the S.S., are highly secretive (Westley, 1956; Reiss, 1968; Savitz, 1970; Stoddard, 1968) which keeps their morally questionable acts shielded from most Americans. This functions to control poor and black Americans in any way necessary while other citizens can continue to believe this is a free democratic society and yet have their property protected at the same time. In fact, the dirty work of policing American slums is so well hidden from the middle classes that even middle class sociologists fail to understand its meaning and function, the function being the maintenance of a highly economically-stratified and racist society.

The police are not a part of the dominant classes of American society, usually being recruited from the lower class or lower middle class (Preiss and Ehrlich, 1966:12; Niederhoffer, 1967:36–38; McNamara, 1967:193; Bayley and Mendelsohn, 1969:6). . . .

Social scientists studying the police have typically assumed that the individual police officer or department is independent to implement social policy much as they see fit. This assumption is reflected in much of the literature reviewed here which stresses the importance of police personalities, discretion, subculture, or police chiefs as determinants of law enforcement style.[4] It is incredible that social scientists would believe that a highly-stratified society would allow lower class or marginally middle class people such as the police to control major social policy.

If social scientists are unable to understand the place of law enforcement in class conflict, then it should not be surprising that other well-educated political liberals, radical students, and many black Americans would see the police as a main source of trouble. Their criticism lends public credence to the social science research which implies that the police are somehow individually or collectively responsible for the way in which laws are enforced. To the degree that police are seen as independent, they will be held responsible to the same degree, of course, for the manner in which they operate.

CONCLUSION

It is sometimes suggested that if police were better organized, this would help them do a better job and would reduce police–community tensions (Wilson, 1968b; Berkley, 1969). Also, the suggestion is sometimes made that better-trained police would solve many of the problems they encounter (Berkley, 1969:87; Skolnick, 1969:290–291; Task Force Report: The Police, 1967:36–37). However, as Terris (1967:63–64) has shown, some cities with very well-trained police still have major police–minority problems. One interpretation for this is that as long as police are used for the purpose of containing economic and racial minorities, police conflicts will not subside. If police are better educated and better organized, they will just become more efficient oppressors.

Since there are obvious differences in law enforcement styles across communities and countries, students of police behavior can profit by directing their research toward an analysis of what effect the presence of large numbers of economic and racial minorities has upon the style of law enforcement in a given jurisdiction. The question involves the relationship between the scope of class conflict and the behavior of the police. The answer to this question would include a description of the exact nature of the structural linkage between the community and local police departments and the kind of theoretical model(s) which would allow us to predict these linkages.

If it is assumed "that the processes of law enforcement serve the interests of dominant groups in the society and either ignore or oppose the interests of those in lower social strata" (Cook, 1967:120), one might make certain predictions for police behavior. Taking such a perspective one might predict, for example, that in heterogeneous communities with large numbers of economic and racial minorities police would behave in an oppressive fashion toward minorities because of the threat these people symbolize to the rest of the community. Following this reasoning this type of police behavior seems less likely to occur in more homogeneous communities.

The argument developed here is not meant to imply that consideration of class conflict is a *sufficient* condition for further understanding of police behavior but only that it is a *necessary* condition. It's not that class conflict alone can help us better understand police behavior but only that it is one element that must be considered.

REFERENCES

Banton, Michael. 1964 *The Policeman in the Community*. New York: Basic Books.

Bayley, David H. and Harold Mendelsohn. 1969 *Minorities and the Police*. New York: The Free Press.

Berkley, George E. 1969 *The Democratic Policeman.* Boston: Beacon Press.

Bittner, E. 1967 "The police on skid-row: a study of peace-keeping." *American Sociological Review* 32 (October):699–715.

Black, D. J. 1970 "Production of crime rates." *American Sociological Review* 35 (August):733–748.

Black, D. J. and A. J. Reiss 1970 "Police control of

[4] An especially clear illustration of this emphasis on the independence of the police is in Skolnick's *The Politics of Protest* (1969).

juveniles." *American Sociological Review* 35 (February):63–77.

Cook, W. 1967 "Policemen in society: which side are they on?" *Berkeley Journal of Sociology* 12 (Summer):117–129.

Fogelson, R. M. 1968 "From resentment to confrontation: the police, the Negroes, and the outbreak of the nineteen-sixties riots." *Political Science Quarterly* 83 (June):217–247.

Gardiner, John A. 1969 *Traffic and the Police, Variations in Law-Enforcement Policy*. Cambridge: Harvard University Press.

Goldman, Nathan. 1963 *The Differential Selection of Juvenile Offenders for Court Appearance*. New York: National Research and Information Center, National Council on Crime and Delinquency.

Hughes, E. C. 1962 "Good people and dirty work." *Social Problems* 10 (Summer):3–11.

Kitsuse, J. I. and A. V. Cicourel. 1963 "A note on the uses of official statistics." *Social Problems* 11 (Fall):131–139.

Klockars, Carl B. 1980 "The Dirty Harry Problem." *The Annals*, 452 (November):42.

McNamara, John H. 1967 "Uncertainties in police work: the relevance of police recruits' backgrounds and training." Pp. 163–252 in David J. Bordua (ed.), *The Police*. New York: John Wiley & Sons.

Merton, Robert K. 1968 "The bearing of sociological theory on empirical research." Pp. 139–155 in Robert K. Merton, *Social Theory and Social Structure*. New York: The Free Press.

Mills, C. W. 1943 "The professional ideology of social pathologists." *American Journal of Sociology* 59 (September):165–180.

Newman, Donald J. 1966 "Sociologists and the administration of criminal justice." Pp. 177–187 in Arthur B. Shostak (ed.), *Sociology in Action*. Homewood, Ill.: Dorsey Press.

Niederhoffer, Arthur. 1967 *Behind the Shield: The Police in Urban Society*. Garden City, N.Y.: Doubleday & Company.

Piliavin, I. and S. Briar. 1964 "Police encounters with juveniles." *American Journal of Sociology* 70 (September):206–214.

Preiss, Jack J. and Howard J. Ehrlich. 1966 *An Examination of Role Theory, The Case of the State Police*. Lincoln: University of Nebraska Press.

Reiss, A. J., Jr. 1968 "Police brutality—answers to key questions." *Trans-action* 5 (July–August):10–19.

Savitz, L. 1970 "The dimensions of police loyalty." *American Behavioral Scientist* (May–June, July–August):693–704.

Schwartz, H. 1967 "Stop and frisk (a case study in judicial control of the police)." *Criminal Law, Criminology and Police Science* 58 (December):433–464.

Skolnick, Jerome H. 1969 *The Politics of Protest*. New York: Simon and Schuster. 1966 *Justice Without Trial*. New York: John Wiley and Sons.

Stinchcombe, A. L. 1963 "Institutions of privacy in the determination of police administrative practice." *American Journal of Sociology* 69 (September):150–160.

Stoddard, E. R. 1968 "The informal 'code' of police deviancy: a group approach to 'blue-coat crime.' " *Criminal Law, Criminology and Police Science* 59 (June):201–213.

Task Force Report: The Police 1967 Washington, D.C.: U.S. Government Printing Office (Number 237–588).

Terris, B. J. 1967 "The role of the police." *The Annals* 374 (November):58–69.

Walker, Daniel. 1968 *Rights in Conflict*. New York: Bantam Books.

Wald, Patricia M. 1967 "Poverty and criminal justice." Pp. 139–151 in Task Force Report: The Courts. Washington, D.C.: U.S. Government Printing Office (Number 239-114).

Westley, William A. 1970 *Violence and the Police: A Sociological Study of Law, Custom, and Morality*. Cambridge: MIT Press. 1956 "Secrecy and the police." *Social Forces* 34 (March):254–257. 1953 "Violence and the police." *American Journal of Sociology* 59 (July):34–41.

Wilson, James Q. 1968a "The police and the delinquent in two cities." Pp. 9–30 in Stanton Wheeler (ed.), *Controlling Delinquents*. New York: John Wiley & Sons. 1968b *Varieties of Police Behavior*. Cambridge: Harvard University Press. 1963 "The police and their problems: a theory." *Public Policy*, A Yearbook of the Graduate School of Public Administration, Harvard University 12, 189–216.

The Detective Task: State of the Art, Science, Craft?

Thomas A. Reppetto

THE DECLINE OF THE DETECTIVE?

Amidst the intellectual and administrative ferment which has characterized American policing since the mid-1960's one major area of change and controversy has been that of criminal investigation. This has been highlighted by a series of sharp attacks on the once premier figure of the detective. A former New York City police commissioner described his detective force (*circa* 1970) in the following words:

> The ambitious ones might be bar-hopping with reporters, politicians, or judges; the shake-down artists, bar-hopping too, might be "shopping"; the lazier ones could be glued to a bar stool ostensibly picking up "information." The real characters, known in the locker rooms as "sock peddlers," would be on the prowl for "discounts" for the boys. Some of the minor crimes besetting the city were sadly of the Bureau's own making.[1]

Recently, another chief declared that some of his detectives "wouldn't know how to make an arrest if a guy walked in and turned himself in."[2] In the operational sphere detective units have been reduced in strength, brought under closer supervision, or had some of their functions and personnel reassigned to the patrol force.

If one surveys the present scene in relation to the not-so-distant past, times have definitely changed. One might recall that as recently as 1954 the Police Commissioner of New York City found it impossible to demote a popular patrolman-detective, an individual who eventually was appointed to a major federal law enforcement post by the President of the United States.[3] In 1956 the Mayor of San Francisco chose a patrolman/detective to be Chief of Police. America's premier law enforcement agency, the F.B.I., headed until 1972 by the nation's foremost police officer, was exclusively a detective force. How then, has the proud detective fallen into decline, if in fact, he has? It is the purpose of this article to examine detective work in America to determine its current state and likely future directions, particularly in light of the view that detectives are on the defensive and their futures clouded.

An understanding of American trends may be afforded by an examination of three major research studies of contemporary detective work. These are the Rand Corporation's national study of criminal investigation conducted for the United States Department of Justice, the Urban Institute study, financed by the Police Foundation, of coordinated team patrol in Rochester, New York, and Harvard professor James Q. Wilson's study of two national law enforcement agencies, the Federal Bureau of Investigation (F.B.I.) and the Drug Enforcement Agency (D.E.A.).

The Rand Report* published in 1975, essentially makes two points about detective work. (1) Criminal investigation is an inherently low-yield undertaking, and (2) It is carried on inefficiently. For example, it notes:

> The single most important determinant of whether or not a case will be solved is the information the victim supplies to the immediately responding patrol officer. If information that uniquely identifies the perpetrator is not presented at the time the crime is reported, the perpetrator, by and large, will not be subsequently identified.
>
> Differences in investigative training, staffing, workload, and procedures appear to have no appreciable effect on crime, arrest or clearance rates.
>
> The method by which police investigators are organized (i.e., team policing, specialists vs. generalists, patrolmen-investigators) cannot be related to variations in crime, arrest, and clearance rates.

All of these tend to support the proposition that detective work is inherently non-productive, i.e., when one

SOURCE: *Police Studies* I, No. 3 (September 1978), pp. 5–10.

* For readers who may be unacquainted with the organization, Rand (an acronym for research and development) was created in the 1940's by the U.S. military to bring to bear top-quality civilian scientific expertise on defense problems. The typical Rand analyst in the police field is a Ph.D. level operations researcher or social scientist of a caliber equivalent to the faculty of institutions such as Harvard or M.I.T.

searches for the needle in the haystack most of the time one will not find it, no matter how hard or systematically one works.

Another finding is the difference between pre- and post-arrest detective work. According to Rand, while the search for the suspect is largely a matter of information available at the crime scene (a condition over which the efforts of the detective have little effect) the post-arrest case preparation stage, if properly done can significantly affect the legal outcome of the case. Not surprisingly, the report calls for:

> Reducing follow-up investigation on all cases except those involving the most serious offenses.
>
> Placing post-arrest (i.e., suspect in custody) investigations under the authority of the prosecutor.

However, the report also declared that:

> Investigative strike forces have a significant potential to increase arrest rates for a few difficult target offenses, provided they remain concentrated on activities for which they are uniquely qualified,

and recommended the establishment of a Major Offenders Unit to investigate serious crimes.[4] These would seem to suggest that detective work is carried on inefficiently and could be made more productive.

Obviously, the findings and recommendations have very different implications. If a particular enterprise is of dubious utility one is well advised not to invest significant resources in it. In contrast, if it is poorly done but has high potential, then a change of personnel or techniques may produce rich dividends. Thus it remains unclear whether pre-arrest investigations are inherently futile or inefficiently carried on.

The Rand Report has attracted considerable public attention by suggesting that half the detective force in any police department could be dispensed with. This in part explains why it has attracted a chorus of critics. For example, in a review of the report, the Los Angeles Police Department concluded that the Rand recommendation, "that half of the investigative effort could be eliminated without lessening the effectiveness of criminal investigation cannot be seriously considered as anything other than the unsubstantiated opinions of researchers who lack the insight and understanding of the police investigation function necessary to draw such a conclusion."[5]

In 1971 the Police Department of Rochester, New York (a city of 300,000 population) began an experiment to test the efficiency of coordinated team patrol (CTP). Prior to this time the police department followed the standard practice of maintaining separate patrol and detective units, the former to conduct preliminary investigations and the latter, follow-up activities. Under CTP, police operations in a particular geographic area were carried out by combined units of patrol and detective officers. After a period of time the experiment was evaluated by the Police Foundation and it was found that in cases of burglary, robbery and larceny, the teams had a substantially higher arrest rate and a higher rate of case clearance. The study also found that the team arrangement increased the amount of communication between patrol and investigative officers and helped to solve the morale problem between patrol officers and investigative personnel.

On the negative side, the researchers found that the teams' on-scene arrests for burglary, robbery and larceny were less likely to result in prosecutions than the non-teams'. The researchers attributed this to the teams' eagerness to make a lot of arrests, and to the fact that the teams were serving low-income areas where people generally were less willing to participate in the process of bringing a case to trial. As a result of the findings the Rochester Police Department organized the entire department into CTP units.[6]

In contrast to the previous studies which concentrated on local police, the study by Professor James Q. Wilson examined federal law enforcement as exemplified by the F.B.I. and the DEA. While the two agencies would appear similar, according to Wilson, their basic field work was quite different. F.B.I. agents functioned as "detectives" (i.e., investigators) in an effort to solve crimes reported to them. In contrast, narcotic agents had to discover crimes and find a means to apprehend criminals actually engaging in drug law violations. Generally this took the form of infiltrating agents into a drug operation so they could make buys and arrest the sellers. As a result Wilson described narcotic agents as "instigators" (in the nonpejorative sense). In essence the F.B.I. was found to follow a reactive strategy while the DEA employed a proactive one. His study also questioned whether drug enforcement aimed at organized narcotic distribution networks might be more effective if the DEA foreswore instigation in favor of intelligence operations designed to produce detailed information which would, over time, lead to prosecutable conspiracy cases.[7]

IMAGES OF THE DETECTIVE

The foregoing review of the three studies suggests a number of values and dimensions to detective work, not all of which are dealt with in each account. Thus the studies are not always looking at the same phenomenon and therefore not in total agreement. As a result, policy-makers would be unwise to apply various recommendations indiscriminately.

In the first instance, one can discern at least four types of detective or criminal investigator. Wilson identifies the detective (that is, the true criminal investigator), the instigator or undercover agent, and the intelligence or analyst-type officer. In contrast, the Rochester study concentrates on the neighborhood level criminal investigator. Over several generations of American policing the organization of detective work has tended to fall into two divisions, territorial generalists and headquarters specialists. The former were usually attached to precinct or neighborhood stations working closely with, or under, the local patrol force and dealt with a wide range of routine crimes. In contrast, the headquarters detectives were organized into special squads such as homicide or robbery and concentrated on major investigations, i.e., those involving large loss, serious assault, or the operations of metropolitan or interstate criminals. Very few American public (as opposed to private) detectives worked under cover—narcotics investigations being the most common instance—and even fewer functioned as intelligence analysts of the type found in the C.I.A. or the military.

To further illuminate or complicate the discussion the present writer would introduce a fifth category of detective, the administrative type. Generally, one assumes that a detective concentrates on investigations related to various criminal offenses. Thus individuals engaged in routine anti-crime patrol or case-preparation, which is essentially clerical, rather than investigatory, are not truly detectives though many persons who perform such functions are in fact, so titled. While at first glance this would seem illogical, the reality of such instances makes it difficult to suggest alternatives. For example, in some police departments the detective post carries extra pay or status so that it is given as a reward to members of aggressive anti-crime patrol squads or officers who are skilled at preparing court papers. Indeed, though the Rand Report recommended replacing detectives with civilians for routine clerical duties, this is not easily accomplished. Every police department maintains "detectives" who never make an arrest or conduct any investigations beyond filling out a simple form. However, this activity may require them to journey at night into a high-crime neighborhood or be alone with a prisoner at headquarters, tasks which are inappropriate for a civilian. If the officers involved are senior members, the detective designation may simply be a courtesy title which serves as a consolation prize for failure to achieve any higher post and as such, is a morale booster.*

In addition to the varying images of what constitutes a detective, the three studies tend to disagree in their findings. For example, the Rochester findings regarding the effectiveness of CTP contradicts the Rand assertion that "The methods by which police investigators are organized cannot be related to variations in crime, arrests, and clearance rates." However, as noted, the Rochester experiment dealt with neighborhood police service of the precinct generalist variety, while the findings of the Rand study may be more applicable to headquarters efforts against major crime.

The dismissal of organizational form also neglects the impact of factors such as specialization. For example, the establishment of a narcotics squad is likely to produce a higher level of arrests for that offense. The reverse is that specialization may also be dysfunctional. A police department with both burglary and narcotics squads may find its burglary detectives giving a "pass" to drug offenders in return for burglary information even though the drug violation is more serious. At the same time the department's narcotics officers may afford similar leniencies to burglars in return for information regarding drugs even though the burglary offense may be of a greater magnitude. A generalized pattern of operation, i.e., the same detectives handle both burglary and drugs, would probably guarantee that no particular preference would be shown to either crime. Thus, a police administrator in a city which perceives drugs as a major problem might wish to create a special narcotics squad whereas an administrator in another city might decide against it.

In respect to the Rand recommendations regarding major case units, certain observations may be in order. The attempt to select cases for special handling is a process complementary to other American law enforcement efforts aimed at particular categories of offenders. For example, the federal government has de-

* In the 1970's the New York City Police Department began to award detective badges and pay to outstanding patrol officers who remained on uniformed duty. While meant to boost morale it has had mixed success.

veloped a career-criminal program designed to identify a corps of repeat offenders who presumably contribute disproportionately to the incidence of crime. Various levels of government have also formed operational strike forces to concentrate on particular types of crime such as narcotics or racketeering, or to "get" some individual such as a Mafia or drug "kingpin." Some prosecutors' offices have established major offenders bureaus to afford special attention to repeat offenders or those who commit serious crimes.

While the discussion of the policy implications of strike forces and major offender programs leads one beyond the dimensions of the present paper, perhaps a few comments are relevant. Besides the obvious civil liberties problems of programs which concentrate on getting particular individuals or types of persons judged socially dangerous, it is also possible that such efforts are not the optimum means of dealing with the problem of reducing the incidence of crime. As Boland and Wilson have pointed out, by the time an offender acquires a significant criminal record he may be in the process of reducing the rate of his criminal activities so that his incarceration would not afford societal relief for more than a few future offenses. In contrast, a relatively young offender at the start of his career, though not identified as a major or career criminal, is likely to be moving into the peak of his criminal activity and therefore from the standpoint of significantly reducing crime, is a better prospect for incarceration.[8] Thus, concentrating on career criminals or major offenders might not be the optimum strategic priority for a detective force.

One might also note that special anti-crime squads of the type cited by Rand have a long history. One thinks of the Los Angeles Police "Crime Crusher" squads of the 1920's, the F.B.I.'s "Get Dillinger" squad of the 1930's, and others. Such units are frequently composed of the most energetic members of an organization backed by the full support of top administrators, so that they frequently achieve spectacular results. However, they may also detract from the achievement of other goals by drawing resources away from more important but less glamorous tasks, while the fact they are "special" means by definition they cannot be institutionalized.

In a similar vein it is possible that overemphasis on management of investigation may have a reverse effect. There is, for example, what might be termed "high public fear" crime. An illustration of this is a recent series of multiple murders in New York City, Los Angeles, and central Ohio attributed respectively to the "Son of Sam," "the Hillside Strangler," and "the 22-Calibre Killer." All three cases had caused vast public alarm in the communities affected particularly since the killers remained uncaught for a long period. In such instances, and they are by no means rare in the United States, the detective bureau is seen in its idealized role, investigating mysterious, sensational crimes amidst the glare of massive publicity. Recent research efforts may unwittingly contribute to a lessening of effectiveness in this area by attempting to compress detective operations into conformity with management systems designed for the lowest common denominators. That is, there may be a tendency to stress quantity over quality in a "numbers game" whereby detective units perceive an advantage in solving many routine cases rather than a few important ones.

Curiously, despite the extensive study and debate, one rather suspects that detective work in most police departments has not been altered as much as the current literature might suggest. A recent survey of 172 police departments which serve cities over 100,000 affords some surprising findings. In the first instance, only 13 per cent of the departments reported a decrease in the proportion of detective strength over the past decade while 31 per cent indicated an increase and the rest, no change. Thus, despite the Rand recommendations, the detective force is not only alive but growing. Fifty-seven per cent reported forming detective task forces along the lines of traditional anti-crime units, and major squads. As with Rochester, ten per cent reported combining patrol and detective operations and 20 per cent assigned some follow-up criminal investigations to patrol officers.[9]

The recent research studies have introduced a new dimension to what might be termed the "scientific" approach to criminal investigation. Previous efforts, primarily by Europeans such as Gross, Locard and Söderman, have concentrated on techniques useful to investigators attempting to solve individual crimes or particular crime categories. In contrast, the American management systems approach as exemplified by Rand, Rochester, and to some extent, Wilson, is directed toward instructing administrators in the optimum organization and operation of a detective force in order to reduce the overall crime rate. While these are somewhat different approaches they share a similar scientific orientation. That is, they seek to utilize empirically derived data to formulate general propositions as a means of prediction.

Competing with the scientific approach are at least two contradictory perspectives. There is, of course, the concept of the detective as an artist, the individual of brilliant insights, a master of interrogation and other skills, who engages in an intuitive exercise which ultimately leads to the solution of a crime. Though this version is usually found in fiction or on the movie or T.V. screen, it is by no means unknown in professional policing. One need only examine the memoirs of a recent New York City detective chief and two admiring books touching the man's career, written by a former deputy commissioner on the same force, to encounter the theory of the detective as an artist.[10] Nor can this be dismissed as an American phenomenon, since it is easy to recall Fabian of Scotland Yard or Vidocq of the Sûreté. While scholars and police professionals are wont to scoff at notions that detective work is an art,*[11] it is useful to recollect the careers of Alan Pinkerton and William Burns, the founding fathers of America's two great private detective agencies. Neither man ever attended a police training course. Instead, they abandoned their trades of cooper or tailor and moved directly into detective work with amazing success both as investigators and then as chiefs.

A second version of detective work is that of the craftsman. Here the detective is seen as the master of a set of practical techniques, not the least of which is the cultivation of informers. In the words of a famous New York detective of yesteryear, "It makes me tired to read how those bulls in books solve mysteries with their deductions. In the honest-to-God story of how the detective gets his man, stool pigeon's the word."[12] It is this model to which most Anglo-American detectives and their crime reporter brethren subscribe.

The artist, craftsman and scientist concepts of detective work obviously have quite different implications for the selection, training, supervising, and operations of individual detectives. In general, Americans local police detectives have been selected from the ranks of the uniformed patrol force while federal agents have largely been drawn from the college-educated civilians. The federal system of direct entrance can be said to assume that detective work is at least somewhat scientific in that it requires a significant amount of education and the passing of an examination geared toward determining an individual's aptitude for investigative work. For example, it is common to require candidates to interpret and apply legal principles and demonstrate an ability to think through complex problems in a logical progression. In contrast, local police selection implicitly assumes the craftsman approach by settling for rather limited formal education, usually high school, and offering an examination to determine applicants' suitability for patrol duty. Indeed, given recent pressures from various sources, the patrolman's exam in many American cities is far from a rigorous intellectual exercise.*[13]

Whether either of the foregoing methods produces effective detectives is not certain. It is likely the answer varies by type. In the instance of the neighborhood or precinct investigator his work probably differs only in degree, not kind, from that of the uniformed patrol officer and therefore the apprentice method provides adequate neighborhood-level detectives. In contrast, one doubts that a good undercover officer who may require "artistic" qualities can be identified and produced by current methods of selection and training, whether federal or local. In his study Wilson noted that most narcotics officers were not able to master the undercover role.[14] It is likely, too, that the present systems of detective production are not geared to turn out intelligence officers.

In terms of organizational patterns it would seem likely that an investigative force such as the DEA must allow greater latitude for its undercover field agents as they practice their art. Thus, it is not surprising that Wilson found the agency highly decentralized with policies frequently being shaped by the cases individual agents were able to make. In contrast, he noted the F.B.I. was highly centralized, and agents invariably responded to headquarters' initiatives.

THE FUTURE

The United States is a vast and diverse country with literally thousands of independent police forces. Thus it is difficult to generalize on its policing arrangements. This is particularly true of the complex field of criminal investigation. Over the past decade a number of ideas have surfaced and at present the more innovative segments of the profession are concerned with the management science aspects of detective work. One suspects that the future will witness several developments.

* Indeed, the Rand report took to task a leading criminal investigation text for describing detective work as an art rather than a science.

* Even federal agents, while selected and trained on a somewhat different basis, are thought to learn their skills primarily via apprenticeship methods in actual field duties. For example, according to Wilson, the primary skill of the F.B.I. agent is interviewing, yet until recently virtually no classroom training was provided in this area.

In the first instance, the research activities will probably produce a more systematic approach to criminal investigation, both in the American sense of management and the European forensic science approach which focuses on investigative techniques in individual cases. As a result of the trends toward science, detectives will be more likely to be selected from the college-educated and required to undergo more intense classroom training in skills such as interrogation and intelligence. They will also be supervised more closely and evaluated according to sophisticated qualitative and quantitative measures. It is expected that the craftsman type detective will be relegated to neighborhood level policing while the artist may become increasingly rare, given the twin pressures of scientific management and restrictions upon police undercover operations. Wilson has noted that even many drug enforcement officers are beginning to doubt the ultimate effectiveness of "buy and bust" methods and may consequently shift more personnel to intelligence operations.

This brief survey suggests that the view that detective work is becoming less important in policing may be incorrect. While present-day American detectives appear to be embattled they are hardly an endangered species. Indeed, they may be moving into a new era of importance.

REFERENCES

1. Patrick V. Murphy and Thomas Plate, *Commissioner: A View From the Top of American Law Enforcement*. (New York, N.Y.: Simon & Schuster, 1977) p. 188.

2. David C. Anderson, "Management Moves in on the Detective," *Police*, March 1978, p. 5.

3. Richard Dougherty, "Requiem for the Center Street Mafia," *Atlantic Monthly*, March 1969, pp. 112–13.

4. See Peter Greenwood and Joan Petersilia, *The Criminal Investigation Process*, 3 volumes (Santa Monica, Cal.: The Rand Corporation, 1975) especially volume 1, pp. VI–XIII.

5. Daryl Gates and Lyle Knowles, "An Evaluation of the Rand Corporation's Analysis of the Criminal Investigation Process," *The Police Chief*, July 1976, pp. 21–22.

6. Peter B. Bloch and James Bell, *Managing Investigations: The Rochester System*, (Washington, D.C.: The Police Foundation, 1976). See especially pp. 1–12.

7. James Q. Wilson, *The Investigators: Managing F.B.I. and Narcotic Agents*, (New York, N.Y.: Basic Books, 1978).

8. Barbara Boland and James Q. Wilson, "Age, Crime and Punishment," *The Public Interest*, Spring 1978, pp. 22–34.

9. *American Policing 1967–77*, (Washington, D.C.: The Police Foundation, forthcoming.)

10. See Albert Seedman and Peter Hellman, *Chief*, (New York, N.Y.: E. P. Dutton, 1974). Robert Daley, *Target Blue* (New York, N.Y.: Delacorte Press, 1973) and same author, *To Kill a Cop*, (New York, N.Y.: 1976).

11. *op. cit.*, Greenwood and Petersilia, p. 147.

12. Michael Fiaschetti, *You Gotta Be Rough*, (New York, N.Y.: Doubleday Doran, 1930) p. 27.

13. *op. cit.*, Wilson, p. 51.

14. *ibid*, p. 50.

The Evolving Role of Women in American Policing

Edith Linn and Barbara Raffel Price

Women constitute fifty-one percent of the population of the United States but, in urban police departments in 1981, only four percent of all sworn personnel.(1) And, this despite the fact that women want to do police work, are needed in police work, and have demonstrated their ability to do the job to police administrators and peers alike.

This article was written expressly for inclusion in this edition.

There are many reasons for a police policy which supports the employment and general assignment of women to all aspects of law enforcement. First, it is illegal for police to discriminate on the basis of sex in their hiring and promotion practices; second, women officers are often especially successful in obtaining essential information from crime victims and informants; third, the presence of women on a police force serves as a reminder to the public that the police are committed to serving the entire community; fourth, diverse views including the voices of women police are needed in formulating law enforcement policy; and finally, women officers provide role models for the general community, demonstrating that women can assume responsible positions of authority and respect, thereby fostering equity for all women.

The case for equality in hiring and promotion is persuasive, but the reality is that women are not yet fully accepted in the majority of American police departments. Yet, in the past when feminism, innovative leadership, and changed crime conditions have converged, women have made inroads into policing. These three forces are once again challenging the basic structure of the policing establishment.

1880–1970: WOMEN GET THEIR "SPECIAL PLACE" IN POLICE WORK (2)

Women's involvement in police work has gone through two periods. The first, dating from around 1880, developed a view that females have a necessary role, but a limited and specialized one. The second, beginning approximately in 1970, saw an end to separate roles and the start of demands for equal participation in what has always been the core of police work: patrol duty.

Women first entered the criminal justice system in response to new social forces. At the outset of women in policing, there was a confluence of factors: a changing crime pattern, an organized women's movement, and an unconventional, eager individual.

White Slavery and "dangers to the morals of young women" emerged as serious concerns in the late nineteenth century.(3) Women's groups, particularly the Women's Christian Temperance Union, initiated in 1880, a successful nationwide campaign for the hiring of police matrons to supervise women and children held in custody. As a result, the first women in police-related work were assigned tasks which were essentially custodial in nature. Between 1877 and 1888, sixteen cities had appointed police matrons to attend to women and children in custody, awaiting trial.(4) In 1893, the Mayor of Chicago appointed Marie Owen to the detective bureau to assist in cases involving women and children. This did not represent a rethinking of the role of women in police work; rather, it appears to have been a way to create a job for a policeman's widow.(5) Nevertheless, Owen served as "patrolman" for thirty years, visiting courts and assisting detective officers in cases involving women and children.

The late 1800s also marked the appearance of the first significant organized women's movement.(6) The suffragettes lobbied for voting rights and questioned the prevailing notion that "a woman's place is in the home." They also began to look outside the home for self-fulfillment and an opportunity to help alleviate some of the mushrooming social problems. The fact that increasingly more criminal offenders were women and children created a need for women professionals. Even in today's more liberated age, there are special problems associated with women in custody when supervised only by male staff.(7) The processing of juveniles, in particular, came to be dominated by the values of therapeutic justice that created jobs for professional social workers, who were mostly women.(8)

At the turn of the century, rapid industrialization accompanied a myriad of problems: the breakdown of the family, endemic poverty, an increase in youthful and female crime, widespread use of child labor, and social disorganization.(9) In the course of these events, women became involved in police work as a part of broader social developments.

The first appointment of a woman with police powers came in 1905 during the Lewis and Clark Expedition in Portland, Oregon.(10) Apparently, large numbers of young women were soliciting the attention of lumbermen, miners, laborers, and vacationers "on sprees." To help cope with the problem, the city fathers of Portland hired Lola Baldwin. Her efforts were so successful that a permanent Department of Public Safety for the Protection of Young Girls and Women was created.(11) Other cities began to hire women police officers, but the scope of the work was generally limited to cases involving children and women. The role of the woman police officer during this period was compatible with progressive movements both for women's rights and humane treatment of young offenders.

In 1910, the first regularly rated policewoman, Alice Stebbins Wells, was appointed. Wells, a graduate theological student and ardent social worker from Los Angeles, believed that protective and preventative work with women and children would be most effective if services were delivered by sworn policewomen.(12) She circulated a petition to this effect; then addressed it to the city council and police commissioner. The result was that the Los Angeles Police Department hired her as a fully empowered policewoman with the rank of detective.(13) The appointment of Wells attracted wide attention, especially from other energetic women searching for solutions to America's social problems. By 1915, at least sixteen cities, recognizing the need for women police officers, had begun to add them to their departments. One woman even became chief of police, in Milford, Ohio.(14) Most of the women hired during this period came from social work backgrounds; their duties generally included supervision of public places of recreation, responsibility for female suspects and work on missing persons cases. Consequently, as a result of their background and assignments, female police officers came to be viewed as specialized social workers.(15)

Feminism (the belief in social, political and economic equality) had become a deeply rooted force in American life by 1915. With women's associations forming in most cities, the idea of organizing a policewomen's society occurred to Wells. In May 1915, the International Association of Policewomen was created with Wells as its first president. The Association dedicated itself to providing police departments and the general public with information on women police, developing standards, and improving the role of policewomen.(16)

With the entrance of the United States into World War I, women were hired to fill newly vacant police positions and to perform quasi-police functions related to their earlier duties, such as keeping prostitutes away from military camps.(17) While America's men were fighting overseas to make the world "safe for democracy," women also became increasingly caught up in the war effort and appeared in even larger numbers in the work force. By the end of World War I, policewomen were employed in over 220 American cities.(18)

During the 1920s, a period of prosperity and economic expansion, the women's movement was strong, the economy was strong and women police appeared to be gaining acceptance. The success of women officers around military camps and the efforts of the International Association of Policewomen, undoubtedly, aided in spreading the idea across the country. In 1922, the International Association of Chiefs of Police passed a resolution stating that policewomen were indispensable to the modern police department.(19) At the same time, the general public became increasingly comfortable with both the notion of crime prevention as a legitimate function of police departments and the presence of female police officers. Yet, female officers, usually relegated to a women's bureau, were promotable only within a specialized unit and received less pay than male officers.(20)

The 1930s were an altogether different time; unemployment soared; poverty and related social ills were rampant. The central focus of President Roosevelt's economic policy, the New Deal, was to reduce poverty by creating jobs for men.(21) The underlying assumptions of the New Deal were that employed wage earners would support their wives and children; widows would receive Aid For Dependent Children. Police jobs for women nearly disappeared, and the International Association of Policewomen disbanded due to lack of funds.(22)

The New York City Police Department, more hospitable to women than others, in 1937, merged its separate matron and youth-clerical employee classes; under the title "Police Woman," the department offered female officers the same salary and benefits as males. Only about fifty of the top scorers on the "Police Woman" exam were hired over a four-year period, limiting this elite cadre to around three hundred.

Many of the New York City policewomen accepted their unequal status, enjoying high salaries, occasional promotions, and acceptance from male colleagues at the price of "keeping their place." But other highly capable women officers wanted to compete with men—for the same promotions and the same "piece of the action."

World War II fueled the economy and turned wage earners into soldiers. America became ripe (again) for policewomen. In the 1940s, however, women were pretty much limited to the role of auxiliary police deployed in specialized capacities (most notably in undercover investigation and in interviewing female victims of crime).(23) On the whole, the 1930s through the late 1960s saw little increase in woman power.(24) Many factors discouraged women from police work, not the least of which was the male, para-military image of the "cop." Women could also be kept off the force by quotas limiting females to one percent, by higher education requirements (a bachelor's or even a master's degree), by height and weight restrictions, and by veterans' preference policies. If they managed to be appointed, they faced limited promotional opportunities, lower pay, fewer benefits, and no uniform allowance or no uniforms at all. And they also faced a corps of men who resented their presence.(25)

WOMEN OFFICERS MOVE TOWARD EQUALITY

In 1963, Felicia Spritzer and Gertrude Schimmel, two "competitive" New York City policewomen, won the right to take male promotional exams.(26) By 1975, Schimmel achieved the rank of inspector, Spritzer, lieutenant, and twenty-three other women were wearing superior officers' shields.(27)

Other women followed Spritzer's strategy, suing their local police agencies for discriminatory employment practices.(28) Their efforts received growing support from the Federal government. Title VII of the 1965 Civil Rights Act banned discrimination by private employers. Not only did the 1967 United States Task Force Report on Police urge greater utilization of women in specialized roles, but also included a line stating that "women should also serve regularly in patrol, vice and investigative divisions."(29) In 1969, Nixon's Executive Order 11478 declared that the Federal government could not use sex as a qualification for hiring. The 1973 Federal report on police, in a large section entitled "Employment for Women," called for an end to the "specialization" orientation and urged abolition of separate hiring and promotion policies.(30) That same year, the Law Enforcement Assistance Administration announced that police, courts, and correctional systems could lose Federal aid if they failed to conform to equal opportunity employment regulations. These stipulated that if a group's representation in a law enforcement agency was less than seventy percent of its representation in the community, that agency must make special recruitment and training efforts to correct the imbalance.(31)

The greatest ally for women seeking equal participation in law enforcement has been the Equal Employment Opportunity Commission (E.E.O.C.)(32) Established in 1972 under an amendment to the Civil Rights Act of 1964, it extended the prohibition on discrimination in employment to state and local civil service. The E.E.O.C. placed the burden on the *employer* to prove that sex was not being used as qualification for a job. As if anticipating the resistance of police departments, it clearly spelled out what were *not* bona fide grounds for discrimination:

1. Preference of co-workers.
2. Tradition.
3. Lack of physical facilities for both sexes.
4. Need to travel, or travel with the opposite sex.
5. Night hours, isolated locations, or unpleasant surroundings.
6. Assumptions about characteristics needed for the job.
7. Assumptions about characteristics of the applicant's sex.(33)

Clearly, the E.E.O.C. put considerable pressure on law enforcement agencies to hire women, not only to bring in females, but also to bring in qualified members of other minority groups. For women to seek the job, and for the public to accept them, however, required both the impetus of a change in the law and a change in consciousness.

The women's movement of the 1970s attacked male hegemony more broadly and more profoundly than at any time in the past. It made people aware of the sexual stereotypes, particularly in the media, that kept "female" and "cop" at opposite conceptual poles. Suddenly, the whimpering woman who could only shriek or faint in the face of danger became offensive and the "macho" man who could rally from a pummeling with perfect aim became ridiculous. Moreover, the glamorized images of frontier marshals and their counterparts who tame the city became suspect—not only for their inaccuracy, but also for their possible contribution to violence in society.

Proponents of women in law enforcement had to literally de-program the public. They needed to point out that for several years English, Swedish, German, and Israeli women had performed police duties competently,(34) that eighty to ninety percent of police contacts are non-violent and service oriented.(35) They needed to publicize the facts: that everyday policing situations demand a knowledge of human behavior and a personal, as opposed to an official authority;(36) that even in violent encounters physical strength is less important than training and quick, clear thinking; and that the major single cause of police deaths is ambush, a situation in which an officer performing a routine duty often does not even see his assailant.(37)

Sociologists added other arguments for women in policing. In writing about the Self-fulfilling Prophecy, Robert Merton documented how the anticipation of a behavior such as aggression can itself produce that behavior.(38) This phenomenon gains importance in the light of studies of police subculture.(39) The policeman must enforce the law *against* the citizens he serves and begins to feel that they are all hostile or apathetic to his efforts. As odd working hours further isolate him from civilians, he grows even closer to other officers. He shares in their "us-versus-them" view of the world, their admiration of firmness and authority, and their desire to "make" the public show a proper respect. In actual contact with civilians, he often perceives any lack of deference as defiance. And civilians, culturally conditioned to expect toughness rather than tact, often act upon *their expectations* rather than the reality of a given situation.(40)

The policewoman, on the other hand, seems neither to possess nor provoke these expectations. Barred from being "one of the boys," she is more likely to identify with the civilian world. One study indicated that women officers, in marked contrast to men, felt that the public "respected and admired them." Other research found that the public had more favorable reports of encounters with women officers than with men.(41) A personality profile of female officers disclosed that they are, indeed, less authoritarian, less alienated, and less conventional than their male colleagues.(42)

With the introduction of greater numbers of females, the police subculture and the inevitable circle of police–community misunderstanding will undoubtedly change. Women have been shown to have a pacifying effect when they assume roles traditionally occupied by men. Studies of such hyper-masculine environments as maximum security mental wards(43) and prisons(44) reveal that inmates become more attuned to social conventions and "normal" behavior with the introduction of females into staff positions. The psychological advantages of a woman's presence have many applications in police work. An offender who in a display of bravado might assault a policeman would instead appear cowardly if he hit a woman. An unruly crowd is more likely to look upon women officers as a legitimate peace-keeping force than as an army of repression.(45) Embattled spouses usually respond better to the female "style of intervention"(46) and are likely to regard a female/male crisis team as more fair-minded and understanding than two stone-faced males. Both suspects and witnesses open up more readily to women during interviews, particularly in sex and juvenile cases.(47) And women from poor communities, who lodge the majority of complaints in these areas(48) and have a wealth of "inside" information to impart, seem infinitely more likely to approach a female officer.

The law enforcement establishment, while rejecting arguments for the undifferentiated deployment of women, has been more willing to concede that their "specialness" gives them a certain usefulness.(49) This became more apparent when the crime pattern shifted in the 1960s. In their war on narcotics, police departments put women on dangerous undercover assignments. In so doing they undermined their own arguments that routine patrol work was too hazardous for females.(50)

Furthermore, there was an increasing number of female offenders. This shattering of stereotype went beyond headlines of terrorists, cult killers, and would-be Presidential assassins. There was also a groundswell of garden-variety burglars, con artists, and muggers.(51) Simple logic said that if women could be criminals, they could also be cops.

THE PATROL STUDIES

In 1968, the Indianapolis Police Department became the first to assign women to routine patrol duty.(52) This, however, did not signal a rush of females into police work. When Title VII was amended in 1972, only two percent of police personnel were female.(53) As late as 1974, of sixty-two municipal departments responding to a survey, fourteen had no women officers and the female representation on the forces of the other forty-eight averaged just four percent.(54) Both this survey and one involving four hundred local, state, and federal agencies answered that same year reported that women remained primarily confined to youth work, community relations, and criminal investigation rather than patrol assignments.(55) Where women did embark on patrol duty in greater numbers, they were closely observed and evaluated. From a research and practical viewpoint this may have been justified, as women on patrol had never before been tested in the United States. On the other hand, it must be remembered that women had heretofore been excluded from police work without any scientific evidence that they could *not* do the job.

The earliest and most thorough patrol study was conducted in Washington, D.C. in 1972.(56) Eighty-six newly-hired women and an equal number of newly-hired men were sent on patrol—on foot and in radio cars, alone, and with partners of either sex. For a full year they were evaluated by supervisors, trained observers, citizens, and fellow officers.

The subjects all had similar educational and job-experience backgrounds and pre-employment interview ratings. When so matched, the female group was sixty-six percent black; the male group, forty-two percent black. In this case then, an equal sexual balance on a police force also produced a better racial balance.

In their *Final Report,* Peter B. Bloch and Deborah Anderson concluded:(57)

> The men and women studied for this report performed patrol work in a generally similar manner. They responded to similar types of calls for police service while on patrol and encountered similar proportions of citizens who were dangerous, angry, upset, drunk, or violent. Both men and women officers were observed to obtain similar results in handling angry or violent citizens. There were no reported incidents which cast any serious doubt on the ability of women to perform patrol work satisfactorily.

Some differences between the two groups did emerge. Women made fewer arrests and issued fewer traffic summonses than men, while the conviction rates of both groups were the same. The researchers were unsure as to whether this might mean that female officers "under-arrest" or male officers "over-arrest" and did not use it as a criterion for performance. Women did not take more sick time than men, but were more apt to be assigned to light duties as the result of injuries. Overprotectiveness by supervisors led to fewer patrol assignments for women, in general, during the probationary period. As a result, the women lost out on supervised patrol experience, and the department lost the opportunity to fully ascertain the rookies' capabilities.

More men than women became involved in serious unbecoming conduct. In the eyes of the public, however, the D.C. police department was highly regarded both before and after the introduction of policewomen. While it was somewhat skeptical of the ability of women to handle violent situations, it was more likely to support the idea of women on patrol than to oppose it.

Bloch and Anderson ventured to predict what effect a large infusion of women might have on police operations:(58)

> A department with a substantial number of women may be less aggressive than one with only men. The presence of women may stimulate increased attention to ways of avoiding violence and cooling violent situations without the use of force.

New York City's first formal study of women on patrol lasted from October 1973 to March 1974. No efforts were made to match the 165 females and 165 males newly on patrol. The results demonstrated no statistically significant differences in arrests, summonses, radio runs, sick time, or performance evaluations.(59)

A more elaborate study was planned by the Vera Institute for a seven-month period in 1975–1976. Unlike the Washington D.C. Study, it used officers with some previous experience who patrolled exclusively in two-person radio cars. Police layoffs stemming from New York's fiscal crisis pared the available subjects down to forty-one matched pairs.

The cutbacks worked against the female group in several ways. It eliminated a disproportionate number of newly-hired women. It increased the risk that women assigned to the patrol study would be called away for matron duty, which many regarded as a "dead end." And it meant that the women were less often assigned to the same patrol partner. Thus, the women's patrol experience was qualitatively and quantitatively inferior to the men's and their morale may have been more adversely affected by job instability and a dwindling number of role models.

The "femaleness" of the subjects made no observable difference in the emotional state of civilians. However, the public rated the women more competent, pleasant, and respectful than their male counterparts. Citizens who encountered mixed patrol teams held a higher regard for the New York City Police Department than did those who encountered teams of only men.(60)

The importance of introducing sufficient numbers of women to patrol duty seems borne out by the experience of New York's 46th Precinct. About twenty-five new women officers were assigned to that troubled section of the Bronx, in order to establish their sense of identity as policewomen, to generate peer pressure, to promote equal treatment, and to gauge the impact on the community of a sizeable group. The women worked around the clock and received their assignments on the basis of a color-blind and sex-blind policy. This group, while consisting of fewer than three percent of the three thousand police officers in the Bronx, had by 1975 amassed sixty-four medals for heroism or exceptional performance. What's more, the women were notably reluctant to take inside jobs that would keep them from patrol.(61)

Policewomen on patrol were also studied in a suburban environment for over six months in 1974. Lewis Sherman compared sixteen women with sixteen men recently recruited into the St. Louis County Police Department and assigned to one-person motor patrol. He found that as in the Washington, D.C. Study, the women's "style" of patrol was less aggressive, with fewer arrests and less "preventive" activity such as car and pedestrian stops. And contrary to Washington D.C. policewomen, they handed out more traffic citations than the men. Sherman noted that although St. Louis County had more female officers than any other suburb (just over four percent), the overwhelming number of men put tremendous pressure on its twenty-six females to mimic the style of male peers.(62) Sherman viewed this as regrettable, for the citizens of St. Louis approved of the greater empathy and sensitivity they perceived in the women officers. The public was satisfied with the responses of policewomen in both service and non-service calls and felt equally safe with either male or female officers. As in both the Washington and New York studies, violent or potentially violent situations occurred too infrequently to permit systematic conclusions about the policewomen's handling of them.(63)

An international seminar was held in Germany in September 1974 to discuss the expanding role of women in policing.(64) It concluded that there are no biological, physiological, or psychological arguments that would rule out the total integration of women into police work; that men and women can be used together in operations to control violence; and that a mixed team specially trained in the use of technical equipment and self-defense is more suitable for more severe situations of violence than are male police officers without this special training.

BLOCKAGES TO SEXUAL INTEGRATION: THE ATTITUDES OF POLICEMEN

Despite every indication that women *can* do police work, skepticism and rejection by the male police establishment continue. Bloch and Anderson found that for the duration of their Washington Study both police brass and patrolmen perceived the women police officers as less capable than the men.(65) Joyce L. Sichel, et al., reported that some New York City precincts gave women a discouraging reception, concerned that the women, when faced with danger, would panic and endanger their male partners. The police felt that women would be more likely to use their guns when threatened and that they would lack the stamina and strength required to chase a suspect for several blocks or carry an injured person to an ambulance.(66) Anthony V. Bouza, a high ranking New York City officer, mentioned that his male colleagues expressed the fear that when the public got over the novelty of seeing a female police officer, she would be in trouble.(67) Sherman noted that supervisory personnel in the St. Louis County Police Department saw the female recruits as less dedicated to a long-term career in law enforcement than men. This view may have some basis in the fact that married women, in particular, said that they could and would give up policing if it conflicted with their family life. On the other hand, the five out of sixteen women officers who had married since joining the force remained on the job through the time of reporting. Both supervisors and male patrol officers were generally negative toward the idea of women on patrol, although less so by the end of the study.(68) A later attitude study by Robert E. Hindman reiterated, "A low acceptance factor for females to be used in all police functions, especially those that could be termed hazardous in nature."(69)

Although policemen are aware that their work is mostly service-oriented, they remain unconvinced that women can deal with the criminal element. They fear that if too many women enter policing, police service might "drift into its having a soft, social therapy image, blurring right and wrong."(70) The most common apprehension is that in violent confrontations, the women will jeopardize the lives of fellow officers. The nightmare of many a male officer is being dependent on a woman in a life-and-death situation. Actual incidents of violence occur too rarely to provide statistical "proof" that females don't "turn tail." All the policeman has to go on is his everyday observation—borne out by research—that women cops often *are* less aggressive.

Male officers may come to realize that female attitudes regarding law and order are not so different from their own, once they have worked alongside women. One study found that both male and female officers shared the views that police should have greater powers to interrogate, that more stringent parole laws should be initiated, and that fewer people should be placed on parole.(71) Furthermore, in working with women, male officers may also see the utility of certain "soft" techniques.

The policeman is by occupational nature resistant to change,(72) perhaps because so little of his world is safe and predictable. His opposition to women on patrol stems in part from his not knowing *how* to treat a woman as a peer. Should he watch his language? Offer to drive? Buy her coffee? Talk about sports? Initiate friendliness? Could he share hours of tension, or even hours of boredom, and not become too involved?

Police officers will build a set of unisex mores, if they have patience, tolerance, and a sense of humor. But the problem of emotional and sexual entanglements is not as easily solved. Patrol partners can develop terrifically intense relationships. Policemen's wives have demonstrated in several cities against mixed patrol teams, ostensibly over concern for their husbands' safety, but also over concern for their fidelity.(73) It can only be noted that both stress and sexual temptation were hazards to police marriages long before women went on patrol.

The outlook for a more favorable attitude among male police personnel is not totally bleak, however. In the Miami Police Department, new women on patrol were reportedly well-accepted by both the public and by male officers.(74) In Dayton, Ohio, the veteran police officers who field-trained ten rookie women were found to have themselves become more attentive and enthusiastic toward police work.(75) Furthermore, in many of the surveys, the subgroups most receptive to women were precisely those that were beginning to occupy greater proportions on police forces—blacks, more educated officers, and younger officers.(76)

It is likely that the next few years will bring in successively more assertive female police candidates, as childhood sexual stereotyping becomes less pronounced. But police departments can take steps *now* to counteract learned passivity. They can assign women instructors to academy and field training, to bring out the aptitudes of new women (and break down the prejudices of new men). They can assign women who are new to patrol to more experienced female partners who can serve as role models. They can provide physical training for women to improve ability and confidence. These actions may reduce the impression male officers have that women can't handle the "rough stuff."

The most effective way sociologists have found to decrease prejudice between hostile groups is to place them in situations that require cooperation to achieve shared goals.(77) And such interdependence can only exist if sufficient numbers of women, in sufficiently active roles are introduced into the police force.

Thus, paradoxically, policewomen's level of acceptance depends on their level of recruitment. Deployment of an adequate number of women ensures a full gamut of policing roles. It decreases the likelihood of special treatment or the formation of a female elite; it creates peer pressure to combat passivity; it provides role models to inspire self-confidence and the confidence of male colleagues. It would make what is novel become what is normal—a peace-keeping force that reflects the community.

THE PRESENT SITUATION

Women officers are making significant inroads into all aspects of police work and in all types and sizes of police jurisdictions—municipal, state, and federal. The number of policewomen employed in the ten largest urban police departments in the United States in 1974 (see *Table 1*) as compared to the female police complement in 1982 (see *Table 2*) documents this gain. And nationwide, women police officers have increased in ranks from 1.5 percent in 1972 to 5.5 percent in 1981.(78) However, while the major city departments

TABLE 1 Women Police Officers in the Ten Major Police Departments in 1974

				Patrol	
Police Department	*Total Size of Dept.*	*Total Women in Dept.*	*Percent of Women in Dept.*	*No. Women on Patrol*	*Percent Women (of Total Personnel)*
New York City	35,653	759	2.10	414	1.20
Chicago	14,935	*	——	*	——
Los Angeles	10,137	148	1.50	0	0
Philadelphia	9,247	69	0.75	0	0
Detroit	6,106	30	0.49	0	0
Washington, D.C.	5,558	268	4.80	161	2.90
Baltimore	4,150	9	0.21	1	0.02
Boston	2,877	14	0.49	11	0.38
St. Louis	2,822	9	0.32	2	0.07
Houston	2,792	*	——	*	——

* Data unavailable.

Note: 1974 data are drawn from *Uniform Crime Reports*, Federal Bureau of Investigation (Washington, D.C.: U.S. Government Printing Office), 1974 and *Deployment of Female Police Officers in the United States*, International Association of Chiefs of Police and the Police Foundation (Washington, D.C.: Police Foundation), 1974. 1974 was used as the comparison year because national figures were not compiled on women on patrol until IACP conducted its survey on female officers that year.

TABLE 2 Women Police Officers in the Ten Major Police Departments in 1982

Police Department	Total Size of Dept.	Total Women in Dept.	Percent of Women in Dept.	Patrol: No. Women on Patrol	Patrol: Percent Women (of Total Personnel)
New York City	24,326	1,405	5.7	687	2.8
Chicago	12,476	620	4.9	303	2.4
Los Angeles	6,900	292	4.2	210	3.0
Philadelphia	7,734	457	5.9	380	4.9
Detroit	4,234	477	11.3	291	6.8
Washington, D.C.	3,644	323	8.8	131	3.6
Baltimore	3,062	211	6.9	131	4.3
Boston	1,670	62	3.7	58	3.5
St. Louis	1,884	66	4.0	*	*
Houston	3,251	224	6.9	72	2.2

* Data unavailable.

Note: 1982 data were collected by the authors using a mail survey in early 1982.

have moved ahead of the law enforcement national average, they still rank well below the percentage of women employed in other fields. For example, among college faculty, women comprise 23 percent, with 9 percent full professors.(79) In law, 32 percent of the students are female.(80) Even the prestigious federal judiciary positions have more women proportionately than policing has. Women make up 6.7 percent of all federal judges.(81) In addition, they hold 6.7 percent of all top level federal government positions.(82) By comparison, law enforcement agencies have neither hired nor promoted women in proportion to other professions.

The most promising indicator of progress in the sexual integration of law enforcement is to be found in the changes in officer deployment from 1974 to 1982 (see *Table 3*). The percentage of women assigned to the patrol function has greatly increased in recent years although the actual numbers are still low; hence the visibility of women police remains limited. However, the fact that about half of the women in large city police forces are now assigned to patrol (Houston reported the lowest percentage with 32 percent of its women out on the street and Boston the highest with 93 percent) suggests a policy commitment in these departments to the fuller utilization and involvement of women.

In the 1960s, when women began to seek remedies for the inferior status they held as members of women's bureaus in police departments, they pressed for promotions commensurate with their years of experience

TABLE 3 Use on Patrol of Available Women Police Officers for 1974 and 1982

Police Department	1974 Patrol %	1974 Number of Women/Patrolling	1982 Patrol %	1982 Number of Women/Patrolling
New York City	54.5	759/414	48.9	1405/687
Chicago	*	——	48.9	620/303
Los Angeles	0	148/0	72.0	292/210
Philadelphia	0	69/0	79.7	457/380
Detroit	0	30/0	61.0	477/291
Washington, D.C.	60.0	161/268	40.5	323/131
Baltimore	11.0	1/9	62.0	211/131
Boston	78.0	11/14	93.5	62/58
St. Louis	22.0	2/9	*	*
Houston	*	——	32.1	224/72

* Data unavailable.

and performance. In response, police administrators maintained that women could only be promoted within their own bureaus because they had not had the full "police experience" of being on the street, i.e., patrol duty. Of course, women had been systematically denied opportunities in the past for general patrol assignments. Energetic women fought to turn this situation around by gaining the right to be assigned to patrol and to work in the same capacity as male officers in order to earn the same pay and the same promotion opportunities. Therefore, the percentage of women in patrol assignments is one critical indicator of the integration of women in policing. Both the percentages of women on patrol and the increase in these percentages over the eight years from 1974 to 1982 are shown in *Table 3*.

Achieving sexually integrated police forces has been made more difficult recently by the fiscal difficulties of many cities. Municipal budgetary problems have forced many departments to reduce their total number of officers. The problem has been most severe in the Northeast but few areas of the country have remained untouched by reduced revenues (see *Table 4*).

The reports from the large city departments show a decrease in sworn personnel as large as 42 percent in Boston and as small as 16 percent in Chicago. Only Houston, situated in the economically strong Southwest, has not experienced a retrenchment of personnel. In fact, Houston has grown 16 percent between 1974 and 1982. The reduction in total officer numbers means that male officers will be competing for even more limited promotion opportunities than in the past and will be less sympathetic to personnel reform measures being pressed by women's groups, minorities, and civil rights commissions. The impact of decreasing opportunities in policing has had an overall conserving effect on hiring procedures and reforms.

It may be that the constriction of police departments is a temporary situation which future recovery of the national economy will reverse. If so, we can anticipate the slow but steady gains of sexual integration in law enforcement to continue in the coming decade. And we can conclude with confidence that women have forged a permanent place for themselves in American policing.

TABLE 4 Large City Police Department Strength: 1974–1982

Police Department	*Sworn Personnel*		*% Change*
	1974	*1982*	
New York City	35,653	24,326	−37
Chicago	14,935	12,476	−16
Los Angeles	10,137	6,900	−32
Philadelphia	9,247	7,734	−32
Detroit	6,106	4,868	−20
Washington, D.C.	5,558	3,644	−34
Baltimore	4,150	3,045	−27
Boston	2,877	1,670	−42
St. Louis	2,822	*	——
Houston	2,792	3,251	+16

* Data unavailable.

REFERENCES

1. *Uniform Crime Reports for the United States* 1981 (Washington, D.C.: Federal Bureau of Investigation, U.S. Department of Justice, (1982), p. 235.

2. Susan Gavin researched the historical materials on women police for an earlier article, "A Century of Women in Policing" in *Modern Police Administration*, Donald O. Schultz (ed.) (Houston: Gulf Publishing Co.), pp. 109–122.

3. Donal E. MacNamara and Edward Sagarin, *Sex, Crime, and the Law* (New York: Free Press, 1977), p. 114.

4. Chloe Owings, *Women Police* (Montclair, N.J.: Patterson Smith, 1969), pp. 98–99.

5. *Ibid.*, p. 99.

6. For a general discussion of the early women's movement, see Eleanor Flexner, *Century of Struggle: The Women's Rights Movement in the United States* (Cambridge: Harvard University Press, 1975).

7. The case of Joanne Little, a poor, black woman from North Carolina, arrested and convicted of breaking and entry is illustrative of the problems which can arise. She was guarded by a male jailor in a small jail in North Carolina and when he attempted to rape her, she killed him in self defense.

8. For a discussion of the therapeutic model, see Anthony M. Platt, *The Child Savers* (Chicago: University of Chicago Press, 1969).

9. Murray Levin and Adeline Levine, *A Social History of Helping Services* (New York: Appleton-Century-Crofts, 1970), p. 24.

10. Peter Horne, *Women in Law Enforcement* (Springfield, IL: Charles C Thomas, 1975), p. 18.

11. *Ibid.*, p. 18.
12. Owings, *op. cit.*, p. 101.
13. *Ibid.*, p. 102.
14. Horne, *op. cit.*, p. 19.
15. Antony Simpson, "The Changing Role of Women in Policing," *Law Enforcement News*, Vol. 1, No. 3 (March 1976), p. 84.
16. *Ibid.*, pp. 21–22.
17. Alice Wells, "Reminiscences of a Policewoman," *The Police Reporter* (September 1929), p. 23.
18. Owings, *op. cit.*, pp. 107–115.
19. Horne, *op. cit.*, p. 19.
20. *Ibid.*, p. 19.
21. *Ibid.*, p. 20.
22. For a discussion of the New Deal see Arthur Schlesinger, *The Age of Roosevelt* (Boston: Houghton Mifflin, 1975).
23. Simpson, *op. cit.*, p. 85.
24. Catherine Milton, *Women in Policing* (Washington, D.C.: Police Foundation, 1972), pp. 16–24.
25. Anthony V. Bouza, "Women in Policing," *F.B.I. Law Enforcement Bulletin* (September 1975).
26. *Spritzer* v. *Lang*, 234 N.Y.S. 2nd, p. 285.
27. Bouza, *op. cit.*, p. 3.
28. See, for example, *Joanne B. Rossi* v. *City of Philadelphia and Fairmont Park Commission*, Docket No. E-3412 (1971) and *Hardy* v. *Stumpf*, Docket No. 415761 (1971), cited in Milton, *op. cit.*, pp. 54–55.
29. U.S. Task Force Report on the Police, *Task Force Report: The Police* (Washington, D.C.: Government Printing Office, 1967), p. 125.
30. U.S. National Advisory Commission on Criminal Justice Standards and Goals, *The Police: A Report* (Washington, D.C.: Government Printing Office, 1973), p. 342.
31. Simpson, *op. cit.*, p. 18.
32. Joyce L. Sichel, Lucy N. Friedman, Janet C. Quint and Michael Smith in *Women on Patrol: A Pilot Study of Police Performance in New York City* (New York: Vera Institute of Justice, 1977), report that the impetus toward placing women on patrol accelerated since March 1972, when the E.E.O.C. began to function, p. 1.
33. Milton, *op. cit.*, pp. 46–49.
34. Lewis Sherman, "A Psychological View of Women in Policing," *Journal of Police Science and Administration* (April 1973), pp. 387–388.
35. Joanna Krukenberg, "Women in Policing: Reflections of a Changing Community," *Police Law Quarterly* (Fall, 1974), p. 24.
36. Bruce J. Terris, "The Role of the Police," *The Ambivalent Force*, edited by Arthur Niederhoffer and Abraham S. Blumberg (San Francisco: Rinehart Press, 1973), p. 47.
37. International Association of Chiefs of Police, *Casualty Summary*, 1971.
38. Robert Merton, "The Self-fulfilling Prophecy," *Antioch Review* (Volume 8, 1948), pp. 193–210.
39. See Joanne McGeorge and Jerome A. Wolfe, "A Comparison of Attitudes Between Men and Women Police Officers: A Preliminary Analysis," *Criminal Justice Review* (February 1974), pp. 21–33, for a synopsis and review of the literature on police occupational subculture.
40. McGeorge and Wolfe, *op. cit.*, p. 27.
41. See Harriet A. Connolly, *Policewomen as Patrol Officers: A Study in Role Adaptation* (Ph.D. dissertation, City University of New York, 1975); Judith Ellen Greenwald, *Aggression as a Component of Police–Citizen Transactions: Differences Between Male and Female Police Officers* (Ph.D. dissertation, City University of New York, 1976); and Sichel et al., *op. cit.*
42. Gary R. Perlstein, *An Exploratory Analysis of Certain Characteristics of Policewomen* (Ph.D. dissertation, Florida State University, 1971).
43. See, for example, Milton Greenblatt, Richard York, and Esther Brown, *From Custodial to Therapeutic Patient Care in Mental Hospitals* (Massachusetts: Russell Sage Foundation, 1955).
44. Milton, *op. cit.*, pp. 31–32.
45. Ronald G. Tenley, "Women in Law Enforcement: An Expanded Role," *Police* (November/December, 1969), pp. 49–51.
46. Sherman, *op.cit.*, p. 388.
47. *Ibid.*, p. 384.
48. Milton, *op. cit.*, p. 37.
49. Anthony Vastola, "Women in Policing: An Alternative Ideology," *The Police Chief*, January 1977, pp. 66–67.
50. Simpson, *op. cit.*, p. 18.
51. Freda Adler, *Sisters in Crime: The Rise of the New Female Criminal* (New York: McGraw-Hill, 1975), pp. 5–30.
52. Simpson, *op. cit.*, p. 16.
53. Milton, *op. cit.*, p. 35.
54. Krukenberg, *op. cit.*, pp. 25–26.
55. Brenda E. Washington, *Deployment of Female Police Officers in the United States* (Washington, D.C.: International Association of Chiefs of Police, 1974).
56. Peter B. Bloch and Deborah Anderson, *Policewomen on Patrol: Final Report* (Washington, D.C.: Police Foundation, 1974).
57. *Ibid.*

58. *Ibid.*, p. 24.
59. Bouza, *op. cit.*, p. 4.
60. Sichel et al., *op. cit.*, pp. xiv–xvi.
61. Bouza, *op. cit.*, p. 5.
62. This phenomenon appears to have occurred in New York's 46th Precinct, where a male officer with whom we spoke complained bitterly of how the introduction of women to patrol duty there had caused them to act "butch" and become too sexually aggressive.
63. Lewis J. Sherman, "An Evaluation of Policewomen on Patrol in a Suburban Police Department," *Journal of Police Science and Administration* (March–April 1975), pp. 434–438.
64. Ilse Mathes and Waltraud Kleinlein, "Women in the Police Force—Reserve or Integration" ("Frauen bei der Polizei—Reservat oder Integration"), *Kriminalistik*, July 1975, pp. 303–305.
65. Bloch and Anderson, *op. cit.*, p. 7.
66. Sichel et al., *op. cit.*, p. 1.
67. Bouza, *op. cit.*, p. 6.
68. Sherman, "An Evaluation," *op. cit.*, p. 437.
69. Robert E. Hindman, "A Survey Related to the Use of Female Law Enforcement Officers," *The Police Chief* (April 1975), pp. 58–59.
70. J. Hilton, "Women in Policing," *Police Journal* (February 1976), p. 95.
71. McGeorge and Wolfe, *op. cit.*, p. 28.
72. McGeorge and Wolfe, *op. cit.*, p. 24.
73. Milton, *op. cit.*, pp. 25–26, reported demonstrations by policemen's wives in Dallas and New Orleans. Diedre Carmody, "Police Divided over Assignment of Women to Street Patrol Here," *New York Times*, July 15, 1974, reported a demonstration of policemen's wives in New York City. Arthur Niederhoffer and Elaine Niederhoffer, *The Police Family* (Lexington, MA: D.C. Heath and Company, 1978), pp. 118–123.
74. John A. Dilucchio, "In Miami: Female Officers in the Department," *The Police Chief* (April 1975), pp. 56–57.
75. W. O. Weldy, "Women in Policing: A Positive Step Toward Increasing Police Enthusiasm," *The Police Chief*, January 1976, pp. 46–47.
76. Bloch and Anderson, *op. cit.*, p. 7; Sherman, "An Evaluation," *op. cit.*, p. 437; and M. Vega and I. J. Silverman, "Women as Peace Officers as Viewed by their Male and Female Counterparts in Three Different Police Departments" (Paper presented to 28th Annual Meeting, American Society of Criminology, Tucson, Arizona) November 4–7, 1976.
77. Elliot Aronson, *The Social Animal* (San Francisco: W. H. Freeman and Company, 1960), p. 199.
78. *Uniform Crime Reports for the United States 1981* (Washington, D.C.,: Federal Bureau of Investigation, U.S. Department of Justice, 1981), p. 239.
79. *Academe: Bulletin of the American Association of University Professors* (1981), 67(4): 218.
80. *Prelaw Handbook*, 1982 (Washington, D.C.: The Association of American Law Schools and The Law School Admissions Council, 1982).
81. Personal correspondence with Susan Ness, author of "A Sexist Judiciary Keeps Women Off the Bench" in *The Criminal Justice System and Women: An Anthology on Women Offenders, Victims and Workers*, Barbara R. Price and Natalie J. Sokoloff (eds.) (New York, NY: Clark Boardman Co., 1982).

A Sketch of the Policeman's Working Personality

Jerome H. Skolnick

A recurrent theme of the sociology of occupations is the effect of a man's work on his outlook on the world.(1) Doctors, janitors, lawyers, and industrial workers develop distinctive ways of perceiving and responding to their environment. Here we shall concentrate on analyzing certain outstanding elements in the police milieu, danger, authority, and efficiency, as they combine to generate distinctive cognitive and behavioral responses in police: a "working personality." Such an analysis does not suggest that all police are alike in "working personality," but that there are distinctive cognitive tendencies in police as an occupational grouping. Some of these may be found in other

SOURCE: *Justice Without Trial: Law Enforcement in a Democratic Society*, pp. 42–49.

occupations sharing similar problems. So far as exposure to danger is concerned, the policeman may be likened to the soldier. His problems as an authority bear a certain similarity to those of the schoolteacher, and the pressures he feels to prove himself efficient are not unlike those felt by the industrial worker. The combination of these elements, however, is unique to the policeman. Thus, the police, as a result of combined features of their social situation, tend to develop ways of looking at the world distinctive to themselves, cognitive lenses through which to see situations and events. The strength of the lenses may be weaker or stronger depending on certain conditions, but they are ground on a similar axis.

Analysis of the policeman's cognitive propensities is necessary to understand the practical dilemma faced by police required to maintain order under a democratic rule of law. We have discussed earlier how essential a conception of order is to the resolution of this dilemma. It was suggested that the paramilitary character of police organization naturally leads to a high evaluation of similarity, routine, and predictability. Our intention is to emphasize features of the policeman's environment interacting with the paramilitary police organization to generate a "working personality." Such an intervening concept should aid in explaining how the social environment of police affects their capacity to respond to the rule of law.

We also stated earlier that emphasis would be placed on the division of labor in the police department, that "operational law enforcement" could not be understood outside these special work assignments. It is therefore important to explain how the hypothesis emphasizing the generalizability of the policeman's "working personality" is compatible with the idea that police division of labor is an important analytic dimension for understanding "operational law enforcement." Compatibility is evident when one considers the different levels of analysis at which the hypotheses are being developed. Janowitz states, for example, that the military profession is more than an occupation; it is a "style of life" because the occupational claims over one's daily existence extend well beyond official duties. He is quick to point out that any professional performing a crucial "life and death" task, such as medicine, the ministry, or the police, develops such claims.(2) A conception like "working personality" of police should be understood to suggest an analytic breadth similar to that of "style of life." That is, just as the professional behavior of military officers with similar "styles of life" may differ drastically depending upon whether they command an infantry battalion or participate in the work of an intelligence unit, so too does the professional behavior of police officers with similar "working personalities" vary with their assignments.

The policeman's "working personality" is most highly developed in his constabulary role of the man on the beat. For analytical purposes that role is sometimes regarded as an enforcement specialty, but in this general discussion of policemen as they comport themselves while working, the uniformed "cop" is seen as the foundation for the policeman's working personality. There is a sound organizational basis for making this assumption. The police, unlike the military, draw no caste distinction in socialization, even though their order of ranked titles approximates the military's. Thus, one cannot join a local police department as, for instance, a lieutenant, as a West Point graduate joins the army. Every officer of rank must serve an apprenticeship as a patrolman. This feature of police organization means that the constabulary role is the primary one for all police officers, and that whatever the special requirements of roles in enforcement specialties, they are carried out with a common background of constabulary experience.

The process by which this "personality" is developed may be summarized: the policeman's role contains two principal variables, danger and authority, which should be interpreted in the light of a "constant" pressure to appear efficient.[1] The element of danger seems to make the policeman especially attentive to signs indicating a potential for violence and lawbreaking. As a result, the policeman is generally a "suspicious" person. Furthermore, the character of the policeman's work makes him less desirable as a friend, since norms of friendship implicate others in his work. Accordingly, the element of danger isolates the policeman socially from that segment of the citizenry which he regards as symbolically dangerous and also from the conventional citizenry with whom he identifies.

The element of authority reinforces the element of danger in isolating the policeman. Typically, the policeman is required to enforce laws representing pu-

[1] By no means does such an analysis suggest there are no individual or group differences among police. On the contrary, most of this study emphasizes differences, endeavoring to relate these to occupational specialties in police departments. This chapter, however, explores similarities rather than differences, attempting to account for the policeman's general disposition to perceive and to behave in certain ways.

ritanical morality, such as those prohibiting drunkenness, and also laws regulating the flow of public activity, such as traffic laws. In these situations the policeman directs the citizenry, whose typical response denies recognition of his authority, and stresses his obligation to respond to danger. The kind of man who responds well to danger, however, does not normally subscribe to codes of puritanical morality. As a result, the policeman is unusually liable to the charge of hypocrisy. That the whole civilian world is an audience for the policeman further promotes police isolation and, in consequence, solidarity. Finally, danger undermines the judicious use of authority. Where danger, as in Britain, is relatively less, the judicious application of authority is facilitated. Hence British police may appear to be somewhat more attached to the rule of law, when, in fact, they may appear so because they face less danger, and they are as a rule better skilled than American police in creating the appearance of conformity to procedural regulations.

THE SYMBOLIC ASSAILANT AND POLICE CULTURE

In attempting to understand the policeman's view of the world, it is useful to raise a more general question: What are the conditions under which police, as authorities, may be threatened?(3) To answer this, we must look to the situation of the policeman in the community. One attribute of many characterizing the policeman's role stands out: the policeman is required to respond to assaults against persons and property. When a radio call reports an armed robbery and gives a description of the man involved, every policeman, regardless of assignment, is responsible for the criminal's apprehension. The *raison d'être* of the policeman and the criminal law, the underlying collectively held moral sentiments which justify penal sanctions, arises ultimately and most clearly from the threat of violence and the possibility of danger to the community. Police who "lobby" for severe narcotics laws, for instance, justify their position on grounds that the addict is a harbinger of danger since, it is maintained, he requires one hundred dollars a day to support his habit, and he must steal to get it. Even though the addict is not typically a violent criminal, criminal penalties for addiction are supported on grounds that he may become one.

The policeman, because his work requires him to be occupied continually with potential violence, develops a perceptual shorthand to identify certain kinds of people as symbolic assailants, that is, as persons who use gesture, language, and attire that the policeman has come to recognize as a prelude to violence. This does not mean that violence by the symbolic assailant is necessarily predictable. On the contrary, the policeman responds to the vague indication of danger suggested by appearance. Like the animals of the experimental psychologist, the policeman finds the threat of random damage more compelling than a predetermined and inevitable punishment.

Something of the flavor of the policeman's attitude toward the symbolic assailant comes across in a recent article by a police expert. In discussing the problem of selecting subjects for field interrogation, the author writes:

A. Be suspicious. This is a healthy police attitude, but it should be controlled and not too obvious.
B. Look for the unusual.

   1. Persons who do not "belong" where they are observed.
   2. Automobiles which do not "look right."
   3. Businesses opened at odd hours, or not according to routine or custom.

C. Subjects who should be subjected to field interrogations.

   1. Suspicious persons known to the officer from previous arrests, field interrogations, and observations.
   2. Emaciated appearing alcoholics and narcotics users who invariably turn to crime to pay for cost of habit.
   3. Person who fits description of wanted suspect as described by radio, teletype, daily bulletins.
   4. Any person observed in the immediate vicinity of a crime very recently committed or reported as "in progress."
   5. Known trouble-makers near large gatherings.
   6. Persons who attempt to avoid or evade the officer.
   7. Exaggerated unconcern over contact with the officer.
   8. Visibly "rattled" when near the policeman.
   9. Unescorted women or young girls in public places, particularly at night in such places as cafes, bars, bus and train depots, or street corners.
   10. "Lovers" in an industrial area (make good lookouts).

11. Persons who loiter about places where children play.
12. Solicitors or peddlers in a residential neighborhood.
13. Loiterers around public rest rooms.
14. Lone male sitting in car adjacent to schoolground with newspaper or book in his lap.
15. Lone male sitting in car near shopping center who pays unusual amount of attention to women, sometimes continuously manipulating rear view mirror to avoid direct eye contact.
16. Hitchhikers.
17. Person wearing coat on hot days.
18. Car with mismatched hub caps, or dirty car with clean license plate (or vice versa).
19. Uniformed "deliverymen" with no merchandise or truck.
20. Many others. How about your own personal experiences?(4)

Nor, to qualify for the status of symbolic assailant, need an individual ever have used violence. A man backing out of a jewelry store with a gun in one hand and jewelry in the other would qualify even if the gun were a toy and he had never in his life fired a real pistol. To the policeman in the situation, the man's personal history is momentarily immaterial. There is only one relevant sign: a gun signifying danger. Similarly, a young man may suggest the threat of violence to the policeman by his manner of walking or "strutting," the insolence in the demeanor being registered by the policeman as a possible preamble to later attack.(5) Signs vary from area to area, but a youth dressed in a black leather jacket and motorcycle boots is sure to draw at least a suspicious glance from a policeman.

Policemen themselves do not necessarily emphasize the peril associated with their work when questioned directly, and may even have well-developed strategies of denial. The element of danger is so integral to the policeman's work that explicit recognition might induce emotional barriers to work performance. Thus, one patrol officer observed that more police have been killed and injured in automobile accidents in the past ten years than from gunfire. Although his assertion is true, he neglected to mention that the police are the only peacetime occupational group with a systematic record of death and injury from gunfire and other weaponry. Along these lines, it is interesting that of the two hundred and twenty-four working Westville policemen (not including the sixteen juvenile policemen) responding to a question about which assignment they would like most to have in the police department,[2] 50 per cent selected the job of detective, an assignment combining elements of apparent danger and initiative. The next category was adult street work, that is, patrol and traffic (37 per cent). Eight per cent selected the juvenile squad,[3] and only 4 per cent selected administrative work. Not a single policeman chose the job of jail guard. Although these findings do not control for such factors as prestige, they suggest that confining and routine jobs are rated low on the hierarchy of police preferences, even though such jobs are least dangerous. Thus, the policeman may well, as a personality, enjoy the possibility of danger, especially its associated excitement, even though he may at the same time be fearful of it. Such "inconsistency" is easily understood. Freud has by now made it an axiom of personality theory that logical and emotional consistency are by no means the same phenomenon.

However complex the motives aroused by the element of danger, its consequences for sustaining police culture are unambiguous. This element requires him, like the combat soldier, the European Jew, the South African (white or black), to live in a world straining toward duality, and suggesting danger when "they" are perceived. Consequently, it is in the nature of the policeman's situation that his conception of order emphasize regularity and predictability. It is, therefore, a conception shaped by persistent *suspicion*. The English "copper," often portrayed as a courteous, easygoing, rather jolly sort of chap, on the one hand, or as a devil-may-care adventurer, on the other, is differently described by Colin MacInnes:(6)

> The true copper's dominant characteristic, if the truth be known, is neither those daring nor vicious qualities that are sometimes attributed to him by friend or enemy, but an ingrained conservatism, and almost desperate love of the conventional. It is untidiness, disorder, the unusual, that a

[2] A questionnaire was given to all policemen in operating divisions of the police force: patrol, traffic, vice control, and all detectives. The questionnaire was administered at police line-ups over a period of three days, mainly by the author but also by some of the police personnel themselves. Before the questionnaire was administered, it was circulated to and approved by the policemen's welfare association.

[3] Indeed, the journalist Paul Jacobs, who has ridden with the Westville juvenile police as part of his own work on poverty, observed in a personal communication that juvenile police appear curiously drawn to seek out dangerous situations, as if juvenile work without danger is degrading.

copper disapproves of most of all: far more, even than of crime which is merely a professional matter. Hence his profound dislike of people loitering in streets, dressing extravagantly, speaking with exotic accents, being strange, weak, eccentric, or simply any rare minority—of their doing, in fact, anything that cannot be safely predicted.

Policemen are indeed specifically *trained* to be suspicious, to perceive events or changes in the physical surroundings that indicate the occurrence or probability of disorder. A former student who worked as a patrolman in a suburban New York police department describes this aspect of the policeman's assessment of the unusual:(7)

> The time spent cruising one's sector or walking one's beat is not wasted time, though it can become quite routine. During this time, the most important thing for the officer to do is notice the *normal*. He must come to know the people in his area, their habits, their automobiles and their friends. He must learn what time the various shops close, how much money is kept on hand on different nights, what lights are usually left on, which houses are vacant . . . only then can he decide what persons or cars under what circumstances warrant the appellation "suspicious."

The individual policeman's "suspiciousness" does not hang on whether he has personally undergone an experience that could objectively be described as hazardous. Personal experience of this sort is not the key to the psychological importance of exceptionality. Each, as he routinely carries out his work, will experience situations that threaten to become dangerous. Like the American Jew who contributes to "defense" organizations such as the Anti-Defamation League in response to Nazi brutalities he has never experienced personally, the policeman identifies with his fellow cop who has been beaten, perhaps fatally, by a gang of young thugs.

SOCIAL ISOLATION

The patrolman in Westville, and probably in most communities, has come to identify the black man with danger. James Baldwin vividly expresses the isolation of the ghetto policeman:(8)

> . . .The only way to police a ghetto is to be oppressive. None of the Police Commissioner's men, even with the best will in the world, have any way of understanding the lives led by the people they swagger about in twos and threes controlling. Their very presence is an insult, and it would be, even if they spent their entire day feeding gumdrops to children. They represent the force of the white world, and that world's criminal profit and ease, to keep the black man corralled up here, in his place. The badge, the gun in the holster, and the swinging club make vivid what will happen should his rebellion become overt. . . .
>
> It is hard, on the other hand, to blame the policeman, blank, good-natured, thoughtless, and insuperably innocent, for being such a perfect representative of the people he serves. He, too, believes in good intentions and is astounded and offended when they are not taken for the deed. He has never, himself, done anything for which to be hated—which of us has? and yet he is facing, daily and nightly, people who would gladly see him dead, and he knows it. There is no way for him not to know it; there are few things under heaven more unnerving than the silent, accumulating contempt and hatred of a people. He moves through Harlem, therefore, like an occupying soldier in a bitterly hostile country; which is precisely what, and where he is, and is the reason he walks in twos and threes.

While Baldwin's observations on police–Negro relations cannot be disputed seriously, there is greater social distance between police and "civilians" in general regardless of their color than Baldwin considers. Thus, Colin MacInnes has his English hero, Mr. Justice, explaining:(9)

> . . . The story is all coppers are just civilians like anyone else, living among them not in barracks like on the Continent, but you and I know that's just a legend for mugs. We *are* cut off: we're *not* like everyone else. Some civilians fear us and play up to us, some dislike us and keep out of our way, but no one—well, very few indeed—accepts us as just ordinary like them. In one sense, dear, we're just like hostile troops occupying an enemy country. And say what you like, at times that makes us lonely.

MacInnes's observation suggests that by not introducing a white control group, Baldwin has failed to see that the policeman may not get on well with anybody regardless (to use the hackneyed phrase) of race, creed, or national origin. Policemen whom one knows well often express their sense of isolation from the public as a whole, not just from those who fail to share their color. Westville police were asked, for example, to rank the most serious problems police have. The category most frequently selected was not racial problems, but some form of public relations: lack of respect for the police, lack of cooperation in enforcement of law, lack of understanding of the requirements of police work:[4] One respondent answered:

> As a policeman my most serious problem is impressing on the general public just how difficult and necessary police service is to all. There seems to be an attitude of "law is important, but it applies to my neighbor—not to me."

Of the two hundred and eighty-two Westville policemen who rated the prestige police work receives from others, 70 per cent ranked it as only fair or poor, while less than 2 per cent ranked it as "excellent" and another 29 per cent as "good." Similarly, in Britain, two-thirds of a sample of policemen interviewed by a Royal Commission stated difficulties in making friends outside the force; of those interviewed 58 per cent thought members of the public to be reserved, suspicious, and constrained in conversation; and 12 per cent attributed such difficulties to the requirement that policemen be selective in associations and behave circumspectly.(10)

A Westville policeman related the following incident:

> Several months after I joined the force, my wife and I used to be socially active with a crowd of young people, mostly married, who gave a lot of parties where there was drinking and dancing, and we enjoyed it. I've never forgotten, though, an incident that happened on one Fourth of July party. Everybody had been drinking, there was a lot of talking, people were feeling boisterous, and some kid there—he must have been twenty or twenty-two—threw a firecracker that hit my wife in the leg and burned her. I didn't know exactly what to do—punch the guy in the nose, bawl him out, just forget it. Anyway, I couldn't let it pass, so I walked over to him and told him he ought to be careful. He began to rise up at me, and when he did, somebody yelled, "Better watch out, he's a cop." I saw everybody standing there, and I could feel they were all against me and for the kid, even though he had thrown the firecracker at my wife. I went over to the host and said it was probably better if my wife and I left because a fight would put a damper on the party. Actually, I'd hoped he would ask the kid to leave, since the kid had thrown the firecracker. But he didn't so we left. After that incident, my wife and I stopped going around with that crowd, and decided that if we were going to go to parties where there was to be drinking and boisterousness, we weren't going to be the only police people there.

Another reported that he seeks to overcome his feelings of isolation by concealing his police identity:(11)

> I try not to bring my work home with me, and that includes my social life. I like the men I work with, but I think it's better that my family doesn't become a police family. I try to put my police work into the background, and try not to let people know I'm a policeman. Once you do, you can't have normal relations with them.

Although the policeman serves a people who are, as Baldwin says, the established society, the white society, these people do not make him feel accepted. As a result, he develops resources within his own world to combat social rejection.

POLICE SOLIDARITY

All occupational groups share a measure of inclusiveness and identification. People are brought together

[4] Respondents were asked, "Anybody who knows anything about police work knows that police face a number of problems. Would you please state—in order—what you consider to be the two most serious problems police have." On the basis of a number of answers, the writer and J. Richard Woodworth devised a set of categories. Then Woodworth classified each response into one of the categories (see table at right). When a response did not seem clear, he consulted with the writer. No attempt was made independently to check Woodworth's classification because the results are used impressionistically, and do not test a hypothesis. It may be, for instance, that "relations with public" is sometimes used to indicate racial problems, and vice versa. "Racial problems" include only those answers having specific reference to race. The categories and results were as follows:

Westville Police Ranking of Number One Problem Faced by Police

	Number	*Per Cent*
Relations with public	74	26
Racial problems and demonstrations	66	23
Juvenile delinquents and delinquency	23	8
Unpleasant police tasks	23	8
Lack of cooperation from authorities (D.A., legislature, courts)	20	7
Internal departmental problems	17	6
Irregular life of policeman	5	2
No answer or other answer	56	20
	284	100

simply by doing the same work and having similar career and salary problems. As several writers have noted, however, police show an unusually high degree of occupational solidarity.(12) It is true that the police have a common employer and wear a uniform at work, but so do doctors, milkmen, and bus drivers. Yet it is doubtful that these workers have so close knit an occupation or so similar an outlook on the world as do police. Set apart from the conventional world, the policeman experiences an exceptionally strong tendency to find his social identity within his occupational milieu.

Compare the police with another skilled craft. In a study of the International Typographical Union, the authors asked printers the first names and jobs of their three closest friends. Of the 1,236 friends named by the 412 men in their sample, 35 per cent were printers.(13) Similarly, among the Westville police, of 700 friends listed by 250 respondents, 35 per cent were policemen. The policemen, however, were far more active than printers in occupational social activities. Of the printers, more than half (54 per cent) had never participated in any union clubs, benefit societies, teams, or organizations composed mostly of printers, or attended any printers' social affairs in the past 5 years. Of the Westville police, only 16 per cent had failed to attend a single police banquet or dinner in the past year (as contrasted with the printers' 5 *years*); and of the 234 men answering this question, 54 per cent had attended 3 or more such affairs *during* the past year.

These findings are striking in light of the interpretation made of the data on printers. Lipset, Trow, and Coleman do not, as a result of their findings, see printers as an unintegrated occupational group. On the contrary, they ascribe the democratic character of the union in good part to the active social and political participation of the membership. The point is not to question their interpretation, since it is doubtlessly correct when printers are held up against other manual workers. However, when seen in comparison to police, printers appear a minimally participating group; put positively, police emerge as an exceptionally socially active occupational group.

Closest Friends of Printers and Police, by Occupation

	Printers N = 1236 (%)	*Police N= 700 (%)*
Same occupation	35	35
Professionals, business executives, and independent business owners	21	30
White-collar or sales employees	20	12
Manual workers	25	22

POLICE SOLIDARITY AND DANGER

There is still a question, however, as to the process through which danger and authority influence police solidarity. The effect of danger on police solidarity is revealed when we examine a chief complaint of police: lack of public support and public apathy. The complaint may have several referents including police pay, police prestige, and support from the legislature. But the repeatedly voiced broader meaning of the complaint is resentment at being taken for granted. The policeman does not believe that his status as civil servant should relieve the public of responsibility for law enforcement. He feels, however, that payment out of public coffers somehow obscures his humanity and therefore, his need for help.[5] As one put it:

> Jerry, a cop, can get into a fight with three or four tough kids, and there will be citizens passing by, and maybe they'll look, but they'll never lend a hand. It's their country too, but you'd never know it the way some of them act. They forget that we're made of flesh and blood too. They don't care what happens to the cop so long as they don't get a little dirty.

Although the policeman sees himself as a specialist in dealing with violence, he does not want to fight alone. He does not believe that this specialization relieves the general public of citizenship duties. Indeed, if possible, he would prefer to be the foreman rather than the workingman in the battle against criminals.

The general public, of course, does withdraw from the workaday world of the policeman. The policeman's responsibility for controlling dangerous and sometimes violent persons alienates the average citizen perhaps as much as does his authority over the average citizen.

[5] On this issue there was no variation. The statement "the policeman feels" means that there was no instance of a negative opinion expressed by the police studied.

If the policeman's job is to insure that public order is maintained, the citizen's inclination is to shrink from the dangers of maintaining it. The citizen prefers to see the policeman as an automaton, because once the policeman's humanity is recognized, the citizen necessarily becomes implicated in the policeman's work, which is, after all, sometimes dirty and dangerous. What the policeman typically fails to realize is the extent he becomes tainted by the character of the work he performs. The danger of their work not only draws policemen together as a group but separates them from the rest of the population. Banton, for instance, comments:(14)

> . . . patrolmen may support their fellows over what they regard as minor infractions in order to demonstrate to them that they will be loyal in situations that make the greatest demands upon their fidelity. . . .
>
> In the American departments I visited it seemed as if the supervisors shared many of the patrolmen's sentiments about solidarity. They too wanted their colleagues to back them up in an emergency, and they shared similar frustrations with the public.

Thus, the element of danger contains seeds of isolation which may grow in two directions. In one, a stereotyping perceptual shorthand is formed through which the police come to see certain signs as symbols of potential violence. The police probably differ in this respect from the general middle-class white population only in degree. This difference, however, may take on enormous significance in practice. Thus, the policeman works at identifying and possibly apprehending the symbolic assailant; the ordinary citizen does not. As a result, the ordinary citizen does not assume the responsibility to implicate himself in the policeman's required response to danger. The element of danger in the policeman's role alienates him not only from populations with a potential for crime but also from the conventionally respectable (white) citizenry, in short, from that segment of the population from which friends would ordinarily be drawn. As Janowitz has noted in a paragraph suggesting similarities between the police and the military, ". . . any profession which is continually preoccupied with the threat of danger requires a strong sense of solidarity if it is to operate effectively. Detailed regulation of the military style of life is expected to enhance group cohesion, professional loyalty, and maintain the martial spirit."(15)

SOCIAL ISOLATION AND AUTHORITY

The element of authority also helps to account for the policeman's social isolation. Policemen themselves are aware of their isolation from the community, and are apt to weight authority heavily as a causal factor. When considering how authority influences rejection, the policeman typically singles out his responsibility for enforcement of traffic violations.(16) Resentment, even hostility, is generated in those receiving citations, in part because such contact is often the only one citizens have with police, and in part because municipal administrations and courts have been known to utilize police authority primarily to meet budgetary requirements, rather than those of public order. Thus, when a municipality engages in "speed trapping" by changing limits so quickly that drivers cannot realistically slow down to the prescribed speed or, while keeping the limits reasonable, charging high fines primarily to generate revenue, the policeman carries the brunt of public resentment.

That the policeman dislikes writing traffic tickets is suggested by the quota system police departments typically employ. In Westville, each traffic policeman has what is euphemistically described as a working "norm." A motorcyclist is supposed to write two tickets an hour for moving violations. It is doubtful that "norms" are needed because policemen are lazy. Rather, employment of quotas most likely springs from the reluctance of policemen to expose themselves to what they know to be public hostility. As a result, as one traffic policeman said:

> You learn to sniff out the places where you can catch violators when you're running behind. Of course, the department gets to know that you hang around one place, and they sometimes try to repair the situation there. But a lot of the time it would be too expensive to fix up the engineering fault, so we keep making our norm.

When meeting "production" pressures, the policeman inadvertently gives a false impression of patrolling ability to the average citizen. The traffic cyclist waits in hiding for moving violators near a tricky intersection, and is reasonably sure that such violations will occur with regularity. The violator believes he has observed a policeman displaying exceptional detection capacities and may have two thoughts, each apt to generate hostility toward the policeman: "I have been trapped," or "They can catch me; why can't they catch crooks as easily?" The answer, of course, lies in the different behavior patterns of motorists and "crooks." The latter do not act with either the frequency or predictability of motorists at poorly engineered intersections.

While traffic patrol plays a major role in separating the policeman from the respectable community, other of his tasks also have this consequence. Traffic patrol is only the most obvious illustration of the policeman's general responsibility for maintaining public order, which also includes keeping order at public accidents, sporting events, and political rallies. These activities share one feature: the policeman is called upon to *direct* ordinary citizens, and therefore to restrain their freedom of action. Resenting the restraint, the average citizen in such a situation typically thinks something along the lines of "He is supposed to catch crooks; why is he bothering me?" Thus, the citizen stresses the "dangerous" portion of the policeman's role while belittling his authority.

Closely related to the policeman's authority-based problems as *director* of the citizenry are difficulties associated with his injunction to *regulate public morality*. For instance, the policeman is obliged to investigate "lovers' lanes," and to enforce laws pertaining to gambling, prostitution, and drunkenness. His responsibility in these matters allows him much administrative discretion since he may not actually enforce the law by making an arrest, but instead merely interfere with continuation of the objectionable activity.(17) Thus, he may put the drunk in a taxi, tell the lovers to remove themselves from the back seat, and advise a man soliciting a prostitute to leave the area.

Such admonitions are in the interest of maintaining the proprieties of public order. At the same time, the policeman invites the hostility of the citizen so directed in two respects: he is likely to encourage the sort of response mentioned earlier (that is, an antagonistic reformulation of the policeman's role) and the policeman is apt to cause resentment because of the suspicion that policemen do not themselves strictly conform to the moral norms they are enforcing. Thus, the policeman, faced with enforcing a law against fornication, drunkenness, or gambling, is easily liable to a charge of hypocrisy. Even when the policeman is called on to enforce the laws relating to overt homosexuality, a form of sexual activity for which police are not especially noted, he may encounter the charge of hypocrisy on grounds that he does not adhere strictly to prescribed heterosexual codes. The policeman's difficulty in this respect is shared by all authorities responsible for maintenance of disciplined activity, including industrial foremen, political leaders, elementary schoolteachers, and college professors. All are expected to conform rigidly to the entire range of norms they espouse.(18) The policeman, however, as a result of the unique combination of the elements of danger and authority, experiences a special predicament. It is difficult to develop qualities enabling him to stand up to danger, and to conform to standards of puritanical morality. The element of danger demands that the policeman be able to carry out efforts that are in their nature overtly masculine. Police work, like soldiering, requires an exceptional caliber of physical fitness, agility, toughness, and the like. The man who ranks high on these masculine characteristics is, again like the soldier, not usually disposed to be puritanical about sex, drinking, and gambling.

On the basis of observations, policemen do not subscribe to moralistic standards for conduct. For example, the morals squad of the police department, when questioned, was unanimously against the statutory rape age limit, on grounds that as late teen-agers they themselves might not have refused an attractive offer from a seventeen-year-old girl.(19) Neither, from observations, are policemen by any means total abstainers from the use of alcoholic beverages. The policeman who is arresting a drunk has probably been drunk himself; he knows it and the drunk knows it.

More than that, a portion of the social isolation of the policeman can be attributed to the discrepancy between moral regulation and the norms and behavior of policemen in these areas. We have presented data indicating that police engage in a comparatively active occupational social life. One interpretation might attribute this attendance to a basic interest in such affairs; another might explain the policeman's occupational social activity as a measure of restraint in publicly violating norms he enforces. The interest in attending police affairs may grow as much out of security in "letting oneself go" in the presence of police, and a corresponding feeling of insecurity with civilians, as an authentic preference for police social affairs. Much alcohol is usually consumed at police banquets with all the melancholy and boisterousness accompanying such occasions. As Horace Cayton reports on his experience as a policeman:(20)

> Deputy sheriffs and policemen don't know much about organized recreation; all they usually do when celebrating is get drunk and pound each other on the back, exchanging loud insults which under ordinary circumstances would result in a fight.

To some degree the reason for the behavior exhibited on these occasions is the company, since the policeman would feel uncomfortable exhibiting insobriety before civilians. The policeman may be likened to other authorities who prefer to violate moralistic norms away from onlookers for whom they are routinely supposed to appear as normative models. College professors, for instance, also get drunk on occasion, but prefer to do so where students are not present. Unfortunately for the policeman, such settings are harder for him to come by than they are for the college professor. The whole civilian world watches the policeman. As a result, he tends to be limited to the company of other policemen for whom his police identity is not a stimulus to carping normative criticism.

CORRELATES OF SOCIAL ISOLATION

The element of authority, like the element of danger, is thus seen to contribute to the solidarity of policemen. To the extent that policemen share the experience of receiving hostility from the public, they are also drawn together and become dependent upon one another. Trends in the degree to which police may exercise authority are also important considerations in understanding the dynamics of the relation between authority and solidarity. It is not simply a question of how much absolute authority police are given, but how much authority they have relative to what they had, or think they had, before. If, as Westley concludes, police violence is frequently a response to a challenge to the policeman's authority, so too may a perceived reduction in authority result in greater solidarity. Whitaker comments on the British police as follows:(21)

> As they feel their authority decline, internal solidarity has become increasingly important to the police. Despite the individual responsibility of each police officer to pursue justice, there is sometimes a tendency to close ranks and to form a square when they themselves are concerned.

These inclinations may have positive consequences for the effectiveness of police work, since notions of professional courtesy or colleagueship seem unusually high among police.[6] When the nature of the policing enterprise requires much joint activity, as in robbery and narcotics enforcement, the impression is received that cooperation is high and genuine. Policemen do not appear to cooperate with one another merely because such is the policy of the chief, but because they sincerely attach a high value to teamwork. For instance, there is a norm among detectives that two who work together will protect each other when a dangerous situation arises. During one investigation, a detective stepped out of a car to question a suspect who became belligerent. The second detective, who had remained overly long in the back seat of the police car, apologized indirectly to his partner by explaining how wrong it had been of him to permit his partner to encounter a suspect alone on the street. He later repeated this explanation privately, in genuine consternation at having committed the breach (and possibly at having been culpable in the presence of an observer). Strong feelings of empathy and cooperation, indeed almost of "clannishness," a term several policemen themselves used to describe the attitude of police toward one another, may be seen in the daily activities of police. Analytically, these feelings can be traced to the elements of danger and shared experiences of hostility in the policeman's role.

Finally, to round out the sketch, policemen are notably conservative, emotionally and politically. If the element of danger in the policeman's role tends to make the policeman suspicious, and therefore emotionally attached to the status quo, a similar consequence may be attributed to the element of authority. The fact that a man is engaged in enforcing a set of rules implies that he also becomes implicated in *affirming* them. Labor disputes provide the commonest example of conditions inclining the policeman to support the status quo. In these situations, the police are necessarily pushed on the side of the defense of property. Their responsibilities thus lead them to see the striking and sometimes angry workers as their enemy

[6] It would be difficult to compare this factor across occupations, since the indicators could hardly be controlled. Nevertheless, I felt that the sense of responsibility to policemen in other departments was on the whole quite strong.

and, therefore, to be cool, if not antagonistic, toward the whole conception of labor militancy.[7] If a policeman did not believe in the system of laws he was responsible for enforcing, he would have to go on living in a state of conflicting cognitions, a condition which a number of social psychologists agree is painful.[8]

REFERENCES

1. For previous contributions in this area, *see* the following: Ely Chinoy, *Automobile Workers and the American Dream* (Garden City, N.Y.: Doubleday, 1955); Charles R. Walker and Robert H. Guest, *The Man on the Assembly Line* (Cambridge: Harvard University Press, 1952); Everett C. Hughes, "Work and the Self," in his *Men and Their Work* (Glencoe, Ill.: The Free Press of Glencoe, 1958), pp. 42–55; Harold L. Wilensky, *Intellectuals in Labor Unions: Organizational Pressures on Professional Roles* (Glencoe, Ill.: The Free Press of Glencoe, 1956); Harold L. Wilensky, "Varieties of Work Experience," in Henry Borow, ed., *Man in a World at Work* (Boston: Houghton Mifflin, 1964), pp. 125–54; Louis Kriesberg, "The Retail Furrier: Concepts of Security and Success," *American Journal of Sociology, 57* (March 1952), pp. 478–85; Waldo Burchard, "Role Conflicts of Military Chaplains," *American Sociological Review, 19* (October 1954), pp. 528–35; Howard S. Becker and Blanche Geer, "The Fate of Idealism in Medical School," *American Sociological Review, 23* (1958), pp. 50–56; and Howard S. Becker and Anselm L. Strauss, "Careers, Personality, and Adult Socialization," *American Journal of Sociology, 62* (November 1956), pp. 253–63.

2. Morris Janowitz, *The Professional Soldier: A Social and Political Portrait* (New York: Free Press, 1964), p. 175.

3. William Westley was the first to raise such questions about the police when he inquired into the conditions under which police are violent. Whatever merit this analysis has, it owes much to his prior insights, as all subsequent sociological studies of the police must. *See* his "Violence and the Police," *American Journal of Sociology, 59* (July 1953), 34–41; also his unpublished Ph.D. dissertation *The Police: A Sociological Study of Law, Custom, and Morality* (University of Chicago, Department of Sociology, 1951).

4. From Thomas F. Adams, "Field Interrogation," *Police* (March–April, 1963), p. 28.

5. *See* Irving Piliavin and Scott Briar, "Police Encounters with Juveniles," *American Journal of Sociology, 70* (September 1964), pp. 206–214.

6. Colin MacInnes, *Mr. Love and Justice* (London: New English Library, 1962), p. 74.

7. Peter J. Connell, "Handling of Complaints by Police," (Unpublished paper for course in Criminal Procedure, Yale Law School, Fall, 1961).

8. James Baldwin, *Nobody Knows My Name* (New York: Dell, 1962), pp. 65–67.

9. Colin MacInnes, *Mr. Love and Justice* (London: New English Library, 1962), p. 20.

10. Royal Commission on the Police, 1962, Appendix IV to *Minutes of Evidence*, cited in Michael Banton, *The Policeman in the Community* (London: Tavistock, 1964), p. 198.

11. Similarly, Banton found Scottish police officers attempting to conceal their occupation when on holiday. He quotes one as saying: "If someone asks my wife, 'What does your husband do?' I've told her to say, 'He's a clerk,' and that's the way it went because she found that being a policeman's wife—well, it wasn't quite a stigma, she didn't feel cut off, but that a sort of invisible wall was up for conversation purposes when a policeman was there." Ibid.

12. In addition to Banton, William Westley and James Q. Wilson have noted this characteristic of police. *See* William Westley, "Violence and the Police," *Ameri-*

[7] In light of this, the most carefully drawn lesson plan in the "professionalized" Westville police department, according to the officer in charge of training, is the one dealing with the policeman's demeanor in labor disputes. A comparable concern is now being evidenced in teaching policemen appropriate demeanor in civil rights demonstrations. *See*, e.g., Juby E. Towler, *The Police Role in Racial Conflicts* (Springfield, Ill.: Thomas, 1964).

[8] Indeed, one school of social psychology asserts that there is a basic "drive," a fundamental tendency of human nature, to reduce the degree of discrepancy between conflicting cognitions. For the policeman, this tenet implies that he would have to do something to reduce the discrepancy between his beliefs and his behavior. He would have to modify his behavior, his beliefs, or introduce some outside factor to justify the discrepancy. . . . *See* Leon Festinger, *A Theory of Cognitive Dissonance* (Evanston, Illinois: Row, Peterson, 1957).

can Journal of Sociology, 59 (July 1953), p. 294; Wilson, "The Police and Their Problems: A Theory," *Public Policy, 12* (1963), 189–216.

13. S. M. Lipset, Martin H. Trow, and James S. Coleman, *Union Democracy* (New York: Anchor Books, 1962), p. 123.

14. Michael Banton, *The Policeman in the Community* (London: Tavistock, 1964), p. 114.

15. Morris Janowitz, *The Professional Soldier: A Social and Political Portrait* (New York: The Free Press, 1964).

16. O. W. Wilson, for example, mentions this factor as a primary source of antagonism toward police. *See* his "Police Authority in a Free Society," *Journal of Criminal Law, Criminology and Police Science, 54* (June 1964), 175–77. In the current study, in addition to the police themselves, other people interviewed, such as attorneys in the system, also attribute the isolation of police to their authority. Similarly, Arthur L. Stinchcombe, in an as yet unpublished manuscript, "The Control of Citizen Resentment in Police Work," provides a stimulating analysis, to which I am indebted, of the ways police authority generates resentment.

17. *See* Wayne R. La Fave, "The Police and Nonenforcement of the Law," *Wisconsin Law Review* (1962), pp. 104–137, 179–239.

18. For a theoretical discussion of the problems of leadership, *see* George Homans, *The Human Group* (New York: Harcourt, Brace, 1950), especially the chapter on "The Job of the Leader," pp. 415–440.

19. The work of the Westville morals squad is analyzed in detail in an unpublished master's thesis by J. Richard Woodworth, *The Administration of Statutory Rape Complaints: A Sociological Study* (Berkeley: University of California, 1964).

20. Horace R. Cayton, *Long Old Road* (New York: Trident Press, 1965), p. 154.

21. Ben Whitaker, *The Police* (Middlesex, England: Penguin Books, 1964), p. 137.

Observations on the Making of Policemen

John Van Maanen

In recent years the so-called "police problem" has become one of the more institutionalized topics of routine conversation in this society. Whether one views the police as friend or foe, virtually everyone has a set of "cop stories" to relate to willing listeners. Although most stories dramatize personal encounters and are situation-specific, there is a common thread running through these frequently heard accounts. In such stories the police are almost always depicted as a homogeneous occupational grouping somehow quite different from most other men.

Occupational stereotyping is, of course, not unknown. Professors, taxicab drivers, used-car salesmen, corporate executives all have mythological counterparts in the popular culture. Yet, what is of interest here is the recognition by the police themselves of the implied differences.

Policemen generally view themselves as performing society's dirty work. As such, a gap is created between the police and the public. Today's patrolman feels cut off from the mainstream culture and unfairly stigmatized. In short, when the policeman dons his uniform, he enters a distinct subculture governed by norms and values designed to manage the strain created by an outsider role in the community.[1]

[1] The use of the term "outsider" in the above context is not intended to invidiously portray the police. Rather, the term simply connotes the widespread conviction carried by the police themselves that they are, of necessity, somehow different, and set-off from the larger society. To most police observers, isolationism, secrecy, strong in-group loyalties, sacred symbols, common language, and a sense of estrangement are almost axiomatic subcultural features underpinning a set of common understandings among police in general which govern their relations with one another as well as with civilians (Bayley and Mendelsohn, 1969; President's Commission, 1967; Skolnick, 1966). Such a perspective emphasizes the necessity to view the world from the eyes of the outsider—a perspective which ideally is empathetic but neither sympathetic or judgmental.

To classify the police as outsiders helps us to focus on several important things: the distinctive social definitions used by persons belonging to such marginal subcultures (e.g., "everybody hates a cop"); the outsider's methods for managing the tension created by his social position (e.g., "always protect brother officers"); and the explicit delineation of the everyday standards of conduct followed by the outsider (e.g., "lay low and avoid trouble"). Furthermore, such a perspective forces a researcher to delve deeply into the subculture in order to see clearly through the eyes of the studied.

CONTEXT

While observation of the police in naturally occurring situations is difficult, lengthy, and often threatening, it is imperative. Unfortunately, most research to date relies almost exclusively upon interview-questionnaire data (e.g., Bayley and Mendelsohn 1969; Wilson 1968), official statistics (e.g., Webster 1970; President's Commission on Law Enforcement and the Administration of Justice 1967), or broad-ranging attitude surveys (e.g., Sterling 1972; McNamara 1967). The very few sustained observational studies have been concerned with specific aspects of police behavioral patterns (e.g., Skolnick 1966—vice activities; Reiss 1971—police-citizen contacts; Bittner 1967, Cicourel 1967—police encounters with "skid row alcoholics" and juveniles, respectively). This is not to say these diverse investigations are without merit. Indeed, without such studies we would not have even begun to see beneath the occupational shield. Yet, the paucity of in-depth police-related research—especially from the outsider perspective—represents a serious gap in our knowledge of a critical social establishment.[2]

In particular the process of becoming a police officer has been neglected.[3] What little data we presently have related to the police socialization process come from either the work devoted to certain hypothesized dimensions of the police personality (e.g., dogmatism, authoritarianism, cynicism, alienation, etc.) or cross-sectional snapshots of police attitudes toward their public audiences. Using a dramaturgic metaphor, these studies have concentrated upon the description of the actors, stage setting, and "on stage" performance of the police production. Little attention has been paid to the orientation of the performers to their particular role viewed from "backstage" perspective. Clearly, for any performance to materialize there must be casting sessions, rehearsals, directors, stagehands, and some form(s) of compensation provided the actors to insure their continued performance. Recognizing that to some degree organizational socialization occurs at all career stages, this paradigm focuses exclusively upon the individual recruit's entry into the organization. It is during the breaking-in period that the organization may be thought to be most persuasive, for the person has few guidelines to direct his behavior and has little, if any, organizationally based support for his "vulnerable selves" which may be the object of influence. Support for this position comes from a wide range of studies indicating that early organizational learning is a major determinant of one's later organizationally relevant beliefs, attitudes, and behaviors (Van Maanen 1972; Lortie 1968; Berlew and Hall 1966; Evan 1963; Hughes 1958; Dornbush 1955). Schein (1971) suggested perceptively that this process results in a "psychological contract" linking the goals of the individual to the constraints and purposes of the organization. In a sense, this psychological contract is actually a modus vivendi between the person and the organizational representing the outcomes of the socialization process.

METHOD

The somewhat truncated analysis that follows was based upon the observation of novice policemen in

[2] If one takes seriously research findings regarding esoteric subcultures, social scientists interested in police behavior are limited in their choice of methodological strategy. If we are to gain insight into the so-called police problem, researchers must penetrate the official smoke screen sheltering virtually all departments and observe directly the social action in social situations which, in the last analysis, defines police work.

[3] One exception is Westley's (1951) insightful observational study of a midwestern police department. However, his research was devoted mainly to the description of the more salient sociological features of the police occupation and was concerned only peripherally with the learning process associated with the police role.

situ. The study was conducted in Union City over a nine-month period.[4] Approximately three months of this time were spent as a fully participating member of one Union City Police Academy recruit class. Following the formal training phase of the initiation process, my fully participating role was modified. As a civilian, I spent five months (roughly eight to ten hours a day, six days a week) riding in patrol units operated by a recruit and his FTO (i.e., Field Training Officer charged with imputing "street sense" into the neophyte) as a back-seat observer.

From the outset, my role as researcher-qua-researcher was made explicit. To masquerade as a regular police recruit would not only have been problematic, but would have raised a number of ethical questions as well (particularly during the field training portion of the socialization sequence).[5]

The conversational data presented below are drawn primarily from naturally occurring encounters with persons in the police domain (e.g., recruits, veterans, administrators, wives, friends, reporters, court officials, etc.). While formal interviews were conducted with some, the bulk of the data contained here arose from far less-structured situations. . . .

[4] Union City is a pseudonym for a sprawling metropolitan area populated by more than a million people. The police department employs well over 1,500 uniformed officers, provides a salary above the national average, and is organized in the classic pyramidal arrangement (see Van Maanen, 1972). Based on interviews with police personnel from a number of different departments and, most importantly, critical readings of my work by policemen from several departments, the sequence of events involved in recruit socialization appears to be remarkably similar from department to department. This structural correspondence among recruit training programs has been noted by others (see Ahern, 1972; Berkeley, 1969; Niederhoffer, 1967).

[5] While it cannot be stated categorically that my presence had little effect upon the behavior of the subjects, I felt I was accepted completely as a regular group member in my particular police academy class and little or no behavior was (or, for that matter, could be) altered explicitly. Furthermore, the lengthy, personal, and involving nature of my academy experiences produced an invaluable carry-over effect when I moved to the street work portion of the study. The importance of continuous observation and full participation as an aid for minimizing distortions and behavior change on the part of social actors has been strikingly demonstrated by a number of social scientists (e.g., see Whyte, 1943; Becker, 1963; Dalton, 1964; Greer, 1964; and, most recently, Schatzman and Strauss, 1973).

THE MAKING OF A POLICEMAN: A PARADIGM

For purposes here, the police recruit's initiation into the organizational setting shall be treated as if it occurred in four discrete stages. While these stages are only analytically distinct, they do serve as useful markers for describing the route traversed by the recruit. The sequence is related to the preentry, admittance, change, and continuance phases of the organizational socialization process and are labeled here as choice, introduction, encounter, and metamorphosis, respectively.

Preentry: Choice

What sort of young man is attracted to and selected for a police career? The literature notes that police work seems to attract local, family-oriented, working-class whites interested primarily in the security and salary aspects of the occupation. Importantly, the authoritarian syndrome which has popularly been ascribed to persons selecting police careers has not been supported by empirical study. The available research supports the contention that the police occupation is viewed by the recruits as simply one job of many and considered roughly along the same dimensions as any job choice.

While my research can add little to the above picture, several qualifications are in order which perhaps provide a greater understanding of the particular choice process. First, the security and salary aspects of the police job have probably been overrated. Through interviews and experience with Union City recruits, a rather pervasive meaningful work theme is apparent as a major factor in job choice. Virtually all recruits alluded to the opportunity afforded by a police career to perform in a role which was perceived as consequential or important to society. While such altruistic motives may be subject to social desirability considerations, or other biasing factors, it is my feeling that these high expectations of community service are an important element in the choice process.

Second, the out-of-doors and presumably adventurous qualities of police work (as reflected in the popular culture) were perceived by the recruits as among the more influential factors attracting them to the job. With few exceptions, the novice policemen had worked several jobs since completing high school and were particularly apt to stress the benefits of working a nonroutine job.

Third, the screening factor associated with police selection is a dominating aspect of the socialization process. From the filling out of the application blank at City Hall to the telephone call which informs a potential recruit of his acceptance into the department, the individual passes through a series of events which serve to impress an aspiring policeman with a sense of being accepted into an elite organization. Perhaps some men originally take the qualifying examination for patrolman lightly, but it is unlikely many men proceed through the entire screening process—often taking up to six months or more—without becoming committed seriously to a police career. As such, the various selection devices, if successfully surmounted, increase the person's self-esteem, as well as buttress his occupational choice. Thus, this anticipatory stage tends to strengthen the neophyte's evaluation of the police organization as an important place to work.

Finally, as in most organizations, the police department is depicted to individuals who have yet to take the oath of office in its most favorable light. A potential recruit is made to feel as if he were important and valued by the organization. Since virtually all recruitment occurs via generational or friendship networks involving police officers and prospective recruits, the individual receives personalized encouragement and support which helps sustain his interest during the arduous screening procedure. Such links begin to attach the would-be policeman to the organization long before he actually joins.

To summarize, most policemen have not chosen their career casually. They enter the department with a high degree of normative identification with what they preceive to be the goals and values of the organization. At least in Union City, the police department was able to attract and select men who entered the organization with a reservoir of positive attitudes toward hard work and a strong level of organizational support. What happens to the recruit when he is introduced to the occupation at the police academy is where attention is now directed.

Admittance: Introduction

The individual usually feels upon swearing allegiance to the department, city, state, and nation that "he's finally made it." However, the department instantaneously and somewhat rudely informs him that until he has served his probationary period he may be severed from the membership rolls at any time without warning, explanation, or appeal. It is perhaps ironic that in a period of a few minutes, a person's position vis-à-vis the organization can be altered so dramatically. Although some aspects of this phenomenon can be found in all organizations, in the paramilitary environment of the police world, the shift is particularly illuminating to the recruit.

For most urban police recruits, the first real contact with the police subculture occurs at the academy. Surrounded by forty to fifty contemporaries, the recruit is introduced to the harsh and often arbitrary discipline of the organization. Absolute obedience to departmental rules, rigorous physical training, dull lectures devoted to various technical aspects of the occupation, and a ritualistic concern for detail characterize the academy. Only the recruit's classmates aid his struggle to avoid punishments and provide him an outlet from the long days. A recruit soon learns that to be one minute late to a class, to utter a careless word in formation, or to be caught walking when he should be running may result in a "gig" or demerit costing a man an extra day of work or the time it may take to write a long essay on, say, "the importance of keeping a neat appearance."

Wearing a uniform which distinguishes the novices from "real" policemen, recruits are expected to demonstrate group cohesion in all aspects of academy life. The training staff actively promotes solidarity through the use of group rewards and punishments, identifying garments for each recruit class, interclass competition, and cajoling the newcomers—at every conceivable opportunity—to show some unity. Predictably, such tactics work—partial evidence is suggested by the well-attended academy class reunions held year after year in the department. To most veteran officers, their police academy experiences resulted in a career-long source of identification. It is no exaggeration to state that the "in-the-same-boat" collective consciousness which arises when groups are processed serially through a harsh set of experiences was as refined in the Union

City Police Department as in other institutions such as military academies, fraternities, or medical schools.[6]

The formal content of the training academy is almost exclusively weighted in favor of the more technical aspects of police work. A few outside speakers are invited to the academy (usually during the last few weeks of training), but the majority of class time is filled by departmental personnel describing the more mundane features of the occupation. To a large degree, the formal academy may be viewed as a didactic sort of instrumentally oriented ritual passage rite. As such, feigning attention to lectures on, for example, "the organization of the Administrative Services Bureau" or "state and local traffic codes" is a major task for the recruits.

However, the academy also provides the recruit with an opportunity to begin learning or, more properly, absorbing the tradition which typifies the department. The novices' overwhelming eagerness to hear what police work is really like results in literally hours upon hours of war stories (alternately called "sea stories" by a few officers) told at the discretion of the many instructors. One recruit, when asked about what he hoped to learn in the academy, responded as follows:

> I want them to tell me what police work is all about. I couldn't care less about the outside speakers or the guys they bring out here from upstairs who haven't been on the street for the last twenty years. What I want is for somebody who's gonna level with us and really give the lowdown on how we're supposed to survive out there.

By observing and listening closely to police stories and style, the individual is exposed to a partial organizational history which details certain personalities, past events, places, and implied relationships which the recruit is expected eventually to learn, and it is largely through war stories that the department's history is conveyed. Throughout the academy, a recruit is exposed to particular instructors who relate caveats concerning the area's notorious criminals, sensational crimes, social-geographical peculiarities, and political structure. Certain charismatic departmental personalities are described in detail. Past events—notably the shooting of police officers—are recreated and informal analyses passed on. The following excerpt from a criminal law lecture illustrates some of these concerns.

> I suppose you guys have heard of Lucky Baldwin? If not, you sure will when you hit the street. Baldwin happens to be the biggest burglar still operating in this town. Every guy in this department from patrolman to chief would love to get him and make it stick. We've busted him about ten times so far, but he's got an asshole lawyer and money so he always beats the rap. . . . If I ever get a chance to pinch the SOB, I'll do it my way with my thirty-eight and spare the city the cost of a trial.

The correlates of this history are mutually held perspectives toward certain classes of persons, places, and things which are the objective reality of police work. Critically, when war stories are presented, discipline within the recruit class is relaxed. The rookies are allowed to share laughter and tension-relieving quips with the veteran officers. A general atmosphere of camaraderie is maintained. The near lascivious enjoyment accompanying these informal respites from academy routine serve to establish congeniality and solidarity with the experienced officers in what is normally a rather harsh and uncomfortable environment. Clearly, this is the material of which memories are made.

Outside the classroom, the recruits spend endless hours discussing nuances and implications of war stories, and collective understandings begin to develop. Via such experiences, the meaning and emotional reality of police work start to take shape for the individual. In a sense, by vicariously sharing the exploits of his predecessors, the newcomer gradually builds a common language and shared set of interests which will attach him to the organization until he too has police experience to relate.

Despite these important breaks in formality, the recruits' early perceptions of policing are overshadowed by the submissive and often degrading role they are expected to play in the academy. Long, monotonous hours of class time are required, a seemingly eternal set of examinations are administered, meaningless as-

[6] Significantly, a recruit is not even allowed to carry a loaded weapon during the classroom portion of his academy training. He must wait until graduation night before being permitted to load his weapon. To the recruit, such policies are demeaning. Yet, the policies "stigmatizing" the recruits-as-recruits (e.g., different uniforms, old and battered batons, allocation of special parking spaces, special scarves, and name plates) were exceedingly effective methods of impressing upon the recruits that they were members of a particular class and were not yet Union City Police Officers.

signments consume valuable off-duty time, various mortifying events are institutionalized rituals of academy life (e.g., each week, a class "asshole" was selected and received a trophy depicting a gorilla dressed as a policeman), and relatively sharp punishments enacted for breaches of academy regulations. The multitude of academy rules make it highly unlikely that any recruit can complete the training course unscathed. The following training division report illustrates the arbitrary nature of the dreaded gigs issued during the academy phase.

> You were observed displaying unofficerlike conduct in an academy class. You openly yawned (without making any effort to minimize or conceal the fact), (this happened twice), you were observed looking out the window constantly, and spent time with your arms lying across your desk. You will report to Sergeant Smith in the communications division for an extra three hours of duty on August 15 (parentheses theirs).

The main result of such stress training is that the recruit soon learns it is his peer group rather than the "brass" which will support him and which he, in turn, must support. For example, the newcomers adopt covering tactics to shield the tardy colleague, develop cribbing techniques to pass exams, and become proficient at constructing consensual ad hoc explanations of a fellow-recruit's mistake. Furthermore, the long hours, new friends, and ordeal aspects of the recruit school serve to detach the newcomer from his old attitudes and acquaintances. In short, the academy impresses upon the recruit that he must now identify with a new group—his fellow officers. That this process is not complete, however, is illustrated by the experience of one recruit during this last week of training before his introduction to the street. This particular recruit told his classmates the following:

> Last night as I was driving home from the academy, I stopped to get some gas. . . . As soon as I shut off the engine some dude comes running up flapping his arms and yelling like crazy about being robbed. Here I am sitting in my car with my gun on and the ole buzzer (badge) staring him right in the face. . . . Wow! . . . I had no idea what to do; so I told him to call the cops and got the hell away from there. What gets me is that it didn't begin to hit me that I WAS A COP until I was about a mile away (emphasis mine).

To this researcher, the academy training period serves to prepare the recruits to alter their initially high but unrealistic occupational expectations. Through the methods described above, the novices begin to absorb the subcultural ethos and to think like policemen. As a fellow recruit stated at the end of the academy portion of training:

> There's sure more to this job than I first thought. They expect us to be dog catchers, lawyers, marriage counselors, boxers, firemen, doctors, baby-sitters, race-car drivers, and still catch a crook occasionally. There's no way we can do all that crap. They're nuts!

Finally, as in other regulated social systems, the initiate learns that the formal rules and regulations are applied inconsistently. What is sanctioned in one case with a gig is ignored in another case. To the recruits, academy rules become behavioral prescriptions which are to be coped with formally, but informally dismissed. The newcomer learns that when The Department notices his behavior, it is usually to administer a punishment, not a reward. The solution to this collective predicament is to stay low and avoid trouble.

Change: Encounter

Following the classroom training period, a newcomer is introduced to the complexities of the "street" through his Field Training Officer (hereafter referred to as the FTO). It is during this period of apprenticeship-like socialization that the reality shock encompassing full recognition of being a policeman is likely to occur. Through the eyes of his experienced FTO, the recruit learns the ins and outs of the police role. Here he learns what kinds of behavior are appropriate and expected of a patrolman within his social setting. His other instructors in this phase are almost exclusively his fellow patrolmen working the same precinct and shift. While his sergeant may occasionally offer tips on how to handle himself on the street, the supervisor is more notable for his absence than for his presence. When the sergeant does seek out the recruit, it is probably to inquire as to how many hazardous traffic violations the "green pea" had written that week or to remind the recruit to keep his hat on while out of the patrol car. As a matter of formal policy in Union City, the department expected the FTO to handle all recruit uncertainties. This traditional feature of police work—patrolmen training patrolmen—insures continuity from class to class of police officers regardless of the content of the academy instruction. In large measure, the flow of influence from one generation to another accounts for the remarkable stability of the pattern of police behavior.

It was my observation that the recruit's reception into the Patrol Division was one of consideration and warm welcome. As near as interviewing and personal experience can attest, there was no hazing or rejection of the recruit by veteran officers. In all cases, the recruits were fully accepted into the ongoing police system with good-natured tolerance and much advice. If anyone in the department was likely to react negatively to the recruits during their first few weeks on patrol, it was the supervisor and not the on-line patrolmen. The fraternal-like regard shown the rookie by the experienced officers stands in stark contrast to the stern greeting he received at the police academy. The newcomer quickly is bombarded with "street wise" patrolmen assuring him that the police academy was simply an experience all officers endure and has little, if anything, to do with real police work. Consequently, the academy experiences for the recruits stand symbolically as their rites de passage, permitting them access to the occupation. That the experienced officers confirm their negative evaluation of the academy heightens the assumed similarities among the rookies and veterans and serves to facilitate the recruit's absorption into the division. As an FTO noted during my first night on patrol:

> I hope the academy didn't get to you. It's something we all have to go through. A bunch of bullshit as far as I can tell. . . . Since you got through it all right, you get to find out what it's like out here. You'll find out mighty fast that it ain't nothing like they tell you at the academy.

During the protracted hours spent on patrol with his FTO, the recruit is instructed as to the real nature of police work. To the neophyte, the first few weeks on patrol is an extremely trying period. The recruit is slightly fearful and woefully ill-prepared for both the routine and eccentricities of real police work. While he may know the criminal code and the rudimentaries of arrest, the fledgling patrolman is perplexed and certainly not at ease in their application. For example, a two-day veteran told the following story to several of his academy associates.

> We were down under the bridge where the fags hang out and spot this car that looked like nobody was in it. . . . Frank puts the spot on it and two heads pop up. He tells me to watch what he does and keep my mouth shut. So I follow him up to the car and just kind of stand around feeling pretty dumb. Frank gives 'em a blast of shit and tells the guy sitting behind the wheel he's under arrest. The punk gets out of the car snivelling and I go up to him and start putting the cuffs on. Frank says, "Just take him back to the car and sit on him while I get the dope on his boyfriend here." So I kind of direct him back to the car and stick him in the backseat and I get in the front. . . . While Frank's filling out a FIR (Field Investigation Report) on the other guy, the little pansy in the backseat's carrying on about his wife and kids like you wouldn't believe. I'm starting to feel sorta sorry for arresting him. Anyway, Frank finishes filling out the FIR and tells the other guy to get going and if he ever sees him again he'll beat the holy shit out of him. Then he comes back to the car and does the same number on the other fag. After we drove away, I told Frank I thought we'd arrested somebody. He laughed his ass off and told me that that's the way we do things out here.

To a recruit, the whole world seems new, and from his novel point of view it is. Like a visitor from a foreign land, the daily events are perplexing and present a myriad of operational difficulties. At first, the squawk of the police radio transmits only meaningless static; the streets appear to be a maze through which only an expert could maneuver; the use of report forms seems inconsistent and confusing; encounters with a hostile public leave him cold and apprehensive; and so on. Yet, next to him in the patrol unit is his partner, a veteran. Hence, the FTO is the answer to most of the breaking-in dilemmas. It is commonplace for the rookie to never make a move without first checking with his FTO. By watching, listening, and mimicking, the neophyte policeman learns how to deal with the objects of his occupation—the traffic violator, the hippie, the drunk, the brass, and the criminal justice complex itself. One veteran reflected on his early patrol experiences as follows:

> On this job, your first partner is everything. He tells you how to survive on the job . . . how to walk, how to stand, and how to speak and how to think and what to say and see.

Clearly, it is during the FTO phase of the recruit's career that he is most susceptible to attitude change. The newcomer is self-conscious and truly in need of guidelines. A whole folklore of tales, myths, and legends surrounding the department is communicated to the recruit by his fellow officers—conspicuously by his FTO. Through these anecdotes—dealing largely with mistakes or "flubs" made by policemen—the recruit begins to adopt the perspectives of his more experienced colleagues. He becomes aware that nobody's perfect and, as if to reify his police academy experiences, he learns that to be protected from his own mistakes, he must protect others. One such yarn told to me by a two-year veteran illustrates this point.

> Grayson had this dolly he'd been balling for quite a while living over on the north side. Well, it seemed like a quiet night so we cruise out of our district and over to the girl's house. I baby-sit the radio while Grayson goes inside. Wouldn't you know it, we get an emergency call right away. . . . I start honking the horn trying to get the horny bastard out of there; he pays me no mind, but the neighbors get kind of irritated at some cop waking up the nine-to-fivers. Some asshole calls the station and pretty soon Sparky and Jim show up to find out what's happening. They're cool but their Sergeant ain't, so we fabricate this insane story 'bout Sparky's girlfriend living there and how he always toots the horn when passing. Me and Grayson beat it back to our district and show up about 45 minutes late on our call. Nobody ever found out what happened, but it sure was close.

Critical to the practical learning process is the neophyte's own developing repertoire of experiences. These events are normally interpreted to him by his FTO and other veteran officers. Thus, the reality shock of being "in on the action" is absorbed and defined by the recruit's fellow officers. As a somewhat typical example, one newcomer, at the prodding of his patrol partner, discovered that to explain police actions to a civilian invited disrespect. He explained:

> Keith was always telling me to be forceful, to not back down and to never try and explain the law or what we are doing to a civilian. I didn't really know what he was talking about until I tried to tell some kid why we have laws about speeding. Well, the more I tried to tell him about traffic safety, the angrier he got. I was lucky to just get his John Hancock on the citation. When I came back to the patrol car, Keith explains to me just where I'd gone wrong. You really can't talk to those people out there, they just won't listen to reason.

In general, the first month or so on the street is an exciting and rewarding period for the recruit. For his FTO, however, it is a period of appraisal. While the recruit is busy absorbing many novel experiences, his partner is evaluating the newcomer's reaction to certain situations. Aside from assisting the recruit with the routines of patrol work, the training officer's main concern is in how the recruit will handle the "hot" or, in the contemporary language of the recruits, the "heavy" call (i.e., the in-progress, or on-view, or help the officer situation which the experienced officer knows may result in trouble). The heavy call represents everything the policeman feels he is prepared for. In short, it calls for police work. Such calls are anticipated by the patrolmen with both pleasure and anxiety, and the recruit's performance on such calls is in a very real sense the measure of the man. A Union City Sergeant described the heavy call to me as follows:

> It's our main reason for being in business. Like when somebody starts busting up a place, or some asshole's got a gun, or some idiot tries to knock off a cop. Basically, it's the situation where you figure you may have to use the tools of your trade. Of course, some guys get a little shaky when these incidents come along, in fact, most of us do if we're honest. But, you know deep down that this is why you're a cop and not pushing pencils somewhere. You've got to be tough on this job and situations like these separate the men from the boys. I know I'd never trust my partner until I'd seen him in action on a hot one.

While such calls are relatively rare on a day-to-day basis, their occurrence signals a behavioral test for the recruit. To pass, he must have "balls." By placing himself in a vulnerable position and pluckily backing-up his FTO and/or other patrolmen, a recruit demonstrates his inclination to share the risks of police work. Through such events, a newcomer quickly makes a departmental reputation which will follow him for the remainder of his career.

At another level, testing the recruit's propensity to partake in the risks which accompany police work goes on continuously within the department. For example, several FTO's in Union City were departmental celebrities for their training techniques. One officer made it a ritual to have his recruit write parking citations in front of the local Black Panther Party headquarters. Another was prominent for requiring his recruit to "shake out" certain trouble bars in the rougher sections of town (i.e., check identifications, make cursory body searches, and possibly roust out customers, à la *The French Connection*). Less dramatic, but nonetheless as important, recruits are appraised as to their speed in getting out of the patrol car, their lack of hesitation when approaching a suspicious person, or their willingness to lead the way up a darkened stairwell. The required behaviors vary from event to event; however, contingent upon the ex post facto evaluation (e.g., Was a weapon involved? Did the officers have to fight the suspect? How many other patrolmen were on the spot?), a novice makes his departmental reputation. While some FTO's promote these climactic events, most wait quietly for such situations to occur. Certainly varying definitions of appropriate behavior in these situations exist from patrolman to patrolman, but the critical and common element is the recruit's demonstrated willingness to place himself in a precarious position while assisting a brother officer. In the police world, such behavior is demanded.

Although data on such instances are inherently difficult to collect, it appears that the behaviorally demonstrated commitment to one's fellow officers involved in such events is a particularly important stage in the socialization process. To the recruit, he has experienced a test and it provides him with the first of many shared experiences which he can relate to other officers. To the FTO, he has watched his man in a police work situation and now knows a great deal more about his occupational companion.

Aside from the backup test applied to all recruits, the other most powerful experience in a recruit's early days on patrol is his first arrest. Virtually all policemen can recall the individual, location, and situation surrounding their first arrest. One five-year veteran patrolman stated:

> The first arrest is really something. I guess that's because it's what we're supposedly out here for. . . . In my case, I'd been out for a couple of weeks but we hadn't done much. . . . I think we'd made some chippies, like standups, or DWI's, but my partner never let me handle the arrest part. Then one night he tells me that if anything happens, I've got to handle it. Believe me, I'll never forget that first arrest, even if it was only a scumbag horn (wino) who had just fallen through a window. . . . I suppose I can remember my first three or four arrests, but after that they just start to blur together.[7]

It is such occurrences that determine the recruit's success in the department. To some extent, both the backup test and the first arrest are beyond the direct control of the newcomer. The fact that they both take place at the discretion of the FTO underscores the orderliness of the socialization process. In effect, these climactic situations graphically demonstrate to the recruit his new status and role within the department. And after passing through this regulated sequence of events, he can say, "I am a cop!"

Continuance: Metamorphosis

This section is concerned broadly with what Becker et al. (1961) labeled the final perspective. As such, the interest is upon the characteristic response recruits eventually demonstrate regarding their occupational and organizational setting. Again, the focus is upon the perspectives the initiates come to hold for the backstage aspect of their career.

As noted earlier, one of the major motivating factors behind the recruit's decision to become a policeman was the adventure or romance he felt would characterize the occupation. Yet, the young officer soon learns the work consists primarily of performing routine service and administrative tasks—the proverbial clerk in a patrol car. This finding seems well-established in the pertinent literature and my observations confirm these reports (e.g., Wilson 1968; Webster 1970; Reiss 1971). Indeed, a patrolman is predominantly an order taker—a reactive member of a service organization. For example, most officers remarked that they never realized the extent to which they would be "married to the radio" until they had worked the street for several months.

On the other hand, there is an unpredictable side of the occupation and this aspect cannot be overlooked. In fact, it is the unexpected elements of working patrol that provide self-esteem and stimulation for the officers. This unpredictable feature of patrol work has too often been understated or disregarded by students of police behavior. To classify the police task as bureaucratically routine and monotonous ignores the psychological omnipresence of the potential "good pinch." It is precisely the opportunity to exercise his perceived police role that gives meaning to the occupational identity of patrolmen. Operationally, this does not imply patrolmen are always alert and working hard to make the "good pinch." Rather, it simply suggests that the unexpected is one of the few aspects of the job that

[7] By "chippies," the officer was referring to normal arrests encountered frequently by patrolmen. Usually, a chippie is a misdemeanor arrest for something like drunkenness. The chippie crimes the officer noted in the quotation, "stand-up" and "DWI's," refer to drunk-in-public and driving-while-intoxicated, respectively.

helps maintain the patrolman's self-image of performing a worthwhile, exciting, and dangerous task. To some degree, the anticipation of the "hot call" allows for the crystallization of his personal identity as a policeman. One Union City patrolman with ten years' experience commented succinctly on this feature. He noted:

> Most of the time being a cop is the dullest job in the world . . . what we do is pretty far away from the stuff you see on Dragnet or Adam 12. But, what I like about this job and I guess it's what keeps me going, is that you never know what's gonna happen out there. For instance, me and my partner will be working a Sunday first watch way out in the north end and expecting everything to be real peaceful and quiet like; then all of a sudden, hell breaks loose . . . Even on the quietest nights, something interesting usually happens.

Reiss noted perceptually the atypical routine enjoyed by patrolmen. After examining the police "straight eight"—the tour of duty—he stated:

> No tour of duty is typical except in the sense that the modal tour of duty does not involve the arrest of a person (Reiss 1971:19).

Still, one of the ironies of police work is that recruits were attracted to the organization by and large via the unrealistic expectation that the work would be adventurous and exciting. In the real world such activities are few and far between. Once a recruit has mastered the various technical and social skills of routine policing (e.g., "learning the district," developing a set of mutual understandings with his partner, knowing how and when to fill out the myriad of various report forms) there is little left to learn about his occupation which can be transferred by formal or informal instruction. As Westley (1951) pointed out, the recruit must then sit back and wait, absorb the subjective side of police work and let his experiences accumulate. The wife of one recruit noted this frustrating characteristic of police work. She said:

> It seems to me that being a policeman must be very discouraging. They spend all that time teaching the men to use the gun and the club and then they make them go out and do very uninteresting work.

It has been suggested that for a newcomer to any occupation, "coping with the emotional reality of the job" is the most difficult problem to resolve (Schein 1963). In police work, the coping behavior appears to consist of the "learning of complacency." Since the vast majority of time is spent in tasks other than real police work, there is little incentive for performance. In other words, the young patrolman discovers that the most satisfying solution to the labyrinth of hierarchy, the red tape and paperwork, the plethora of rules and regulations, and the "dirty work" which characterize the occupation is to adopt the group norm stressing staying out of trouble. And the best way in which he can stay out of trouble is to minimize the set of activities he pursues. One Union City veteran patrolman explained:

> We are under constant pressure from the public to account for why we did or did not do this or that. It's almost as if the public feels it owns us. You become supersensitive to criticisms from the public, almost afraid to do anything. At the same time, the brass around here never gives a straightforward answer about procedures to anyone and that creates a lot of discontent. All communication comes down. But, try and ask a question and it gets stopped at the next level up. It gets to the point where you know that if you don't do anything at all, you won't get in trouble.

In a similar vein, another veteran officer put it somewhat more bluntly. He suggested caustically:

> The only way to survive on this job is to keep from breaking your ass . . . if you try too hard you're sure to get in trouble. Either some civic-minded creep is going to get outraged and you'll wind up with a complaint in your file; or the high and mighty in the department will come down on you for breaking some rule or something and you'll get your pay docked.

These quotations suggest that patrolman disenchantment has two edges. One, the police with the general public—which has been well-substantiated in the literature—and two, the disenchantment with the police system itself. In short, a recruit begins to realize (through proverb, example, and his own experience) it is his relationship with his fellow officers (particularly those working the same sector and shift—his squad) that protects his interests and allows him to continue on the job—without their support he would be lost.[8]

To summarize, the adjustment of a newcomer in police departments is one which follows the line of least resistance. By becoming similar in sentiment and behavior to his peers, the recruit avoids censure by the department, his supervisor and, most important, his brother officers. Furthermore, since the occupational rewards are to be found primarily in the unusual situation which calls for "real" police work, the logical situational solution is for the officers to organize their activities in such a way as to minimize the likelihood of being sanctioned by *any* of their audiences. The low visibility of the patrolman's role vis-à-vis the department allows for such a response. Thus, the pervasive adjustment is epitomized in the "lie low, hang loose, and don't expect too much" advice frequently heard within the Union City Police Department. This overall picture would indicate that the following tip given to me by a Union City veteran represents a very astute analysis of how to insure continuance in the police world. He suggested:

> There's only two things you gotta know around here. First, forget everything you've learned in the academy 'cause the street's where you'll learn to be a cop; and second, being first don't mean shit around here. Take it easy, that's our motto.

The above characterization of the recruit socialization process, while necessarily a drastic condensation of a much more complex and interdependent process, does delineate the more important aspects of becoming a policeman. Furthermore, this descriptive narrative hints that many of the recent attempts to alter or reform police behavior are likely to meet with frustration and failure.

A CODA FOR REFORMERS

Most police reformers view the behavior of individual patrolmen as a problem for the department or society, not vice versa. I have, in a small way, tried to correct this bias by describing the point of view of the entering recruit. This emphasizes the intelligibility of the newcomer's actions as he works out solutions to his unique problems. In short, we "looked up" at the nature of the network above the recruit rather than using the usual approach which, in the past, has "looked down" on the "outsider." Perhaps this approach indicates the dilemma in which our police are indeed trapped.

In a very real sense, this article suggests a limit upon the extent to which the police can be expected to solve their own problems. Regardless of how well-educated, well-equipped, or professional the patrolman may become, his normative position and task within society will remain unchanged. From this perspective, the characteristic response of police officers to their present situation is indeed both rational and functional. Clearly, the police subculture—like subcultures surrounding bricklayers, lawyers, or social workers—will probably exist in even the most reformed of departments. To change the police without changing the police role in society is as futile as the labors of Sisyphus.

The long-range goal should be a structural redefinition of the police task and a determination of ways in which the external control principle—so central to the rule of law—may be strengthened. Of course, ways must be found to make the policeman's lot somewhat more tolerable, both to him and to the general citizenry. Organizational change can aid this process by designing training programs which place less stress on the apprenticeship relationship. However, it is doubtful

[8] In most ways, the patrolmen represent what Goffman (1959) calls a team. In Goffmanesque, a team is "a set of individuals whose intimate co-operation is required if a given projected definition of the situation is to be maintained" (1959:104). The situational definition to be sustained in the patrol setting is that "all-is-going-well-there-are-no-problems." The covert rule for patrolmen is to never draw attention to one's activities. An analysis I conducted on written weekly FTO progress reports illustrates this point convincingly. Of over 300 report forms, only one contained an even slightly negative evaluation. Uniformly, all forms were characterized by high praise for the recruit. The topics the FTO's chose to elaborate upon were typified by such concerns as the recruit's driving skill, the recruit's pleasing personality, the recruit's stable home life, and so on. The vast majority of reports contained no reference whatsoever to the types of activities engaged in by the recruits. The point is simply that in no case was an FTO report filed which might result in departmental attention. It should be clear that such behavior does not pass unnoticed by the recruit. Indeed, he learns rapidly the importance and value of his team as well as the corresponding definition of the police situation.

that without profound alterations in the definition and structural arrangement of the police task (and in the implied values such arrangements support), significant change is possible.

Thus, plans to increase the therapeutic and operational effectiveness of police institutions by "in-house" techniques must be judged in terms of what is being done now and what might be done—and, given the features of the police institution as described here, the difference is painfully small. The particular pattern of police practices is a response to the demands of the larger complex and, as such, reflects the values and norms prevalent throughout society. The extent to which the police system undermines the rule of law; the extent to which the public is willing to alter the crime fighter image of police; the extent to which the police bureaucracy will allow change; and ultimately, the extent to which the police system as presently constructed can operate under strict public accounting—these are the major issues confronting the police, not the degree to which the individual policeman can be professionalized.[9]

REFERENCES

Ahern, J. F., (1972) Police in Trouble. New York: Hawthorn Books.

Bayley, P. H., and H. Mendelsohn, (1969) Minorities and the Police. New York: The Free Press.

Becker, H. S. (1963) Outsiders: Studies in the Sociology of Deviance. New York: The Free Press.

Becker, H. S., B. Greer, E. C. Hughes, and A. Strauss, (1961) Boys in White: Student Culture in Medical School. Chicago: University of Chicago Press.

Berkeley, G. E., (1969) The Democratic Policeman. Boston: Beacon Press.

Berlew, D. E., and D. T. Hall, (1966) The socialization of managers: effects of expectations on performance. Administrative Science Quarterly 11:207–23.

Bittner, E., (1967) The police on skid row. American Sociological Review 32:699–715.

Cicourel, A. V., (1967) The Social Organization of Juvenile Justice. New York: John Wiley and Sons.

Dalton, M., (1964) Preconceptions and methods in men who manage. *In* Sociologists at Work, P. Hammond, ed. New York: Doubleday.

Dornbush, S. M., (1955) The military academy as an assimilating institution. Social Forces 33:316–21.

Evan, W. M., (1963) Peer group interaction and organizational socialization: a study of employee turnover. American Sociological Review 28:436–40.

Goffman, E., (1959) The Presentation of Self in Everyday Life. New York: Doubleday.

Greer, B., (1964) First days in the field. *In* Sociologists at Work, P. Hammond, ed. New York: Doubleday.

Hughes, E. C., (1953) Men and Their Work. Glencoe, Illinois: The Free Press.

Laing, R. D., (1964) The obvious. *In* Dialectics of Liberation, D. Cooper, ed. London: Institute of Phenomenological Studies.

Lortie, D. C., (1968) Shared ordeal and induction to work. *In* Institutions and the Person, H. S. Becker, B. Greer, D. Riesman, and R. T. Weiss, eds. Chicago: Aldine.

McNamara, J., (1967) Uncertainties in police work: the relevance of police recruits' background and training. *In* The Police: Six Sociological Essays, D. J. Bordura, ed. New York: John Wiley and Sons.

Niederhoffer, A., (1967) Behind the Shield. New York: Doubleday.

President's Commission on Law Enforcement, (1967) Task Force Report: The Police. Washington, D.C.: Government Printing Office.

Reiss, A. J., (1971) The Police and the Public. New Haven: Yale University Press.

Schatzman, L., and A. Strauss, (1973) Field Research: Strategies for a Natural Sociology. Englewood Cliffs, New Jersey: Prentice-Hall.

Schein, E. H., (1963) Organizational socialization in the early career of industrial managers. Paper presented at the New England Psychological Association, Boston, Massachusetts. (1971) Organizational socialization and the profession of management. Industrial Management Review 2:37–45.

[9] I have attempted to suggest in this article that the intelligibility of social events requires they be viewed in a context which extends both spatially and in time. Relatedly, social actors must be granted rationality for their behavior. Given the situational imperatives faced by patrolmen, is it any wonder our police recoil behind a blue curtain? Perhaps we have reached what R. D. Laing (1964) calls the "theoretical limit of institutions." According to Laing, this paradoxical position is characterized by a system which, when viewed as a collective, behaves irrationally, yet is populated by members whose everyday behavior is eminently rational.

Skolnick, J., (1966) Justice Without Trial: Law Enforcement in a Democratic Society. New York: John Wiley and Sons.

Sterling, J. W., (1972) Changes in Role Concepts of Police Officers. Washington, D.C.: International Association of Chiefs of Police.

Van Maanen, J., (1972) Pledging the police: a study of selected aspects of recruit socialization in a large, urban police department. Ph.D. Dissertation, University of Calilfornia, Irvine. (1976) Breaking-in: socialization to work. *In* Handbook of Work, Organization, and Society, R. Dubin, ed. Chicago: Rand-McNally.

Webster, J. A., (1970) Police task and time study. Journal of Criminal Law, Criminology and Police Science 61:94–100.

Westley, W. A., (1951) The police: a sociological study of law, custom and morality. Ph.D. Dissertation, University of Chicago, Chicago, Illinois.

Whyte, W. F., (1943) Street Corner Society. Chicago: University of Chicago Press.

Wilson, J. Q., (1968) Varieties of Police Behavior. Cambridge, Massachusetts: Harvard University Press.

The Black Police Officer: An Historical Perspective

Jack L. Kuykendall and David E. Burns

INTRODUCTION

This paper is a descriptive examination of the utilization and role of black Americans as police officers from the early 1860's through the mid-1960's. This 100 year period begins with the so-called "freeing" of slave blacks and ends with the domestic and official violence of the 1960's influenced, in part, by prolonged and extensive racial discrimination. These riots, like their predecessors (e.g., East St. Louis in 1917, Chicago in 1919, New York in 1935 and Detroit in 1943), indicated that many blacks had continued to believe that they were slaves of social, economic and political oppression. As the Skolnick Report to the Violence Commission states (Skolnick, 1969: 129):

> The history of black protest is the history of the temporary decline, fall, and resurgence of almost every conceivable means of achieving black well-being and dignity within the context of a generally hostile polity, and in the face of unremitting white violence, both official and private.

Several recurring recommendations can be found in every major riot commission report in the twentieth century. One of these concerns is improving community–police relations.

SOURCE: *Journal of Contemporary Criminal Justice* I, No. 4 (November 1980). Reprinted by permission.

One approach in responding to black militancy and crime has been an increased emphasis on employing blacks as police officers. Lack of proportional representation in police organizations was viewed as *de facto* evidence of discrimination, and black police were thought to be more effective in working in black communities because of their unique cultural identification and insight. Supposedly, the combination of more black police and blacks policing blacks would alleviate community–police tension. (See: President's Commission on Law Enforcement, 1967; President's Commission on Civil Disorders, 1968.)

The increasing number of blacks working as police officers since the mid-1960's has resulted in problems of organizational integration and role conflict (see: Alex, 1969; Palmer, 1973, Cooper, 1975). It would, however, be incorrect to assume that these problems do not have important historical antecedents. Blacks have been employed as municipal police officers in the United States since at least 1861 (Johnson, 1947). The purpose of this paper is to examine the extent of this employment, the effectiveness of black officers in policing black communities and strategies of discrimination confronting blacks as they become employed as police officers. As noted previously, the time frame for consideration is approximately a 100 year period between the early 1860's and the mid-1960's.

BLACK POLICE EMPLOYMENT: 1861–1970[1]

The earliest date found for blacks serving as police officers was 1861 in Washington, D.C. (Johnson, 1947: 54). In that same city in 1873, President U. S. Grant was arrested for driving a team of horses at a dangerous pace. The arresting officer was black (Landis, 1958). One year earlier, in 1872, Chicago, Illinois employed that city's first black officer (Sloan, 1965).

Other cities with black officers prior to 1890 include Galveston, Texas in 1870 (Jefferson County, 1953), several other Texas communities in the 1870's and 1880's (Rice, 1971), Philadelphia, Pennsylvania in 1874 (Du Bois, 1899), Columbia and Charleston, South Carolina in 1873 (Bennett, 1968), and Meridian, Jackson, and Clinton, Mississippi in 1871, 1874 and 1875, respectively. In 1874, the Chief of Police in Jackson, Mississippi was black (Wharton, 1947; Bennett, 1968: 253).

A visitor to New Orleans, Louisiana in 1872 remarked on the " . . . polite but consequential . . . black officers" (Bennett, 1968: 303). In 1874, General James H. Clanton, the head of the Alabama Klan, said, "I see Negro police—great black fellows—leading white girls around the streets of Montgomery, and locking them up in jail" (Bennett, 1968: 319–20). As late as September 6, 1890, a visitor to Charleston, South Carolina reported ". . . white and black policemen walking together in friendly converse" (Tindall, 1952: 305).

In 1890, there were an estimated 74,629 "watchmen, policemen and firemen," in the United States. Of these, 2,019 were black. Other cities employing blacks as police after 1890 include St. Louis, Missouri as early as 1907 (and perhaps before) (Johnson, 1947: 54), Dayton, Ohio in 1913 (Quillin, 1913), Berkeley, California in 1919 (Danielson, 1964); and Los Angeles, California as early as 1927 (U.S. Commission on Civil Rights, 1960).

From 1930 to 1940 while the number of black police increased in the United States, the percentage declined. However, by 1950 the percentage had more than doubled (see Table 1). In 1952, of all cities in the United States with over 5,000 population, 252 employed black policemen (Guzman, 1952). In 1962, in a survey of all cities with over 5,000 black residents, 106 cities outside the south had black police. The average was one black policeman to every 1,361 black residents compared with one white officer for every 443 white residents (Ebony, 1966).

The above provides an overview of black police employment of selected cities. Table 1 presents data from U.S. *Census Reports* for the period, 1860–1970. Racial groupings were first utilized in 1890. Related occupations were included in the police category until 1920

TABLE 1 Black and White Police (and Related Occupations): 1860–1970

Year	*Total*	*White*	*Black*	*W:B Ratio*	*B.% of Total*
1860	4,759[1]	—	—	—	—
1870	No listing	—	—	—	—
1880	13,384[2]	—	—	—	—
1890	74,629[3]	72,610	2,019	36:1	2.70
1900	129,259[4]	126,308	2,951	43:1	2.28
1910	60,749[5]	60,209	540	111:1	.88
1920	80,716[6]	79,727	989	81:1	1.22
1930	129,341[6]	128,077	1,264	101:1	.97
1940	169,502[6]	167,969	1,533	110:1	.90
1950	216,735[6]	212,340	4,395	48:1	2.02
1960	281,224[6]	271,215	10,009	27:1	3.55
1970	374,623[7]	350,808	23,815	15:1	6.35

[1] Listed as "watchmen, policemen and firemen." Also includes "messengers" (i.e., errand and office boys).
[2] Listed as "watchmen (private) and detectives." No racial breakdown provided.
[3] Listed as "watchmen, policemen and firemen."
[4] Listed as "watchmen, policemen, and firemen."
[5] Several mixed occupational group listings (e.g., marshall, sheriff, watchmen, doormen, detectives, etc.). This total is for police only.
[6] Listed as "police."
[7] Listed as "police and detectives."

and in 1970 "police and detectives" were grouped together.

Table 2 provides an analysis of police growth from 1920–1970 by ten periods. From 1920 to 1930, the estimated number of police increased by about 60 percent while black police employment increased about 28 percent. Between 1960 and 1970 the number of police increased about 33 percent while the black increase was about 138 percent. Between 1920 and 1930 this growth in black police employment represented less than 1 percent of the decade increase; however, between 1960 and 1970 it represented about 15 percent of total growth. Said another way, between 1920 and 1930 for every additional 177 police officers, one was black; between 1960–70, this was one black officer for every seven additional police.

To illustrate the circumstances associated with the increasing utilization of blacks as police officers, events in Chicago and in southern states will be briefly described.

Chicago, Illinois

Blacks have been continuously employed as police officers in Chicago, Illinois since 1872 except for the two year period, 1877–1879. In the late nineteenth century, appointments to the police department were based on political influence. One black officer described his experiences in this regard (Gosnell, 1935: 248).

> When I came to Chicago I got a job working for the flour company of Swanson and Eckhart. I worked very hard and made a good reputation for myself. But I saw that I wasn't getting any place working for them so I decided to try to get into the Police Department. There had been a few Negroes appointed and I thought that maybe through the influence of my white friends I could get an appointment. So I spoke to Mr. Eckhart about it. He referred me to his brother, Barney Eckhart who was in politics. Barney Eckhart spoke to several others until I finally reached a man who gave me a letter to Chief Hubbard and I was appointed.

The pressure of the black community beginning in the 1890's was significant in increasing the number of black officers. Black citizens complained frequently of the "stupidity, prejudice and brutality" of white officers. A black controlled newspaper, the Chicago Defender noted (Gosnell, 1935: 245):

> There is no law, municipal or otherwise which calls for the insulting of respectable Race people by these big, rawboned sapheads, who are maintained by taxpaying citizens of which class thousands of our people form a part. It is hard to understand on what basis these "hounds" of the law are accorded encouragement in their dastardly practices by station house superiors, by word of mouth, and by their chief himself, by his ignoring of protests made by their victims. Something will and must be done. Bulldozers should have no place in Chicago's police department. . . .

The number of black police officers continued to increase in Chicago after the turn of the century and by 1930 there were 137 black officers (Gosnell, 1935: 244–53); by 1967 there were approximately 1,800 (Citizens Committee, 1967).

The South

In southern states,[2] prior to 1921 but after reconstruction, there were black police in approximately ten cities including Knoxville and Memphis, Tennessee; Wheeling, West Virgina; Tampa, Florida; and Houston, Texas (Rudwick, 1962). By 1924 several additional cities began to employ blacks but, according to Rudwick (1962), there were still less than fifty black officers in 1940.

After 1940 black police utilization increased as a result of the "emerging political participation" of blacks.

TABLE 2 An Analysis of Changes in Black Police: 1920–1970

Time Periods	*Total Numerical Change*	*Total Percent Change*	*Black Numerical Change*	*Black Percent Change*	*Black Percent of Total Change*	*W:B Ratio in Change*
1920–1930	48,625	60.24	275	27.80	.56	176:1
1930–1940	40,161	31.05	269	21.28	.67	148:1
1940–1950	47,233	27.86	2,862	186.69	6.05	16:1
1950–1960	64,489	29.75	5,614	127.73	8.70	11:1
1960–1970	93,399	33.21	13,806	137.93	14.78	6:1

Organized movements were often supported by liberal whites (Rudwick, 1962: 3). By 1944, there were an estimated 230 black officers in forty-two cities in ten southern states.

Apparently, the employment of blacks as police followed a similar pattern in many cities. At some point a church or civic group became concerned over crime rates, law enforcement in black areas, or race relations, either because of racial tension or a desire for integration. It was believed that the utilization of blacks as police officers in the black areas would contribute substantially to the reduction of the black hostility toward police. Studies were then made of other municipalities that had utilized black police and the results tended to be favorable. Recommendations to appropriate city leaders were made followed by an attempt to educate the public to insure a favorable reception. These programs of education usually took place through church, civic organizations, and the press. The leaders of a community usually agreed to make a few experimental appointments (Johnson, 1947: 56).

Black police increases continued in southern and border states and by 1954 there were an estimated 822 black police in 143 cities in thirteen states (Southern Regional Council, 1955: 35). By 1962 there were an estimated 1,128 black police in 124 cities (Ebony, 1966: 102). Even though fewer cities were surveyed than in 1954 the number of black police increased.

It is apparent from the data presented in this section that in the approximate 100 year period covered by this study, the number of black police in the United States increased substantially. However, black initial acceptance and organization integration are important problems for consideration. Frequently, blacks were confronted with discriminatory barriers before, and after, employment. The next section examines some strategies of discrimination utilized against black police.

Strategies of Discrimination. Discrimination is a form of aggression. An act can be considered aggressive if as a consequence of the act an individual suffers physical, psychological or social injury. Frequently, the act is not accidental and is committed even though it will injure another. If the aggressive act arbitrarily excludes an individual from a status or position valued by society the act is discriminatory (Hamblin, 1962). Historically, the forms of discrimination that have been utilized against black police have been numerous and varied.

At times, white citizens would not accept the black officer. After a black police–white citizen confrontation that led to a Meridian, Mississippi riot in 1871, a white official noted ". . . Negroes ought not be put in a position to discharge constabulary functions which it is proper for white men to exercise" (Wharton, 1947: 167–68). In Clinton, Mississippi, in September, 1875, a black officer and an intoxicated white came into conflict. In the general shooting precipitated by this incident, three whites and between ten and thirty blacks were killed. For four days following the incident, armed whites roamed the areas, murdering an estimated ten to fifty black leaders (Wharton, 1947: 191).

In Jackson County, Texas, in 1876, a black constable was unable to post the required security bond. Perhaps the reason was similar to the one in Huntsville, Texas, where a black, Joshus (sic) Green was elected constable but in order to dissuade him, the county judge raised the bond requirement to twenty thousand dollars. However, even after raising satisfactory securities for that amount, residents "intervened" and"persuaded" Green not to assume his duties (Rice, 1971: 89). In other Texas communities whites refused to work or cooperate with black public officials, including police.

Bennett (1968: 421) writing of the reconstruction period in the south, states:

> As the years wore on, the area of black expressiveness narrowed, and by World War I it was considered subversive for black men to hold public office. By that time, the whole black population had been redirected to a form of group servitude and the south, with the approval of the Supreme Court and every structure of power in the north, was grinding out Jim Crow laws of increasing severity.

The indirect impact of these laws will be discussed later when the limitations on the authority of the black police officer are considered.

Beginning in about 1915 blacks from southern states began to migrate in large numbers to urban areas. In Chicago, Illinois, this resulted in a tendency to assign black officers to black neighborhoods. In 1919, the black community became aroused when three black officers were taken before a police merit committee because they would not utilize what were referred to as "Jim Crow" sleeping quarters (Chicago Commission, 1922).

In the 1930's in Chicago, black officers were restricted in type and location of assignments, and efficiency ratings were negatively manipulated by superior officers. Apparently, dismissal because of race was also a possibility (Gosnell, 1935:256).

> I was working under a hard-boiled sergeant. He and the sergeant at the station wanted to get me . . . They wanted to get me for two reasons, first, I was a Negro and they didn't like Negroes, and second, I didn't stand for any foolishness.

This officer was brought before a "trial board" of the police department on "charges" made by one of the sergeants. The results are not recorded. Other areas of concern during this period include use of black officers as honor guards in special events, in parades and specialized assignments such as motorized patrol and traffic enforcement. Few blacks were given these types of assignments. In addition, black and white officers rarely worked together (Gosnell, 1935:257–59).

One of the most sensitive areas in Chicago in the 1930s was that of promotions (Gosnell, 1935:263).

> I passed all three examinations and was among the highest in my rating for patrol sergeant. After the examinations were graded the chief of police called me in and asked me to waive my right for promotion to patrol sergeant. He told me I didn't have to unless I wanted, but that if I did he would look after me when it came time to appointments for detective sergeants. I hesitated. I didn't want to waive any right that was mine, but on the other hand, I knew that the chief would have the right to refuse me three times if I didn't waive the right. As he had promised to appoint me to detective sergeant, I thought better to get that job for sure than take a chance standing on my rights. So I agreed to waive my right for promotion to patrol sergeant.

This officer later regretted waiving his right for promotion because the chief of police did not promote him to detective sergeant. Even when promotion was received it was not always cause for elation. Promoted blacks were not often congratulated by white officers and they were not given duties involving active command. In one instance, black lieutenants were even assigned to walk a beat as patrol officers (Gosnell, 1935:263).

The material presented above was based upon studies of the Chicago Police Department during the 1930's and earlier. Apparently, problems of discrimination still existed in 1966 as it was necessary to integrate squad cars on the basis of a direct order from the head of the department because integration had not taken place on a voluntary basis (National Center, 1967).

Historically, there are also other community police agencies with evidence of discriminatory behavior toward black police. In Philadelphia, Pennsylvania, the first black officers were assigned "in or near" black areas and were limited in opportunities for promotion (Du Bois, 1899:132). In a 1950's study of Philadelphia a "hurt, bitter, resentful and puzzled," feeling was found among blacks, concerning promotions (Kephart, 1954). In a related study, it was discovered that 59.9 percent of the white officers objected to riding in patrol cars with black officers and 76.5 percent believed black officers should be assigned only to black areas. In a question concerning supervision, 57.2 percent of the white commanders objected to having black subordinates and some of these commanders stated they were "stricter" in their treatment of such officers (Kephart, 1957). In a 1966 study, a survey of white officers indicated that 80 percent had "all the way" prejudices toward blacks. Some white officers believed that blacks should be excluded from the police force (University of California, 1967).

In Los Angeles, California, prior to 1959 blacks were restricted in geographical assignments and at one point, all non-whites were assigned to an industrial district in one division of the city. Even when the restrictions on assignments were eliminated, black officers were assigned to specific patrol cars that would not be dispatched on certain types of calls in white neighborhoods unless officers were not available (Conot, 1967). There were also accusations of discrimination by social organizations within the department as recently as the mid-1960's (Conot, 1967:157–160).

In 1967, in Washington, D.C., a black newspaper reporter noted the following concerning discrimination within the police department (Raspberry, 1967: Sec. B., p. 1):

> The real causes are myriad, sometimes substantial, sometimes not. There is, for example, the widespread feeling that Negro officers do not get a fair shake in promotions or efficiency ratings; that whites are given preference in station house jobs, special assignments and other "plums"; that whites do not want Negro scout-car partners and that white officers' preference often is decisive in making such assignments.

In addition to the strategies of discrimination apparent in individual cities, there is also evidence of limitations on black police authority in southern states. In 130 cities and counties in the south (including Oklahoma and Kentucky) in 1959, 69 required black officers to call white officers in arresting white suspects. In six of the cities, the black officer could make felony arrests (Rudwick, 1962:13–14). In a 1966 survey of southern states, 28 police departments reported restrictions on arrest powers (Ebony, 1966:102).

In a 1959 survey 107 cities, of 130 contacted, indicated black officers patrolled only in black neighborhoods, 6 reported that black officers worked primarily in black areas, 16 reported no restrictions and 1 city did not respond (Rudwick, 1962:8–13).

Individual cities in southern states have also engaged in various strategies of discrimination against black officers. In 1930 the black police in Louisville, Kentucky were not permitted to wear their uniforms to their homes as did white police (Rudwick, 1961). In Charlotte, North Carolina, prior to civil service, black officers received a lower salary than did white officers (Johnson, 1947:56). In Birmingham, Alabama, until the mid-1950's, police examinations were not given to black applicants (Morgan, 1964; Greenberg, 1959). In 1962, in some southern communities, black officers were not allowed access to police headquarters and, at times, were not permitted to attend training programs (New York Times, 1962).

In Memphis, Tennessee, the first black officer was employed in 1948 and by 1966 there were 50 blacks on the 750 person force. In 1966 patrol cars were segregated and black lieutenants were not permitted to supervise uniformed subordinates. Efforts were made to recruit blacks but once employed they were trained separately from whites. Black police were also assigned to black neighborhoods and white officers were usually called to "take over" when a black officer arrested a white suspect (U.S. Commission on Civil Rights, 1967; 1962).

In Atlanta, Georgia, blacks were first employed as police in 1948. Initially, they were forbidden to wear their uniforms to and from work and had to testify in court in plain clothes. When in court they answered to their first names but were required to address all whites as "mister." Black officers did not report to work at the police department but to the Young Men's Christian Association in a black neighborhood to change into their police uniforms. They were frequently called "YMCA" cops (Thomas, 1967).

In the mid-1960's in Atlanta there were indications that black detectives worked primarily in black neighborhoods. The traffic division was supposedly closed to blacks and black and white officers did not compete against each other for promotions. Black officers believed a quota existed in promotions and that blacks were promoted only to "black positions" (Thomas, 1967:4–5).

This section has attempted to identify historic strategies of discrimination involving black police. It is possible that some of the evidence provided lends itself to other interpretations but there is little doubt that discrimination against black police was extensive and took many forms. One police official stated in 1966 (President's Commission on Civil Disorders, 1968):

> I think one of the serious problems facing the police in the nation today is the lack of adequate representation of Negroes in police departments. I think the police have not recruited enough Negroes in the past and are not recruiting enough of them today. I think we would be less than honest if we didn't admit that Negroes have been kept out of police departments in the past for reasons of discrimination.

As noted in the introduction, one of the reasons often given for employing black police is their "special" effectiveness in relating to black citizens. The next section is concerned with that subject area.

Effectiveness of Black Police. As noted previously, the race riots of the mid-1960's resulted in an increased demand for black police. The President's Commission stated that (Task Force Report: The Police, 1967:162).

> Police officers have testified to the special competence of Negro officers in Negro neighborhoods. The reasons given include: they get along better and receive more respect from the Negro residents; they receive less trouble . . .; they can get more information; and they understand Negro citizens better.

Historically, this has been a common belief among some police officials (Johnson, 1935:56). This opinion has also been shared by some citizens. Banner (1946), in discussing the black citizen's attitude towards black officers, states:

> In selected places, he even feels safer because of the addition of colored police to the force, in other places, too well does he know how white officers, without warrant, violate the sanctity of his inner chambers at will.

In a 1952 study conducted in several southern states, 100 of 162 citizens stated that black citizens would not object to or resist black officers to the degree they would white officers. In response to a question concerning black officers employed in their respective communities, 134 citizens believed the officers to be well qualified. The majority of the respondents believed black officers were more effective in obtaining information and in finding wanted persons in black areas. One Georgia Chief of Police commented that: "The colored officers are doing an excellent job of educating the colored population to avail themselves of the full protection of the law" (Jefferson County, 1953:3–7).

However, not all citizens and police have supported the utilization of black officers. Some white citizens believed that white officers were as effective as black officers in black communities. One chief of police stated that blacks diluted the strength of the force because they could not be assigned with white officers. Another stated that blacks were lax in meeting their responsibilities and that the only advantage to their employment was political.

Despite some reservations, the response to black police officers in southern states was generally favorable (Price, 1947:2). One student of race relations has said that one of the most effective contributions in terms of respect for the law made in the south in years was when blacks were employed as police officers and placed in black neighborhoods (Johnson, 1947:52).

The response of black citizens to black police has been mixed. Many black citizens wanted them because it would provide an opportunity for more public jobs, more understanding, less white police brutality and more effective supervision of black criminals (Landrum, 1947; Myrdal, 1944). Less favorable responses were also recorded: "Colored people . . . (will) not have any respect for a Negro policeman. It takes a white policeman to have any authority in a colored section" (Fleming, 1947). Rudwick (1960) has suggested that blacks from lower socio-economic classes preferred white to black officers. He found that poorer, uneducated blacks frequently asked for white officers when in need of help, and were more likely to plead guilty to a charge made by a white officer (Rudwick, 1962:11).

In contrast, a Los Angeles police officer testifying before the McCone Commission in 1965 admitted that most white patrolmen couldn't distinguish between law-abiding and lawless blacks (Platt, 1971:316).

As is the case with white police, black police have also had a record of behavioral excess by some officers (Gosnell, 1935:258–259).

> Some Negro detectives are bad. They are full of ego and simply want to walk down the street and everybody point them out as a plainclothesman. In the Negro districts they are sometimes overbearing and hard on the other Negroes and in white districts they are sometimes too timid . . . There are four or five colored plainclothesmen that are the dirtiest and biggest crooks, regardless of comparison anywhere. These crooks are . . . using their guns and badges to rob people.

In Chicago, the community resentment against one black officer was so great that a theater audience applauded when it was announced that he had been dismissed from the force (Gosnell, 1935:271).

Similar feelings were expressed by black residents of New York following the riots in 1935 (Locke in Platt, 1971:194).

> A surprising and convincing reason for suspecting police brutality and intimidation is the fact that many in the Harlem community feel as much resentment toward Negro police as toward white police, and even toward the Negro police lieutenant, who sometime back was a popular hero and a proud community symbol.

Also, some black officers have apparently held, or developed, prejudicial attitudes toward black citizens. In a mid-1960's study conducted in Boston, Washington and Chicago, it was found that 28 percent (N = 43) of the black officers working in a predominantly black neighborhood had negatively prejudicial attitudes toward black citizens. . . . In an area with a mixed black-white population, 10 percent (N = 51) had negatively prejudicial attitudes, 36 percent were neutral and, 24 percent had positive prejudices. The attitudes of the remaining black officers could not be determined. In this study almost one in ten black officers exhibited extreme negative attitudes toward black citizens. Comments from several black officers are provided below (University of Michigan, 1967:135–37):

> I'm talking to you as a Negro, and I'm telling you these people are savages. And they're real dirty. There have always been jobs for Negroes but those . . . people are too stupid to go out and get an education. They all want the easy way out. Those people are animals. They don't do anything for themselves.

Prejudicial attitudes of black officers can result in inappropriate police behavior. There is some evidence that black officers have been "harder" on black citizens than have white officers. In a 1950's study in Philadelphia some officers believed this to be true but some also felt that black officers were "easier" in their treatment of black citizens. The majority of black officers believed it was necessary to be "stricter" with their "own" people than they were with non-blacks (Kephart, 1957:60–62).

In the mid-1960's, and perhaps before, the apparent desire of many black citizens for black police was modified somewhat. Studies conducted in San Diego and Philadelphia indicate that some black citizens saw black police as "finks" who were "selling them out" (University of California, 1967:76, 93). This opinion was shared by the Student Non-violent Coordinating Committee in 1967 (Letter, 1967):

> . . . In the minds of black people in this country any color police . . . represents a repressive element in our communities . . . It is of little relevance to us whether a cop is black or white. To black people, they are all enemies.

Another less militant view, indirectly related to the issue of black police, was expressed by a black staff member of the McCone Commission in discussing black leaders (Platt, 1971:300).

> (The) . . . whole concept of leadership disturbs me. I think he [McCone], like the majority community, think they help build Negro leaders. And to the extent that they do, their Negro leaders are going to have certain built-in defects; because in order for a Negro to be acceptable as a leader to (white citizens) . . . you have to meet certain standards of the white community, you have to make sure you stay in your place and do all the other things which have always been characteristics of the "Uncle Tom." And once you build this kind of person, one who can communicate with the white power structure, he can't communicate with his own people because he's out of touch with their real problems. And so it's just a fantastic vicious circle. . . .

CONCLUSION

Even with the limitations identified concerning the data utilized in this paper, it is apparent that the employment of blacks as police officers has increased steadily since 1940. Since 1950 employment percentage gains have surpassed total police growth and in the 1960's for every seven police officers added, one was black. Using the somewhat arbitrary, but perhaps necessary, criterion of proportional employment (i.e., blacks shall be employed in proportion to their numbers in the population) blacks were not proportionally represented by 1970. But in the 1960's they were being employed at a rate (14.78 perecent) of growth higher than their numbers in the population (11.11 percent according to the 1970 census).

Assuming a 30 percent increase per decade for police after 1970, with blacks constituting 15 percent of the increase,[3] blacks will represent approximately 11 percent of police in the United States by the year 2000. Given recent court and Equal Employment Opportunity Commission affirmative action rulings, the authors are inclined to believe that blacks will be proportionately represented as police by the mid-1980's.[4]

Strategies of discrimination utilized against black police historically have been numerous and varied. These strategies include discrimination in appointments, testing procedures, white acceptance, promotions, duty assignments, areas assignments, efficiency ratings, use of departmental facilities, treatment by supervisors, arrest powers, and salaries. By the mid-1960's, the organizational practices of overt discrimination had been altered but replaced by the overt and covert discrimination of some individual officers. In several instances, departments have and are inadvertently utilizing non-job related practices, procedures and standards which have a disparate effect on recruitment, employment and promotion of black officers.

The evidence of the special effectiveness of the black officer in working in black communities remained largely unresolved by the mid-1960's. It was a rather common belief on the part of some citizens that black police would be more effective but apparently a substantial number of black officers held either positive or negative prejudicial attitudes toward black citizens and treated them either "harder" or "easier" than did white officers. Reiss (1971) corroborated this finding in his 1966 research that concluded that "both negro and white policemen . . . (are) more likely to exercise force unduly against members of their own race."

The measurement of effectiveness, of course, is a function of definition. Compared to white performance, and treatment of black citizens, black police may have been an improvement. However, if effectiveness is defined in terms of due process of law and situationally consistent behavior, more black police were not necessarily a positive step toward democratic police behavior. The increasing impetus for black police employment resulting from affirmative action after the

1960's may reflect more of a concern for the democratic precept of equality of equity, than it does a concern for improved effectiveness through excellence. Equality of opportunity should exist but excellence must be the goal if democratic police professionalism is to be fully, and finally, realized.

NOTES

1. The introduction indicates that the paper covers through the mid-1960's. This is true for most of the research; however, the 1970 census data is utilized because it is more comprehensive than any available for mid-1960 years. Unless indicated otherwise, census data is the source of police statistics. The volumes utilized are *Compendium of the Census* for 1860–1890, *Population: Occupational Statistics* for 1910 and 1920, *Population: Occupations by State* for 1930, *Population: The Labor Force* for 1940 and *Characteristics of the Population* for 1960 and 1970.

In reading this section it is important to consider the accuracy of census data. Census statistics are subject to error in categories with small numbers (i.e., occupations by race) therefore care must be exercised when interpreting this data. Errors are also caused by human and mechanical processing, incorrect or missing data, sampling size bias, and sampling variability. Prior to 1940, occupational statistics were based on a total in-residence self reporting count. Since 1950, occupational statistics have been based on a 20 percent sample. There are problems in obtaining accurate data when using self reporting procedures and samples. For example, the 1970 census reports 374,623 "police and detectives" in the United States; however, according to the U. S. Department of Justice, Law Enforcement Assistance Administration, *Expenditure and Employment Data for the Criminal Justice System,* 1970–79, U. S. Department of Commerce, Bureau of the Census (Washington, D.C.: U. S. Government Printing Office, 1973), p. 11, there were 528,594 police employees for all levels of government in the United States in October 1971. Even assuming some growth, there were probably more police in the United States in 1970, and perhaps other years, than those listed in the census. This, however, does not necessarily mean that the relationships of black to total police, and black to white police would be altered. The authors can think of no reason why more or less black or whites would or would not engage in self reporting to a degree that would substantially influence relationships in recent years.

2. Southern states include Mississippi, South Carolina, Louisiana, Georgia, Alabama, Arkansas, Virginia, North Carolina, Florida, Tennessee and Texas.

3. From 1930 to 1970, the mean decade increase for police was 30.47 percent.

4. The Civil Rights Act of 1964 as amended by the Equal Employment Opportunity Act of 1972 provides that upon finding that a respondent has engaged in an unlawful employment practice the U. S. District Court has the authority not only to enjoin continuation of the practice but also to order "affirmative action" which may include such "equitable relief" as the court deems appropriate.

Although there is some inconsistency between judicial districts, the courts have tended to construe the delegation of broad equitable power under Title VII as authorizing the establishment of goals for the purpose of remedying the discriminatory effects of the past as well as bar like discrimination in the future.

REFERENCES

Alex, N. (1969). *Black in Blue*. New York: Meredith.

Banner, W. M. (1946). "Southern Negro Communities." *Phylon, 7* (Third Quarter), p. 255.

Bennett, L. (1968). *Black Power U. S. A.: The Human Side of Reconstruction 1867–1877*. Baltimore: Penguin Books, p. 212.

Chicago Commission on Race Relations. (1922). *The Negro in Chicago: A Study of Race Relations and a Race Riot.* Chicago: The University of Chicago Press, p. 34.

Citizen's Committee to Study Police–Community Relations in the City of Chicago. (1967). *Police and Public: Critique and a Program*. Chicago: Citizen's Committee, p. 74.

Conot, R. (1967). *Rivers of Blood, Years of Darkness.* New York: Bantam Books, pp. 157–60.

Cooper, L. (et al.) (1975). *The Iron Fist and the Velvet Glove*. Berkeley: Center for Research on Criminal Justice.

Danielson, W. F. (1964). "Employment of Minority Group Persons in the Berkeley Fire Department and in the Berkeley Police Department." Report prepared for the members of the Personnel Board of Berkeley, (Mimeographical), p. 33.

Du Bois, W. E. B. (1899). *The Philadelphia Negro*. Philadelphia: University of Pennsylvania, p. 132.

Ebony Magazine. (ed). (1966). *The Negro Handbook*. Chicago: Johnson Publishing, p. 102.

Fleming, H. C. (1947). "How Negro Policemen Worked Out in One Southern City." *New South*, II, pp. 3–7.

Gosnell, H. F. (1935). *Negro Politicians: The Rise of Negro Politics in Chicago*. Chicago: University of Chicago Press, pp. 245–47.

Greenberg, J. (1959). *Race Relations and American Law*. New York: Columbia University Press, p. 164.

Guzman, J. P. (ed.) (1952). *The Negro Yearbook: A Review of Events Affecting Negro Life*. (11th ed.). New York: William H. Wise and Company, p. 275.

Hamblin, R. L. (1962). "The Dynamics of Racial Discrimination." *Social Problems*, X, pp. 103–105.

Jefferson County Coordinating Council. (1953). *A Study of Negro Police*. Birmingham, Alabama: Coordinating Council, p. 1.

Johnson, C. S. (1947). *Into the Mainstream: A Survey of Best Practices in Race Relations in the South*. Chapel Hill: University of North Carolina Press, p. 54.

Kelly, C. M. (1974). *Crime in the United States: Uniform Crime Reports*. Washington, D.C.: Government Printing Office.

Kephart, W. M. (1954). "The Integration of Negroes into the Urban Police Force." *The Journal of Criminal Law, Criminology, and Police Science*, XLV, pp. 325–335.

Kephart, W. M. (1957). *Racial Factors and Urban Law Enforcement*. Philadelphia: University of Pennsylvania Press, pp. 23–98.

Landis, K. M. (1958). *Segregation in Washington*. Chicago: National Committee on Segregation in the Nation's Capital, p. 86.

Landrum, L. W. (1947). "The Case of Negro Police." *New South*, II, pp. 5–6.

Locke, A. (1971). "Dark Weather-Vane." in Platt, A. M. (ed.). *The Politics of Riot Commissions*. New York: Collier Books, p. 194.

Morgan, C. (1964). "Segregated Justice in Birmingham." in Alan Westin (ed.), *Freedom Now*. New York: Basic Books, pp. 210–15.

Myrdal, G. (1944). *An American Dilemma: The Negro Problem and Modern Democracy*. New York: Harper and Brothers, p. 542.

National Center on Police and Community Relations. (1967). *A National Survey of Police and Community Relations, Field Survey V, Report of the President's Commission on Law Enforcement and Administration of Justice*. Washington, D.C.: Government Printing Office, p. 261.

New York Times, January 24, 1962, p. 8.

Palmer, E. (1973). "Black Police in America." *The Black Scholar*, Vol. 5.

Platt, A. M. (1971) (ed.). *The Politics of Riot Commissions*. New York: Collier Books, p. 316.

President's Commission on Civil Disorders. (1968). *Report of the Advisory Commission on Civil Disorders*. New York: Bantam Books.

President's Commissison on Law Enforcement and Administration of Justice. (1967). *Task Force Report: The Police*. Washington, D.C.: Government Printing Office.

Price, M. (1947). "South Finding Negro Policeman Valuable." *New South*, II, p. 2.

Quillin, F. V. (1913). *The Color Line in Ohio*. Ann Arbor, Michigan: George Wahr, pp. 134–138.

Raspberry, W. (1967). "Police Rift Widens Here Among White and Negro Officers." *Washington Post*, (September 23), Sec. B., p. 1.

Reiss, A. J. (1971). *The Police and the Public*. New Haven: Yale University Press, p. 147.

Rice, L. D. (1971). *The Negro in Texas: 1874–1900*. Baton Rouge: Louisiana State University Press.

Rudwick, E. (1960). "The Negro Policeman in the South." *The Journal of Criminal Law, Criminology and Police Science*, II, pp. 273–276.

Rudwick, E. (1961). "The Southern Negro Policeman and the White Offender." *The Journal of Negro Education*, XXX, pp. 426–31.

Rudwick, E. (1962). *The Unequal Badge: Negro Policemen in the South, Report of the Southern Regional Council*. Atlanta: Southern Regional Council, pp. 3–14.

Skolnick, J. (ed.). (1969). *The Politics of Protest*. New York: Simon and Schuster, p. 129.

Sloan, I. J. (1965). *The American Negro: A Chronology and Fact Book*. Atlanta: Southern Regional Council, pp. 33–35.

Student Non-violent Coordinating Committee (Letter, 1967).
Thomas, D. (1967). "The Color Line—Why." *Denver Post Bonus*, October 24, pp. 4–5.
Tindall, G. B. (1952). *South Carolina Negroes: 1877–1900*. Columbus: University of South Carolina Press, p. 305.
United States Commission on Civil Rights. (1960). *Los Angeles and San Francisco Hearings: January 25–28*. Washington, D.C.: Government Printing Office, p. 32.
United States Commission on Civil Rights (Tennesssee State Advisory Committee). (1967). *Employment, Administration of Justice and Health Services in Memphis—Shelby County, Tennessee*. Memphis: State Advisory Committee, pp. 31–37.
United States Commission on Civil Rights. (1962). *Memphis, Tennessee, Hearings, June 1962*. Washington, D.C.: Government Printing Office, pp. 83–90.
University of California. (1967). *The Police and the Community: The Dynamics of Their Relationship in a Changing Society, Field Survey VI*. Report of the President's Commission on Law Enforcement and Administration of Justice, Washington, D.C.: Government Printing Office, p. 189.
University of Michigan. (1967). *Studies in Crime and Law Enforcement in Major Metropolitan Areas, Field Survey III*. Report of the President's Commission on Law Enforcement and Administration of Justice, Washington, D.C.: Government Printing Office, p. 135–37.
Wharton, V. L. (1947). *The Negro in Mississippi: 1865–1890*. Chapel Hill: University of North Carolina Press.

The Jewish Patrolman

Arthur Niederhoffer

The Great Depression was mainly responsible for the entry of a number of Jews into the classically Irish police force.(1) In those days Jews faced prejudice. The prevailing attitudes toward them were of thinly disguised contempt, and disbelief that they would make good cops. Jewish policemen were forced to prove themselves worthy.

One Jewish patrolman finally convinced the opposition. He won so many awards for his police work that his nickname became "Medals." But his finest hour came when the other policemen, and his personal friends outside the force, started calling him "Reilly." There were not many Jewish "Reillys" at the beginning.

Jewish policemen faced more than prejudice. A high percentage of these newcomers were college men. They naturally became the target for the anti-intellectualism that policemen shared with many other Americans. A Jewish policeman with a college degree soon realized that for him the police world was out of joint. His handling of police situations often seemed feasible by college standards, but frequently was impractical according to the standards of traditional police practice. With middle-class antecedents, and his Jewish heritage, he almost inevitably attempted to solve problems verbally rather than by force.

There are several recurrent, unpleasant situations that confront the Jewish policeman. Often the non-Jewish policeman tries to be friendly by hailing him with *"Mach a leben?"* To the non-Jew this remark is equivalent to saying, "How are things?" To the Jew it not only is bad grammar, but also covertly insinuates that Jews are mainly interested in making money. It is also difficult for the Jewish policeman to deal with an anti-Semitic civilian. The problem is complicated by the fact that anti-Semites are reputedly sensitive to Jewishness and able to recognize a Jew quickly but are fooled by the police uniform which they associate with the Irish, or at least non-Jewish policemen. Repeatedly an anti-Semite will sidle up to the Jewish policeman and "out of a clear sky" start blaming the evils of the world on the Jews. Only a little less irritating to his pride as a policeman is the reaction of the Jewish occupants of a car that he has stopped for a traffic violation. The officer will hear them say in Yiddish, "Give him a few dollars to forget the ticket, and let's get out of here."

SOURCE: Arthur Niederhoffer, *Behind the Shield: The Police in Urban Society* (Garden City, N.Y.: Doubleday, 1967).

Today relative deprivation describes the state of Jewish patrolmen. A generation ago Jewish policemen, compared with members of different faiths or ethnic groups, had real grievances; they were discriminated against and treated as inferiors. Deprivation was not at all relative but absolute. Except in isolated instances this is no longer true. If the Jewish policeman experiences frustration today, it is probably due to his commitment to the traditional Jewish *Weltanschauung* from which he is not completely emancipated. This tradition is typified by the advice their leaders gave Jewish immigrants near the end of the nineteenth century.

> Select a goal and pursue it with all your might. No matter what happens to you, hold on. You will experience a bad time but sooner or later you will achieve your goal. . . . A bit of advice for you: Do not take a moment's rest. Run, do, work, and keep your own good in mind. . . . A final virtue is needed in America—called cheek. . . . Do not say, I cannot; I do not know.(2).

Jewish mothers-in-law have learned subtle techniques to disguise their disappointment at having gained a policeman son-in-law when they lost their daughter in marriage. For example, one mother-in-law bravely surmounted her loss of status by introducing her policeman son-in-law as a college graduate with two degrees. Others try to conceal the police blemish by describing the policeman relative as "in youth work" or, if he is lucky enough to be attached to the Police Academy, as "a teacher."

Jewish parents look forward to the wonderful day when they can proudly introduce their offspring with the ritual words, "My son, the doctor." It cannot give them the same degree of satisfaction to present, "My son, the cop." They suspect their friends of translating the words "My son, the cop" into an altogether different phrase "My cop-son." It is one of those ironical coincidences that in the Yiddish colloquial speech the term of mild contempt commonly used to signify "a person who will never amount to anything" is pronounced phonetically *"cop son."*

While contemporary Jews have no high regard for police work as an occupation, older Jewish people remember the old-country ghettos, and the respect they were forced to display to policemen. On the other hand, since several European nations barred Jews from the police force, émigré Jews are often secretly proud that in America a Jew can become an influential official with the power of life and death over others. This ambivalence is mirrored in the attitude of Jewish policemen who sometimes feel like failures, but are often inwardly proud that they have succeeded in an occupation that once had this particular significance for their forebears.

REFERENCES

1. Nathan Glazer and Daniel P. Moynihan, *Beyond the Melting Pot* (Cambridge, Mass.: The M.I.T. Press, 1963), p. 261.

2. Moses Rischin, *The Promised City: New York's Jews 1870–1914* (Cambridge: Harvard University Press, 1962), p. 75.

3

POLICE ORGANIZATION AND CONTROL

Police systems occupy a unique position in our democratic society. More than any other institutions and professions they have been subjected to strong control by civil authority. Furthermore, they have been dispersed and fragmented to insure their weakness. The benchmark of most professions is their autonomy and relative freedom from external controls. Striving to move toward professional status, the police can hardly hope to achieve this kind of independence. Instead, because of the political traditions of our nation, they meet a wall of resistance. And this may constitute the greatest barrier to genuine police professionalism.

The one exception where police have been able to maintain autonomy is in connection with the processing of certain complaints against the police. In our larger cities, when a civilian board for the review of citizens' complaints against the police has been established, police organizations have been uniformly successful in neutralizing the claims. This phenomenon is a testimonial to the ability of the police to orchestrate highly sophisticated techniques involving political and judicial strategies. The success of police resistance to this variety of external control may be the result of a coalition consisting of community power centers and the police, whose mutual interests appear to coincide regarding the issues and threats symbolized by a civilian review board. The most sophisticated police leaders never lose sight of the fact that their power and organizational autonomy can only be asserted up to a point, at which time the external political forces and other community power centers are aroused.

Another type of police adminstrator, entranced by the glowing illusion of police professionalism, fails to perceive these limits. The administrator works ardently for the autonomy and self-governance of his or her organization and is rudely disillusioned at failure to attain these goals. Not only administrators, but also rank-and-file police officers who misinterpret the stress on education and technology as the fulfillment rather than the timorous first step on the road to professionalism, equally share the misconceptions that lead to their frustration and disenchantment.

Police officers, who must deal with the challenges of the urban arena, cannot afford to be simplistic. The seemingly straightforward administrative problems such as recruitment, training, education, disposition of the force, problems of productivity, community relations, and cost–benefit issues are really much more complex; and all these administrative issues are fraught with potential political repercussions. The police administrator must be alert to the political dimensions that may require compromise or modification of a department's priorities and performance agenda.

If police leaders are insensitive to the external environment that we have described, then they may fail to comprehend the equally turbulent internal organizational milieu and its accompanying dynamics of struggles for power and the new directions of policing.

We recognize that it is extremely taxing to walk the rather narrow line required by the foregoing contingencies without becoming a cynic, a Machiavellian, or, at worst, a political hack. But that is the art of being a police administrator. Unless police officers and their superiors come to grips with this underlying reality that governs their organizations, they will not be able to advance toward the status and goals they seek.

The Traffic Violator: Organizational Norms

Richard J. Lundman

An essential interpretation to be drawn out of the existing literature on police exercise of discretion is that police officers routinely violate norms emphasizing the consistent or equitable treatment of citizens. The bulk of the existing literature suggests that factors such as demeanor, social class, sex, age, and race routinely influence the decisions made by police patrol officers (Bittner, 1967a, 1967b; Black, 1970; Black and Reiss, 1970; Gardiner, 1968; Goldman, 1963; La Fave, 1965; Lundman, 1974; Lundman et al., 1978; Marshall and Purdy, 1972; Petersen, 1971; Piliavin and Briar, 1964; Rubinstein, 1973; Skolnick, 1975; Wilson, 1968).[1]

Also present within the existing literature, however, is evidence of disagreement as to the origins or causes of differential police practices. Piliavin and Briar (1964), for example, explained the higher rates of arrest of black juveniles in terms of the attitudes and prejudices of individual police officers. Black (1970), by contrast, reported that report writing by police was largely a function of the preferences of the citizens involved. According to Black (1970), race is unrelated to report writing.

Despite this disagreement, common to nearly all explanations of police exercise of discretion is a focus on the actors involved in the decision-making situation. And it must be admitted that such a focus is seemingly logical. Police organizations are somewhat unique in that low-level members, street-level patrol officers, possess a great deal of latitude in their action. To a large extent, the work of the patrol officer is unsupervised and, to a lesser extent, it is unsupervisable. The individual police officer, therefore, is relatively free to act on the basis of individual attitudes and prejudices. Equally, the literature suggests that police officers are sensitive to the attitudes and preferences of the citizens involved in an encounter (Sykes and Clark, 1975) and that their actions frequently reflect compliance with the stated preferences of citizens (Lundman et al., 1978). Police exercise of discretion, therefore, would appear to reflect the result of some type of compromise between the preferences of the officers and citizens involved in an encounter.

SOURCE: Richard J. Lundman, "The Traffic Violator: Organizational Norms," *Criminology*, Vol. 17 (August 1979), pp. 159–171. Reprinted by permission of Sage Publications, Inc.

The fundamental purpose of the present study, however, is to suggest an expanded imagery. Specifically, it is the thesis of the present study that police exercise of discretion is a function of relations between organizational norms and employee concerns with autonomy. This thesis will be advanced in the context of an examination of police work with traffic law violators.

ORIENTATION

Traffic law violations are the single most frequent reason for contacts between police patrol officers and citizens (Ross, 1960; Skolnick, 1966; Gardiner, 1968). However, citizen conceptions of the police mission, the perceived innocuousness of the offense, and the circumstances in which traffic law violations occur contribute to the individual's dismay when cited for a traffic offense. As a result, citizens frequently offer opposition to a traffic citation and traffic stops are major sources of friction between police officers and citizens (Skolnick, 1966: 55, Rubinstein, 1973: 153–155).

Further, traffic stops and citations appear to have little or no effect on accident rates or subsequent driving practices. Campbell and Ross (1968), for example, found that an unprecedented crackdown on speeding in an eastern state had no discernible impact on automobile fatality rates. Gardiner (1968: 171) noted that there exists little evidence that police enforcement practices have any influence on traffic law violations or accident rates. Ross reached an essentially similar conclusion reporting that there seems to be "no effect on subsequent driver history of appearing in one of the best reputed traffic courts in America, as compared to paying a small fine to a clerk, or even with merely receiving a warning from a policeman" (1973: 79).

Despite citizen opposition and the lack of evidence that strict enforcement of traffic laws prevents accidents, traffic stops and citations for offenses are an integral element of the work expectations surrounding most uniformed, motorized police patrol officers. Police administrators, as is true of administrators of other large-scale bureaucracies (Blau and Scott, 1962: 65), require easily codifiable evidence that their subordinates are working. And, unlike felony arrests which are largely a matter of assignment, good fortune, and rarely a result of individual effort,[2] traffic law violations are easily discovered. As a consequence, administrators of most police organizations establish citation quotas for patrol officers (Gardiner, 1968; La Fave, 1965; Petersen, 1971; Rubinstein, 1973).[3]

Citation quotas, however, only direct patrol officers to issue a certain number of traffic tickets. They do not determine the types of individuals to whom citations will be issued in order to meet organizational expectations. It is necessary, therefore, to consider an additional set of organizational norms in order to understand police exercise of discretion in the context of traffic law violations.

Central to the norms of many watch-style (Wilson, 1968: 140–171) police organizations are negative typifications of, and associated recipes for actions against, minority, lower class, and disrespectful citizens. It has frequently been observed that police officers in watch-style departments maintain negative stereotypical images of minority citizens (cf. Kirkham, 1975; Reiss, 1971: 147; Skolnick, 1975: 256; Westley, 1970: 99; Wilson, 1968: 43). Similarly, negative typifications of relatively powerless citizens are characteristic of most watch-style police organizations (Reiss, 1971: 151; Westley, 1970: 99; Williams, 1975: 137). Finally, patrol officers in these departments routinely emphasize that disrespectful citizens are to be treated differently than polite and respectful citizens (Reiss, 1971: 136; Rubinstein, 1973: 318; Skolnick, 1975: 42; Westley, 1970: 119; Wilson, 1968: 37). In addition to citation requirements, then, organizational norms emphasizing differential treatment of certain types of citizens would also appear to play an important role in police work with traffic law violators.

As is true of all employees, however, police patrol officers attempt to retain some degree of autonomy or independence in the face of organizational norms intended to guide their actions (Olsen, 1968). Petersen (1971: 358–359), for example, reports that on "one occasion an officer and the writer sat in an immobile patrol car in a deserted parking lot in the city for more than three hours because the officer had already filled his citation quota."

In the context of police work with traffic law violators, therefore, it is suggested that police exercise of discretion is a function of relations between organizational norms and employee concerns with autonomy. Specifically, if an officer is constrained to act by reference to organizational norms, then police exercise of discretion should result in a disproportionate number of citations for minority, lower class, and disrespectful citizens. If, however, an officer is momentarily free of organizational constraints, then there should be evidence of action undertaken by reference to other than organizational factors. Their observations sensitize analysis of the data which follow.

METHOD

During a 15-month period beginning in June 1970, a participant-as-observer study of police-citizen encounters was conducted in a midwestern city of more than 500,000 located in a standard metropolitan statistical area of over two million. A group of seven observers, trained over three months, traveled with the police on a random-time sample basis, using portable electronic coding equipment and an interaction process code. During the 15 months, observers appeared at precinct stations and observed officers in randomly selected patrol cars for full shifts. Interaction between police and citizens was simultaneously and sequentially content analyzed and coded using the portable equipment.

To isolate traffic law violations from other activities, the encounters selected for analysis in this study met the following four criteria: (1) the offense was a moving rather than a parking violation; (2) the motorist possessed a valid driver's license; (3) did not have any outstanding warrants; and (4) was sober.[4] Of the 1,978 encounters observed, 293 or approximately 15% met these four criteria.

RESULTS

The police department studied represented a blend of the watch and legalistic departments described by Wilson (1968) and maintained a formal quota of two traffic citations per officer shift. In order to emphasize the importance of traffic citations, police administrators made and posted citation tallies in precinct roll call rooms at the end of each month. In practice, many patrol officers resisted these quotas by postponing "working traffic" until the later portions of each month. They then worked aggressively to meet their quota. For the analysis, therefore, each of the 15 months of observation were divided in half with the first 15 days representing a period of low-quota saliency and the last half a period of high-quota saliency. This operationalization serves as a measure of the importance of the quota system.

Table 1 shows the zero-order relationships of the independent variables to the percent of encounters ending with a traffic citation: 52% of the traffic stops made during periods of high-quota saliency ended with a traffic citation as compared to 42% of the encounters occurring during periods of low-quota saliency. Additionally, more traffic stops were made during the last days of each month than the first.

The other zero-order relationships in Table 1 are, with two exceptions,[5] in the directions expected on the basis of previous study of police exercise of discretion (Piliavin and Briar, 1964; Black and Reiss, 1970). Thus, more male than female motorists received traffic citations as did more black than white motorists. Similarly, more lower- than middle-class motorists received citations and citizens who offered verbal resistance received more citations than citizens who offered no verbal resistance.[6] Type of offense, a crude indicator of offense seriousness, plays a minor role in citation decisions as traffic stops made for moving violations were somewhat more likely to end in a ticket than stops made for equipment violations.[7]

TABLE 1 Percent of Traffic Law Violation Encounters Ending with a Traffic Citation According to Selected Characteristics of the Encounter[a]

Condition	Number	Percent Ending in a Citation
I Quota saliency		
Low	125	42
High	168	52
II Social and demographic		
A Sex		
Male	252	48
Female	40	43
B Race		
Black	29	55
White	256	47
C Social class		
Lower	169	49
Middle	116	44
D Age		
Adult	105	47
Young adult	143	48
Adolescent	39	46
E Style of dress		
Conventional	260	48
Unconventional	33	48
F Verbal resistance		
None, some	256	47
Above average	37	51
III Type of offense		
Equipment violation	98	44
Moving violation	195	49
IV Totals	293	47

[a] Encounters were excluded from the analysis when an observer was unable to classify a citizen along a specific dimension.

A final observation to be drawn from Table 1 is that none of the independent variables or predictors exerts a particularly strong effect on the decision to issue a traffic citation. Many of the differences are minor and, with the exception of the quota predictor, all are substantively insignificant. It is possible, however, that predictors may occasion interaction effects under varying quota conditions. This possibility is explored next.

Table 2 shows the first-order relationships of the independent variables to the percent of encounters ending with a traffic citation with the effect of the quota predictor controlled. As can be seen, a number of in-

TABLE 2 Percent of Traffic Law Violation Encounters Ending with a Traffic Citation According to Selected Characteristics of the Encounter and Quota Saliency[a]

	Quota saliency				*Totals*	
	Low		*High*			
Selected Characteristics	*N*	*%*	*N*	*%*	*N*	*%*
I Social and demographic						
A Sex						
Male	(106)	42	(146)	52	(252)	48
Female	(19)	42	(21)	43	(40)	43
B Race						
Black	(12)	42	(17)	65	(29)	55
White	(111)	43	(145)	50	(256)	47
C Social class						
Lower	(66)	35	(103)	57	(169)	49
Middle	(58)	50	(58)	38	(116)	44
D Age						
Adult	(39)	44	(6)	48	(105)	47
Young adult	(67)	42	(76)	54	(143)	48
Adolescent	(19)	42	(20)	50	(39)	46
E Style of dress						
Conventional	(108)	42	(152)	52	(260)	48
Unconventional	(17)	47	(16)	45	(33)	48
F Verbal resistance						
None, some	(110)	45	(146)	49	(256)	47
Above average	(15)	27	(22)	68	(37)	51
II Type of offense						
Equipment	(43)	37	(55)	49	(98)	44
Moving	(82)	45	(113)	52	(195)	49
III Totals	(125)	42	(168)	52	(293)	47

[a] Encounters were excluded from the analysis when an observer was unable to classify a citizen along a specific dimension.

teraction effects emerge once this control is introduced. Most, however, are substantively insignificant. There is some evidence that gender interacts with quota saliency to produce somewhat higher citation rates for males during periods of high-quota saliency. Similarly, there is some evidence that age, style of dress, and type of offense interact with the quota predictor to produce somewhat higher citation rates for younger, conventionally dressed, and moving violators during periods of high-quota saliency.

Table 2 also contains evidence of complex and substantively important interactions between organizational norms and employee concerns with autonomy. Under periods of low-quota saliency, essentially equal proportions of black and white traffic law violators received traffic citations. Under periods of high-quota saliency, however, race interacts with the quota predictor producing higher citation rates for black traffic law violators.

The effects of social class on citation rates also vary dependent upon the saliency of the quota predictor. Under periods of low-quota saliency, more middle- than lower-class violators received citations; under periods of high-quota saliency, however, more lower- than middle-class violators received citations.

Finally, the effects of verbal resistance are also found to vary dependent upon quota saliency. Thus, under periods of low-quota saliency, violators who verbally resist the citation receive fewer tickets than violators who offered little or no verbal resistance. The reverse is true during periods of high-quota saliency.

These three interactions would appear to be supportive of the earlier discussion of the importance of organizational norms and employee concerns with autonomy. Patrol officers resisted quota demands during the first half of each month by making fewer traffic stops and issuing proportionately fewer citations. In addition, officers acted apart from organizational norms emphasizing the differential treatment of minority, powerless, and disrespectful citizens. During the last half of each month, however, it appears that the police patrol officers paid for their earlier autonomy. They made more traffic stops and issued proportionately more citations. In addition, the data suggest that they acted by reference to organizational norms emphasizing the differential treatment of minority, lower-class, and disrespectful citizens. The tentative interpretation attached to these data is that police exercise of discretion in the context of traffic law violations appears to be a function of relations between organizational norms and employee concerns with autonomy.

DISCUSSION

This analysis of police exercise of discretion in the context of traffic law violations raises a number of issues that deserve further attention. However, it must first be recognized that although the findings regarding the importance of race, social class, and demeanor are essentially similar to those reported by others, the interpretation advanced is limited to traffic stop encounters. It is obvious, therefore that organizationally sensitive study of other types of encounters (e.g., public drunkenness or juvenile rowdiness) as well as replication must be undertaken to assess the generalizability of the present argument. For purposes of discussion, however, it will be assumed that the present interpretation is at least partially valid.

To begin, it can be noted that these data suggest that it may no longer be sufficient to explain police exercise of discretion solely by reference to the characteristics of citizens (Goldman, 1963), the preferences of complainants (Black and Reiss, 1970), or the prejudices of individual police officers (Piliavin and Briar, 1964). While it is likely that these, and other, factors play a role in police decision making, it is also likely that their priority and intensity are established by reference to organizationally generated constraints. It therefore appears necessary to explore the possibility that organizational norms may be at least as important as the individualistic and situational contingencies previously identified as important in the context of police exercise of discretion.

Further, it must also be recognized that police officers are employees who possess concerns essentially similar to those of other types of persons. As a consequence, it is likely that certain of their actions reflect a preference for less work rather than more. Police administrators, of course, recognize this and that is one of the reasons for quota systems, radio-equipped patrol cars, and the elaborate paperwork which surrounds most police work. It is perhaps useful for sociological students of police and policing to adopt a similar perspective.

CONCLUSION

Keeping in mind the limits of the present analysis, it does not appear unreasonable to conclude by suggesting that these observations provide certain of the elements necessary for an expanded image of police exercise of discretion. Minimally, it would appear that it is now necessary to recognize that police decision making is also shaped by organizational norms and employee concerns with autonomy. It is also possible that it is within the constraints imposed by these factors that the effects of individualistic and situational contingencies are likely to be manifested.

NOTES

1 This is not to suggest that all of these factors are uniformly reported in each of these studies. Instead, what is being suggested is that variables such as these are routinely reported in the bulk of the existing literature.

2 The fortuitous nature of felony arrests is reflected in the conversation of patrol officers at the scene of an arrest. Thus, it is not at all unusual to observe officers deciding who will get credit for the arrest. Officers who have had a run of bad luck are likely to be included and several officers are typically credited for a single arrest.

3 In operation, these systems closely resemble the "service" expectations surrounding professors at large universities. Thus, patrol officers and their precincts are rarely rewarded for meeting or exceeding their quo-

tas: they are, however, sanctioned for regular failure to meet ticket expectations.

4 Driving while intoxicated encounters are being examined in a separate analysis now underway. They are being analyzed separately because they represent a more serious violation of the traffic laws and, therefore, police officers are ostensibly more constrained in the types of actions they can take.

5 The two exceptions are the absences of any relationships between the age and style of dress of traffic law violators and percent receiving a traffic citation.

6 Verbal resistance was defined as statements involving aggressive noncompliance, attempts to embarrass, heated argument, name calling, ridicule, or personal vituperation. Motorists were divided into groups on the basis of frequency of these statements: those showing above average levels of verbal resistance and those showing below average levels of verbal resistance. Since the modal level was zero, the latter group is more numerous.

7 Included in the moving violation category is speeding, illegal turns, U-turns, and the like. Equipment violations include faulty mufflers and tail or head light failures.

REFERENCES

Bittner, E. (1967a) "The police on skid row: a study of peace-keeping." Amer. Soc. Rev. 32:699–715.

——— (1967b) "Police discretion in the emergency apprehension of mentally ill persons." Social Problems 14:278–292.

Black, D. J. (1970) "Production of crime rates." Amer. Soc. Rev. 35:733–747.

——— and A. J. Reiss, Jr. (1970) "Police control of juveniles." Amer. Soc. Rev. 35:63–77.

Blau, P. M. and W. Scott (1962) Formal Organizations. San Francisco: Chandler.

Campbell, D. and H. L. Ross (1968) "The Connecticut crackdown on speeding." Law and Society Rev. 3:33–53.

Gardiner, J. A. (1968) "Police-enforcement of traffic laws: A comparative analysis," in J. Wilson (ed.), City Politics and Public Policy. New York: John Wiley.

Goldman, N. (1963) The Differential Selection of Juvenile Offenders for Court Appearance. Washington, D.C.: National Council on Crime and Delinquency.

Kirkham, G. (1975) "On the etiology of police aggression in black communities," pp. 167–173 in J. Kinton (ed.), Police Roles in the Seventies. Aurora, IL: Social Science and Sociological Resources.

LaFave, W. (1965) Arrest: The Decision to Take a Suspect into Custody. Boston: Little, Brown.

Lundman, R. J. (1974) "Routine police arrest practices: A commonweal perspective." Social Problems 22:127–141.

——— R. E. Sykes and J. P. Clark (1978) "Police control of juveniles: a replication." J. of Research in Crime and Delinquency 15:74–91.

Marshall, H. and R. Purdy (1972) "Hidden deviance and the labeling approach: the case for drinking and driving." Social Problems 19:541–553.

Olsen, M. E. (1968) The Process of Social Organization. New York: Holt, Rinehart and Winston.

Petersen, D. (1971) "Informal norms and police practices: The traffic quota system." Sociology and Social Research 55:354–362.

Piliavin, I. and S. Briar (1964) "Police encounters with juveniles." Amer. J. of Sociology 70:206–214.

Reiss, A. J., Jr. (1971) The Police and the Public. New Haven: Yale Univ. Press.

Ross, H. (1973) "Folk crime revisited." Criminology 11:71–85.

——— (1960) "Traffic law violation: a folk crime." Social Problems 8:231–241.

Rubinstein, J. (1973) City Police. New York: Ballantine Books.

Skolnick, J. (1975) Justice Without Trial. 2nd ed. New York: John Wiley.

——— (1966) Justice Without Trial. New York: John Wiley.

Sykes, R. E. and J. P. Clark (1975) "A theory of deference exchange in police-civilian encounters." Amer. J. of Sociology 81:584–600.

Westley, W. (1970) Violence and the Police: Cambridge, MA: MIT Press.

Williams, F. P. (1975) "Toward a theory of police behavior: some critical comments," pp. 133–147 in J. Kinton (ed.), Police Roles in the Seventies. Aurora, IL: Social Science and Sociological Resources.

Wilson, J. Q. (1968) Varieties of Police Behavior. Cambridge, MA: Harvard Univ. Press.

The Paramilitary Model of Police and Police Professionalism

James H. Auten

The precise nature of early policing is clouded sufficiently to obscure the exact structure of the organizations that provided police services. However, we do know that in many instances the early policing responsibilities of order maintenance and the protection of life and property were quite likely fulfilled by the military. For example, in 27 B.C., a military police unit, the Praetorian Guard, was created to maintain security at the palace of the Emperor Augustus.[1] Not only was such the case in Rome, but policemen, as such, ". . . were known in ancient China and Egypt thousands of years ago but were usually military men under military command. . . ."[2] It seems safe to presume that if the policing services were being provided by military personnel, then they were working within the framework of a military organizational structure. We may also presume that if police services were being provided elsewhere in the world, although unrecorded, then they were also being provided by military personnel who were also functioning within a military organizational environment.

The "modern" police era was ushered in with the creation of the London Metropolitan Police in 1829. Two commissioners, one a barrister and the other a former officer in the British army, were selected to oversee the organization and operation of the agency. If one considers the organizational form assumed by the London Metropolitan Police it is evident that the agency was organized along military or paramilitary lines. In looking at the history of the early British police, one recognizes that the literal definition of paramilitary is an exact description of the organization founded by Sir Robert Peel in 1829. It is quite likely that this organizational structure emerged for several reasons. The first of these is directly related to Peel himself. Not only did Peel create the Metropolitan Police Act of 1829–1830, but he also developed the principles that guided the organization and operation of the "new" police. In looking at these principles, we find that the initial one listed by Peel states, "The police must be stable, efficient and organized along military lines."[3] Additionally, Peel singled out former non-commissioned officers in the military as being particularly suited for inclusion in the department.

SOURCE: *Police Studies*, Summer 1981. Reprinted by permission.

The second reason relates to the fact that there was virtually no other organizational model to emulate. The various organizational and management theories that exist today did not exist in 1829. The only other organizational model in existence, other than the military, with a proven track record was the Roman Catholic Church or the Anglican Church. Even though the church is not a military organization in the strict sense of the term, one would be hard pressed to find a more paramilitary organization, then and today.

Third, one must recognize the role and setting into which the London Metropolitan Police were cast. Prior to their creation, Great Britain had been racked by a serious depression, vast unemployment, widespread civil disorder, and a crime rate that was running wild. In London in 1828, it is estimated that one person in every 383 was a criminal.[4] the government had tried several measures to deal with the various factors that were destroying the fabric of society, one of which was the application of military force. None of these measures seemed to have the desired results and the London Metropolitan Police emerged as a possible solution to part of the problem, the excessive incidence of crime. This overriding objective was clearly set forth in the early Instructions and Police Orders issued to members of the force. These stated, "It should be understood, at the outset, that the principal object to be attained is the prevention of crime."[5] Therefore, the "new" police were cast into the role of preventing crime and were in part replacing the military to remedy at least some of the ills afflicting British society.

Finally, we should consider that one of the first commissioners of the Metropolitan Police was a former British Army officer. The military had long been established and had a long standing organizational tradition. Someone coming from such an organization would naturally look to the military organizational model when creating an organization in the setting described previously. Further, the policing done in England prior to this time had been done, to a large extent, by private organizations which, in some cases, could best be described as unstructured, disorganized, and ineffective. One of the important objectives in staffing the Metropolitan Police was to hire personnel who could be relied on to do the law enforcement job. Police corruption had been a glaring defect under the old police system. Such was not to be the case with the Metropolitan Police. For example, between 1829 and 1831, 8,000 men had been enrolled in the ranks of the police department and over 3,000 had been discharged for unfitness, incompetence, or drunkenness.[6] One obvious way to establish control over a body of men, and at the same time to create a disciplined organization, was to employ a military organizational structure and management philosophy. In the circumstances, it was the only alternative.

An unusual situation was occurring in the United States at the same time the London Metropolitan Police emerged. It seems that virtually the same ills that were afflicting British society were also evident in the United States. To an extent, the same remedies had been applied in both countries with the same degree of limited success. Perhaps because they had no other model to turn to, or perhaps because of the origins of this country, the model presented by the Metropolitan Police was closely examined. Apparently those examining the model liked what they saw for in the 1840s the British model of policing was brought to this country. Even though the model was adopted in the United States there was not exact duplication. As Walker (1976) points out, "While the American police were modeled after the London Metropolitan Police . . . the American police were far less centralized, less militarized, less 'professional,' and far more political than the London Police."[7] Even though the early American police were less military in their organizational structure than their British counterparts, the political consideration soon changed that.

In the early part of the twentieth century in the United States, police departments were part of the patronage system that was ingrained in urban politics. Corruption in many police departments was widespread and most agencies were grossly inefficient. Laxity in the adherence to departmental regulations was commonplace. To correct these deficiencies in organization and operations, police reformers turned to the military organizational model as the foundation upon which to establish police discipline and eliminate corruption.[8] As a result, the legacy of the Peelian model has continued to dominate American policing; most notable are its distinctive quasi-military features emphasizing discipline and hierarchical control.[9] Thus began the long-standing tradition of paramilitary organizations within police departments in the United States.

The term "paramilitary" has several definitions.

1. Organized military, but not part of or in cooperation with the official armed forces of a country; having to do with a military force so organized in its tactics.
2. Existing where there are no military services, or existing alongside the military services and professionally non-military but formed on an underlying military pattern as a potential auxiliary or diversionary military organization.

If an organization is structured along paramilitary lines then it will exhibit most, if not all, of the following characteristics:

1. A centralized command structure with a rigidly adhered to chain of command.
2. A rigid superior-subordinate relationship defined by prerogatives of rank.
3. Control exerted through the issuance of commands, directives, or general orders.
4. Clearly delineated lines of communication and authority.
5. The communications process primarily vertical from top to bottom.
6. Employees who are encouraged to work primarily through threats or coercion.
7. Initiative at the supervisory and operational levels neither sought, encouraged, nor expected.
8. An authoritarian style of leadership.
9. Emphasis on the maintenance of the status quo.
10. Highly structured system of sanctions and discipline procedures to deal with nonconformists within the organization.
11. Usually a highly centralized system of operations.
12. Strict adherence to organizational guidelines in the form of commands, directives, general orders, or policy and procedure.
13. Lack of flexibility when confronted with problems or situations not covered by existing directives, general orders, or policy and procedure.
14. Promotional opportunities which are usually only available to members of the organization.
15. An impersonal relationship between members of the organization.
16. Feelings of demoralization and powerlessness in the lower levels of the organization.
17. Concept of the administration and top command as being arbitrary.

18. Growing level of cynicism among supervisory and operational level personnel.
19. Development of a we-they attitude among supervisory and operational level personnel toward top management.

Naturally, not all paramilitary organizations will exhibit all of these characteristics; however, most will be quite evident within the typical police agency in the United States.

The prevailing belief in the United States among police administrators is clearly that the goals of law enforcement can best be attained if the police agency is organized along paramilitary lines. To quote several scholars in the field:

> There is an ample supply of evidence that the paramilitary style of management in police organizations is the rule and not the exception.[10]
>
> The majority of American police departments today . . . are managed in the same antiquated fashion that they were in the 1800s.[11]
>
> Most (American police departments) were organized on the principle of fixed and official jurisdictional lines which were ordered within the organization by rules and administrative regulations. They were structured with strong hierarchies and semi-military levels of graded authority and very rigidly defined superior-subordinate relationships.[12]
>
> . . . the military or semi-military structure which characterizes the organization of most current police agencies.[13]
>
> Traditional policing emphasizes the paramilitary command structure . . .[14] The organization and discipline of modern police departments have been modeled after the military services.[15]
>
> Traditionally, police departments have thought of themselves as quasi-military organizations which "enforce the law."[16]
>
> The traditional model of police administration in America has been military and autocratic.[17]

In addition, in a survey recently conducted by the author of Illinois police administrators, command officers, and supervisors, over 87 percent of the respondents agreed with the statement that a police agency functions most effectively if it is organized along paramilitary lines, and that their departments were so structured.

Considering its long-standing tradition, this emphasis upon the police agency being organized paramilitary should not surprise anyone. However, this emphasis is abhorrent, considering the demands placed on law enforcement by today's society. This is particularly true if we consider only the lowest level of the organization, the operational level. In attempting to attain its goals in the community, the police agency must rely on one primary source of activity, the patrol officer. It is the nature, frequency, and scope of the patrol officer's activities that determine whether the organization attains its goals and objectives. The payoff in terms of how well the organizational structure functions, how appropriate the paramilitary structure is, can be found in the performance of the "street" cop. Does the paramilitary organization allow the patrol officer to function effectively?

To answer this question we need to turn to the military organizational model, particularly at its operational level, that of the individual soldier, because the soldier is analogous to the patrol officer in the police agency. Specifically, we need to examine what the military has traditionally expected of the individual soldier. Putting the obvious exception aside, that of effectively killing the enemy, we see that the individual soldier is expected:

1. To obey the orders of superior officers.
2. Not to display a wide range of initiative or discretion in the performance of his/her duties.
3. To function effectively as part of a larger unit, e.g., squad, platoon, company, etc.
4. To perform tasks in a precisely prescribed manner, i.e., the "army" way.
5. To be uniform in his/her appearance, conduct, and behavior.

These are the traditional expectations of the individual soldier. However, today they can probably be further qualified to say that they are the expectations in a conflict setting. The military recognized some time ago that it would have to modify its traditional organizational structure and expectations as society changed and the individual soldier's job became more technical. Specialist ranks were created in recognition of the technical skills required for certain jobs. In some cases, the standards of appearance were relaxed. The use of individual initiative and discretion is expected in some jobs. In other words, the military modified its organizational structure and expectations to "get into step" with the rest of society. This is the nature of the military organization in the non-conflict setting. Should a conflict arise, then the traditional expectations will probably come to the fore. At least the military recognized that society was changing around them and that they would have to change if they were to properly fulfill their mission. Unfortunately, the same cannot be said for law enforcement in the United States.

Before looking more closely at the analogy between the individual soldier and the patrol officer, we need to examine the managerial/administrative philosophy that the paramilitary organization represents since it also directly influences the performance of the patrol officer. Those who administer or manage within an organization structured along paramilitary lines represent a very distinct philosophy. Whether they realize it or not, their style of management reflects certain values regarding human beings, and in fact, forms their expectations of human behavior in the work environment. This is significant because these expectations are not unknown to the workers and in turn affect their work behavior. The following are examples of what can happen as a result of these usually unstated expectations:

> Other serious problems arise from the paramilitary form of organizational structure. For one, the member of the organization is exposed to a conflicting set of expectations. On the one hand, outside the organization, he is constantly making on-the-spot decisions, carries a weapon and is capable of power over life and death. On the other hand, within the organization, he experiences himself as being treated like a child who is not even permitted to decide on his own uniform to wear when the weather changes.[18]

> Even more important . . . is the stifling of innovation produced by the (paramilitary) organizational structure. First, the rigidity of the chain of command tends to block the upward flow of ideas at the middle management level. . . . Secondly, there is a tendency to "cover yourself" by acting only when so ordered . . . because actions of supervisors and top command are viewed as arbitrary, members anticipate a lack of support for any risks they do take.[19]

The best description of the managerial/administrative philosophy reflected by the paramilitary organization is contained in Douglas MacGregor's Theory X. MacGregor's Theory X describes humans as follows:

1. The average human being has an inherent dislike of work and will avoid it if he can.
2. Because of this human characteristic of dislike of work, most people must be coerced, controlled, directed, and threatened with punishment to get them to put forth adequate effort toward the achievement of organizational objectives.
3. The average human being prefers to be directed, wishes to avoid responsibility, has relatively little ambition, wants security above all.[20]

These expectations about human beings may sound familiar to a student of management, a member of a typical police agency, or both. It is important to remember that police tend to work up to the level that is expected of them. The management philosophy of an organization becomes a self-fulfilling prophecy.

With the foregoing in mind, let's return to the analogy between the patrol officer and the individual soldier, remembering that both are the fundamental end products of the organizational structure and philosophy no matter what form it happens to take. Remember also, they are the people who do the basic job of the organization and largely determine whether it accomplishes its mission. Consider too that the expectations of the organization regarding the individual soldier will closely coincide with those of the police agency concerning the individual patrol officer since they are products of virtually the same organizational structure and management philosophy.

Essentially, what the military has expected of the individual soldier within its traditional organizational structure is a predictable, obedient, blindly unquestioning response. The individual soldier does not, and is not expected to, decide how to dress—it is prescribed. He/she does not decide when to march, when to eat, when to take a break, what equipment to carry, how to address superior officers, or make most of the decisions common daily to civilian life. The fact notwithstanding that we are talking about human beings, what the traditional military organization produced was a machine. The individual soldier has often been referred to as a "fighting machine," and the phrase is accurate in terms of the desired outcome. If the police agency is a paramilitary organization and the foregoing analogy is accurate, is this really what we expect of the individual patrol officer? If the individual patrol officer is performing the job according to military expectations, can the job of providing effective law enforcement in the community really be accomplished?

Applying these expectations to the job of policing in our society, let us address these questions. Beginning with a military expectation to obey orders, we find that within police organizations "orders" are issued/presented in a format or setting that is somewhat different from that of the military. The effective supervisor in a police agency, even though he is functioning in a paramilitary environment, usually does not give orders in the military sense for several reasons. First, since his direct contact with his subordinates during their working day is limited, there is little opportunity to do so. Second, the job performance of the patrol officer is such that "orders" are rarely required for completion. Most of what a patrol officer does during a tour of duty is undertaken either as the result of a radio dispatch or at his/her own initiative. The good supervisor will most likely control and direct the activities of his subordinates through the use of guidance or in giving proper instructions. The orders that exist in police organizations take the form of directives, policy and procedure, or general orders. It is through the development and issuance of these that the police administrator attempts to direct and control the work activities of members of the organization.

Unfortunately, this use of directives, policy and procedure, and general orders to control and direct the work activities of subordinates fails for several reasons. First, they are usually not structured or interpreted as guidelines, which they should be. They come to be interpreted by members of the organization as "rules" to be followed irrespective of the circumstances. They eliminate the flexibility of judgment and latitude of initiative required by the job of policing. In point of fact, it is highly probable that the typical patrol officer, if he/she is trying to do the job right, spends as much time covering up his/her violations of the "rules" as in complying with them.

Next, it is impossible to develop a set of directives, policy and procedure, or general orders that would adequately encompass all facets of the policing job, particularly at the patrol officer's level. It is senseless to attempt to develop "rules" to be applied to situations where the "rules" cannot be applied. Nonetheless, many police organizations continue to pursue the impossible dream of producing the all-encompassing book of "rules" in a variety of forms. As John Gardner, former Secretary of HEW, said, "The last act of a dying organization is to produce a better and more comprehensive version of the rule book."[21] If this is true, then some police organizations are about to expire.

The third reason for the failure of this approach is that it assumes that MacGregor's Theory X is correct in describing human beings in the work environment. Police officers, like most of us, are more effective in doing a job if they are led, not pushed. In terms of the law enforcement operation in our society today, it is both unreasonable, except in unusual cases, and impractical to expect the patrol officer to obey orders like his/her military counterpart.

Another military expectation is that the patrol officer will not have to display a wide range of initiative or discretion in performing his/her duties; this is totally unrealistic. It is impossible for the patrol officer to do the job without being able to exercise initiative and discretion, two qualities that are at the foundation of the job. Since directives, policy and procedure, and general orders cannot be formulated to cover all aspects of the job, the individual initiative and discretion of the officer must be relied on to deal effectively with the variety of situations faced each working day. Not only must the patrol officer display initiative and discretion in performing the job, but so must the first-line supervisor, the middle manager, and the police administrator. Without the ability to exercise initiative and discretion in doing the job we have the beginnings of a "police state." If one were to consider *only* this aspect of the paramilitary organization and management philosophy, it would be sufficient to cause the abandonment of it as a model for the police.

While the individual soldier is expected to function effectively as part of a larger unit, such is certainly not the case with the individual patrol officer. In the military, the individual soldier is deployed as part of a squad, platoon, company, battalion, etc., against the enemy. When the patrol officer is deployed to do the job, he/she is usually expected to do the job alone. The vast majority of police operational problems or tasks consist of those that can be handled by one or perhaps two people. Remember, too, that while the patrol officer is working, he/she is working with loose or infrequent supervision. This fact alone makes it essential that the officer be able to exercise initiative and discretion. Except in some unusual situations, e.g., riots, hostages, etc., the patrol officer never really works as part of a larger unit in the military sense. Officers are assigned to a platoon/shift/watch, but usually do not function in this environment in a collective or team sense in the organization.

The expectation that the individual soldier will perform tasks in a prescribed manner is certainly reasonable within the military environment, but such an expectation has no substantial application to the real world of police work. If initiative and discretion are required in doing the job, then the patrol officer can't operate "by the book" most of the time. As previously pointed out, the "book" is impossible to write anyway. The patrol officer cannot function effectively within a precisely prescribed set of task procedures most of the time, but he/she can function very effectively, if properly led with intelligently prepared guidelines. Give the officer the parameters within which to do the job and it will get done properly. This is not to say that the application of procedures has no place in law enforcement because it certainly has. Certain tasks can be performed most efficiently and effectively if set procedures are followed, e.g., administering first-aid, completing a report form, conducting a traffic stop, filling out a traffic ticket, etc. However, we get into serious trouble when this development of set procedures is carried too far, e.g., establishing a set procedure to universally apply to handling the domestic disturbance. Guidelines, yes; set procedure, no.

A final expectation, that the individual soldier will be uniform in his/her appearance, conduct, and behavior, only applies in part to the patrol officer, and it has an implication that has become a real obstacle to effective law enforcement. The implication is in the concept of a uniform appearance. One of the important considerations in the creation of the London Metropolitan Police was their appearance. To avoid any suspicion that they were a military police, the police uniform was carefully chosen. When the New Police appeared on the streets of London on September 29, 1829, they wore blue suits of civilian cut and top hats.[22] Thus was born the concept that police officers should wear distinctive uniforms. This is an altogether appropriate concept if one is concerned with the public being able to readily identify the police officer, especially if they are in need of one.

How could this traditional concept (and anyone who doesn't think it is traditional might try suggesting that uniformed officers discard their uniforms and wear blazers), that seems so reasonable, be an obstacle to effective policing? Simply because of the mind set that it has created, i.e., that patrol officers must accomplish their duties while wearing a distinctive uniform and usually riding in a distinctly marked vehicle. Not only have we adopted and made traditional how the officer should look, but we have adopted and made traditional how the officer should do the job. If such isn't the case, then how frequently do patrol officers conduct patrol activities in something other than their uniforms and marked patrol cars? The patrol officer can no more meet the responsibilities of the job by patrolling all the time in uniform in a marked vehicle than if he/she were to patrol all the time in plainclothes in an unmarked car. Both assumptions are equally ludicrous. What is required, if the job is to be done effectively, is flexibility: flexibility to deploy the patrol officer in a manner that most effectively deals with the situation being faced, whether it be in uniform, plainclothes, on a bicycle, foot patrol, surveillance, whatever it takes.

It is appropriate to expect that the conduct and behavior of the patrol officer be uniform within certain limitations. We should expect that the officer will present an example of honesty, objectivity, and compliance with the law. We should expect that the officer will be polite, courteous, patient, and tactful in interacting with the public. All this is reasonable but not as an absolute. By the very nature of the job and the variety of people involved, the exercise of initiative and discretion are once again called for. Interacting with a professional criminal calls for a type of behavior that is very difficult from that called for in taking a burglary report from a citizen. Arresting a felon is very different from issuing a traffic ticket. The expectations are different and so should be the conduct and behavior of the officer. If the patrol officer were to treat everyone encountered during the course of a tour of duty in exactly the same manner, the job would never get done. Although officers must recognize the basic rights and dignity of each person, they must also recognize that people are very different and that they must be dealt with individually.

As posed at the outset, the question really is not whether police agencies in the United States are organized along paramilitary lines, but why are they so organized. The most apparent answer is tradition. Since the emergence of the "modern" police era in 1829, police agencies have been organized along paramilitary lines.

Another possible answer relates to tradition, although the relationship may not be obvious. Those charged with running police agencies and those charged with the responsibility of supervising the work activities of the patrol officer are products of the paramilitary system. They have spent their careers learning to function within the system. Not only have they learned to function within and to manipulate the system, but the only role models they have to emulate are also products of the system. They quite simply don't know any other way to do the job of policing. Further, the vast majority of the training that law enforcement personnel receive, from the recruit level onward, is predicated on the assumption that they will be working within a paramilitary organization. Even if a supervisor should be trained in something other than the paramilitary management philosophy, he would probably be viewed as a pariah should he attempt to integrate what he had learned into organizational operations. Police organizations, because of their paramilitary structure and other factors, have tended to resist change more than other types of organizations. This resistance to change can be immense.

Unquestionably, many police administrators sincerely believe that the law enforcement agency can best meet its responsibilities within the community by operating as a paramilitary organization. The widespread existence of this organization seems to establish this. The sincerity of their belief notwithstanding, the facts should indicate to them otherwise. As the American police trace their origins to the London Metropolitan Police, we should return to them to determine how the effectiveness of the police should be evaluated. To quote from the Instructions and Police Orders, "The absence of crime will be considered the best proof of the complete efficiency of the Police."[23] The existence of this criterion is still in evidence today as most police departments have identified crime prevention as one of their major goals. Since the organizational structure and management philosophy have a direct influence on the ability of an organization to attain its goals, we should be able to evaluate the effectiveness of the paramilitary organizational model by looking at its operational efficiency, i.e., the impact of the police agency on crime. If the organization is properly organized, then it should manifest some degree of success in attaining its goals.

The continually and rapidly rising crime rate in the United States certainly rules out classifying the police operation as completely efficient. If there was some evidence of a sustained reduction in the crime rate, perhaps we could view the police operation as somewhat efficient. If the crime rate just stayed the same we could call the police operation marginally efficient. In the absence of either a sustained reduction or a maintenance of the status quo in the crime rate, however, the only term we can use to accurately describe the police operation is *inefficient*. If an organization is inefficient in attaining one of its major goals then one of the primary reasons, if not the single most important reason, has to be the work environment created by the structure and administrative/management philosophy of that organization. To continue to hold tenaciously to the belief that being a paramilitary organization is the most efficient way to run a police agency, or more accurately the best way to meet the policing responsibilities within the community, is, quite simply, to be totally out of touch with reality.

Others would hold that the paramilitary way is the best because, like it or not, MacGregor's Theory X accurately describes human beings. For the majority of us, however, Theory X neither describes us or the conditions under which we want our work efforts directed or supervised. MacGregor's Theory Y applies much more to most of us:

1. The expenditure of physical and mental effort in work is as natural as play or rest.
2. External control and threat of punishment are not the only means for bringing about effort toward organizational objectives. Man will exercise self-direction and self-control in the service of objectives to which he is committed.
3. Commitment to objectives is a function of the rewards associated with their achievement.
4. The average human being learns, under proper conditions, not only to accept but to seek responsibility.
5. The capacity to exercise a relatively high degree of imagination, ingenuity, and creativity in the solution of organizational problems is widely, not narrowly, distributed in the population.
6. Under the conditions of modern industrial life, the intellectual potentialities of the average human being are only partially utilized.[24]

Surely these expectations about humans are better than those of the paramilitary position.

Another possible answer to the "why" question could be that there is no other way to organize the police agency other than along paramilitary lines. This position is also against the facts. The military recognized some time ago that their traditional structure was inappropriate and incorporated some elements of contemporary management philosophy. Not only is it well established that there are other organizational models and management philosophies available to choose from, but the variety of choices is almost overwhelming.

One last reason which might explain why police agencies in the United States are models of the paramilitary organization is that although some police administrators see the futility in maintaining the paramilitary structure and management philosophy it represents, they are unwilling or afraid to implement the steps necessary to bring about change. As stated previously, resistance to change in a police organization can be immense. Only the most carefully thought out, researched and planned change process has the possibility of success. Courage of convictions is called for, but courage has always been one of the obvious attributes of the police officer. Some police departments are beginning to move away from the traditional paramilitary organizational structure with a variety of approaches such as "team" policing. These approaches do not always epitomize alternatives, but they are movements in the right direction. It would be much easier to forget about needed change and simply maintain the status quo if the following could be reconciled: the concept of law enforcement as a profession, a professional self-perception, a value system, a self-concept as a police administrator, the responsibilities of the police agency within the community, and the rapidly rising crime rate. To maintain the status quo, to stand still, also spells retrogression, for society is moving forward. Nothing remains the same except change.

After examining the possible positions in support of maintaining the paramilitary organizational model within law enforcement, we should look elsewhere to seek what justification can be found for adopting something other than the paramilitary model. In doing so, the negative implications just outlined should come to mind first. They are significant, but putting them aside for a moment, let us look at what some of the scholars in the field see as the limitations of the paramilitary model as it applies to policing:

> . . . the evidence that is available seems to indicate that the traditional police organization with a long scalar chain of command is dysfunctional.[25] Every effort should be made to ensure that the men and women in this new profession are products of psychologically healthy organizations which no longer employ the bureaucratic paramilitary management style that pervades police organizations today.[26]

> Certainly the educated police professional will not for long tolerate the present antiquated and authoritarian structures which neither allow for effective policing of the community, nor the personal growth of the officer.[27]

> Another complex of mischievous consequences arising out of the military bureaucracy relates to the paradoxical fact that while this kind of discipline ordinarily strengthens command authority, it has the opposite effect in police departments. This effect is insidious rather than apparent. Because police supervisors do not direct the activities of officers in any important sense, they are perceived as mere disciplinarians. Contrary to the army officer who is expected to lead his men into battle—even though he may never have the chance to do so—the analogously ranked police official is someone who can only do a great deal to his subordinates and very little for them. For this reason, supervisory personnel are often viewed by the line personnel with distrust and even with contempt.[28]

> The old police "orders" cannot cover the broad discretionary areas in which an individual officer's judgment has to be exercised. Many of the functions of the officer's job demand self-directed personnel.[29]

> There is an ample supply of evidence that the paramilitary style of management is the rule and not the exception. It is not the model for the proper motivation of the personnel who will be joining the police profession in the next 15 years.[30]

> The new police of the next two decades will need to employ positive rewards rather than the adverse controls that are frequently found in the paramilitary police organizations of today.[31]

> Many police departments defend the need to operate on a quasi-military basis. While military organizations have many superlative qualities, they also have several features which are counterproductive when applied to civilian, non-combat police situations.[32]

> . . . many large police departments seem to cling most tenaciously to the least productive aspects of the military model and resist military organizational techniques which might prove most beneficial.[33]

> By self-conception, organization and training, the police function is paramilitary. It virtually ignores the vital interpersonal relationship between police and the public.[34]

> Evidence is mounting that traditional police methods do not have a significant impact on crime.[35]

> Police managers have recognized for some time that there is an incredible amount of untapped and under-used talent in the lower ranks—talent that traditional, centralized methods of management tend to waste.[36]

> . . . the adherence to the quasi-military model by our police forces is largely a self-defeating pretense. Its sole effect is to create obstacles in the development of a professional police system.[37]

> The military managerial philosophy, which has been used by the police for the past 150 years, probably was inappropriate shortly after the New Police were formed, and, at least at the present time, it is completely inconsistent with the American concept of the police function.[38]

> The American counterpart to Peel's police, as it exists today, is not an effective alternative to the use of armed forces, hence the police have no reason to maintain the term paramilitary as a description of their organization.[39]

> . . . the police as a semimilitaristic bureaucracy have been largely ineffective.[40]

The rigid, military approach does not seem to fit the demanding, variable, discretion-laden nature of the police job today.[41]

The most serious roadblock preventing the use of enlightened management in the police is the erroneous concept that they are a paramilitary organization.[42]

One of the first changes (in reorganizing the police operation) would be the abandonment of the quasi-military structure of police organizations.[43]

Such recommendations (supporting paramilitary organizations) seem to run counter to findings regarding the complexity of police work and the necessity for individual discretion.[44]

. . . the [paramilitary] organization itself suffers from the vast human resource which is left untapped by the paramilitary form of decision-making and communication. Under this form of organization, it is precisely those members who are in direct contact with clients and who control implementation of policy who are eliminated from the process.[45]

For many years police organizations have imposed on their members a rigid set of narrowly defined standards which are always defended on the grounds that they are the proper and traditional way of doing things in police work. . . . this imposed dogma has stagnated meaningful change within American police departments since the 19th century.[46]

. . . as long as policemen will be treated like soldier-bureaucrats, they cannot be expected to develop professional acumen, nor value its possession.[47]

. . . [under a paramilitary organization] officers often become unwilling to fully utilize their discretionary powers, as a result, a more legalistic style tends to develop.[48]

The foregoing have not been presented as a test for enduring a long series of quotes, but in the hope that the end of an era of paramilitary police organization may soon be realized. These are not just a few "radicals" calling for change, but a consensus of rational, concerned, and committed professionals who earnestly seek the improvement of the police.

One final thought on the paramilitary organization and its impact upon the police operation: By their very nature the paramilitary organization and management philosophy dictate a reactive approach to policing. Primarily, this results because of the stifling of both initiative and discretion throughout the organization. The adoption of something other than a reactive approach to policing calls for the following, all of which are virtually impossible within the paramilitary framework:

1. The exercise of initiative and discretion within the organization, particularly at the supervisory and operational levels.
2. Control exerted through the use of guidance techniques rather than directives, orders, coercion, and the threat of punishment.
3. A communication process that is not only vertical in both directions, but horizontal as well.
4. The incentive to accomplish organizational objectives provided through the use of positive rewards.
5. Flexibility in operations, particularly at the supervisory and operational levels.
6. To the extent possible, a decentralized system of operations.
7. Decision-making at the lowest possible level in the organization.
8. A non-authoritarian style of leadership which emphasizes participative management.
9. An emphasis on the need and desirability of change in the organization.
10. The development and distribution of guidelines delineating organizational expectations.

Unless the organizational structure and management philosophy can be changed, we are locked into a reactive philosophy of policing, a philosophy that doesn't work. The rapidly rising crime rate is sufficient proof of that.

What type of organizational structure and management philosophy *is* best suited for the law enforcement agency if it is going to adequately meet its policing responsibilities in the community? Rather than attempt to label such an organization, or to recommend a specific model, it is probably more appropriate simply to list the desirable characteristics of an alternative organizational approach and management philosophy. Such a "shopping list" can offer suggestions that are most appropriate to a particular organization. It is important to consider in reviewing the following list that the primary task of the police administrator is to create a work environment that will bring together, as much as possible, the goals of both individuals and the organization insofar as common means will serve diverse ends.

1. A managerial style/philosophy reflecting MacGregor's Theory Y.
2. Organizational goals and objectives that are attainable, jointly established, and universally defined and understood.
3. Participative management to the fullest extent possible.

4. As few levels as possible within the organizational hierarchy.
5. Increased autonomy given to middle managers, supervisors, and operational level personnel.
6. Increased interaction with, and utilization of, other governmental resources.
7. A concept of power within the organization that is based upon the principles of reason and cooperation rather than threat or coercion.
8. Control exercised through the issuance of broad guidelines and the application of guidance techniques.
9. The adoption of a proactive philosophy toward law enforcement operations.
10. A recognition of the need for, and the opportunity to apply, initiative and discretion throughout the organization, particularly at the supervisory and operational levels.
11. A communications and planning process that seeks the widest possible variety of appropriate input.
12. To the fullest extent possible, a decentralized system of operations.
13. A viable and effective system for evaluation, research, and planning.
14. A willingness and ability to change with the changes in society and the community.

The reasons for the existence of the paramilitary organizational structure and management philosophy are understandable; however, it is not as easy to understand the resistance to change. Certainly, some traditions are worthwhile and needed for stability in our lives, but the paramilitary organization of the police agency isn't one of them. Law enforcement in the United States can no longer remain mired in the nineteenth century any more than we as citizens can. The process of change is inevitable in our lives just as it is in the police organization. Although, historically, law enforcement has been slow to adapt to changes in society, we can be instrumental in effecting a new image for law enforcement. It is time to take some positive steps toward really making law enforcement a profession today.

REFERENCES

1. A. C. German, Frank Day and Robert Gallati, *Introduction to Law Enforcement and Criminal Justice* (Springfield, Illinois: Charles C Thomas, 1970), p. 4.

2. Norman Clowers, *Patrolmen Patterns, Problems, and Procedures* (Springfield, Illinois: Charles C Thomas, 1962), p. 20.

3. James Waters and Sheree McGrath, *Introduction to Law Enforcement* (Columbus, Ohio: Charles E. Merrill, 1974), p. 7.

4. A. C. C. Ramsey, *Sir Robert Peel* (London: 1928), p. 87.

5. J. L. Lyman. "The Metropolitan Police Act of 1829," *The Journal of Criminal Law, Criminology and Police Science* (March 1964):151.

6. Ibid., p. 153.

7. Samuel Walker, "The Urban Police in American History: A Review of the Literature," *The Journal of Police Science and Administration* 4, no. 3:255.

8. Project Star. *The Impact of Social Trends on Crime and Criminal Justice* (Los Angeles: Anderson-Davis, 1976), p. 154.

9. Thomas Reppetto, "Bachelors on the Beat: Organizational Design of the Educated Police Department," *The Journal of Police Science and Administration* 7, no. 1 (1979):2.

10. Richard Staufenberger and Glen Stahl, *Police Personnel Administration* (North Scituate, Mass.: Duxbury Press, 1974), p. 153.

11. Calvin Swank, "The Police in 1980: Hypotheses for the Future," *The Journal of Police Science and Administration* 6, no. 4 (1974):297.

12. Gary Cordner, "Open and Closed Models of Police Organizations: Traditions, Dilemmas, and Practical Considerations," *The Journal of Police Science and Administration* 6, no. 1 (1978):30.

13. Richard Ward and Thomas Curran, *Police and Law Enforcement 1973–1974* (New York: A.M.S. Press, 1975), p. 119.

14. Victor Cizanckas and Donald Hanna, *Modern Police Management and Organization* (Englewood Cliffs, N.J.: Prentice-Hall, 1977), p. 36.

15. Project Star, p. 217.

16. Harlan Hahn, *Police in Urban Society* (Beverly Hills: Sage Publications, 1971), p. 267.

17. Stanley Vanagunas and James Elliott, *Administration of Police Organizations* (Boston: Allyn and Bacon, 1980), p. 273.

18. Georgette Sandler and Ellen Mintz, "Police Organizations: Their Changing Internal and External Relationships," *The Journal of Police Science and Administration* 2, no. 4 (1974):459.

19. Ibid.

20. Douglas MacGregor, *The Human Side of Enterprises* (New York: McGraw-Hill, 1960), p. 34.
21. *Innovation in Law Enforcement* (Washington, D.C.: Government Printing Office, 1973), p. 87.
22. Lyman, p. 152.
23. Ibid., p. 154.
24. MacGregor, p. 35.
25. James Munro, *Administrative Behavior and Police Organizations* (Cincinnati: W. H. Anderson, 1974), p. 180.
26. Staufenberger and Stahl, p. 98.
27. Munro, p. 184.
28. Egon Bittner, *The Functions of Police in Modern Society* (Chevy Chase, Md.: National Clearinghouse for Mental Health, 1970), p. 59.
29. V. A. Lubans and J. M. Edgar, *Policing by Objectives* (Hartford: Social Development Corp., 1979), p. 2.
30. Staufenberger and Stahl, p. 153.
31. Ibid., p. 164.
32. John Angell and Fontaine Hagedorn, "A Municipal System for Improving Local Police," *The Journal of Police Science and Administration* 4, no. 2 (1976):219.
33. Ibid.
34. Ramsey Clark, *Crime in America* (New York: Simon and Schuster, 1970), p. 140.
35. Angell and Hagedorn, p. 217.
36. Lubans and Edgar, p. 18.
37. Bittner, p. 47.
38. James Elliott, *The New Police* (Springfield, Illinois: Charles C Thomas, 1973), p. 57.
39. Ibid.
40. Joseph Fink and Lloyd Sealy, *The Community and the Police: Conflict or Cooperation?* (New York: John Wiley and Sons, 1967), p. 144.
41. Robert Sheehan and Gary Cordner, *Introduction to Police Administration* (Reading, Mass: Addison-Wesley, 1979), p. 8.
42. Elliott, p. 57.
43. *Police Practices and the Preservation of Civil Rights* (Washington, D.C.: Government Printing Office, 1978), p. 131.
44. Reppetto, p. 6.
45. Sandler and Mintz, p. 459.
46. Swank, p. 299.
47. Bittner, p. 61.
48. Cordner, p. 30.

Discipline in American Policing

Donal E. J. MacNamara

Police discipline is the most publicized, yet least researched area of American police administration and management. Certainly any analysis of police news (in newspapers, popular periodicals, on radio and television) will document the disproportionate coverage of charges of police corruption, brutality, discrimination against minorities, and violations of constitutional protections. The crimes and peccadilloes of police officers are heavily reported compared either to the attention given these matters by police textbooks and professional journals or the attention given by the media to similar infractions by physicians, lawyers, public officials, businessmen, and blue-collar workers. Perhaps this occupational inequity is understandable on the basis of the "man bites dog" yardstick of the media, but the reluctance of those who undertake to educate the law enforcement officers and commanders of the future to come to grips clearly and forcibly with this important problem of police management and community relations is obviously less defensible.

The very nature of the police officer's job (its responsibilities, powers, opportunities, temptations, dangers, pressures, and frustrations) creates disciplinary problems unlikely to develop in most other occupations. Acton tells us that "power corrupts," and the individual police officer at the very base of the command hierarchy exercises, for the most part unsupervised, a degree of direct power (discretion) over the lives, liberties, reputations, behaviors, and incomes of thousands of his fellow citizens unequaled by many with much more imposing titles and at much higher levels of the public and private power pyramids.

SOURCE: from *Modern Police Administration*, by Donald O. Schultz.

Alexander Pope tells us that "vice is a monster of so frightful mien . . . that to be hated needs but to be seen. Yet seen too oft, familiar with her face, We first endure, then pity, then embrace." One would have to scan the *Dictionary of Occupational Titles* at great length before discovering a calling so continually exposed as that of the police officer to man at his most vicious, immoral, dishonest, and unethical worst; and the police officer is not exposed to just a small and easily identifiable criminal element but all too frequently to public officials, professionals, and esteemed citizens of the community. Certainly no other occupation combines so maximally temptation with opportunity—and at least until very recently little risk of exposure and punishment.

Perhaps we should not ask ourselves why some police officers embrace vice but rather how it is that so many of our more than 500,000 full-time police officers remain faithful to their oaths of office and with courage and dedication protect the lives and properties of their more than 200 million fellow citizens.

There are to be sure two perspectives: the first, favored by most police or police-oriented writers, is the "bad apple" school which avers that the rogue cop is the atypical exception and that once we identify and eliminate him the problem is solved; the second perspective is from the increasing number of critics from outside the police establishment, with some support from mavericks within. These critics see a more systemic infection communicated to succeeding generations of police officers through a process of in-group socialization, with ostracism and sometimes harsher penalties visited on those whose consciences do not permit them to participate or to consent by their silence.

FRAGMENTATION OF AMERICAN POLICE

It might be best once again to emphasize the decentralized character of the American police operation. In no other country has the shibboleth of local autonomy and the fear of strong central authority combined to produce so anarchic a police structure. There are some 40,000 police agencies (many with only a handful of officers) on five governmental levels. They frequently have overlapping jurisdictions with no formal machinery to provide inspection and supervision, to mandate coordination, or even to promote cooperation.

Among these many agencies and departments, there are always some officers who maintain the highest of ethical standards and uncompromising disciplinary codes and others in whom brutality, corruption, discrimination, and job-shirking are minor. Still others (and not always just the highly publicized big-city forces) are so undisciplined, standards are so low, and supervision is so lax that they are involved in scandals. They often create headlines just as the participants in a previous scandal are being transported to the penitentiary (or in all too many cases drawing the first pension checks of an ill-earned retirement).

No specific agencies, bureaus, or departments will be mentioned in this essay, nor will any invidious comparisons between federal and state levels, sheriffs and county police, or big-city and small-town law enforcement be attempted. There are outstanding police agencies at all levels, of all sizes, and in all geographical regions of the country, and there is blame enough and to spare for police agencies in each category which have either throughout their history—or more frequently, for limited periods—failed to measure up to the standards of police conduct which both their fellow police officers and the citizenry have every right to expect.

APPROACHES TO POLICE DISCIPLINE

An analysis of the infrequent discussions of police disciplinary problems in the professional literature reveals three major approaches to discipline: the *preventive*, the *positive*, and the *punitive*.

Preventive discipline emphasizes (1) the recruitment and probationary processes to prevent the appointment or tenuring of potentially troublesome officers, (2) alert supervision to detect difficulties in time so that they can be dealt with before they reach unmanageable proportions, and (3) the elimination of as many temptations and opportunities as possible. Included among the preventive disciplinary techniques are: intensive character and background investigations of recruits; polygraph and psychiatric screening; relatively long probationary periods under intensive supervision with rigorously administered separation proceedings against those who fail to measure up; and deterrent attention during recruit training to the ethical code and the punitive consequences of violations. Douglas Kelley and others have documented that a great number of the disciplinary infractions involve a relatively small percentage of the total police work force. Early identification and elimination of those unsuited for police duties and responsibilities should reduce the overall disciplinary problem to more manageable proportions. In the past decade, partly as the result of efforts to open police ranks to a greater number of minority officers (a goal with which I am in complete sympathy), the effective use of the recruitment and probationary processes to prevent the appointment and tenuring of officers with criminal records, emotional difficulties, deviant lifestyles and other potentially troublesome characteristics has been curtailed—and, as we shall see, their later elimination from police agencies even after serious overt misbehavior has become much more difficult.

Positive discipline emphasizes training, leadership, example, development of esprit de corps, professionalism and a system of rewards and recognition. Modeled on the military approach, it entails command interest in the morale and well-being of the force (including their pay and fringe benefits, working conditions, and family welfare) and highly publicized incentives for valued behavior (commendations, medals, extra days off, desirable assignments, and promotions). Special attention is given to the example (appearance and behavior) set by supervisory and command officers and to their training in leadership techniques. Opportunity and encouragement (salary increments, additional promotion credits, time off, and tuition reimbursements) are provided for officers seeking college degrees, and police personnel are encouraged to identify themselves as professionals—not workers. While there is little doubt that the *positive* approach has many values both to the agency and the individual officers (and indeed to the community), it is equally obvious that over reliance on this optimistic view of human reaction to good leadership, good example and good treatment rests on undemonstrated psychological hypotheses and may open a department to serious misbehavior by a perhaps small minority of officers who would interpret such a positive disciplinary emphasis as naiveté or command weakness.

Punitive discipline is by far the most widespread disciplinary approach. Here, there is an emphasis on rules and regulations, on attempts to surprise (or even entrap) officers in violations, on intensive investigation of complaints, and on the imposition of penalties for disvalued and nonconforming behaviors. Although only a few police administrators publicly acknowledge that this is their principal disciplinary model, examination of many administrators' procedures and records—and interviews with their police officers and union delegates—make abundantly clear the predominance of the punitive approach to the discipline of police personnel. Comparison of the number of commendations with the number of charges and penalties recorded in a department over a one- or two-year period will convincingly demonstrate its dependence on negative, punitive disciplinary measures.

DISCIPLINARY RESPONSIBILITY OF THE POLICE ADMINISTRATOR

The chief executive of a law enforcement agency is as responsible for its discipline as for its effectiveness; the two are related but neither is synonymous nor wholly interrelated. This is not to say that every police administrator is accorded either the legal authority, the political support, or the necessary facilities to effectively carry out his disciplinary responsibilities. Civil service laws, veterans' rights, police unions, political interference, public pressures and, paradoxically, the *occasional* opposition of the communications media at times severely limit his capacity to discipline or remove undesirable officers; and criminal charges all too frequently fail for want of aggressive prosecution, technical difficulties with the proofs, or overly sympathetic juries whose members will later decry police dishonesty.

Police administrators often sit uneasily atop pressure boilers with no warning or cut-off valves. Although they have great need for information as to what is going on in the ranks below, they are frequently last to know of a developing scandal, learning of it only when the headlines blazon a grand jury investigation and their jobs and reputations are in jeopardy.

While in some instances the police chief is the victim of a conspiracy of silence among his subordinates, more frequently, he is self-victimized, neither seeking nor welcoming unpleasant information. Many chiefs neither read the papers nor have a staff aide abstract news relating to their departments; others do not cultivate contacts either with their colleagues in the criminal justice system or with those knowledgeable about community affairs; some cut themselves off from communication with their subordinate officers; and others unfortunately are themselves part of the problem because they are brutal, corrupt, and contemptuous of the Constitution, court decisions, and legislative fiats.

POLICE DISCIPLINARY OFFENSES

The components of the police disciplinary problem might well be classified into four general categories:

1. Offenses committed by an officer in a personal, nonjob-related capacity (wife-beating, assaulting a neighbor, drunken driving, adultery, nonpayment of debts, smoking marijuana, or shoplifting);
2. Administrative offenses (late report, drunk on duty, off post, improper uniform, disrespect to a superior);
3. Excess of zeal (use of excessive force, warrantless search or seizure, coercive interrogation, illegal detention—where no malice or personal profit was involved);
4. Abuse of police status (extortion, prejudiced actions against minorities, deliberate false arrest or false charges, faked evidence, perjury, selling, destroying, or divulging police information).

There are some who hold that an officer's nonjob-related personal offenses are not cognizable by the police disciplinary system, but maturer reflection on the disproportional publicity accorded a police officer's misdemeanor or felony and the resultant negative impact on the good name of the department and profession should convince us that a police agency, not unlike the military services, must insist on a standard of personal conduct somewhat higher than that perhaps required of a worker in private industry—or a public employee not empowered to enforce the laws against his fellow citizens.

A much more difficult disciplinary problem to deal with concerns the tradition of "professional courtesy," which is either limited to members of the local department or extended rather broadly to all who carry police identification. While such "courtesy" is usually restricted to minor violations (traffic offenses, drunkenness, disorderly conduct), in some cases it is rationalized as necessary to maintain good interdepartmental working relationships. It should be obvious that such preferential treatment of police officer violations is illegal, illogical, unprofessional, and likely to exacerbate police–community irritations.

Violations of departmental rules constitute by far the greatest number of disciplinary infractions (in some departments almost 100 percent). These are usually handled within the chain of command, and only in unusual circumstances do they arouse widespread public interest. However, failure to monitor this important disciplinary area will soon produce a sloppy, inefficient, undependable force with low morale, no sense of professional pride, and a vulnerability to much more serious infractions.

Excess-of-zeal offenses can result from many different causes: inadequate training and supervision; undue pressure on officers for speedy results; pressure to meet quotas; improper personnel assignments; a perception among officers that administrators and commanders are giving only lip service to the constitutional limitations on police procedures; and occasionally an overly judgmental, moralistic, almost missionary zeal (or highly competitive instinct) in a police officer. While policemen must necessarily be encouraged to zealously pursue their sworn duties to enforce the laws, apprehend offenders, control disorders, and faithfully fulfill their many responsibilities, commanders must equally insist that officers scrupulously observe the limitations imposed on their choice of methods and procedures by the Constitution, the legislature, the courts, and the agency's policies—even if such limitations are in their opinion undesirable, unnecessary, unwise, or make the officer's tasks more dangerous, difficult, and time-consuming. When excessive zeal is repeatedly and selectively utilized against persons of a particular minority (e.g., ethnic, ideological, or lifestyle groups) to the extent that it is demonstrably a manifestation of an officer's bias or prejudice against that minority, the offense must be reclassified into the much more serious "abuse of police status" category of disciplinary infractions.

Abuse-of-police-status offenses constitute the most serious disciplinary problem because they are subversive of the essential and fundamental mores of the police service. There should be little doubt or controversy as to the need for prompt, rigorous disciplinary action in the following offenses by law enforcement officers: shakedowns of numbers runners, bookies, dope pushers, afterhours clubs, peddlers, pimps, and prostitutes; operation of systematic "pads" to give protection to continuing illegal activities; cooperation with organized crime by destroying records, divulging information, and providing warnings of impending raids or arrests; changing testimony in criminal prosecutions; maliciously framing innocent persons or protecting guilty ones; and burglarizing premises on their patrol beats instead of protecting property.

BRUTALITY, CORRUPTION, AND DISCRIMINATION

The three serious charges repeatedly leveled against police officers and/or agencies over the past decades might well be subsumed under this heading—with perhaps, as regards certain agencies, the additional allegation of arrogant invasion of constitutional protections. That many of these charges are self-serving, exaggerated, false, even malicious, is demonstrable. That all too many have been amply documented by official investigations which resulted in criminal penalties and civil damages is equally incontestable.

The overuse of force (or the use of any force in situations not authorized by law), discriminatory actions against minorities, and invasions of constitutionally protected rights are often interrelated and stem in the opinion of some commentators from identifiable police attitudes and ideologies. Without attempting to psychoanalyze or stigmatize so large, so varied, and on the whole so competent and dedicated an occupational grouping, some studies have indicated that police, as compared to other occupational cohorts, tend to be more conformist and conservative, more judgmental and moralistic, more intolerant of deviation and more resistant to change than many if not most of those with whom they at times come into adversary contact (civil rights and antiwar demonstrators, hippies and college students, rock fans and nude bathers, gay liberationists, and left-wing ideologues). They also have been found to share to a greater or lesser extent the antiminority prejudices of the lower middle-class blue-collar families from which so many of them originate. Thus oriented, they are easily irritated and angered by the often deliberately provocative conduct of their adversaries. The police at times overreact physically.

This tendency to physical overreaction to stress situations is complicated by the fact that, unlike the military, most police officers are neither experienced in nor trained for small unit tactics in controlling crowds, mobs, demonstrators, pickets, sit-ins, passive resisters, and/or mutinous prisoners. Nor are they used to acting under verbal commands from on-the-scene superior officers. The police officer's experience is in acting alone or with a long-time partner without supervision; confronted with a hostile crowd, and sometimes incompetently commanded by superior officers not personally known to him (or perhaps from another police agency), he quite humanly at times out of anger, hate, frustration, and perhaps even fear, lashes out with fists or night stick against those whom he perceives as his tormentors, his enemies. With a few notorious exceptions in recent decades, his violent reaction has rarely included the misuse of firearms.

Corruption, however, is quite different, both as to the type of police likely to be involved and as to the circumstances in which it flourishes. Here, the adversary confrontation between the forces of social protection and the enemies of society breaks down, and an unholy alliance between good and evil is negotiated. The officers involved may be inherently dishonest (we have no validated screening devices for identifying such a character weakness in prospective police recruits), or they may have developed what might be called a situational dishonesty stemming from a negative socialization by their police peers into the mysterious distinction between "clean" and "dirty" graft. They may be following the herd instinct ("everybody does it"), or they may be participating because they fear peer pressure, the threat of ostracism, or, worse, being identified as a stooge for the bosses. Or they may have over the years become cynical of society's commitment to honesty, having witnessed the "best and the brightest" grab with impunity; and they may have noted the few rewards for resisting the temptation of immediate and sometimes very lush payments for breaking one's oath of office. Recurrent disclosures of widespread corruption in police agencies of all sizes and in all areas have, moreover, not been consistently followed up with policies and procedures designed to eliminate this evil.

SOURCES OF COMPLAINTS AND AGENCY ATTITUDES TOWARD COMPLAINANTS

Complaints of police misconduct may be initiated by widely divergent sources, and the source of the complaint rather than its nature or its seriousness frequently influences agency response, as does with some lesser frequency the identity or rank of the officer complained of. One might classify sources as *internal* (police supervisors, commanders, special inspectional or disciplinary control units, and, very rarely, fellow officers) or *external* (the victim of the abuse complained of, pressure groups, politicians or public office holders, civil liberties organizations, journalists, prosecutors and other officers of the criminal justice system, and occasionally disinterested citizens who claim to have witnessed the misconduct). By far, the greatest number of disciplinary actions are initiated by police superior officers who have observed misconduct on the part of a subordinate or who have had a violation of the rules, regulations, or procedures brought to their attention. Analysis of complaint files (where they exist) indicates only a minimal number of external complaints, yet it is these complaints which all too frequently elicit an aggressively hostile agency response which might be characterized as harassment of the complainant rather than investigation of the complaint.

It is axiomatic that some complainants (individual and organizational) are antipolice or out to "get" an individual police officer, that some politicians and pressure groups seek publicity and advantage in making false or exaggerated charges, and that sensational newspapers disproportionately headline undocumented and unproved scandals. However, these abuses do not justify negative agency response. The ulterior motivations of the complainant are less important than the substance of the complaint.

DEPARTMENTAL HANDLING OF COMPLAINTS

Every complaint, from whatever source, should be *acknowledged, recorded, investigated, reported on*, and if found valid, *acted on* to prevent reoccurrence. Few agencies until recent years maintained satisfactory complaint and disciplinary files . . . complaints were often ignored, "lost," bucked from one unit to another with little possibility of fixing responsibility. Annual reports contained inadequate information for either chronological or cross-departmental disciplinary comparisons, and the individual files of police personnel often were so cavalierly secured that information about disciplinary matters could easily be altered or removed.

I devised a very simple disciplinary record system many years ago. It is now employed by many smaller police departments, with some larger departments adapting it to fit their more complex needs. Basically, it consists of three things. There is a *complainant's file card* (a 5 × 8 card made up for each complaint source, i.e., individual, organizational, or anonymous) recording the following in columnar format:

Date of complaint
Complainant's name, address, and identifying material
Officer or unit being complained about
Date acknowledged
Nature of the complaint (brutality, shakedown, drunk on duty)
File number assigned
Investigating officer
Result of investigation (unfounded, upheld, etc.)
Disposition

There is also an *officer's* or *unit disciplinary record card* (also in columnar format) which will show the following at a glance:

Number and type of complaints against the officer
Identity of the complainants
Disposition in each case

The third record is an *offense record card* showing the following for each type of offense (discrimination, late report, unnecessary use of firearm, etc.):

Number of such complaints
Repeat complainants
Repeat offenders
Level of validity (founded complaints) for or against each

Analysis annually would clearly identify complainants who repeatedly level false or exaggerated charges or who are out to crucify an individual officer. It would also reveal which officers should be retrained, reassigned, or separated from the department, and which areas require intensified command and supervisory attention. Agency policy should provide for a "statute of limitations" so that after an appropriate period (perhaps three to five years) complaints might be removed from an officer's disciplinary record.

"QUIS CUSTODIET IPSOS CUSTODES?"—JUVENAL*

While the departmental or agency chain of command is usually quite adequate and efficient in investigating and processing internal complaints of minor misconduct, a more formal system and more specialized mechanisms have proved necessary to ferret out corruption and to process complaints of serious misconduct. Many large agencies have set up internal security or intelligence units to police their police officers; some have appointed carefully selected integrity officers to report serious offenses by officers within their

* Who watches the watchman? Who polices the police?

units (and a few departments have encouraged turnarounds by apprehended rogue police officers who escape severe punishment by informing on their fellow officers). In other areas the processing of certain types of complaints has been turned over to special prosecutors, grand juries, crime commissions, and/or civilian complaint units. No method has proved so demonstrably successful as to merit a recommendation for general acceptance. Indeed, the personality, integrity, determination, and ability of the agency head, rather than the organizational structure of the tactics employed, seem to be the key to the elimination of abuses.

RIGHTS OF POLICE OFFICER DEFENDANTS IN DISCIPLINARY CASES

The emergence of strong police organizations (unions in fact if not in name) and the cumulative effect of judicial reviews of administrative disciplinary proceedings have eliminated the grosser violations of due process which until a decade ago characterized the trials of police officer defendants. Today, by law or by policy, the police officer charged with an offense is entitled to timely, written notice specifically setting forth the charges of misconduct. He may be represented by counsel. He is entitled to process for securing witnesses and records necessary for his defense. He may cross-examine the complainant and witnesses against him (even impute discreditable motives or actions on the part of a superior officer). He is entitled to a record of the proceedings and to an avenue of appeal from its determinations. Summary dismissals and punishments are now seldom encountered, and the tribunal (whether a trial commissioner or administrative judge, a civil service panel or the public safety committee of the municipal legislature, a court-martial-type board of superior officers, or a specially appointed hearing officer) is well aware that the record will have to support the findings and disposition.

Nevertheless, there are many problems which continue to cause difficulty. Space precludes consideration of all of them but certainly several demand attention:

Suspension of police officer defendants
Double jeopardy
Impact of administrative proceedings on possible civil action against either the governmental unit or the individual officer
Waiver of immunity
Employment of the polygraph or psychological stress evaluator

Suspension of a police officer against whom serious charges have been brought seems at first consideration to be proper and necessary. Yet, maturer consideration raises some questions. Suspending a police officer increases the burdens on his fellow officers and, if the suspension is without pay, punishes his family. If the suspension is prolonged (and even administrative proceedings can take weeks or months), not only are these conditions exacerbated, but should he be exonerated, the police officer will have to be paid in full for all the period of his suspension. Depending on the nature of the charges and the potential for separating the defendant officer from the force, it might be better to find some assignment for him, pending the final disposition of his case, which will not bring him into direct contact with the public nor entail the employment of his police authority.

Should the nature of the charges indicate that the defendant officer might face indictment and a criminal trial, as well as administrative disciplinary action, some jurisdictions postpone the latter until final disposition of the case in the criminal justice system, rationalizing that a finding of guilt in the disciplinary hearing might prejudice the officer's defense in the criminal trial. It should be quite clear that separate determination of the administrative charges and the criminal indictment (even if they grow out of the same alleged misconduct) does not constitute double jeopardy, and it seems quite clear to me that the agency should process its case independently and with dispatch. A finding of guilt by the agency does not bind the criminal court, nor does an acquittal in court preclude agency disciplinary action.

Much the same reasoning applies to situations when either the municipality or the defendant-officer faces the prospect of civil action for damages growing out of the alleged misconduct. Civil trials in many jurisdictions take even longer than criminal court cases and with appeals may go on for years. To delay resolution of administrative disciplinary charges until final disposition in such a case would entail either long-term suspension of the officer, months or even years of limited duty assignment, or dismissal of the complaint for violation of the speedy-trial requirement.

Some jurisdictions require public employees against whom charges have been brought to waive immunity at least insofar as their testimony (before a grand jury or other official investigating commission) relates to their official duties. Such jurisdictions provide for dismissal of officers who refuse to sign a waiver. While there is some dispute as to the constitutionality of such involuntary waivers, there is a strong case in law, logic, and necessity for retaining the requirement that a public officer must answer before any lawful tribunal for his stewardship or forfeit his public office or employment. This can be distinguished from the compulsory self-incrimination prohibited by the Constitution in criminal cases.

Many law enforcement agencies employ instrumental detection of deception in connection with their investigations of criminal charges against nonpolice officers. Yet, there is strong opposition to employing either the polygraph or the psychological stress evaluator to assist in determining whether a police officer took a bribe, committed perjury, or engaged in other alleged misconduct. Without addressing the scientific arguments as to the validity of instrumental detection or the legal arguments as to its admissibility in criminal trials, I must confess a strong leaning toward a contractual waiver which would require as a condition of continued employment in a police agency submission to polygraph interrogation, under full safeguards, in specifically designated cases of serious misconduct. The imperatives of the public good and of the agency's needs in such cases seem to me superior to the alleged malefactor's individual interests.

PENALTIES FOR OFFICERS ADJUDICATED GUILTY

The penalties which may be imposed on law enforcement officers adjudicated guilty in an administrative disciplinary proceeding range from dismissal to an admonition or reprimand. Among the interpolated penalties are monetary fines (in a recent case as high as $30,000), demotion (seldom used), suspension without pay for definite periods, disciplinary transfers (a questionable penalty with grave administrative consequences), forced retirement or resignation, removal from promotion consideration, and extra duty (assignment to work on holidays or loss of vacation). Penalties should, of course, be proportionate to the offense and should, as Beccaria tells us, be swift, certain, and consistent. They should, however, also have some positive attributes, either deterring reoccurrence of the offense by the defendant-officer or by the example of his punishment deterring others. Sentencing authorities should consider, either as alternatives or as additions to the penalty imposed, recommending counselling (particularly in cases related to alcohol abuse or family troubles), retraining (especially in cases of excessive zeal or ignorance of proper procedures or techniques), restitution (in cases involving injury, property damage, or monetary loss growing out of the officer's misconduct), special supervision, and/or a period of special probation. By and large, despite the stereotype of the tough police administrator and the general police paranoid perception of themselves as a persecuted minority, penalties in police disciplinary procedures are heavily skewed to the lenient end of the punishment spectrum.

CONCLUDING REMARKS

Although the decades from August Vollmer through J. Edgar Hoover and O. W. Wilson to Pat Murphy, Ed Davis, Frank Rizzo, and Tony Bouza have produced reams of rhetoric on police professionalism, codes of police ethics, tens of thousands of college-educated law enforcement officers, judicial and legislative limitations on the police abuses of the past, and an alert and intelligent public appreciation of the need for a controlled and disciplined police, the reality is that the battle is far from won. Police officers are human beings subject to the weaknesses inherent in the human condition. They are subjected to strong temptations and enjoy unique opportunities to succumb. Their work requires them to deal with criminals, and their authority induces those who wish to cut corners or operate outside the law to attempt to purchase favorable treatment. They observe others of higher station, with greater perquisites (the white-collar criminals) stealing millions with impunity; and they frequently see the moral lapses of those who hypocritically condemn what seem to the police either necessary circumventions of the law (wiretapping, excessive force, or warrantless searches) or minor peccadilloes (sharing the profits of the bookmaker, numbers runner, or afterhours bar). They also see the many unnecessary and unenforceable laws enacted by legislators anxious to win votes and the resistance of pressure groups to decriminalizing conduct which the mores and folkways of the society have decreed acceptable. In many jurisdictions they also experience public hostility and noncooperation, neglect of their legitimate needs for increased pay and fringe benefits, little recognition of their courageous and dedicated service, and overreaction to their failings; and within their own agencies, preferment and promotion are given to those whom they know to be untrue to the ethics of the profession.

No approach to police discipline and the elimination of abuses of police authority will be effective if it concentrates on sporadic investigations, emphasizes changes in organizational patterns and personnel assignments, makes an example of a dozen or a score of low-ranking scapegoats, and ignores the very real truth that a police agency stems from a societal milieu. The police agency is in itself a microcosm of that society and is unlikely to ever exhibit a higher standard of dedication, ethics, morals, and professionalism than is the mode for the population it controls and protects.

4

POLICE VALUES AND CULTURE

Police, who have already been socialized and shaped in one society, are required to adapt to a new world when they enter the police culture. When former stabilized values and the values of their new police world coincide, there is no conflict and consequently no problem. When the old style of life runs counter to the imperatives of their new culture, there is a need for resolution of the resultant conflict. The nature of the resolution will in large measure depend on such variables as the degree of commitment one has to the old or new, the age of entry for socialization into the new culture, the personality resistance or flexibility of the individual, and the strength of the value in the total hierarchy of values of the police culture.

The special structural qualities of the police culture include: the uniform, ceremonials, etiquette, power and authority, a unique set of duties, strong kinship and solidarity among police officers, a sense of isolation from the rest of the community and other occupations, and a perception of common hazards and dangers that are shared by all police officers. This combination endows the police organization with an irresistible psychological power, so that most officers internalize the traditional values of the police culture.

Many of these values have been identified by scholars. There is wide agreement that the basic traits of the police culture are:

1. Respect for power and authority.
2. Secrecy, especially in those matters where it may affect their colleagues and organization.
3. Loyalty to the organization even when it may mean compromises of all kinds.
4. A sense of minority group status and all that implies.
5. Political conservatism.
6. A broad cynicism that is rationalized in terms of knowing the real world and "what the score is."
7. Yet in spite of the cynicism there is an unquestioning belief in and loyalty to country, flag, family, and religion; an unswerving conviction that police do an exemplary job in combating crime, but are hamstrung by judges, courts, and corrections officials; an assumption that the trouble with America is lack of respect for the law, police, and constituted authority; and an associated doctrine that the cause of crime and related social problems is a widespread permissiveness.

As the police system changes, the values undergo transformation. With the unprecedented spurt in growth of the phenomenon of the college-educated police officer comes a questioning and reappraisal of police values. These individuals are more willing and better prepared to challenge the older police values, which are seen as somewhat narrow in scope and not necessarily valid in many instances. Education, higher salaries, and fringe benefits have moved many police officers well into middle-class status. Their immersion in a new class position causes them to be receptive to a competing set of values that is at odds with a number of the traditional police values. Finally, the introduction in substantial numbers of minority groups, including women, to the police world has already had and will continue to have an impact on police culture.

Bob Patrick

Studs Terkel

Harold's son. He is thirty-three, married, and has a child. He has been a member of the city police force for six years. For the past three years he has been an emergency service patrolman.

"Emergency service is like a rescue squad. You respond to any call, any incident: a man under a train, trapped in an auto, bridge jumpers, psychos, guys that murdered people and barricaded themselves in. We go in and get these people out. It is sometimes a little too exciting. I felt like I wasn't gonna come home on two incidents."

He finished among the highest in his class and at the police academy, though he was "eleven years out of high school." Most of his colleagues were twenty-one, twenty-two. "I always wanted to be with the city. I felt that was the best job in the world. If I wasn't a cop, see, I don't think I could be anything else. Oh, maybe a truckdriver."

I got assigned to foot patrolman in Bedford-Stuyvesant. I never knew where Bedford-Stuyvesant was. I heard it was a low, poverty-stricken area, and it was a name that people feared. It's black. Something like Harlem, even worse. Harlem was where colored people actually grew up. But Bedford-Stuyvesant is where colored people migrated from Harlem or from North Carolina. They were a tougher class of people.

Myself and two friends from the neighborhood went there. We packed a lunch because we never really ventured outside the neighborhood. We met that morning about six o'clock. We had to be in roll call by eight. We got there a quarter after six. We couldn't believe it was so close. We laughed like hell because this is our neighborhood, more or less. We were like on the outskirts of our precinct. It was only ten minutes from my house.

When we got our orders, everybody said, "Oh wow, forget it." One guy thought he was going there, we had to chase him up three stories to tell him we're only kidding. He was ready to turn in his badge. Great fear, that was a danger area.

I was scared. Most people at Bedford-Stuyvesant were unemployed, mostly welfare, and they more or less didn't care too much for the police. The tour I feared most was four to twelve on a Friday or Saturday night. I'm not a drinker, I never drank, but I'd stop off at a bar over here and have a few beers just to get keyed up enough to put up with the problems we knew we were gonna come up against.

I would argue face to face with these people that I knew had their problems, too. But it's hard to use selective enforcement with 'em. Then get off at midnight and still feel nervous about it. And go for another few drinks and go home and I'd fall right to sleep. Two or three beers and I would calm down and feel like a husband again with the family at home.

I rode with a colored guy quite a few times. They would put you in a radio car and you'd be working with an old-timer. One of the calls we went on was a baby in convulsions, stopped breathing. The elevator was out of order and we ran up eight flights of stairs. This was a colored baby. It was blue. I had taken the baby from the aunt and my partner and I rushed down the stairs with the mother. In the radio car I gave the baby mouth to mouth resuscitation. The baby had regurgitated and started breathing again. The doctor at the hospital said whatever it was, we had gotten it up.

The sergeant wanted to write it up because of the problem we were having in the area. For a white cop

SOURCE: From *Working: People Talk about What They Do All Day and How They Feel about What They Do*, by Studs Terkel. New York: Random House, 1975, pp. 739–748.

doin' what I did. But I didn't want it. I said I would do it for anybody, regardless of black or white. They wrote it up and gave me a citation. The guys from the precinct was kidding me that I was now integrated. The mother had said she was willing to even change the baby's name to Robert after what I did.

The guy I worked with had more time on the job than I did. When we went on a family dispute, he would do all the talking. I got the impression that they were more aggressive than we were, the people we were tryin' to settle the dispute with. A husband and wife fight or a boyfriend and a husband. Most of the time you have to separate 'em. "You take the wife into the room and I'll take the husband into the other room." I looked up to my partner on the way he settled disputes. It was very quick and he knew what he was doing.

I've been shot. The only thing I haven't been in Bedford-Stuyvesant is stabbed. I've been spit at. I've been hit with bottles, rocks, bricks, Molotov cocktails, cherry bombs in my eye . . . I've gotten in disputes where I've had 10-13s called on me. That would be to assist the patrolman on the corner. Called by black people to help me against other black people.

After three years at Bedford-Stuyvesant he was assigned to the emergency service patrol. "Our truck is a $55,000 truck and it's maybe $150,000 in equipment. We have shotguns, we have sniper rifles, we have tear gas, bullet-proof vests, we have nets for jumpers, we have Morrissey belts for the patrolman to hold himself in when he gets up on a bridge, we have Kelly tools to pry out trapped people, we give oxygen . . ."

Fifty to seventy-five percent of our calls are for oxygen. I had people that were pronounced DOA by a doctor—dead on arrival. We have resuscitated them. I had brought him back. The man had lived for eight hours after I had brought him back. The doctor was flabbergasted. He had written letters on it and thought we were the greatest rescue team in New York City. We give oxygen until the arrival of the ambulance. Most of the time we beat the ambulance.

We set up a net for jumpers. We caught a person jumping from twenty-three stories in Manhattan. It musta looked like a postage stamp to him. We caught a girl from a high school four stories high. If it saves one life, it's worth it, this net.

A young man was out on a ledge on a six-story building. He was a mental patient. We try to get a close friend to talk to him, a girl friend, a priest, a guy from the old baseball team . . . Then you start talkin' to him. You talk to him as long as you can. A lot of times they kid and laugh with you—until you get too close. Then they'll tell you, "Stop right where you are or I'll jump." You try to be his friend. Sometimes you take off the police shirt to make him believe you're just a citizen. A lot of people don't like the uniform.

You straddle the wall. You use a Morrissey belt, tie it around with a line your partner holds. Sometimes you jump from a ledge and come right up in front of the jumper to trap him. But a lot of times they'll jump if they spot you. You try to be as cautious as possible. It's a life . . .

Sometimes you have eleven jobs in one night. I had to shoot a vicious dog in the street. The kids would curse me for doin' it. The dog was foaming at the mouth and snapping at everybody. We come behind him and put three bullets in his head. You want to get the kids outa there. He sees the cop shooting a dog, he's not gonna like the cop.

We get some terrible collisions. The cars are absolutely like accordions. The first week we had a head-on collision on a parkway. I was just passing by when it happened and we jumped out. There were parents in there and a girl and a boy about six years old. I carried the girl out. She had no face. Then we carried out the parents. The father had lived until we jacked him out and he had collapsed. The whole family was DOA. It happens twenty-four hours a day. If emergency's gonna be like this, I'd rather go back to Bedford-Stuyvesant.

The next day I read in the papers they were both boys, but had mod haircuts. You look across the breakfast table and see your son. My wife plenty times asked me, "How can you do that? How can you go under a train with a person that's severed the legs off, come home and eat breakfast, and feel . . . ?" That's what I'm waiting for: when I can go home and not feel anything for my family. See, I have to feel.

A patrolman will call you for a guy that's DOA for a month. He hanged himself. I'm cuttin' him down. You're dancing to get out of the way of the maggots. I caught myself dancing in the middle of the livingroom, trying to get a ring off a DOA for a month, while the maggots are jumping all over my pants. I just put the damn pants on, brand-new, dry cleaned. I go back to the precinct and still itch and jump in the shower.

And to go under a train and the guy sealed his body to the wheel because of the heat from the third rail.

And you know you're gonna drop him into the bag. A sixteen-year-old kid gets his hand caught in a meat grinder. His hand was comin' out in front. And he asks us not to tell his mother. A surgeon pukes on the job and tells you to do it.

One time we had a guy trapped between the platform and the train. His body was below, his head was above. He was talking to the doctor. He had a couple of kids home. In order to get him out we had to use a Z-bar, to jack the train away from the platform. The doctor said, "The minute you jack this train away from the platform, he's gonna go." He was talkin' and smokin' with us for about fifteen minutes. The minute we jacked, he was gone. (Snaps fingers.) I couldn't believe I could snuff out life, just like that. We just jacked this thing away and his life. And to give him a cigarette before it happened was even worse.

While you're en route to the job, to build yourself up, you say, This is part of the job that has to be done. Somebody's gotta do it. After this, there couldn't be nothing worse. No other job's gonna be as bad as this one. And another job comes up worse. Eventually you get used to what you're doin'.

Homicides are bad. I seen the medical examiner put his finger into seventeen knife wounds. I was holding the porto-light so he could see where his finger was going. Knuckle deep. And telling me. "It's hit the bone, the bullet here, the knife wound through the neck." I figure I've seen too much. Jeez, this is not for me. You wouldn't believe it. Maybe I don't believe it. Maybe it didn't hit me yet.

I'm afraid that after seein' so much of this I can come home and hear my kid in pain and not feel for him. So far it hasn't happened. I hope to God it never happens. I hope to God I always feel. When my grandmother passed away a couple of months ago, I didn't feel anything. I wonder, gee, is it happening to me?

One time a guy had shot up a cop in the hospital and threw the cop down the stairs and his wheel chair on top of him. He escaped with a bullet in him. He held up a tenement in Brownsville. They called us down at three o'clock in the morning, with bullet-proof vests and shotguns. I said to myself, This is something out of the movies. The captain had a blackboard. There's eight of us and he gave each of us a job: "Two cover the back yard, you three cover the front, you three will have to secure the roof."

This guy wasn't gonna be taken alive. Frank and me will be the assault team to secure the roof. We're loaded with shotguns and we're gonna sneak in there. We met at four o'clock in the morning. We're goin' up the back stairs. On the first stairway there was a German shepherd dog outside the doorway. The dog cowered in the corner, thank God. We went up three more stories. We secured the roof.

We could hear them assaulting in each apartment, trying to flush this guy out. He fled to the fire escape. As he was comin' up, we told him to freeze. Tony, it was all over. He started to go back down. We radioed team one in the back yard. We heard shots. The rooftops had actually lit up. The assault man had fired twenty-seven bullets into this guy and he recovered. He's still standing trial from what I heard. This was one of the jobs I felt, when I was goin' up the stairs, should I give my wife a call? I felt like I had to call her.

If a perpetrator's in a building, you either talk to him or contain him or flush him out with tear gas rather than runnin' in and shoot. They feel a life is more important than anything else. Most cops feel this, yes.

I went on the prison riots we had in the Tombs. I was the first one on the scene, where we had to burn the gates out of the prison, where the prisoners had boarded up the gates with chairs and furniture. We had to use acetylene torches. My wife knew I was in on it. I was on the front page. They had me with a shotgun and the bullet-proof vest and all the ammunition, waiting to go into the prison.

I wonder to myself, Is death a challenge? Is it something I want to pursue or get away from? I'm there and I don't have to be. I want to be. You have chances of being killed yourself. I've come so close . . .

I went on a job two weeks ago. A nineteen-year-old, he just got back from Vietnam on a medical discharge. He had ransacked his parents' house. He broke all the windows, kicked in the color television set, and hid upstairs with a homemade spear and two butcher knives in one hand. He had cut up his father's face.

We were called down to go in and get this kid. He tore the bannister up and used every pole for a weapon. We had put gas masks on. All the cops was there, with sticks and everything. They couldn't get near him. He kept throwing down these iron ash trays. I went up two steps and he was cocking this spear. We cleared out all the policemen. They just wanted emergency, us.

If you wait long enough, he'll come out. We had everybody talk to him, his mother . . . He didn't come out. The sergeant gave orders to fire tear gas. I could hear it go in the windows. I went up a little further and I seen this nozzle come out of his face. I said, "Sarge, he's got a gas mask on." We fired something like sixteen cannisters in the apartment. When he went back to close one of the doors, I lunged upstairs. I'm very agile. I hit him in the face and his mask went flying. I grabbed his spear and gave him a bear hug. He just didn't put up any resistance. It was all over.

The patrol force rushed in. They were so anxious to get this guy, they were tearing at me. I was tellin' him, "Hey, fella, you got my leg. We got him, it's all over." They pulled my gas mask off. Now the big party starts. This was the guy who was agitating them for hours. "You bum, we got you." They dragged him down the stairs and put him in a body bag. It's like a straitjacket.

When we had him face down a patrolman grabbed him by the hair and slammed his face into the ground. I grabbed his wrist, "Hey, that's not necessary. The guy's handcuffed, he's secure." I brushed the kid's hair out of his eyes. He had mod long hair. My kid has mod hair. The guy says, "What's the matter with you?" I said, "Knock it off, you're not gonna slam the kid."

The neighbors congratulated me because the kid didn't get a scratch on him. I read in the paper, patrolman so-and-so moved in to make the arrest after a preliminary rush by the emergency service. Patrolman so-and-so is the same one who slammed the kid's face in the ground.

I'm gonna get him tonight. I'm gonna ask if he's writing up for a commendation. I'm gonna tell him to withdraw it. Because I'm gonna be a witness against him. The lieutenant recommended giving me a day off. I told my sergeant the night before last the lieutenant can have his day off and shove it up his ass.

A lot of the barricade snipers are Vietnam veterans. Oh, the war plays a role. A lot of 'em go in the army because it's a better deal. They can eat, they can get an income, they get room and board. They take a lot of shit from the upper class and they don't have to take it in the service.

It sounds like a fairy tale to the guys at the bar, in one ear and out the other. After a rough tour, a guy's dead, shot, people stabbed, you go into a bar where the guys work on Wall Street, margin clerks, "How ya doin? What's new?" You say, "You wouldn't understand." They couldn't comprehend what I did just last night. With my wife, sometimes I come home after twelve and she knows somethin's up. She waits up. "What happened?" Sometimes I'm shaking, trembling. I tell her, "We had a guy . . ." (Sighs.) I feel better and I go to bed. I can sleep.

The one that kept me awake was three years ago. The barricaded kid. The first night I went right to sleep. The second night you start thinking, you start picturing the kid and taking him down. With the kid and the tear gas, the sergeant says, "Okay fire." And you hear the tear gas . . . Like you're playing, fooling around with death. You don't want to die, but you're comin' close to it, to really skin it. It's a joke, it's not happening.

I notice since I been in emergency she says, "Be careful." I hate that, because I feel jinxed. Every time she says be careful, a big job comes up. I feel, shit, why did she say that? I hope she doesn't say it. She'll say, "I'll see you in the morning. Be careful." Ooohhh!

Bad accidents, where I've held the guys' skulls . . . I'm getting used to it, because there are younger guys comin' into emergency and I feel I have to be the one to take charge. 'Cause I seen a retired guy come back and go on a bad job, like the kid that drowned and we pulled him out with hooks. I'm lookin' to him for help and I see him foldin'. I don't want that to happen to me. When you're workin' with a guy that has eighteen years and he gets sick, who else you gonna look up to?

Floaters, a guy that drowns and eventually comes up. Two weeks ago, we pulled this kid out. You look at him with the hook in the eye . . . You're holdin' in because your partner's holdin' in. I pulled a kid out of the pond, drowned. A woman asked me, "What color was he?" I said, "Miss, he's ten years old. What difference does it make what color he was?" "Well, you pulled him out, you should know." I just walked away from her.

Emergency got a waiting list of three thousand. I have one of the highest ratings. I do have status, especially with the young guys. When a guy says, "Bob, if they change the chart, could I ride with you?" that makes me feel great.

I feel like I'm helpin' people. When you come into a crowd, and a guy's been hit by a car, they call you. Ambulance is standing there dumbfounded, and the people are, too. When you give orders to tell this one to get a blanket, this one to get a telephone book, so I can splint a leg and wrap it with my own belt off my gun, that looks good in front of the public. They say, "Gee, who are these guys?"

Last week we responded to a baby in convulsions. We got there in two minutes. The guy barely hung up the phone. I put my finger down the baby's throat and pulled the tongue back. Put the baby upside down, held him in the radio car. I could feel the heat from the baby's mouth on my knuckles. At the hospital the father wanted to know who was the guy in the car. I gave the baby to the nurse. She said, "He's all right." I said, "Good." The father was in tears and I wanted to get the hell out of there.

This morninig I read the paper about that cop that was shot up. His six-year-old son wrote a letter: "Hope you get better, Dad." My wife was fixin' breakfast. I said, "Did you read the paper, hon?" She says, "Not yet." "Did you read the letter this cop's son sent to his father when he was in the hospital?" She says, "No." "Well, he's dead now." So I read the part of it and I started to choke. I says, "What the hell . . ." I dropped the paper just to get my attention away. I divided my attention to my son that was in the swing. What the hell. All the shit I seen and did and I gotta read a letter . . . But it made me feel like I'm still maybe a while away from feeling like I have no feeling left. I knew I still had feelings left. I still have quite a few jobs to go . . .

The Asshole

John Van Maanen

I guess what our job really boils down to is not letting the assholes take over the city. Now I'm not talking about your regular crooks . . . they're bound to wind up in the joint anyway. What I'm talking about are those shitheads out to prove they can push everybody around. Those are the assholes we gotta deal with and take care of on patrol. . . . They're the ones that make it tough on the decent people out there. You take the majority of what we do and it's nothing more than asshole control.

A VETERAN PATROLMAN[1]

SOURCE: *Policing: A View from the Street,* John Van Maanen and Peter K. Manning, Eds. Goodyear Publishing Co., 1978, pp. 221–238.

[1] All police quotes are taken from field notes I compiled of conversations and observations taking place during a year of participant observation in what I have referred to anonymously in my writings as the Union City Police Department (a large, metropolitan force employing over 1,500 uniformed officers). The quotes are as accurate as my ear, memory, and notes allow. I should note, also, that in this essay I use the terms "police," "police officer," "patrolman," and "policemen" somewhat interchangeably. However, unless I indicate otherwise, my comments are directed solely toward the street-level officer—the cop on the beat—and not toward his superiors, administrators, or colleagues in the more prestigeful detective bureaus.

I. POLICE TYPIFICATIONS

The asshole—creep, bigmouth, bastard, animal, mope, rough, jerkoff, clown, scumbag, wiseguy, phony, idiot, shithead, bum, fool, or any of a number of anatomical, oral, or incestuous terms—is a part of every policeman's world.[2] Yet the grounds upon which such a figure stands have never been examined systematically. The purpose of this essay is to display the interactional origins and consequences of the label asshole as it is used by policemen, in particular, patrolmen, going about their everyday tasks. I will argue that assholes represent a distinct but familiar type of person to the police and represent, therefore, a part of their commonsense wisdom as to the kinds of people that populate their working environment. From this standpoint,

[2] I chose the term "asshole" for the title of this essay simply because it is a favorite of working policemen (at least in Union City). The interested reader might check my assumption by a casual glance at what several others have to say about this linguistic matter. Most useful in this regard are the firsthand accounts police have themselves provided and can be found, for example, in Terkel (1968, 1974); Droge, (1973); Maas (1972); Olsen (1974); Whittemore (1973); Walker (1969). I should note as well that such labeling proceeds not only because of its functional use to the police but also because it helps officers to capture perceptual distinctions (i.e., labels are "good to think"). Thus assholes are conceptually part of the ordered world of police—the statuses, the rules, the norms, and the contrasts that constitute their social system.

assholes are analytic types with whom the police regularly deal. More importantly, however, I will also argue that the label arises from a set of situated conditions largely unrelated to the institutional mandate of the police (i.e., to protect life and property, arrest law violators, preserve the peace, etc.) but arises in response to some occupational and personal concerns shared by virtually all policemen.

According to most knowledgeable observers, nothing characterizes policing in America more than the widespread belief on the part of the police themselves that they are primarily law enforcers—perpetually engaged in a struggle with those who would disobey, disrupt, do harm, agitate, or otherwise upset the just order of the regime. And, that as policemen, they and they alone are the most capable of sensing right from wrong; determining who is and who is not respectable; and, most critically, deciding what is to be done about it (if anything). Such heroic self-perceptions reflecting moral superiority have been noted by numerous social scientists concerned with the study of the police. Indeed, several detailed, insightful, and thoroughly accurate mappings of the police perspective exist.[3] For instance, learned discussions denote the various "outgroups" perceived by the police (e.g., Harris, 1973; Bayley and Mendelsohn, 1969); or the "symbolic assailants" which threaten the personal security of the police (e.g., Skolnick, 1966; Niederhoffer 1967; Rubinstein, 1973); or the "suspicious characters" recognized by the police via incongruous (nonordinary) appearances (e.g., Sacks, 1972; Black, 1968). These reports provide the background against which the pervasive police tropism to order the world into the "for us" and "against us" camps can most clearly be seen.

Yet these studies have glossed over certain unique but altogether commonsensical properties of the police situation with the attendant consequence of reifying the police position that the world is in fact divided into two camps. Other than noting the great disdain and disgust held by many police officers toward certain predefined segments of the population they presumably are to serve, these studies fail to fully describe and explain the range and meaning attached to the various labels used by the police themselves to affix individual responsibility for particular actions occurring within their normal workaday world. Furthermore, previous studies do not provide much analytic aid when determining how the various typifications carried by the police are recognized as relevant and hence utilized as guides for action by a police officer in a particular situation. In short, if police typifications are seen to have origins as well as consequences, the popular distinction between "suspicious" or "threatening" and the almost mythologized "normal" or "respectable" is much too simple. It ignores not only the immediate context in which street interactions take place, but it also disregards the critical signs read by the police within the interaction itself which signify to them both the moral integrity of the person with whom they are dealing and the appropriate recipe they should follow as the interaction proceeds.[4] Therefore, any distinction of the "types" of people with whom the police deal must include an explicit consideration of the ways in which the various "types" are both immediately and conditionally identified by the police. Only in this fashion is it possible to accurately depict the labels the police construct to define, explain, and take action when going about their routine and nonroutine tasks.

To begin this analysis, consider the following typology which suggests that the police tend to view their occupational world as comprised exhaustively of three types of citizens (Van Maanen, 1974). These ideal types are: (1) "suspicious persons"—those whom the police have reason to believe may have committed a serious offense; (2) "assholes"—those who do not accept the police definition of the situation; and (3) "know nothings"—those who are not either of the first two categories but are not police and therefore, according to the police, cannot know what the police are about.

[3] See, for example: Rubinstein's (1973) report on the Philadelphia police; Westley's (1970) study of a midwestern police department in the late 1940s; Wilson's (1968) global accounting of the police perspective; Reiss's (1971) research into police-community interactions; LaFave's (1965) treatment of the police decision to arrest; Cain's (1973) and Banton's (1964) observations on the British police; and Berkeley's (1969) cross-cultural view of policing in democratic societies. What comes out of these excellent works is tantamount to a reaffirmation of Trotsky's famous dictum, "There is but one international and that is the police."

[4] For example, Skolnick's (1966) idea that policemen are "afraid" of certain categories of persons distorts the nature of the occupational perspective. More to the point, policemen are disgusted by certain people, envious of others, and ambivalent toward most. At times they may even vaguely admire certain criminals—those that the British police call "good villains" (Cain, 1971). Fear must, of course, be given its due, but the occasion of fear hangs more upon unforeseen situational contingencies (the proverbial dark alley, desolate city park, or underlife tavern) than upon certain individuals.

This everyday typification scheme provides a clue to the expectations, thoughts, feelings, and behaviors of the police. For example, "suspicious persons" are recognized on the basis of their appearance in public surroundings. Such an appearance is seen as a furtive, nonroutine, *de trop*, or, to use Sacks's (1972) nicely turned phrase, "dramatically torturous." Crucially, such persons, when they provide the police reason to stop and interrogate them, are treated normally in a brisk, though thoroughly professional, manner. It is not their moral worth or identity which is at issue, but rather it is a possible illegal action in their immediate or not-so-immediate past which is in question. From the patrolman's point of view, he is most interested in insuring that formal procedural issues are observed. Hence the personal production of a professional police performance is called for and is presented—at least initially.[5] On the other end of the continuum reside the "know nothings," the "average" citizens, who most generally come under police scrutiny only via their request for service. The "know nothing" may be the injured or wronged party or the seeker of banal information and as such is treated with a certain amount of deference and due respect by the patrolman.

"Assholes," by way of contrast, are stigmatized by the police and treated harshly on the basis of their failure to meet police expectations arising from the *interaction situation itself.* Of course, street interaction may quickly transform suspicious persons into know nothings and know nothings into assholes, or any combination thereof. But it is the asshole category which is most imbued with moral meaning for the patrolman—establishing for him a stained or flawed identity to attribute to the citizen upon which he can justify his sometimes malevolent acts. Consequently, the asshole may well be the recipient of what the police call "street justice"—a physical attack designed to rectify what police take as personal insult. Assholes are most vulnerable to street justice, since they, as their title implies, are not granted status as worthy human beings. Their actions are viewed by the police as stupid or senseless and their feelings as incomprehensible (if they can even be said to have feelings). Indeed, as I will show, the police consistently deny an asshole a rationale or ideology to support their actions, insisting that the behavior of an asshole is understandable only as a sudden or lifelong character aberration. On the other hand, suspicious persons are less likely candidates for street justice because, in the majority of cases, their guilt may still be in question, or, if their guilt has been in fact established, their actions are likely to seem at least comprehensible and purposeful to the police (i.e., a man steals because he needs money; a man shoots his wife because she "two-timed" him; etc.). Also, there are incentives for the suspicious person to cooperate (at least nominally) when subject to police attention. The suspicious person may well be the most cooperative of all the people with whom the police deal on a face-to-face basis. This is, in part, because he is most desirous of presenting a normal appearance (unafraid, unruffled, and with nothing to hide), and, in part, because if he is in fact caught he does not want to add further difficulty to his already difficult position. Finally, know nothings are the least likely candidates for street justice since they represent the so-called client system and are therefore those persons whom the police are most interested in impressing through a polished, efficient, and courteous performance.

At this point, I should note that the above ideal types are anything but precise and absolute. One purpose of this paper is to make at least one of these categories more explicit. But since I am dealing primarily with interior, subjective meanings negotiated in public with those whom the police interact, such typifications will always be subject to severe situational, temporal, and individually idiosyncratic restriction. Hence, an asshole in one context may be a know nothing in another, and vice versa. In other words, I am not arguing in this essay that a general moral order is shared by all policemen as their personalized but homomorphic view

[5] Certainly this may not always be the case. For example, some "suspected persons," due to the nature of their alleged crime (e.g., child molestation, drug dealing, indecent exposure, political sabotage, assault [or worse] upon a police officer, etc.) are likely to provide a strong sense of moral indignation on the part of the arresting (or stopping) officers. In such cases, once identity has been established to the satisfaction of the police (and it should be noted that errors are not unknown—particularly in these volatile cases), the person suspected is transformed immediately into an asshole and is subject to a predictably harsh treatment. Thus, in effect the label arises from an offense which occurred outside the immediate presence of the officers. However, since the spoiled identity must be reestablished anew in the immediate surroundings, the properties of the "affront" correspond analytically to the more familiar case outlines in the text. And while the distinction has theoretical value regarding the norms of the police culture (i.e., that it is not the denounced per se that is important, but rather it is the denouncer that matters—"say's who?"), its practical implications are questionable because patrolmen rarely encounter such situations.

of the world. Indeed, the moral order subscribed to by police is complex, multiple, and continually shifts back and forth between that which is individual and that which is collective. What I will argue, however, is that particular situational conditions (i.e., provocations) predispose most policemen toward certain perceptions of people which lead to the application of which can be shown to be rule-governed police actions. My objective, then, is simply to begin teasing out the underlying structure of police thought and to denote the features of what might be called the secondary reality of police work.

The remainder of this essay is divided into four sections. The next section, "Patrol Work," describes very briefly certain understandings shared by street-level patrolmen as to what is involved in their work. In a sense, these understandings are akin to behavioral rules that can be seen to mobilize police action; hence they represent the grounds upon which the figure of the asshole is recognized. The following section, "Street Justice," deals with the characteristic processes involved in discovering, distinguishing, and treating the asshole. Some conclusions revolving around the relationship between the police and the asshole are suggested in the next section. And, finally, a few of the broad implications that flow from this analysis are outlined in the last section.

II. PATROL WORK

Policing city streets entails what Hughes (1958) refers to as a "bundle of tasks." Some of these tasks are mundane; many of them are routine; and a few of them are dangerous. Indeed, patrol work defies a general job description since it includes an almost infinite set of activities—dogcatching, first-aid, assisting elderly citizens, breaking up family fights, finding lost children, pursuing a fleeing felon, directing traffic, and so forth. Yet, as in other lines of endeavor, patrolmen develop certain insider notions about their work that may or may not reflect what outsiders believe their work to be. Such notions are of course attached firmly to the various experientially based meanings the police learn to regularly ascribe to persons, places, and things—the validity of which is established, sustained, and continually reaffirmed through everyday activity. Because these meanings are, to some degree, shared by patrolmen going about similar tasks, their collective representation can be detailed and linked to certain typical practices engaged in on the street by the police. Thus, to understand the police perspective on, and treatment of, the asshole, it is necessary also to understand the manner in which the policeman conceives of his work. Below is a very short summary of certain interrelated assumptions and beliefs that patrolmen tend to develop regarding the nature of their job.

Real Police Work

Many observers have noted the pervasive police tendency to narrowly constrict their perceived task to be primarily—and to the exclusion of other alternatives—law enforcement. As Skolnick and Woodworth (1967:129) suggest evocatively, "when a policeman can engage in real police work—act out the symbolic rites of search, chase and capture—his self-image is affirmed and morale enhanced." Yet, ironically, opportunities to enact this sequence are few and far between. In fact, estimates of the time police spend actually in real police work while on patrol vary from 0 percent (as in the case of the quiet country policeman for whom a street encounter with a bona fide "criminal" would be a spectacular exception to his daily tour of duty) to about 10 or 15 percent (as in the case of the busy urban patrolman who works a seamy cityside district in which the presence of pimps, dealers, cons, and burglars, among others, are the everyday rule). Nonetheless, most of the policeman's time is spent performing rather dry, monotonous, and relatively mundane activities of a service nature—the proverbial clerk in a patrol car routinely cruising his district and awaiting dispatched calls (see Cain, 1971; Reiss, 1971; Webster, 1970; and Cumming, Cumming and Edell, 1965, for further discussion on how the police spend their time).

Within these boundaries, notions of real police work develop to provide at least a modicum of satisfaction to the police. To a patrolman, *real police work* involves the use of certain skills and special abilities he believes he possesses by virtue of his unique experience and training. Furthermore, such a perspective results in minimizing the importance of other activities he is often asked regularly to perform. In fact, an ethos of "stay-low-and-avoid-trouble-unless-real-police-work-is-called-for" permeates police organizations (Van Maanen, 1973, 1974, 1975). Only tasks involving criminal apprehension are attributed symbolic importance. For the most part, other tasks, if they cannot be avoided, are performed (barring interruption) with ceremonial dispatch and disinterest.

Territoriality

A central feature of policing at the street level is the striking autonomy maintained (and guarded jealously) by patrolmen working the beat. All patrol work is conducted by solo officers or partnerships (within a squad to whom they are linked) responsible for a given plot of territory. Over time, they come to know, in the most familiar and penetrating manner, virtually every passageway—whether alley, street, or seldom-used path—located in their sector. From such knowledge of this social stage comes the corresponding evaluations of what particular conditions are to be considered good or bad, safe or unsafe, troubled or calm, usual or unusual, and so on. Of course, these evaluations are also linked to temporal properties associated with the public use of a patrolman's area of responsibility. As Rubinstein (1973) suggests, the territorial perspective carried by patrolmen establishes the basic normative standard for the proper use of place. And those perceived by patrolmen to be beyond the pale regarding their activities in space and time are very likely to warrant police attention.

Maintaining the Edge

Charged with enforcing ambiguous generalized statutes and operating from an autonomous, largely isolated position within the city, it is not surprising that police have internalized a standard of conduct which dictates that they must control and regulate all situations in which they find themselves. At one level, police feel they have the right to initiate, terminate, or otherwise direct all encounters with members of the public. Yet such perceptions penetrate more broadly into the social scheme of things, for police feel, furthermore, that the public order is a product of their ability to exercise control. The absence of trouble on their beat becomes, therefore, a personalized objective providing intimate feedback as to one's worth as a patrolman. Activity which may threaten the perceived order becomes intolerable, for it signifies to the patrolman that his advantage over the conduct of others (his "edge") is in question. It is a source of embarrassment in front of a public audience, and sometimes it is considered a disgrace to the police uniform if it is viewed by one's peers or departmental superiors. Clearly, such activity cannot be allowed to persist, for it may indicate both to a patrolman's colleagues and to his superiors that the officer no longer cares for his job and has, consequently, lost the all-important respect of those he polices (endangering, it is thought, other policemen who might work the same district). Hence, to "maintain one's edge" is a key concept vis-à-vis the "how to" of police work. And, as all policemen know, to let down the facade (for they do recognize the contrived nature of the front) is to invite disrespect, chaos, and crime.

The Moral Mandate

In light of the above three features of the police frame, it should be clear that police are both representatives of the moral order and a part of it. They are thus committed ("because it is right") to maintain their collective face as protectorates of the right and respectable against the wrong and the not-so-respectable. Situations in which this face is challenged—regardless of origin—are likely to be responded to in unequivocal terms. For example, Cain (1971) writes that when the authority of an officer is questioned by a member of the nonpolice public, the officer has three broad responses available to him. He may (1) physically attack the offender; (2) swallow his pride and ignore the offender; or (3) manufacture a false excuse for the arrest of the offender. What this suggests is a highly personalized view on the part of the police as to their moral position and responsibility, one in which an attempt on the part of the citizen to disregard the wishes of a policeman may be viewed by the police as a profaning of the social and legal system itself. Such an act can also be seen to provoke moral and private indignation on the part of the officer as an individual, thus providing him with another *de rigueur* excuse to locate an appropriate remedy. Since the police personally believe that they are capable of making correct decisions regarding the culpability of an involved party, justice is likely, in the case of an offense to the moral sensibilities of a police officer, to be enacted quickly, parsimoniously, and self-righteously—whether it be the relatively trivial swift kick in the pants or the penultimate tragedy involved in the taking of a life. Thus, the moral mandate felt by the police to be their just right at the societal level is translated and transformed into occupational and personal terms and provides both the justification and legitimation for specific acts of street justice.

This truncated picture of the occupational frame involved in the doing of police work provides the rubric upon which we now can examine the making of an asshole. As one would expect, assholes are not afforded the protection of the more structured relationships police maintain with other of their categories of persons—the suspicious and the know nothings. Rather, they fall outside this fragile shelter, for their actions are seen as "senseless," so "aimless" and "irrational" that recognizable and acceptable human motives are difficult for the police to discover (i.e., from the patrolmen's perspective, there are not legitimate reasons to distrust, disagree with, make trouble for, or certainly hate the police). In this sense, it is precisely the "pointlessness" of an individual's behavior that makes him an asshole and subjects him to the police version of street justice.

III. STREET JUSTICE

Policeman to motorist stopped for speeding:
"May I see your driver's license, please?"
Motorist:
"Why the hell are you picking on me and not somewhere else looking for some real criminals?"
Policeman:
"Cause you're an asshole, that's why . . . but I didn't know that until you opened your mouth."

The above sea story represents the peculiar reality with which patrolmen believe they must contend. The world is in part (and, to policemen, a large part) populated by individuals to whom an explanation for police behavior cannot be made, for, as the police say, "assholes don't listen to reason." The purpose of this section is to explore the commonplace and commonsense manner in which the tag asshole arises, sticks, and guides police action during a street encounter. This stigmatization process is divided into three stages which, while analytically distinct, are highly interactive and apt to occur in the real world of policing almost simultaneously. For convenience only, then, these phases are labeled *affront, clarification*, and *remedy*.

Throughout this discussion it should be remembered that the asshole is not necessarily a suspected law violator—although the two often overlap, thus providing double trouble, so to speak, for the labeled. Importantly, the police view of the asshole as deviant is a product of the immediate transaction between the two and not a product of an act preceding the transaction. This is not to say, however, that certain classes in society—for example, the young, the black, the militant, the homosexual—are not "fixed" by the police as a sort of permanent asshole grouping. Indeed, they are. Yet such bounded *a priori* categories can do policemen little good—except perhaps when dealing with the racial or bohemian obvious—for such stereotypes are frequently misleading and dysfunctional (e.g., the "hippie" who is a detective's prized informant; the black dressed in a purple jumpsuit who happens to be a mayor's top aide; the sign carrying protestor who is an undercover FBI agent). And, even in cases in which *a priori character* judgments are a part of the decision to stop an individual, the asshole label, if it is to play a determining role in the encounter, must arise anew. That is to say, if the asshole distinction is to have a *concrete* as opposed to *abstract* meaning, it must in some manner be tied fundamentally and irresolutely to observable social action occurring in the presence of the labeling officer.

Certainly, a policeman's past experience with an individual or with a recognizable group will influence his street behavior. For example, a rookie soon discovers (as a direct consequence of his initiation into a department) that blacks, students, Mexicans, reporters, lawyers, welfare workers, researchers, prostitutes, and gang members are not to be trusted, are unpredictable, and are usually "out-to-get-the-police." He may even sort these "outsiders" into various categories indicative of the risk he believes they present to him or the implied contrast they have with his own life-style and beliefs. Yet, without question, these categories will never be exhaustive—although the absolute size of what patrolmen call their "shit lists" may grow over the years. Consequently, to understand the police interpretation and meaning of the term "asshole" we must look directly into the field situations in which it originates.

Affront: Challenge

When a police officer approaches a civilian to issue a traffic citation or to inquire as to the whys and wherefores of one's presence or simply to pass the time of day, he directly brings the power of the state to bear on the situation and hence makes vulnerable to disgrace, embarrassment, and insult that power. Since the officer at the street level symbolizes the presence of the Leviathan in the everyday lives of the citizenry, such interactions take on dramatic properties far different from ordinary citizen-to-citizen transactions (Manning, 1974a; Silver, 1967). In a very real sense, the patrolman-to-citizen exchanges are moral contests in which the authority of the state is either confirmed, denied, or left in doubt. To the patrolman, such contests are not to be taken lightly, for the authority of the state is also his personal authority, and is, of necessity, a matter of some concern to him. To deny or raise doubt about his legitimacy is to shake the very ground upon which his self-image and corresponding views are built.

An affront, as it is used here, is a challenge to the policeman's authority, control, and definition of the immediate situation. As seen by the police, an affront is simply a response on the part of the other which indicates to them that their position and authority in the interaction are not being taken seriously. It may occur with or without intent. Whether it is the vocal student who claims to "know his rights," the stumbling drunk who says he has had "only two beers," or the lady of the evening who believes she is being questioned only because she is wearing "sexy clothes," the police will respond in particular ways to those who challenge or question their motive or right to intervene in situations that they believe demand police intervention. Clearly, overt and covert challenges to police authority will not go unnoticed. In fact, they can be seen to push the encounter to a new level wherein any further slight to an officer, however subtle, provides sufficient evidence to a patrolman that he may indeed be dealing with a certifiable asshole and that the situation is in need of rapid clarification. From this standpoint, an affront can be seen, therefore, as disrupting the smooth flow of the police performance. The argumentative motorist, the pugnacious drunk, the sometimes ludicrous behavior of combatants in a "family beef" all interfere, and hence make more difficult, the police task. Of course, some officers relish such encounters. In this sense, ironically, the asshole gives status to the police rather than takes it away. However, since the label is itself a moral charge (and it need not be made salient or verbally expressed), it is open theoretically for rebuttal, and evidence may or may not be forthcoming which will substantiate or contradict the charge. Such evidence is gathered in the next analytic stage.

Clarification: Confrontation

Based upon a perceived affront, the patrolman must then attempt to determine precisely the kind of person with whom he is engaged. It is no longer an idle matter to him in which his private conceptions of people can be kept private as he goes about his business. But the patrolman is now in a position wherein he may discover that his taken-for-granted authority on the street is not exactly taken for granted by another. Two commonsensical issues are critical at this point in an encounter. *First*, the officer must determine whether or not the individual under question could have, under the present circumstances, acted in an alternative fashion. To wit, did the perceived affront occur by coercion or accident through no fault of the person? Did the person even know he was dealing with a police officer? Was he acting with a gun at his head? And so on. *Second*, and equally important, given that the person could have acted differently, the officer must determine whether or not the individual was aware of the consequences that might follow his action. In other words, was the action frivolous, naive, unserious, and not meant to offend? Did the person know that his actions were likely to be interpreted offensively by the police? The answers to these two questions provide patrolmen with material (or lack of it) to construct and sustain an asshole definition. Let us examine in some depth these questions, for they raise the very issue of personal responsibility which is at the nexus of the asshole definition.[6]

McHugh (1969) argues persuasively that the social construction of deviant categories is a matter of elimination which proceeds logically through a series of negotiated offers and responses designed to fix responsibility for a perceived deviant act (i.e., a deviant act requires a charge before it can be said to have happened). Police follow a similar paradigm when filling, emptying, or otherwise attending to their person categories. Again, the first item to be determined in this process is the issue of whether or not the person had alternative means available to him of which he could reasonably be expected to be aware. For example, the speeding motorist who, when pulled to the side of the road, could be excused for his abusive language if it were discovered by the officer that the motorist's wife was at the same time in the back seat giving birth to a child. Similarly, juveniles "hanging out" on a public street corner at certain times of the day may be sometimes overlooked if the police feel that "those kids don't have anyplace to go." On the other hand, if it can be determined that there is no unavoidable reason behind the affronting action, the

[6] In most regards, the asshole is a classic case of the deviant—although not transituationally so. See Matza (1969), Becker (1963), and Cohen (1965) for a systematic elaboration of the ideas which underpin this analysis.

individual risks being labeled an asshole. The drunken and remorseless driver, the wife who harangues the police officer for mistreating her husband after she herself requested police service to break up a family fight, or the often-warned teenager who makes a nuisance of himself by flagrantly parading in public after curfew are all persons whom the police believe could have and should have acted differently. Their acts were not inevitable, and it could be expected that they had available to them conventional alternatives.

Given that there are no compelling deterministic accounts readily available to the patrolman to excuse a particular affront, the officer must still make a judgment about the offender's motive. In other words, as the second issue listed above suggests, the policeman must decide whether or not the person knows what he is doing. Could the person be expected to know of the consequences which follow an affront to an officer of the law? Indeed, does the person even realize that what he is doing is likely to provoke police action? Could this particular person be expected to know better? All are questions related to the establishment of a motive for action. For example, the stylized and ceremonial upright third finger when attached to the hand of the thirty-year-old man is taken by the police very differently from the same gesture attached to the hand of a four-year-old child. Loud and raucous behavior in some parts of a city may be ignored if the police feel "the people there don't know any better." Or the claim that one is Jesus Christ resurrected and is out to do battle with the wages of sin may indicate to the police that they are either in the presence of a "dope-crazed radical hippie freak" or a "soft-brained harmless mental case," depending, perhaps, on the offender's age. If the person is young, for instance, responsibility is likely to be individualized—"it is his fault"; however, if the person is old, responsibility is likely to be institutionalized—"he can't help it, he's a nut."

Summarily, the police have available to them two principles of clarification. One concerns the means available to a person guilty of an affront, and the other concerns the purposes behind the affront itself. If the affront is viewed as unavoidable or unintended, the person is unlikely to be subjected to shabby or harsh treatment at the hands of the police. The asshole, however, is one who is viewed as culpable and blameworthy for his affronting action, and, as the next section details, he will be dealt with by the police in ways they feel appropriate.

Remedy: Solution

The above portrait of the clarification principles utilized by police in labeling assholes suggests that certain typical police responses can be displayed by a simple fourfold typology. Table 1 depicts the relationship between the police officer's assessment of responsibility for the affront and denotes, within each cell, the typical police response given the various possible assessments.

Cell A represents the subject case of this essay since it involves a flagrant (inexcusable) disregard for the sentiments of the police. To the police, those falling into this category are unmistakably assholes and are therefore prominent candidates to be the recipients of street justice—the aim of which is to punish or castigate the individual for a moral transgression. Persons placed in this category are also the most likely to be placed under questionable arrest. This is not so because of the original intent of the encounter (which often, by itself, is trivial) but rather because of the serious extralegal means utilized by the police to enforce their particular view of the situation upon the recalcitrant asshole—"hamming-up" or "thumping" (beating).[7] And, as Reiss (1971) suggests, the use of force is not a philosophical question to the police but rather one of who, where, when, and how much.

The use of such means requires, of course, that the officer manufacture post facto a legally defensible account of his action in order to, in the vernacular of the day, "cover his ass."[8] Such accounts in legalese most

TABLE 1

	Does the Person Know What He Is Doing?	
	Yes	*No*
Could the person act differently under the circumstances? Yes	A Castigate	B Teach
No	C Ignore	D Isolate

[7] By the term "extralegal" I am merely implying that the formal police mandate excludes such moral considerations from actions inducing decisions made by officers on the street. The notion of professional policing makes this explicit when it is suggested that patrolmen must act impersonally without regard to individual prejudice.

[8] The "cover-your-ass" phenomena associated with urban policing is described in more depth in Van Maanen (1974). See also Manning (1974b) for a theoretical view of the more general construct, the police lie; and Chevigny (1968) for a presentation of numerous disturbing case studies.

often take the form of "disorderly conduct," "assaulting a police officer," "the use of loud and abusive language in the presence of women and children," "disturbing the peace," or the almost legendary—due to its frequent use—"resisting arrest." The asshole from this position is subject to a police enactment of double jeopardy—justice without trial in the streets and justice, perhaps with trial, in the courts. And regardless of the outcome in the latter case, there is usually only one loser. I should emphasize, however, that I am not saying the behavior of the asshole may not be brutish, nasty, and itself thoroughly vicious. I am simply suggesting that behavior violating extralegal moral codes used by police to order their interactions—whether it be inconsiderate, barbarous, or otherwise—will be responded to in what police believe to be appropriate ways.

Cell B of Table 1 also represents serious affront to police integrity, and it too may be an affront which calls for an extralegal response. An illustration provided by the remarks of a patrolman is useful in this context:

> Those goddamn kids got to learn sooner or later that we won't take a lot of shit around Cardoza (a local college campus). Next time I see one of those punks waving a Viet Cong flag I'm gonna negotiate the little bastard back into an alley and kick his rosy red ass so hard he ain't gonna carry nothing for a while. Those kids gotta be made to see that they can't get away with this type of thing.

Whether or not such a prediction was actually carried out does not matter, for the quotation itself indicates that "teaching" occupies a particularly prominent position in the police repertoire of possible responses. Thus, the uncooperative and surly motorist finds his sobriety rudely questioned, or the smug and haughty college student discovers himself stretched over the hood of a patrol car and the target of a mortifying and brusque body search. The object of such degradation ceremonies is simply to reassert police control and demonstrate to the citizen that his behavior is considered inappropriate. Teaching techniques are numerous, with threat, ridicule, and harassment among the more widely practiced. Other examples are readily available, such as the morally-toned lectures meted out to those who would attempt to bribe, lie, or otherwise worm their way out of what a policeman sees to be a legitimate traffic citation, the traditional—but vanishing—"kick in the ass" administered to a youngster caught stealing an apple or cutting school. The intent in all these cases is clear. The person must be taught a lesson. And whether the teaching occurs in public or in the back of an alley, the person must be shown the error of his ways. He has acted perhaps out of ignorance, but nevertheless the police feel they must demonstrate that they will not casually overlook the action. However, I should note that the person in this category will remain an asshole in the eyes of the police until he has apparently learned his lesson to the satisfaction of the officers on the scene. Here a display of remorse is no doubt crucial to the police.[9]

Cell C represents the case in which the police are likely to excuse the affront due to the extenuating circumstances surrounding the affront. When it is clear to the police that there are indeed mitigating conditions, their response is to ignore the error—to pretend, as it were, that such an affront never happened. For example, it is understandable to the police that the victim of a mugging may be somewhat abusive toward them when they interrogate him just after the crime (although there is a fine line to be drawn here). Similarly, if a teenage male vigorously defends the chaste and virtuous intentions of his and his girl friend while questioned by the police in a concealed and cozy corner of a public park, it is understood by the police that the boy has few other acceptable alternative lines available. The police response is typically to adopt a somewhat bemused tolerance policy toward actions which under different circumstances may have produced the orb and scepter.

Finally, cell D in Table 1 concerns the case of an affront which police take to lie beyond the responsibility of the actor. While such action cannot normally be allowed to continue, the moral indignation felt by police is tempered by the understanding that the person is not aware nor could be easily made aware of the rule-breaking nature of his actions. The police response is to isolate the offender, not to punish him. Thus, the

[9] Arrests are, of course, sometimes used to teach someone a lesson. However, police believe that in many cases the asshole will arrange his release before the patrolman will have completed the paperwork necessitated by the arrest. And since the affront was moral, the legal justification to "make the case" in court may be lacking. Thus, the classroom more often than not is in the street. Given the opportunity to teach the asshole either by "turning him in" or "doing him in," most police would choose the latter.

"mental case" is shipped to the county hospital for observation and treatment; the "foul-mouthed child" is returned to those responsible for his behavior; the out-of-state tourist prowling an area close to his hotel but frequented by prostitutes is informed of his "oversight" and told in unmistakable terms to vacate the territory. It is important to note that police feel justified in using only enough force or coercive power to seal off the offender from public (and, by implication, their own) view. To use more force would be considered unreasonable.

It has been my purpose here to suggest that much of what the general public might see as capricious, random, or unnecessary behavior on the part of the police is, in fact, governed by certain rather pervasive interpretive rules which lie close enough to the surface so that they can be made visible. Certain police actions, following the model presented above, can be seen, then, to be at least logical if not legal. Furthermore, much of the power of these rules stems from their tacit or taken-for-granted basis. Indeed, were the rules to be questioned, the game could not continue. However, while these rules are applied in a like fashion by all police in a given interactional episode, the specific situated behavior of a citizen that is taken as a sign which leads to isolating, ignoring, teaching, or castigating a given individual is no doubt quite different across patrolmen. Here, the police game continues as it does because, in part, the asshole label swallows up and hides whatever individual differences exist across patrolmen. Thus, language neatly solves the problem of misunderstanding that would arise among the police were the rules to be articulated and standards sought as to how they should be applied.

IV. SOME CONCLUSIONS

It is possible, of course, to see the preceding ritualized sequence as an isolated and rarely indulged propensity of the police. However, in this section, I will argue that indeed such a sequence and the corresponding identification and treatment of the asshole is intimately related to the police production and represents an aspect of policing that is near the core of the patrolman's definition of his task. In essence, the existence of an asshole demonstrates and confirms the police view of the importance and worth of themselves both as individuals and as members of a necessary occupation. However, several other, somewhat more practical and everyday features of police work insure the ominous presence of the asshole in the police world.

First, the labeling of individuals as assholes can be seen as a technique (although invisible to most) useful to patrolmen in providing distance between themselves and their segmented audiences—to be liked by the people in the street is, in the defensive rhetoric of patrolmen, a sign of a bad cop. By profaning and degrading the actions of another, social distance can be established and maintained—a guarantee, so to speak, that the other will not come uncomfortably close. Thus, the asshole simplifies and orders the policeman's world and continually verifies his classification scheme regarding those who are "like him" and those who are "unlike him." Relatedly the labeling serves also as an immediate call to action, denoting a consensually approved (by the police culture) means for remedying "out-of-kilter" situations.

Second, the label not only describes and prescribes but it also explains and makes meaningful the statements and actions of others. In fact, an entire set of action expectations (i.e., "they are out to make the police look bad") can be ascribed as motives to the asshole. In this sense, the police function in street interaction is not unlike that of a psychiatrist diagnosing a patient. Both explain perceived deviancy in terms of a characterological genesis. Hence, the label implies that a different, inappropriate, and strange motivational scheme is used by the "type of person" known as an asshole. In this manner, an act is made understandable by stripping away whatever meaning might be attributed to it by the actor. Thus, to make sense of the act is to assume that it does not make sense—that it is stupid, irrational, wrong, deranged, or dangerous. Any other assumption would be too threatening.

Third, the labeling process must be viewed as serving an occupational purpose. I suggested previously that the urban policeman is primarily a keeper of the peace yet he defines his job in terms of law enforcement. Furthermore, as others have noted, many patrolmen try to convert peacekeeping situations to those of law enforcement (e.g., Bittner, 1967, 1970; Wilson, 1967; Piliavin and Briar, 1964). Since real police work is seldom available, marginally legitimate arrests of assholes provide a patrolman excitement and the opportunity to engage one's valued skills. Perhaps the police cliché," a good beat is full of deadbeats," reflects structural support for the asshole-labeling phenomena.

Fourth, the discovery and subsequent action taken when the police encounter the asshole provides an expressive outlet—almost ceremonial in its predictability—for much of the frustration policing engenders. To the patrolman, one particular asshole symbolizes all those that remain "out there" untouched, untaught, and unpunished. Such emotional outbursts provide, therefore, a reaffirmation of the moral repugnance of the asshole. Whether the officer responds by placing the handcuffs on the person's wrists such that they cut off circulation (and not incidentally cause intense, almost excruciating pain) or pushes a destitute soul through a shop window, these actions release some of the pent-up energies stored up over a period in which small but cumulative indignities are suffered by the police at the hands of the community elites, the courts, the politicians, the uncaught crooks, the press, and numerous others. The asshole stands, then, as a ready ersatz for those whom the police will never—short of a miracle—be in a position to directly encounter and confront.

Finally, the asshole can be seen as a sort of reified other, representing all those persons who would question, limit, or otherwise attempt to control the police. From this standpoint, knowing that there are assholes at large serves perhaps to rally and solidify police organizations around at least one common function. Thus, the police are, to a limited degree, unified by their disdain of those who would question their activities. Perhaps one could say that the police represent what Simmel (1950) referred to as an "invisible church" in which the faithful are fused together through their common relation to an outside phenomenon.

Consequently, assholes are not simply obscure and fanciful figments of the bedeviled imagination of the police. On the contrary, they define to a surprising degree what the police are about. And while the internal satisfactions and rewards involved in "slamming around" an asshole may seem esoteric if not loathsome to the outsider, to the patrolman who makes his living on the city streets it is not.

V. POSTSCRIPT

The foregoing description and explanation of an overlooked aspect of urban policing highlight the fact that the police officer is anything but a Weberian bureaucrat whose discretion and authority are checked rigidly. The collective myth surrounding the rulebound "policeman-as-public-servant" has no doubt never been very accurate. By virtue of their independence from superiors, their carefully guarded autonomy in the field, their deeply felt notions about real police work and those who would interfere with it, and their increasing isolation from the public they serve (as a result of mobile patrol, rotating shifts, greater specialization of the police, and the growing segmentation of the society at large with its own specialized and emerging subcultures), police-community "problems" will not disappear. And, since the police view their critics as threatening and as persons who generally should be taught or castigated, one could argue that the explosive potential of citizen-police encounters will grow.

Additionally, if the police become more sensitive to public chastisement, it could be expected that something of a self-fulfilling prophecy may well become a more important factor in the street than it is presently. That is to say, if the police increasingly view their public audience as foes—whose views are incomprehensible if not degenerate or subversive—it is likely that they will also magnify clues which will sustain the stereotype of citizen-as-enemy escalating, therefore, the percentage of street interactions which result in improper arrest and verbal or physical attack. Thus, the fantasy may well become the reality as stereotypes are transformed into actualities. In fact, the future may make prophetic Brendan Behan's half-jesting remark that he had never seen a situation so bad that a policeman couldn't make it worse.

To conclude, this essay has implied that there is a virtual—if unintended—license in this society granted to police. In particular, when it comes to the asshole, police actions are not governed at all, given the present policies of allowing the watchers to watch themselves. It would seem that something is amiss, and, if the practical morality in urban areas is not exactly inverted, it is at least tilted. If the asshole is indeed a critical aspect of policing, then there is a serious risk involved in the movement to "professionalize" the police. As other observers have remarked, successful occupational professionalization inevitably leads to increased autonomy and ultimately increased power for members of the occupation (Becker, 1962; Hughes, 1965). Professionalism may well widen the police mandate in society and therefore amplify the potential of the police to act as moral entrepreneurs. From this perspective, what is required at present is not professional police but accountable police.

REFERENCES

Banton, Michael, (1964) *The Policeman in the Community*. New York: Basic Books.

Bayley, P. H. and H. Mendelsohn, (1969) *Minorities and the Police: Confrontation in America*. New York: Free Press.

Becker, Howard S., (1962) "The Nature of a Profession," in *Education for the Professions*, 61st Yearbook of the Society for the Study of Education, Part 2. Chicago: University of Chicago Press. (1963) *Outsiders*. New York: Free Press.

Berkeley, George E., (1969) *The Democratic Policeman*. Boston: Beacon Press.

Bittner, Egon, (1970) *The Functions of the Police in Modern Society*. Washington, D.C.: United States Government Printing Office. (1967) "The Police on Skid Row," 32, *American Sociological Review*, 699–715.

Black, Donald, (1968) "Police Encounters and Social Organization: An Observational Study." Unpublished Ph.D. Dissertation, University of Michigan.

Cain, Maureen, (1973) *Society and the Policeman's Role*. London: Kegan Paul. (1971) "On the Beat: Interactions and Relations in Rural and Urban Police Forces," in S. Cohen (ed.) *Images of Deviance*. Middlesex, England: Penguin Books.

Chevigny, Paul, (1968) *Police Power: Police Abuses in New York*. New York: Pantheon.

Cohen, Albert K., (1965) "The Sociology of the Deviant Act," 30, *American Sociological Review*, 5–14.

Cumming, E., I. Cumming and L. Edell, (1965) "The Policeman as Philosopher, Guide and Friend," 12, *Social Problems*, 276–286.

Droge, Edward F., (1973) *The Patrolman: A Cop's Story*. New York: New American Library.

Harris, Richard N., (1973) *The Police Academy: An Inside View*. New York: John Wiley and Sons.

Hughes, Everett C., (1965) "Professions," in K. S. Lynn (ed.) *Professions in America*. Boston: Beacon Press. (1958) *Men and Their Work*. Glencoe, Ill.: Free Press.

LaFave, W. R., (1965) *Arrest: The Decision to Take a Suspect into Custody*. Boston: Little, Brown and Company.

Maas, Peter, (1973) *Serpico*. New York: The Viking Press.

Manning, Peter K., (1971) "The Police: Mandate, Strategies and Appearances," in J. Douglas (ed.) *Crime and Justice in America*. Indianapolis: Bobbs-Merrill. (1974a) "Dramatic Aspects of Policing: Selected Propositions," *Sociology and Social Research*, 59 (October). (1974b) "Police Lying," *Urban Life* 3 (October).

Matza, David, (1969) *Becoming Deviant*. Englewood Cliffs, N.J.: Prentice-Hall.

McHugh, Peter, (1969) "A Common-Sense Perception of Deviancy," in J. Douglas (ed.) *Deviance and Respectability*. New York: Basic Books.

Niederhoffer, Arthur, (1967) *Behind the Shield*. Garden City, N.Y.: Doubleday.

Olsen, Jack, (1974) *Sweet Street*. New York: Simon and Schuster.

Piliavin, I. and S. Briar, (1964) "Police Encounters with Juveniles." 70, *American Journal of Sociology*, 206–214.

Reiss, Albert J., (1971) *The Police and the Public*. New Haven, Conn.: Yale University Press.

Rubinstein, Jonathan, (1973) *City Police*. New York: Farrar, Straus and Giroux.

Sacks, Harvey, (1972) "Notes on Police Assessment of Moral Character," in D. Sudnow (ed.) *Studies in Social Interaction*. New York: The Free Press.

Silver, Allen, (1967) "The Demand for Order in Civil Society," in D. Bordua (ed.) *The Police: Six Sociological Essays*. New York: John Wiley and Sons.

Simmel, Georg, (1950) *The Sociology of Georg Simmel*. Translated, edited, and with an introduction by Kurt H. Wolff. New York: The Free Press.

Skolnick, Jerome, (1966) *Justice Without Trial*. New York: John Wiley and Sons.

Skolnick, Jerome and J. R. Woodworth, (1967) "Bureaucracy, Information and Social Control," in D. Bordua (ed.) *The Police: Six Sociological Essays*. New York: John Wiley and Sons.

Terkel, Studs, (1968) *Division Street: America*. New York: Random House. (1974) *Working*. New York: Pantheon.

Van Maanen, John, (1972) "Pledging the Police: A Study of Selected Aspects of Recruit Socialization in a Large Police Department." Unpublished Ph.D. Dissertation, University of California, Irvine. (1973) "Observations on the Making of Policemen," 32, *Human Organizations*, 407–418. (1974) "Working the Streets: A Developmental View of Police Behavior," in H. Jacobs (ed.) *Reality and Reform: The Criminal Justice System*, Beverly Hills, California:

Sage Publications. (1975) Police Socialization. *Administrative Science Quarterly*, 20, 207–228.

Walker, T. Mike, (1969) *Voices from the Bottom of the World: A Policeman's Journal*. New York: Grove Press.

Webster, J. A., (1970) "Police Task and Time Study," 61 *Journal of Criminal Law, Criminology and Police Science*, 94–100.

Westley, William, (1970) *Violence and the Police*. Cambridge, Mass.: MIT Press (originally a Ph.D. Dissertation, University of Chicago, 1951).

Whittemore, L. H., (1973) *The Super Cops*. New York: Stein and Day.

Wilson, James Q., (1967) "Police Morale, Reform and Citizen Respect: The Chicago Case," in D. Bordua (ed.) *The Police: Six Sociological Essays*. New York: John Wiley and Sons. (1968) *Varieties of Police Behavior*. Cambridge, Mass.: Harvard University Press.

Police Misconduct

Richard J. Lundman

POLICE MISCONDUCT AS ORGANIZATIONAL DEVIANCE

All police officers are exposed to opportunities for misconduct. In even the sleepiest of suburban patrol districts, there exists opportunities to accept money for not issuing a traffic citation and to render "street justice" to verbally aggressive citizens. Given the rates of work-based deviance by persons in occupations ranging from factory work to medicine,[1] it should not surprise us that police officers also engage in occupational misconduct.

However, the frequency and patterning of police misconduct vary between departments. In some departments there are only a few officers who accept bribes and render street justice. They do these things alone and hide their actions from most colleagues and superiors. In these departments police misconduct is infrequent and unpatterned, and is a form of individual or subcultural deviance.

In other departments large numbers of officers engage in misconduct. Patrol officers routinely accept bribes and involve themselves in other types of corrupt activities. Officers also routinely assault verbally aggressive citizens. They do these things together and do not attempt to shield their actions from most colleagues and superiors. In these departments police misbehavior is frequent and patterned, a form of organizational deviance. This is the type of misconduct of concern in this chapter.

SOURCE: From *Police and Policing: An Introduction* by Richard J. Lundman. Copyright © 1980 by Holt, Rinehart and Winston. Reprinted by permission of Holt, Rinehart and Winston, CBS College Publishing.

Police Corruption

Police corruption exists when officers accept money, goods, or services for actions they are sworn to do anyway.[2] It also exists when police officers accept money, goods, or services for ignoring actions they are sworn to invoke legal procedures against.

Types of Police Corruption. Of the various typologies of police corruption that have been advanced, one developed by Thomas Barker and Julian Roebuck is most useful.[3] As compared to other typologies, Barker and Roebuck's is less unwieldy: it contains only eight categories.[4] The Barker and Roebuck model also contains an indicator of seriousness and it was developed in an organizationally sensitive manner. It emphasizes that most forms of corruption are supported by internal operating norms, socialization, peers, and administrative personnel. For these reasons the Barker and Roebuck paradigm will be used to lay the groundwork for our analysis of police misconduct as organizational deviance.

Barker and Roebuck identify eight types of police corruption.[5] These types, arranged on a continuum from least to most serious, are as follows:

1. Acceptance of free or discount meals and services
2. Acceptance of kickbacks for referrals for services
3. Opportunistic theft from helpless citizens or unsecured premises

4. Shakedowns
5. Protection of illegal activities
6. Acceptance of money to fix cases
7. Planned theft

The eighth type of corruption, "assignment and promotion based upon internal payoffs," is not part of their seriousness continuum. It does, however, represent an extreme form of corruption, one that involves only police. We now will consider examples of each form of corruption.

Meals and Services.[6] Free or discount meals are available to police in most cities. Certain nationwide restaurant chains have a policy of giving police free meals. Other nationwide restaurant chains offer police meals at half price. Owners of many local restaurants also offer police free or discount meals. Police in most cities find it difficult to pay for meals in these restaurants. They literally are told either that they cannot pay at all or that they cannot pay full price for a meal.

Owners and operators at a variety of other commercial establishments also offer "police discounts." Next to restaurants, dry cleaning shops are probably the type of establishment which most routinely offers police discounts. Many other businesses desire police patronage and make special efforts to attract it. Officers readily exchange information on these establishments prior to roll call and over coffee.

It is likely that many of the people who provide police meals and services do so out of respect and gratitude. It is equally likely that many are simply buying the "deterrent presence"[7] of uniformed officers. They believe that a robbery is unlikely when a marked squad car is parked outside and an officer in uniform inside. They also believe that well-fed and dressed police are more likely to respond quickly to their calls for assistance and to make themselves available during higher risk times such as closing.

These strategies are generally effective. It is highly doubtful that a person would decide to rob a restaurant or store when a police officer is present. Police officers also acknowledge their obligations. They attempt to respond more quickly to calls and make themselves available at closing.

Kickbacks. Acceptance of money in exchange for referrals also is available for patrol officers in most large cities. Towing companies, for instance, stand to benefit from police referrals and some are willing to pay police officers for doing so. Former New York City police officer Edward F. Droge, Jr., reports that officers received two types of kickbacks from towing companies.[8] The first was for ignoring illegal attempts to solicit repair work at the scene of an accident. The second and more lucrative kickback was received when patrol officers reported accidents directly to towing companies. According to Droge, this was worth between $20 and $30.

Other opportunities for kickbacks exist, including those from undertakers. Chicago newspaper journalist Mike Royko describes this type of kickback:

> On Skid Row, somebody had died—an old pensioner in a flophouse. The paddy wagon men hauled him into their van and drove as fast as they could to a funeral home about two miles away. They went past a couple of funeral homes along the way. The one they were going to paid the best prices for stray bodies.[9]

Opportunistic Theft. James Spradley asked men in the Seattle city jail who had been arrested for public drunkenness: "Have you ever personally witnessed the Seattle police rolling, clipping, or stealing from a drunk or someone picked up for drunk?"[10] Of those interviewed, exactly one-third said they had witnessed this type of opportunistic theft. In one situation, an offender reported that a friend had cashed a check and the two had gone drinking. As they were leaving a bar, two police officers stopped and searched the pair, relieving the one of his money. When he objected, he was told to forget the incident or go to jail. He withdrew his objection and the suddenly more affluent police went on their way.

The possibility of opportunistic or unplanned theft from unsecured premises also is frequent for patrol officers. The actions of several officers provide an example of this type of activity.

It had been a relatively quiet middle watch and the officers had every reason to believe that it would continue to be quiet. It was a weekday and they were working a comfortable working-class area. At about 7:00 P.M. they received a call to "check some unclaimed property" at the rear of a beer warehouse. The night before the warehouse had been broken into and some beer had been taken. The call seemed to suggest that perhaps some beer had been left behind. At least, the officers hoped that was the case.

The officers in one other squad apparently thought the same thing and the two squads arrived almost simultaneously. A brief search of the tall weeds in the rear of the warehouse yielded a "treasure": 13 cases of malt liquor apparently left behind the night before. Without hesitation one officer said, "Let's split it." The beer was carried to the squad cars and exactly six and one-half cases of malt liquor were placed in the trunk of each squad. The next step was to transfer the cases to their personal cars, and they began to drive to the precinct station.

As the cars drove off, one of the officers noticed that an officer in the other squad had left his keys in the lock of the trunk of the car. Failing to recognize the consequences of his upcoming action, he picked up his microphone and said, "______, your keys are still in the trunk." Once off the air, the officer then said, "Oh, shit," realizing what he had done. The dispatcher, quick to confirm his worst fears, came on the air and said, "I take it there will be a property report on that call?" The officer was quick to recover and respond by saying, "Yep, could I have the number for it?" The officer received the number and both squads proceeded to the precinct station. Now, however, the malt liquor would be placed in the property room, where it would be claimed by a representative of the warehouse.

Upon arriving at the station, several of their colleagues and a lieutenant greeted them. One said, "On the air he says 'your keys.' " Another observed, "It was a dumb piece of police work." The officers essentially agreed; after all, they *had* blown an opportunity for some free malt liquor.

The problem was that the officer who told the other squad that the keys were still in the trunk also told anybody else who was listening, including superiors, that *something* (most probably beer, given the location and the burglary of the night before) had been placed in the trunk. The dispatcher immediately recognized the problem and gave the officers a way out by assuming that a report would be forthcoming. And the officers who greeted the squad at the precinct were absolutely correct: it had been dumb to put something like that out over the air. Of such mistakes are opportunistic thefts blown.[11]

Shakedowns. Police officers shake down citizens by accepting money from them for withdrawing an arbitrary threat to enforce the law. Chicago police routinely shake down tavern owners by threatening to enforce obscure liquor laws. Herbert Beigel and Alan Beigel provide a description of the "club's" operation and how it affected one tavern owner:

> She had been approached . . . by . . . [police] . . . and told that a club was being formed to service the . . . taverns. If she wanted to . . . avoid problems that could cause the loss of her liquor license, she would be wise to pay a reasonable sum of money once a week—$25. Each week an officer stopped by . . . to collect the payment.[12]

At this point in the Barker–Roebuck typology, it is necessary to note that it is possible for individual police officers to engage in each of these first four types of corruption in the absence of organizational support. Most patrol officers work alone or with a trusted partner. Most routine policing remains outside the scrutiny of immediate superiors, and especially, administrative elites. Many citizens who "suffer" from corrupt practices either encourage these actions (for example, restaurant and tow company owners) or are in a poor position to effectively object to them (such as public drunkenness offenders). And the "code of secrecy" which surrounds police and policing protects individually corrupt officers. The result is that it is possible for individual police officers who are so inclined to become individual entrepreneurs by soliciting kickbacks and engaging in opportunistic thefts and shakedowns on their own.

Entrepreneurial corruption is possible but it is not easy. Partners periodically change because of illness, different days off, and vacations. Sergeants occasionally observe patrol officers as they work and they may acquire evidence of corrupt activities. Citizens sometimes complain to administrators about the amount of money and services they are providing police. The individually corrupt officer must therefore be constantly alert lest new partners, inquisitive sergeants, or knowledgeable administrators acquire discrediting information. It is difficult to keep one's eyes and ears open, but it is possible.

Kickbacks, opportunistic theft, and shakedowns are both possible and easy when an officer is a member of a deviant department. Nearly all partners can be trusted; the least that can be expected is silence. Sergeants and administrators also can be trusted, either because they share their subordinates' improper income or they are busy creating and maintaining their own. The other types of corruption identified by Barker and Roebuck are also both possible and easy in a deviant department.

Protection of Illegal Activities. Effective protection of illegal activities, such as gambling and narcotics, requires that officers in divisions other than patrol be involved. This is because the other divisions are largely responsible for policing these activities.[13] Vice and narcotics officers ostensibly function to control, if not eliminate, organized gambling and narcotics operations. Moreover, citizens frequently complain of illegal activities located in their neighborhoods.[14] Consequently, administrative superiors in police organizations inevitably know about these activities. Because of this division of labor and input from citizens, individual patrol officers can offer little more than the promise that *they* will not intervene. That is not a very effective system of protection.

But when officers in special function divisions such as vice and narcotics and administrative superiors agree to protect illegal activities along with patrol officers, then effective protection can be guaranteed. The price, however, is generally steep. In New York, for instance, the Knapp Commission found that plainclothes officers in five divisions "collected regular biweekly or monthly payments amounting to as much as $3,500 from each of the gambling establishments in the area under their jurisdiction, and divided the take in equal shares."[15] In the area of narcotics "enforcement," payments were said to be less systematic but more lucrative: a single payment totalled $80,000.[16]

William J. Chambliss has presented an essentially similar portrait of police in Seattle.[17] The owner of a restaurant (legal) and card room (illegal but protected) told Chambliss of the price of his "pay to stay" protection. Each month, a patrol officer collected $250 for distribution to appropriate officers. Administrators had their own "bag man," and he too appeared monthly. Chambliss also reports that Seattle police were paid to protect prostitution, drug distribution, pornography, and usury operations.

Case Fixing. Traffic ticket fixing is likely the most common form of case fixing and often it does not even involve a monetary payment. According to John Gardiner, tickets are fixed in Massachusetts in one of several ways.[18] The cited motorist's "best bet" is to know someone who is a member of the police department which issued the ticket. Failing that, calls to "any" chief of police, police officer, or politician are said to be effective. Friends of these people are a last but sometimes effective resort.

Ticket fixing also is the least offensive type of case fixing. It pales by comparison with case fixing of organized crime. Nicholas Gage described case fixing in the state of New York:

> Paul Vahio, who is listed by the Justice Department as a captain in the Mafia family of the late Thomas Luchese, pleaded guilty before Supreme Court Justice Domenic S. Rinaldi to commercial bribery of a police officer. Vahio, whose criminal record dates back to 1925 . . . could have been given up to a year in jail. Instead, Judge Rinaldi fined him $250.00. . . . Vahio is not the only Mafioso who has fared better than ordinary defendants in New York State courts. . . . [The] rate of dismissals and acquittals for racketeers was five times that of other defendants.[19]

Although it is likely that case fixing by police and other members of the criminal justice system has declined since the era of Prohibition,[20] it remains a fixture in certain police jurisdictions.

Planned Theft. Direct involvement by police in criminal activities is not as uncommon as one might imagine. What follows is only a partial list of cities since 1960 in which police burglary rings and other forms of direct criminal activity by police have been reported: Denver, Colorado; Chicago, Illinois; Nassau County, New York; Des Moines, Iowa; Nashville, Tennessee; Birmingham, Alabama; Cleveland, Ohio; Bristol, Connecticut; Burlington, Vermont; Miami, Florida;[21] "Mid-City";[22] New York City; Philadelphia, Pennsylvania; Buffalo, New York; New Orleans, Louisiana;[23] and Newburgh, New York.[24]

The extent of organizational support for police burglary rings and other forms of direct criminal activity by police is unclear.[25] It seems accurate to suggest that passive support is present in most situations. However, if knowledge of these activities becomes public, even deviant departments generally respond in a forceful manner. As Barker and Roebuck note, "departments that tolerate other forms of corruption will usually prosecute and send to prison officers discovered engaging in forms of direct criminal activities."[26]

Assignment and Promotion Based upon Payoffs. In this circumstance, police activities and rewards are bought and sold by police officers; there are no outside corruptors. Barker and Roebuck describe this type of corruption:

> Officers who administer the distribution of assignments and personnel . . . collect fees for assigning officers to certain divisions, precincts, units, details, shifts, and beats and for insuring that certain personnel are retained in, transferred from or excluded from certain work assignments . . . officers in certain assignments have little opportunity to engage in other types of corrupt activities. Internal pay-offs provide these officers with an illegitimate opportunity structure.[27]

Barker and Roebuck thus identify eight types of corruption. Their typology contains an indicator of seriousness and also allows for entrepreneurial corruption. They emphasize, however, that most of the types of misbehavior identified involve the active or passive support of patrol officers, special function police, and administrative superiors. They therefore encourage analysis of police corruption as organizational deviance.

Factors Related to the Incidence and Seriousness of Police Corruption

Few police organizations display all or even most of the types of corruption identified by Barker and Roebuck. Observation of patrol officers in a large midwestern city several years ago revealed that they routinely and unhesitatingly took advantage of the numerous opportunities for free or discount meals and services. They also "liberated" the meager resources and unopened hard liquor of chronic drunkenness offenders. Least frequently, they took advantage of burglary and break-in calls by helping themselves to a variety of items. The other types of corruption identified by Barker and Roebuck were not evident.

An early journalist, however, described this city as "wide-open." The city administration and the police department were said to have been "sold" to racketeers. It was only after a reform mayor was elected that the rackets were closed down. Since that time, corruption apparently has remained at the level described.

Other police departments evidence signs of more serious and persistent corruption. The New York City Police Department (NYCPD) is an example. At remarkably regular 20-year intervals, starting in 1894 and ending in 1971 with the Knapp Commission, NYCPD officers have been found to be extensively involved in corrupt activities.[28] This situation has been serious and persistent.

Still other departments present strong evidence that it is possible to eliminate chronic corruption. In the early 1950s, Oakland's police were as thoroughly corrupt as those in New York.[29] Their actions ranged from acceptance of free meals to planned theft. By 1960, however, corruption had been completely eliminated and the department has remained free of corruption.[30]

This contrast shows the variation in the amount of wrongdoing in police departments. The questions that emerge are several:

1. What factors determine whether or not a department is corrupt (for example, Oakland versus New York)?
2. If corrupt, what factors determine the seriousness of corruption (for instance, the midwest city versus New York)?
3. What factors relate to persistence in patterns of corruption (Oakland versus New York)?

Review of the available literature suggests that *partial* answers to each of these three questions arise when one examines the environment external to police organizations and the internal responses to that environment.

External Factors. Sociologist Lawrence W. Sherman has studied police corruption in Europe and the United States, and is author of two books on the topic.[31] Sherman suggests that three factors external to police organizations help determine the presence and seriousness of police corruption. He develops his suggestion by advancing three propositions:

1. There will be less police corruption in a community with little anomie. . . .
2. There will be less police corruption in communities with a more public-regarding ethos (among elected officials).
3. There will be less corruption in a community with less culture conflict.[32]

Let us briefly examine the content and implications of each of these propositions.

Community Anomie. The role of anomie in the generation of social deviance has been considered by a number of social scientists, including Émile Durkheim and Robert K. Merton. Their ideas will be used to lay the groundwork for an analysis of Sherman's description of the role of anomie in the generation of police corruption.

Durkheim coined and applied the notion of anomie in the context of his study of suicide rates.[33] Durkheim observed that a number of factors were related to increases in rates of suicide. They included economic catastrophes as well as sudden economic gains, declines in the control afforded persons by traditional religions, and increases in the proportion of persons working in industry or in professions such as teaching.

Durkheim then sought to determine what was common or central to each of the factors causing increases in suicide rates. The answer Durkheim advanced was that each represented a condition or situation in which the social controls which surround the members of a society have been weakened. He termed this condition anomie or normlessness and argued that anomic suicide "results from man's activity's lacking regulation and his consequent sufferings."[34]

Robert K. Merton's essential contribution was to broaden the meaning of anomie and to extend it to forms of deviance other than suicide.[35] Merton defines anomie as a gap between important goals and legitimate means of reaching those goals. Merton then argues that rates of criminality and deviance are higher among groups of persons denied easy access to legitimate means of reaching cultural goals; the gap leads some individuals to use illegitimate or criminal means of achieving societal or situationally important goals.

What Lawrence W. Sherman is suggesting is that rates of police corruption may be higher in communities where large numbers of people are denied easy access to legitimate means of attaining goals. As Merton predicts, groups of persons in communities such as this frequently turn to innovative means. Gambling, prostitution, and narcotics services represent three of these means.

Outlook of Elected Officials. Sherman notes that the level of anomie characteristic of a community affects the outlook or perspective of elected officials. Community anomie frequently produces a sense of normlessness among officials. Instead of attempting to serve in the best interests of the public-at-large, there exists a privatization or segmentation of commitment among local leaders. They are responsive to elite community members and to the persons who provide illegal but widely demanded services such as gambling and prostitution. Frequently elected officials are responsive to this latter group of persons because they are paid to ignore their actions. Richard J. Daley's Chicago was such a community:

> The city's dramatic physical redevelopment has been a boon to the political world as well as the private investors. There are so many deals involving ranking members of the Machine that it has been suggested that the city slogan be changed from *Urbs In Horto*, which means, "City in a Garden," to *Ubi Est Mea*, which means "Where's mine?"[36]

Sherman is suggesting that in Chicago, Philadelphia, Seattle, and other cities characterized by a privatization of perspective among governmental officials, police corruption may be present. This is because elected leaders are concerned with protecting and promoting special interests. As long as the activities of others, including those that are illegitimate, do not interfere with the interests of another group, they are tolerated or ignored. Police corruption may flourish in such a situation because the opportunities for it are present and because police are seen as simply another privatized or segmented interest group.

Culture Conflict. Sherman is here sensitizing us to the differences in the *sentiments* attached to certain laws. The state has traditionally attempted to use the law to define and control the "morality" of its citizenry. Biblical injunctions against sodomy, for instance, guided English and Puritan laws which attempted to regulate the sexual activities and preferences of consenting adults.[37] Currently, most communities try to control the sale of intoxicating beverages,[38] and many still seek to restrain the sexual activities of consenting adults.[39] Laws governing gambling, prostitution, and drug use constitute additional examples of contemporary efforts to define and regulate morality.

The problem is that laws intended to govern morality are almost always met with mixed reaction. Many citizens, and especially those personally affected by these laws, resent and resist state attempts to control their actions. Other citizens believe that the state should not be in the business of attempting to regulate morality. Still others see these laws as creating opportunities to provide for the many citizens who desire these services. Since provision of most of these illegal services requires police tolerance, culture conflict creates additional opportunities for police corruption.

As a consequence of Sherman's three propositions, we are now in a position to identify the circumstances in which police misdeeds may be present. In communities characterized by anomie, privatization or segmentation of interest, and culture conflict over the propriety of certain laws, numerous opportunities for police corruption exist.

However, most of our large cities fit the above description. The urban poor, black, and young routinely experience problems in gaining easy access to legitimate means of reaching their goals. Many of our cities are governed by less than public-minded officials. And many citizens disagree over whether the state has the right to direct their morality. Obviously something more is needed to explain organized police corruption.

Internal Factors. In cities characterized by anomie, segmentation of interest, and culture conflict, police departments generally display either a legalistic or watch style of policing.[40] It is a department's type of policing which is the prime determinant of its response to external opportunities for corruption.

Legalistic Departments. Officers in legalistic departments generally fail to respond in an organized fashion to opportunities for corruption. Legalistic departments typically do not contain internal operating norms supportive of corruption. Police socialization emphasizes adherence to the law for both police and citizens. And administrators are intolerant of improper actions of either citizens or police. The corruption which does exist is of the entrepreneurial or "rotten pocket" variety.[41]

It is important to recognize, however, that legalistic policing does not mean that external opportunities for corruption have been eliminated or even lessened.[42] In communities rich in opportunities for corruption, legalistic policing frequently emerges in the wake of scandal and it represents an attempt at reform. But reform policing of a legalistic nature cannot and does not change community patterns of anomie. Large numbers of citizens continue to be denied access to legitimate means of achieving goals. Reform policing of a legalistic nature also cannot and does not bring consensus to community sentiments about laws intended to define and regulate public morality. Large numbers of people still wish to engage in these actions and others remain willing to serve those so inclined. The successful and largely legalistic reforms of policing in Oakland, California, Newburgh, New York, and New York City can hardly be said to be the result of lessened anomie or culture conflict.[43]

Extensive opportunities for corruption are thus available to police in large cities. Officers in legalistic departments, however, do not respond to these opportunities in an organized manner. Their failure to respond reflects membership in a nondeviant department.

Watch Departments. The internal characteristics of watch-style departments encourage organized responses to external chances for misbehavior. Internal operating norms are supportive of involvement in corruption and they provide justifications for such action. Police socialization involves introduction to and evaluation in terms of the norms supportive of corruption. And watch department administrators are involved in their own dishonest activities, supportive of the corrupt activities of subordinates, or both. We will now briefly examine the ways in which these internal factors facilitate the organized corruption characteristic of watch-style departments.

In these departments, the internal operating norms of the department provide patrol officers and others with rationalizations and justifications for corrupt actions. Officers learn that it is acceptable to utilize free or discount services or to accept kickbacks because of their deterrent presence, more frequent proactive observation, quick responses to calls for police presence, and more frequent referrals. From this perspective, store owners and others are simply paying for a level of service over and above that received by other citizens.[44]

Police officers who opportunistically steal from citizens or shake them down do so because of additional rationalizations. Officers who illegally confiscate the property of chronic drunkenness offenders *explain* that the items were almost certainly obtained illegally. Officers who release beer-drinking juveniles, but not their beer (it is saved for consumption after work in a backroom of the precinct station), note that they are giving the released juveniles a break.[45]

The most serious forms of corruption characteristic of watch departments require other rationalizations. In the context of protecting or fixing arrests for illegal gambling operations and liquor law violations, the distinction between these "clean" sources of corrupt income (as compared to the "dirty" money associated with narcotics and gun sales) appears to have been an important justification for this type of activity. Writing in 1965, Jerome Skolnick noted that police in the watch department he studied ("Eastville") took protection money from bookmakers and numbers operators. They did not take money from those who sold narcotics because they "felt that narcotics use posed a serious danger to the community and restrictions upon its use were not nearly severe enough."[46]

However, the traditional distinction between clean and dirty money in watch departments appears to be changing. In the words of the Knapp Commission Report of Police Corruption in New York:

> More relaxed attitudes toward drugs, particularly among young people, and the enormous profits to be derived from

> drug traffic have combined to make narcotics-related payoffs more acceptable to more and more police. . . .[47]

In watch departments narcotics money is increasingly being rationalized as clean.

The most serious form of corruption—planned theft—as well as internal payoffs appear to be less a function of specific norms supportive of these activities. Instead, related but more general factors are of paramount importance.

The emergence of planned theft and internal payoffs appears to require the existence of most, if not all, of the other forms of corruption we have examined. Planned theft is an extreme action, engaged in by what some have called the "evil fringe" of a thoroughly corrupt department. It is a risky undertaking since its discovery by outsiders almost always creates scandal and forces even a watch department to undertake disciplinary action. Internal payoffs work to the detriment of patrol officers and other subordinate members of a department. They advantage only those few officers in positions to allocate assignments or shifts. It is unlikely that patrol norms or the more general police subculture support either planned theft or internal payoffs. How, then, does the existence of most or all of the other types of corruption give rise to these most serious types?

Two tentative answers suggest themselves. For those officers who engage in planned theft, the existence of other types of misbehavior acts as a kind of insurance for their own activities. Officers involved in other forms of corruption are unlikely to take action against colleagues involved in planned theft for fear of a retaliatory exposure of their own actions. They also may decide not to take action for fear that the resulting investigation by outsiders might not stop at planned theft but instead be expanded to include additional types of corruption.

This is precisely what happened in three cities: Chicago,[48] Newburgh, New York,[49] and New York City.[50] In Chicago and Newburgh, the discovery of police burglary rings resulted in major scandals which ultimately exposed the other forms of corruption also characteristic of these two departments. In New York City, the Knapp Commission investigation had already begun but many remained uncertain of the seriousness of police corruption. In the course of their investigation, Knapp Commission agents inadvertently stumbled upon a police burglary. Agents watched as police broke into a meat warehouse and began carting parts of cows to their cars. The onlookers anonymously called the local precinct station several times to report that the burglary was literally in progress as they observed. No squads were sent to investigate. This incident understandably received extensive publicity. It prompted reform administrator Patrick V. Murphy to take even sterner actions. It also helped convince a sometimes skeptical citizenry of the need to thoroughly investigate the extent of police corruption.

The development of internal payoffs, which benefit only a few officers, also would appear to require the existence of the other types of corruption. When these other types exist, a *department* anomie or sense of normlessness emerges, one which mirrors the anomie of the community "served" by the department. In such a department, distinctions between proper and improper behavior, police officers and criminals, and fair and unfair advantages become blurred and, with time, meaningless. With few norms other than "where's mine?" to guide individual actions, officers in a position to control assignments feel entirely justified in "getting theirs" through internal payoffs. The officers who make these payments also find themselves in an anomic or normless situation, with compliance as the only alternative.

The first point, then, is that officers in watch-style departments take advantage of the extensive opportunities for corruption available to them because of rationalizations and justifications embedded within the police subculture(s) of their departments. Across time there emerges norms protective of *all* types of police corruption.

Also fundamental to the maintenance of patterns of corruption in watch-style departments is the effective socialization of new members. Without complete socialization, corruption is necessarily and precariously confined to particular cohorts of officers. Additionally, unless new members are thoroughly socialized, police corruption ultimately slips to the level of subcultural deviance within an organizational context.

However, all police organizations are effective socializers of new members. This is especially true of corrupt watch-style departments, for three reasons. First, such departments tend to recruit locally. The people who join corrupt watch-style departments are generally well aware of the patterns of corruption characteristic of the department. For example, newspaper journalist Robert H. Williams was born and raised in East St. Louis, Illinois, a city with a thoroughly corrupt watch-style department during Williams' childhood. Growing up in East St. Louis, Williams took police corruption for granted as did many other residents, including those who later became East St. Louis police officers. Williams recalls: "I never really knew until I left there that all cops didn't get paid off by gangsters and ordinary businessmen, or even that they weren't *supposed* to."[51]

A second reason that corrupt watch-style departments are especially effective socializers of new members is that selection procedures tend to be stacked in favor of the maintenance of corruption. Because line officers, administrators, and the segments of the community which benefit from police corruption all stand to lose a great deal should a "do-gooder" somehow manage to slip through, new recruits are selected by reference to the signs they give of their willingness to participate in or at least be silent about corruption.[52]

Lastly although many police administrators would prefer to think of policing as a science, it remains a folk art taught and learned on the streets. In all police academies recruits are sent (reluctantly in academies where instructors seek to give at least an initial appearance of integrity) to observe and work with experienced officers. After completion of recruit training, the new police officer generally spends a probationary period under the guidance of a field training officer.

The result is that new officers in corrupt watch-style departments are quickly exposed to the routine corruption characteristic of their department. It is likely that while still at the academy recruits consume the first of many free or discount meals. In addition, they are exposed to the rationalizations and justifications for the corruption characteristic of their department. Finally, they are judged by field and other supervisors by reference to departmental norms, including those supportive of corruption. Although new officers may elect not to engage in these activities, they must at least evidence a willingness to abide by subculture norms emphasizing secrecy.

However, even in corrupt watch-style departments a minority of officers elect to stay straight. Occasionally, this commitment to ethical action leads them to violate the "no rat" rule and alert superiors or outsiders to the existence of police corruption. In Birmingham, Alabama, four young police officers went public about a police burglary ring in their precinct. The officers involved in the ring were ultimately fired, but the consequences for the officers who violated norms emphasizing secrecy were almost as severe:

> Even four months later, the four officers say, half of the [police] in the . . . precinct will not speak to them. They work together, in adjacent beats, because they said other officers would not back them up on dangerous calls. . . .[53]

A final element fundamental to an organizational understanding of the origins of police corruption is administrative involvement. This involvement may be active, as when superiors engage in actions essentially similar to those of their subordinates. In Philadelphia, New York, and Chicago, police administrators were found to be actively involved in the widespread corruption characteristic of these departments. The Pennsylvania Crime Commission, for instance, concluded that "patterns of corruption exist within the Philadelphia Police Department . . . [that] . . . are not random or isolated but systematic and . . . citywide . . . [and] these patterns are not restricted to low ranking officers."[54] In Chicago, money is "filtered . . . from the lowest ranks of the department to the highest levels of command."[55]

Alternatively, involvement of members of the dominant administrative coalition may be passive, as when superiors elect to ignore or tolerate the corrupt activities of their subordinates. James C. Parsons, a reform chief in Birmingham, Alabama, reports "attending a conference with several nationally noted police chiefs and during a dinner discussion the conversation turned to police corruption. . . . [T]he chiefs were reluctant even to discuss the issue."[56] James F. Ahern notes one reason for this:

> Most police chiefs . . . having come up through the ranks of their own departments, alleviate their insecurity—as much as possible—years before they become chiefs. They protect their own, they play politics, and they survive. If they serve in cities where crime machines hold the real power and lubricate police departments with illicit funds, the chiefs function in ways that perpetuate machine power and cut off police from broad democratic controls.[57]

In summary: we have reviewed the various types of police corruption and identified and discussed the external and internal factors productive of this type of police misconduct. The essential conclusion to be drawn is that the opportunities for corruption available in jurisdictions characterized by community anomie, segmentation of interest, and culture conflict are taken advantage of when watch-style departments police these areas. More precisely, opportunities for corruption are seized by watch-style departments because of the presence of rationalizations supportive of corruption; selection, socialization, and evaluation procedures which emphasize involvement in unethical actions; and active or passive support by members of the dominant administrative coalition. In such departments, police corruption is an organizational rather than purely individualistic phenomenon.

REFERENCES

1. See Clifton Bryant (ed.), *Deviance: Occupational and Organizational Bases* (Chicago: Rand McNally, 1974).

2. Based upon Lawrence W. Sherman (ed.), *Police Corruption: A Sociological Perspective* (Garden City, N.Y.: Doubleday/Anchor Books, 1974), p.6.

3. Thomas Barker and Julian Roebuck, *An Empirical Typology of Police Corruption: A Study in Organizational Deviance* (Springfield, Ill.: Charles C Thomas, 1973), pp. 26–27.

4. Herbert Beigel and Alan Beigel, *Beneath the Badge: A Story of Police Corruption* (New York: Harper & Row, 1977), pp. 277–278.

5. Barker and Roebuck, *An Empirical Typology*, pp. 21–41.

6. Jonathan Rubinstein, *City Police* (New York: Ballantine, 1973), pp. 405–406; and personal observation.

7. Lawrence W. Sherman, *Scandal and Reform: Controlling Police Corruption* (Berkeley, Calif.: University of California Press, 1978), p. 138.

8. Edward F. Droge, Jr., *The Patrolman: A Cop's Story* (New York: Signet, 1973), p. 110.

9. Mike Royko, *Boss: Richard J. Daley of Chicago* (New York: Signet, 1971), p. 111.

10. James P. Spradley, *You Owe Yourself a Drunk* (Boston: Little, Brown, 1969), p. 286.

11. This is a paraphrase of Albert J. Reiss, Jr.'s statement: "of such evenings is much police work made." See Albert J. Reiss, Jr., *The Police and the Public* (New Haven, Conn.: Yale University Press, 1971), p. 21.

12. Beigel and Beigel, *Beneath the Badge*, p. 32; also, see Royko, *Boss*, p. 113.

13. See Robert H. Williams, *Vice Squad* (New York: Crowell, 1973) for a description of special function units.

14. Reiss, *The Police and the Public*, p. 86.

15. *The Knapp Commission Report on Police Corruption* (New York: Braziller, 1972), p. 1.

16. *Knapp Commission Report*, p. 2.

17. William J. Chambliss, "Vice, Corruption, Bureaucracy, and Power," in William J. Chambliss and Milton Mankoff (eds.), *Whose Law, What Order?* (New York: Wiley, 1976), p. 173.

18. John A. Gardiner, "Ticket Fixing," in John A. Gardiner and David J. Olson (eds.), *Theft of the City* (Bloomington, Ind.: Indiana University Press, 1974), p. 160.

19. Nicholas Gage, "Organized Crime in Court," in Gardiner and Olson, *Theft of the City*, p. 165.

20. Rubinstein, *City Police*, p. 375.

21. Barker and Roebuck, *An Empirical Typology*, p. 36.

22. Ellwyn R. Stoddard, "The Informal 'Code' of Police Deviancy: A Group Approach to 'Blue-Coat Crime,' " *Journal of Criminal Law, Criminology and Police Science, 59* (1968): 201–213.

23. Williams, *Vice Squad*, passim.

24. Sherman, *Scandal and Reform*, pp. 74–75. Also see Fred J. Cook, *The Corrupted Land: The Social Morality of Modern America* (New York: Macmillan, 1966), p. 243.

25. See Beigel and Beigel, *Beneath the Badge*, p. 277.

26. Barker and Roebuck, *An Empirical Typology*, p. 36.

27. Barker and Roebuck, *An Empirical Typology*, p. 37.

28. *Knapp Commission*, pp. 61ff.

29. Jerome Skolnick, *Justice Without Trial* (New York: Wiley, 1966), p. 28. Peter K. Manning identified "Westville" as Oakland. See Peter K. Manning, "The Researcher: An Alien in the Police World," in Arthur Niederhoffer and Abraham S. Blumberg (eds.), *The*

Ambivalent Force (Hinsdale, Ill.: The Dryden Press, 1976), p. 105.

30. Jerome Skolnick, *Justice Without Trial*, 2nd ed. (New York: Wiley, 1975), p. 269; and Sherman, *Scandal and Reform*, pp. xxx–xxxiv.

31. Sherman, *Police Corruption*; and Sherman, *Scandal and Reform*.

32. Sherman, *Police Corruption*, p. 31. Sherman also lists several additional factors, pp. 31ff.

33. See Émile Durkheim, *Suicide*, John A. Spalding and George Simpson (trans.) (New York: Free Press, 1951).

34. Durkheim, *Suicide*, p. 258.

35. Robert K. Merton, "Social Structure and Anomie," *American Sociological Review, 2* (October 1938): 672–682.

36. Royko, *Boss*, p. 73.

37. See George Lee Haskins, *Law and Authority in Early Massachusetts* (New York: Macmillan, 1960).

38. See Norman K. Denzin, "Notes on the Criminogenic Hypothesis: A Case Study of the American Liquor Industry," *American Sociological Review, 42* (December 1977): 905–920.

39. See Charles H. McCaghy, *Deviant Behavior: Crime, Conflict and Interest Groups* (New York: Macmillan, 1976), pp. 345–381.

40. See James Q. Wilson, *Varieties of Police Behavior* (Cambridge, Mass.: Harvard University Press, 1968), pp. 140–199, for a discussion of watch and legalistic departments.

41. Sherman, *Police Corruption*, p. 115.

42. I am grateful to William B. Sanders for alerting me to this point and for convincing me that it needed to be covered.

43. Sherman, *Scandal and Reform*, passim.

44. Sherman, *Scandal and Reform*, p. 41; and Rubinstein, *City Police*, pp. 407–409.

45. Personal observations.

46. Skolnick, *Justice Without Trial*, p. 208.

47. *Knapp Commission Report*, p. 7.

48. Royko, *Boss*, pp. 116–120.

49. Sherman, *Scandal and Reform*, pp. 74–75.

50. Sherman, *Scandal and Reform*, pp. 123, 222, and 225.

51. Williams, *Vice Squad*, p. 6.

52. See Stoddard, "The Informal Code"; and Beigel and Beigel, *Beneath the Badge*, p. 272.

53. Steve Gettinger, "Profile: Birmingham Police," *Police Magazine* (Prototype Issue, April 1977): 42.

54. Williams, *Vice Squad*, p. 55.

55. Beigel and Beigel, *Beneath the Badge*, p. x.

56. James C. Parsons. "A Candid Analysis of Police Corruption," in Jerome H. Skolnick and Thomas C. Gray (eds.), *Police in America* (Boston: Little, Brown, 1975), p. 255.

57. James F. Ahern, *Police in Trouble* (New York: Hawthorn Books, 1972), p. 96.

5

POLICE DISCRETION

Probably no other area has received as much attention in professional journals, books, and newspapers as that of police discretion. Despite the attendant voluminous writing and discussion, police discretion remains the most confounded subject.

Practitioners of virtually every occupation and profession are charged to a greater or lesser degree with the responsibility for making decisions. Inherent in that responsibility is discretion, which is defined by the degree of freedom to make choices.

Police decision making differs markedly from other professions in two major areas:

1. In most other professions the limits of discretion are proportionate to the rank held in the professional hierarchy. Thus lower-level workers and practitioners are usually circumscribed in the ambit of their power of discretion. And the power and possibilities of discretion are magnified with rank in the hierarchical structure. In the case of the police, however, the power of discretion that most affects individual members of the public is exercised by the lower-ranking field personnel, typically the police officer on patrol. Usually it is the patrol officers whose discretion is called into play in individual cases. At their discretion they may choose to use force, or to arrest, or to issue a summons, or instead, perhaps, to desist from engaging in any of the foregoing actions. Of course, it would be a mistake to ignore the sweeping discretionary powers of the top administrators in any police organization. They make the "big" decisions with reference to tables of organization, budget, enforcement priorities, and overall departmental policy, as well as management of related housekeeping functions. Discretion is involved in all of these overarching issues.

2. The second critical difference is the time frame available for the making of crucial decisions. In most other professions, the practitioner often has the time and is indeed obliged to consult with fellow professionals, to research an area in order to reconcile uncertainties, and to rule out inappropriate or dangerous courses of action. In medicine, for example, the medical student and the intern are roughly equivalent to the police officer working under stress, harried, functioning in a hostile environment, suffering from sleep deprivation, and making life-and-death decisions involving the fate of others. The important difference, however, is that the medical student and intern have available as immediate resources at the bedside of a patient the resident, chief resident, experienced nurses, their professors, and a variety of other clinical consultants, including their fellow students and interns. A sound teaching hospital prides itself on the fact that discretion and decision making are group efforts also monitored by senior colleagues who possess a vast reservoir of theo-

retical and clinical experience. In many instances clinical decisions are not only arrived at by team effort, but they can be modified or even reversed as necessitated by subsequent data. Further, medical practitioners have available to them, even in emergencies, the possibilities of obtaining hard data through the use of instruments, laboratory procedures, and a variety of diagnostic tests.

In the field of law, the student, the junior associate, or the senior partner can, even in a trial court situation, request an adjournment to consult, research, or to seek the resources of other practitioners in order to explore possible courses of action in a troublesome case. It is rare for even the most accomplished or renowned practitioner to try or argue an important case without the assistance of a team of experts. In addition, every legal transaction is preceded by intricate and often monumental preparation for trial or appeal.

The police officer is one of the few professionals who either works alone or with one partner who probably has no greater resources or experience than he or she. Officers must often make a decision in the most controversial cases without the benefit of precedent, extensive consultation, or research. They cannot pause for extended, sober reflection; nor can they ask for a delay in order to consult with a more experienced or supervisory administrator. Their range of options is ambiguously defined by a melange of laws, customs, precedents, and departmental regulations. They have a limited technology available to them for a genuinely sophisticated diagnosis, as do practitioners of law or medicine. Their clients are not on an admitting table or seated in an office, but may often be a vague shadow in the darkness, dimly perceived in some kaleidoscopic scene problematic in its import. Often they must decide which is the transgressor needing restraint and which the victim needing succor. There is no detector to tell them whether the flash of metal they see is a gun, a cigarette lighter, a knife, or a ball point pen. In some cases they may be able to ask questions, like a physician or lawyer. But the many conflicting claims made by the parties, the misleading statements by witnesses, and the demands of the situation requiring precipitous action, eliminate the possibilities of evaluating evidence and judicious weighing of alternatives. Keenly aware that there are no fail-safe devices to absolve them, police officers are especially bothered by the finality and irreversibility of their most critical decisions. Their courses of action cannot be altered or even reversed. Their actions are indelibly recorded and witnessed; and they become the subject of future review, litigation, and possible grounds for dismissal or even criminal prosecution.

Explanations that purport to illuminate the concept of police discretion have utilized lines of inquiry ranging from police personality, social class, race, and ideological factors, as well as situational determinants, such as the type of crime, the relative social standing of the complainants and offenders, and a host of other variables. On the one hand, police are accused of making too many arrests of minority, lower-class groups; on the other hand, they are accused of not making enough arrests of more powerful groups. For some, police discretion is an evil that is to be eliminated because of its potential for wrongdoing; yet others contend that the real art of police work is defined by the legal and structural limits of police discretion.

We believe it is impossible, as well as inadvisable, to contemplate the elimination of police discretion. The proper use of discretion, in most cases, can be taught as part of an overall training process. The excesses can be limited by adequate professional supervision. There will always be cases requiring the use of force where the police officer's discretion will be the basis for controversy. Police departments must accept this fact as a basic condition of their existence; and police officers must learn to live with this risk and the implications for being second-guessed.

Discretion to arrest or not to arrest is usually the central concern of the literature. There are some general guidelines that are connected with the police function and the officer's concept of his or her role. Generally, in serious cases involving a felony or certain misdemeanors, there will nearly always be an arrest. In trivial cases there will hardly ever be an arrest. Police discretion as it pertains to arrest is connected largely to a group of middle-level offenses, neither too serious nor too trivial. It is really this rather narrow range of cases that has produced the greatest controversies over police discretion. Even with young delinquents whose actions are not legally crimes, the police officer defines the act in terms of adult criteria. A forcible rape by a fifteen-year-old is interpreted as a serious adult felony, and the child is taken into custody. A petty larceny by a fourteen-year-old, however, is likely to be considered a minor offense, and the child will probably receive a warning.

When one understands the police culture in all its ramifications, one is less inclined to attribute arrest decisions to such variables as values, class differences, personality factors, ideological considerations, and racial or ethnic components, all of which appear prominently in the literature explaining police discretion. Community definitions as to what constitutes a case serious enough to call for an arrest govern a great deal of local police actions. These definitions are informal and tacit, rather than legally prescribed. In this area police officers are in the same position as an anthropologist, relying on cultural relativity to shape their judgment so that they may behave appropriately.

The other range of variables that we consider important are such things as the police officer's record of performance. Also, does each officer have to meet an arrest quota for that month? What time of day does an incident take place? Is it near the end of a shift or at the beginning of a tour? Will the police officer have to spend hours after duty in processing an arrest? Will this interfere with a social or a family engagement? Does the department pay overtime for additional hours of work? Does the officer need the additional compensation? Although rarely taken into account, these seemingly prosaic factors loom as controlling and compelling determinants of action.

In the section that follows we have selected articles that seem to us to be clearly representative of the various positions with regard to police discretion.

A Socio-Legal Theory of Police Discretion

Richard E. Sykes, James C. Fox, and John P. Clark

INTRODUCTION

The Problem

The literature on police delineates two distinct perspectives on the factors associated with the decision to take a suspect into custody. One approach has focused on the decision to arrest as limited by legal and judicial criteria with the conclusion that many of the serious problems of discretion are associated with the decision not to arrest (H. Goldstein 1967; J. Goldstein 1960; LaFave 1962, 1965a, b; Livermore 1970). The other has emphasized extralegal criteria (Black 1968, 1970; Black and Reiss 1970; Goldman 1963; Hartjen 1972; Peterson 1972; Piliavan and Briar 1964; President's Commission 1967; Westley 1953). This perspective is apt to emphasize problems of discretion associated with the decision to arrest.

The difference between these two perspectives is greater than is generally acknowledged in the literature. Those who emphasize decisions *not to arrest* suggest that more arrests should take place. Police should not have so much discretion to let suspects go. Those who emphasize decisions *to arrest* suggest that citizens are being apprehended for extralegal, personal reasons. Arrest is sometimes a conscious, sometimes an unconscious, exercise of harassment. The first group

Note: This research was supported by the Center for Studies of Crime and Delinquency, National Institute of Mental Health, Grant No. R01 MH17917-02. Opinions expressed herein are the authors' and do not necessarily reflect those of the research sponsors or monitors.

decries lax enforcement; the second group, unfair enforcement. Both groups see a violation of the rule of law since it is enforced differentially across the population.

The goals of the authors are:

1. To formulate a theory of police discretion which takes both these perspectives into account
2. To assess the weight officers give to factors emphasized in each perspective by analyzing data on situational dispositions of police-civilian encounters
3. To integrate both viewpoints into one *and* assess which viewpoint more accurately reflects actual police practice

Some Definitions

Discretion exists whenever an officer is free to choose from two or more task-relevant, alternative interpretations of the events reported, inferred, or observed in a police-civilian encounter. Alternatives include (1) definition of an event as one of official interest to police or not, (2) identification of a citizen as incumbent in a role of official interest to police or not, and (3) choice of actions towards events and citizens so defined and identified. "Official" implies the use of reports to recognize the commission of an offense, or special actions by means of which a citizen identified as a violator has imposed upon him a new status vis-à-vis the legal system. Such a status is usually assumed after initiatory arrest procedures.

The theory will be tested using data gathered by field observers who quantitatively coded the nature of a random sample of more than 3,000 police-citizen encounters, their outcomes, and more than a thousand hours of interaction between the participants. The intent of the research was to gather descriptive data on the nature of police activities as well as to collect data on the factors which influenced police decision making. The data make it possible to compare the demeanor of officers and citizens across encounters, *statement by statement*, as well as by other cues, and to create profiles of such encounters. Such information permits study of the association of many variables with the decision whether or not to arrest.

A THEORY OF DECISION MAKING

Role Attribution

In a police-citizen encounter the problem of the actors is to decide what position each is to occupy and what behavior the occupant of that position is expected to display. Role attribution and role-appropriate behavior are the result of the information exchanged by the participants in the encounter.[1] As a result a violator may be labelled. Subsequent behavior as policeman is contingent on this previous decision. When there is no predetermined agenda the most important variables seem to be those criteria by which actors decide to attribute identities and expectations to one another and then act in terms of such attributions. The questions then are (1) in police-citizen interactions how do actors decide on identities, and (2) once identities are decided, what behavior follows?

We shall limit ourselves to answering those questions only insofar as officers' decisions about citizens are concerned. How do officers decide that someone is to be given the identity of violator? We conceptualized this problem of identity in terms of the decisions which the officers had to make. We proposed that officers identify the actors by a set of criteria henceforth termed *decision criteria*.

Decision Criteria

Integrating the legal and extralegal traditions of scholarship mentioned in the introduction yields four such criteria: (1) the law, (2) official or unofficial departmental policy, (3) the demeanor of the suspect toward the officer, and (4) the potential threat the suspect poses to the officer's safety. By these criteria officers decide whether or not to define a situation as one in which a violation has taken place and to identify in-

[1] In his comments a reviewer makes some very pertinent suggestions which would expand information to include previous knowledge as well as information gathered during the encounter itself. Essentially we agree with this and later suggestions concerning the importance of other actors. However, our data indicate that over a *large* number of encounters, most of which occur in private places, relatively few involve people or places known to police either personally or by reputation. While such knowledge is apt to be decisive in individual cases, it does not account for much of the variance over a large number of cases.

Basically, however, our problem is methodological. Previous literature on police addresses the importance of psychological and demographic variables. The model we propose pertains to a different set of variables and a different level of explanation. For this reason we view it as complementing rather than competing with other explanations. Not only this, but were we to include as many factors as probably influence decisions, there would be no analytic technique capable of handling either the number of dimensions or the limited size of our sample.

dividuals as violators. By comparing information to each criterion the officers can decide whether or not the criterion is satisfied.

Law

The state and municipal law establish various limits upon citizen behavior. If the behavior of citizens exceeds these limits and is known, that behavior may be defined as criminal by either the police or citizen public, and the legal criterion becomes salient. In most cases, police respond to citizen judgments (Black 1968:188–92, Clark 1965:309–10, LaFave 1962:210–19, Reiss 1971:69–70). Once requested by a citizen, information is sought by the officer to determine the covariance of his and the citizen's judgment. Except for motor vehicle offenses, which are primarily a function of departmental policy (Gardiner 1969), the uniformed patrolman directly witnesses and takes action on a violation in only a small percentage of cases (Reiss 1971:19–20, Wilson 1968:19). Information is sought from witnesses to determine whether or not an offense has occurred, and if it has occurred, whether it is a felony or a misdemeanor.

Policy

Police departments differ in the extent to which goal-relevant policy is official or unofficial. Official policy is that which is written and communicated by regularized means to department members (cf. Goldstein 1960, Parnas 1967). In the largest department included in this research, policy was often not explicit but might be inferred from official documents. The official policy was that offense reports were to be written for all complaints pertaining to crimes against persons or property, implying that other violations were not necessarily considered offenses, nor their perpetrators technically considered violators. Since policy often reflects administrative priority in the face of limited resources, such policy establishes a hierarchy among the multitude of goals. An officer's knowledge of policy may not involve so much a set of separate goals as a set of legally relative hierarchies. In a sense the organization predetermines the probabilities of certain identities being attributed within the broader mandate of law.

Respect

To a certain extent, law establishes rights and obligations of role incumbents. Historically an officer may use deadly force for self-protection or for apprehending a felon. With certain limitations the officer may seek legally relevant information, but the law is vague in regard to citizen behavior vis-à-vis an officer's role behavior. Verbal behavior which would be in clear contempt of court is often tolerated by a law officer (Reiss 1971:179–80). While the legal literature on police decisions gives only limited attention to the goal of maintaining respect for the uniform (cf. LaFave 1962:231–32) sociological literature emphasizes this factor considerably more (Bittner 1970, Piliavin and Briar 1964, Reiss 1971). Respect includes recognition or obedience to the legitimate exercise of authority by an officer. The brief and problematic nature of the officer's relation to the citizen makes this an area of concern from the officer's perspective. A citizen who does not display such respect may be labelled a violator.

Safety

An officer is vulnerable to attack by hostile, abnormal, or emotionally distraught persons. Personal strategies are often adopted for self-protection. Were safety not important, officers would not draw their weapons *before* many encounters, and therefore before any disrespect for their role has occurred. Indeed, police training literature emphasizes the need for caution, prudence, and superior force in the face of danger in order to maximize safety (Leonard and More 1971, Wileman 1970, 1971).

The officer makes decisions within legal and police constraints. If he decides to ignore these constraints he will do so either at serious risk to himself, or else by creatively using legal and policy criteria pretextually for violations that do not normally result in arrest. The possible combinations of legal and policy criteria are illustrated in Figure 1. Generally it will be hypothesized that the more criteria are congruent with one another the more likely a particular outcome. For instance, the cell 1 cases, where a felony has been committed and policy encourages arrest, are very apt to end in arrest, while cell 6 cases are very unlikely to end in arrest. While it is possible for departmental policy not to require arrest for a felony, in the departments we studied this was not the case. It is also possible for arrest to occur by policy directive where no legal offense occurred, but such a policy if overt would make officers liable for false arrest. In the departments studied, as far as we are aware, no such policies existed at least insofar as the normal activities of uniformed police are concerned. In these data there is also no case in which the characteristics of cell 6 were satisfied and an arrest occurred.

FIGURE 1 Combinations of Legal and Policy Criteria

Legal criterion	*Policy directive* Arrest (+)*	Do not arrest (−)
Felony (+)	1. + +	2. + −
Misdemeanor (±)	3. ± +	4. ± −
No violation (−)	5. − +	6. − −

*Where signs are the same, congruency exists.

Legal and policy criteria will henceforth be termed "formal constraints." They combine with respect and safety criteria as in Figure 2. Six groups of goal criteria configurations were evident (Figure 2). In groups 1 and 2 the officer had reason to believe felonies had taken place and that departmental policy directed that an arrest be made. In groups 3 and 4 misdemeanors have been committed. In groups 5 and 6 the officer's information led him to conclude that no legal violations had occurred.

Generally we would hypothesize that the greater the number of positive signs that exist, the more likely a citizen is to be identified as a violator; and the more negative signs, the less likely. If a felony has occurred we would expect that fact to outweigh all other criteria. Where there is no legal violation we would expect likelihood of arrest to increase as signs for other criteria are positive, but we would also expect that arrests would be pretextual.

FIGURE 2 Possible Configurations of Decision Criteria

Possible cells

Group	FC*	R†	S††
1.	+ +	+	+
	+ +	+	−
	+ +	−	+
	+ +	−	−
3.	± +	+	+
	± +	+	−
	± +	−	+
	± +	−	−
5.	− +	+	+
	− +	+	−
	− +	−	+
	− +	−	−
2.	+ −	+	+
	+ −	+	−
	+ −	−	+
	+ −	−	−
4.	± −	+	+
	± −	+	−
	± −	−	+
	± −	−	−
6.	− −	+	+
	− −	+	−
	− −	−	+
	− −	−	−

*Formal constraints

†Respect (+indicates disrespect)

††Safety (+ indicates danger to the person of the officer)

Theoretically, a distinction must be made between arrest (official identification of a citizen as a violator) and enforcement of the law, since arrest is only one means of enforcement. An adequately broad perspective must encompass means other than those specifically prescribed by law or departmental policy, otherwise police behavior cannot be accounted for in most instances.

A flow chart of the series of decisions the officer must make (Figure 3) delineates the process as follows: The officer, receiving information either directly or indirectly from evidence or testimony, compares this to decision criteria. If any information is relevant to criteria (i.e., a law has been broken, a policy is relevant, respect for the role is lacking, or his safety is threatened) the officer may take action, since by these criteria a violation may be defined or a violator identified. His action will be compared to criteria of means (criteria of behavior *after* a person is identified) at the same time that a citizen's reaction is judged. Thus, there is a continuous feedback cycle to both decision criteria and criteria of means.

For an outcome of arrest to occur, at least the legal criterion must be satisfied. If a minor violation, other criteria must be satisfied in addition. So-called "good pinches" occur when the legal violation is serious; or if not serious, the other criteria are satisfied as well. Generally, except for felony violations, we would predict that the more criteria satisfied, the more likely the arrest. These additional criteria are not necessary for arrest for most felony violations of the type with which uniformed patrolmen usually deal. Identification as a felon is sufficient for official labelling to take place.

Proceeding from this perspective we shall now examine its fit to the particular data collected in this study.

DATA COLLECTION

Observers gathered data while riding with police officers. These data were gathered by systematic observation of police-citizen encounters using an interaction coding system. Briefly, this coding schema permitted the observers to do the following:

FIGURE 3 Dynamics of Process of Law Enforcement

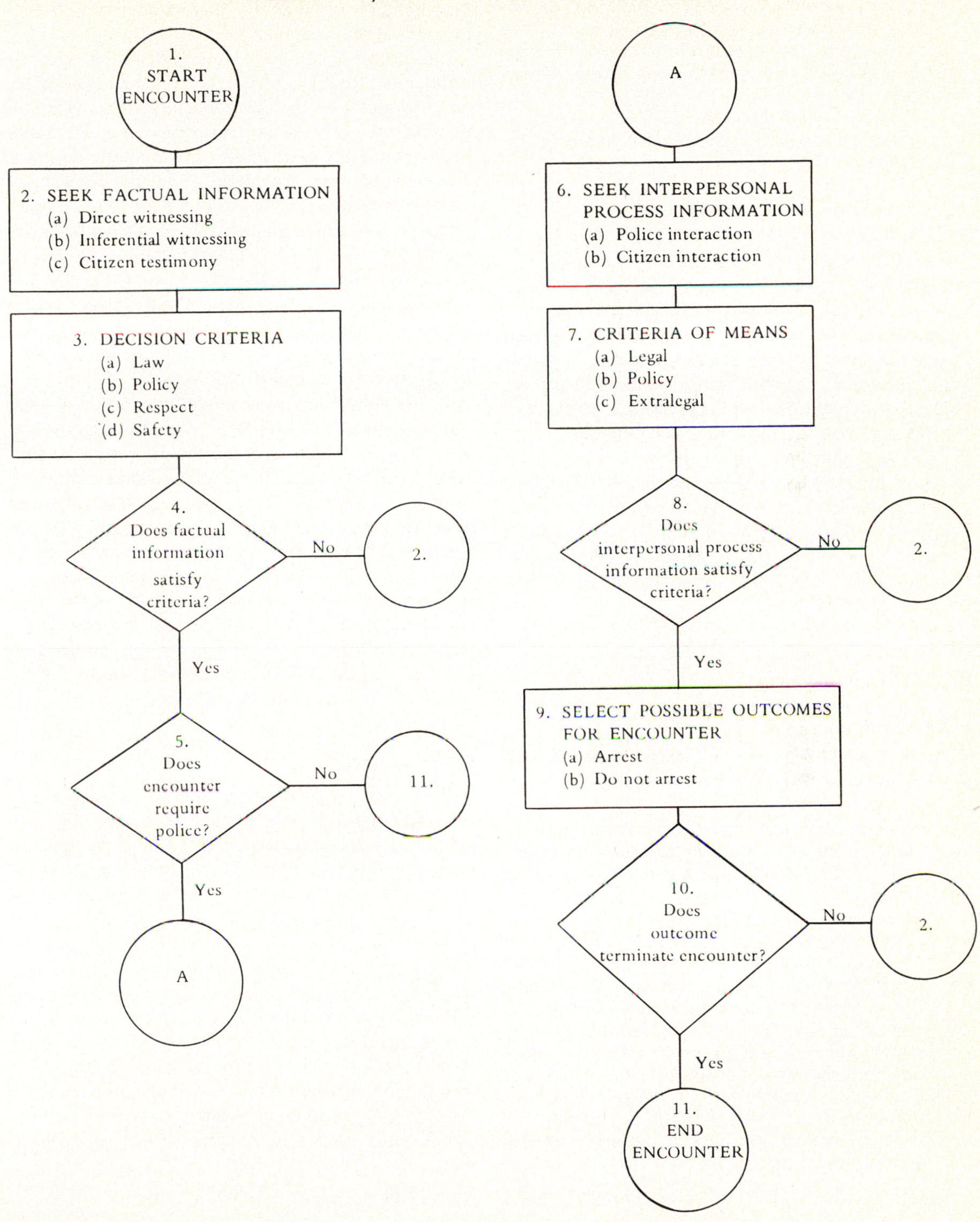

1. To record the nature of the encounter, e.g., crime against person or property, a violation of private or public decorum, service needed;
2. To rate every encounter-relevant verbal interaction of police and citizens along several dimensions;
3. To code certain nonverbal behaviors as well as outcomes, and descriptions of citizen-actors involved.

A full description of the code may be found in Sykes 1972.

Five observers rode for more than a year in one city of about half a million and in two residential suburbs of about 25,000 population each. The full data base consisted of 3,323 police-citizen encounters observed during randomly sampled shifts of police departments in the three midwest communities. In about 15 percent of these encounters (N = 520) an alleged violator was present who was not a routine traffic offender.

Consistent with the above theory we will look at the effects of these factors in the decision to officially define a citizen as a violator. Arrest was the criterion for official labelling as a violator. The "fit" of the factors to the criteria was decided by the observers. Interobserver reliability using Scott's coefficient ranged from 0.70 to 0.80 (Scott 1955).

ANALYSIS

Legal Criteria

Most alleged violator-present police-citizen encounters fall into four of five legal categories:

1. From the officer's perspective, information indicates no apparent legal violation has occurred, or if it has, the violation was not witnessed by an officer.
2. From the officer's perspective, information indicates a misdemeanor has occurred which was witnessed by an officer.
3. From the officer's perspective, information indicates a felony has occurred or is occurring.
4. The officer is performing a ministerial function in making an arrest, e.g., serving a warrant or transporting a shoplifter arrested by someone else.
5. An additional but very small category consists of situations in which some action by the police is required, though not necessarily arrest; for example, threatened suicide.

Information includes not only that relayed through the communication net, but that information gathered after arrival at the scene.

The subject encounters, when ordered by legal criterion, reveal that 146 of 520, or more than one-fourth, involved either no technical violation or no violation for which the officers had the choice of arrest (Table 1). Many of these encounters were domestic disputes, arguments between neighbors, or calls about vaguely suspicious persons. In such cases the process of inquiry led to the conclusion that what was initially alleged by either officer or citizen as illegal behavior actually involved no violation. On the other hand, more than half involved situations where there was a violation of the law but no felony. Common in this category were loud parties, barking or unleashed dogs, unwanted guests, and many cases of public drunkenness.

If law enforcement were limited to arrest, and legal criteria were all that an officer used in his decision to place a suspect into custody, then it would be self-evident that the law is dramatically underenforced. In more than two-thirds of our cases (374) arrest could have been the outcome; but, in fact, arrest was the outcome in only slightly more than one-fourth of those cases (102 of 374) (Table 1). Since nonarrest decisions accounted for a much greater proportion of the cases than arrest decisions did, there must have been other factors than legal criteria which affected the decision to arrest. On the other hand, where a felony was involved, arrest almost always occurred.

Policy Criteria

The police departments studied had few official policy guidelines that were explicit other than the ones previously referred to. The former guidelines required offense reports in cases of possible crimes against property or persons. We might expect that officers would have treated these cases more seriously and thus arrest outcomes would have been more frequent.

It would appear from an examination of Table 2 that where minor technical offenses occurred, even in regard to property or persons, arrests were not made. In that regard, legal criteria and policy criteria together are inadequate to account for outcomes of arrest. On the other hand, where a felony had occurred or where the officers were serving a warrant or acting in a ministerial function, the legal criterion was adequate in itself.

TABLE 1 Arrest Outcomes and Apparent Technical Status of Violation after Receipt of Information by Officer (N = 520)

	Technical Status					
Outcome	1 No violation within authority of officer	2 Probable misdemeanor	3 Probable felony	4 Ministerial	5 Special cases	6 Totals
No arrest	146	241	3*	15†	13	418
Misdemeanor arrests	0	37	16	15	2	70
Felony arrests	0	4	23	5	0	32
Total	146	282	42	35	15	520
Percentage	28.0	54.2	8.1	6.7	2.9	99.9

* 2 citizen arrests and 1 escape

† 11 citizen arrests, 3 special cases involving transporting juveniles to a detention home, and 1 case in which a store owner who had arrested a juvenile for shoplifting was persuaded not to press charges after the juvenile was reprimanded by officers

Respect and Safety Criteria

Scholars have identified other extralegal criteria than those of safety and respect for the police officer's role, which influence the labelling of the violator. Briefly, these criteria include identification of the alleged violator as a minority group member, or as lower-class. Our data confirm that arrest is more likely for lower-class, nonwhite males. A subsequent article will deal with these data, but meantime, we have found that of the observed encounters, nearly half (Table 1) were either legal or policy relevant (146 involved no violations, 39 involved felony arrests, 20 involved arrests in ministerial capacity). Thus, these criteria accounted for the situational disposition of the violator. In the remaining violator-present encounters, legal or policy criteria were important in defining the behavior as illegal. Whether or not the offender was arrested, however, was undefined, since in only 12 percent (Table 2) of these encounters was arrest the outcome (41 of 282 misdemeanors).

This permits us to make an important distinction: there was a difference in our findings between inter-

TABLE 2 Arrests and Nonarrests by Type of Violation (N = 359)‡

	Status of Violation						
	2 ***Probable misdemeanor***		**3** ***Probable felony***		**4** ***Warrant or transport***		
Type of Violation	*A**	*NA†*	*A*	*NA*	*A*	*NA*	*5* *Totals*
Against property	5	29	12	0	7	0	53
Against person	2	6	1	1	4	0	14
Domestic dispute	3	11	3	0	1	1	19
Public decorum	29	174	10	0	2	0	215
Other	2	21	13	2	6	14	58
Total	41	241	39	3	20	15	359
Percentage	11.4	67.1	10.9	0.8	5.6	4.2	100.0

* Arrest

† No arrest or no arrest by the officers themselves

‡ Does not include 146 cases in which no violation occurred and 15 special cases (see Table 1)

personal behavior between officers and citizens *incidental* to arrest, and interpersonal behavior which *led* to arrest. Where legal or policy criteria were adequate or where the police were acting in a ministerial function, interaction itself, except as information relative to criterion, should not have been used to explain the decision to take a suspect into custody. Interaction incidental to felony arrest may have been polite or impolite, hostile or friendly, aggressive or not, and offenders may have been any class, color, and so forth, but in each case these factors did not ordinarily contribute to arrest outcomes. This modification has generally been ignored by previous scholars, but we found that it is important if police behavior is to be accounted for.

This distinction revealed that after officers had collected sufficient information, alleged violator-present encounters would fall into one of three categories:

1. Discretion without arrest option
2. Discretion with arrest option
3. Discretion limited to arrest

In the first case, information available to officers indicated that no violation had occurred, that no legal criteria were relevant, and thus, arrest was extremely unlikely. In the second case, a violation had occurred and arrest was one option that officers may have exercised. In the third case, the violation was so serious that officers had almost no choice but to make an arrest and thus, legal or policy criteria accounted for arrest outcomes. Strictly speaking there was no arrest discretion in the last instance.

In the first and third cases interpersonal factors could not have accounted for arrest but may have affected strategies of officers. Since arrest was problematic in the second category, extralegal factors may have affected arrest because legal or policy criteria already defined the behavior as illegal. At the same time, however, arrest on those criteria alone was unlikely.

Since so many violators of the law escaped arrest, *what conditions had to be present for a suspect to be arrested?* We will examine 282 encounters in which legal or policy criteria were relevant but did not themselves determine arrest (Table 4).

Our data in this regard were utilized in several ways. First, we wished to determine if the frequency of impoliteness, or noncompliance, or the expression of anger, or the threat of violence, changed the chances that an alleged violator would be arrested. Secondly, we wished to determine if mutual or unilateral anger altered the probabilities of arrest.

In Table 4 the distribution of impolite statements by citizens in encounters is divided into four groups depending on the degree of displayed impoliteness. It is evident that in any given encounter, as the violator increased his level of impoliteness, his chances of being arrested increased dramatically. When this distribution is compared with nonarrest outcomes, the difference is statistically significant ($\chi^2 = 19.07$, d.f. = 3, $P > 0.001$).

A similar tendency was evident in regard to the effect of displays of anger on the officer's decision to take a suspect into custody (Table 5). Arrest rates were significantly higher when the citizen alone was angry or when both citizen and officer were angry than when neither was angry or the officer alone was angry.

When politeness was examined together with ordering and complying behavior, similar results were obtained (data not included here). Where no impoliteness by either officer or citizen was displayed, the arrest rate was about 11.3 percent. If the officer initiated an impolite order or command, however, the arrest rate increased to slightly less than 15.8 percent. When the citizen initiated impoliteness or coupled that

TABLE 3 Mean Number of Impolite Statements per Discretion Category (N = 505)*

Discretion Category	$\overline{X}$	*S*	S^2	*N*
Discretion without arrest	1.64	4.71	22.19	146
Discretion with arrest	2.30	5.96	35.54	282
(No arrest)	1.79	5.31	28.16	241
(Arrest)	5.29	8.37	70.01	41
Discretion limited to arrest	6.92	18.06	326.26	77

* Does not include 15 special cases (see Table 1)

TABLE 4 Arrest Rates by Level of Citizen Impoliteness (N = 282)*

Level of Impoliteness	*Arrest rate (%)*
1. None	9.7
2. Less than average	23.4
3. Greater than average	11.1
4. Much greater than average†	40.9

* Cases in which only a technical violation occurred (see Table 1)
† More than one standard deviation greater than the average level of impoliteness

TABLE 5 Arrest Percentages by Anger (N = 282)*

Anger	*Arrest rate (%)*
None displayed	8.6
Officer only	12.8
Citizen only	23.1
Mutual display	24.3

* Cases of probable misdemeanor, in which only a technical violation occurred (see Table 1)

with noncompliance to the officer's legitimate authority, the rate of arrest increased to about 24.4 percent. And finally, if the impolite orders and impolite noncompliance were mutual, the rate rose dramatically to 40 percent regardless of who initiated the action.

Our evidence was very limited with regard to the probabilities of arrest when an officer's safety was threatened, if we did not consider impoliteness or anger as implicitly threatening. While citizen anger occurred in a third of all encounters observed, and officer or citizen anger occurred in nearly half the encounters, the incidence of violence or threatened violence was so low as to make conclusions difficult.

Our impression is that the actual commission of violence against an officer automatically led to arrest. The reverse was not necessarily true, since sometimes an officer may have attacked a citizen without arresting him and may have approached an encounter with his gun drawn as a precaution but with no further effect.

CONCLUSIONS

1. Careful documentation of police patrol activities has provided a basis for some empirically grounded criteria which police in three midwestern communities used in deciding whether or not to identify a citizen as a violator. The thrust of current police literature (and even the rhetoric of the police occupation itself) is that patrol officers have considerable arrest discretion. On the contrary, however, our studies indicate that in approximately half such cases, patrol officers in contact with alleged violators had little, if any, arrest discretion. Officers were not allowed to make an arrest because statutes and/or departmental policy did not encourage arrest; on the other hand, officers had no other option but to make an arrest because other authorities (e.g., the courts) or departmental policy so directed.

2. In any comprehensive explanation of a police officer's decision to arrest, one must first examine the real restraints which impinge upon the latitude of his decision making. One such significant restraint in our study was the requirement of law which often acted primarily as a suppressant of arrest relative to the demands of police by complainants. Another restraint was the finer distinctions made by the informal and formal policies of a particular police department. Patrol officers on rare occasions may have ignored such restraints, but direct observational data impressively attested to the impact of such restraints.

3. Outcomes of police-citizen contact could best be predicted by us by first employing legal or organizational policy models. These were, in effect, rules for defining the situation and identifying citizen roles, not extralegal models, such as those used for sociologically oriented research. Only after this large portion of nonarrest and arrest outcomes was removed did it seem advisable to utilize models which incorporated such variables as use of abusive language and failure to show respect for the uniform. Legal and organizational policy criteria generally had to be taken into account before extralegal variables had a chance to affect arrest decisions. But once these criteria were satisfied, the chances of arrest fell rather heavily on those who showed disrespect for the officer's role or threatened his safety.

4. One last general conclusion must be drawn from the data and the strong impression of our observations of police patrol activities. The overwhelming atmosphere of alleged violator-present police-citizen encounters was relatively calm, routine, and not particularly entangling for all parties concerned. In spite of the circumstances which generated the presence of police officers with their uniforms and weapons—the high incidence of drunkenness, the presence of adversaries, and the occasional presence of known past offenders—one must be impressed with the high degree of civility all parties accorded each other. This in no way is meant to diminish the role of uncivil behavior and its consequences, but is stated in order to accurately describe the observable character of most of the police-citizen encounters in our study.

SOME SUGGESTED PERFORMANCE CRITERIA

Our data clearly show that a substantial proportion of our encounters involve either discretion without arrest option or discretion limited to arrest. In both cases the so-called nonvisibility problem is less crucial, since in the first instance there is probably no legal violation, and in the second instance there is virtually always an arrest. The crucial cases are discretion with arrest-option cases. What criteria now seem to govern these cases?

We have distinguished enforcement from arrest. Enforcement is a broad category comprising techniques by means of which persons are brought into compliance with the law. In practice, arrest may be a means of enforcement or a means of punishment, two functionally different ends. If a person commits a crime of sufficient seriousness he will be arrested although he ceases and desists. In the case of a homicide an officer does not merely warn the suspect not to do it again or to stop murdering people. But in the case of a loud party, arrest normally follows the *refusal* of the suspect to hold a quiet party. However the law may read, in a great many cases, the arrest is not so much for having a loud party as for refusing to cease having a loud party. As our data show, noncompliance, especially impolite noncompliance, increases likelihood of arrest to 40 percent. No doubt this percentage would be higher if our data base distinguished degrees of seriousness of noncompliance.

We suggest that the law might more openly recognize the distinction between arrest as a means of enforcement and arrest as a punishment for an act by explicitly providing a formal "warning" and "compliance" stipulation. We suggest that most misdemeanors should be considered as instances where the officer's first duty is to enjoin the citizen to cease from his activity. He would issue a warning ticket and request that the citizen sign an indication of compliance. If the citizen were then to desist there would be no further legal hassle. Such a procedure would formalize present practice to a degree and make visible the great bulk of low-visibility decisions without overloading the jail house. It would also provide a record, should a citizen refuse to sign the compliance, to which both citizen and officer could refer. If, later in his shift, an officer were called back to the scene, he would have a record of a compliance and, given this record and a repetition of the original act, reason to arrest the citizen. If the citizen refused to sign the original compliance, either because he felt he was innocent, or for other reasons, then the alternative of arrest would be clear to both himself and to the officer. Generally the compliance should be specific—that, for instance, the suspect agrees to leave the Triangle Bar, and not return there that evening, or that the suspect agrees to turn down his radio to a level acceptable to his neighbors. The warning-and-compliance procedure would be somewhat different from the issuing of tickets for misdemeanors now being tried in some departments.

A compliance would be somewhat like a "fix-it" ticket, but more immediate, since in most cases it would involve immediate compliance through ceasing an activity which is an annoyance to some other person(s) in the vicinity. Here we should note that all studies of uniformed police agree that more than three-quarters of police work is in response to citizen complaints, and that (unlike a speeder) unless the person complies the interpersonal annoyance is likely to continue and cause renewed complainant dissatisfaction. Compliances would be encounter-specific, not long-term contracts, and they would not become a matter of permanent record. They would be discarded and destroyed by officers at the end of some specific period of time, probably within the week.

The use of compliances would minimally formalize and make visible what is now practiced informally and invisibly. The amendment of many present laws pertaining to misdemeanors would formalize the warning function of the officer and make it mandatory, thus eliminating those inequities which result from an officer's directly arresting a person for an act in one case, while another officer negotiates or imposes some other outcome than arrest for the same act in another case.

The second factor which seems to influence discretion with arrest-option situations is the interpersonal respect which characterizes officer-civilian interaction during the encounter. When such respect is not displayed, arrest percentages increase dramatically. We have already commented on the lack of formal sanctions available to police in such situations and therefore their resort to informal punishment. We suggest that perhaps the law and the courts ought to take more notice of these relations. After proper warning, as with cases referred to above, officers should be able to ticket a citizen for certain specifically described acts of disrespect, notably for the use of gratuitous insult, especially that involving gutter language and insulting labels, or, alternately, such acts should be taken cognizance of by the prosecutor and/or the court should a case come to trial and ultimate conviction on some other ground.

The same rules should apply to police officers. It should be expected that they would exercise their authority with decent language, and that a citizen should have the same right to make a complaint against the officer as the officer does against him. One possible means of impartial evidence collection might be a requirement that officers carry small, portable recording devices in their shirt pockets which would record both their words to the civilians and the civilians' to them. The recordings would be erased within forty-eight hours unless a complaint by either a citizen or an officer was heard.

A third controversy relates to violence. The traditional right of an officer to use deadly force to apprehend a felon is now recognized by many to be an unwisely broad mandate, since the outcome may be equivalent to capital punishment for a theft. It is less widely recognized that violence is still used beyond the point of necessity and as an informal punishment by officers, mainly because of indifference or lack of control by their superiors. Generally, the law should make the use of violence against any person who is restrained, either physically or by handcuffs, grounds for immediate dismissal of an officer, as well as for civil and criminal action. An impartial officer of the court might be present at the jail when prisoners are brought in to determine whether either the prisoner or the officer is injured and to make a report in all such cases.

Fourth, police departments should develop new methods to control and to evaluate personnel. Our data indicate that a supervisor is present less than 5 percent of the time, and that he takes an active part in an encounter much less often than that. Generally, dispatchers can anticipate a situation which is likely to be "hot." Street sergeants should be present at the scene to control their men, especially in those situations where tempers fray and angry words are exchanged.

Additionally, departments should formally recognize that one characteristic of a good officer in cases of "discretion with arrest option" is that he is usually able to settle the situation short of arrest. Too many arrests for minor offenses suggest that the officer is ineffective in negotiating or imposing street solutions. Similarly, if an officer needs to use violence frequently this also indicates lack of interpersonal skill, for violence occurs in probably less than 2 or 3 percent of police-civilian encounters.

Perhaps one monitoring method would be for each officer to carry a book of precoded forms, one of which would be filled out for each call. On it the officer would indicate the original nature of the call; whether a legal violation appeared to have occurred over which he had power; whether alternatives to arrest were offered; whether any physical contact occurred between himself and any civilian during the encounter, and if so, the reason for it; what he assessed the nature of the human relations during the encounter to be; and what the final outcome of the encounter was. Such a card would simply require making checkmarks, but it would enable the department to maintain a continuous monitoring of officer activities, as well as require the officer to do some monitoring of his own activities and manner. Whenever aggressive physical contact occurred, a further explanation of the reason for and nature of the contact should be required. Each encounter report would be entered into the department's data system and would be utilized in personnel evaluations, as well as in evaluations of the nature of departmental activities and studies of the exercise of discretion.

Utilization of procedures similar to those recommended above would make low-visibility decisions more visible, but would permit the continuance of many of the informal practices which result in a much lower arrest rate than would occur with a slavish adherence to the letter of the law. Such procedures would further introduce control features into the patrol system, a system which presently suffers from lack of supervision.

REFERENCES

1. R. L. Ackoff and T. Emery, *On Purposeful Systems* (Chicago: Aldine-Atherton, 1972).

2. American Bar Association Project on Standards for Criminal Justice, *Standards Relating to the Urban Police Function* (Chicago: American Bar Association, 1973).

3. W. Ross Ashby, *An Introduction to Cybernetics* (London: Chapman and Hall, 1956).

4. E. Bittner, "The Police on Skid Row: A Study of Peace Keeping," *American Sociological Review, 32* (October 1967), pp. 699–715.

5. E. Bittner, *The Function of the Police in Modern*

Society (Washington, D.C.: U.S. Government Printing Office, 1970).

6. D. J. Black, "Police Encounters and Social Organization: An Observational Study." (Ph.D. dissertation, University of Michigan, 1968).

7. D. J. Black, "Production of Crime Rates," *American Sociological Review, 35* (August 1970), pp. 733–48.

8. D. J. Black and A. J. Reiss, Jr., "Police Control of Juveniles," *American Sociological Review, 35* (February 1970), pp. 63–77.

9. Walter Buckley, *Sociology and Modern Systems Theory* (Englewood Cliffs, N.J.: Prentice-Hall, 1967).

10. J. P. Clark, "Isolation of the Police: A Comparison of the British and American Situations," *Journal of Criminal Law, Criminology and Police Science, 56* (September 1965), pp. 307–19.

11. E. Cumming, I. Cumming, and L. Edell, "Policeman as Philosopher, Guide and Friend," *Social Problems, 12* (Winter 1965), pp. 276–86.

12. John A. Gardiner, *Traffic and the Police: Variations in Law-Enforcement Police* (Cambridge, Mass.: Harvard University Press, 1969).

13. N. Goldman, *The Differential Selection of Juvenile Offenders for Court Appearance*, National Research and Information Center, National Council on Crime and Delinquency (New York: National Council on Crime and Delinquency, 1963).

14. H. Goldstein, "Administrative Problems in Controlling the Exercise of Police Authority," *Journal of Criminal Law, Criminology and Police Science, 58* (June 1967), pp. 160–72; J. Goldstein, "Police Discretion Not to Invoke the Criminal Process: Low Visibility Decisions in the Administration of Justice," *Yale Law Journal, 69* (March 1960), pp. 543–94.

15. Neal Gross, Ward S. Mason, and Alexander W. McEachern, *Explorations in Role Analysis* (New York: John Wiley & Sons, 1958).

16. C. A. Hartjen, "Police-Citizen Encounters: Social Order in Interpersonal Interaction," *Criminology* (May 1972), pp. 61–84.

17. W. R. LaFave, "The Police and Nonenforcement of the Law," parts 1 and 2, *Wisconsin Law Review* (January, March 1962), pp. 104–37 and 179–239; *Arrest: The Decision to Take a Suspect Into Custody* (Boston: Little, Brown, 1965); "Improving Police Performance Through the Exclusionary Rule," parts 1 and 2, *Missouri Law Review, 30* 3, 4 (1965), pp. 391–458 and 566–610.

18. W. R. LaFave and F. S. Remington, "Controlling the Police: The Judge's Role in Making and Reviewing Law Enforcement Decisions," *Michigan Law Review, 63* (1965), pp. 987–1012.

19. U. A. Leonard and H. W. More, *Police Organization and Management* (Mineola, N.Y.: Foundation Press, 1971).

20. E. W. Linse, Jr., *Due Process in Practice: A Study of Police Procedures in Minneapolis* (Minneapolis: University of Minnesota, 1965).

21. J. M. Livermore, "Policing," *Minnesota Law Review, 55* (1970), pp. 649–729.

22. R. J. Lundman, "Police and the Maintenance of Propriety" (Ph.D. dissertation, University of Minnesota, Minneapolis, 1972); "Domestic Police-Citizen Encounters" (mimeograph, University of Delaware, 1973).

23. James G. March and Herbert A. Simon, *Organizations* (New York: John Wiley & Sons, 1958).

24. R. I. Parnas, "The Police Response to the Domestic Disturbance," *Wisconsin Law Review* (Fall 1967), pp. 914–60.

25. I. Piliavin and S. Briar, "Police Encounters with Juveniles," *American Journal of Sociology, 70* (September 1964), pp. 206–14.

26. D. M. Peterson, "Police Disposition of the Petty Offender," *Sociology and Social Research, 56* (April 1972), pp. 320–30.

27. President's Commission on Law Enforcement and Administration of Justice, *Task Force Report: The Police* (Washington, D.C.: U.S. Government Printing Office, 1967).

28. A. J. Reiss, Jr., *The Police and the Public* (New Haven: Yale University Press, 1971).

29. R. E. Sykes, "Police III: A Code for the Study of Police-Citizen Interaction," *Observations, 3* (November 1972), pp. 20–40.

30. James D. Thompson, *Organization in Action* (New York: McGraw-Hill, 1967).

31. Stanley H. Udy, Jr., "Administrative Rationality, Social Setting and Organizational Development," *American Journal of Sociology, 68* (1962), pp. 299–308.

32. Ludwig von Bertalanffy, *General Systems Theory: Foundations, Development, Applications* (New York: George Braziller, 1968).

33. P. Watslawick, H. H. Beavin, and D. D. Jackson, *Pragmatics of Human Communication* (New York: Norton, 1967).

34. W. A. Westley, "Violence and the Police," *American Journal of Sociology, 59* (July 1953), pp. 34–41.

35. F. A. Wileman, ed., *Guidelines for Discretion: Five Models for Local Law Enforcement Agencies.*

36. ——— and F. J. Crisafi, eds., *Guidelines for Discretion: Twelve Models for Local Law Enforcement Agencies.*

37. J. Q. Wilson, *Varieties of Police Behavior* (Cambridge, Mass.: Harvard University Press, 1968).

38. Thomas P. Wilson, "Normative and Interpretive Paradigms in Sociology," *Understanding Everyday Life*, Jack Douglas, ed. (Chicago: Aldine, 1970).

Causes of Police Behavior: The Current State of Quantitative Research

Lawrence W. Sherman

This paper is a first attempt to organize and codify the findings of quantitative research on four aspects of police behavior: detection, arrest, service, and violence. A framework of five explanatory approaches is used to organize the findings: individual characteristics of police officers; situational, organizational, and community characteristics; and legal variables. The findings generally show weak relationships between a wide range of the hypothesized causes and police behavior, the implications of which for building a substantive theory of policing are briefly considered.

The quantitative study of police behavior has been largely focused on four major aspects of police work, primarily in uniformed patrol. One aspect is detection activities, including style of uniformed patrol, decisions to take crime reports from a complainant, and decisions to stop and question someone. Another is the decision to arrest. A third is police "service" behavior, a residual category that includes such diverse items as the manner in which police settle disputes and their demeanor in interacting with citizens. Police violence, the justified and unjustified use of any physical force (including deadly force) against citizens, has also been studied quantitatively. All four aspects of police behavior exhibit considerable variety in both frequency and form.

SOURCE: *Journal of Research in Crime and Delinquency*, January 1980, pp. 69–100. (This article has been excerpted to include only the *individual* and *situational* approaches to police behavior.)

The approaches to explaining the variation in these aspects of police behavior can be classified into five levels of analysis: individual, situational, organizational, community, and legal. The individual approach attempts to explain variation in the behavior of police officers with the characteristics of the officers themselves, such as length of service, race, and sex. The situational approach attempts to explain the outcomes of citizen-police encounters with the characteristics of the situation, such as relationship between complainant and suspect, number of police officers present, whether the encounter was initiated by a citizen request or a police decision to intervene, and demeanor, race, class, and other characteristics of the suspect and complainant. The organizational approach attempts to explain rates of police behavior across either suborganizational units or entire police organizations with such characteristics as patrol strategy or percentage of college graduates in a police department. The community approach attempts to explain rates of police behavior across municipal police departments with the characteristics of the communities they police, such as economic and demographic composition, political ethos, or structure of government. Finally, the legal approach attempts to explain police behavior at various levels with the constraints of procedural and substantive law that the written legal system attempts to impose on the police.

None of these approaches constitutes a substantive theory of police behavior, although the research findings have been used to help construct more general theories of law and social control (e.g., Black, 1976). The present state of the field is best characterized as a series of bivariate assertions about the impact of certain variables on police behavior about which a moderate amount of empirical evidence has accumulated.[1] After reviewing that evidence at each level of explanation, the article examines the even more limited evidence about multivariate relationships and briefly assesses the adequacy of the current approaches.

First, however, some notes on methodology: This article does not represent an exhaustive review of all studies that meet the criteria described above. A review of all relevant indexes and an effort to find more unpublished reports are in progress; this article should be treated as an interim report on that work. And while this article contains some comments about the methodological weaknesses and interpretation issues in some of the studies, thorough methodological critiques of each of the studies are beyond its scope.[2] That does not mean that all studies are of equal value, however, and conclusions based on a "democratic vote" of the available studies on each issue would clearly be inappropriate.

INDIVIDUAL EXPLANATIONS

Police reformers since Theodore Roosevelt have assumed that who a police officer is makes a difference in how the officer acts (Fogelson, 1977). Recent research has tested that proposition with at least eight specific characteristics of the individuals performing police roles: age, length of service, sex, height, race, education, job satisfaction, and racial attitudes. Some of these characteristics are ascribed; others are actively achieved or passively developed, either before or after entering police work. All of them are assumed to influence behavior regardless of the influences of other variables. Most have substantial policy implications, since the decision about who will become a police officer is a more "tractable" variable (Scott and Shore, 1974; Davis, 1975) than are most of the other factors thought to influence police behavior. Table 1 summarizes the available findings to date.

Officer Age

Conventional police wisdom holds that younger officers are more aggressive, and also more likely to make mistakes, than older officers. Yet it is difficult to test that proposition in a way that separates biological age from length of service in policing, since most police departments only hire officers between the ages of twenty-one and thirty. The limited evidence from one archival study shows that when controlling for length of service there is no difference among officers of different ages in their likelihood to gather sufficient evidence (or do whatever is necessary) for the arrests they make to lead to a conviction (a detection measure) or in their overall quantity of arrests (Forst, Lucianovic, and Cox, 1977:50). Another archival study did find, however, that officers in a single cohort who were oldest at time of appointment were less likely than average to have civilian complaints filed against them for such offenses as discourtesy, racial slurs, or excessive use of force—best treated as a measure of service (Cohen and Chaiken, 1972:15). Younger officers were also assaulted more often in the thirteen southwestern cities investigated in one archival study, but this may be a spurious result of their more frequent assignment to patrol duties in high-crime areas (Hale and Wilson, 1974:8).

Length of Service

Both archival and observation research supports the proposition that more experienced officers do less police work, but the work they do is often "better" than that of their less experienced colleagues. Friedrich's (1977:278–284) reanalysis of the Black-Reiss data (1967) found that less experienced officers do more to detect crime: They initiate more citizen contacts, do more active preventive patrolling, and record crime reports from citizens more often than do officers with more experience, particularly than those with more than eight years of service. Yet Forst, Lucianovic, and Cox (1977:48–49) found that more experienced officers, when they made arrests, were more likely to have the arrest result in conviction. Both Forst et al. and Friedrich found that less experienced officers made more arrests. The Freidrich finding was more significant since it examined only patrol officers; Forst and his col-

[1] The term *moderate* is, of course, relative. In comparison with the 231 studies of the effectiveness of correctional treatment (Lipton, Martinson, and Wilks, 1975), the 62 studies discussed in this article seem rather scanty; in comparison with the 30,000 studies reviewed in the most recent Surgeon General's report on cigarette smoking, the study of police behavior is just beginning.

[2] For a discussion of the methodology of the two major observation studies from which many of the findings are drawn, see Reiss (1971b) and Sykes (1972).

TABLE 1 Individual Officer Characteristics and Police Behavior

	Police Behavior							
	Detection Finding		*Arrest Finding*		*Service Finding*		*Violence Finding*	
Officer Characteristic	*Relationship*	*No. of Findings*	*Relationship*	*No. of Findings*	*Relationship*	*No. of Findings*	*Relationship*	*No. of Findings*
Age	b	1	b	1	a	1	d	1
Length of service	a	2	a	2	c	2	e	
Sex	c	3	c	5	b	3	e	
Height	e		b	1	b	5	b	6
Race	a	1	a	1	c	2	c	2
Education	a	1	a	1	a	2	c	2
Job satisfaction	a	1	a	1	b	1	e	
Racial attitudes	b	1	a	1	b	1	e	

[a] Consistent relationship(s) found
[b] No relationship found
[c] Mixed findings
[d] Relationship found, but possibly spurious
[e] No data available

Note: Directions of relationships are not specified because different measures within categories may have relationships in opposing directions, although consistently so for each measure.

leagues did not control for assignment, and more experienced officers are more likely to get desk jobs.

This pattern is more complicated in the area of service, however. Friedrich (1977:278) found that more experienced officers were more likely than their juniors to be friendlier to nonoffenders and "tougher" with offenders. But an observation study in Miami found more senior officers to be more sympathetic and less threatening with citizens generally (Cruse and Rubin, n.d.:157).

Generational differences might well be the underlying cause of these apparent effects of differences in the length of service. Differences in the nature of early socialization into police work, specific events that transpired over the years in which the older cohort served, or other factors unique to those years rather than the simple passage of time might cause the observed differences. The agreement between the Forst et al. analysis of Washington, D.C., officers in 1974 and Friedrich's (1977:467) analysis of the same city (along with Boston and Chicago) in 1966, however, shows the relationships holding up across generations in one city and therefore tends to refute this rival hypothesis.

Officer Sex

Although interpretations of the findings may differ, the evaluations of women newly assigned to patrol duties in recent years show that they do generally differ from men in both their detection and arrest behaviors. An observation study in Washington, D.C., of the first eighty-six women assigned to patrol after recruit training (with eighty-six comparison male recruits) found that the female officers initiated fewer citizen encounters (detection) and made fewer felony and misdemeanor arrests than the male officers (Bloch and Anderson, 1974:5, 14). An observation study of sixteen females and sixteen males on patrol in St. Louis County (Sherman, 1975) confirmed both the patrol style and arrest findings of the Washington study. Archival research in the Philadelphia Police Department (Bartell Associates, n.d.) and the New York City Police Department (Sichel et al., 1977) also found that women made fewer arrests, in the latter study by a difference of four to one. One exception to the "less arrest" pattern is an earlier study of a much smaller sample in New York, where no difference in arrest frequency was found (reported in Melchionne, 1974:356). One exception to the different detection pattern is the Washington, D.C., finding that arrests made by "new women" and comparison men were equally likely to result in conviction (Bloch and Anderson, 1974:25–26), a finding confirmed by a later archival study of all officers in that city that controlled for length of service (Forst, Lucianovic, and Cox, 1977:52).

These studies do not show many differences in the kind of service female officers provide, nor do they offer enough data to test the hypothesis that women have more of a calming effect on violent or emotionally upset citizens than male officers do (Sherman, 1973), since so few incidents in this category were observed (but see Bloch and Anderson, 1974:18–19). All the studies are limited by the lack of experienced females to compare with experienced males, as well as by the possibility that male officers are intentionally limiting the detection and arrest activity of their female partners.

Officer Height

The closely related proposition that shorter officers (including most females) do police work differently (or less well, in policy terms) is generally unsupported by recent research on male patrol officers, most of which has been conducted by police departments themselves. No evidence is available on the issue of detection, but a study of San Diego officers found that there was no relationship between height and frequency of arrest (Hoobler and McQueeny, 1973). A review and reanalysis of research in several other police departments (White and Bloch, 1975) found either no differences or inadequately controlled data on citizen complaints (a service measure) and assaults on the police officer (which usually means the officer has used force as well). The latter finding received further support from an archival study of thirteen Southwestern police departments (Swanson and Hale, 1975). So despite the biological and psychological arguments about the influence of officer height on police conduct, the evidence suggests height actually has little influence.

Officer Race

Theorists of many persuasions have argued that black police officers behave differently from white officers. The recent research supports the general argument, although some of the findings are unexpected. Black officers in three large cities in 1966 patrolled more aggressively, initiated more citizen contacts, and recorded crime reports more often than white officers. They also made more arrests than white officers regardless of citizen race (although the black officers in only one of the three cities, Chicago, were responsible for all of this difference in the aggregated data; it is not clear whether they faced more serious offenses). But when faced with black suspects, black officers were more likely to make an arrest than when they were faced with white suspects. This disparity in favor of the opposite race was shown by white officers as well (Friedrich, 1977:300–319, 453).

The same study found black officers to be slightly more neutral (less frequently friendly or unfriendly) in their manner toward citizens than white officers were (Friedrich, 1977:314), but an observation study in Miami in 1970–71 found that the two older black officers in the sample the study observed for six months were less "threatening" in their behavior toward blacks than older white officers were (Cruse and Rubin, n.d.:157). Black officers hired in New York in 1957 received the same number of citizen complaints as white officers, on average, throughout their careers (Cohen and Chaiken, 1972:14). Most unexpected was the finding that black officers in 1966 used unjustified force more often than white officers, both in general and especially against black citizens (Reiss, 1972:303). An archival study of police use of deadly force in New York City (1971–75) also found that black officers used force more often than whites, but concluded that the relationship was a spurious result of overrepresentation of black officers' assignment and residence in high-crime neighborhoods (Fyfe, 1978:ix).

Officer Education

The theory that college-educated officers behave differently from less educated officers (see Sherman, 1979) has generally been unsupported by studies of indirect performance indicators such as attitudes and supervisory evaluations (Smith, 1978). The four studies that directly measured (through archival research) those aspects of police work considered in this discussion, however, all show college-educated officers to behave differently. McGreevy (1964) found college-educated officers in the St. Louis Police Department to be more active in such detection practices as stopping vehicles and checking businesses. Bozza (1973) found that better educated officers (in a sample of 24) in a California police department made more arrests. Cohen and Chaiken (1972) found that officers who had some college education when they joined the New York City Police in 1957 were the subjects of fewer citizen complaints than were those who had no college upon joining. Cascio (1977) replicated that finding in a study of 940 officers in Dade County, Florida, and also found that more educated officers suffered fewer injuries from assaults and were the subjects of fewer allegations of having used excessive force. A study of thirteen Southwestern police agencies, however, found that more educated officers ($n = 1{,}745$) were more likely to be assaulted than were those with less education (Hale and Wilson, 1974:20).

All of these studies, unfortunately, suffer from a number of flaws. Most important is the failure to control for other factors, such as motivation or I.Q., that might be the true cause of both educational achievement and job performance. Additional considerations, even though they do not affect the interpretation of the findings, are the failure to examine the kind of education officers receive; the erroneous assumption that a year of education is a fungible property at an interval level of measurement; and an absence of sufficient variance in levels of education so that if an interval level of measurement is assumed it may be used with its full potential. While we may be fairly confident that education is at least a correlate of these aspects of police behavior, we are much less certain whether and to what degree it is a cause.

Job Satisfaction

Police morale is a prime concern of both police union leaders and police administrators, but only one study of its effect on aspects of police behavior could be found. Friedrich (1977:292–299) found support in the Black-Reiss data for the assumption that job satisfaction influences performance. More satisfied officers initiated more citizen contacts, patrolled more aggressively, and took crime reports more often. They also made arrests more often than their less satisfied colleagues, but their manner toward citizens was no different.

Racial Attitudes

Black and Reiss's (1967:138) original conclusion that racial attitudes are generally unrelated to police behavior was based on separate analyses of attitudes, which were generally prejudiced, and behavior, which they concluded was not discriminatory. An analysis of their data linking the attitudes and behavior of specific officers, however, found that the more white officers disliked blacks, the more likely they were to arrest black suspects (Friedrich, 1977:321). Yet the analysis also found that racial attitudes were unrelated to white officers' decisions to take crime reports from black complainants. The relationship reappears in the area of service quality, with negative behavior toward black citizens more frequent among white officers whose dislike of blacks is more pronounced (Friedrich, 1977:329). Yet all of these relationships are weak (percentage differences no greater than 15 percent; gammas no greater than .2), as they are for many of the correlations of police behavior and individual officers' characteristics.

SITUATIONAL EXPLANATIONS

The second approach to explaining police patrol behavior assumes that the structural attributes of police-citizen encounters will determine their outcomes regardless of the characteristics of the officers involved. Four types of structural attributes have been examined in systematic observation studies: the way police enter an encounter, the characteristics and behavior of the suspect and of the complainant, and the visibility of the encounter. Table 2 summarizes the findings to date on the influence of the specific variables studied within each of these categories.

Police Entry

One hypothesis about police entry into citizen encounters is that when they enter on their own initiative (proactively) they will be granted less legitimacy than when they enter at the request of a citizen (reactively); this, in turn, will shape their behavior (Reiss, 1971a:47). Proactive encounters, which comprise as little as 13 percent of all citizen contacts and are most often concerned with legally petty offenses (Black, 1971:1091), appear to differ substantially from reactive encounters. Citizens are generally more antagonistic to the police in proactive encounters (Reiss, 1971a:51) and police are correspondingly harsher in their manner, but only toward suspects (Friedrich, 1977:411). Both the Black-Reiss data (Black, 1971:1102; Friedrich, 1977:377) and the Sykes-Clark data (Lundman, 1974:130) show that police make arrests more often in proactive encounters (although the latter report was limited to encounters with drunks). Proactive encounters are also more likely to result in an injury to a police officer—an indication that violence is more likely to emerge (Reiss, 1971a:61).

Another hypothesis about police entry in reactive encounters is that the speed with which officers respond to a call for service will make a difference in its outcome. Although there is some evidence that arrests leading to conviction are more likely when the arrest takes place shortly after the offense occurs (Forst, Lucianovic, and Cox, 1977), there is little evidence that the speed with which police travel to the scene makes any difference. Two studies in Kansas City found that the time interval between citizens calling the police and the arrival of the police usually makes little difference in the result. One study (Kansas City, Missouri, Police Department, 1977) found that the time from the receipt of a call by a police operator to the dispatch of a car is unrelated to both the likelihood of an arrest

TABLE 2 Situational Characteristics and Police Behavior

	Police Behavior							
	Detection Finding		*Arrest Finding*		*Service Finding*		*Violence Finding*	
Situational Characteristics	*Relationship*	*No. of Findings*	*Relationship*	*No. of Findings*	*Relationship*	*No. of Findings*	*Relationship*	*No. of Findings*
1. Police entry								
Proactive-reactive	c		a	2	a	1	a	1
Response time	b	1	c	2	e		e	
Number of officers	a	1	a	2	a	1	c	1
2. Suspect								
Race	a	4	c	4	c	2	c	5
Demeanor	e		a	8	a	2	a	2
Relation to victim	a	2	a	2	a	1	e	
Age	a	1	a	2	a	2	c	2
Sex	a	1	a	2	a	1	a	4
Social class	c	2	a	3	a	1	a	1
3. Complainant								
Preference	a	2	a	4	e		e	
Demeanor	a	2	e		a	1	e	
Race	c	2	e		e		e	
Social class	a	1	e		e		e	
4. Visibility								
Public-private setting	b	1	c	2	a	1	a	1
Number of citizens	e		a	1	a	1		

[a] Consistent relationship(s) found
[b] No relationship found
[c] Mixed findings
[d] Relationship found, but possibly spurious
[e] No data available

Note: Directions of relationships are not specified because different measures within categories may have relationships in opposing directions, although consistently so for each measure.

being made. The amount of time from dispatch to police arrival was also unrelated to finding a witness, as well as to the likelihood of arrest for most crimes, with the major exception of burglary (Kansas City, Missouri, Police Department, 1977:45, 72, 75). An earlier, less comprehensive study with many fewer observations found similar results for arrest outcomes (Pate et al., 1976a).

The number of officers present at a citizen encounter has also been hypothesized to affect police behavior: An officer is purportedly more cautious and less threatening when alone than when accompanied by one or more other officers (Wilson, 1963; Banton, 1964:151–152). The recent evidence provides some support for that hypothesis and refutes the claim of some police union leaders that two-officer cars are safer for police officers. The Black-Reiss data show that a lone officer is more likely to take a crime report and less likely to make an arrest (Friedrich, 1977:377, 380). An archival study in San Diego (Boydstun, Sherry, and Moelter, 1977:5) also found lone officers are more likely to take crime reports, but found lone officers more likely to make arrests. The Black-Reiss data, however, also show single officers more likely to make arrests when other situational variables are controlled (Friedrich, 1977:389), as they probably are by the experimental design of the San Diego study. Incidents handled by lone officers produced fewer citizen complaints than those with two officers in San Diego, and lone officers had fewer incidents involving "resisting arrest," an indicator of violence. Lone officer and two-officer encounters, however, were equal on two other indicators of violence, injury to and assault on the officer.

Suspect Characteristics

Race. The argument that the police do not treat all citizens the same is most often made in relation to the race of the suspects they encounter. A fair amount of evidence has now accumulated on this question, but the interpretations of the data vary substantially. Four findings on detection are consistent. An archival study of some 6,000 proactive field interrogations in one city in 1973 (Bogomolny, 1976:571) found that police were more likely to stop black males than the presence of black males in either the city population or the city's arrest population would predict. A small-scale observation study, contrary to the widely cited view that it found blacks more likely to be interrogated (e.g., Ferdinand and Luchterhand, 1970:510), actually found that 70 percent of the "innocent," but only 30 percent of the "guilty," youths stopped by juvenile officers were black—or that blacks who were stopped were more likely to be innocent than whites who were stopped (Piliavin and Briar, 1964:212). The Black and Reiss (1967:81) observation data show that blacks are more likely to be both searched and interrogated once they have been identified as suspects.

The observation studies of arrest decisions also consistently show higher rates of arrest for black suspects, but the primary analyses of those data conclude that the relationship is spurious. The Black-Reiss data on encounters with adult suspects were originally interpreted to show that blacks are more likely to be arrested, even controlling for seriousness of offense (i.e., felony or misdemeanor), because they are more often disrespectful to the police (Black, 1971:1103). The Black-Reiss data on juvenile suspects were originally interpreted to show that black juveniles are arrested more often (controlling for seriousness of offense) because complainants who prefer arrest are more often present at encounters with black juveniles (Black and Reiss, 1970:70–71), a finding and interpretation replicated in the Sykes-Clark data (Lundman, Sykes, and Clark, 1978:84).

But the Black-Reiss adult data fail to show whether the disrespect emerged before or after the arrest was made; the Sykes-Clark data suggest that arrest may cause disrespect as much as disrespect causes arrest (Sykes, Fox, and Clark, 1976:177–178). Even if disrespect does precede arrest, the Sykes-Clark data set (at least for drunken adults) fails to replicate the explaining away of the racial differences in arrest with differences in suspect demeanor (Lundman, 1974:136). Finally, a reexamination of the juvenile data in Black and Reiss (1970:81) shows that, even when controlling for the complainant's preference for an arrest, blacks are arrested more often than whites. This finding did not appear in the Sykes-Clark replication, but the replication data have as few as four cases in some of the categories.[3]

[3] Two other kinds of studies, while not strictly "situational" in focus, are of related interest here. Hindelang's (1978:100) national sample comparison of the race of arrestees and offenders (as reported through victimization surveys) found that blacks are overrepresented in the arrestee population, relative to their size in the offender population (from 8 to 11 percent difference), for the crimes of rape, aggravated assault, and simple assault, but not for robbery. Many decisions (such as allocation of police resources, patrol strategies) other than the decision to arrest, per se, however, could contribute to this disparity. The data from several archival studies of police juvenile officers' decisions to refer in-custody juveniles to juvenile court (which could be taken as a different definition of "arrest") also tend to show black suspects being referred more often, but here again interpretations can vary. Both Goldman (1963) and Williams and Gold (1972) found the police more likely to refer black suspects, but the absence of statistically significant differences led them to conclude that suspect race did not affect police decisions. Both studies feature small (41 or less) numbers of blacks in the analyses, however, which could explain the absence of statistical significance; when Goldman (1963:42) pooled his data from all four cities ($n = 71$ blacks, 1,165 whites), a significant ($p < .01$) black-white difference did emerge. Terry (1967a:178, 1967b) reported no association between the ethnicity of juveniles and police referrals, but the Racine, Wisconsin, police may not be typical of urban police generally—a problem all these studies face. Two of the three most elaborate studies on this question (Ferdinand and Luchterhand, 1970; Wolfgang, Figlio, and Sellin, 1972) both concluded that juvenile court referral is significantly more likely for blacks than for whites even when crime seriousness (both studies), age (Ferdinand and Luchterhand), prior offenses, and socioeconomic status (Wolfgang, Figlio, and Sellin) are held constant; but a third study (McEachern and Bauzer, 1967) found no relationship to race. The third study did, however, pool data from a large number of police departments, and if the departments with more black juveniles referred juveniles generally at a lower rate than the departments with a predominantly white clientele, racial bias in departments with both white and black clientele could be suppressed in the findings based on pooled data.

Suspect race may make less difference in the area of service. The Black-Reiss data show police as more cautious and neutral, but not more harsh, toward black suspects (Friedrich, 1977:305). On the other hand, the data show that police use a more coercive approach to settling disputes among blacks than they do among whites (Black, 1979:115). In the area of excessive force, those data show that black suspects are victims of brutality at less than half the rate of white suspects (Reiss, 1972:303). For deadly force, however, two studies have found blacks to be shot or killed by the police more often than their presence in the arrest population would predict (Knoohuizen, Fahey, and Palmer, 1972; Sherman, 1980); those studies that find, to the contrary, that the proportion of deadly force victims who are black closely matches the proportion of arrestees for Part I index crimes who are black (Milton et al., 1977; Fyfe, 1978) fail to explain the disparity, since the same studies show that up to 40 percent of the incidents in which deadly force is used are less serious than Part I index crimes.

Demeanor. The evidence on suspect demeanor is far more consistent. At least eight separate analyses of observational data have concluded that "disrespectful" or "uncooperative" suspects are more likely to be arrested than "civil" suspects (Piliavin and Briar, 1964; Black and Reiss, 1970; Black, 1971; Petersen, 1972; Lundman, 1974; Sykes, Fox, and Clark, 1976; Friedrich, 1977; Lundman, Sykes, and Clark, 1978). Several of these studies also found that very deferential behavior was more likely to be followed by arrest than merely civil behavior, both for juveniles (Black and Reiss, 1970; Lundman, Sykes, and Clark, 1978) and for adults (Friedrich, 1977:372). Whether the observed demeanor precedes or follows arrest, however, is only reported by Sykes, Fox, and Clark (1976:178), who also found that "impoliteness" when no arrest had been made increased the chances of an arrest.

Similar patterns have been found in the *manner* of police toward very deferential, civil, and antagonistic suspects (Black and Reiss, 1967:34; Friedrich, 1977:407), and elaborated in relation to the relative status of suspect and police officer (Sykes and Clark, 1975). The Black-Reiss demeanor data have never been analyzed with respect to violence, but if only 16 percent of all offenders are antagonistic to the police (Black and Reiss, 1967:tab. 12) and 48 percent of the offenders subjected to excessive force verbally or physically challenged police authority (Reiss, 1971a:49), it would seem that suspect demeanor also predicts police violence.

Relational Distance. The more distant the relationship of the suspect to the victim, the evidence suggests, the more vigorously the police seem to respond. They are more likely to take a crime report (Black, 1970:741), more likely to make an arrest (Black, 1971:1107; Friedrich, 1977:377), less conciliatory and more penal in their approach to settling disputes (Black, 1979:115), and generally more likely to obtain witness testimony needed for the arrest to result in conviction (Forst, Lucianovic, and Cox, 1977:43) when the suspect is a stranger to the victim than when the suspect is an acquaintance or relative.

Age. Relatively young and very old suspects seem to be treated differently by the police from other suspects, but in complex ways. People under twenty-five are more likely to be stopped by police for field interrogation than their proportions in the general, arrest, or street (as measured by a roadblock sample) populations would predict (Bogomolny, 1976). Once they have been defined as suspects, however, the young may be better off in the hands of the police.[4] The Sykes-Clark observation data show that drunks under twenty-five are less likely to be arrested (Lundman, 1974). The Black-Reiss observation data show the likelihood of street arrest to increase steadily across the three age categories leading up to age twenty-five, after which arrest chances decline until jumping to their highest level (33 percent of suspects encountered) in the sixty-or-above category (Friedrich, 1977:366). On the other hand, those data also show that the manner of police is most often negative to ten to eighteen year olds and least often negative to one to ten year olds. In settling disputes, those data show that police favor adults over juveniles (Black, 1979:115). Archival studies consistently find that the majority of the people shot or killed by police are under age thirty (Robin, 1963; Kobler, 1975), but the studies that compare the age of shooting victims with the age of arrestees obtain conflicting results on the question of whether the proportions match (Milton et al., 1977:21; Fyfe, 1978:xv).

Sex. There is little doubt that police discriminated in favor of women at the time the available data on the question were collected. Both black and white women were stopped for field interrogation in one city in 1973 less often than their presence in the arrest

[4] See also Goldman (1963:45), McEachern and Bauzer (1967:155), Williams and Gold (1972:223), Ferdinand and Luchterhand (1970:514), and Terry (1967a:179) for findings on age of suspect and police referrals to juvenile court.

population would predict (Bogomolny, 1976:571).[5] Observation data from 1966 (Friedrich, 1977:366) and 1971 (on drunks only; Lundman, 1974:130) show that female suspects are generally less likely than males to be subjected to street arrest. The 1966 data also show that female suspects receive more polite treatment from police (Friedrich, 1977:400). No white woman and only two black women (5 percent) were found among the thirty-seven victims of excessive force in the 1966 data (Reiss, 1972:305), whereas females comprised 17 percent of the suspects the police encountered (Friedrich, 1977:366). Archival studies show women comprise only 0 to 4 percent of those shot or killed by police, less than their presence in the arrest population would predict (Robin, 1963; Milton et al., 1977:17; Fyfe, 1978:viii).

Social Class. The frequent observation in the qualitative studies of policing that lower-class suspects receive harsher treatment from the police (e.g., Banton, 1964:186–187) is generally supported by the limited quantitative observational evidence. Both the Black-Reiss (Black and Reiss, 1967:80; Friedrich, 1977:366) data and the Sykes-Clark data (for drunk suspects only; Lundman, 1974:136) show lower-class suspects more likely to be arrested.[6] The police treat lower-class suspects in a negative manner more often than higher-status suspects (Friedrich, 1977:401), devote less time and energy to settling lower-class disputes, and treat lower-class disputants in a more penal and less conciliatory fashion than they do middle-class disputants (Black, 1979:115). And while lower-class suspects comprised 100 percent of those subjected to excessive force (Reiss, 1972:305), they constituted only 68 percent of the suspects police encountered (computed from Friedrich, 1977:401).

The one exception to this pattern is the relationship between class and detection. In reactive encounters, blue-collar blacks are more likely to be searched than white-collar blacks, but there are no class differences among whites (Black and Reiss, 1967:81). In proactive encounters, however, blue-collar whites are five times more likely to be searched than white-collar whites; the Black-Reiss data had too few cases to analyze social class differences for blacks in proactive encounters. Interrogations show still a different pattern: White-collar whites are less likely than blue-collar whites to be interrogated in both proactive and reactive encounters, but white-collar blacks are *more* likely than blue-collar blacks to be interrogated, at least in reactive encounters.

Complainant Characteristics

Attentive as they may be to the suspects they make decisions about, police officers may be even more guided by the actions and identities of the citizens (if any) who complain about or are victimized by the suspects: their preference (if any) for police action, their demeanor, race, and social class.

Preference. A polite complainant can generally exert substantial influence on police behavior. The Black-Reiss data show that police rarely took a crime report if the complainant asked them not to, and explicit complainant requests for a report also increased the likelihood the police would write one (Black, 1970:738; Friedrich, 1977:374). Complainant preferences for arrest decisions were also followed for both adults (Black, 1971:1085; Friedrich, 1977:371) and juveniles (Black and Reiss, 1970:71), with the latter finding replicated in the Sykes-Clark data (Lundman, Sykes, and Clark, 1978:80, 82).

Demeanor. A complainant's influence may be easily lost, however, through disrespect. When complainants are antagonistic, police are one-third as likely to fill out crime reports as they are when complainants are very deferential (Black, 1970:743; see also Friedrich, 1977:374). Police are also less likely to give any citizen who is not a suspect harsh treatment if the citizen is not antagonistic. Unfortunately, the relationship of complainant demeanor to arrest decisions in the Black-Reiss data has never been reported.

Race and Class. The polite complainant may also lose some influence over police behavior by being black, lower class, or both. Friedrich (1977:303), unlike Black (1970:745), found black complainants significantly less

[5] Archival studies of juvenile court referrals in the late 1940s (Goldman, 1963:44) show females less likely to be referred, although data for 1958–62 (Terry, 1967a), 1964 (Ferdinand and Luchterhand, 1970), and 1964–67 (Williams and Gold, 1972) fail to replicate the finding. McEachern and Bauzer (1967) found a relationship that disappeared when the offense was controlled.

[6] Archival studies of police decisions to refer juvenile suspects to court are less supportive of the hypothesis. Terry (1967b), Weiner and Willie (1971), and Williams and Gold (1972) all failed to find a relationship, with the exception of the latter study's observation that lower-status white girls were more likely to be referred than higher-status white girls (p. 225).

likely to have the police write crime reports when a larger portion[7] of the Black-Reiss data are examined. Black, however, controlled for class (which Friedrich did not do) and found that even the insignificant zero-order difference he observed by race disappeared. Black did find that blue-collar felony complainants were less likely to have crime reports taken than white-collar complainants were, and Friedrich (1977:304) found that black nonoffenders[8] (like black suspects) were treated more neutrally than whites. But once again, the race and class of complainants in relation to arrest decisions in the Black-Reiss data have not been reported.

Visibility

Police behavior also seems to vary according to the visibility of police-citizen encounters, but in surprising ways. Friedrich (1977:377, 381) found that while police are equally likely to take crime reports and make arrests in public and private settings, they are more likely to behave harshly toward suspects in public settings. Lundman (1974:130), on the other hand, found police more likely to arrest drunks in public places and in the more visible downtown area (as contrasted with other areas). Friedrich (1977:377) also found arrest decisions to be more likely when more than ten citizens were present, although the likelihood of arrest decreased monotonically as the number of citizens grew larger up to ten. Reiss (1972:305) found that most instances of excessive police use of force took place in private places. And though bystanders were present in three-fourths of those instances, the bystanders' lack of sympathy for the victim of the excessive police force (in all but one of the thirty-seven cases) suggests that it may be the *quality* of the audience rather than its size or presence that makes a difference in police behavior.

REFERENCES

Aaronson, D. E., C. T. Dienes, and M. Musheno, 1978, "Changing the Public Drunkenness Laws: The Impact of Decriminalization." *Law and Society Review* 12 (3): 405–436.

Banton, M., 1964, *The Policeman in the Community*. New York: Basic Books.

Bartell Associates, n.d., "The Study of Policewomen Competency in the Performance of Sector Police Work in the City of Philadelphia." Report submitted to the Philadelphia Police Department.

Black, D., 1970, "The Production of Crime Rates." *American Sociological Review* 35 (August): 733–748.

———, 1971, "The Social Organization of Arrest." *Stanford Law Review* 23 (June): 1087–1111.

———, 1976, *The Behavior of Law*. New York: Academic Press.

———, 1979, "Dispute Settlement by the Police." New Haven, Conn.: Yale University.

[7] Black (1970:736–737) examined 554 cases, excluding all those initiated proactively or by complainants who approached police other than by telephone, and all those incidents in which a suspect was present. Friedrich (1977) analyzed 862 cases, apparently not excluding the categories Black discarded in order to achieve a more homogeneous sample.

[8] Friedrich collapsed all citizen roles in police encounters other than suspect (bystanders, complainants, etc.) into the broader category of "nonoffender" for much of his analysis.

Black, D., and A. J. Reiss, Jr., 1967, *Studies of Crime and Law Enforcement in Major Metropolitan Areas*, Vol. 2, Field Surveys III. Section I: "Patterns of Behavior in Police and Citizen Transactions." Washington, D.C.: Govt. Printing Office.

———, 1970, "Police Control of Juveniles." *American Sociological Review* 35 (February): 63–77.

Bloch, P., and D. Anderson, 1974, *Policewomen on Patrol: Final Report*. Washington, D.C.: Police Foundation.

Bogomolny, R., 1976, "Street Patrol: The Decision to Stop a Citizen." *Criminal Law Bulletin* 12 (5): 544–582.

Boydstun, J. E., and M. E. Sherry, 1975, *San Diego Community Profile: Final Report*. Washington, D.C.: Police Foundation.

Boydstun, J., M. Sherry, and N. P. Moelter, 1977, *Patrol Staffing in San Diego: One- or Two-Officer Units*. Washington, D.C.: Police Foundation.

Bozza, C. M., 1973, "Motivations Guiding Policemen in the Arrest Process." *Journal of Police Science and Adminstration* 1 (4): 468–476.

Campbell, D. T., and J. C. Stanley, 1963, *Experimental and Quasi-Experimental Designs for Research*. Chicago: Rand-McNally.

Cascio, W. F., 1977, "Formal Education and Police Officer Performance." *Journal of Police Science and Administration* 5 (1): 89–96.

Cohen, B., and J. M. Chaiken, 1972, *Police Background Characteristics and Performance: Summary*. New York: Rand Institute.

Cruse, D., and J. Rubin, n.d., "Determinants of Police Behavior." The Psychiatric Institute.

Davis, J. A., 1975, "On the Remarkable Absence of Nonacademic Implications in Academic Research: An Example from Ethnic Studies." In *Social Policy and Sociology*, N. J. Demerath, O. Larsen, and K. F. Schuessler, eds. New York: Academic Press. Pp. 233—241.

Ferdinand, T., and E. G. Luchterhand, 1970, "Inner City Youth, the Police, the Juvenile Court, and Justice." *Social Problems* 17 (4): 510–526.

Fogelson, R. M., 1977, *Big City Police*. Cambridge, Mass.: Harvard University Press.

Forst, B., J. Lucianovic, and S. J. Cox, 1977, *What Happens after Arrest? A Court Perspective of Police Operations in the District of Columbia*. Washington, D.C.: Institute for Law and Social Research.

Friedrich, R. J., 1977, "The Impact of Organizational, Individual, and Situational Factors on Police Behavior." Ph.D. diss., Department of Political Science, University of Michigan.

Fyfe, J. J., 1978, "Shots Fired: An Examination of New York City Police Firearms Discharges." Ph.D. diss., School of Criminal Justice, State University of New York at Albany.

Gardiner, J. A., 1969, *Traffic and the Police*. Cambridge, Mass.: Harvard University Press.

Gay, W., H. T. Day, and J. P. Woodward, 1977, *Neighborhood Team Policing*. Washington, D.C.: National Institute of Law Enforcement and Criminal Justice.

Goldman, N., 1963, *The Differential Selection of Juvenile Offenders for Court Appearance*. Hackensack, N.J.: National Council on Crime and Delinquency.

Hale, C. D., and W. R. Wilson, 1974, *Personal Characteristics of Assaulted and Non-Assaulted Officers*. Norman, Okla.: Bureau of Government Research, University of Oklahoma.

Heaphy, J. F., ed., 1978, *Police Practices: The General Administrative Survey*. Washington, D.C.: Police Foundation.

Hindelang, M. J., 1978, "Race and Involvement in Common Law Personal Crimes." *American Sociological Review* 43 (February): 93-109.

Hoobler, R. L., and J. A. McQueeney, 1973, "A Question of Height." *The Police Chief* (November): 42–48.

Jacobs, D., and D. Britt, 1979, "Inequality and Police Use of Deadly Force: An Empirical Assessment of a Conflict Hypothesis." *Social Problems* 26 (4): 403–412.

Kania, R. E., and W. C. Mackey, 1977, "Police Violence as a Function of Community Characteristics." *Criminology* 15 (1): 27–48.

Kansas City, Missouri, Police Department, 1977, *Response Time Analysis*. Kansas City, Mo.: Board of Police Commissioners.

Kelling, G. L., et al., 1974, *The Kansas City Preventive Patrol Experiment*. Summary Report. Washington, D.C.: Police Foundation.

Knoohuizen, R., R. Fahey, and D. J. Palmer, 1972, *The Police and Their Use of Fatal Force in Chicago*. Chicago: Chicago Law Enforcement Study Group.

Kobler, A., 1975, "Figures (and Perhaps Some Facts) on Police Killing of Citizens in the United States." *Journal of Social Issues* 31: 185–191.

Lipton, D., R. Martinson, and J. Wilks, 1975, *The Effectiveness of Correctional Treatment*. New York: Praeger.

Lundman, R., 1974, "Routine Police Arrest Practices: A Commonweal Perspective." *Social Problems* 22 (October): 127–141.

Lundman, R., R. E. Sykes, and J. P. Clark, 1978, "Police Control of Juveniles." *Journal of Research in Crime and Delinquency* 15 (1): 74–91.

Manning, P., and J. Van Maanen, 1978, *Policing: A View From the Street*. Santa Monica, Calif.: Goodyear.

McEachern, A. W., and R. Bauzer, 1967, "Factors Related to Disposition in Juvenile Police Contacts." In *Juvenile Gangs in Context*, M. W. Klein and B. G. Myerhoff, eds. Englewood Cliffs, N.J.: Prentice-Hall. Pp. 148–160.

McGreevy, T. J., 1964, "A Field Study of the Relationship between the Formal Education Levels of 556 Police Officers in St. Louis, Missouri, and Their Patrol Duty Performance Records." Master's Thesis. School of Public Administration and Public Safety, Michigan State University.

Melchionne, T. M., 1974, "The Changing Role of Policewomen." *Police Journal* 47 (4): 340–358.

Merton, R. K., 1968, *Social Theory and Social Structure*. New York: Free Press.

Milner, N., 1970, "Comparative Analysis of Patterns of Compliance with Supreme Court Decisions: Miranda and the Police in Four Communities." *Law and Society Review* 4 (August): 119–134.

Milton, C. M., et al., 1977, *Police Use of Deadly Force*. Washington, D.C.: Police Foundation.

Muir, W. K., Jr., 1977, *Police: Streetcorner Politicians*. Chicago: University of Chicago Press.

Pate, T., R. A. Bowers, and R. Parks, 1976, *Three Approaches to Criminal Apprehension in Kansas City: An Evaluation Report*. Washington, D.C.: Police Foundation.

Pate, T., et al., 1976a, *Police Response Time: Its Determinants and Effects*. Washington, D.C.: Police Foundation.

Pate, T., et al., 1976b, *Kansas City Peer Review Panel: An Evaluation Report*. Washington, D.C.: Police Foundation.

Petersen, D. M., 1972, "Police Disposition of the Petty Offender." *Sociology and Social Research* 56 (3): 320–330.

Piliavin, J., and S. Briar, 1964, "Police Encounters with Juveniles." *American Journal of Sociology* 70 (September): 206–214.

Reiss, A. J., Jr., 1971a, *The Police and the Public*. New Haven, Conn.: Yale University Press.

———, 1971b, "Systematic Observation of Natural Social Phenomena." In *Sociological Methodology 1971*, H. L. Costner, ed. San Francisco: Jossey-Bass. Pp. 3–33.

———, 1972, "Police Brutality." In *The Criminal in the Arms of the Law*, Vol. 2, Crime and Justice, L. Radzinowicz and M. E. Wolfgang, eds. Pp. 293–308.

Reiss, A. J., Jr., and D. J. Bordua, 1967, "Environment and Organization: A Perspective on the Police." In *The Police: Six Sociological Essays*, D. J. Bordua, ed. New York: John Wiley. Pp. 25–55.

Reppetto, T. A., 1975, "The Influence of Police Organizational Style on Crime Control Effectiveness." *Journal of Police Science and Administration* 3 (3): 274-279.

Robin, G. D., 1963, "Justifiable Homicides by Police." *Journal of Criminal Law, Criminology and Police Science* 54 (2): 225–231.

Rossi, P. H., R. A. Berk, and B. K. Eidson, 1974, *The Roots of Urban Discontent: Public Policy, Municipal Institutions, and the Ghetto*. New York: John Wiley.

Scott, R. A., and A. Shore, 1974, "Sociology and Policy Analysis." *The American Sociologist* 9: 51–58.

Sherman, L. J., 1973, "A Psychological View of Women in Policing." *Journal of Police Science and Administration* 1 (4): 383–394.

———, 1975, "An Evaluation of Policewomen on Patrol in a Suburban Police Department." *Journal of Police Science and Administration* 3 (4): 434–438.

Sherman, L. W., 1979, "College Education for Police: The Reform that Failed?" *Police Studies: The International Review of Policy Development* 1 (4): 32–38.

———, 1980, "Execution without Trial: Police Homicide and the Constitution." *Vanderbilt Law Review*.

Sherman, L. W., C. H. Milton, and T. Kelley, 1973, *Team Policing: Seven Case Studies*. Washington, D.C.: Police Foundation.

Sichel, J., et al., 1977, *Women on Patrol: A Pilot Study of Police Performance in New York City*. Washington, D.C.: Govt. Printing Office.

Smith, D.C., 1978, *Empirical Studies of Higher Education and Police Performance*. Washington, D.C.: Police Foundation.

Swanson, C., 1978, "The Influence of Organization and Environment on Arrest Policies in Major U.S. Cities." *Policy Studies Journal* 7: 390–398.

Swanson, C., and C. D. Hale, 1975, "A Question of Height Revisited: Assaults on Police." *Journal of Police Science and Administration* 3 (2): 183–188.

Sykes, R. E., 1972, "Police III: A Code for the Study of Police-Citizen Interaction." *Observations* 3 (November): 20–40.

Sykes, R. E., and J. P. Clark, 1975, "A Theory of Deference Exchange in Police-Civilian Encounters." *American Journal of Sociology* 81 (3): 584–600.

Sykes, R. E., J. C. Fox, and J. P. Clark, 1976, "A Socio-Legal Theory of Police Discretion." *The Ambivalent Force: Perspectives on the Police*, 2d ed., A. Blumberg and A. Niederhoffer, eds. Hinsdale, Ill.: Dryden Press. Pp. 171–183.

Terry, R. M., 1967a, "The Screening of Juvenile Offenders." *Journal of Criminal Law, Criminology and Police Science* 58 (2): 173–181.

———, 1967b, "Discrimination in the Handling of Juvenile Offenders by Social Control Agencies." *Journal of Research in Crime and Delinquency* 4 (2): 218–230.

Toch, H., D. Grant, and R. Galvin, 1975, *Agents of Change: A Study in Police Reform*. Cambridge, Mass.: Schenkman.

Wald, M., et al., 1967, "Interrogations in New Haven: The Impact of *Miranda*." *Yale Law Journal* 76 (8): 1519–1616.

Wasby, S., 1976, *Small Town Police and the Supreme Court*. Lexington, Mass.: D. C. Heath.

Webb, K. W., et al., 1977, *Specialized Patrol Projects*.

Washington, D.C.: National Institute of Law Enforcement and Criminal Justice.

Weiner, N. L., and C. V. Willie, 1971, "Decisions by Juvenile Officers." *American Journal of Sociology* 77 (2): 199–210.

White, T. W., and P. B. Bloch, 1975, *Police Officer Height and Selected Aspects of Performance*. Washington, D.C.: Police Foundation.

Williams, J. R., and M. Gold, 1972, "From Delinquent Behavior to Official Delinquency." *Social Problems* 20: 209–229.

Wilson, J. Q., 1967, "The Police and the Delinquent in Two Cities." In *Controlling Delinquents*, S. Wheeler and H. M. Hughes, eds. New York: John Wiley. Pp. 9–30.

———, 1968, *Varieties of Police Behavior*. Cambridge, Mass.: Harvard University Press.

Wilson, J. Q., and B. Boland, 1978, "The Effect of the Police on Crime." *Law and Society Review* 12 (3): 367–390.

Wilson, O. W., 1963, "One Man Patrol Cars." *The Police Chief* (May): 18–24.

Wolfgang, M. E., R. M. Figlio, and T. Sellin, 1972, *Delinquency in a Birth Cohort*. Chicago: University of Chicago Press.

Wycoff, M. A., and G. L. Kelling, 1978, *Organizational Reform*, Vol. 1, The Dallas Experience. Washington, D.C.: Police Foundation.

A Typology of Operational Styles

Michael K. Brown

A patrolman's operational style is based on his responses to the central problem of a professional police force, the difficulties and dilemmas he encounters in attempting to control crime. Yet an operational style is more than a mere set of strategies to cope with crime, for it encompasses not only a patrolman's considered reflections on the difficulties of crime fighting but also the ways in which he accommodates himself to the pressures and demands of the police bureaucracy. An operational style thus defines both how a patrolman will go about working the street and how he adapts to the contradictory requirements of behaving as a professional performing an uncertain task and as a bureaucrat subject to the stringent but uncertain discipline of the police bureaucracy.

An operational style initially derives from the choices a patrolman must make about how to work the street. Our observations of crime fighting revealed that patrolmen could be differentiated in terms of two characteristics: how *aggressive* they were in pursuit of the goal of crime control, and how *selective* they were in the enforcement of the law. Beliefs toward aggressiveness and selectivity are the core elements of a patrolman's operational style.

The ideal of many patrolmen is that of the inner-directed, aggressive policeman. Aggressiveness is both a matter of taking the initiative on the street to control crime and a preoccupation with order that legitimizes the use of illegal tactics. A patrolman must also make some decision in regard to priorities, and the most common basis for such a choice is a distinction between enforcement of felonies and misdemeanors. Selectivity thus distinguishes between patrolmen who believe that all the laws should be enforced insofar as possible, and those who consciously assign felonies a higher priority.

An operational style structures a patrolman's responses to three kinds of incidents in addition to crime fighting: the enforcement of minor violations; serious order-maintenance incidents in which the police are required to contain violence and disorder; and service order-maintenance calls which merely require that the police provide minor services of one kind or another. Crime fighting, of course, refers not to the reaction of a patrolman to a single, concrete event, as in the other sorts of incidents, but how he patrols the street in light of the objective of crime control. All of these types of incidents pose different legal requirements, imply dif-

SOURCE: From *Working the Street* by Michael K. Brown.

ferent kinds of organizational goals, and often involve different kinds of people. The use of discretion in two of them—crime fighting and the enforcement of minor violations—initially turns on the decision of a patrolman to intervene; discretion in the other two, in which a patrolman normally becomes involved through a call for service, turns on the character of a patrolman's response.[1]

By combining the attitudinal dimensions of aggressiveness and selectivity it is possible to derive a fourfold typology of operational styles (see Table 1). There are two types of patrolmen who are highly aggressive, dedicated crime fighters: the *Old Style Crime Fighter* who is selective, and the *Clean Beat Crime Fighter* who is not. The other two styles are much more aggressive; the *Professional Style*, like the Clean Beat Crime Fighter, is not selective, while the *Service Style* is. This typology was developed inductively, largely on the basis of the field observations. Individual patrolmen who "fit" any one of these styles were observed in all three departments, but only a few patrolmen perfectly exemplify any of these styles. These operational styles are analytical types that highlight the distinctive characteristics of a particular approach to police work.

The differences between these styles may be clarified by describing in greater detail the characteristics of each, the typical responses to different kinds of incidents, and related attitudes associated with each style. The discussion that follows is based upon data derived from the field observations. I have classified all patrolmen for whom sufficient information about beliefs and behavior on the street is available into one of the four categories. It was possible to classify 82 of the 95 patrolmen observed.[2]

OLD STYLE CRIME FIGHTERS

This patrolman is very aggressive but selective: felonies are believed to be the only violation worth pursuing; minor violations and service activities are not "real" police work, and if possible they are avoided. "Real" police work is not the fortuitous arrest of a burglary suspect, but rather the *skillful* application to crime problems of techniques learned on the street: the assiduous cultivation of informants; the uncanny ability to spot a narcotics suspect walking down the street; a rough but effective method of interrogation; and above all a wealth of knowledge about people and their foibles, and the area in which they work. These officers have "street sense," the ability to judge people and situations quickly and deftly. If the Old Style Crime Fighter attempts to practice the art of police work in its highest form, he does not hesitate to solve problems on the street by whatever means are necessary, legal or otherwise. From his point of view, society must decide whether or not it wants to protect its members from predators; legal restrictions sometimes do more harm than good, and it is often the case that curbstone justice does more to deter an offender than the courts.

What strikes the observer about these patrolmen is the depth of their preoccupation with crime and the assiduous application of the tools and skills of their craft to the task at hand. They are never unprepared. One Old Style Crime Fighter, upon entering the patrol car, produced a pair of high-power binoculars, black leather gloves, and a fat notebook containing the names, crimes, and dates last encountered of resident heroin addicts, burglars, and thieves. The stress placed upon the meticulous use of sheer skill is most apparent in the way these cops go about accumulating information about suspects and crimes. Any stop is worked for information about the area and activities of various individuals. For instance, after investigating a call about some juveniles disturbing the peace, one Old Style Crime Fighter stopped to talk to some juveniles sitting in front of a house, and proceeded to make small talk about a football team the police were organizing. Under the guise of recruiting one juvenile for the football team as a tackle, the patrolman obtained a very good description of him, his name, his address, and what he was doing. The patrolman's interest derived from his suspicion that the juvenile was a potential suspect in some strong-arm purse snatches that had recently occurred. Often the use of skill amounts to nothing more than the straightforward application of "textbook" principles to situations on the street. Patrolmen are notorious for the perfunctory way they handle burglar alarms, yet two avowed Old Style Crime Fighters always took plenty of time to check a building with a

TABLE 1 Typology of Operational Styles

Selectivity of Enforcement	*Aggressiveness on the Street*	
	High Aggressiveness	*Low Aggressiveness*
Selective	Old Style Crime Fighter	Service Style
Non-selective	Clean Beat Crime Fighter	Professional Style

ringing burglar alarm. They made more than their share of burglary arrests as a result.

Beyond the skill these men display, what stands out is their ruthless and aggressive demeanor on the street. Most of their free time is spent prowling down darkened streets, often with the car lights out, and stopping any vehicle or individual that looks even remotely suspicious. While these patrolmen pride themselves on their ability to separate the innocuous from the deviant—an acquired skill in their estimation—their aggressiveness often gets the better of them and diminishes the salience of skill. Some of their stops, especially those made for narcotics, are outright sloppy, based on the flimsiest of criteria or the ever present inclination to play the slot machine. On the other hand, there is a measure of truth in their frequent assertion that they are stopping people on the basis of justifiable suspicions. They are frequently right when they pick a man out of a crowd on a street corner as a possible "hype," and there is less randomness in their stops than with the Clean Beat Crime Fighters.

The aggressiveness of these patrolmen does not extend to minor violations, which most of them regard with disdain. One said he would never waste his time on trivial violations such as misdemeanors or arrests that involve juveniles; only felonies are important, and of these, burglaries and narcotics are the preferred offenses. He was observed to act on his beliefs. In one instance, this patrolman saw three juveniles looking under the hood of a stalled car at 3:30 A.M. He stopped, the juveniles were interrogated, the car searched, and then they were released. None of the juveniles had any identification; there was no conclusive evidence the car was theirs (though the patrolman believed it was) and there were several different charges that could have been used to make an arrest had the patrolman wanted to. But he took no action because, in his opinion, juveniles take too much time to process and nothing ever comes of it.

Traffic violations are also regularly ignored by Old Style Crime Fighters. It was rare to observe them stopping a car for any kind of traffic violation, and one of them admitted that he usually wrote no more than five tickets a month. Similar attitudes prevail in regard to drunks and drunk drivers. On the whole, these patrolmen are far more likely than any of the other styles to believe that violations they regard as trivial can safely be ignored. Yet it is safe to say that if nothing else turned up after a long night on the street, a "good" drunk driver would be arrested.

Data drawn from the field observations bear out these impressions. Seventy-two percent of the on-view stops made by those patrolmen who could be justifiably classified as Old Style Crime Fighters were for field interrogations; only 28 percent were for minor violations. Of those individuals they stopped for a minor violation, only one-third were cited or arrested.

The aggressiveness of Old Style Crime Fighters in the street is complemented by a taste for controlled violence. Violence and the use of coercive tactics are accepted as a necessary element of routine police work, not an indulgence. The objective on the street is to maintain control, but tactics are proportional to the end. Here again the accent is on skill. If these patrolmen were frequently involved in altercations on the street, they insist that when they use force it is necessary. One Old Style Crime Fighter claimed to have been involved in a lot of fights on the street but said he had never had a brutality complaint since he only "decks" people when they deserve it—and they know, he insists, they deserve it. Despite the bravado, this patrolman characterizes both the acceptance and skill that is attached to violence by the Old Style Crime Fighter. What they regard as necessary, however, and what the department regards as necessary often differ, and these patrolmen invariably come into conflict with supervisors. But their attitude toward the department on the question of tactics is openly disdainful, for they believe that most supervisors and administrators are hopelessly out of touch with the realities of the street.

Driven by a preoccupation with crime, the Old Style Crime Fighter regards most order-maintenance calls as trivial matters to be avoided if at all possible. In handling order-maintenance incidents, the Old Style Crime Fighters are far more predisposed than other patrolmen to resolve matters informally, to rely on a warning rather than an arrest. The standards these patrolmen bring to bear derive from their assessment of the character and intentions of the individuals involved rather than an assessment of the intent and requirements of the law. The victim's culpability is always at issue and a justification for ignoring the dispute. And there is a propensity to apply particularistic standards: people are often treated by the Old Style Crime Fighter according to his interpretation of the differing moral standards that might prevail among different groups of individuals.

The Old Style Crime Fighters usually attempt to avoid these calls through engineering, indeed they appear to engage in engineering more frequently and with more skill than other patrolmen. If they cannot avoid a trivial order-maintenance call—and much of the time they cannot—these patrolmen handle them in as perfunctory a manner as possible. What they are often unwilling to do is to act as "philosopher, guide, and friend." Sometimes incidents are handled with a brutal callousness. In one instance, two avowed Old Style Crime Fighters answered a family dispute call between an elderly couple in an old dilapidated apartment building. The woman who answered the door immediately began talking in a rambling, desultory manner. She explained that her husband, who was lying on a dirty bed across the room, was extremely sick and needed help. She then switched tracks and said her husband always beat her and she couldn't take it any more. The response of these two patrolmen was to advise her in a jocular manner to get a divorce, and then to leave as quickly as possible. Clearly, there was no police "problem" involved; all the woman really wanted was a few moments of compassion which they were unwilling to extend. It was as much the way they dismissed her as anything else that signified their attitude toward these incidents. The woman's plight was not ignored because of other pressing demands or the tough choices between compassion and responsibility that any professional concerned with human affairs must often make; she was literally dismissed, her plight treated as insignificant.

Yet there are exceptions. Order-maintenance calls in which there is or has been violence will bring forth a more skillful and thorough response. The aggressiveness and the acceptance of violence characteristic of these officers often result in a willingness to resolve a serious order-maintenance incident. If they chose to rise to the occasion, some of these patrolmen could be awesomely effective in coping with the ambiguities of family disputes and the like. Perhaps the decisive fact about the Old Style Crime Fighter's stance toward order-maintenance incidents is that he draws distinctions, and those incidents regarded as trivial are ignored while more serious incidents are treated with all the skill and street sense he can muster.

The Old Style Crime Fighter is frequently found in a large department like the LAPD, where his emergence is facilitated by the surfeit of resources which permit independent action, and by a departmental tradition which legitimizes sleuthing. Yet both his style of action and his attitudes bring the Old Style Crime Fighter into conflict with the department and the values of professionalism. He manages this conflict partly through the respect he has acquired by virtue of his skill, by his ability to do the job. In a way, the Old Style Crime Fighters earn the right to flout rules to which other policemen are subject.[3] Failing this, they survive by dint of sheer skill in outmaneuvering supervisors. But this kind of police work comes at a high price; Joseph Wambaugh is correct when he suggests, as he did in his sentimental recreation of a crime fighter in the *Blue Knight*, that this style represents both the best and the worst that the police have to offer. These men dominated law enforcement when there were fewer constraints on police action than now; and despite their skill, they were (and are) brutal and often given to the worst abuses of police power.

CLEAN BEAT CRIME FIGHTER

These patrolmen are as aggressive and preoccupied with controlling crime as the Old Style Crime Fighters, and like them, exhibit the same dislike of order-maintenance and service calls. What is different is a legalistic frame of mind, and a different view of crime control. The Clean Beat patrolman believes in the rigid and unrelenting enforcement of the law. If he believes, like the Old Style Crime Fighter, that the primary function of street patrol is to prevent and control crime, he thinks this can be done only through aggressive enforcement of minor violations and through stopping and interrogating suspicious individuals. An effective patrolman, in his opinion, looks for all kinds of violations on his beat, from jaywalking to homicide, and makes as many stops as he can. In a sense, Clean Beat patrolmen are more consciously preventative than Old Style Crime Fighters. Their justification for aggressive enforcement of all laws is not that the law should be enforced impartially; it is the presumption that crime can be deterred only through aggressive enforcement. Crime is really controlled, they think, by keeping a clean beat, by establishing a reputation for consistent, hard-nosed enforcement.

Like the Old Style Crime Fighter, the Clean Beat patrolman is quite willing to violate procedural rules or to bend the law to serve his immediate purposes, and is prone to complain about the limitations placed on a policeman's activity by the courts and police administrators. What distinguishes the two is that the Clean Beat patrolman fails to bring the skill and subtlety to encounters on the street that is characteristic of the Old Style Crime Fighter. The Clean Beat patrolman acts like a rampaging Don Quixote in his efforts to suppress crime. He is something of a rogue elephant in a police department, the kind of officer who will make a lot of felony arrests but will be consistently in trouble. The Clean Beat patrolman thus lives in a continual state of tension: his proclivity for aggressive action conflicts with the demands imposed by an increasingly watchful department and a hostile public. He is, in a word, frustrated.

The most striking thing about the Clean Beat patrolman is the pace of his activity; he is continually on the move, stopping cars, interrogating people, always trying "to dig something up." Consider the activities of a patrolman I shall call Appleby (the name is fictitious), who is representative of this style of police work. On the tour of duty that I observed, Appleby's frustration at being unable to turn up anything reached a crescendo, and culminated in an ever more frenzied search for a crime. The first four hours had been taken up with service calls, and as the night wore on Appleby and his partner became increasingly aggressive. Driving down a major thoroughfare, Appleby saw a man jaywalking; he stopped the man, who had been drinking but was not especially drunk. Deciding he needed an arrest, Appleby booked him. After more frenetic driving, Appleby stopped to investigate a parked car in a vacant lot. Finding a young Mexican-American and his girl friend in the front seat, Appleby rousted them out, and proceeded to thoroughly interrogate them and search the car from top to bottom. All this effort produced only a meager packet of Zig Zag cigarette papers. Angry that once again his efforts were to no avail, Appleby let the young man go only after impressing upon him that the police meant business. The aggressive search for crime continued, and the final incident of the evening was, in many ways, the most instructive. Driving down a major street Appleby observed a young man with long hair walk across the street, in the crosswalk but against the "Don't Walk" sign. The time was just after 2:00 A.M. Appleby told his partner to pull over to the curb, and as they stopped, he leaned out of the window and yelled at the top of his lungs, "You sir, have committed a violation of the law, stop!" The man, who revealed that he had just arrived in Los Angeles from Hawaii, was utterly perplexed by the whole incident. For his carelessness he received a citation for jaywalking and a warning that he had better watch his step because "this is how things are done in Los Angeles."

Not all patrolmen who adopt the Clean Beat style are as aggressive and frustrated as Appleby, but their pace is just as furious. To take another example, two Clean Beat patrolmen in the course of an evening cited one jaywalker; made three traffic stops, two of which resulted in citations; arrested six drunks, although two were the result of a backing up a vice unit in a bar; stopped and interrogated one suspected heroin addict; and made two other investigative stops in "suspicious" circumstances. This was in addition to handling a moderate number of calls for service. Clean Beat patrolmen make as many, if not more, stops for field interrogations than the Old Style Crime Fighters, but they make far more stops to enforce minor violations. A fairly equal mix between stops for field interrogations and for minor violations is characteristic of this style. Calculations based on the field observations reveal that just over half the stops Clean Beat patrolmen make are to enforce minor violations (55 percent), and two-thirds of these result in citations or an arrest.

Clean Beat patrolmen evidence a distinct distaste for order-maintenance calls, though they are less prone to avoid them through engineering than the Old Style Crime Fighters, preferring to simply handle a call as quickly as possible. Unlike the Old Style Crime Fighters, the rigid legalism of the Clean Beat patrolmen precludes the use of particularistic standards. They do, however, treat a victim's claims with suspicion, and the plight of a victim they think is somehow culpable will be treated with complete indifference much of the time. What does distinguish the Clean Beat Crime Fighters is that they often go to extremes in handling disputes. Minor disputes are often handled abruptly and crudely. Two Clean Beat patrolmen answered a disturbing-the-peace call in which a lady in an apartment complained that her neighbor was making so much noise she could not sleep. The patrolmen went to the door of the neighbor's apartment, banged loudly, and when the occupant, a young black woman, answered, she was told that they had a complaint she was making noise and she had better stop. The woman denied making any noise, and the patrolmen replied that she and the "male object" (her boyfriend) in the room had better "shape up" since they did not want to come back. Clearly, in some sense, the problem was solved, but with what consequences? In a more serious situation, the tendency of the Clean Beat patrolmen is to resort to an arrest rather than mediation. The aggressiveness and the frenzy that is characteristic of these patrolmen on the street carries over into their handling of order-maintenance problems.

The core of the Clean Beat approach, the dedication to crime suppression and the penchant for aggressive, strict law enforcement, is not regarded as harassment, or as an extreme policing style, but as sound law enforcement. Clean Beat patrolmen are slaves to the values of police professionalism, and it often seems as if they have taken the rhetoric of police professionalism too literally. They have no proportion, and some are inevitably consumed by the means they employ. This is vividly illustrated by their attitude toward tactics on the street. Unlike the Crime Fighters, they often appear to have no comprehension of the limits to violence, and their choice of tactics often reveals no understanding of the necessity for measured responses. Their aggressiveness simply outstrips any sense of proportion. Clean Beat patrolmen thus tend to apply coercion spontaneously and very often indiscriminately.

These officers are unable to reconcile the dilemma between the instrumental and substantive goals of police work and the numerous moral choices patrolmen routinely confront. Often it is not the sacrifice of someone's civil rights that gets them into trouble, but their single-minded, rigid approach to law enforcement. Innocuous incidents have a way of blowing up in their hands. Yet because they wholeheartedly accept the canons of professionalism and display an undue sense of obedience and deference toward supervisors, these men come to feel a deep sense of betrayal when supervisors fail to support their decisions and their tactics. Unable to reconcile their aggressive style of patrol with the external limits imposed upon them, these men are reduced to frustration. Appleby, whose frustration stands out from that of others only in its virulence, is an extreme instance of this. As he put it toward the end of the evening:

> You come on the job with balls, you want to act like a man, you want to burn the world up, you want to put guys in jail, you want to solve problems and do something for people. But you find out that you can't act like a man, that you can't be the man you once were until after twenty years on the job [that is, after retirement].

PROFESSIONAL STYLE

If the Clean Beat style denotes extreme aggressiveness and the frequent use of illegal tactics, the Professional Style denotes an active but not overly aggressive patrolman. There is no reluctance to stop people for purposes of a field interrogation, but it is done less often and usually with somewhat more justification. These patrolmen are legalistic without being rigid. Perhaps flexibility is the adjective that best describes their attitude. If they believe that control of crime is the major function of the police, they also accept—some with more, some with less equanimity—the legitimacy of competing goals. Family disputes may often be trivial and petty (adults behaving like children), but people have a right to assistance and courteous treatment from the police. According to the Professional Style, although the law should be enforced and a patrolman does not have the right to presume innocence or guilt, the act of enforcement should be tempered with a judicious understanding of the foibles of human nature. Yet flexibility does not mean that a patrolman should let things go by; even if a citation is not issued, a person who breaks the law should be stopped and warned. These patrolmen are often tough and firm, but they are not obsessively preoccupied with order.

The attitudes and views of the Professional Style are vividly illustrated by a young patrolman with four years experience whom I shall call Joe Fisher. Unlike Appleby, he is not overpowered by the compulsion to control crime; indeed Fisher is overtly hostile to Appleby's style of police work. He has a strong aversion to what he calls "415 police officers," men whom he describes as "badge heavy": they rush to every hot call, they drive at excessive rates of speed, they throw their weight around, and they are usually sarcastic and abrupt with people. Fisher's training officer was like this, and as he reflected on his experiences he observed, "I hated him; I thought the job was to help people."

Yet the law is there to be enforced; there are criminals on the street, and they have to be apprehended. The difference between the Professional Style and the two types of Crime Fighters is the steadfast belief that law enforcement is tantamount to serving people, provided it is done in the proper way. Two incidents involving Fisher and his rookie partner illustrate this belief. In the first, Fisher and his partner stopped in front of a house where they observed a car raised on jacks parked in the street. They contacted the owner and told him that the car was illegally parked and dangerous; it could fall and injure someone, especially a child. They ordered the owner to move the car by the next day or they would issue a citation. The second incident concerned a young man stopped for speeding who talked Fisher out of a ticket. In not issuing the ticket, Fisher said he was being "compassionate," even though giving the man a warning might not have been in his best interests. A ticket, Fisher suggested, may have been more effective in suggesting to him the errors of his ways. While Fisher would let people off with a warning, he was not averse to hard-nosed law enforcement when he thought it necessary and justified.

Nonetheless, field interrogations and like tactics are the exception rather than the rule with these patrolmen. If anything, they are preoccupied with traffic offenses. Where the Old Style Crime Fighter virtually ignores traffic and the Clean Beat Crime Fighter uses traffic enforcement as an instrument to maintain order, the Professional enforces traffic laws in order to prevent accidents and because, after all, it is the law and ought to be enforced as often as necessary and as impartially as possible. Some of these patrolmen were observed to spend a large proportion of their free time patrolling for traffic violations and, what is most unusual, issuing parking citations on their own initiative. At the same time, they are less likely to "play the slot machine," to stop someone just to find out if something is amiss. This is partly because these patrolmen are not inclined to make a stop except in light of fairly compelling evidence that it is justified. Whether this results from an unwillingness to disregard probable cause or a reluctance to take the risks that an aggressive style of patrol entails is not clear. In any event, the legalism and the lack of aggressiveness that is characteristic of the Professional Style are readily apparent among these patrolmen. Judging from the field observations, these patrolmen make far more stops for minor violations than either type of Crime Fighter. Seventy-nine percent of the on-view stops made by the Professionals were made to enforce minor violations; the other 21 percent were for field interrogations. Like the Clean Beat style, however, these patrolmen cite about two-thirds of those individuals stopped for minor violations.

The Professional's perspective on disturbances and service calls is that every call should be treated as unique, and even the trivial ones should be thoroughly handled. These patrolmen rarely engaged in engineering, did not display the disdain for these affairs so characteristic of the Crime Fighters, and were not reluctant to spend as much time as necessary to resolve a dispute. Upon arriving at a routine dispute between two neighbors, two Professionals were told by the complainant that the man living next door had torn down a fence in the backyard near a garden he was cultivating with the permission of the landlord. He wanted action. He was told by the policemen that they would have to learn to live together, but they said they would talk to the man next door. The other man's version of the dispute was much different: he said that the complainant was a hostile man, always fighting and arguing with him and his wife. He admitted tearing down the fence in the garden but said that had to do with an argument over the boundaries of their gardens. The dispute was not serious, and there was good reason to doubt both stories. But both patrolmen took quite a bit of time to talk to both parties and made a concerted effort to resolve the dispute. They later explained that if they are often reluctant to make arrests in disturbances, neither are they willing to ignore them. Not every Professional patrolman is willing to be quite so patient, but the inclination to do so if possible is what distinguishes this patrolman from both Crime Fighters.

Like the Clean Beat approach, the Professional Style incorporates many of the essential beliefs and values of police professionalism. The differences between the two turn on the emphases they give to the elements of police professionalism, and the ways they accommodate themselves to organizational and community pressures. The Professionals adhere as much as possible to departmental rules and policies. They are preoccupied with doing a good job as that is defined by their supervisors. As one of them said in the midst of issuing parking tickets, "I'm out here for eight hours and I might as well give the city its money's worth." They firmly enforce the law, but they believe they are flexible enough to know when not to; they vigorously pursue felons, but they are less likely to indulge themselves in the frequent and wanton use of illegal tactics; in short, they believe that a policeman can enforce the law and cope with crime while maintaining rapport with the people in the community. For these officers the conflicts inherent in police work are either sublimated or do not exist.

SERVICE STYLE

There are two distinct groups of patrolmen who exhibit the two basic characteristics of this style, which are selectivity in enforcement of the law and a lack of aggressiveness. The attitude of one group was concisely summed up by a patrolman who said, "I don't want to chase every asshole on the street, I'm just as happy if things don't come up." These patrolmen neither worked very hard to enforce the law nor paid much attention to people's problems; their actions were calculated to keep the sergeant happy and do the minimal amount of work necessary to get by. They were notorious for ignoring violations and treating disturbances in as perfunctory a manner as possible. Some of these individuals were merely using police work as a means to another occupation, as they either went to school or worked at another job. Others were "burnt out" patrolmen; at one time in their career they may have been "hustlers," now they were coasting and hoping to make twenty years and retirement in one piece. Their code was to take problems as they occur and above all stay out of trouble.[4]

The second group, those few individuals who advocate the Service Style as a positive method, are quite different, for they advocate a qualitatively unique approach to police work. What distinguishes them from the other three styles is their belief that crime suppression is *not* the most important goal of a police department. They argue that the police should take a positive role in assisting people to solve their problems. Consequently, impersonal and legalistic law enforcement is deemphasized, and one of the defining characteristics of this approach is the belief that the exercise of discretion ought to be based on a sensitivity to community values and needs. In one sense this style attempts to return to the concept of the beat cop; but if it stresses the beat cop's sensitivity to community values and his selectivity, it is modern in its emphasis upon legality, especially in regard to due process, and a code of professional conduct. It seeks to combine the best of the beat cop and the professional policeman.

The implications of this style are manifold. It prescribes a definite set of priorities: vice laws are deemphasized and crimes of violence become the fundamental concern. Enforcement is selective in that it is based on the presence of an identifiable problem. The utility of an arrest or citation is often questioned on the grounds that perhaps other techniques would be more effective. To this extent these officers find themselves pushing for diversionary approaches in handling family disputes, and while they stress strict enforcement in regard to serious crimes the strategy of crime control advocated is quite different. The approach moves away from aggressive patrol to more traditional police techniques, business checks and the like, and to more modern but indirect methods, for example, neighborhood watch programs.

Yet as a whole this style is ill-defined; the bits and pieces of the beliefs described here have been taken from comments and observations of a number of patrolmen. Rather than a coherent approach, what unites these patrolmen is a skepticism of present approaches to police work and a good deal of criticism of many of their fellow officers. Consider a patrolman whom I shall call Ralph Williams. Williams is severely critical of the kind of law enforcement practiced by the men in his department, and he caustically refers to other patrolmen as "order-freaks." He frequently challenges their conduct on the street, especially the propriety of strictly enforcing some minor violations such as drunk in public, and the way some members of a minority group were being treated. At this point, however, Williams can only articulate his criticism of professional police work, for he has not yet defined a working alternative.

The Service Style, more than anything else, reflects submerged ideological conflicts which presently animate the practitioners of the police craft. This is partly a matter of the changing values among young policemen, but it is also indicative of the responses of policemen to the social and political turmoil of the late sixties. Be that as it may, what unites the few individuals who, to a greater or lesser degree, practice this style is a singular distaste for the doctrines of police professionalism and many of the practices endemic to contemporary police. But whether this portends far-reaching changes in American police work is unclear.

In sum, there is strong empirical justification for concluding not only that patrolmen have the latitude to fashion diverse approaches to police work but also that they actually do so. There are first clear differences in the propensity to conduct field interrogations and to intervene to enforce minor violations. Calculations based on the field observations show that the ratio of stops for field interrogations to stops for minor violations (the higher the ratio the more stops for field interrogations in relation to minor violations) is 2.55 for Old Style Crime Fighters, .83 for the Clean Beat Crime Fighters, .27 for the Professional Style, and .38 for the Service Style. Clean Beat patrolmen are by far the most active, and make the most stops for either kind of incident, while the Service Style is the least active. Both the Clean Beat and Professional patrolmen cite 67 percent of the individuals they stop for minor violations; in contrast the Old Style Crime Fighters cite only 33 percent and the Service Style only 25 percent. Differences in the way order-maintenance and service calls are handled are more difficult to discern, but both types of Crime Fighters exhibited less tolerance for these calls than either Professional or Service patrolmen.

THE DEVELOPMENT OF OPERATIONAL STYLE

If it is clear that patrolmen manifest distinctive operational styles, two important questions remain. First, to what extent is operational style influenced by the expectations of police administrators, and do patrolmen who adopt different operational styles react in distinctive ways to the conflicts and pressures of the police bureaucracy—to the conflict between the values of police professionalism and those of the police culture? And, second, how are we to explain the origins of a patrolman's beliefs?

In order to provide some tentative answers to these questions, I have used the survey data to construct a serviceable but crude measure of operational style based on two attitudinal scales that measure aggressiveness and selectivity. The aggressiveness scale combines questions that measure a patrolman's inclination to take the initiative on the street and to take extra-legal factors into account in making a decision. A patrolman who is high on this scale is one who has presumably adopted an aggressive style of patrol. The selectivity scale measures whether a patrolman emphasizes felony violations over misdemeanors. A patrolman who is high on this scale is one who believes that traffic laws, drunkenness and the like are not as important as felonies. Each scale has been dichotomized at the mean and then recombined into the four different types. For example, all those patrolmen with a score *higher* than the mean on the aggressiveness and selectivity scales were classified as Old Style Crime Fighters. On the other hand, those patrolmen with a score *lower* than the mean on the aggressiveness and selectivity scales were classified as Professionals.[5]

A patrolman develops an operational style in response to the exigencies of controlling crime and coping with the ambiguities and conflicts inherent in working the street. The development of operational style is partly dependent on the kind of community in which a patrolman first learns his craft. Patrolmen who first learn what it means to be a cop in the harsh environment of a crime-ridden, lower-class community are probably more preoccupied with crime fighting than those who begin in a more affluent community. But an operational style also grows out of the way a patrolman interprets and reacts to his experiences within the department. This raises the question of whether the traditions, training practices, and administrative policies of a police department lead to a single operational style unique to that department. James Q. Wilson argues that the beliefs (operational style) and hence decisions of patrolmen are shaped by the administrative style of the chief of police.[6] In general, then, a single, unique operational style will be associated with different police departments.

Neither the field observations nor the survey evidence show that any of the three departments are characterized by a single distinctive style (see Table 2). Yet there are some differences worth noting. Almost three-fifths of the patrolmen in the two divisions of the LAPD can be classified as either Clean Beat or Professional patrolmen, a slightly higher proportion than in either of the small departments. Inglewood, in contrast, has the highest concentration of Old Style Crime Fighters, almost twice as many as the other departments, and a slightly higher proportion of Clean Beat patrolmen. At the other extreme, Redondo Beach is dominated by the Professional and Service Styles. The traditions and policies of a department are not irrelevant to the formation of operational style, but the beliefs of patrolmen cannot be explained simply in terms of the expectations of the chief of police. The rising crime rate in Inglewood and the placid environs of Redondo Beach may have more to do with the concentration of Crime Fighters in the former and of less aggressive patrolmen in the latter than with the expectations of administrators. The matter is clearly more complex than Wilson's argument would suggest.

Regardless of the expectations of administrators, every patrolman must still come to terms with the pressures

TABLE 2 Operational Style by Department

	Small Departments		*LAPD*	
Operational Style:[a]	*Inglewood* (%)	*Redondo Beach* (%)	*Rampart* (%)	*Northeast* (%)
Old Style Crime Fighters	42	24	20	24
Clean Beat Crime Fighters	32	12	26	28
Professional Style	8	38	29	28
Service Style	18	27	26	22
Number of Respondents	(62)	(34)	(51)	(51)

[a] Significant @ $P \leq .01$

of the police bureaucracy—the disjuncture between rewards and performance, the punitive style of supervision and control, and the pressure to reconcile the substantive and instrumental goals of police work. Our discussion of the four styles suggests that each handles these conflicts in a different way. Yet it is also clear that the impact of departmental controls is related to the size of the department, and the pressures generated by the system of administrative controls are more intense in Inglewood and Redondo Beach than in LAPD. The immediate empirical question is whether all patrolmen experience these pressures in much the same way, notwithstanding the differences in operational style, or if operational style makes a difference in the way a patrolman reacts to the police bureaucracy. Table 3, which displays the relationship between operational style and attitudes toward the process of administrative control, offers some evidence on this score.

The perceptions of patrolmen toward administrative control are measured by three attitudinal scales, and table 3 presents the mean score on each scale for each operational style. The first scale measures the degree to which patrolmen believe that supervision in the department is strict and punitive (the lower the score the more the patrolman believes supervision is punitive). Patrolmen in the LAPD are slightly more likely to believe that supervision is punitive, though the difference is not large. The other two scales measure the extent to which patrolmen believe their discretion is constrained by departmental controls (the lower the score the greater the perception that discretion is constrained). The "Perception of Supervisor's Behavior" scale measures the frequency with which patrolmen believe supervisors observe and actually intervene in incidents they are handling. The "Perceived Limits on Discretion" scale is an overall measure of the degree to which patrolmen believe their actions are limited by departmental controls.[7] On this latter scale patrolmen in the small departments perceive greater constraints on their actions than patrolmen in the LAPD. On the "Perception of Supervisor's Behavior" scale patrolmen in Inglewood sense the greatest monitoring of their actions by supervisors.

There are clear-cut differences in the perceptions of the four operational styles of the process of administrative control. Old Style Crime Fighters in all three departments are the most likely to believe that supervision is punitive (their mean score on this scale is 47.21), and the most likely to believe that administrative controls are severely confining (their mean score on the "Perceived Limits on Discretion" scale is 46.00). They are also highly inclined to believe that supervisors aggressively observe their behavior on the street. If the Old Style Crime Fighters have the darkest view of supervision, the Professionals are the best integrated. They stand at the other extreme from the Crime Fighters, as they have the highest mean scores on all three scales. The Clean Beat and Service Styles stand in between, though the Clean Beat patrolmen, largely those in the small departments, are the most likely to believe that supervisors frequently observe their behavior. The Service Style, mostly because it is more selective, is more likely to perceive departmental limits on choices than either the Clean Beat or Professional Style.

TABLE 3 Operational Style by Attitudes Toward Supervision

Attitudes toward Supervision:	*Old Style Crime Fighter*	*Clean Beat Crime Fighter*	*Professional Style*	*Service Style*
Punitiveness of Supervision:				
Small Departments	49.29	51.79	51.78	52.45
LAPD*	44.00	46.96	53.17	50.63
Perception of Supervisor's Behavior:				
Small Departments*	46.47	43.30	53.94	47.45
LAPD	52.08	52.00	52.69	54.08
Perceived Limits on Discretion:				
Small Departments	44.62	48.38	49.17	47.55
LAPD**	48.14	54.00	54.38	53.75

* Difference in means significant @ $P \leq .02$

** Difference in means significant @ $P \leq .06$

This pattern, as Table 3 clearly indicates, holds up in both the small departments and the LAPD, although there are some exceptions and in some cases the differences are not large (for example, there is little difference among patrolmen in the LAPD in their perception of supervisors' behavior). Moreover, length of experience makes little difference. In other words, despite differences in experience and the differing impact of administrative controls in the small departments and the LAPD, the four types of patrolmen—especially the Old Style Crime Fighters and the Professionals—have radically different perceptions of the impact of administrative controls. Thus, operational style entails consequences not only for a patrolman's decisions on the street but for his relationship to the department as well.

In a way these findings are not at all surprising. Both the Clean Beat and Professional Styles incorporate the essential beliefs and values of professionalism, and both are at root bureaucratic styles of action. Both, especially in their legalistic view of the world, are far more responsive to administrative controls than either of the other types of patrolmen. The Professional, in particular, is the consummate organization man. If any of these patrolmen have molded themselves in the image of the department it is the Professional. In his exaggerated legalism and his penchant for aggression, the Clean Beat patrolman is a caricature of a professional policeman. Administrators may not always like the results of this approach, but judging from their own attitudes they often believe that the risk entailed by tolerating a Clean Beat patrolman is worth it.

If administrators accept, and even encourage, aggressiveness they are reluctant to tolerate selectivity. This partly explains the perceptions of the Old Style Crime Fighters and the Service Style. But the reasons for the apparent estrangement of the Crime Fighters go deeper: these men are above all individuals, craftsmen in an increasingly rationalized world. Unlike either the Clean Beat Style or the Professional, the Crime Fighter is profoundly anti-bureaucratic. In a way they are anachronisms; their style of police work was far more pervasive in an earlier era of policing. Their inclination is to do police work the way it used to be done, and to have little truck with (as they see it) the petty concerns of departmental bureaucrats.

For slightly different reasons the Service Style is also in conflict with the department. For some of these men the reluctance to work hard and take risks incurs the enmity of supervisors, often for very good reason. Most supervisors hardly think they should tolerate a man who cannot measure up to the street or a man who has quit. Aside from these cases, those men who profess the Service Style, who are critical of contemporary police work, feel the hostility of supervisors for many of the same reasons as the Old Style Crime Fighters. Like them, they have rejected much of police professionalism.

Thus, one of the crucial attributes that distinguishes these styles is the way they react to the vision of police work expressed in the doctrines of police professionalism. In their own ways both the Clean Beat and Professional patrolmen have succumbed to the ideology of professionalism. The Crime Fighters seek to return to an older style of policing when there were fewer constraints on a patrolman's actions. And the Service Style, looking to the future, seeks to redefine the role of the police.

If the kind of community in which a patrolman first works and the pressures generated by administrative controls shape the caliber of patrolman's experiences and thus influence the development of an operational style, why does a patrolman adopt one operational style rather than another? One possible explanation is that formal training and socialization within a police department do little to offset deeply ingrained attitudes learned while growing up in particular social environments, and these attitudes and the accompanying psychological attributes are the determinant forces in police behavior. In this view, the adopted style is to be explained in terms of background and psychological characteristics. Alas, with a couple of minor exceptions, none of the salient background characteristics for which I have measures (social class, ethnicity, education, religion, prior military service, region of birth) are related to the measure of operational style.[8] While it is possible, indeed probable, that deeply rooted psychological attributes contribute to the development of different operational styles—these cannot and should not be ruled out—the weight of the evidence here suggests that an alternative explanation, the role of occupational socialization, may be more significant and ought to be explored.[9]

If it is the process of occupational socialization into the department that is decisive for the development of an operational style, and if this process cannot be understood solely as a response to the expectations of the chief of police, how does a patrolman learn an operational style? What must be understood is that a patrolman doesn't grapple with his initial experiences alone; they are interpreted for him by his immediate peers. Patrolmen undergo an intensive rite of passage in which they acquire some general precepts of police work and learn the norms that govern the police culture.[10] Through this experience a patrolman not only comes to share the burden of performing an arduous task, but he also acquires a distinctive set of values and beliefs, and learns to be not just a policeman but a particular kind of policeman. A patrolman's initial experiences are mediated and interpreted by a significant elder officer, usually the field training officer, who assumes the role of father confessor and guide to the rookie. What happens, I suspect, is that rookie patrolmen model their style after that of an older officer, though they may sometimes react negatively to these initial experiences, as Fisher did, and adopt a style which is just the opposite. In any event, the field training officer passes on not just the "tricks of the trade" but a distinctive way of working the street.

The elder policeman who mediates a rookie's experiences need not always be a field training officer. A watch commander or sergeant can fulfill this role just as well, and there were sergeants in all three departments who had this kind of reputation among patrolmen. But not every supervisor can command this kind of respect and influence. Field supervisors are not ordinarily in a position to influence a patrolman's beliefs the way a field training officer can, and, more important, they must overcome the chasm between patrolmen and management. What often distinguished the more influential supervisors, aside from their personal qualities, was their overt identification with the plight of patrolmen. The limits to the influence of supervisors over the development of patrolmen's operational style is revealed by the fact that the attitudes of the large number of highly aggressive patrolmen in Inglewood and the equally significant number of selective patrolmen in Redondo Beach run counter to the desires and expectations of the field supervisors in those departments.[11]

By the time a patrolman finishes his second or third year on the street he will have more or less developed an operational style, though his behavior and perhaps some of his attitudes may be modified by further experiences on the street and with administrators. To what extent do patrolmen change their attitudes as they gain more experience? There is no appreciable difference between the lesser and more experienced patrolmen in their attitude toward selectivity, but their attitudes toward aggressiveness are modified. After five years on the street, aggressiveness drops off sharply: 43 percent of the patrolmen with two to four years experience are highly aggressive compared to just 18 percent of those with five years or more. By and large, it is the younger patrolmen who display a preference for the Clean Beat approach, while both the Professional and Service Style patrolmen have more experience. Though one cannot be absolutely sure in the absence of data that trace the development of patrolmen over time, it is a plausible hypothesis that the Clean Beat patrolmen (and the Old Style Crime Fighters to a lesser extent) shift toward a less aggressive style after five years. This is not really surprising, and it is probably the pervasive sense of frustration, especially among Clean Beat patrolmen, that accounts for this apparent shift in attitudes. After years of being asked to meet contradictory responsibilities and to take risks for meager rewards, some of these patrolmen lose their élan and retreat to a more subdued style.[12]

THE RELEVANCE OF OPERATIONAL STYLE FOR POLICE DISCRETION

An operational style represents a patrolman's initial response to the uncertainties of attempting to control crime and the demands of police administrators. A patrolman develops a predisposition toward aggressiveness and selectivity as he attempts to balance the conflict between crime fighting and providing services, as he confronts the contradictory impulses of police professionalism, and as he deals with unique citizens, hostile or otherwise, in a specific community. An operational style structures action, it leads a patrolman toward some alternatives and away from others, and it is frequently the decisive factor in determining his choices. But if a patrolman's operational style is influential in determining his choices, there are nevertheless limits on the ability of patrolmen to practice their craft in a way that is fully consistent with the dictates of their operational style. If patrolmen clearly have different ideas about how they should carry out their task, and if they vary in their motivation and sheer ambition, all of them must take account of the reactions of administrators and supervisors to their decisions. The question now is, What difference does the web of bureaucratic controls on patrolmen make for the exercise of discretion?

REFERENCES

1. My distinctions between different types of incidents is somewhat similar to the distinction between the law enforcement and order-maintenance functions drawn by James Q. Wilson, but the use is rather different. Wilson argues that most of the variation in discretion is a result of two factors: the mode of intervention in an incident and whether it involves a law enforcement or order-maintenance problem. Here the point is that these incidents impose different constraints on patrolmen but that discretion is determined by operational style and the impact of departmental controls. See James Q. Wilson, *Varieties of Police Behavior: The Management of Law and Order in Eight Communities* (New York: Atheneum, 1970), pp. 84–85.

2. Additional support for this typology comes from William Ker Muir's, Jr. recent study of policemen and an earlier study by Susan O. White. All three studies were *conducted independently and in different departments*, and all arrived, to some degree, at remarkably similar types of policemen. White's categories are very close to mine, while two of Muir's types (the Professional and Enforcer) are almost identical to two of mine (the Old Style and Clean Beat Crime Fighters). See William Ker Muir, Jr., *Police: Streetcorner Politicians* (Chicago: University of Chicago Press, 1977), pp. 13–36; and Susan O. White, "A Perspective on Police Professionalization," *Law and Society Review* (Fall 1972): 61–85, especially pp. 70–79.

3. For a description of an Old Style Crime Fighter doing just that, see Joseph Wambaugh, *The Onion Field* (New York: Delacorte Press, 1973), pp. 229–233.

4. A few of these patrolmen are similar to those Muir has dubbed avoiders, men who simply cannot measure up to the responsibilities of police work. See Muir, *Police: Streetcorner Politicians*, pp. 31–36.

5. For a complete description of the items in each scale see Michael K. Brown, *Working the Street* (New York: Russell Sage Foundation, 1981), pp. 145–146; 163–167 and Appendix. Both scales have been normalized with a mean of 50 and a standard deviation of 10.

6. Wilson, *Varieties of Police Behavior*, pp. 138–39; 230–6.

7. See Brown, *Working the Street*, pp. 120, 124–126 and Appendix for a full discussion of the items in each scale and the method used in constructing them.

8. The only exception to this generalization worth mentioning is that patrolmen who adopt the Service Style tend to be slightly better educated than the others. But the difference is not large and not statistically significant.

9. I do not wish to appear to be arbitrarily ruling out the importance of deeply rooted psychological traits. The significance of operational style for police discretion clearly suggests that the psychology of individual policemen, and the link between psychological traits and an operational style, ought to be investigated in more depth than it so far has been. The question must remain open for the moment, for I have neither the data nor the expertise to pursue it here. For some provocative hints along these lines see Muir, *Police: Streetcorner Politicians*, passim.

10. On the process of socialization in police departments, see John Van Maanen, "Working the Street: A Developmental View of Police Behavior," in *The Potential for Reform of Criminal Justice*, ed. Herbert Jacob (Beverly Hills: Sage Publications, 1974), pp. 83–103; and "Police Socialization: A Longitudinal Examination of Job Attitudes in an Urban Police Department," *Administrative Science Quarterly* 20 (1975): 207–28.

11. Cf., Muir, *Police: Streetcorner Politicians*, pp. 184–87; 235–57. Muir believes sergeants to be far more influential in shaping the behavior of patrolmen than I do. I do not doubt that some sergeants are influential nor do I doubt that they can be. But my observations lead me to believe that in most cases they are not terribly influential, partly because a lot of them are not interested, but mostly because of the bifurcation of internal control in police departments.

12. Such a development is entirely consistent with Van Maanen's data. See "Police Socialization: A Longitudinal Examination of Job Attitudes in an Urban Police Department," especially pp. 220 ff.

Police Cynicism

Arthur Niederhoffer

In the police world, cynicism is discernible at all levels, in every branch of law enforcement. It has also characterized police in other times and places. During the French Revolution and then under Napoleon, Joseph Fouché, the minister of police, concluded that with a few exceptions the world was composed of scoundrels, hypocrites, and imbeciles.(1) Many years later, reviewing the American police scene in 1939, Read Bain found that policemen were committed to the belief that the citizen was always trying "to get away with something," and that all men would commit crimes except for the fear of the police.(2)

In an interview conducted by the Center for the Study of Democratic Institutions, the late Chief William Parker of the Los Angeles Police Department was asked, "Are you inclined to be pessimistic about the future of our society?"

> I look back [he replied] over almost thirty-five years in the police service, thirty-five years of dealing with the worst that humanity has to offer. I meet the failures of humanity daily, and I meet them in the worst possible context. It is hard to keep an objective viewpoint. But it is also hard for me to believe that our society can continue to violate all the fundamental rules of human conduct and expect to survive. I think I have to conclude that this civilization will destroy itself, as others have before it. That leaves, then, only one question—when?(3)

A female store detective, with fifteen years of police experience to support her conclusions, states emphatically, "I am convinced that we are turning into a nation of thieves. I have sadly concluded that nine out of ten persons are dishonest."(4)

As noted before, it is possible to distinguish between two kinds of police cynicism. One is directed against life, the world, and people in general; the other is aimed at the police system itself.(5) The first is endemic to policemen of all ranks and persuasions—including the professionals. The second, common among patrolmen, is by definition excluded from the ideology of the professional policeman. The professional wants to transform and eventually control the system. This hope keeps him from cynicism.

Cynicism may be a by-product of *anomie* in the social structure; at the same time it may also prepare the way for personal *anomie* or anomia. Anxious over a personal failure, the individual policeman often disguises his feelings with a cynical attitude, and thus negates the value of the prize he did not attain. Frequently, he includes in his cynicism all persons who still seek that prize or have succeeded in winning it, and, occasionally, deprecates the entire social system within which the failure occurred.

As the cynic becomes increasingly pessimistic and misanthropic, he finds it easier to reduce his commitment to the social system and its values. If the patrolman remains a "loner," his isolation may lead to psychological *anomie* and even to suicide. . . .

Anomie is not the inevitable outcome of police cynicism. Instead a policeman may be absorbed by the "delinquent" occupational subculture, dedicated to a philosophy of cynicism. This group may be deviant, but it is not anomic. It has a code of values and a clear, consistent ideology that function well in the police world. The members may be alienated from their former groups and goals, but they can be completely incorporated into this new reference group.

The third adaptation to cynicism is to overcome it, to regain commitment to the ideal of a decent and honorable career within the police force. Typically, there are two critical points in the advanced career of a policeman when he may discard cynicism. One crisis occurs when he considers retrospectively the many risks his career has involved. Fearing investigation, he may surrender his disaffection and resolve to do his job to the best of his ability. The second opportunity for reassessment comes when a man who is near retirement seeks another job and is often rebuffed. When this happens, a policeman's present situation understandably will seem more attractive to him.

The process leading to cynicism and *anomie* may be viewed as a continuum stretching from commitment at one end to *anomie* at the other, with cynicism as the critical intervening stage. Since police professionals are committed to the highest ideals of police work, they belong at the commitment end; the cynics around the opposite pole. The following model illustrates the typical *stages* that succeed one another as the policeman moves from commitment to cynicism and *anomie*.

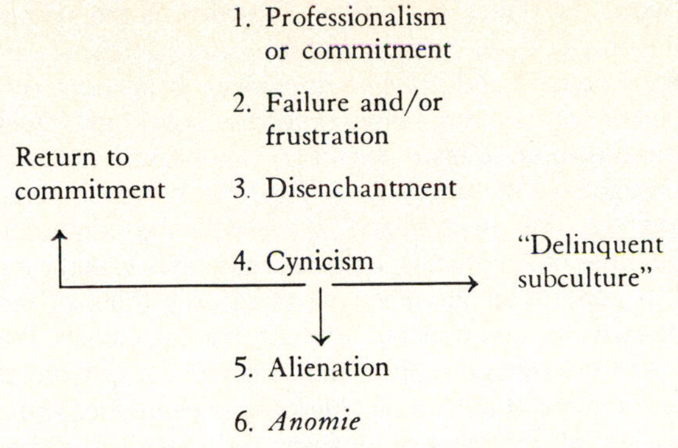

Differences in the patterns of cynicism are apparently related to a policeman's age and experience. The following classification scheme indicates that there is a succession of typical stages in the growth of cynicism that runs parallel to the occupational career. (I am indebted to Professor Joseph Bram of New York University for his help with this typology.)

The preliminary stage, pseudo-cynicism, is recognizable among recruits at the training school. This attitude barely conceals the idealism and commitment beneath the surface.

The second stage, romantic cynicism, is reached in the first five years of the police career. The most idealistic young members of the force are precisely the ones who are most disillusioned by actual police work, and most vulnerable to this type of cynicism.

The third stage, aggressive cynicism, depends on the conjunction of individual cynicism and the subculture of cynicism. It corresponds to *ressentiment* because resentment and hostility become obvious in this period, most prevalent at the ten-year mark.

In the last few years of the police career, resigned cynicism replaces the former, more blatant type. This detachment may be passive and apathetic or express itself as a form of mellow if mild good will. It accepts and comes to terms with the flaws of the system.

Because these stages represent ideal types, there will probably be practical variations in style and degree. Cynicism as an orientation to life depends for proof of its existence upon inferences drawn from human behavior. I have included descriptive material that indicates the likelihood of a correlation between police work and cynicism.

A more acceptable method is what Kenneth Clark has termed that of the "involved observer."(6) Because I was a policeman for more than twenty years, and have read a large portion of the police literature, I am convinced that there is a great deal of cynicism among my former colleagues.

Even so, the scientific method is most persuasive. The sociologist tries to emulate the rigor of the physical scientist: he observes and describes, collecting data; he classifies and compares, moving from the empirical to the conceptual. Thus he constructs hypotheses that cannot usually be tested by scientifically controlled experiment. The compromise solution is to prepare a questionnaire, most likely to evoke forthright responses, submit it to a well-chosen sample, and then analyze the results to see whether the hypotheses are substantiated. In this fashion research may be lifted to theory. I have utilized all these methods, emphasizing the last, formulating and testing the following hypotheses in my study of police cynicism. . . .

1. For the first few years of a police career one's degree of cynicism will increase in proportion to his length of service, but it will tend to level off at some point between the fifth and tenth year of service. Generally, cynicism is learned as part of socialization into the police occupation, a process likely to take at least five years.
2. Newly appointed men will show less cynicism than more seasoned Police Academy recruits. In turn, the recruit group will be less cynical than the more experienced patrolmen: not only will the average degree of cynicism be lower, but there will be fewer cynics in the group.
3. Superior officers will be less cynical than patrolmen. According to my theory, cynicism is commonly a mode of adaptation to frustration. Cynicism should therefore vary positively according to the degree of failure and frustration. Men in the lower ranks have more reason to feel frustrated than do their superiors.
4. Among patrolmen, those with college educations will reveal a higher level of cynicism than other patrolmen because their expectations for promotion (still unfulfilled) were greater.
5. Patrolmen with preferred assignments (details) will be less cynical than other patrolmen.
6. Because foot patrolmen are of low status, they will be more cynical than patrolmen assigned to other duties.
7. Patrolmen who receive awards for meritorious duty will be less cynical. Patrolmen who were the subjects of departmental charges (complaints) will be more cynical.

8. Jewish patrolmen will be more cynical than non-Jewish patrolmen. Jewish tradition stresses that true success in life lies in becoming a professional man. A Jewish policeman who remains a patrolman is thus a double failure: he did not become a doctor or lawyer, and he has been unable to rise from the low rank of patrolman.

9. When members of the force have served for seventeen or eighteen years, and are approaching retirement, they will exhibit less cynicism. When policemen near retirement search for employment outside the police system, they find opportunities distinctly limited. As a result, their appreciation of, and commitment to the police occupation revives.

10. Members of the Vice Squad will be more cynical than members of the Youth Division. The specific work situation within the organization plays its part in shaping attitudes.

11. Middle-class patrolmen will be less cynical than working-class patrolmen. Their receptivity to professionalism should insulate against cynicism. The middle-class ethic is more sympathetic to the ideas of professionalism than is the ideology of the working class.

So far I have tried to establish the relationship between the police system and cynicism. Is the system the only or even the principal source of cynicism? Perhaps police candidates were cynical, or at least vulnerable to cynicism, before becoming policemen. Does this possibility weaken the theory? In one sense anyone brought up in America, by the time he reaches his twenties, has internalized, along with the admirable qualities of Americans, a host of materialistic and cynical patterns of thought. We need only think of the distrust of "do-gooders," the anti-intellectualism, the "I'm from Missouri. Show me!" stance, the proverbial wisdom that there is a bit of larceny in everyone. Thus, we are all mixtures of idealism and cynicism. Other things being equal, we can expect the cynicism to be outweighed by the more attractive qualities. The question then arises, "Why is the police system with all its concentrated effort incapable, in so many cases, of dissipating that cynicism or encouraging the potent idealism?"

Still the lingering doubt persists. Is it not likely that there is something unusual about an individual who chooses to become a policeman? If he is not clearly cynical, is he not typically authoritarian? And, then once more, is it not true that authoritarianism and cynicism are strongly connected?

REFERENCES

1. Louis Madelin, *Fouché* 1759–1820 (Paris: Plon-Nourrit et Cie., 1903), p. 394.

2. Read Bain, "The Policeman on the Beat," *Scientific Monthly, 48* (1939), p. 451.

3. *The Police: An Interview by Donald McDonald with William H. Parker, Chief of Police of Los Angeles* (Santa Barbara: Center for the Study of Democratic Institutions, 1962), p. 169. His view is that "The police departments have been demoralized by political control, poor leadership, and low rates of pay. The life of many districts seems competitive and raw; individuals pursue their own ends with little regard for public morality, and the policeman sees the ugly underside of outwardly respectable households and businesses. Small wonder then, that many American policemen are cynics."

4. Dorothy Crowe, "Thieves I Have Known," *Saturday Evening Post, 234* (Feb. 4, 1961), pp. 21, 78.

5. An index of this attitude is the nearly universal desire to get out of uniform—the most visible sign of the police occupation. For this reason, there is not only a quest to become a detective, but also a refusal to wear the police uniform when off duty although a policeman has a right to do so. It is also revealed by the denigration of the police job. In a relevant published study the author found that "For example, many of the Illinois police officers perceive their occupation to be a cause of ridicule to their children." John P. Clark, "Isolation of the Police: A Comparison of the British and American Situations." *Journal of Criminal Law, Criminology and Police Science, 56* (September, 1965), p. 313.

6. Kenneth Clark, *Dark Ghetto* (New York: Harper and Row, 1965), pp. xv–xviii.

6

POLICE AND SOCIETY

The police act as a barometer of the current state of a society, gauging the pressures and forces that are arrayed in the uneasy equilibrium that characterizes any social structure. It follows that the greater the stresses and points of conflict that appear in a given society, the greater the concomitant growth in the dependence upon the power of the police. When civil disorders and related disturbances become a real threat to existing institutional arrangements, more resources, greater funding, increased personnel, and significant augmentation of both technology and authority are granted to police departments.

Inevitably, because of the real function of the police, social critics can label the police "the strategic arm of the ruling class." Claims for the validity of this observation are in large measure based on the obvious fact that the police are legally mandated to act as the defenders and protectors of existing political, economic, and property relationships. Historically, one of the least recognized, but perhaps the most vital role of the police in any large-scale society, is that of social lightning rod or institutional scapegoat. Every attack upon an institution or a power center in society is deflected or defused by a phalanx of police who absorb the shock that originally motivated the attack. In this fashion a good deal of explosive anger and aggressive behavior is ventilated, shunted away, and displaced from the original objects of hostility.

Despite our own use of the generic phrase "police and society" we must warn students of law enforcement against excessive generalization, against the use of clichés such as "police and the community" or "police role in society," which are usually employed as "umbrella" concepts. Instead the student must focus on more explicit contexts such as the particular police officer, and a given beat, precinct, school, or any small segment of a community in which that officer has a significant impact. In other words, it is best to view the relationships between the police and society in microscopic rather than macroscopic terms. This is a more valid approximation of the true state of affairs.

Within one precinct, the same corps of officers might be considered friendly servants within a three-block, upper-middle-class area; a security force there to protect against burglaries and undesirable outsiders in a nearby residential area; or even the enemy, occupying still another zone of the same precinct.

Policeman as Philosopher, Guide, and Friend

Elaine Cumming, Ian Cumming, and Laura Edell

This is the fourth report from a group of studies designed to throw some light upon the division of labor among the social agents whose central role is concerned with maintaining social integration by controlling various forms of deviant behavior.(1)

In earlier reports, we have adopted the convention of looking at social agents and agencies in terms of their relatively supportive or relatively controlling character. We have assumed that it is difficult for an agent to exercise both support and control at the same time and that any agent tends, therefore, to specialize in one or the other aspect of the integrative process.(2) Even when he is specialized, such an agent may be considered controlling when he is compared with some agents, and supportive when compared with others. Thus, the probation officer is more on the client's side, that is, supportive to him, than the policeman, but less so than the psychiatrist. Furthermore, the agent may be seen as supportive by the layman but experienced as controlling by the client, and *vice versa*. For example, the prisoner remanded by the court for psychiatric treatment may well experience his hospitalization as incarceration. Conversely, a chronic alcoholic may be grateful, in mid-winter, for a night in prison.

There is another aspect to this duality in the handling of deviance. While it is probably impossible to perform acts of support and control simultaneously, support without control is over-protection and invites passivity and dependency, while control without support is tyranny and invites rebellion. While the agent may specialize in one aspect of social control of deviance, the other must, nevertheless, be part of his repertoire.(3) Thus, while physicians and clergymen are generally supportive of people in pain or trouble, such people are expected, in return, to perform appropriately the role of patient or parishioner. The support is overt, the control is latent. In general, the agent's training and professional ethics focus on the skills needed for the overt part of his role; the latent aspects are derived from and governed by general norms and values. Role conflict can be avoided in part by keeping the "contradictory" side of a role latent.

SOURCE: *Social Problems, 12, 3* (1965), published by The Society for the Study of Social Problems.

The policeman's role in an integrative system is, by definition and by law, explicitly concerned with control—keeping the law from being broken and apprehending those who break it—and only latently with support. For example, if you break the law, you can expect to be arrested, but if you go along quietly, you can, unless there is a special circumstance, expect to be treated reasonably.(4) In the course of controlling one member of society, moreover, the policeman often provides indirect support to another. For example, when he apprehends, and thus controls a wife-beating husband, he supports the wife, just as, in a reverse situation, the doctor controls the behavior of those attending a patient when he prescribes rest and sympathy. Finally, besides latent support, the policeman often gives direct help to people in certain kinds of trouble. When he does this, the balance between support and control has shifted, and he is acting overtly as a supportive agent and only latently in his controlling role. He has, at the same time, changed from a professional to an amateur. This paper reports a study of the requests for help received by a city police department and the policeman's response to them, with special attention to what is assumed here to be the latent side of his role.

METHODS OF STUDY

Because there seems to be no systematic account of the day-to-day activities of policemen, two specific questions were posed: (1) What kinds of calls for help do policemen get, and (2) How do they answer them? Two kinds of data were collected. First, a total of 801 incoming telephone calls at the police complaint desk in a metropolitan police department were observed over a total of 82 hours. These hours were not evenly distributed around the 24 hours, for reasons connected with the field worker, not with the Police Department. As each complaint was received and disposed of, a description was dictated into a tape recorder. Fourteen selected prowl car calls were then observed. At the end of this phase of the study, the worker submitted field notes concerned with the general culture of the police station. Secondly, interviews were conducted with detectives concerning their special assignments. A formulation of the nature of the policeman's supporting role was then constructed from these data.

RESULTS

The Complaint Desk. Figure 1 shows the hourly distribution of police calls. The daily peak activity is between the evening hours of seven and eight o'clock excepting for Thursday, Friday, and Saturday when it is between nine and ten. Because of the gaps in the data, there is a possibility that there is a peak at about noon in the first part of the week, but on both theoretical and common-sense grounds, it seems unlikely. The last part of the week also shows a greater volume of calls than the first. In general, the high rate of calls in the evening and on weekends suggests that problems arise when the social pulse is beating fast—when people are coming and going, regrouping, and, of course, engaging in informal rather than formal activities.

In order to interpret these rhythms further, the 801 calls were classified according to their content, as Table 1 shows. One hundred forty-nine, or 18.6 percent of the calls, were excluded from analysis; 88 of these were call-backs on earlier complaints, 33 were requests for information only, and 28 were outside this police department's jurisdiction.[1] The remaining 652 calls were for service within the purview of these police. They are treated as independent, but the unit of analysis is the call, and not the caller, and results must be interpreted with this in mind.

The 652 calls included in the study were divided into two major groups: the first included calls for service in connection with things or possessions, while the second included calls for support or assistance with regard to problems of health, safety, or interpersonal relationships.[2]

The first (nearly one-third of the total of 801 calls) include traffic violations, reports of losses or thefts, calls about unlocked doors, fallen power wires, and so on. These are part of the regular controlling function of the police and are not the main focus of this paper. The second major group (about one-half of all calls) is concerned with personal problems and therefore may reasonably be expected to include the need or desire

[1] The latter two groups (61 calls) were excluded because there was no chance of a car being sent, and therefore they could not be compared with the remainder.

[2] It was surprisingly easy to classify the calls on these two major dimensions and coders had no trouble getting over 90 percent agreement. Differences were reconciled in conferences.

FIGURE 1 Average Police Calls per Hour, First Part of the Week (6 A.M. Sunday–5 A.M. Thursday) and Second Part of the Week (6 A.M. Thursday–5 A.M. Sunday)

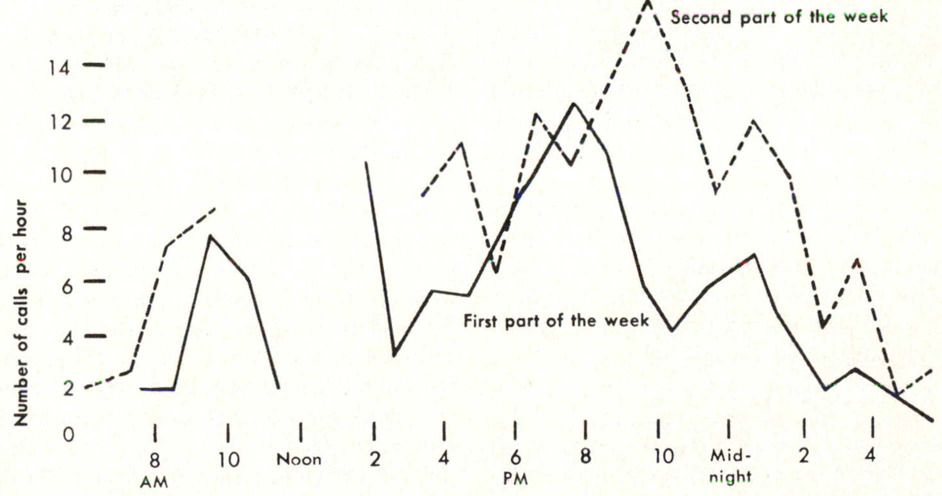

TABLE 1 Classification of Calls to the Complaint Desk of a Metropolitan Police Department during 82 Selected Hours in June and July 1961

Type of Call	*Number of Calls*	*Percent of Total*
Total	*801*	*100.0*
Calls included in analysis	652	*81.4*
1. Calls about "things"	255	31.8
2. Calls for support	397	49.6
Persistent personal problems	*230*	*28.7*
a. Health services	81	10.1
b. Children's problems	83	10.4
c. Incapacitated people	33	4.1
d. Nuisances	33	4.1
Periodic personal problems	*167*	*20.9*
a. Disputes	63	7.9
b. Violence	43	5.4
c. Protection	29	3.6
d. Missing persons	11	1.4
e. Youths' behavior	21	2.6
Calls excluded from analysis	*149*	*18.6*
Information only	33	4.1
Not police business	28	3.5
Feedback calls	88	11.0

for some form of support. These calls were subdivided into two types: (1) persistent problems occurring throughout the week; and (2) periodic problems occurring mainly on the weekend.

As Table 1 shows, the first type comprises 230 calls, of which about one-third are requests for health services, that is, ambulance escorts, investigation of accidents, suicide attempts, and so on; another third are children's problems, usually complaints about trespassing or destructive behavior; and the remainder are divided equally between incapacitated people, usually described over the phone as drunk or "psycho," and nuisances, usually noisy behavior.

Periodic problems comprise 167 calls of which more than a third are about disputes and quarrels of all kinds, both in families and among unrelated people. Almost half are concerned with violence or protection from potential violence[3] and the remainder are about missing persons or gangs of youths and hot-rodders.

[3] Most "protection" calls are for a "clothing escort," that is, for a policeman to accompany a person who has left his home, or been thrown out of it, into the house to get his clothing.

Table 2 shows the distribution of the calls, by type, through the days of the week and the period of the day. It now appears that the heaping up of calls in the last part of the week is made up of two effects: first, routine police business and persistent interpersonal calls occur most frequently on Thursday, while periodic interpersonal problems heap up on Friday night. The meaning of this finding is not clear, but it may be that the tensions associated with the instrumental activity of the working week are increasing by Thursday and are then let go on Friday—payday—and on the weekend, when formal constraints are fewer. Because fewer of the other agents are available at these times, the policeman takes over many emergency health and welfare services, a kind of division of labor through time.

Almost three-quarters of all 652 calls were answered by dispatch of a patrolman in a squad car to the scene, while about eight percent received various kinds of advice or information, and about four-and-one-half percent were referred to another source of help. Of the 29 referrals, one was to a medical service, one to a social service, 19 to other legal services and the remaining eight to commercial concerns, such as the Telephone Company. Almost 15 percent of the calls were terminated—that is, service was withheld for reasons not determined, occasionally because no car was available.

In Table 3, we see that the probability of a car being sent out is inversely related to the rate at which calls are coming in. During the six time periods in which a total of 235 calls were received at a rate of fewer than eight calls per hour, 78 percent of them were responded to with cars. During the five time periods in which 417 calls were received at a rate of more than eight calls per hour, cars were sent only 68 percent of the time. This difference is highly significant ($\chi^2 = 7.54$, d.f. $= 1$), and suggests that cars are sent on a simple supply-and-demand basis. Furthermore, there is no difference among the three major categories with regard to the likelihood of a car being sent. Nevertheless, certain sub-categories of complaint are more likely to get service than others. As Table 4 shows, calls regarding violence (control), children and youths (support and control), and illness (support) are the most likely to be responded to with a car although the likelihood of the law being broken—which defines the police mandate—is greater for some of these complaints than for others.

When the complainant reports a nuisance or a dispute, he has only one chance in two of getting more

TABLE 2 Number of Calls to the Complaint Desk of a Metropolitan Police Department by Type of Problem,* Day of Week, Time of Day, and Hours of Observation during 82 Selected Hours in June and July 1961

Time of Day, Hours of Observation, and Type of Call	*Total*	*Sun.*	*Mon.*	*Tue.*	*Wed.*	*Thur.*	*Fri.*	*Sat.*
All calls	*652*	*50*	*69*	*55*	*76*	*95*	*54*	*253*
(hours observed)	(82)	(8)	(14)	(9)	(9)	(9)	(6)	(27)
12:01 A.M.–5:00 A.M.	*91*	*16*	*18*					*57*
(hours observed)	(14)	(2)	(5)	(0)	(0)	(0)	(0)	(7)
Routine	*28*	4	8					16
Persistent	*21*	4	4					13
Periodic	*42*	8	6					28
5:01 A.M.–noon	*52*		9	*19*		*17*		*7*
(hours observed)	(13)	(0)	(4)	(3)	(0)	(3)	(0)	(3)
Routine	36		6	11		15		4
Persistent	*10*		2	4		2		2
Periodic	6		1	4		0		1
12:01 P.M.–6:00 P.M.	*187*	*18*		*36*	*38*	*38*	*31*	*26*
(hours observed)	(26)	(4)	(0)	(6)	(5)	(3)	(4)	(4)
Routine	*88*	9		12	18	18	16	15
Persistent	*68*	6		17	11	16	12	6
Periodic	*31*	3		7	9	4	3	5
6:01 P.M.–midnight	*322*	*16*	*42*		*38*	*40*	*23*	*163*
(hours observed)	(29)	(2)	(5)	(0)	(4)	(3)	(2)	(13)
Routine	*103*	4	13		17	15	2	52
Persistent	*131*	5	22		18	17	7	62
Periodic	*88*	7	7		3	8	14	49

* Departures from uniformity:

1. Periodic interpersonal calls occur more often than chance would indicate on Friday evening ($\chi^2 = 24.1$, d.f. $= 5$, $P < .01$) and the early hours of Saturday ($\chi^2 = 8.4$, d.f. $= 2$, $P = .02$).

2. Both routine police calls and persistent interpersonal calls occur more frequently than chance would indicate on Thursday, the former in the morning ($\chi^2 = 12.3$, d.f. $= 3$, $P < .01$) and the latter in the afternoon ($\chi^2 = 13.1$, d.f. $= 5$, $P = .05$).

than advice—albeit philosophical advice. Thus, a man calls to say that he has had a fight with his girl and she hasn't come to see him, although he knows she is off duty from the hospital; the policeman says he can't make her come to his house—perhaps she doesn't want to—and goes on to advise the man that that's the way life is sometimes.

It is possible that some of the calls about violence are later stages of these unanswered dispute calls. For example, to one complaint, "My boy friend is mad at me and is going to beat me up," the answer was, "Call us again when he does."[4]

It is quite apparent that the policeman must often exercise a kind of clinical judgment about these complaints, and that this judgment reflects his own values.

[4] Police Chief Murphy describes this entry as "poor police practice."

The field notes suggest, for example, that policemen are sincerely, if sentimentally, concerned about children, and that negligent parents are likely to find the police at their most truculent. The following example is taken from the notes:

> A call came from a very kindly-sounding Italian man at about 11 o'clock in the evening. He was reporting that he had found a little boy from next door wandering in the street . . . and he thought the police ought to know about the situation. A car was dispatched and reported that there was nobody home, and in fact, there were three smaller children in the house. . . . The captain dispatched a camera crew, child placement was notified and the children were immediately placed in a temporary placement home. A stake-out was set for the parents. Meanwhile the pictures had been developed and they showed four under-nourished, under-clothed little children lying in their own feces on a mattress on the floor. The refrigerator contained two

TABLE 3 Percent of Calls to Which Cars Sent by Hours of the Day, Days of the Week and Type of Call, and Number of Calls Received per Hour (82 Selected Hours at the Complaint Desk of a Metropolitan Police Department, June and July 1961)

	Total		***Sun.–Wed.****		***Thursday***		***Fri.–Sat.****	
Time of Day, Type of Call, and Calls/Hr.	*Calls*	*Percent to Which Car Sent*	*Calls*	*Percent to Which Car Sent*	*Calls*	*Percent to Which Car Sent*	*Calls*	*Percent to Which Car Sent*
Total calls	*652*	*72.1*	*250*	*72.8*	*95*	*71.6*	*307*	*70.0*
(Total/hr.)	(8.0)		(6.3)		(10.6)		(9.3)	
12:01 A.M.–5:00 A.M.	*91*	*80.2*	*34*	*85.3*			*57*	*77.2*
(calls/hour)	(6.5)		(4.9)				(8.1)	
Routine	28	85.7	12	91.7			16	81.3
Persistent	21	71.4	8	87.5			13	61.5
Periodic	42	81.0	14	78.6			28	82.1
5:01 A.M.–noon	*52*	*86.5*	*28*	*89.3*	*17*	*88.2*	*7*	*71.4*
(calls/hour)	(4.0)		(4.0)		(5.7)		(2.3)	
Routine	36	88.9	17	94.1	15	86.7	4	75.0
Persistent	10	90.0	6	83.3	2	100.0	2	100.0
Periodic	6	66.7	5	80.0	0	—	1	—
12:01 P.M.–6:00 P.M.	*187*	*73.8*	*92*	*70.7*	*38*	*71.0*	*57*	*80.7*
(calls/hour)	(7.2)		(6.1)		(12.7)		(7.1)	
Routine	88	69.3	39	66.7	18	66.7	31	74.2
Persistent	68	80.9	34	76.5	16	75.0	18	94.4
Periodic	31	71.0	19	68.4	4	75.0	8	75.0
6:01 P.M.–midnight	*322*	*66.5*	*96*	*65.6*	*40*	*65.0*	*186*	*67.2*
(calls/hour)	(11.1)		(8.7)		(13.3)		(12.4)	
Routine	103	60.2	34	58.8	15	40.0	54	66.7
Persistent	131	72.5	45	73.3	17	76.4	69	71.0
Periodic	88	64.8	17	58.8	8	87.5	63	57.1

* Calls grouped because of similar distribution.

TABLE 4 Disposition of 397 Calls to the Complaint Desk of a Metropolitan Police Department Regarding Interpersonal Problems, by Sub-Category of Complaint (82 Selected Hours in June and July 1961)

Type of Call	*Total Calls*	*Percent Car Sent*
Total calls	*397*	*76.8*
Persistent problems	*230*	*79.1*
a. Health services	81	86.4
b. Children's problems	83	85.5
c. Incapacitated people	33	75.8
d. Nuisances	33	48.5
Periodic problems	*167*	*73.7*
a. Disputes	63	50.8
b. Violence	43	95.3
c. Protection	29	79.3
d. Missing persons	11	81.8
e. Youths' behavior	21	85.7

cans of condensed milk and some rotten vegetables; the place was filthy and unheated. As the time went by, anger began to rise and when at about four o'clock in the morning the parents were brought in to the station everybody was in an ugly mood. . . . Had they been the least bit smart, glib, or said almost anything other than "yes" or "no" while they were issued tickets, they would have gotten poked.

All-out support for the children is accompanied by the barest minimum of support to the parents in the form of approval for appropriately docile behavior.

The Squad Car. Certain calls are considered serious enough to warrant a captain following the squad car to the scene.[5] The following thumbnail summaries rep-

[5] The field worker could not go with the regular prowl car owing to a rule forbidding the officers to carry passengers. It is also possible that the captain did not want the field worker to see episodes that he did not himself monitor.

resent 14 calls made by the captain in a 23-hour period. Half of them were not considered serious but the field worker asked the captain to go to the scene.

1. A man, reported by his ex-wife as dangerous and perhaps mentally ill, is found asleep; his ex-wife and her mother are in an agitated state. They report that when the ex-wife came to the home the husband shook his fist under her nose and said, "I have divorced you, I want you out of this goddam house by morning." The police officer woke up the man, who once again threatened his ex-wife, and the officer then told her that since it was his house and she was legally divorced from him, she and her mother should "please leave, and not cause any more trouble."

2. A car accident severely injures a woman and the police supervise her removal to hospital.

3. A bartender asks for, and receives, help in closing up so that there will be no problems—a routine "preventive" police service usually given by the car on the beat.

4. A man has beaten up his female neighbor earlier in the day and she has called the police and preferred charges. At the time of this call, the man's wife had threatened this woman with a knife. All are drunk and are taken to the station for further investigation.

5. A call from a woman about neighborhood children bullying a small boy who wears glasses. The field notes read, "There was a lot of argument and a lot of screaming back and forth, nothing was particularly accomplished, the three policemen (captain and two officers from a squad car) stood around for awhile, questioned people, did a little shouting, got shouted at, then the whole thing sort of dissolved and was resolved in a manner that I don't understand."

6. A woman complains that her husband doesn't bring home enough of his money to feed the kids. She is advised to go to Children's Court.

7. Field notes read: "Husband destroying property at his house. He's drunk and he and his wife got in an argument over the children . . . the wife smashed the gift he had given her for Mother's Day. This set the incident off. He fought the officers, they handcuffed him, and is taken to the station—a psycho."

8. A slightly drunk man is an unwelcome visitor in his ex-wife's home. Police send him home in a cab.

9. An ex-patient from a mental hospital is missing from her relative's home. They will broadcast a missing persons call.

10. A drunk man claims he has been slugged, but cannot amplify so no action is taken. "This is a low IQ street," says the policeman.

11. A woman in her pajamas and covered with mud says her husband threw her out. He is at home drunk with the children. As he has a police record, two cars are dispatched, one with a tear-gas gun. The house is found in a shambles. The wife is taken to hospital, children to a shelter, and the husband is booked for investigation and possible psychiatric treatment.

12. Fight in a third floor apartment between a man and his wife. Policeman settles it in some undiscernible fashion.

13. A man has "gone out of his mind over a girl" and has gone berserk with a gun. The man is shipped to hospital and witnesses are taken in because the gun makes the affair a felony.

14. The call is "see if an ambulance is needed." A young Negro in a filthy crowded house appears to be in agony. Police examine him for knife wounds and being satisfied that he has not been stabbed, and that no further investigation is needed, send him to hospital in an ambulance.

There seem to be three types of cases here. In the first, the police act as guides or conveyors to the courts and hospitals, giving indirect support meanwhile. In the second, they appear to resolve problems by giving concrete information and guidance about what is and is not possible under the law. Here both indirect and overt support are given. In the third type, they appear to settle problems through some consensual method based on mutual understanding between the police and the people involved. Here support is fairly overt but control is, of course, latent because of the policeman's representation of law and order. Occasionally, the police give outright friendly support, as in the following incident from the field notes:

Sitting in the police station is an old man, a citizen wanderer who is on his way to Oregon, and has become dissatisfied with the Rescue Mission and walked out. He's going to spend the night out of the rain until the morning when he's going over to the Salvation Army.

It is, of course, not possible to say what proportion of the policeman's responses to citizens fall into these three types, nor indeed, to know what other types there may be, because of the method of selecting the squad car calls.

Detectives. Four detectives of the twenty in the department, selected only because they were on duty at the time of the field worker's visit, were asked to describe their ten most recent cases. It was felt that they might be assigned the more "professional" and hence controlling tasks. Two of them were specialists in theft and forgery and so their cases were, indeed, of this character. However, fifteen out of twenty cases described by the two general detectives fell into our two personal-problem categories, and were similar to the complaint calls except that they were being further investigated because of more serious breaches of the law.

Another detective, in charge of services to alcoholics, reported that in 1956 the police department sent him to Yale for training in the handling of alcoholics. He says, "As a police officer I saw people being arrested for drunk and re-arrested for drunk and I thought it was a pretty medieval way of going about trying to help a person with a basic problem and illness that the public was just kicking in the corner and that's how I wound up here." This officer handles about 900 alcoholics a year. Of these, he takes about 150 charged persons on suspended sentence from the court and tries to arrange for some agency to carry them—an outright supportive service.

Missing Persons. The sergeant in charge of this service estimates that he locates about 600 missing people from his area in a year, about half of them children. He further estimates that from three to five percent are mentally disturbed adults. This particular officer says that he sometimes counsels with children that he has traced after they have been returned home. At the same time, he complains to the interviewer that children don't respect police officers the way they did when he was young.

Detectives in charge of homicide and those on duty with the vice squad were not interviewed, so it is impossible to say what proportion of all detective work is supportive. These data suggest that it is similar to the patrolman's.

Police Culture. The field worker reports several impressions that are relevant to our interests. Although they cannot be demonstrated from these data, some of them are similar to findings from other studies. First, poor, uneducated people appear to use the police in the way that middle-class people use family doctors and clergymen—that is, as the first port of call in time of trouble. Second, the policeman must often enforce unpopular laws among these poor people at the same time that he sees these laws being flouted by those in positions of power.[6] Third, many policemen are themselves recruited from and sympathetic to the class of people from whom most of the "interpersonal" calls for assistance come.[7]

Fourth, the police have little knowledge of, and liaison with, social or even medical agencies, and seem to feel that these agencies' activities are irrelevant to the problems they, themselves, face.

Fifth, the police appear to have a concern not only for children but also for those they define as disturbed and ill. They are tolerant, for example, about many crank calls, and will, if a car is available, help a paranoid old lady search her house for the malignant intruder she feels sure is hiding there. Nevertheless, it is possible to see, both in episodes of prejudice against minorities, and in less dramatic ways, how their own values transcend the individual's rights. A field note says, for example, "A woman wants protection from her doctor who is trying to commit her to a mental institution; the officer replies, 'That's not police business, lady. The police cannot go against any doctor.' "[8]

Finally, many policemen are bitter about their low pay, the label "punitive" applied to them in a world that values "warmth," the conflicting demands of their jobs, and the ingratitude of the public. This bitterness is reflected, in this police force, in a catch phrase, "I hate citizens."[9]

[6] This seems to be most true of the vice squad and it was not covered here. Nevertheless, a lot of police station conversation was on this topic.

[7] This becomes less true, of course, as the police department becomes more professionalized, and is probably less true of this department now than it was in 1961 when these data were collected.

[8] This attitude is, of course, construed by some as a denial of the basic rights of the mentally ill person. *See*, in this regard, Thomas Szasz, *The Myth of Mental Illness* (New York: Harper, 1961). A trickle of manifestly disturbed people may be turned down for other reasons at the complaint desk. One agitated man complained that his back yard was full of snails; the officer replied, "What do you want me to do, come and shoot them?" Even so, the field worker reports that if the complaint officer had had a car available, he would probably have sent it out.

[9] It may be that the higher respect for policemen in England is related to the higher value on order and the lower value on warmth.

SUMMARY AND DISCUSSION

We return now to our starting questions: What calls are made to the police and how do they respond? More than one-half of the calls coming routinely to the police complaint desk, and perhaps to detectives, appear to involve calls for help and some form of support for personal or interpersonal problems. To about three-quarters of these appeals, a car is sent. When the policeman reaches the scene, the data suggest that he either guides the complainant to someone who can solve his problem or tries to solve it himself. To do this, he must often provide support, either by friendly sympathy, by feeding authoritative information into the troubled situation, or by helping consensual resolution to take place. We started with the assumption that these activities belonged to the latent aspect of his role, and he is certainly an amateur—these policemen have no training for this kind of service. Why then, are they called upon to exercise their amateur talents half of the time?

The reasons are probably complex. First, the policeman has to do much of what he does because he is on duty at times of the day when no other agent is available. Second, he deals with the problems of a group of people—the poor and the ignorant—that studies of our own and others have shown no other agent to be anxious to serve(5) and, third, he has knowledge of, and access to, very few other agents. In other words, he is part of an integrative system in which the labor is divided not so much on the basis of function as on the basis of the time of day and the nature of the target population. All citizens can count on emergency help from the police when there is sudden illness at night, but only a certain kind of citizen takes his marital troubles to them.

The policeman's supportive acts are not only the latent and hence amateur part of his role, they are also latent in not being recognized and legitimated by the other agents in the integrative system. These others, our own studies show, prefer to recognize the policeman's professional controlling function, which they both need and often call upon.[10] Thus, it is as an agent of control that the policeman participates in a divided labor with social workers, doctors, clergymen, lawyers and teachers in maintaining social integration. The problems he faces appear to be a *failure of integration within the integrative system*, so that he cannot mobilize the other agents when he needs them.

Some modern advocates of "professionalization" of police work recognize that the policeman on the beat spends about half his time as an amateur social worker and they hope, instead of improving the referral process, to equip him with the skills of a professional. The policeman will then have a role containing both overtly supportive and overtly controlling elements. If our assumption that these are incompatible activities is correct, this development would tend once more to segregate these elements. This, in turn, would result in a basic shift in the relationship of the police to the rest of the integrative system. All of this might remove the policeman's present reasons for hating citizens, but it would not guarantee that they would not be replaced with others.

REFERENCES

1. Earlier reports include: Elaine Cumming, "Phase Movement in the Support and Control of the Psychiatric Patient," *Journal of Health and Human Behavior, 3* (Winter 1962), pp. 235–41; Isabel McCaffrey, Elaine Cumming and Claire Rudolph, "Mental Disorders in Socially Defined Populations," *American Journal of Public Health, 53* (July 1963), pp. 1025–30; Elaine Cumming and Charles Harrington, "Clergyman as Counselor," *American Journal of Sociology, 69* (November 1963), pp. 234–43.

2. This assumption is derived in part from studies of the division of labor in small groups—*see*, for example, Bales' "The Equilibrium Problem in Small Groups," in T. Parsons and R. F. Bales, *Working Papers in the Theory of Action* (Glencoe, Ill.: The Free Press of Glencoe, 1953)—and upon theories of role conflict—*see*, for example, W. J. Goode, "A Theory of Role Strain," *American Sociological Review, 25* (August 1960), pp. 483–95. At another level of analysis, of course, we all control and support one another—by

[10] There is reason to believe that most social workers, clergymen, and doctors have no conception of the amount of support policemen give during a day's work. There is also reason to believe that they do not want the burden of the "unmotivated" poor and ignorant, whom they believe to be increasing in number.

showing disapproval when our expectations are not met and by friendliness, responsiveness, understanding and sympathy when they are.

3. Certain highly skilled agents, such as psychoanalysts, may be able to phase their activities so that they are supportive in certain phases of the treatment and controlling in others. It is doubtful if this is feasible in the ordinary run of events because of the ambiguity it would generate in social interaction; *see*, for example, Gregory Bateson, D. D. Jackson, J. Haley, and J. Weakland, "Toward a Theory of Schizophrenia," *Behavioral Science, 1* (October 1956), pp. 251–64.

4. For an excellent discussion of the many problems inherent in the controlling function of the police, *see* Claude R. Sowle, ed., *Police Power and Individual Freedom* (Chicago: Aldine, 1962).

5. *See*, for a discussion of this problem in this community, Claire Rudolph and John Cumming, "Where Are Psychiatric Services Most Needed?" *Social Work, 7* (July 1962), pp. 15–20.

Broken Windows: The Police and Neighborhood Safety

James Q. Wilson and George L. Kelling

In the mid-1970s, the state of New Jersey announced a "Safe and Clean Neighborhoods Program," designed to improve the quality of community life in twenty-eight cities. As part of that program, the state provided money to help cities take police officers out of their patrol cars and assign them to walking beats. The governor and other state officials were enthusiastic about using foot patrol as a way of cutting crime, but many police chiefs were skeptical. Foot patrol, in their eyes, had been pretty much discredited. It reduced the mobility of the police, who thus had difficulty responding to citizen calls for service, and it weakened headquarters control over patrol officers.

Many police officers also disliked foot patrol, but for different reasons: it was hard work, it kept them outside on cold, rainy nights, and it reduced their chances for making a "good pinch." In some departments, assigning officers to foot patrol had been used as a form of punishment. And academic experts on policing doubted that foot patrol would have any impact on crime rates; it was, in the opinion of most, little more than a sop to public opinion. But since the state was paying for it, the local authorities were willing to go along.

Five years after the program started, the Police Foundation, in Washington, D.C., published an evaluation of the foot-patrol project. Based on its analysis of a carefully controlled experiment carried out chiefly in Newark, the foundation concluded, to the surprise of hardly anyone, that foot patrol had not reduced crime rates. But residents of the foot-patrolled neighborhoods seemed to feel more secure than persons in other areas, tended to believe that crime had been reduced, and seemed to take fewer steps to protect themselves from crime (staying at home with the doors locked, for example). Moreover, citizens in the foot-patrol areas had a more favorable opinion of the police than did those living elsewhere. And officers walking beats had higher morale, greater job satisfaction, and a more favorable attitude toward citizens in their neighborhoods than did officers assigned to patrol cars.

These findings may be taken as evidence that the skeptics were right—foot patrol has no effect on crime; it merely fools the citizens into thinking that they are safer. But in our view, and in the view of the authors of the Police Foundation study (of whom Kelling was one), the citizens of Newark were not fooled at all. They knew what the foot-patrol officers were doing, they knew it was different from what motorized officers do, and they knew that having officers walk beats did in fact make their neighborhoods safer.

But how can a neighborhood be "safer" when the crime rates has not gone down—in fact, may have gone up? Finding the answer requires first that we understand what most often frightens people in public places. Many citizens, of course, are primarily frightened by crime, especially crime involving sudden, violent attack by a

SOURCE: From *Thinking about Crime*, by James Q. Wilson.

stranger. This risk is very real, in Newark as in many large cities. But we tend to overlook or forget another source of fear—the fear of being bothered by disorderly people. Not violent people, nor, necessarily, criminals, but disreputable or obstreperous or unpredictable people: panhandlers, drunks, addicts, rowdy teenagers, prostitutes, loiterers, the mentally disturbed.

What foot-patrol officers did was to elevate, to the extent they could, the level of public order in these neighborhoods. Though the neighborhoods were predominantly black and the foot patrolmen were mostly white, this "order-maintenance" function of the police was performed to the general satisfaction of both parties.

One of us (Kelling) spent many hours walking with Newark foot-patrol officers to see how they defined "order" and what they did to maintain it. One beat was typical: a busy but dilapidated area in the heart of Newark, with many abandoned buildings, marginal shops (several of which prominently displayed knives and straight-edged razors in their windows), one large department store, and, most important, a train station and several major bus stops. Though the area was rundown, its streets were filled with people, because it was a major transportation center. The good order of this area was important not only to those who lived and worked there but also to many others, who had to move through it on their way home, to supermarkets, or to factories.

The people on the street were primarily black; the officer who walked the street was white. The people were made up of "regulars" and "strangers." Regulars included both "decent folk" and some drunks and derelicts who were always there but who "knew their place." Strangers were, well, strangers, and viewed suspiciously, sometimes apprehensively. The officer—call him Kelly—knew who the regulars were, and they knew him. As he saw his job, he was to keep an eye on strangers, and make certain that the disreputable regulars observed some informal but widely understood rules. Drunks and addicts could sit on the stoops, but could not lie down. People could drink on side streets, but not at the main intersection. Bottles had to be in paper bags. Talking to, bothering, or begging from people waiting at the bus stop was strictly forbidden. If a dispute erupted between a businessman and a customer, the businessman was assumed to be right, especially if the customer was a stranger. If a stranger loitered, Kelly would ask him if he had any means of support and what his business was; if he gave unsatisfactory answers, he was sent on his way. Persons who broke the informal rules, especially those who bothered people waiting at bus stops, were arrested for vagrancy. Noisy teenagers were told to keep quiet.

These rules were defined and enforced in collaboration with the "regulars" on the street. Another neighborhood might have different rules, but these, everybody understood, were the rules for *this* neighborhood. If someone violated them, the regulars not only turned to Kelly for help but also ridiculed the violator. Sometimes what Kelly did could be described as "enforcing the law," but just as often it involved taking informal or extralegal steps to help protect what the neighborhood had decided was the appropriate level of public order. Some of the things he did probably would not withstand a legal challenge.

A determined skeptic might acknowledge that a skilled foot-patrol officer can maintain order but still insist that this sort of "order" has little to do with the real sources of community fear—that is, with violent crime. To a degree, that is true. But two things must be borne in mind. First, outside observers should not assume that they know how much of the anxiety now endemic in many big-city neighborhoods stems from a fear of "real" crime and how much from a sense that the street is disorderly, a source of distasteful, worrisome encounters. The people of Newark, to judge from their behavior and their remarks to interviewers, apparently assign a high value to public order, and feel relieved and reassured when the police help them maintain that order.

Second, at the community level, disorder and crime are usually inextricably linked, in a kind of developmental sequence. Social psychologists and police officers tend to agree that if a window in a building is broken *and is left unrepaired*, all the rest of the windows will soon be broken. This is as true in nice neighborhoods as in run-down ones. Window-breaking does not necessarily occur on a large scale because some areas are inhabited by determined window-breakers whereas others are populated by window-lovers; rather, one unrepaired broken window is a signal that no one cares, and so breaking more windows costs nothing. (It has always been fun.)

Philip Zimbardo, a Stanford psychologist, reported in 1969 on some experiments testing the broken-window theory. He arranged to have an automobile without license plates parked with its hood up on a street in the Bronx and a comparable automobile on a street in Palo Alto, California. The car in the Bronx was attacked by "vandals" within ten minutes of its "abandonment." The first to arrive were a family—father, mother, and young son—who removed the radiator and battery. Within twenty-four hours, virtually everything of value had been removed. Then random destruction began—windows were smashed, parts torn off, upholstery ripped. Children began to use the car as a playground. Most of the adult "vandals" were well-dressed, apparently clean-cut whites. The car in Palo Alto sat untouched for more than a week. Then Zimbardo smashed part of it with a sledgehammer. Soon, passersby were joining in. Within a few hours, the car had been turned upside down and utterly destroyed. Again, the "vandals" appeared to be primarily respectable whites.

Untended property becomes fair game for people out for fun or plunder, and even for people who ordinarily would not dream of doing such things and who probably consider themselves law-abiding. Because of the nature of community life in the Bronx—its anonymity, the frequency with which cars are abandoned and things are stolen or broken, the past experience of "no one caring"—vandalism begins much more quickly than it does in staid Palo Alto, where people have come to believe that private possessions are cared for, and that mischievous behavior is costly. But vandalism can occur anywhere once communal barriers—the sense of mutual regard and the obligations of civility—are lowered by actions that seem to signal that "no one cares."

We suggest that "untended" behavior also leads to the breakdown of community controls. A stable neighborhood of families who care for their homes, mind each other's children, and confidently frown on unwanted intruders can change, in a few years or even a few months, to an inhospitable and frightening jungle. A piece of property is abandoned, weeds grow up, a window is smashed. Adults stop scolding rowdy children; the children, emboldened, become more rowdy. Families move out, unattached adults move in. Teenagers gather in front of the corner store. The merchant asks them to move; they refuse. Fights occur. Litter accumulates. People start drinking in front of the grocery; in time, an inebriate slumps to the sidewalk and is allowed to sleep it off. Pedestrians are approached by panhandlers.

At this point it is not inevitable that serious crime will flourish or violent attacks on strangers will occur. But many residents will think that crime, especially violent crime, is on the rise, and they will modify their behavior accordingly. They will use the streets less often, and when on the streets will stay apart from their fellows, moving with averted eyes, silent lips, and hurried steps. "Don't get involved." For some residents, this growing atomization will matter little, because the neighborhood is not their "home" but "the place where they live." Their interests are elsewhere; they are cosmopolitans. But it will matter greatly to other people, whose lives derive meaning and satisfaction from local attachments rather than worldly involvement; for them, the neighborhood will cease to exist except for a few reliable friends whom they arrange to meet.

Such an area is vulnerable to criminal invasion. Though it is not inevitable, it is more likely that here, rather than in places where people are confident they can regulate public behavior by informal controls, drugs will change hands, prostitutes will solicit, and cars will be stripped. That the drunks will be robbed by boys who do it as a lark, and the prostitutes' customers will be robbed by men who do it purposefully and perhaps violently. That muggings will occur.

Among those who often find it difficult to move away from this are the elderly. Surveys of citizens suggest that the elderly are much less likely to be the victims of crime than younger persons, and some have inferred from this that the well-known fear of crime voiced by the elderly is an exaggeration: perhaps we ought not to design special programs to protect older persons; perhaps we should even try to talk them out of their mistaken fears. This argument misses the point. The prospect of a confrontation with an obstreperous teenager or a drunken panhandler can be as fear-inducing for defenseless persons as the prospect of meeting an actual robber; indeed, to a defenseless person, the two kinds of confrontation are often indistinguishable. Moreover, the lower rate at which the elderly are victimized is a measure of the steps they have already taken—chiefly, staying behind locked doors—to minimize the risks they face. Young men are more frequently attacked than older women, not because they are easier or more lucrative targets but because they are on the streets more.

Nor is the connection between disorderliness and fear made only by the elderly. Susan Estrich, of the Harvard Law School, has recently gathered together a number of surveys on the sources of public fear. One, done in Portland, Oregon, indicated that three-fourths of the adults interviewed cross to the other side of a street when they see a gang of teenagers; another survey, in Baltimore, discovered that nearly half would cross the street to avoid even a single strange youth. When an interviewer asked people in a housing project where the most dangerous spot was, they mentioned a place where young persons gathered to drink and play music, despite the fact that not a single crime had occurred there. In Boston public housing projects, the greatest fear was expressed by persons living in the buildings where disorderliness and incivility, not crime, were the greatest. Knowing this helps one understand the significance of such othewise harmless displays as subway graffiti. As Nathan Glazer has written, the proliferation of graffiti, even when not obscene, confronts the subway rider with the "inescapable knowledge that the environment he must endure for an hour or more a day is uncontrolled and uncontrollable, and that anyone can invade it to do whatever damage and mischief the mind suggests."

In response to fear, people avoid one another, weakening controls. Sometimes they call the police. Patrol cars arrive, an occasional arrest occurs, but crime continues and disorder is not abated. Citizens complain to the police chief, but he explains that his department is low on personnel and that the courts do not punish petty or first-time offenders. To the residents, the police who arrive in squad cars are either ineffective or uncaring; to the police, the residents are animals who deserve each other. The citizens may soon stop calling the police, because "they can't do anything."

The process we call urban decay has occurred for centuries in every city. But what is happening today is different in at least two important respects. First, in the period before, say, World War II, city dwellers—because of money costs, transportation difficulties, familial and church connections—could rarely move away from neighborhood problems. When movement did occur, it tended to be along public-transit routes. Now mobility has become exceptionally easy for all but the poorest or those who are blocked by racial prejudice. Earlier crime waves had a kind of built-in self-correcting mechanism: the determination of a neighborhood or community to reassert control over its turf. Areas in Chicago, New York, and Boston would experience crime and gang wars, and then normalcy would return, as the families for whom no alternative residences were possible reclaimed their authority over the streets.

Second, the police in this earlier period assisted in that reassertion of authority by acting, sometimes violently, on behalf of the community. Young toughs were roughed up, people were arrested "on suspicion" or for vagrancy, and prostitutes and petty thieves were routed. "Rights" were something enjoyed by decent folk, and perhaps also by the serious professional criminal, who avoided violence and could afford a lawyer.

This pattern of policing was not an aberration or the result of occasional excess. From the earliest days of the nation, the police function was seen primarily as that of a night watchman: to maintain order against the chief threats to order—fire, wild animals, and disreputable behavior. Solving crimes was viewed not as a police responsibility but as a private one. In the March 1969, *Atlantic*, one of us (Wilson) wrote a brief account of how the police role had slowly changed from maintaining order to fighting crimes. The change began with the creation of private detectives (often ex-criminals), who worked on a contingency-fee basis for individuals who had suffered losses. In time, the detectives were absorbed into municipal police agencies and paid a regular salary; simultaneously, the responsibility for prosecuting thieves was shifted from the aggrieved private citizen to the professional prosecutor. This process was not complete in most places until the twentieth century.

In the 1960s, when urban riots were a major problem, social scientists began to explore carefully the order-maintenance function of the police, and to suggest ways of improving it—not to make streets safer (its original function) but to reduce the incidence of mass violence. Order-maintenance became, to a degree, coterminous with "community relations." But, as the crime wave that began in the early 1960s continued without abatement throughout the decade and into the 1970s, attention shifted to the role of the police as crime-fighters. Studies of police behavior ceased, by and large, to be accounts of the order-maintenance function and became, instead, efforts to propose and test ways whereby the police could solve more crimes, make more arrests, and gather better evidence. If these things could be done, social scientists assumed, citizens would be less fearful.

A great deal was accomplished during this transition, as both police chiefs and outside experts emphasized the crime-fighting function in their plans, in the allocation of resources, and in deployment of personnel. The police may well have become better crime-fighters as a result. And doubtless they remained aware of their responsibility for order. But the link between order-maintenance and crime-prevention, so obvious to earlier generations, was forgotten.

That link is similar to the process whereby one broken window becomes many. The citizen who fears the ill-smelling drunk, the rowdy teenager, or the importuning beggar is not merely expressing his distaste for unseemly behavior; he is also giving voice to a bit of folk wisdom that happens to be a correct generalization—namely, that serious street crime flourishes in areas in which disorderly behavior goes unchecked. The unchecked panhandler is, in effect, the first broken window. Muggers and robbers, whether opportunistic or professional, believe they reduce their chances of being caught or even identified if they operate on streets where potential victims are already intimidated by prevailing conditions. If the neighborhood cannot keep a bothersome panhandler from annoying passersby, the thief may reason, it is even less likely to call the police to identify a potential mugger or to interfere if the mugging actually takes place.

Some police administrators concede that this process occurs, but argue that motorized-patrol officers can deal with it as effectively as foot-patrol officers. We are not so sure. In theory, an officer in a squad car can observe as much as an officer on foot; in theory, the former can talk to as many people as the latter. But the reality of police–citizen encounters is powerfully altered by the automobile. An officer on foot cannot separate himself from the street people; if he is approached, only his uniform and his personality can help him manage whatever is about to happen. And he can never be certain what they will be—a request for directions, a plea for help, an angry denunciation, a teasing remark, a confused babble, a threatening gesture.

In a car, an officer is more likely to deal with street people by rolling down the window and looking at them. The door and the window exclude the approaching citizen; they are a barrier. Some officers take advantage of this barrier, perhaps unconsciously, by acting differently if in the car than they would on foot. We have seen this countless times. The police car pulls up to a corner where teenagers are gathered. The window is rolled down. The officer stares at the youths. They stare back. The officer says to one, "C'mere." He saunters over, conveying to his friends by his elaborately casual style the idea that he is not intimidated by authority. "What's your name?" "Chuck." "Chuck who?" "Chuck Jones." "What'ya doing, Chuck?" "Nothin'." "Got a P.O. [parole officer]?" "Nah." "Sure?" "Yeah." "Stay out of trouble, Chuckie." Meanwhile, the other boys laugh and exchange comments among themselves, probably at the officer's expense. The officer stares harder. He cannot be certain what is being said, nor can he join in and, by displaying his own skill at street banter, prove that he cannot be "put down." In the process, the officer has learned almost nothing, and the boys have decided the officer is an alien force who can safely be disregarded, even mocked.

Our experience is that most citizens like to talk to a police officer. Such exchanges give them a sense of importance, provide them with the basis for gossip, and allow them to explain to the authorities what is worrying them (whereby they gain a modest but significant sense of having "done something" about the problem). You approach a person on foot more easily, and talk to him more readily, than you do a person in a car. Moreover, you can more easily retain some anonymity if you draw an officer aside for a private chat. Suppose you want to pass on a tip about who is stealing handbags, or who offered to sell you a stolen TV. In the inner city, the culprit, in all likelihood, lives nearby. To walk up to a marked patrol car and lean in the window is to convey a visible signal that you are a "fink."

The essence of the police role in maintaining order is to reinforce the informal control mechanisms of the community itself. The police cannot, without committing extraordinary resources, provide a substitute for that informal control. On the other hand, to reinforce those natural forces the police must accommodate them. And therein lies the problem.

Should police activity on the streets be shaped in important ways, by the standards of the neighborhood rather than by the rules of the state? Over the past two decades, the shift of police from order-maintenance to law enforcement has brought them increasingly under the influence of legal restrictions, provoked by media complaints and enforced by court decisions and departmental orders. As a consequence, the order-maintenance functions of the police are now governed by rules developed to control police relations with suspected criminals. This is, we think, an entirely new development. For centuries, the role of the police as watchmen was judged primarily not in terms of its compliance with appropriate procedures but rather in terms of its attaining a desired objective. The objective was order, an inherently ambiguous term but a condition that people in a given community recognized when they saw it. The means were the same as those the community itself would employ, if its members were sufficiently determined, courageous, and authoritative. Detecting and apprehending criminals, by contrast, was a means to an end, not an end in itself; a judicial determination of guilt or innocence was the hoped-for result of the law-enforcement mode. From the first, the police were expected to follow rules defining that process, though states differed in how stringent the rules should be. The criminal-apprehension process was always understood to involve individual rights, the violation of which was unacceptable because it meant that the violating officer would be acting as a judge and jury—and that was not his job. Guilt or innocence was to be determined by universal standards under special procedures.

Ordinarily, no judge or jury ever sees the persons caught up in a dispute over the appropriate level of neighborhood order. That is true not only because most cases are handled informally on the street but also because no universal standards are available to settle arguments over disorder, and thus a judge may not be any wiser or more effective than a police officer. Until quite recently in many states, and even today in some places, the police make arrests on such charges as "suspicious person" or "vagrancy" or "public drunkenness"—charges with scarcely any legal meaning. These charges exist not because society wants judges to punish vagrants or drunks but because it wants an officer to have the legal tools to remove undesirable persons from a neighborhood when informal efforts to preserve order in the streets have failed.

Once we begin to think of all aspects of police work as involving the application of universal rules under special procedures, we inevitably ask what constitutes an "undesirable person" and why we should "criminalize" vagrancy or drunkenness. A strong and commendable desire to see that people are treated fairly makes us worry about allowing the police to rout persons who are undesirable by some vague or parochial standard. A growing and not-so-commendable utilitarianism leads us to doubt that any behavior that does not "hurt" another person should be made illegal. And thus many of us who watch over the police are reluctant to allow them to perform, in the only way they can, a function that every neighborhood desperately wants them to perform.

This wish to "decriminalize" disreputable behavior that "harms no one"—and thus remove the ultimate sanction the police can employ to maintain neighborhood order—is, we think, a mistake. Arresting a single drunk or a single vagrant who has harmed no identifiable person seems unjust, and in a sense it is. But failing to do anything about a score of drunks or a hundred vagrants may destroy an entire community. A particular rule that seems to make sense in the individual case makes no sense when it is made a universal rule and applied to all cases. It makes no sense because it fails to take into account the connection between one broken window left untended and a thousand broken windows. Of course, agencies other than the police could attend to the problems posed by drunks or the mentally ill, but in most communities—especially where the "deinstitutionalization" movement has been strong—they do not.

The concern about equity is more serious. We might agree that certain behavior makes one person more undesirable than another, but how do we ensure that age or skin color or national origin or harmless mannerisms will not also become the basis for distinguishing the undesirable from the desirable? How do we ensure, in short, that the police do not become the agents of neighborhood bigotry?

We can offer no wholly satisfactory answer to this important question. We are not confident that there *is* a satisfactory answer, except to hope that by their selection, training, and supervision, the police will be inculcated with a clear sense of the outer limit of their discretionary authority. That limit, roughly, is this—the police exist to help regulate behavior, not to maintain the racial or ethnic purity of a neighborhood.

Consider the case of the Robert Taylor Homes in Chicago, one of the largest public-housing projects in the country. It is home for nearly 20,000 people, all black, and extends over ninety-two acres along South State Street. It was named after a distinguished black who had been, during the 1940s, chairman of the Chicago Housing Authority. Not long after it opened, in 1962, relations between project residents and the police deteriorated badly. The citizens felt that the police were insensitive or brutal; the police, in turn, complained of unprovoked attacks on them. Some Chicago officers tell of times when they were afraid to enter the Homes. Crime rates soared.

Today, the atmosphere has changed. Police–citizen relations have improved—apparently, both sides learned something from the earlier experience. Recently, a boy stole a purse and ran off. Several young persons who saw the theft voluntarily passed along to the police information on the identity and residence of the thief, and they did this publicly, with friends and neighbors looking on. But problems persist, chief among them the presence of youth gangs that terrorize residents and recruit members in the project. The people expect the police to "do something" about this, and the police are determined to do just that.

But do what? Though the police can obviously make arrests whenever a gang member breaks the law, a gang can form, recruit, and congregate without breaking the law. And only a tiny fraction of gang-related crimes can be solved by an arrest; thus, if an arrest is the only recourse for the police, the residents' fears will go unassuaged. The police will soon feel helpless, and the residents will again believe that the police "do nothing." What the police in fact do is to chase known gang members out of the project. In the words of one officer, "We kick ass." Project residents both know and approve of this. The tacit police–citizen alliance in the project is reinforced by the police view that the cops and the gangs are the two rival sources of power in the area, and that the gangs are not going to win.

None of this is easily reconciled with any conception of due process or fair treatment. Since both residents and gang members are black, race is not a factor. But it could be. Suppose a white project confronted a black gang, or vice versa. We would be apprehensive about the police taking sides. But the substantive problem remains the same: how can the police strengthen the informal social-control mechanisms of natural communities in order to minimize fear in public places? Law enforcement, per se, is no answer. A gang can weaken or destroy a community by standing about in a menacing fashion and speaking rudely to passersby without breaking the law.

We have difficulty thinking about such matters, not simply because the ethical and legal issues are so complex but because we have become accustomed to thinking of the law in essentially individualistic terms. The law defines *my* rights, punishes *his* behavior, and is applied by *that* officer because of *this* harm. We assume, in thinking this way, that what is good for the individual will be good for the community, and what doesn't matter when it happens to one person won't matter if it happens to many. Ordinarily, those are plausible assumptions. But in cases where behavior that is tolerable to one person is intolerable to many others, the reactions of the others—fear, withdrawal, flight—may ultimately make matters worse for everyone, including the individual who first professed his indifference.

It may be their greater sensitivity to communal as opposed to individual needs that helps explain why the residents of small communities are more satisfied with their police than are the residents of similar neighborhoods in big cities. Elinor Ostrom and her co-workers at Indiana University compared the perception of police services in two poor, all-black Illinois towns—Phoenix and East Chicago Heights—with those of three comparable all-black neighborhoods in Chicago. The level of criminal victimization and the quality of police–community relations appeared to be about the same in the towns and the Chicago neighborhoods. But the citizens living in their own villages were much more likely than those living in the Chicago neighborhoods to say that they do not stay at home for fear of crime, to agree that the local police have "the right to take any action necessary" to deal with problems, and to agree that the police "look out for the needs of the average citizen." It is possible that the residents and the police of the small towns saw themselves as engaged in a collaborative effort to maintain a certain standard of communal life, whereas those of the big city felt themselves to be simply requesting and supplying particular services on an individual basis.

If this is true, how should a wise police chief deploy his meager forces? The first answer is that nobody knows for certain, and the most prudent course of action would be to try further variations on the Newark experiment, to see more precisely what works in what kinds of neighborhoods. The second answer is also a hedge—many aspects of order-maintenance in neighborhoods can probably best be handled in ways that involve the police minimally, if at all. A busy, bustling shopping center and a quiet, well-tended suburb may need almost no visible police presence. In both cases, the ratio of respectable to disreputable people is ordinarily so high as to make informal social control effective.

Even in areas that are in jeopardy from disorderly elements, citizen action without substantial police involvement may be sufficient. Meetings between teenagers who like to hang out on a particular corner and adults who want to use that corner might well lead to an amicable agreement on a set of rules about how many people can be allowed to congregate, where, and when.

Where no understanding is possible—or if possible, not observed—citizen patrols may be a sufficient response. There are two traditions of communal involvement in maintaining order. One, that of the "community watchmen," is as old as the first settlement of the New World. Until well into the nineteenth century, volunteer watchmen, not policemen, patrolled their communities to keep order. They did so, by and large, without taking the law into their own hands—without, that is, punishing persons or using force. Their presence deterred disorder or alerted the community to disorder that could not be deterred. There are hundreds of such efforts today in communities all across the nation. Perhaps the best known is that of the Guardian Angels, a group of unarmed young persons in distinctive berets and T-shirts, who first came to public attention when they began patrolling the New York City subways but who claim now to have chapters in more than thirty American cities. Unfortunately, we have little information about the effect of these groups on crime. It is possible, however, that whatever their effect on crime, citizens find their presence reassuring, and that they thus contribute to maintaining a sense of order and civility.

The second tradition is that of the "vigilante." Rarely a feature of the settled communities of the East, it was primarily to be found in those frontier towns that grew up in advance of the reach of government. More than 350 vigilante groups are known to have existed; their distinctive feature was that their members did take the law into their own hands, by acting as judge, jury, and often executioner as well as policeman. Today, the vigilante movement is conspicuous by its rarity, despite the great fear expressed by citizens that the older cities are becoming "urban frontiers." But some community-watchmen groups have skirted the line, and others may cross it in the future. An ambiguous case, reported in *The Wall Street Journal*, involved a citizens' patrol in the Silver Lake area of Belleville, New Jersey. A leader told the reporter, "We look for outsiders." If a few teenagers from outside the neighborhood enter it, "we ask them their business," he said. "If they say they're going down the street to see Mrs. Jones, fine, we let them pass. But then we follow them down the block to make sure they're really going to see Mrs. Jones."

Though citizens can do a great deal, the police are plainly the key to order-maintenance. For one thing, many communities, such as the Robert Taylor Homes, cannot do the job by themselves. For another, no citizen in a neighborhood, even an organized one, is likely to feel the sense of responsibility that wearing a badge confers. Psychologists have done many studies on why people fail to go to the aid of persons being attacked or seeking help, and they have learned that the cause is not "apathy" or "selfishness" but the absence of some plausible grounds for feeling that one must personally accept responsibility. Ironically, avoiding responsibility is easier when a lot of people are standing about. On streets and in public places, where order is so important, many people are likely to be "around," a fact that reduces the chance of any one person acting as the agent of the community. The police officer's uniform singles him out as a person who must accept responsibility if asked. In addition, officers, more easily than their fellow citizens, can be expected to distinguish between what is necessary to protect the safety of the street and what merely protects its ethnic purity.

But the police forces of America are losing, not gaining, members. Some cities have suffered substantial cuts in the number of officers available for duty. These cuts are not likely to be reversed in the near future. Therefore, each department must assign its existing officers with great care. Some neighborhoods are so demoralized and crime-ridden as to make foot patrol useless; the best the police can do with limited resources is respond to the enormous number of calls for service. Other neighborhoods are so stable and serene as to make foot patrol unnecessary. The key is to identify neighborhoods at the tipping point—where the public order is deteriorating but not unreclaimable, where the streets are used frequently but by apprehensive people, where a window is likely to be broken at any time, and must quickly be fixed if all are not to be shattered.

Most police departments do not have ways of systematically identifying such areas and assigning officers to them. Officers are assigned on the basis of crime rates (meaning that marginally threatened areas are often stripped so that police can investigate crimes in areas where the situation is hopeless) or on the basis of calls for service (despite the fact that most citizens do not call the police when they are merely frightened or annoyed). To allocate patrol wisely, the department must look at the neighborhoods and decide, from first-hand evidence, where an additional officer will make the greatest difference in promoting a sense of safety.

One way to stretch limited police resources is being tried in some public-housing projects. Tenant organizations hire off-duty police officers for patrol work in their buildings. The costs are not high (at least not per resident), the officer likes the additional income, and the residents feel safer. Such arrangements are probably more successful than hiring private watchmen, and the Newark experiment helps us understand why.

A private security guard may deter crime or misconduct by his presence, and he may go to the aid of persons needing help, but he may well not intervene—that is, control or drive away—someone challenging community standards. Being a sworn officer—a "real cop"—seems to give one the confidence, the sense of duty, and the aura of authority necessary to perform this difficult task.

Patrol officers might be encouraged to go to and from duty stations on public transportation and, while on the bus or subway car, enforce rules about smoking, drinking, disorderly conduct, and the like. The enforcement need involve nothing more than ejecting the offender (the offense, after all, is not one with which a booking officer or a judge wishes to be bothered). Perhaps the random but relentless maintenance of standards on buses would lead to conditions on buses that approximate the level of civility we now take for granted on airplanes.

But the most important requirement is to think that to maintain order in precarious situations is a vital job. The police know this is one of their functions, and they also believe, correctly, that it cannot be done to the exclusion of criminal investigation and responding to calls. We may have encouraged them to suppose, however, on the basis of our oft-repeated concerns about serious, violent crime, that they will be judged exclusively on their capacity as crime-fighters. To the extent that this is the case, police administrators will continue to concentrate police personnel in the highest-crime areas (though not necessarily in the areas most vulnerable to criminal invasion), emphasize their training in the law and criminal apprehension (and not their training in managing street life), and join too quickly in campaigns to decriminalize "harmless" behavior (though public drunkenness, street prostitution, and pornographic displays can destroy a community more quickly than any team of professional burglars).

Above all, we must return to our long-abandoned view that the police ought to protect communities as well as individuals. Our crime statistics and victimization surveys measure individual losses, but they do not measure communal losses. Just as physicians now recognize the importance of fostering health rather than simply treating illness, so the police—and the rest of us—ought to recognize the importance of maintaining, intact, communities without broken windows.

Controlling People

Jonathan Rubinstein

A policeman's principal concern is to physically control the people he is policing. While he sometimes wants to hurt or humiliate them, that is not nearly so often his purpose as it is the consequence of his efforts to control them. When he intervenes in a person's life, his attitude is basically instrumental. He mainly wants to place himself as quickly as possible in a position that will allow him to control the person, if that is required, or hopefully to discourage any inclinations to resist him or his orders. That is why he ignores the risks he takes in driving and violates departmental regulations by refusing to use the safety belt provided for him. The idea of being confined and prevented from moving quickly out of his car terrifies him.

Policemen act as though all people are right-handed. If he has any choice in the matter, the patrolman tries to move in a leftward direction toward a person in order to control his fighting arm. This allows him to stand at the person's right, at a slight angle, when he is facing him, which keeps his gun away from the man he is seeking to dominate. He consistently violates the normal distances which people seek to maintain when they are engaged in friendly conversation, often causing discomfort and nervousness when he does not mean to. He is not formally trained to do this, nor does he do it consciously, but an understanding of his actions would not deter him, since his objective is the maintenance of his personal security and not the discomfort of others. By constantly crowding people, he reduces their opportunities for kicking and punching him effectively. When he can, the patrolman stands slightly at an angle to the person he is confronting to avoid a crippling blow to the groin. Naturally he can be grabbed and wrestled with; this is the main reason why most policemen wear clip-on ties and hate any gear that offers someone a handhold on them.

The first and sometimes the only thing a policeman looks at when approaching someone is his hands. Recruits are warned repeatedly to train themselves to check people's hands first ("If the guy's got a brick, he better be building a house"). But he must do more than just look—he must learn to expect to see things. A policeman is frequently called into the presence of people who are distressed, depressed, angry, or fearful. It is not surprising that many of them are holding some kind of weapon, which they do not necessarily intend for use against him. He must be prepared to disarm them swiftly without resorting to force. Often he sees boys walking down the street carrying sticks or boards; he usually disarms them and sends them on their way, unless there has been a specific call or an order to bring them in. Anyone who comes into his presence is unceremoniously disarmed. A boy carrying a bow and arrow has the toy taken from him, and given to his mother after the policeman finishes talking with them. A suicidal woman wielding weapons opens her door for an officer who quickly grabs a butcher knife and a pistol. He enters the house, unloads the gun, places the knife in a drawer, sits down for a cup of coffee and a little conversation, and leaves after the woman has had a good cry and he is reasonably sure she will not commit suicide. People often tell him of weapons in their houses and offer to get them, but the experienced patrolman will not let anyone handle a gun in his presence. People holding paper bags are looked at carefully, because every policeman knows that it is not an elegant manner of transporting a gun, but it is one that is used often enough. He is not concerned about hurting the feelings of the people whom he handles unceremoniously in these moments. He only cares about disarming them, for there are occasions when the door opens and he is looking directly into the barrel of a shotgun, and then he is stripped of everything he is but his blue suit.[1]

Anyone whose hands are concealed, wittingly or not, risks serious injury or worse when he attracts the attention of a policeman. Hidden hands imply danger to a policeman, and he must decide in a few seconds what course of action to take. Whatever he decides to do, he must continue until he has succeeded or failed, because there is no possibility of mediation with a policeman intent on assuring his security, and he will be satisfied only by seeing empty hands.

A young white officer noticed a man standing near a street corner turn away as the patrol car approached. He stopped his car and rolled down the window to look at the elderly Negro man. Instead of getting out of the car, he yelled across the deserted street to him, "Take your hand out of your coat." The man had turned back toward the car when it stopped, and he had his right hand jammed inside. He did not react to the command. They were frozen for several seconds; then the patrolman repeated his demand. When the man remained silent, the officer drew his pistol, continuing to remain seated in his car. He placed his gun in plain view and again ordered the man to show his hand. The man was very agitated but he remained silent. Slowly he began to extract his hand, but he gave the appearance of concealing some intention which threatened the patrolman, who cocked his gun and pointed it directly at the man. Suddenly the old man drew out his hand and threw a pistol to the ground. He stood trembling. The patrolman uncocked his gun with a shaking hand and approached. He was on the verge of tears, and in a moment of confusion, fear, and anxiety, he struck the man with the butt of his pistol. "Why didn't you take your hand out when I told you? I almost shot you, you dumb bastard." The man protested the treatment he had received, complaining that there was no reason to hit him. He said he had had no intention of using the gun but was carrying it for self-protection. The patrolman recovered from his fright, but despite his regret for striking the man in anger, he refused to acknowledge any responsibility. "Are you wearing a sign? How the fuck am I supposed to know what you're gonna do?"

From a purely technical point of view, the patrolman had initially made an error by failing to close the dis-

[1] A 26-year-old man armed with a Luger pistol and a rifle disarmed three policemen early today and held them at bay for nearly two hours. . . . The man finally gave up his weapons and surrendered after having a cup of coffee with two of the policemen. The drama started when police received a report of a 'disturbance.' . . . The first officer to respond was Policeman Robert Patrick . . . who said he saw Hansen standing at the front door, his back toward the street. 'Did you call, sir?' Patrick asked. Hansen turned around and according to Patrick, 'The next thing I knew I had a rifle to my head.' " *Philadelphia Daily News* (July 27, 1971).

tance between himself and the suspect, allowing himself no alternative but to leave or to use his gun. If he had charged the man immediately upon suspecting him of some misdeed, any passer-by might have "seen" an elderly black man being "assaulted" by a policeman, but the patrolman would have avoided the chance of a much more serious incident. The presumption here is that the policeman was behaving correctly in having suspicions about the man and stopping to make any kind of investigation. Nobody obliged him to stop the man, and if he had continued on his patrol, his superiors and colleagues would not have known. But the patrolman makes these stops because they are his job. He knows colleagues who do not make them, or seldom do so, to avoid moments like the ones he had passed through, but if his morale is high and if he treats his job in a serious way, he has little choice but to exercise the skills he has developed. Whether these stops should be allowed is a political issue. They have tactical value to the police, but the use of suspicion stops as a police tactic cannot be decided from a simple, technical viewpoint but must be made in terms of the political values of the people who pay the police.

The positioning and distance of a patrolman in relation to the person he is seeking to control are absolutely critical. When they are separated by many feet, the chances of the policeman drawing his gun are considerable. But even if he is in close proximity to the suspect, the policeman can still fail unless he positions his body to do what he wants it to. He uses his gun infrequently when he is close to a suspect, relying instead on his hand weapons and his physical assets. When he commits himself to this kind of action and fails, he is in serious trouble.

Consider the predicament of the patrolman turning off his fifteenth hydrant on a hot, steamy day. He approached the gushing hydrant, wrench in hand, watching the children splashing and a young man washing his Irish setter. He asked them to stand back, but the man continued to wash his dog, splashing water freely about and entirely ignoring the presence of the officer. He was told again to move, this time forcefully but without insult. The fellow looked up and said, "Fuck you, pig!" In that split second the patrolman committed himself. He lunged in anger, but trying to avoid the water, he arched his body and limited his reach. The fellow leaped back into the middle of the street and taunted the policeman with obscene gestures and remarks. If the policeman gave chase, he might capture him, but the chances were not good. Every time he took a step forward, the fellow sprang back, yelling louder and attracting larger and larger numbers of onlookers. The policeman grew angrier by the moment and was very reluctant to withdraw, although he realized his situation was untenable. He concluded the incident by vowing to "get" the fellow.

The policeman had every intention of settling the "score" with the young man and mentioned him to his sergeant and several colleagues, who urged that he remain away. The policemen did not find the young man, although one night he found them. When they were answering a call at another house, the fellow allegedly dropped a jug of water out of a second-floor window, narrowly missing a patrolman. The officer called an assist, broke into the man's house, and arrested him after an altercation. A number of law suits erupted out of this event, and the fellow moved out of the district.

The policeman's intense concern with position, his ability to see a suspect's hands and to make some judgment about his physical capacity and inclinations combine to make all car stops potentially explosive moments. A policeman usually stops a car because he thinks that it is stolen, that the occupants are trying to avoid him, or that there has been some kind of traffic violation. He has used his power to stop the car. He can see the driver and the other occupants, but he cannot make any judgments about what they are doing. He cannot see their hands or how big they are, or determine what they might do. All the unknowns he fears are present as he proceeds to investigate.

The patrolman is under orders—often disregarded—not to make suspicion car stops when he is working alone. Each time he makes a car stop, he is supposed to inform his dispatcher and, before getting out of his car, give his location and the color, make, and license number of the car. If he is alone and his stop is on suspicion, he is supposed to await the arrival of a back-up before proceeding. If his suspicion is strong and the stop is made at night, the patrolman tries to blind the driver by shining his spotlight directly onto the car's rear-view mirror. He does not take his eyes off the car once he has signaled the stop. He counts the number of occupants he sees and makes sure that they all remain visible. If he is alone and waiting for another officer, he will stay in his car and order anyone trying to get out to remain seated.

If two men are making a suspicion stop, they use speed and position to overcome the deficiencies in their situation. Both patrolmen emerge quickly, stepping out with one leg so that their bodies do not turn away from the car they are going to approach. The recorder stations himself at the right rear of the car, looking through the back windows to make sure nobody is hiding on the floor or concealing something under a seat. The driver approaches the front of the car and positions himself to maximize his advantage over the occupants. He stands to the rear of the front door and well away from it, to avoid the possibility of someone opening the door and knocking him down. By standing back, he obliges the person to turn around to him, an awkward and uncomfortable position. Policemen are urged to adopt this posture without seeming aggressive. Few policemen walk directly to a car window without first making some judgment about the driver.

There is no way for the policeman completely to settle his anxieties when making a car stop. The people he is seeking to control are right before him; he is close to them, but he cannot get near enough to place them under his physical control. His personal estimate of his own vulnerability greatly increases his tension. Many patrolmen not only unlatch the strap on their holsters before approaching a car but actually pull their guns. At night it is not uncommon to see policemen unholster their guns and conceal them behind a thigh as they approach a suspicious car. There is relatively little the occupants of a car can do to ease the situation. Occasionally people who have considerable experience with the police place their hands on top of the steering wheel to indicate their peaceful intentions. But this does not calm him; rather it tells the officer that he is approaching someone who is cop-wise and his wariness increases.

The policemen's unease does not result from the attitudes of the people but from the constraints of the situation. Even when he sees people who give every appearance of peace, he is unlikely to relax his wariness. Two patrolmen approached a parked car with a running motor. It was very early on a frosty Sunday morning. The white policeman walked directly toward the driver, but his black partner restrained him. "Sleeping like a baby, right? Made a load and can't get home, so he pulls over and parks. Well, you want to check 'em out, see he ain't dead. But before you open the door or knock on the window, look inside first. You gotta make sure the car is in park and the guy don't have a knife in his hand. A lot of these dudes have been rolled so many times they keep an open knife on their lap before they doze off, for protection, you know. That's O.K., you know, but you don't want no surprises when you wake him up. Some of 'em been rolled by guys in blue suits, too, and you can't forget that neither."

A car stop combines the anxieties of entry into an enclosed space where concealment is possible with the frustrations of being unable to control people who are visible and in some sense publicly available. The policeman must try to balance his need to give a stern and forceful appearance, his "I mean business" manner, with a recognition that most stops turn into nothing, that they are false alarms that can get out of hand if he acts too aggressively or, in his desire to control the people, is insulting. In moments of extreme tension, when the police are mobilized in search of "cop killers" or feel that the department is being besieged and threatened, some men cast caution to the wind and openly use their guns to control car stops. A faultlessly polite patrolman pointed his revolver directly at a person's head, saying, "Sir, would you please stand out of your car?" But even having a gun ready is not always a guarantee of success.

Two patrolmen stopped a car they knew to be stolen. The plate was listed on the hot sheet and they had checked it with the dispatcher before moving. They were on special patrol in search of some men who the day before had murdered a policeman. Both policemen had their revolvers out as they approached the car, which held two men. The driver had his hands on the steering wheel and was looking back over his shoulder at the advancing officer. According to the patrolman, the fellow smiled and said to him, "Shit, man, you don't need that." He suckered the officer, who hesitated and then holstered his gun. He later claimed that he knew he had made an error the moment he did it. The man dropped his hand and came up with a .45, shooting the policeman twice, while the other man wounded the second officer. The two men were captured a short while later. There is no point in a policeman having his gun out unless he is prepared to shoot someone, and the police cannot be allowed to think of shooting except in defense. Their assailant must be allowed the first move, however slight, but the police have to be able to protect themselves. If they are not allowed to approach people closely, carefully controlling their movements and even violating their bodies, the only way they can make suspicion stops is with their guns unhooked and their sticks ready to hit.

A patrolman with twenty years' experience had recently arrested two robbery suspects on a car stop. He recalled that although he had drawn his gun several times, he had never shot anyone. "I don't know, they were just bad, the way they were acting. The detectives found a gun under the seat. I was real close to them, working alone. I had my gun pointed right at the driver's head. If one of them had bent down, I would have shot him. It would have been too bad for me if it had been a handkerchief under there, but I would have shot him."

The policeman knows that he does not have an unrestricted right to interfere with people's privacy, but his decision to violate their bodies is not made with regard either to their feelings or to their rights. At the police academy the distinctions between a frisk and a search are carefully explained to him, and the limitations of his authority are defined as clearly as the law allows, but his instructors stress that he should not hesitate to frisk anyone if he feels it is necessary.[2] "Any judgment you make is gonna have to be backed up in court, but if you think you should, do it." Body control is treated as a technical issue; considerable time is spent teaching recruits how to efficiently violate the privacy of fellow citizens.

Several recruits at the academy were arbitrarily selected to enact a stop and frisk in class. They were given a situation; first one and then the other played the officer and the suspect. Almost everyone failed. They spoke in muffled tones, asked politely for some identification, and muttered questions about why he was loitering in the alley at so late an hour. "You just gonna stand there and ask him to put his hand in his coat pocket? Hey, boy, you're up an alley, it's dark, and we ain't here," the instructor piped in. Everyone, including a few ex-policemen back for a refresher, failed badly and knew it. How do you frisk someone? How do you not violate him? He's your friend and buddy.

The instructor concealed several guns and knives on a student collaborator and arranged to demonstrate frisking. "O.K., it ain't so easy. Half you guys would be on your ass by now, and this guy's gonna play football with your head, remember that. So now, we learn how to frisk." The collaborator and another student were called to the front of the room. Two others were called up to frisk them. "O.K. Put 'em on the wall and frisk 'em down," the black instructor ordered. The recruits mumbled their orders, and without using their hands or stepping in close to the men, they positioned the "suspects" on the wall. Both men used their feet to kick at the subjects' legs, spreading them to keep the man off balance. "Hey, wait a minute. Why all this kickin'? Everybody starts kickin' the guy's legs. Why all the rough stuff?" The men finished their frisk and were followed by two other recruits. Throughout the hour nobody found any of the weapons, and each man commenced his frisking by kicking or roughing up his classmate.

The instructor exhibited his mock displeasure (his students rarely find any weapons the first time) and demonstrated a proper frisk on his collaborator. "When you frisk someone, it is for your own protection. You don't have to kick him. You have to put him under your control and frisk him systematically." The instructor used his entire body, placing the man in the position he wanted him, feet back and spread wide, every muscle tensed to keep his head, which was far forward, from slipping down and causing him to fall. "You want to stand right in there. Don't be afraid of him. You gonna be afraid when he ain't in this position. Now you got him. Put your leg inside his, and if he moves you can trip him up. If he takes a few bumps, that's resisting. Frisk him systematically. Don't use your fingertips. Use your palms. Start with the palms on his head and work one side of his body and then the other. Look at his hair, and don't be afraid to put your hands in his crotch, it won't bite. And if the guy gives you any shit, why you can give him a little shot to remember you while you're there."

The instructor showed them the concealed knives and guns and told them, "They were hardly hidden. But you are gonna learn. And listen, the rough stuff is for nothing. It doesn't help you find anything. If you're

[2] A policeman may examine the outer clothing of any person he stops on suspicion if he feels the person means him harm or may be concealing a weapon. If he feels anything that might be a weapon, he may go into the person's clothing and extract the object for examination. If in the course of the frisk he discovers any contraband or evidence implicating the person in some crime, it is not considered to be legally seized since the policeman has conducted what amounts to a search without reasonable grounds. The distinctions between stop and frisk are discussed in Lawrence P. Tiffany, Donald M. McIntyre, Jr., and Daniel L. Rotenberg, *Detection of Crime* (Boston, Little, Brown, 1967), pp. 44–57. The stop-and-frisk authority of the police in a number of other countries is discussed in Sowle, *Police Power and Individual Freedom*. In no country do the police appear to have less formal power than they do in America, although the actual practices may differ. A cursory discussion of police frisking in London and the negative responses of people is in Peter Laurie, *Scotland Yard* (London, Bodley Head, 1970), pp. 62–5.

nervous, the guy out there is gonna know it. He may have more experience at this than you. You give him a chance, he'll take it. Don't talk to him or let him distract you, just frisk him. Then if he don't stand still, you make him, but don't get tough just because you're nervous or don't like the guy's color or looks or whatever."

After several weeks of practicing and discovering the many places a weapon can be concealed (one student sliced open his finger on a razor blade stuck behind a belt), the students' admiration for their instructor was unbounded and their efficiency at frisking vastly improved. Most of the kicking had disappeared, and the recruits were beginning to use their bodies to place people on the wall and to control them while they were there. But even using loaded guns (with blanks) and switchblades did not create the necessary ingredients to make it all real—fear and anger.

Most frisking is actually done casually and in an offhand manner. When a policeman is working alone, he is reluctant to bend down, which he must do in a full frisk from the rear, and he will forgo it unless he has strong reasons to believe the person is armed. A decision to frisk is also affected by the relative size of the people involved. Few policemen frisk youngsters (unless they are quite large), because an officer assumes that if he gets any trouble from a kid, he can put him down. He contents himself with casually feeling the outer pockets of his jacket and his waist area. But the experienced man does not waste these few motions. He is not delicate in poking his hands about while he is making conversation.

A frisk usually occurs after a stop is made and the patrolman has made some determination about his initial suspicions, but there are numerous occasions when the frisk and stop occur almost simultaneously.

Two patrolmen were searching an area for suspects in the shooting of a police officer. There was little information about the killers except that they were young. Driving slowly down an almost deserted street, they passed a young man walking in the opposite direction. "Did he turn away? Yeah, let's get him. Shit, I hate backin' up on these dudes," he muttered to his recorder, throwing the car into reverse. He jumped out, ran between two parked cars, grabbed the man, and turned him about. He was frisking his midriff when the man said, "Hey, Hank, what's the matter, man?" The patrolman, surprised at hearing his name, looked up and noticed that he had stopped the brother of a close friend. He stopped the frisk and apologized. They smoked a cigarette, chatted, and parted. He had been so intent on quickly approaching the suspect without losing sight of the man's hands that he did not even look at his face. He was not embarrassed but considered the action an excellent example of how to do his job properly. "He might have been a killer. When you go up on someone like that, you got no business lookin' at his face," he said.

If the policeman has not stopped a person on suspicion or encountered him under circumstances that suggest involvement in disorder or crime, he will not frisk him unless in the course of conversation something is said suggesting violence or resistance. He does not search everyone he meets or everyone he stands next to on a dark street. He is never relaxed in the presence of strangers, and he assumes that his alertness and readiness are sufficient to handle surprises, but if there is a hint of a weapon present, his entire manner changes abruptly.

Two patrolmen were interviewing a man who claimed that two acquaintances had robbed him of a thousand dollars. "Wow, that's like a million bucks in this neighborhood. You must be a number writer, pal," one officer said, with a grin. The alleged victim did not think it funny, and the more he talked of his loss, the angrier he became. He was quite vague in giving a description of the robbers, and the patrolmen began to think the man was just another drunk. "I'm gonna kill them motherfuckers!" he mumbled, and in a second one officer had grabbed him by the arm, twisted him about, and started frisking him. From inside the man's overcoat he extracted an ice pick. "I didn't like the way he said 'kill.' You hear that kinda shit all the time, but he really meant it. An ice pick is the worst, too, because there's no hole when you pull it out. All the bleeding is on the inside," he said to his inexperienced partner.

Whenever he is making a suspicion stop, the patrolman conducts some kind of frisk. How he proceeds depends on whether he is working alone or with a partner. If he is alone, he will not bother to back-frisk anyone he thinks has no chance of overpowering him. But if the person appears to be strongly built and willing to "give it a go," he will turn him about, often accompanying his commands with a few threats, but he will not bend down to do a thorough search. Instead he uses his stick to feel the man's legs or, if he has no stick, does not bother to do a complete job. If he bends down, the policeman is vulnerable, and while the man may not hurt him, he has a chance to "make it"; no policeman wants to give anyone the opportunity of involving him in a chase.

When patrolmen work in pairs, their approach alters completely. Two men who work together regularly come to understand each other's attitudes and routines. They divide responsibilities, and each knows what he is going to do when they make a stop or go into a place where there is some kind of trouble. Whether they are stopping one man or five, one officer conducts the interrogation and the frisk, and the other stands back and controls the scene. If they have stopped a group of men, the patrolman does not hesitate to unholster his gun in order to make them more responsive to his commands. Working in pairs, one man can focus his attention on the frisk and does not have to worry about the chances of assault or flight.

Working alone, the patrolman's control of the situation is slight and tenuous. If he is working one to one, only fear prevents the person he has stopped from proceeding. The degree of force the policeman must use to make him obey depends as much on his willingness to appear forceful as it does on the actual use of force. There are many policemen who rarely use force for the simple reason that they appear willing (and possibly are) to do almost anything to subdue resistance. Other patrolmen, who misjudge their power (or like to abuse it), often find themselves in situations where they are risking serious danger for little reward.

A young, aggressive patrolman told of a problem he had encountered when he stopped six men outside a bar. "I had all six on the wall, you know, and I was gonna search the one on the end when one guy said they should rush me. I cocked my gun and nobody moved, and I told him if they came, I'd burn him. What else could I do? I started to frisk the one guy when the guys at the other end started drifting around the corner. I lost two, but I finished the other four." If he had expected solace and comfort from his colleagues, he was disappointed. "Carl, you are a dumb motherfucker. You keep up that crazy shit, you are gonna be in the hospital or dead."

Even if the policeman is careful not to exceed the limits of his capacity to safely control suspects, he cannot focus his attention closely on what he is doing when he frisks someone. Most frisks are done quickly and informally to assure the officer that the suspect does not have anything on him which might be used against the policeman. Patrolmen who fancy themselves specialists in gun pinches frisk people very thoroughly, but they are exceptional. Every time a person is arrested he is usually frisked twice, first by the arresting officer and then by the wagon crew, before he is transported to the station, but weapons are still overlooked, concealed behind belt buckles, in armpits, and even in a folded wallet.

A patrolman recalled a time when he was working plainclothes and was arrested during a raid on a speakeasy. The police missed the small revolver he had stuck behind his belt buckle. "I was sittin' on the bench in the station, waitin', you know, to tell 'em who I was when we was in private, but I was worried if they noticed the gun they'd kick the shit outta me. So I called a cop over and real quiet I told him I was still carryin'. He almost shit." On another occasion, a young man was sitting in a station, handcuffed, waiting for some detectives to come for him. He acted quite nervous, kept looking about and fidgeting. Finally a patrolman approached and told him to keep quiet. He apologized and said he was very nervous because he had a gun in his pocket that the policeman had not taken from him. The patrolman seized him by the lapels, twisted him about as he raised him from the bench, and grabbed the gun.

Frisking is much more common in some parts of the city than in others, and it is not an activity engaged in exclusively by the police. There are bars and restaurants where regular patrons "bump" into strangers, checking whether or not they are armed. Prostitutes who work out of bars frequently seek to protect themselves from entrapments by plainclothesmen by holding hands and pretending affection for a potential client while actually checking to see if the man's hands match what he claims to do for a living and if he is carrying a small gun or a jack somewhere about his middle. These people frisk for protection, as a policeman does. An officer is forbidden by regulation to frisk a woman except in an extreme emergency; he must turn her over to a matron or a policewoman. Undoubtedly the number of complaints against the police would increase if this restriction were lifted, but so, too, would the number of stops and arrests. There are many reasons why a policeman does not look with suspicion on women in public places (except in areas where prostitutes work), but one of them certainly is his inability to protect himself. Not only can he not frisk a woman, a policeman is reluctant to hit a woman, and even when he has justification (from his point of view), he recalls doing so with regret and chagrin.

Although a policeman views frisking as a defensive act devoid of personal comment, those he stops cannot help but feel angered by their powerlessness, if for no other reason. Regardless of how the policeman behaves or what he says, he is compelling the person to submit to him and to turn his body over for examination. Younger men in some parts of the city are so familiar with the routine that when they are hailed by the police, they stop and spread their arms to the side before the officer has asked a question or even approached. They understand that this signal of submission will gain them more gentle and circumspect treatment. Sometimes a patrolman runs his hands absentmindedly over a man's pockets while engaging in conversation, not really meaning to frisk him but just letting him know that he is in control, that for the moment the man belongs to the patrolman. It is not a consciously hostile or aggressive act. It is an expression of the policeman's belief that regardless of the momentary tone of the interaction, his place in that relationship is supported ultimately by his personal will and readiness to exercise all of the authority invested in him. There is no way he can make this point without causing discontent, because the authority given to him can be exercised only by restraining the liberty of some persons and violating their autonomy. A policeman does not enjoy frisking people. During a busy tour he may wash up several times because many of the people he stops are filthy. He constantly grumbles about the dirt and the odors, but they do not cause him to keep his distance or to avoid intimate contact. He knows that when he is on the street, it is only his readiness to demonstrate his power that maintains the edge necessary for him to do his work and come home safely each day.

The Effect of the Police on Crime

James Q. Wilson and Barbara Boland*

The effect of police practices on the rate of robbery in 35 large American cities is estimated by a set of simultaneous equations. The measures of police resources (patrol units on the street) and police activity on the street (moving citations issued) are more precise than anything thus far available in studies of this kind and permit the use of identification restrictions that allow stronger inferences about the causal effect of arrests on crime rates than has heretofore been possible. Police resources and police activity independently affect the robbery rate after controlling for various socioeconomic factors. The political arrangements that lead to the use of aggressive patrol strategies are discussed and their effect estimated. The implications for, and limitations upon, policy are also discussed.

SOURCE: "The Effect of the Police on Crime," by James Q. Wilson and Barbara Boland. *Law and Society Review* 12, No. 3 (Spring 1978), pp. 367–390. *The Law and Society Review* is the official publication of the Law and Society Association. (The appendix and footnotes have been omitted.)

* The authors wish to thank Ralph Gants and Olsen Lee for their able assistance in gathering and processing data and Jan Chaiken, Robert Crain, Franklin Fisher, Robert Gillespie, David F. Greenberg, Zvi Griliches, Richard Muth, and William Scanlon for their comments on an earlier version. The research for this paper was supported by a grant to The Urban Institute from the Law Enforcement Assistance Administration (LEAA). Neither the Institute nor LEAA is responsible for the views presented here.

This is an attempt to estimate the effect of police practices on the rate of robbery in 35 large American cities and to set forth some reasons why those practices vary from city to city. Several previous studies have dealt with police effects on crime but all have been criticized: some for the measures used, others for the estimation procedures employed. Differences in police practices among cities have sometimes been explained, but usually as a result of differences in resources (expenditures on the police). We shall present data that are consistent with the view that police patrol strategies have an effect on the rate at which robberies are committed, that this effect is a causal one and not the result of a spurious statistical correlation, and that the existence of a given patrol strategy is affected by bureaucratic decisions as well as by levels of resources.

We conjecture that these decisions about police practices can be altered independently of expenditures on the police, within certain unmeasured political constraints.

I. PRIOR STUDIES

A number of studies have found a strong negative correlation between the rate at which persons are arrested for an offense and the rate at which that offense occurs. The results of these studies are by no means unambiguous but they broadly suggest that police behavior, as measured by either clearance rates (the proportion of those offenses known to the police that are "cleared" by an arrest) or arrest rates (the ratio of arrests for a given offense to the number of such offenses reported), affects the crime rate independent of other social factors. Tittle and Rowe (1974), for example, found that among cities and counties in Florida, the higher the clearance rate the lower the total index crime rate,[1] at least for those jurisdictions in which 30 percent or more of the reported crimes are cleared by arrest. (The authors argued that there is a "tipping effect" such that differences in clearance rates only affect crime rates when the former exceed a certain minimum level.) Bailey (n.d.) reanalyzed the Florida data, looking at each major crime separately, and found that the negative relationship between clearance rates and crime rates persisted for certain offenses (primarily those committed for gain) but not for others. Block (1972) found a negative correlation between clearance rates and property crime rates among police precincts in Los Angeles; Phillips and Votey (1972) also found such a relationship using national data for the years 1952–67. Logan (1975) compared clearance rates with reported index offenses and found a negative relationship for property crimes using statewide data for five successive years.

There is a problem in employing the clearance rate in measuring police effect on crime: a crime "cleared by arrest" is whatever the police say it is. Some departments and officers conscientiously report offenses as cleared only when they have taken into custody a person against whom they have sufficient evidence to bring charges. Such arrested persons may, and often do, admit that they have committed offenses other than that for which they were arrested; the police are entitled to count these as having been cleared. But obviously the suspect will be influenced by many things in admitting other offenses: his memory and eagerness to boast, confess, or please his captors, and the interest of the police in eliciting additional admissions (Skolnick, 1966). Clearance rates may vary substantially among departments for reasons having nothing to do with the objective probability of getting caught.

A few studies of the police employ arrest ratios rather than clearance rates. Though there are difficulties with this index as well, at least it introduces less measurement error—an arrest is a more or less concrete, easily counted event not dependent on the vagaries of memory and interrogation. Sjoquist (1973) examined 53 middle-sized American cities in 1968 and found that the arrest ratios for property crimes (robberies, burglaries, and larcenies) were negatively related to the rates at which those crimes were reported, independent of various socioeconomic factors. Wilson and Boland (1976) compared arrest ratios and the rate at which serious robberies were recounted to Census Bureau interviewers in 26 large cities and found the same strong, negative association reported in other studies even though they used victimization surveys rather than Federal Bureau of Investigation (FBI) crime reports.

In sum, there is a good deal of evidence that supports the assertion that differences in the risk of arrest are associated with differences in the rate of crime. But there are at least two difficulties that stand in the way of drawing any policy conclusions from this observed association.

The first is the familiar problem known to economists as "simultaneity." Crime rates and arrest probabilities may be negatively associated either because high arrest rates cause lower crime rates or because higher crime rates cause lower arrest rates. The latter would be the case if a high and rising level of reported crime swamped police resources so that the rate at which criminals were arrested went down. Crime and arrest rates influence each other; they are "simultaneously determined." The observed negative association in the studies mentioned may mean either that arrests deter crime or that crime "deters" arrests.

The second problem arises from the fact that changes in police practices may affect the crime rate through causal linkages that do not increase the chances of being arrested. It may be difficult or impossible to increase this probability because the police have little or

[1] The total index crime rate, as defined by the FBI, is the total number of murders, rapes, robberies, aggravated assaults, burglaries, auto thefts, and larcenies reported to the police per 100,000 population.

no control over such decisive factors as the willingness of citizens to report a crime, offer information to the police, or identify suspects. But the police may be able to do other things that affect the crime rate and affect it only indirectly, or not at all, by altering the chances of being arrested. These direct deterrence effects depend on the number and activity of patrol officers. An offender may alter the rate at which he commits crime not because the *actual* chance of being caught has increased but because he *perceives* that it has, perhaps because he sees more officers than usual or more activity among them.

Thus far efforts to see if crime rates are affected by differences in police presence—usually measured by the number of police per capita—have proved unavailing. Cross-sectional statistical studies have found either no relationship between police per capita and crime rates or a perverse one: the greater the police presence, the higher the rate of crime. But such studies are clearly defective in that they do not measure how many police are *on the street*, only how many are on the payroll and, as we shall see, there is only a weak relationship between the size of a police force and the number of officers it deploys on patrol. Studies like the Kansas City Preventive Patrol experiment suggest that simply increasing the number of patrol units in a given beat will not have any effect on crime rates (Kelling *et al.*, 1974). Moreover, some of the studies that purport to discern a perverse relationship between police per capita and crime rates (e.g., Pressman and Carol, 1971; Allison, 1972) fail to take into account the obvious fact that cities hire more officers because their crime rates are high; in other words, the causal direction of the relationship may be reversed.

But the police may affect crime rates less by *how many* of them are on patrol than by *what* they do there. What they do includes many things in addition to, and perhaps more important than, making arrests. Though patrol behavior is complex, we can distinguish two extreme strategies: "aggressive" and "passive." By an aggressive strategy we do not mean that the officer is hostile or harsh but rather that he maximizes the number of interventions in and observations of the community. In another study, Wilson (1968) has referred to this as the "legalistic" police style. An officer follows a passive strategy when he rarely stops motor vehicles to issue citations for moving violations or to check for stolen cars or wanted fugitives, rarely stops to question suspicious persons, and does not employ "decoy" or stake-out procedures in areas with high crime rates. When an officer acts in the opposite manner, he is employing an "aggressive" strategy.

In San Diego, a well-designed experiment showed that one component of an aggressive patrol strategy—field interrogations or "street stops"—is associated with a significant decline in certain kinds of crime. In one area of the city, field interrogations were eliminated, whereupon the number of "suppressible" crimes rose by about a third; when field interrogations were resumed the number of such crimes dropped. ("Suppressible" crimes were defined as robbery, burglary, theft, auto theft, assault, sex crimes, malicious mischief, and disturbances.) There was no change in the frequency of suppressible crimes in control areas where field interrogation practices continued unchanged. The presence or absence of field interrogations did not, however, affect the number of arrests in the experimental areas (Boydstun, 1975). So far as we know, there is no study that attempts to see whether other components of aggressive or passive patrol strategies are associated with changes in the level of reported crime.

To achieve an aggressive patrol strategy a police executive will recruit certain kinds of officers, train them in certain ways, and devise requirements and reward systems (traffic ticket quotas, field interrogation obligations, promotional opportunities) to encourage them to follow the intended strategy. This used to be, and for many officers still is, the core of the concept of "police professionalism." Some police chiefs have developed a new theory of professionalism that emphasizes community service, but the choice of an aggressive patrol strategy is still quite common.

The major problem in testing a theory that relates crime rates and police strategies is to find valid and systematic measures of an aggressive strategy and the procedural arrangements that sustain it. These data are not readily available and efforts to gather them may be hindered by the fact that many departments are unaware of, or reluctant to comment on, the relationship between reward systems and patrol strategies. We have selected a measure we believe is a reliable, though not complete, proxy for the existence of an aggressive strategy: the number of citations for moving traffic violations issued per sworn officer.

In an earlier study, one of the present authors (Wilson, 1968) found that where one element of a "legalistic" (or aggressive) patrol style was present, other elements were likely to be present as well. From our experience and that of others whom we have consulted, departments in our sample with high rates of traffic citations are generally thought by both their members and outside observers to display a strong commitment to "police professionalism" as conventionally defined. It is possible, of course, that the police in some cities may be aggressive about enforcing the traffic laws but lax about making street stops, checking suspicious persons, or employing other specialized patrol techniques. We think this unlikely, and we believe our statistical results, taken as a whole, suggest that this is not generally the case, but the reader should be aware that this is a possible limitation on the study.

II. THE MODELS

We shall investigate in two ways the possible effect of police practices on crime. First, we shall ask whether patrol strategies affect the probability of arrest for robbery and whether this probability in turn affects the rate at which robberies are committed. (We selected robbery for examination because we, and probably most citizens, think it an especially serious and fearsome offense.) In this first line of inquiry we assume that the probability of an arrest for any given robber is affected by, among other things, the level of police resources (measured by the number of patrol units on the street per capita) and the degree of aggressiveness of those units (measured by the number of moving traffic citations issued per patrol unit). Because the number of arrests that can be made will be constrained by the number of patrol units available, it is possible that any negative association between robbery rates and arrest rates can have either of two meanings: high rates of robbery have "swamped" police resources or high rates of arrest have lowered the robbery rate. We therefore estimate the effect of police strategies on arrests and of arrests on crime by means of simultaneous equations that explicitly take police resources into account. The model we estimate contains four separate equations: a crime rate equation that measures the effect of arrest rates on crime rates; an arrest productivity equation that measures the effect of an aggressive strategy, resources, and crime levels on arrest rates; a police deployment equation that explains the number of patrol units (per 100,000 population) on the street; and a resource equation that explains the number of police employees. Like most economic models of police behavior, this one assumes that communities respond to increased crime rates by hiring more police in the expectation that such hiring will lead to an increase in the arrest rates and a concomitant reduction in crime. According to the economic view of arrest productivity, what actually happens depends on how fast and to what extent police resources are increased relative to the crime rate. If the increase in the number of police is not proportional to the increase in the crime rate, or the hiring and training of additional police officers take a significant amount of time to implement, an increase in crime results in an overload on the police and a decline in arrest rates and deterrence, at least temporarily. In this model, departmental choice of a patrol strategy is viewed not as a response to high or rising crime rates or to community demands that the police do something about crime, but rather as an organizational decision influenced by factors unrelated to crime; these latter will be investigated in a later section.

In estimating models of this sort where two variables, X and Y, are thought to affect each other mutually it becomes necessary to make defensible assumptions that there are additional factors that will affect one of the variables but not the other. These assumptions, called "identification restrictions," ensure that the estimating techniques can separate the effect of X on Y from the effect of Y on X. In the present case, since we are particularly interested in identifying the deterrent effect of arrests on crime, the critical identification restriction is a justifiable assumption that there are one or more factors that affect the arrest rate but not the crime rate (Nagin, 1978; Fisher and Nagin, 1978). If such factors can be found, we can develop logically and empirically separate equations to estimate the deterrent effect of arrests. We are then entitled to say that the observed negative association between the crime rate and the arrest rate cannot be wholly the result of crimes overloading the police because other factors, independent of the crime rate, also determine the arrest rate.

Drawing on our analysis in the preceding section, we suggest that the arrest ratio is affected by the choice of a patrol strategy, which is itself the result of various organizational and political decisions that are independent of the crime rate. We do not mean that police administrators create and sustain an aggressive patrol strategy without regard to its effect on crime—they will certainly justify it on that ground, among others. Rather, we argue that a city's patrol strategy cannot be predicted from its crime rate but can be explained by the political arrangements (governmental structure and animating ethos) within which police decisions are made.

In an earlier study, we crudely approximated these independent "police strategy" factors by a subjective measure of "police effectiveness" as judged by outside observers and found that it was significantly, and negatively, correlated with the crime rate (Wilson and Boland, 1976).

We assume, in estimating this model, that patrol strategy affects the robbery rate only by changing the probability that an arrest will be made. It is easy to see how this might occur. By stopping, questioning, and otherwise closely observing citizens, especially suspicious ones, the police are more likely to find fugitives, detect contraband (such as stolen property or concealed weapons), and apprehend persons fleeing from the scene of a crime. But it is also possible that an aggressive patrol strategy will affect the crime rate directly, and not through its effect on the arrest rate, if it leads would-be offenders to believe that their chances of being arrested have increased, even though they have not. If this occurs, then patrol strategy cannot be used to identify the crime rate by excluding it from the crime-rate equations, and thus we will not be able to say whether a higher arrest rate will drive down the robbery rate or a higher robbery rate will drive down the arrest rate. We know of no way to demonstrate the validity of our assumption, though we believe it is reasonable, for we have no information on the perceptions of would-be offenders and find it difficult to imagine how one would acquire such information.

To deal with this problem, we shall develop a second line of inquiry based on the assumption that patrol strategies may affect crime rates indirectly or directly—that aggressive patrolling reduces robberies either by increasing the actual chances of being caught or by misleading would-be offenders into believing that this has happened. In designing this model, we shall argue that the effect of patrol strategy on crime does not face the problem of simultaneity and thus can properly be estimated using ordinary least squares.

The first model is a set of four equations estimated using 1975 data gathered from 35 large American cities. . . . The unpublished data (patrol units on the street per capita and the number of moving traffic citations issued per patrol unit) were gathered by the authors from the cities in the sample. The results, estimated using two-stage least-squares procedures, are presented in Table 1.

Equation 1(a) states that the rate at which robbery occurs is a function of sanctions (the arrest ratio for robbery), demography (the proportion of males ages 15–29 in the population, the proportion of the population nonwhite, and the unemployment rate), and opportunity (population density). Equation 1(b) states that the arrest ratio used in the preceding equation is a function of aggressive patrol (moving violations cited per patrol unit), the level of police resources relative to crime or workload (crimes per patrol unit) and demography (proportion of population nonwhite). Equation 1(c) states that the number of patrol units on the street (per 100,000 people) is a function of the level of police resources (number of sworn officers per 100,000 people), the proportion of officers assigned to two-officer cars, the housing density of the city, and the population. Equation 1(d) states that the level of police resources is a function of the rates of property and personal crime, available municipal resources (equalized property tax base per capita), the cost of adding additional police manpower (the starting salary of sworn officers), and a northeast regional dummy variable to control for the frequently observed tendency of large cities located in the northeast to spend more on municipal services.

The results are consistent with expectations. Controlling for demographic and opportunity variables, the robbery crime rate is strongly and negatively correlated with the robbery arrest ratio. This, in turn, is affected by both the deployment measures and the workload variable. The number of patrol units on the street is affected by the number of officers, the proportion in two-officer cars, and the population of the city. Police resources are determined by the rate of personal crime (but not by the rate of property crime) and by the available tax base.

Alternative versions of the crime equation 1(a) were estimated using different socioeconomic variables, including measures of income distribution, poverty, proportion of families on welfare, and the like. These other variables were not statistically significant and did not increase the explanatory power of the model. The unemployment variable is included in equation 1(a) though it is not significant; other economic variables do even less well (to our surprise).

Many of the cities with an aggressive patrol strategy are located in the western part of the United States. Cultural factors associated with the region may have an effect on arrest ratios independent of an aggressive patrol strategy. To ensure that the moving citations variable is not just a proxy for these other factors, we inserted in equation 1(b) a regional dummy variable. This regional control variable is not significant.

TABLE 1 Estimating Robbery-Arrest-Police Relationships

Dependent Variables	*Constant*	*Independent Variables*					*R^2 (Corrected)*[a]
		Robbery-Arrest Ratio	*Age/Sex*	*Percent Nonwhite*	*Unemployment Rate*	*Population Density*	
(a) Robbery Crime Rate							
Coefficient	730.82	−11.6	−39.3	12.7	28.6	.024	.74
(t-ratio)[b]	(1.49)	(−2.02)	(−1.62)	(5.74)	(1.42)	(2.90)	
		Moving Citations Per Patrol Unit (log)	*Crimes Per Patrol Unit*	*Percent Nonwhite*	*West*		
(b) Robbery Arrest Ratio							
Coefficient	12.3	6.54	−.10	.04	1.17		.25
(t-ratio)[b]	(.80)	(2.43)	(−3.74)	(.51)	(.34)		
		Sworn Officers Per Capita	*Percent Two-Officer Patrol Cars*	*Housing Density*	*Population*		
(c) Patrol Units Per Capita							
Coefficient	38.4	.17	−.46	−0.16	−.005		.72
(t-ratio)[b]	(1.65)	(3.91)	(−5.04)	(−.72)	(−2.63)		
		Property Crime Rate	*Personal Crime Rate*	*Per Capita Tax Base*	*Officers' Salary*	*Northeast*	
(d) Sworn Officers Per Capita							
Coefficient	113.70	−.018	.169	.010	.002	58.0	.50
(t-ratio)[b]	(.45)	(−1.03)	(5.43)	(2.42)	(.19)	(1.18)	

Data: 35 largest cities in 1975.
Method: Two-stage least squares.
[a] R^2s are not a valid measure of goodness of fit in simultaneous equation models estimated by two-stage least squares. They are reported as an item of interest to many readers.
[b] t-ratio: Ratio of estimated coefficients to asymptotic standard errors.

We have repeated this analysis for two other crimes, burglary and auto theft, but without obtaining significant results for 1975 data. The poor results for burglary do not surprise us: it is a crime of stealth, rarely has eye-witnesses, leaves few clues, and is not visible to police patrol. The results for auto theft are harder to explain, since we had expected this to be a patrol-suppressible crime. The same model was estimated using 1970 crime and arrest data for auto theft, and the results were as predicted and quite robust: the auto theft rate was strongly and negatively associated with the auto arrest ratio, which was strongly and positively associated with the rate at which moving citations were issued. We do not know why high arrest ratios lowered the auto theft rate in 1970 but not in 1975, nor why aggressive patrolling increased the arrest ratio in 1970 but not in 1975. One possibility is that by the early 1970s an increasing proportion of cars on the road were equipped with steering locks and other antitheft devices. These devices will not defeat a professional auto thief but they will frustrate, or at least discourage, casual auto thieves, mostly juveniles seeking joy-rides rather than income (Zimring, 1975). The proportion of juveniles among persons arrested for auto theft began to decline in the early 1970s, probably as a result of their decreased participation in the crime. This pattern may have proceeded unevenly, with a different mix of professional and casual auto thieves in different cities.

Such a trend could explain the decline between 1970 and 1975 in the sensitivity of auto theft rates to arrest ratios and patrol methods.

Equation 1(b) suggests that the arrest ratio is influenced by both the level of resources (crimes per patrol unit) and how those resources are deployed (moving citations per sworn officer). Defining police resources in terms of patrol units on the street eliminates the paradoxical findings of other studies that use police expenditures or total police personnel as indices (cf. Greenwood and Wadycki, 1973; Swimmer, 1974). The reason some of these latter studies reach the implausible conclusion that police resources either have no effect on crime rates or a perverse effect is that the correlation in our sample between the total number of sworn officers and the number of patrol units on the street at a given time is only .48; if two extreme cases are eliminated (Boston and Washington, D.C.), the correlation falls to .24.

Equation 1(c) suggests that the number of patrol units per capita will depend on the number of sworn officers per capita, the proportion of the force assigned to two-officer rather than one-officer cars, and the population of the city (the larger the city, the *smaller* the proportion of the force on the street). A police administrator cannot easily increase the size of his or her force (city councils and mayors will have something, often negative, to say about that) but can, in principle, decide what proportion of the patrol force will be in two-officer cars. And that decision, as suggested by Equation 1(b), may have an important effect on the ratio of arrests to robberies.

The total size of the police force (sworn officers per 100,000 persons) is largely explained in Equation 1(d) by the rate of crimes against the person, and the funds available (per capita tax base). Other things being equal, cities with a higher rate of *personal* crime (homicide, rape, assault, robbery) will devote more resources to police services than those with lower rates; cities with larger tax bases will employ more officers per capita than cities with smaller bases. Officers' starting salary, the rate of property crime, and the region in which the city is located are less important explanatory factors as indicated by the low value of the associated t-ratios.

In sum, the results of the simultaneous equations are consistent with the following theory: Cities that experience high rates of personal crime and have higher than average tax bases will hire more police employees in proportion to their populations. That it should be the rate of personal, not property, crime that generates this response is understandable: personal crimes apparently induce greater anxieties and thus fuel political demands in a way that property crimes, such as burglary and auto theft, do not. Some departments assign a high proportion of officers to patrol in one-man patrol cars and encourage them to adopt an aggressive patrol strategy, as evidenced by their tendency to issue disproportionately high numbers of traffic tickets for moving violations. These patterns of deployment and behavior increase the arrest rates for robbery. We would expect to find that police in such "aggressive" departments also make many "street stops" or field interrogations of suspicious persons, have a quicker than usual response time to citizen calls for service, and resort to arrest in a larger proportion of police-citizen encounters.

In those cities that manage to produce higher arrest ratios by employing an aggressive patrol strategy or increasing the number of patrol units, the robbery rates are lower than one would predict knowing only the socioeconomic composition of the city and the density of criminal opportunities. Thus, citizens do not necessarily have to spend more money to get more law enforcement; they can get it by having police organizations capable of devising and maintaining a personnel, incentive, and management system that delivers more law enforcement (Leibenstein, 1976).

III. EXPLAINING PATROL AGGRESSIVENESS

In addition to deciding what proportion of his personnel to put on the street and to deploy in one-officer units, the police administrator can choose a patrol strategy that will have an effect on arrest ratios independent of resources levels, and thus (if one accepts the assumptions stated earlier in this paper) on robbery rates.

On the basis of prior research (Wilson, 1968), we suggest that cities with a certain political culture will be more likely to select and support police administrators strongly committed to conventional doctrines of "police professionalism," among which will be an aggressive patrol strategy. By "political culture" we mean those widely shared expectations about how issues will be raised, governmental objectives defined, and the administration of public affairs conducted. One such culture, frequently described in the literature of urban politics, is what is loosely called "good" or "reformed" government (Banfield and Wilson, 1963). Among the attitudes contributing to this culture are the belief that the "best person" should be hired to perform each administrative job, even if that person is politically an outsider; that police administrators should not be subject to political interference as long as they act in accordance with prevailing professional doctrine; and that public decisions ought to be made on the basis of what is best for the community "as a whole," and should not favor particular neighborhoods, constituencies, or interests (Wilson and Banfield, 1964, 1971). Historically, this political culture has been institutionalized in the council-manager form of government operating on the basis of nonpartisan, at-large elections. At any given time, the culture will most likely animate such institutions when they are placed in the hands of a "professional" city manager—someone with advanced training in urban management and experience in governing other cities—in short, a specially trained cosmopolitan.

Since we cannot measure directly the presence of attitudes that correspond to a particular political culture without costly opinion surveys, and since the mere presence of nonpartisan, council-manager institutions may tell one little about how decisions are really made, we take as our measure of the underlying political culture the presence of a "professional" city manager. In an earlier study, Wilson showed that police forces in such cities were more likely to have high arrest rates in those routine cases—larceny, drunkenness, driving while intoxicated, disorderly conduct, and simple assault—that an officer could easily ignore or handle by means other than an arrest should he wish to do so (1968:275).

We now wish to see if our "political culture" variable—the presence of a professional city manager—can help us explain why some of our large cities have an aggressive patrol strategy as measured by the number of moving traffic violations cited per sworn officer. In Equation 2 we suggest that moving citations are a function of opportunity (the number of automobiles per capita) and politics (whether or not the city has a professional city manager) (see Table 2). We also test the possibility that aggressiveness is stimulated by police reactions to the presence of a large number of nonwhites: it is possible that the police might stop, question, and ticket nonwhites out of prejudice or suspicion.

The results of ordinary least-squares regression are about as predicted. Both opportunity and political culture contribute significantly and independently to high rates of traffic ticketing. The correlation with proportion nonwhite is not significant.

TABLE 2 Estimating the Number of Moving Traffic Citations per Sworn Officer

Independent Variables	*Coefficient*	*t-statistic*	*Elasticity*
Professional City Manager	0.49	2.2	
Automobiles per capita	0.028	2.4	0.25
Percent nonwhite	−0.0067	−1.09	−0.04

Constant = 3.15; corrected R^2 = .32; F = 6.2
Method: Ordinary least squares . . .
Sample: 35 largest U.S. cities in 1975

In sum, a city with a "reformed" or professionalized municipal management system will be more likely to have a police department with an aggressive patrol strategy, though not necessarily one with many patrol units on the street. Aggressiveness and a larger number of patrol units, separately and in combination, will lead to a higher arrest ratio for robbery, and this higher ratio, in turn, leads to a lower robbery crime rate.

We now relax somewhat the assumption we made at the outset that aggressiveness lowers the crime rate by changing the probability of arrest for that crime. Suppose that aggressiveness also affects crime directly, by making would-be offenders more apprehensive of the chances of being arrested, as well as indirectly, by making them worried. There is no way we can test the extent to which police activity affects crime through direct rather than indirect deterrence. But we do not believe that such a test is necessary given our purpose, which is to show the effect of police practices generally on robbery rates. The model estimated in Equation 1 is consistent with both theories. Police practices do affect crime rates, directly or indirectly, and these practices are, so far as we can tell, the product of decisions made over the long term and not in response to short-term changes in crime rates or resource levels.

In our earlier study we used a different and admittedly more subjective measure of police style: three expert judges rated 23 big-city police departments as "professional" or "nonprofessional" in terms of their adherence to norms of efficiency and legalism. We entered this rating as a dummy variable in an ordinary least squares equation that estimated the rate of serious robberies. We repeat the results in Table 3.

The consistency between this model and the one presented earlier in this paper, despite the use of different measures of the crime rate and of police style, strengthens our confidence that the police do make a

TABLE 3 Estimating the Effects of Police Style and Three Demographic Variables on the Rate of Serious Robberies in 23 Cities in 1973

Independent Variables	*Coefficient*	*t-statistic*	*Elasticity*
Police professionalism (0,1)	−2.37306	−2.5967	
Percent nonwhite	0.06234	2.2598	0.28657
Labor force participation rate	0.06152	0.1431	0.16067
Density	0.00040	3.5974	0.48416

Constant = 1.887; corrected R^2 = .68; F = 13.529

Method: Ordinary least squares

Data sources and definitions:

Rate of Serious Robberies: number of robberies in which more than $10 was stolen per 1000 population. Unpublished data from the LEAA victimization surveys provided by the National Criminal Justice Information and Statistics Service.

Police Professionalism: cities judged professional were: Cincinnati, Dallas, Los Angeles, New York, Oakland, Portland, St. Louis, San Diego, and Washington, D.C. Other cities in the sample were: Atlanta, Baltimore, Boston, Chicago, Cleveland, Denver, Detroit, Houston, Miami, Milwaukee, Newark, Philadelphia, Pittsburgh, and San Francisco. Unpublished data collected by the authors.

Percent Nonwhite: U.S. Department of Justice (1974a, 1974b).

Labor Force Participation Rate: labor force participation rate of men ages 16–34 living in low income areas (U.S. Department of Commerce 1972c).

Density: central city population per square mile (U.S. Department of Commerce, 1972d).

difference and that this is not entirely dependent on resources.

IV. DOES IT REALLY WORK THAT WAY?

Two things are missing from this study that would be important to anyone wishing to change police practices in order to change crime rates. First, this study looks at many cities during one year whereas more might be learned by looking at a few cities over time. Differences among cities may not be the result of underlying factors we have not measured or factors that, if measured, would prove quite resistant to change. If it could be shown, however, that in several cities the arrest rate changed over a five- or ten-year period and that this was associated with changes in the crime rate (controlling for population change), then we could be more confident both that the correlation between crime and arrests is real and that we can change the former by changing the latter.

Second, this study does not investigate in detail how arrests are made or what happens on patrol when different strategies are employed. This sort of fine-grained analysis would be particularly valuable but it is especially hard to carry out. The day-to-day work of the patrol officer is no more visible to the academic observer than it is to the police administrator. Ideally, we would like systematic knowledge about the circumstances confronting an officer whenever he encounters an opportunity to make a street stop or an arrest, together with detailed information about what the officer did and the result. Obviously, such information would be very difficult to collect.

Unpublished data gathered by researchers from the Police Foundation are suggestive but permit few definite conclusions. For two large cities, all the arrests for major property crimes (robbery, burglary, larceny from the person) and stranger-to-stranger crimes of violence (aggravated assault) were tabulated for a period of time, together with available information on what the officer was doing just before the arrest and what happened to the arrestee after he was brought to the station. In one city, nearly 60 percent of the arrests occurred when an officer answered a call for help. About 60 percent of the arrests were dismissed before being presented to the prosecutor, usually for lack of sufficient evidence. What is most intriguing is that officers differed greatly in the extent to which their arrests survived this review process: of those officers who made 3 or more arrests, all the arrests made by 31 officers went to prosecution, whereas none of those made by 89 other officers was prosecuted. In Washington, D.C., another study found that fewer than 10 percent of the officers made over half the arrests; indeed, nine accounted for more arrests than 450 of their fellows (Forst *et al.*, 1977). What explains these differences and whether we can change the behavior of officers who make few arrests, or whose arrests do not lead to prosecution, is beyond our present knowledge.

What are required to settle these issues are not more statistical analyses of current police practices and crime rates, but carefully designed experiments that measure the effect of innovations in police strategies on crime rates. Though there have been experiments on policing, most have attempted to measure only the effect of a greater or lesser police *presence* on crime, as in the Kansas City patrol experiment (Kelling *et al.*, 1974) and various quasi-experiments in New York City involving the 20th Precinct (Press, 1971) and Transit Authority police in the subway (Chaiken *et al.*, 1974). None of these made a significant effort to monitor what the police actually did. The San Diego field interrogation experiment, which analyzed the effect of street stops on crime and community attitudes, is the closest approximation in the existing literature (Boydstun, 1975; Boydstun *et al.*, 1977). The next step would be to introduce a generally aggressive patrol strategy (street stops, high traffic citation rates, quick response time) in an experimental area of a city and compare the crime rate with that of a control area where the same number of officers follow a passive patrol strategy.

Two studies of police response time contain some evidence that aggressiveness can make a difference. Isaacs (1967), studying the Los Angeles police, and Clawson and Chang (1977), studying the Seattle police, came to similar conclusions: a greater proportion of patrol unit responses to citizen calls resulted in arrests as response time decreased. There are limits, of course, to how much the arrest productivity of police units can be raised by accelerating their response: once a certain minimum has been achieved (roughly three minutes) differences in response time cease to affect arrests. We believe that our studies, together with other research findings, are consistent with the view that police activity can reduce the rates of some serious property crimes, and at least offer a compelling case for experiments designed to test this conclusion and identify the processes by which arrest rates can be increased.

Suppose that statistical studies and experiments do confirm our beliefs. A police chief may still be unable to obtain the additional resources or change his deployment strategy so as to achieve more aggressive patrols and higher arrest ratios. It may turn out that the principal constraints on arrest ratios are community attitudes that the police cannot alter: citizens may be tolerant of minor crimes, reluctant to call the police or offer evidence, unwilling to report suspicious activities or assist officers in pursuit of suspects, or irritated by frequent street stops and high rates of traffic tickets. Police unions may successfully resist efforts to redeploy the patrol force so as to put more units on the street in high-risk periods (such as the evening) or more officers in one-officer patrol cars. For though a recent carefully executed experiment suggests that officers who patrol alone produce as many arrests, and are as safe, as those who patrol with a partner (Boydstun *et al.*, 1977), we are not optimistic that police who believe differently will be persuaded by its evidence.

We cannot offer any advice on how to deal with these problems. Social scientists can, ideally, tell practitioners what will happen *if* some changes are made, but they can rarely give scientific guidance about the political and human processes that might bring about these changes. Indeed, social scientists are likely to ignore or underestimate the unanticipated consequences—both good and bad—of any change, especially since the studies they conduct (like this one) typically consider only two kinds of results—crime rates and police practices.

REFERENCES

Allison, John P. (1972) "Economic Factors and the Rate of Crime," 48 *Land Economics* 193.

Bailey, William C. (no date) "Certainty of Arrest and Crime Rates for Major Felonies." Cleveland State University, mimeo.

Banfield, Edward C., and James Q. Wilson (1963) *City Politics*. Cambridge, Mass.: Harvard University Press.

Block, Michael K. (1972) *An Economic Analysis of Theft with Special Emphasis on Household Decisions under Uncertainty*. Ph.D. Dissertation, Department of Economics, Stanford University.

Boydstun, John E. (1975) *San Diego Field Interrogation: Final Report*. Washington, D.C.: Police Foundation.

Boydstun, John E., Michael E. Sherry, and Nichalos P. Moelten (1977) *Patrol Staffing in San Diego*. Washington, D.C.: Police Foundation.

Chaiken, Jan M. (1977) *What's Known about Deterrent Effects of Police Activity*. Santa Monica, California: Rand Corp. (mimeo).

Chaiken, Jan M., Michael W. Lawless, and Keith A. Stevenson (1974) "The Impact of Police Activity on Subway Crime," 3 *Urban Analysis* 173.

Chapman, Jeffrey I. (1973) *The Impact of Police on Crime and Crime on Police*. Los Angeles: UCLA Institute of Government and Public Affairs (mimeo).

Clawson, Calvin, and Samson K. Chang (1977) "The Relationship of Response Delays and Arrest Rates," 5 *Journal of Police Science and Administration* 53.

Federal Bureau of Investigation (1976) *Crime in the United States, 1975*. Washington, D.C.: Government Printing Office.

Fisher, Franklin M., and Daniel Nagin (1978) "On the

Feasibility of Identifying the Crime Function in a Simultaneous Model of Crime Rates and Sanction Levels," in Alfred Blumstein, Jacqueline Cohen and Daniel Nagin (eds.), *Deterrence and Incapacitation: Estimating the Effects of Criminal Sanctions on Crime Rates*. Washington, D.C.: National Academy of Sciences.

Forst, Brian, Judith Lucianovic, and Sarah J. Cox (1977) *What Happens after Arrest*. Washington, D.C.: Institute for Law and Social Research.

Greenwood, Michael J., and Walter J. Wadycki (1973) "Crime Rates and Public Expenditures for Police Protection: Their Interaction," 31 *Review of Social Economy* 138.

International City Management Association (1971) *The Municipal Yearbook, 1971*. Washington, D.C.: International City Management Association.

Isaacs, Herbert (1967) "A Study of Communications, Crimes and Arrests in a Metropolitan Police Department," in President's Commission on Law Enforcement and Administration of Justice, *Task Force Report: Science and Technology*. Washington, D.C.: Government Printing Office.

Kelling, George L., Tony Pate, Duane Dieckman, and Charles E. Brown (1974) *The Kansas City Preventive Patrol Experiment*. Washington, D.C.: Police Foundation.

Leibenstein, Harvey (1976) *Beyond Economic Man*. Cambridge, Mass.: Harvard University Press.

Logan, Charles H. (1975) "Arrest Rates and Deterrences," 55 *Social Science Quarterly* 376.

McPheters, Lee R., and William B. Stronge (1974) "Law Enforcement Expenditures and Urban Crime," 27 *National Tax Journal* 644.

Nagin, Daniel (1978) "General Deterrence: A Review of the Empirical Evidence," in Alfred Blumstein, Jacqueline Cohen, and Daniel Nagin (eds.), *Deterrence and Incapacitation: Estimating the Effects of Criminal Sanctions on Crime Rates*. Washington, D.C.: National Academy of Sciences.

Phillips, Llad, and Harold L. Votey, Jr. (1972a) "An Economic Analysis of the Deterrent Effect of Law Enforcement on Criminal Activity," 63 *Journal of Criminal Law, Criminology, and Police Science* 330.

——— (1972b) "Police Effectiveness and the Production Function for Law Enforcement," 1 *Journal of Legal Studies* 423.

Pogue, Thomas F. (1972) "Effect of Police Expenditures on Crime Rates: Some Evidence," 3 *Public Finance Quarterly* 14.

Press, S. James (1971) *Some Effects of an Increase in Police Manpower in the 20th Precinct of New York City*. New York: Rand Corp.

Pressman, I. and A. Carol (1971) "Crime as a Diseconomy of Scale," 29 *Review of Social Economy* 227.

Sjoquist, David Lawrence (1973) "Property Crime and Economic Behavior: Some Empirical Results," 63 *American Economic Review* 439.

Skolnick, Jerome H. (1966) *Justice Without Trial*. New York: John Wiley.

Swimmer, Gene (1974) "The Relationship of Police and Crime," 12 *Criminology* 293.

Tittle, Charles R., and Alan R. Rowe (1974) "Certainty of Arrest and Crime Rates: A Further Test of the Deterrence Hypothesis," 52 *Social Forces* 455.

U.S. Department of Commerce (1972a) "Housing Characteristics for States, Cities, and Counties," in I(1) *1970 Census of Housing*. Washington, D.C.: Government Printing Office.

——— (1972b) "Characteristics of the Population," in I (1–52) *1970 Census of Population*. Washington, D.C.: Government Printing Office.

——— (1972c) *Employment Profiles of Selected Low Income Areas* Washington, D.C.: Government Printing Office.

——— (1972d) *Statistical Abstract of the United States*. Washington, D.C.: Government Printing Office.

——— (1973a) "Taxable Property Values and Assessment—Sales Price Ratios," in II(2) *1972 Census of Government*. Washington, D.C.: Government Printing Office.

——— (1973b) *County-City Data Book, 1972*. Washington, D.C.: Government Printing Office.

——— (1977) *Population Estimates and Projections*. Washington, D.C.: Government Printing Office.

U.S. Department of Justice (1974a) *Crime in Eight American Cities*. Washington, D.C.: Government Printing Office.

——— (1974b) *Crime in the Nation's Five Largest Cities*. Washington, D.C.: Government Printing Office.

U.S. Department of Labor (1976) *Area Trends in Employment and Unemployment*. Washington, D.C.: Government Printing Office.

Wilson, James Q. (1968) *Varieties of Police Behavior*. Cambridge, Mass.: Harvard University Press.

Wilson, James Q., and Edward C. Banfield (1964) "Public-Regardingness as a Value Premise in Voters' Behavior," 58 *American Political Science Review* 876.

——— (1971) "Political Ethos Revisited," 65 *American Political Science Review* 1048.

Wilson, James Q., and Barbara Boland (1976) "Crime," in William Gorham and Nathan Glazer (eds.), *The Urban Predicament*. Washington, D.C.: Urban Institute.

Zimring, Franklin (1975) *Dealing with Youth Crime*. Chicago: University of Chicago Law School (mimeo).

The Seven Deadly Sins of Terrorism

Paul Johnson

The wrong approach to terrorism is to see it as one of many symptoms of a deep-seated malaise in our society, part of a pattern of violence that includes juvenile delinquency, rising crime rates, student riots, vandalism, and football hooliganism, that can be attributed to the shadow of the H-bomb, rising divorce rates, inadequate welfare services, and poverty. This analysis usually ends in the meaningless and defeatist conclusion that society itself is to blame: "We are all guilty."

International terrorism is not part of a general human problem. It is a specific and identifiable problem on its own. And because it is specific and identifiable, because it can be isolated from the context that breeds it, it is a remediable problem. That is the first point to get clear.

To say it is remediable is not to underestimate the size and danger of the problem. On the contrary: it is almost impossible to exaggerate the threat that terrorism poses for our civilization. Take some recent examples: suicidal bombing attacks in Lebanon—against the United States marines headquarters and an Israeli military compound—and a time bomb, exploded in a United States Senate chamber hallway (despite a 1,200 member Capitol police force) remind us that the threat is more immediate. And, therefore, in a sense it is more serious than the risk of nuclear war, the population explosion, global pollution, or the exhaustion of the earth's resources. These dangers to our civilization can be, are being, or have been, contained. The threat of terrorism is not being contained. Quite the reverse. It is increasing steadily, and one reason why it constitutes such a grave and growing threat is that very few people in the civilized world—government and parliaments, TV and newspapers, and public generally—take terrorism seriously enough.

SOURCE: *The New Republic*, Sept. 15, 1979, pp. 19–21.

Most people, lacking an adequate knowledge of history, tend to underestimate the fragility of a civilization. They do not appreciate that civilizations fall as well as rise. Civilizations can be, and have been, destroyed by malign forces. In our recoverable history there have been at least three dark ages. One occurred in the third millenium BC and smashed the civilization of the Egyptian Old Kingdom, the culture that built the pyramids. Another occurred toward the end of the second millenium BC and destroyed Mycenaean Greece, Minoan Crete, the Hittite Empire, and much else. We are more familiar with the third, which destroyed the Roman Empire in the West in the fifth century AD. It took Europe 800 years to recover, in terms of organization, technical skills, and living standards, from that disaster. There was a common factor in all these great catastrophes. They occurred when the spread of metals technology and the availability of raw materials enabled the forces of barbarism to equal or surpass the civilized powers in the quality and quantity of their weapons. For in the last resort, civilization stands or falls not by covenants, but by the sword.

Edward Gibbon wrote at the end of his great book, *The Decline and Fall of the Roman Empire*: "The savage nations of the globe are the common enemies of civilized society, and we may well inquire with anxious curiosity whether Europe is still threatened with a repetition of those calamities which formerly oppressed the arms and institutions of Rome." Writing in the 1780s, on the threshold of the industrial revolution, Gibbon thought he could answer his own question with a reasonably confident negative. He rightly estimated the strength of the civilized world to be increasing, and he believed the scientific and rational principles on which that strength was based were becoming more firmly established with every year that passed.

Now, nearly 200 years later, we cannot be so sure. The principles of objective science and human reason, the notion of the rule of law, the paramountcy of politics over force, are everywhere undergoing a fierce and purposeful challenge. The forces of savagery and violence that constitute this challenge are becoming bolder, more numerous, and, above all, better armed. The arms available to terrorists, their skills, and, not least, the organizational techniques with which they deploy these weapons and skills, are all improving at an accelerating rate—a rate much faster than the counter measures available to civilized society.

These menacing improvements in terrorism have been brought about by the international availability of terrorist support, supply, and training services. Terrorism is no longer a purely national phenomenon, which can be destroyed at national level. It is an international offensive—an open and declared war against civilization itself—which can only be defeated by an active alliance of the civilized powers. The impact of terrorism—not merely on individuals, not merely on single nations, but on humanity as a whole—is intrinsically evil. It is so for a number of demonstrable reasons—what I call the seven deadly sins of terrorism.

First, terrorism is the deliberate and cold-blooded exaltation of violence over all forms of political activity. The modern terrorist employs violence not as a necessary evil, but as a desirable form of action. There is a definite intellectual background to the present wave of terrorism. It springs not only from the Leninist and Trotskyist justification of violence, but from the postwar philosophy of violence derived from Nietzsche through Heidegger, and widely popularized by Sartre, his colleagues, and disciples. No one since 1945 has influenced young people more than Sartre and no one has done more to legitimize violence on the left. It was Sartre who adapted the linguistic techniques, common in German philosophy, of identifying certain political arrangements as the equivalent of "violence," thus justifying violent correctives or responses. In 1962 he said: "For me the essential problem is to reject the theory according to which the left ought not to answer violence with violence."

Some of those influenced by Sartre went much further—notably Franz Fanon. His most influential work, *Les Damnés de la Terre*, which has a preface by Sartre, has probably played a bigger part in spreading terrorism in the third world than any other tract. Violence is presented as liberation, a fundamental Sartrean theme. For a black man, writes Sartre in his preface, "to shoot down a European is to kill two birds with one stone, to destroy an oppressor and the man he oppresses at the same time." By killing, the terrorist is born again—free. Fanon preached that violence is a necessary form of social and moral regeneration for the oppressed. "Violence alone," he writes, "violence committed by the people, violence organized and educated by its leaders, makes it possible for the masses to understand social truths and gives the key to them." The notion of "organized and educated violence," conducted by elites, is the formula for terrorism. Fanon goes further: "At the level of individuals, violence is a cleansing force. It frees the oppressed from his inferiority complex and from his despair and inaction."

It is precisely this line of thought, that violence is positive and creative, that enables the terrorists to perform the horrifying acts for which they are responsible. The same argument—almost word for word—was used by Hitler, who repeated endlessly, "Virtue lies in shedding blood." Hence the first deadly sin of terrorism is the moral justification of murder not merely as a means to an end but for its own sake.

The second deadly sin is the deliberate suppression of the moral instincts in man. Terrorist organizers have found that it is not enough to give their recruits intellectual justifications for murder: the instinctive humanity in us all has to be systematically blunted, or else it rejects such sophistry. In the Russia of the 1870s and 1880s, the Neznavhalie terror groups favored what is called "motiveless terror" and regarded any murder as a "progressive action." Once indiscriminate terror is adopted, the group rapidly suffers moral disintegration—indeed the abandonment of any system of moral criteria becomes an essential element in its training. The point is brilliantly made in Dostoevsky's great anti-terrorist novel, *The Possessed*, by the diabolical Stavrogin, who argues that the terror group can be united only by fear and moral depravity: "Persuade four members of the circle to murder a fifth," he says, "on the excuse that he is an informer, and you will at once tie them all up in one knot by the blood you have shed. They will be your slaves." This technique is undoubtedly used by some terror groups today. In these, women recruits are subjected to repeated rapes, or forced to take part in communal acts of sexual depravity, to anesthetize moral reflexes and to prepare them for the gross travestying of their natures that their future "duties" will entail. The theory is based on the assumption that neither man nor woman can be an effective terrorist as long as he or she retains the moral elements of a human personality. The second deadly sin of terrorism is a threat not merely to civilization but to humanity as such.

The third deadly sin is the rejection of politics as the normal means by which communities resolve conflicts. To terrorists, violence is not a political weapon, to be used *in extremis*: it is a substitute for the entire political process. The Arab terrorists, the IRA, the Bader-Meinhof gang, the Red armies or brigades in Japan, Italy, and elsewhere have never shown any desire to engage in the democratic political process. They reject the notion that violence is a technique of last resort, to be adopted only if all other attempts to obtain justice have failed. In doing so, they reject the mainstream of civilized thought, based, like so much of our political grammar, on the social-contract theorists of the 17th century. Hobbes and Locke rightly treated violence as the antithesis of politics, a form of action characteristic of the archaic realm of the state of nature. They saw politics as an attempt to create a tool to avoid barbarism and make civilization possible: politics makes violence not only unnecessary but unnatural to civilized man. Politics is an essential part of the basic machinery of civilization, and in rejecting politics, terrorism seeks to make civilization unworkable.

Terrorism, however, is not neutral in the political battle. It does not, in the long run, tend toward anarchy: it tends toward despotism. The fourth deadly sin of terrorism is that it actively, systematically, and necessarily assists the spread of the totalitarian state. The countries that finance and maintain the international infrastructure of terrorism—that give terrorists refuge and havens, training camps and bases, money, arms, and diplomatic support as a matter of deliberate state policy—are, without exception, despotic states. The governments of all these states rule by military and police power. The notion that terrorism is opposed to the "repressive forces" in society is false—indeed, it is the reverse of the truth. International terrorism, and the various terrorist movements it services, is entirely dependent on the continuing good will and active support of police states.

Which brings us to the fifth deadly sin. International terrorism poses no threat to the totalitarian state. That kind of state can always defend itself by judicial murder, preventive arrest, torture of prisoners and suspects, and complete censorship of terrorist activities. It does not have to abide by the rule of law or any other consideration of humanity or morals. Terrorism can only get a foothold in a state where the executive is under some kind of restraint, legal, democratic, and moral. The shah's regime in Iran was overthrown—and terrorists played a central part in that operation—not because it was ruthless but because it hesitated to be ruthless. The effect of such terrorist victories is not the expansion but the contraction of freedom and law. Iran is now a totalitarian state, where the rule of law no longer exists, and a state from which terrorists can operate safely and with active official assistance. Hence, the fifth deadly sin is that terrorism distinguishes between lawful and totalitarian states in favor of the latter. It can destroy a democracy, as it destroyed Lebanon, but it cannot destroy a totalitarian state.

The base of terrorism is in the totalitarian worlds—that is where its money, training, arms, and protection come from. But at the same time, it can only operate effectively in the freedom of a liberal civilization. Terrorists are the advance scouts of the totalitarian armies. The sixth deadly sin of terrorism is that it exploits the apparatus of freedom in liberal societies, and thereby endangers it.

In meeting the threat of terrorism, a free society must arm itself. But that very process of arming itself against the danger within threatens the freedoms, decencies, and standards that make the society civilized. Terrorism is a direct and continuous threat to all the protective devices of a free society. It is a threat to the freedom of the press and TV. It is a threat to the rule of law, necessarily damaged by emergency legislation and special powers. It is a threat to *habeas corpus*, to the process of humanizing the legal code and civilizing our prisons. It is a threat to any system to curb excesses by the police or prison authorities or any other restraining force in society.

Yet the seventh deadly sin of terrorism operates, paradoxically, in the reverse direction. A free society that reacts to terrorism by invoking authoritarian methods necessarily damages itself. But an even greater danger—and a much more common one today—is that free societies, in their anxiety to avoid authoritarian excesses, *fail* to arm themselves against the terrorist threat, and so abdicate their responsibility to uphold the law. The terrorists succeed when they provoke oppression, but they triumph when they are met with appeasement. The seventh and deadliest sin of terrorism is that it saps the will of a civilized society to defend itself. We have seen it happen. We find governments negotiating with terrorists—negotiations aimed not at destroying or disarming the terrorists, for such negotiations may sometimes be necessary, but negotiations whose natural and inevitable result is to concede part of the terrorists' demands. We find goverments providing ransom money to terrorists, or permitting private individuals to provide ransom money, even assisting in the process whereby such funds reach terrorist hands. We find governments releasing convicted criminals in response to terrorist demands; according terrorists the status, rights, and advantages, and above all the legitimacy, of negotiating partners. We find governments conceding to terrorist convicts the official and privileged status of political prisoners, always a major blunder and a surrender. We find governments surrendering to demands—an invariable part of terrorist strategy—for official inquiries, or international investigations, into alleged ill-treatment of terrorist suspects, or convicts. We find newspapers and TV networks —often, indeed, state TV networks—placing democratic governments and the terrorists on a level of moral equality. We find governments failing, time and again, in their duty to persuade the public that terrorists are not misguided politicians. They are criminals. They are extraordinary criminals, indeed, in that they pose a threat not merely to the individuals they murder without compunction but to the whole fabric of society, but criminals just the same.

In short, the seventh and deadliest sin of terrorism is its attempt to induce civilization to commit suicide.

7

POLICE AND THE LEGAL SYSTEM

Our country's founders with great relief had overcome a foreign oppressor. Consequently, they were most diligent in avoiding a repressive domestic police system that might replicate their unfortunate colonial experience. They rejected the concept of a national police force, reposing their confidence in the individual states to establish appropriate police and peace-keeping systems. The original conceptualizations of our country's founders have come down to us almost intact. And the legal system in America has been the principal instrument in the control of the police.

Although police power and authority are defined by law and the strictures imposed by appellate courts, police organizations have been highly successful in gaining judicial support for an increasing variety of aggressive police activities. Given the widespread fear of crime, courts have tended to support those police practices that are thought to prevent and control crime. In the process, police field behavior that heretofore had been tactics and strategies of informal, de facto police power and authority have been formally recognized by the courts as constituting proper police conduct. Thus, the circumstances under which police searches can take place have been greatly expanded, the stopping and questioning of suspicious persons, warrantless searches, the use of informants, the employment of "sting" operations, monitoring of telephone conversations, the seizure of evidence—which may include body fluids—have all been recognized by the appellate courts as legitimate police conduct under the appropriate circumstances.

Historically, the police occupational role was peace-keeping—dealing with derelicts, drunkenness, exuberant youths, marauding animals, or other socially disruptive behavior. However, early in this century the police role evolved to that of crime control and its accompanying emphasis on solving crimes, making arrests, and preparing cases for court adjudication. As the public fear of crime mounted in the 1960s and 1970s, the appellate courts tended to reach an accommodation with the police in terms of judicial ratification of police decision making that had the effect of diluting strict standards of "probable cause." In addition, for example, recent appellate decisions have begun to erode the Exclusionary Rule, which bars the introduction of illegally seized evidence, and the requirements of a *Miranda* warning in a number of instances where it appeared that invoking those rules would impact adversely on police efficiency in dealing with crime. As the composition of the U.S. Supreme Court changes in the near future due to the advanced age of a majority of its members, it is likely there will be even greater support and sympathy for the police world-view. A more sympathetic Supreme Court may deflect the police from a service-oriented role to retrogress to an older, cruder style of policing that was bereft of the niceties of legalism and due process of law.

In this section we have also included material about the civil, criminal, and administrative liabilities of police officers, an area that merits greater attention in the police literature. Further, because in large measure judicial oversight and decision making with regard to the police are grounded in the intellectual rationale of the often asserted police role in the control and deterrence of crime, a systematic review of this issue concludes that such a police role may be problematic.

Liberty and Justice: Fair Play and Fair Trial

Leo Pfeffer

FROM MAGNA CARTA TO BILL OF RIGHTS

The First Amendment . . . concerns laws that government in our democracy may not make: laws respecting an establishment of religion or prohibiting its free exercise, or abridging freedom of speech or of the press or of the right of the people peaceably to assemble and to petition for a redress of grievances. The other Amendments in the Bill of Rights deal mainly with laying down the rules of fair play in accordance with which laws that may constitutionally be made shall be enforced. Lawyers, as we have seen, call the rights secured by the First Amendment "substantive," those secured by the other Amendments "procedural."

Mention of procedures and methods of enforcing laws gives rise to images of lawyers quibbling over technicalities, throwing rules of pleading and evidence at each other—rules generally unintelligible to the nonlawyer—and apparently doing everything to avoid coming to grips with the simple question to be decided: Is the accused guilty or innocent of the crime with which he is charged? Particularly when the accused is charged with an especially heinous crime, such as committing a violent sex offense against a child . . . is there likely to be popular impatience with procedural technicalities.

The popular image is false, and the popular impatience lacks understanding. Neither appreciates the tremendous stake all Americans have in making sure that the accused rapist . . . receives the full protection of all procedural requirements. It was such impatience with technicalities and procedures that for centuries justified the use of torture to exact a speedy confession from an accused person who everyone well knew was guilty—so why waste time on long-drawn-out trials? As Justice Frankfurter had sagely noted, the "history of liberty has largely been the history of observance of procedural safeguards."

Nor is the story of how these procedural safeguards developed a dull, uninteresting chronicle. On the contrary, it is one of the most fascinating chapters in human history. The temptation is great to recount it in detail here, but to accord it even minimal justice would require a volume at least as large as this book, whose purpose, after all, is to portray the contemporary scene. We must therefore content ourselves here with little more than a bare mention of the highlights of the struggle.

That part of the story which concerns procedural safeguards is generally considered to have begun at Runnymede on the Thames in 1215, when the rebellious barons and clergy of England, under the leadership of Stephen Langton, Archbishop of Canterbury, exacted the Magna Carta—the great Charter—from King John. But the story goes back long before that. The Mosaic code imposed a number of procedural safeguards, such as public trial and the right of confrontation. Some of these were even more stringent than those imposed under our present constitutional system; Moses required at least two eyewitnesses for conviction in any capital case; our Constitution imposes this requirement only in trials for treason.

SOURCE: *The Liberties of an American* (Boston: Beacon Press, 1963). Reprinted by permission of the Beacon Press,

The Romans too enjoyed certain procedural safeguards now included among the liberties of Americans. According to the Acts of the Apostles, Porcius Festus, Roman procurator of Judea, deemed it "unreasonable to send a prisoner and not withal to signify the crimes laid against him." "It is not," Festus reported, "the manner of the Romans to deliver any man to die, before that he which is accused have the accusers face to face, and have license to answer for himself concerning the crime laid against him."

Thus, when King John consented to the thirty-ninth article of the Magna Carta—that "No freeman shall be taken, or imprisoned, outlawed, or exiled, or in any way harmed, nor will we go upon or send upon him, save by the lawful judgment of his peers or by the law of the land"—he was establishing no new precedent. This article itself was apparently taken from an earlier Continental source and reflected usages well established in England when the Great Charter was given.

The importance of the Charter in the history of the struggle for civil liberties is not primarily intrinsic. The Charter had its greatness thrust upon it; it was not born great. Indeed it was to some extent a reactionary instrument. Its purpose was to insure feudal rights and protect baronial privileges against royal encroachment. Little in the seventy articles protected the vast majority of Englishmen, the villeins and the tenants. The intended beneficiaries of Article 39 and Article 40 ("To none will we sell, to none deny or delay right or justice") were not the common people but the noblemen.

Even to the limited extent that it sought to regulate governmental relations the Charter was largely ineffectual. No sooner had the barons returned to their castles than John repudiated it as having been obtained under duress. Pope Innocent III, with whom John had made his peace, sided with John as against the Pope's own appointee Langton, and released John from its observance. The committee of barons set up to insure the king's adherence to the Charter never had an opportunity to function, since civil war broke out again shortly after the Charter was granted.

To infer, nevertheless, that the Charter was a completely reactionary document and without intrinsic significance in the struggle for democratic liberties would be unfair and inaccurate. It did, for the first time in England, give written, constitutional form to libertarian advances that had been achieved. It recognized the rightful existence of representatives of those protected, with authority to insure observance of the guarantees. It constituted an acknowledgement by a divinely appointed monarch that he could be required to judge not according to his own will but according to "the law of the land." Repudiated by John, the Charter was reissued after his death in the name of his young son—although with some of its libertarian provisions conspicuously omitted. In 1354 its protection, limited as it may have been, was extended by statute to every man "of what estate or condition that he be," a statute that first used the modern equivalent for "law of the land" in assuring that no man should be harmed in any way except by "due process of law."

But the real importance of the Charter is extrinsic to it. Its greatness was ascribed to it by succeeding generations, and therein lies its real significance. For the Charter, whether as the result of bad historical research, romanticism, wishful thinking, or any other reason, in time came to be looked upon as truly the Charter of liberties of free Englishmen. Through the centuries Englishmen in trouble with the authorities invoked the Charter as guarantor of rights—such as trial by jury and habeas corpus—whose relationship with it was, if not fanciful, then certainly remote and tenuous. English public opinion was quick to rally around any claim for liberty made in the name of the Charter. By the time Madison and his colleagues added the Bill of Rights to the American Constitution, the Charter had acquired a gloss of centuries that made of it a world of liberties which the barons at Runnymede never dreamed of, and which would have shocked and terrified them if they had.

The one figure most responsible for this development was Sir Edward Coke, one of England's greatest jurists, whose writing and thinking were known to every American lawyer of the eighteenth century and profoundly influenced American constitutional development. As Chief Justice of the Common Pleas, Coke became the champion of Parliament against James I and Charles I, attacking the royal prerogative and setting the precedent for judicial supremacy in the United States by declaring that royal decrees contrary to law were null and void. His arguments and reasoning were based upon history as he saw it and upon historical documents such as the Magna Carta as he interpreted them. Although neither his history nor his historical interpretations were entirely accurate; his reasoning was brilliant and his arguments impressive—in no small measure because they harmonized so well with the growing libertarian spirit of seventeenth-century England and with the democratic libertarianism of eighteenth-century America. Coke's *Institutes*, published in 1628, contained a commentary upon the Magna Carta in which he showed to the satisfaction of the American colonists the identity in meaning between the Charter's "law of the land" and the prevalent "due process of law" and that the purpose of these provisions was to protect the citizen from governmental oppression. Coke it was also who, in the same year, was probably chief draftsman of the Petition of Right, sent by Parliament to Charles I, which reaffirmed the principle of habeas corpus by asserting that no person might be imprisoned without cause shown, and declared that martial law might not be employed in time of peace.

The only other figure we can mention in this brief chronicle is the radical Puritan pamphleteer, John Lilburne—"Freeborn John"—as obnoxious a character as one is likely to come across in history. (How much civilization owes to obnoxious characters!) It was Lilburne who contributed much to the abolition in 1641 of the Star Chamber, that secret tribunal of judges, clergy, lawyers, and laymen that for a century and a half acted as the Crown's instrument for tyranny and oppression. The Star Chamber's proceedings were totally devoid of the procedural safeguards that later became the liberties of Americans. One who incurred the displeasure of the Crown could be arrested in secret and tried in secret. He had no right to be informed of the charges leveled against him nor to face or examine his accusers. He could be tortured to exact a confession. If by any chance the jury should acquit him, the members of the jury could themselves be fined and imprisoned. If he was convicted, his nose could be slit, his ears cut off, his tongue drilled, and his cheeks branded. Whipping, pillory, and staggering fines were imposed. The Star Chamber could (and did) impose any penalty short of death.

Lilburne's troubles began in 1637, when he was barely twenty. Accused of importing unlicensed Puritan books from Holland, he was brought before the Star Chamber and ordered to take the usual inquisitorial oath. This he refused to do, claiming the right not to incriminate himself. For this he was sentenced to be publicly whipped and placed in the pillory. While this was going on he exhorted his hearers to resist the tyranny of the bishops and threw among them copies of the condemned books. The Star Chamber ordered him gagged and placed in solitary confinement, and immediately decreed that persons thereafter sentenced to whipping or pillory be searched before the sentence was carried out.

The Long Parliament, which abolished the Star Chamber, voted Lilburne £300 reparation (little of which was ever paid), declaring that his punishment had been "illegal and most unjust, against the liberty of the subject, and the law of the land and Magna Carta." But Lilburne—of whom it was said that "if the world was emptied of all but John Lilburne, Lilburne would quarrel with John and John with Lilburne"—soon found himself at odds with Oliver Cromwell and his Puritan Commonwealth. A left-wing Puritan himself, he nevertheless protested the illegal court that condemned Charles I to death. For this he was tried for treason and, though acquitted, later banished. Returning to England, he was again tried and, though again acquitted, placed in confinement as a dangerous character. Indeed, most of his adult life was spent shuttling between the prison walls and the courtroom chamber. But throughout his many trials, he continually and loudly asserted his procedural rights (such as the privilege against self-incrimination, the right to be informed of the crime charged against him, assistance of counsel, and public trial) and by doing so helped secure them for succeeding generations of Englishmen and Americans.

The long but ultimately successful struggle for procedural safeguards in criminal proceedings was an integral part of the long and ultimately successful struggle for constitutional democracy. These procedural safeguards rest upon two underlying assumptions of democracy, the integrity of the individual and government by law rather than men.

When Sir Walter Raleigh was tried for treason in 1603 he claimed that he was entitled to acquittal unless two eyewitnesses testified against him. To this one of the judges replied: ". . . many horse stealers may escape if they may not be condemned without witnesses." Both before that time and since then, every assertion by an accused of the benefits of a procedural safeguard not established by ancient precedent—from the assertion of the right not to be tortured into confessing, to an accused Communist's claim of the right to confront secret informers—has been met with the same objection: that, if it is granted, many guilty persons may escape. The fact that, notwithstanding this objection, procedural safeguards have developed and have become part of our legal system manifests the deliberate judgment of the people that the integrity of the individual in a democracy is so valuable that it is more important that he be accorded a fair trial than that every culprit be punished.

It is clear that observance of the procedural safeguards designed to insure a fair trial assumes the supremacy of laws over the arbitrary will of men. Under the Anglo-American legal system a criminal case is entitled "*The King* v. *Jones*," or "*State* v. *Jones*"; and it is prosecuted in exactly that way—a contest between the government and the individual. But, with all its power, the government, whether king or state, must abide by the rules of the game. When Edward Coke contested the claimed right of James I to remove from the law courts and to judge for himself whatever cases he wished, the king replied that, if Coke was correct, then the king was "under the law, which was treason to affirm." But Coke stood his ground and replied that the king "ought not be under men but under God and the law." The inclusion in the Bill of Rights of the procedural safeguards deemed necessary to insure fair play for accused Americans constituted a recognition that in our democracy the state, like the king, is not above the law.

DUE PROCESS—FEDERAL AND STATE

By the time the colonies declared their independence of the king, the struggle for fair play in criminal trials had long been won in England. Indeed, one grievance against the king listed in the Declaration of Independence was that he had deprived the colonists of a number of important elements of fair play in criminal cases, such as trial by jury and trial at the place of commission of the charged offense. The concept of fair trial had been slow in developing and had come about by the gradual and erratic accretions of seemingly unrelated procedural safeguards. When, therefore, the Constitution and the Bill of Rights were framed here, the framers included specifically the more important components of fair trial that had by that time become established as liberties of Englishmen and Americans. These were:

1. Privilege of habeas corpus (Constitution, Art. I, sec. 9)
2. No bills of attainder (Art. I, sec. 9,10)
3. No ex post facto laws (Art. I, sec. 9,10)
4. Trial by jury (Art. III, sec. 2; Amendment 6)
5. No unreasonable searches and seizures (Amend. 4)
6. Right to indictment by grand jury and to be informed of crime charged (Amend. 5,6)
7. No double jeopardy (Amend. 5)
8. No compulsory self-incrimination (Amend. 5)
9. Speedy and public trial at place of crime (Amend. 6)
10. Confrontation of witnesses (Amend. 6)
11. Compulsory process for defense witnesses (Amend. 6)
12. Right to counsel (Amend. 6)
13. Reasonable bail (Amend. 8)
14. No cruel and unusual punishment (Amend. 8)

These, of course, are not all the components of fair play in criminal proceedings. For example, while Amendment 6 guarantees trial by an "impartial jury," there is no specific guarantee that the *judge* be impartial. Nor is there any express abolition of the judge's power, which had survived to Freeborn John's day, of fining a jury for bringing in a verdict with which he disagreed. Nor is there anything expressly prohibiting a State from rushing an accused to trial immediately after indictment without affording him a reasonable time in which to prepare his defense. These unmentioned procedural safeguards are surely important elements of fair trial.

To provide for unmentioned established safeguards and perhaps for those not yet established, Madison and his colleagues who drafted this Bill of Rights included an omnibus guarantee. No person, the Fifth Amendment states, shall "be deprived of life, liberty or property without due process of law." The phrase "due process of law" is much broader than its Magna Carta ancestor "law of the land," which guaranteed only that no person should be proceeded against except for violation of an existing law. "Due process of law" includes this but goes much further; it guarantees that, when a person is proceeded against for violation of a law, the government will act fairly and will accord him all the procedural safeguards comprising fair play and within the concept of ordered liberty. The short phrase "due process of law" thus leaves unlimited room for the evolution and expansion of the Anglo-American concept of fair play.

Before the Civil War the requirements of fair play were applicable only to the Federal government. The only exception was the ban on bills of attainder and ex post facto laws, which Article I, Section 10, of the Constitution made applicable to the States as well as to Congress. The Fourteenth Amendment, enacted after the Civil War to secure the rights of Americans against infringement by the States, incorporated the "due process" clause but did not expressly declare that the specific procedural safeguards set forth in the Bill of Rights should be applicable to the States. . . . Justices Black and Douglas believed that this was the purpose of the Amendment, but the majority of the Supreme Court has never accepted this view. The position of the Court is that the "due process" clause of the Fourteenth Amendment requires the States to accord defendants only such procedural safeguards as are at the particular time considered essential components of ordered liberty or fair play.

In most cases this interpretation will not result in any practical difference between State and Federal procedures. Thus, a "third degree" confession is barred to the States as outside the limits of fair play, and barred to the Federal government by the express ban on compulsory self-incrimination. On the other hand, there are many instances where permissible State procedures may differ from those in the Federal courts.

Since the Federal government is also subject to the "due process" clause, which in the Fifth Amendment means all that it means in the Fourteenth, the net result is that the States have substantially more leeway than the Federal government in the conduct of criminal proceedings, and correspondingly an accused American's procedural liberties are less comprehensive in the State courts than in the Federal courts. To a substantial degree the practical difference is lessened by the fact that most State constitutions themselves contain many of the specific guarantees of the Bill of Rights, and the State courts generally interpret these in the same way that the Supreme Court interprets those in the Bill of Rights.

. . . It is only because of historical accident that the procedural safeguards developed in criminal proceedings; there is nothing inherent in criminal proceedings that makes procedural safeguards relevant only there. Procedural safeguards evolved in criminal proceedings as part—and only part—of the development of constitutional democracy out of despotism and tyranny. Democracy differs from despotism in that in the former the government deals fairly with the people in all its relations with them—not in a selected few. A government that adheres to fair play only part of the time is only a part-time democracy.

United States, Petitioner *v.* Albert Ross, Jr.
456 U.S. 798 (1982)

Supreme Court of the United States

Justice Stevens delivered the opinion of the Court.

In *Carroll v. United States*, 267 U.S. 132, the Court held that a warrantless search of an automobile stopped by police officers who had probable cause to believe the vehicle contained contraband was not unreasonable within the meaning of the Fourth Amendment. The Court in *Carroll* did not explicitly address the scope of the search that is permissible. In this case, we consider the extent to which police officers—who have legitimately stopped an automobile and who have probable cause to believe that contraband is concealed somewhere within it—may conduct a probing search of compartments and containers within the vehicle whose contents are not in plain view. We hold that they may conduct a search of the vehicle that is as thorough as a magistrate could authorize in a warrant "particularly describing the place to be searched."[1]

I

In the evening of November 27, 1978, an informant who had previously proved to be reliable telephoned Detective Marcum of the District of Columbia Police Department and told him that an individual known as "Bandit" was selling narcotics kept in the trunk of a car parked at 439 Ridge Street. The informant stated that he had just observed "Bandit" complete a sale and that "Bandit" had told him that additional narcotics were in the trunk. The informant gave Marcum a detailed description of "Bandit" and stated that the car was a "purplish maroon" Chevrolet Malibu with District of Columbia license plates.

Accompanied by Detective Cassidy and Sergeant Gonzales, Marcum immediately drove to the area and found a maroon Malibu parked in front of 439 Ridge Street. A license check disclosed that the car was reg-

[1] "The right of the people to be secure in their persons, houses, papers, and effects, against unreasonable searches and seizures, shall not be violated, and no warrants shall issue, but upon probable cause, supported by Oath or affirmation, and particularly describing the place to be searched, and the persons or things to be seized." U.S. Const., Amdt. 4.

istered to Albert Ross; a computer check on Ross revealed that he fit the informant's description and used the alias "Bandit." In two passes through the neighborhood the officers did not observe anyone matching the informant's description. To avoid alerting persons on the street, they left the area.

The officers returned five minutes later and observed the maroon Malibu turning off Ridge Street onto Fourth Street. They pulled alongside the Malibu, noticed that the driver matched the informant's description, and stopped the car. Marcum and Cassidy told the driver—later identified as Albert Ross, the respondent in this action—to get out of the vehicle. While they searched Ross, Sergeant Gonzales discovered a bullet on the car's front seat. He searched the interior of the car and found a pistol in the glove compartment. Ross then was arrested and handcuffed. Detective Cassidy took Ross' keys and opened the trunk, where he found a closed brown paper bag. He opened the bag and discovered a number of glassine bags containing a white powder. Cassidy replaced the bag, closed the trunk, and drove the car to Headquarters.

At the police station Cassidy thoroughly searched the car. In addition to the "lunch-type" brown paper bag, Cassidy found in the trunk a zippered red leather pouch. He unzipped the pouch and discovered $3,200 in cash. The police laboratory later determined that the powder in the paper bag was heroin. No warrant was obtained.

Ross was charged with possession of heroin with intent to distribute, in violation of 21 U. S. C. §841(a). Prior to trial, he moved to suppress the heroin found in the paper bag and the currency found in the leather pouch. After an evidentiary hearing, the District Court denied the motion to suppress. The heroin and currency were introduced in evidence at trial and Ross was convicted.

A three-judge panel of the Court of Appeals reversed the conviction. It held that the police had probable cause to stop and search Ross' car and that, under *Carroll* v. *United States, supra*, and *Chambers* v. *Maroney*, 399 U. S. 42, the officers lawfully could search the automobile—including its trunk—without a warrant. The court considered separately, however, the warrantless search of the two containers found in the trunk. On the basis of *Arkansas* v. *Sanders*, 442 U. S. 753, the court concluded that the constitutionality of a warrantless search of a container found in an automobile depends on whether the owner possesses a reasonable expectation of privacy in its contents. Applying that test, the court held that the warrantless search of the paper bag was valid but the search of the leather pouch was not. The court remanded for a new trial at which the items taken from the paper bag, but not those from the leather pouch, could be admitted.

The entire Court of Appeals then voted to rehear the case en banc. A majority of the court rejected the panel's conclusion that a distinction of constitutional significance existed between the two containers found in respondent's trunk; it held that the police should not have opened either container without first obtaining a warrant. The court reasoned:

> No specific, well-delineated exception called to our attention permits the police to dispense with a warrant to open and search "unworthy" containers. Moreover, we believe that a rule under which the validity of a warrantless search would turn on judgments about the durability of a container would impose an unreasonable and unmanageable burden on police and courts. For these reasons, and because the Fourth Amendment protects all persons, not just those with the resources or fastidiousness to place their effects in containers that decision-makers would rank in the luggage line, we hold that the Fourth Amendment warrant requirement forbids the warrantless opening of a closed, opaque paper bag to the same extent that it forbids the warrantless opening of a small unlocked suitcase or a zippered leather pouch.

. . . , since its earliest days Congress had recognized the impracticability of securing a warrant in cases involving the transportation of contraband goods. . . It is this impracticability, viewed in historical perspective, that provided the basis for the *Carroll* decision. Given the nature of an automobile in transit, the Court recognized that an immediate intrusion is necessary if police officers are to secure the illicit substance. In this class of cases, the Court held that a warrantless search of an automobile is not unreasonable . . .

. . . In short, the exception to the warrant requirement established in *Carroll*—the scope of which we consider in this case—applies only to searches of vehicles that are supported by probable cause. In this class of cases, a search is not unreasonable if based on facts that would justify the issuance of a warrant, even though a warrant has not actually been obtained.

. . . A lawful search of fixed premises generally extends to the entire area in which the object of the search may be found and is not limited by the possibility that separate acts of entry or opening may be required to complete the search . . . Thus, a warrant that authorizes an officer to search a home for illegal weapons also provides authority to open closets, chests, drawers, and containers in which the weapon might be found. A warrant to open a footlocker to search for marijuana would also authorize the opening of packages found inside. A warrant to search a vehicle would support a search of every part of the vehicle that might contain the object of the search. When a legitimate search is under way, and when its purpose and its limits have been precisely defined, nice distinctions between closets, drawers, and containers, in the case of a home, or between glove compartments, upholstered seats, trunks, and wrapped packages, in the case of a vehicle, must give way to the interest in the prompt and efficient completion of the task at hand.

. . . an individual's expectation of privacy in a vehicle and its contents may not survive if probable cause is given to believe that the vehicle is transporting contraband. Certainly the privacy interests in a car's trunk or glove compartment may be no less than those in a movable container. An individual undoubtedly has a significant interest that the upholstery of his automobile will not be ripped or a hidden compartment within it opened. These interests must yield to the authority of a search, however, which—in light of *Carroll*—does not itself require the prior approval of a magistrate. The scope of a warrantless search based on probable cause is no narrower—and no broader—than the scope of a search authorized by a warrant supported by probable cause. Only the prior approval of the magistrate is waived; the search otherwise is as the magistrate could authorize.

The scope of a warrantless search of an automobile thus is not defined by the nature of the container in which the contraband is secreted. Rather, it is defined by the object of the search and the places in which there is probable cause to believe that it may be found.

We hold. . . . If probable cause justifies the search of a lawfully stopped vehicle, it justifies the search of every part of the vehicle and its contents that may conceal the object of the search.

The judgment of the Court of Appeals is reversed. The case is remanded for further proceedings consistent with this opinion.

It is so ordered.

Justice Marshall, with whom Justice Brennan joins, dissenting.

The majority today not only repeals all realistic limits on warrantless automobile searches, it repeals the Fourth Amendment warrant requirement itself. By equating a police officer's estimation of probable cause with a magistrate's, the Court utterly disregards the value of a neutral and detached magistrate. For as we recently, and unanimously, reaffirmed:

> The warrant traditionally has represented an independent assurance that a search and arrest will not proceed without probable cause to believe that a crime has been committed and that the person or place named in the warrant is involved in the crime. Thus, an issuing magistrate must meet two tests. He must be neutral and detached, and he must be capable of determining whether probable cause exists for the requested arrest or search. This Court long has insisted that inferences of probable cause be drawn by "a neutral and detached magistrate instead of being judged by the officer engaged in the often competitive enterprise of ferreting out crime." *Shadwick* v. *City of Tampa*, 407 U. S. 345, 350 (1972), citing *Johnson* v. *United States*, 333 U. S. 10, 13–14 (1948).

A police officer on the beat hardly satisfies these standards. In adopting today's new rule, the majority opinion shows contempt for these Fourth Amendment values, ignores this Court's precedents, is internally inconsistent, and produces anomalous and unjust consequences. I therefore dissent.

I

According to the majority, whenever police have probable cause to believe that contraband may be found within an automobile that they have stopped on the highway, they may search not only the automobile but also any container found inside it, without obtaining a warrant. The scope of the search, we are told, is as broad as a magistrate could authorize in a warrant to search the automobile. The majority makes little attempt to justify this rule in terms of recognized Fourth Amendment values. The Court simply ignores the critical function that a magistrate serves. And although the Court purports to rely on the mobility of an automobile and the impracticability of obtaining a warrant, it never explains why these concerns permit the warrantless search of a *container*, which can easily be seized and immobilized while police are obtaining a warrant.

The new rule adopted by the Court today is completely incompatible with established Fourth Amendment principles, and takes a first step toward an unprecedented "probable cause" exception to the warrant requirement. In my view, under accepted standards, the warrantless search of the container in this case clearly violates the Fourth Amendment.

. . . The warrant requirement is crucial to protecting Fourth Amendment rights because of the importance of having the probable cause determination made in the first instance by a neutral and detached magistrate. Time and again, we have emphasized that the warrant requirement provides a number of protections that a post-hoc judicial evaluation of a policeman's probable cause does not.

The requirement of prior review by a detached and neutral magistrate limits the concentration of power held by executive officers over the individual, and prevents some overbroad or unjustified searches from occurring at all.

. . . Furthermore, even if a magistrate would have authorized the search that the police conducted, the interposition of a magistrate's neutral judgment reassures the public that the orderly process of law has been respected:

> The point of the Fourth Amendment, which often is not grasped by zealous officers, is not that it denies law enforcement the support of the usual inferences which reasonable men draw from evidence. Its protection consists in requiring that those inferences be drawn by "a neutral and detached magistrate instead of being judged by the officer engaged in the often competitive enterprise of ferreting out crime." *Johnson* v. *United States*, 333 U. S. 10, 13–14 (1948).

. . . The majority's rule masks the startling assumption that a policeman's determination of probable cause is the functional equivalent of the determination of a neutral and detached magistrate. This assumption ignores a major premise of the warrant requirement—the importance of having a neutral and detached magistrate determine whether probable cause exists. The majority's explanation that the scope of the warrantless automobile search will be "limited" to what a magistrate could authorize is thus inconsistent with our cases, which firmly establish that an on-the-spot determination of probable cause is *never* the same as a decision by a neutral and detached magistrate.

. . . The only convincing explanation I discern for the majority's broad rule is expediency: it assists police in conducting automobile searches, ensuring that the private containers into which criminal suspects often place goods will no longer be a Fourth Amendment shield. . . .

. . . This case will have profound implications for the privacy of citizens traveling in automobiles, as the Court well understands. "For countless vehicles are stopped on highways and public streets every day and our cases demonstrate that it is not uncommon for police officers to have probable cause to believe that contraband may be found in a stopped vehicle." . . . A closed paper bag, a tool box, a knapsack, a suitcase, and an attache case can alike be searched without the protection of the judgment of a neutral magistrate, based only on the rarely disturbed decision of a police officer that he has probable cause to search for contraband in the vehicle. The Court derives satisfaction from the fact that its rule does not exalt the rights of the wealthy over the rights of the poor. . . . A rule so broad that all citizens lose vital Fourth Amendment protection is no cause for celebration.

I dissent.

The Supreme Court and the Police: Constitutional Searches and Seizures

David N. Atkinson

I. INTRODUCTION

The language of the Fourth Amendment invites controversy. It consists of only one sentence: "The right of the people to be secure in their persons, houses, papers, and effects, against unreasonable searches and seizures, shall not be violated, and no Warrants shall issue, but upon probable cause, supported by Oath or affirmation, and particularly describing the place to be searched, and the persons or things to be seized." The Amendment seems, as a matter of first impression, to be uncomplicated. It reflects a preference to be "left alone," it emphasizes the importance the colonists attached to their privacy, and it confirms the importance the early common law attached to a person's home.

This article was written expressly for inclusion in this edition.

But a closer reading of the Amendment discloses numerous limitations and ambiguities. For instance, the scope of the right to search is limited to only "persons, houses, papers, and effects" and only "persons and things" may be seized. The words "effects" and "things" become important because, if the Amendment is to be applicable to new situations (like automobiles and intangibles like wiretaps), it is because of an inclusive interpretation given "effects" and "things."

Second, only "unreasonable searches and seizures" are prohibited by the Amendment. Consequently, if the search and seizure is conducted in a reasonable manner by the police, there is no constitutional difficulty. But who determines what is reasonable? Should the Supreme Court Justices make this determination? Or should they exercise deference to the Congress or the state legislatures and then withdraw from such controversies? The language of the Amendment offers no guide.

A third ambiguity arises from the impression given by the Amendment that all searches and seizures without warrant are unreasonable and therefore prohibited. But should reasonableness be equated with warrants? There is no express prohibition of warrantless searches and seizures, even though warrants are clearly favored by the Amendment.

Fourth, "probable cause" is required to support a warrant, but the Amendment contains no definition of probable cause. Is suspicion an equivalent term? Or are there circumstances in which the terms mean roughly the same thing?

A fifth source of litigation has concerned the permissible scope of the search. The Amendment states only that the warrant shall "particularly" describe the place of the search and the persons or things to be seized. How exact must this description be? And how much latitude do the police have when they act without warrants?

And finally, what exactly does the Amendment protect? Property interests? Personal expectations of privacy? Societal expectations of privacy?

These are some of the problems suggested by the language of the Amendment. They have been answered and reanswered many times by the Supreme Court, but each time in a slightly different way.[1] This means that the search and seizure law is subject to continuous modification, to an even greater degree than in most other areas of constitutional law. It means also that any changes in Court personnel are likely to be felt immediately because of the extent of disagreement in recent cases.

II. SEARCH OF PERSONS

A search of the person is considered reasonable if conducted by the police in accordance with a warrant issued for probable cause. Probable cause has been defined, however inexactly, by the Court:

> Under the Fourth Amendment, an officer may not properly issue a warrant to search a private dwelling unless he can find probable cause therefore from facts or circumstances presented to him under oath or affirmation. Mere affirmance of belief or suspicion is not enough.[2]

In effect, probable cause requires that the police will present facts, before a neutral magistrate, that will satisfy a reasonable, prudent person that illegal activity has occurred. The police are most likely to be sustained when acting under the authority of a warrant.

There are, however, circumstances in which the police are permitted to search in the absence of a warrant. For example, a person may be searched without warrant at the time of a valid arrest. The usual reasons given for the warrant exception are that they are needed to protect the police from concealed weapons, to protect the arrestee from self-inflicted injury or escape, and to prevent the destruction of evidence.

Two areas of recent interest involving warrantless searches of the person are strip searches (which have been curtailed by most police departments as a result of public indignation and many lawsuits) and stop and frisk laws. The police have had the authority to stop and frisk persons who act suspiciously since 1968, when the Court adopted the view that police safety justified a departure from the probable cause standard.[3] Chief Justice Earl Warren's opinion for the Court emphasized the legitimate law enforcement interest at issue and the narrowness of the exception. The police were strictly limited to a weapons search.

Recent cases have tended to enlarge state authority. A Detroit stop and identify ordinance which was later declared unconstitutional nonetheless was held to justify a search which revealed the suspect possessed illegal drugs.[4] Chief Justice Warren Burger, speaking for the Court, was persuaded that the police had probable cause to make the arrest under the ordinance that, at the time, was presumed valid, even though the statute required only "reasonable cause" for a citizen to be stopped by the police.

Justice Harry Blackmun acknowledged the risk that police might use a stop and identify ordinance as an excuse to arrest persons for improper identification and then subject them to a thorough search for contraband, thereby circumventing the probable cause requirement. He could find, however, no evidence the Detroit police had used the ordinance as a pretext for avoiding probable cause.

In dissent, Justice William Brennan diverted attention from the good faith of the police and the validity of the ordinance at the time of the search. The question, he contended, was not whether the state authorized the search, nor whether the police acted reasonably, but whether the search was reasonable under the Fourth Amendment. Justice Brennan concluded that police authority to accost citizens was strictly limited to the stop and frisk statutes. Searches, with or without warrants, cannot be conducted in the absence of probable cause.

The rights protected by the Fourth Amendment are violated only when the illegal conduct concerns one's own privacy interests. Thus, where a defendant falsified a federal income tax return by denying he had funds abroad, he could not suppress damaging evidence illegally obtained from a foreign bank by United States agents.[5] The search was not considered unreasonable as to the defendant, although Justice Thurgood Marshall unsuccessfully urged the Court to suppress the evidence because to do otherwise would encourage the government to invade one person's rights in order to acquire evidence against another person.

III. SEARCH OF PREMISES

Warrants are required for the police to lawfully search premises unless one of several recognized exceptions are present. A warrantless search will be sustained if contraband is about to be destroyed, or if there is an emergency requiring immediate action, or if the police are in "hot pursuit" of an escaping suspect, or if the search is incidental to a lawful arrest.

Although warrantless searches are most likely to be controversial, a widely publicized recent case involved a search, with warrant, of the *Stanford Daily* (Stanford University's student newspaper) even though the newspaper was not suspected of criminal involvement.[6] The police had been assaulted at the Stanford University Hospital by a group of demonstrators and they had reason to believe that the student newspaper office contained photographs that would assist in identifying the persons involved in the assault. Justice Byron White's majority opinion discounted the First Amendment freedom of the press issue and emphasized the Fourth Amendment's reference to "things" that may reasonably be sought. It was considered unimportant that the photographs were located on the property of an innocent third party; the photographs could be sought wherever they might be. The Court rejected an alternative suggestion that the photographs could simply be subpoenaed. The delay occasioned by this procedure might have resulted in the loss or destruction of the photographs by potentially uncooperative members of the newspaper staff.

The fact that a newspaper office was searched complicated the case, inasmuch as the burden on the right of press freedom was substantial. In the first place, the normal procedures of the newsroom were thoroughly disrupted. And, beyond that, the police could ransack every file in the newsroom, prying into any confidential material available, until the sought-for evidence was discovered or found not to be there.

Nonetheless, the *Stanford Daily* case sanctioned third party searches where the police have probable cause to believe the sought-after evidence is located on certain property even though there is no probable cause to believe the owner or possessor of the property is implicated. The inevitable Fourth Amendment tension between privacy and public need was resolved in favor of the latter interest.

Justice John Paul Stevens, who dissented in the *Stanford Daily* case, wrote for a Court majority in *Payton* v. *New York* where the police were disallowed entry into a suspect's home in order to make a felony arrest without a warrant.[7] Where there is ample opportunity to obtain a warrant, the police are obliged to do so, even though there was probable cause to arrest the suspect on a felony charge. As the Court emphasized: "The zealous and frequent repetition of the adage that a 'man's house is his castle,' made it abundantly clear that both in England and in the Colonies 'the freedom of one's house' was one of the most vital elements of English liberty."[8]

The result in *Payton* was challenged by Justice White on two principal grounds: the majority misrepresented common law history on the subject of warrantless entries and had overestimated the police intrusiveness involved in the procedure. In the first place, there should be no significance attached to where an arrest occurs because the Fourth Amendment protects people not places. Moreover, the police were carefully monitored. There are "four restrictions on home arrests—felony, knock and announce, day-time, and stringent probable cause—" all of which "constitute powerful and complementary protections for the privacy interests associated with the home."[9] All of the restrictions were observed in *Payton*.

The Supreme Court was also sharply divided in *Dalia* v. *United States*, where a majority upheld a covert entry into an office for the purpose of installing bugging equipment authorized by a warrant.[10] Justice Lewis Powell concluded that, inasmuch as the electronic surveillance was properly authorized, it followed that the covert entry was also authorized by implication. To hold otherwise "would promote empty formalism."[11] On the other hand, Justice Brennan took particular exception to the majority's willingness to characterize permission to install a bug as tantamount to a warrant authorization. The privacy invasion is substantial and, of equal importance, the covert entry practically amounts to an independent search and seizure.

A narrower question was presented in *Steagald* v. *United States*, where the issue was whether the police could "legally search for the subject of an arrest warrant in the home of a third-party without first obtaining a search warrant."[12] The Court concluded they could not, in the absence of special circumstances or consent, because the probable cause used to justify the issuance of an arrest warrant is distinguishable from the probable cause needed to issue a search warrant. Moreover, the interests involved are not the same: the arrest warrant is required to safeguard against unreasonable seizures whereas the search warrant is required to safeguard "an individual's interest in the privacy of his home and possessions against the unjustified intrusion of the police."[13] The two interests are not interchangeable. Nor was the Court persuaded that numerous practical problems would necessarily follow from this particular restriction on the police. After all, a suspect can easily be apprehended while leaving or entering the house of a third-party. And the warrant requirement would not be required if there were special circumstances, as when the police are in "hot pursuit" of a suspect.

Although Justice William Rehnquist, dissenting, agreed that the case rested on a narrow set of facts, he found the case to be of special interest because of the "pristinely simple manner" in which Justice Marshall proceeded for the majority.[14] He charged that Justice Marshall assumed, with no reason to do so, that the petitioner's residence could not have been searched without a warrant. Moreover, the majority ignored the fact that the police already had a search warrant to arrest the fugitive who had taken sanctuary within the petitioner's house. The police concluded they had probable cause to believe the fugitive was in the house, which, of course, Justice Marshall considered irrelevant because the controlling principle behind the probable cause requirement is to substitute the judgment of a neutral magistrate for that of the police.

Nonetheless, Justice Rehnquist may have been correct when he insisted that recent decisions suggested a contrary result. For example, *Dalia* did not require that the police obtain a separate warrant prior to the covert entry needed to plant an electronic bug. And *Payton* rejected the contention that the police needed a separate search warrant before they could enter a suspect's house with an arrest warrant. Was the police behavior in *Steagald* unreasonable simply because an arrest warrant does not address the privacy interest of a third-party homeowner? Justice Rehnquist thought not, largely because of the fugitive's mobility in such circumstances. While the police seek a warrant, the fugitive may escape. The costs of stakeouts are high, fugitives who know they are being sought are unlikely to return home, and the arrest warrant precludes any general search of a third-party dwelling. Because of these considerations, the government interest was viewed as sufficiently compelling to justify the warrantless search of a third-party home.

No warrant was required in *Washington* v. *Chrisman*, where Chief Justice Burger justified a seizure of contraband that was in plain view of a police officer who had followed a student into his dormitory room after a valid arrest for possessing alcohol when underage.[15] The student was arrested on the street, but had asked to return to his dormitory room in order to get his identification. Was it necessary for the officer to follow the student into the room in order to either protect himself or maintain control over him? Justice White's dissent emphasized that neither reason appeared important to the officer at the time because, until he saw the contraband, he did not bother to follow the student into the room. Thus, it is apparent that the discovery of the contraband was the sole reason why he entered the room without a warrant.

Both the Court's majority and the dissenters agreed that the officer acted consistently with the requirements of the Fourth Amendment only if he had a right to be with the student inside the room. Of course, the officer could have stayed with the student throughout the proceedings, but since he did not, is it appropriate to conclude that any incriminating evidence that is seen inside a house may be seized by the police without a warrant? *Chrisman* extends warrantless seizure doctrine beyond what has been permissible in the past. In effect, Chief Justice Burger considered "the arresting officer's authority to maintain custody over the arrested person" equivalent to the warrant requirement.

IV. SEARCH OF VEHICLES

As always, a warrant is required when it is practicable to obtain it. Therefore, if a vehicle is in a garage, or if it is expected to be at a certain place each day, a search warrant must be acquired. Many vehicle searches, however, will occur under circumstances where no warrant has been issued. The law pertaining to warrantless vehicle searches has been sufficiently Byzantine to cause Justice Powell to observe "that the law of search and seizure with respect to automobiles is intolerably confusing. The Court apparently cannot agree even on what it has held previously, let alone on how these cases should be decided."[16]

The Court, in *Rakas* v. *Illinois*, divided over whether the Fourth Amendment protects persons who are only passengers from warrantless searches.[17] Following a robbery report, the petitioners were stopped and told to get out of the automobile. A rifle was then discovered under the seat and rifle shells were found stored in the glove compartment. Justice Rehnquist, for the majority, concluded that inasmuch as the petitioners did not own the car they had no legitimate expectation of privacy that was violated by the search. The Fourth Amendment protects personal rights, the Court continued, and the petitioners—as passengers—were in no position to vicariously exercise the rights of the driver, who owned the car. Nor (perhaps understandably) did the petitioners lay claim to the ownership of the gun and rifle shells. Since they owned nothing that was searched, they had no cause to object to the search and seizure that later resulted in their conviction for armed robbery.

The principal objection raised by the dissenters was that the Court had reduced the protection against warrantless searches to a property interest, thus diminishing the privacy interest thought to be protected by the Fourth Amendment. In fact, Justice White accused the majority of declaring an "open season" on automobiles whenever there are persons other than the owner present.[18] When incriminating evidence is found—however unreasonable the search—only the owner will be in a position to object to the evidence, which then will be used against the other occupants. The risk of abuse is high, especially in those situations where it is the passenger in whom the police are really interested.

The Court also has disagreed over the scope of searches that are incidental to custodial arrests. How much of an automobile may properly be searched? Although the Justices agreed that "the area within the immediate control of the arrestee" may be searched, the definition has been variously interpreted.[19] In *New York* v. *Belton*, the Court sustained a search that encompassed a jacket lying on the back seat of an automobile which was found to have cocaine in one of its pockets. Moments before the search the petitioner had been arrested for possession of marijuana. The Court's conclusion was that articles within the general area of the passenger compartment may properly be searched for weapons or evidence that might be destroyed by the arrestee.

The dissenters insisted that warrantless searches be confined to the arrestee or the area under his immediate control after the arrest, which would not include the entire passenger compartment. Indeed, Justice Brennan believed a grant of broad discretion to the police would generate more questions than it would answer.

> Would a warrantless search incident to arrest be valid if conducted five minutes after the suspect left his car? Thirty minutes? Three hours? Does it matter whether the suspect is standing in close proximity to the car when the search is conducted? Does it matter whether the police formed probable cause to arrest before or after the suspect left his car? And *why* is the rule announced today necessarily limited to searches of cars? What if a suspect is seen walking out of a house where the police, peering in from outside, had formed probable cause to believe a crime was being committed? Could the police then arrest that suspect and enter the house to conduct a search incident to arrest? Even assuming today's rule is limited to searches of the "interior" of cars—an assumption not demanded by logic—what is meant by "interior"? Does it include locked glove compartments, the interior of door panels, or the area under the floorboards? Are special rules necessary for station wagons and hatchbacks, where the luggage compartment may be reached through the interior, or taxicabs, where a glass panel might separate the driver's compartment from the rest of the car?[20]

In a case decided the same day, *Robbins* v. *California*, the Court reached a contrary result because the police searched an automobile trunk (as distinguished from the passenger compartment), where they found wrapped packages containing bricks of marijuana.[21]

Closed luggage or sealed packages imply an expectation of privacy, although Justice Powell, concurring, expressed concern that warrants might be required of the police in order to examine containers in which no one might reasonably have an expectation of privacy.

Justice Rehnquist emphatically denied the petitioner had any reasonable expectation of privacy in the two green plastic garbage bags containing the marijuana. Prior to the trunk search, the police had discovered marijuana in the passenger compartment; the petitioner had volunteered that: "What you are looking for is in the back"; and one of the officers knew that marijuana was often wrapped in the manner in which it was discovered. "Surely, given all the circumstances," Justice Rehnquist concluded, "the contents of the garbage bags 'could be inferred from their appearance.' "[22]

Were the two cases, *Belton* and *Robbins*, decided inconsistently? Justice Stevens believed they were. His position has the advantage of clarity and ease of application: in both cases the petitioners were lawfully stopped and arrested, and the police had probable cause to suspect contraband was present. He concluded that "the 'automobile exception' to the warrant requirement therefore provided each officer the authority to make a thorough search of the vehicle—including the glove compartment, the trunk, and any containers in the vehicle that might reasonably contain the contraband."[23] Accordingly, Justice Stevens saw no reason to provide a plastic garbage bag filled with contraband with "a mantle of constitutional protection."[24] Applying this analysis to *Belton*, the officer had smelled marijuana, which had provided him with probable cause to believe contraband was present. This is entirely distinguishable, Justice Stevens explained, from the totally indefensible situation where a traffic violator is stopped and, on the pretext of an arrest, a briefcase is searched. Such an act is clearly unconstitutional.

Justice Stevens' position eventually prevailed in *United States* v. *Ross*, where the police, acting on an informant's tip, had probable cause to believe Ross was selling narcotics which he kept in his automobile trunk.[25] Acting without warrant, the police were nonetheless authorized to make a full search of the automobile, including packaged contraband in the trunk. The decision overruled *Robbins*, decided in the previous year. The doctrinal shift reflected in *Ross* was in part attributable to a change in Court personnel. Justice Potter Stewart had been replaced by Justice Sandra O'Connor, who joined the new majority. Moreover, Justice Powell and Chief Justice Burger had unenthusiastically joined the majority decision in *Robbins*, and they joined in easily with the new coalition.

Although *Ross* has clarified Fourth Amendment requirements insofar as automobiles are concerned, it has not been immune from criticism. Justice Marshall's dissent charged that the majority had, in effect, made warrants unnecessary. The police, not a neutral magistrate, decide whether or not to make a search. One may ask, following *Ross*, if further exceptions to the warrant requirement may be forthcoming. Clearly, police efficiency has been assisted and the Court has implicitly acknowledged the special difficulties law enforcement officials confront when dealing with mobile items. But the warrant requirement was intended to discourage general searches, which now are likely to be used more frequently by the police because of *Ross*.

V. CONCLUSIONS

Search and seizure law has moved unmistakably during the past several years toward an increased acceptance of police decision making in situations where warrants have not been issued by neutral magistrates based on probable cause. The police increasingly have been allowed to act on their own assessment of probable cause. This may have several consequences. First, the police will be inclined to act, as a practical matter, on the basis of reasonable suspicion instead of the more rigorous showing of proof traditionally required by probable cause. Police are not constitutionalists, nor should they be expected to routinely act as if they are. Second, there will be more warrantless searches than ever before because it is easier and less time consuming for the police to make judgments in the field. The Constitution's warrant requirement is deliberately burdensome. The police may be expected to excuse themselves from its application to the full extent permitted by the Court.

[As of fall 1984, decisions of the Supreme Court have narrowed the application of the exclusionary rule in situations where the police have acted in good faith, *U.S.* v. *Leon*, 104 S.Ct. 3405 (1984); *Mass* v. *Sheppard*, 104 S.Ct. 3424 (1984), and where there is an independent source for seizing challenged evidence apart from any illegal police conduct, *Segura* v. *U.S.*, 104 S.Ct. 3380 (1984). These cases suggest that warrants, when acquired, will be more likely than before to withstand judicial scrutiny.]

The discretion intrusted to law enforcement officials, even before the recent cases, was extensive. What accounts for the Court's willingness to be even more deferential to police judgments reached in the field as to what is constitutionally appropriate? One answer may lie with the vagueness of the Fourth Amendment. As has been shown, it is one of the least precise provisions in the Bill of Rights. There has always been judicial discord as to its meaning. Another factor in the Court's recent decisions may be its perception of the extent of the seriousness and extent of contemporary crime. Because evidence obtained in violation of the Fourth Amendment is suppressed, it is not unlikely that the Court has "watered down" the Amendment in order to avoid retrials (minus important evidence) or dismissals of persons apprehended with evidence that was clearly incriminating. By focusing on whether the search was conducted in a reasonable manner rather than on whether the police had obtained a warrant, it is less likely the police will be second guessed and obviously guilty persons released.

The recent decisions make the traditional checks on police indiscretion more important than ever. An indispensable first check is a vigilant and informed public opinion which, in a free society, is deceptively important. For example, widespread indignation over strip searches resulting from relatively minor automobile offenses only recently emphasized the extent of police dependence on public approval. Additionally, instances of police lawlessness can be appealed in the courts. This important check on the police may be illustrated by the *Ross* case. After *Ross*, there will be appeals based on whether or not the police had probable cause to suspect an automobile contained contraband. Official judgments will still be contested in the courts.

Although a police assessment of probable cause was sustained in *Ross*, the Court reached a contrary result in the so-called "drug courier profile" case, *Florida* v. *Royer*. [26] Royer, who was in fact transporting illegal drugs, fit the "drug courier profile" almost exactly. He was carrying heavy American Tourister luggage, appeared young (between 25–35), was casually dressed, was pale and nervously looked about, paid for his airline ticket in cash, and wrote only a name and destination on his luggage identification tab. Royer was also travelling to New York City, a major narcotics distribution center. With these facts in mind, the police approached Royer as he neared the boarding concourse, identified themselves, and asked to speak with him for a moment. Royer agreed. When asked, he produced a driver's license which carried his correct name. His airline ticket, however, was in another name. When questioned about the discrepancy, he became visibly nervous and unsettled. At this point, police interest in him increased. Thereupon, the police revealed they suspected him of involvement in the narcotics traffic and asked that he accompany them to a small room nearby, where his luggage was brought. When asked if he consented to a search of his luggage, Royer said nothing but produced a key and unlocked one of the suitcases. The police opened the suitcase and found marijuana. When asked if he minded whether the second suitcase was opened, Royer said "no, go ahead."[27] It also contained marijuana. With this evidence the State obtained a felony conviction.

The Supreme Court's response to the case highlights many of the present uncertainties surrounding the search and seizure area. The plurality opinion by Justice White agreed with the Florida Court of Appeal that Royer had been involuntarily confined within the small room without probable cause, that the limited restraint justified by earlier stop and frisk cases had been exceeded, and that the consent obtained from Royer was invalid inasmuch as it had been obtained while he was unlawfully confined.

One of the detectives admitted at the suppression hearing that until the suitcases were opened, there had been no probable cause to arrest Royer. The police had simply overreached. The implications were enormous, for if the conviction remained intact "every nervous young man paying cash for a ticket to New York City under an assumed name and carrying two heavy American Tourister bags may be arrested and held to answer for a serious felony charge."[28]

In the course of the opinion, Justice White attempted to summarize the present search and seizure law as it related to *Royer*. His major conclusions, with which Justices Marshall, Powell, and Stevens agreed, were as follows:

First, without probable cause or exigent circumstances, and without his consent, Royer's luggage could not be searched in the absence of a search warrant. And the State must show that consent was given freely and voluntarily.

Second, the police can approach a person in a public place and ask questions, if the person is willing to listen.

Third, in the years since the stop and frisk exception was established, the exception has grown so that now "certain seizures are justifiable under the Fourth Amendment if there is articulable suspicion that a person has committed or is about to commit a crime."[29]

Fourth, the stop and frisk cases still constitute a very limited exception to the general rule that persons cannot be seized without probable cause. There must be a strong public interest present in order to justify an exception to the general rule.

Fifth, even voluntary statements cannot be used in evidence if they are obtained as a result of an illegal detention.

Sixth, voluntary consent can be obtained from a suspect after a police encounter in a public place or after a brief detention based on less than probable cause. However, consent is no longer voluntary when, as in *Royer*, the proceeding amounts to a confinement rather than an investigation.

Although he agreed with this summary of the present rules, Justice Powell wrote separately to indicate that he had no difficulty with the initial "stop for questioning" but, thereafter, it was apparent Royer was not free to walk away. Under the circumstances, consent was no longer voluntary.

Justice Brennan, who provided the decisive fifth vote, considered the entire proceeding unlawful, beginning when the police first stopped Royer to question him. They had no right to do so. They had no warrant and they had no probable cause with which to get one. Effective law enforcement, Justice Brennan insisted, is less important than the "peril to our free society"[30] encouraged by a disregard for Fourth Amendment protections.

In stark contrast with Justice Brennan's assessment, and at the opposite pole of the constitutional spectrum, was that offered by Justice Rehnquist. Joined by Chief Justice Burger and Justice O'Connor, he accused the "plurality's meandering opinion" of betraying "a mindset more useful to those who officiate at shuffleboard games" than "to those who are seeking to administer a system of justice whose twin purposes are the conviction of the guilty and the vindication of the innocent."[31] Everything the police did was reasonable under the circumstances. Royer voluntarily cooperated fully at every step in the proceedings, there was no evidence of coercion, and Royer's willing entry into a small room off the concourse did "not transform a voluntary consent to search into a coerced consent."[32]

Disassociating himself from the Rehnquist opinion, Justice Blackmun believed the "conduct should not be subjected to a requirement of probable cause" because of "society's interest in overcoming the extraordinary obstacles to the detection of drug traffickers."[33] In perhaps the most analytically sophisticated of the five opinions, Justice Blackmun emphasized that the police intrusion was minimum and a serious assessment of privacy expectations is required.

> Here, Royer was not taken from a private residence, where reasonable expectations of privacy are perhaps at their greatest. Instead, he was approached in a major international airport where, due in part to extensive anti-hijacking surveillance and equipment, reasonable privacy expectations are of significantly lesser magnitude, certainly no greater than the reasonable privacy expectations of travelers in automobiles. As in the automobile stop cases, and indeed as in every case in which the Court has upheld seizures upon reasonable suspicion, Royer was questioned where he was found, and all questions were directly related to the purpose of the stop.[34]

In short, the individual interest in being left alone must be balanced against the societal interest in "uncovering illicit drug couriers."[35] In certain kinds of cases—for example, the illicit drug traffic, illegal immigration, and airline hijacking—where police intrusion is minimal, where both individual and public privacy expectations are significantly lessened, and where the societal interest in surveillance is substantial, police procedures based on "particularized suspicion" are reasonable within the limited context in which they are developed.

The *Royer* case illustrates, as does much of the recent case law, the extent to which the Supreme Court is thoroughly divided over how the Fourth Amendment should be construed. Even *Ross* mustered only a six Justice majority. Only Justices Brennan and Rehnquist at present can be said to be wholly predictable, although the former is often joined by Justice Marshall and the latter is often joined by Chief Justice Burger and Justice O'Connor. The other Justices have tended to rely on pragmatic situational decision making with no particular agreement on criteria and a general mistrust of "bright line" rules in the cases. Consequently, any changes in the membership of the Court (which is now one of the century's oldest) could easily have an important and immediate impact on the resolution of search and seizure issues.

REFERENCES

1. For an excellent brief overview of search and seizure law up to the point where the present discussion begins, see Congressional Quarterly's *Guide to the U.S. Supreme Court* 539–53 (1979).

2. *Nathanson* v. *United States*, 290 U.S. 41 at 47 (1933).

3. *Terry* v. *Ohio*, 392 U.S. 1 (1968). See also, *Sibron* v. *New York*, 392 U.S. 40 (1968) and *Peters* v. *New York*, 392 U.S. 40 (1968).

4. *Michigan* v. *De Fillippo*, 443 U.S. 31 (1979).

5. *United States* v. *Payner*, 448 U.S. 911 (1980).

6. *Zurcher* v. *Stanford Daily*, 436 U.S. 547 (1978).

7. 445 U.S. 573 (1980).

8. *Id.* at 596–97.

9. *Id.* at 616.

10. 441 U.S. 238 (1979).

11. *Id.* at 237.

12. 451 U.S. 204, 205 (1981).

13. *Id.* at 213.

14. *Id.* at 223.

15. 455 U.S. 1 (1982).

16. *Robbins* v. *California*, 453 U.S. 420, 430 (1981).

17. *Rakas* v. *Illinois*, 439 U.S. 128 (1978).

18. *Id.* at 157.

19. *New York* v. *Belton*, 453, 460 (1981), where the rule in *Chimel* v. *California*, 395 U.S. 752 (1969) is cited with approval.

20. *Id.* at 470.

21. 453 U.S. 420 (1981).

22. *Id.* at 442.

23. *Id.* at 444.

24. *Id.* at 448.

25. 456 U.S. 798 (1982).

26. 103 S.Ct. 1319 (1983).

27. *Id.* at 1322.

28. *Id.* at 1329.

29. *Id.* at 1324.

30. *Id.* at 1332.

31. *Id.* at 1336.

32. *Id.* at 1332.

33. *Id.* at 1342.

34. *Id.* at 1333–34.

35. *Id.* at 1335.

DOUBLE STANDARD—"There is a law for the poor and a law for the rest of us"—and, says the author, a judge, that means inequities in housing, employment and the ability to defend oneself in court.

Drawing by JAMES FLORA

Legal Aspects of Police Administration

Jack Call and Donald Slesnick

The person who talks of an unalterable law is probably an unalterable fool.

Sydney Smith

SOURCE: Reprinted with permission of Macmillan Publishing Company from *Police Administration: Structure, Processes, and Behavior* by Charles R. Swanson and Leonard Territo. Copyright © 1983 by Macmillan Publishing Co., Inc. Excerpted from pp. 305–320 and pp. 322–325; footnotes have been deleted.

ADMINISTRATIVE DISCIPLINE: DUE PROCESS FOR POLICE OFFICERS

The Fifth Amendment to the U.S. Constitution states that "no person shall be . . . deprived of life, liberty, or property, without due process of law." Early decisions of the U.S. Supreme Court held that this amendment and the rest of the Bill of Rights applied only to actions of the federal government. However, the Fourteenth Amendment uses identical language to impose a due process requirement upon the states also.

The question of due process for police officers falls into two categories: what the law calls procedural due process and substantive due process. The former, as its name implies, refers to the legality of the procedures used to deprive police officers of something of significant value, such as dismissal or suspension from their job, promotion, demotion, or loss of pay or vacation time. Substantive due process is a difficult and more elusive concept. For our purposes, we will simply define substantive due process as the requirement that government disciplinary action be based upon reasonable, relevant, and justifiable cause.

Procedural Due Process

There are two general types of situations in the disciplinary process in which a police officer (or any other government employee) can claim the right to be protected by the guarantees of due process. The first type involves those situations in which the disciplinary action taken by the government employer threatens liberty rights of the officer. The second type involves a threat to property rights.

Liberty rights have been defined loosely as those involving the protection and defense of one's good name, reputation, and position in the community. It has, at times, been extended further to include the right to preserve one's future employment opportunities as well. Thus, where an officer's reputation, honor, or integrity are at stake because of government-imposed discipline, procedural due process must be extended to the officer.

It should be pointed out that the use of the "liberty rights" approach as a basis for requiring procedural due process has always proven extremely difficult. Only recently the Supreme Court restricted the use of this legal theory further by holding that it can be utilized only when the employer is shown to have created and disseminated a false and defamatory impression about the employee.

The more substantial and meaningful type of due process guarantee is that pertaining to the protection of one's property. However, not all employees are entitled to its protection. Although the general concept of property extends only to real estate, houses, and other such tangible possessions, the courts have developed the concept that a person's property also includes the many valuable intangible belongings acquired in the normal course of business (e.g., monetary credits and right-of-way privileges across land owned by others).

Certainly the most important intangible piece of property that a person owns is his or her job and its accompanying benefits. However, the courts have consistently held that an employee acquires a protected interest in a job only when it can be established that there exists a justifiable expectation that employment will continue without interruption except for dismissal or other discipline based on "proper cause." This expectation of continued employment is sometimes called tenure or "permanent status."

In 1972, the Supreme Court issued two landmark decisions on tenure. In one of these cases, the plaintiff was a state university professor who had been hired under a one-year contract and had been dismissed at the end of that year without notice or a hearing. The Court held that the professor was not entitled to notice or a hearing because under the circumstances the professor had no tenure since he had no justifiable expectation of continued employment after his contract expired and therefore had no vested property interest protected by the Fourteenth Amendment. The other case also involved a state university professor employed on a one-year contract, but this professor had taught previously in the state college system for ten years. Under these circumstances, the Court held that the professor had acquired de facto tenure—a justifiable expectation of continued employment—and therefore possessed a vested property interest protected by the Fourteenth Amendment.

Since property rights attach to a job when tenure has been established, the question of how and when tenure is established becomes crucial. Public employment has generally used certain generic terms, such as "annual contract," "continuing contract," and "tenure" in the field of education or "probationary" or "permanent" in civil service employment to designate the job status of employees. However, the cases indicate that it is the definition of these terms as established by the employer rather than the terms themselves that determines an employee's legal status. Thus, the key to the establishment of the rights of an employee is the specific wording of the ordinance, statute, rule, or regulation under which that person has been employed.

Traditionally, federal courts have made their own independent determination as to whether a state-created interest in employment amounted to a property interest that was entitled to due process protection.

However, two recent Supreme Court decisions suggest that federal courts should defer to the judgments of lower courts as to the status of the state-created interest in employment because the lower courts have greater expertise in local law. These cases also suggest that, since the state created the interest, the employee is only entitled to the procedural protections that the state intended to confer in conjunction with public employment.

The more recent of these decisions, *Bishop* v. *Wood*, is of particular importance to police officials because it involved a police officer who had served for three years but was dismissed summarily by the city manager without a hearing. The primary issue in the case was whether the city ordinance provided for termination of the officer at will or only for proper cause. The Supreme Court found that the ordinance was ambiguous enough that it could have been read either way, but since the federal district court that heard the case originally had ruled that the officer was "terminable at will," the Supreme Court deferred to that interpretation.

Bishop emphasizes the point that merely classifying job holders as "probationary" or "permanent" does not resolve the property rights question. Whether or not a property right to the job exists is not a question of constitutional dimension; rather, the answer lies in a careful analysis of the applicable state and local laws that might create legitimate mutual expectations of continued employment.

Despite the result in *Bishop*, lower federal courts have been inclined to read employment laws liberally so as to grant property rights whenever possible. For example, the Fifth Circuit Court of Appeals found that a city employment regulation that allows termination "only for cause" created a constitutionally protected property interest. A federal district court in Florida held that a Florida statute, known as the "Police Officer's Bill of Rights," created a property interest in employment for Florida law enforcement employees because of its disciplinary notice provisions. That approach is consistent with other jurisdictions in which state statutes have been interpreted to give property interests in a job to local government employees.

Once a liberty or property right has been established, certain due process guarantees attach to protect the employee. The question becomes, "What process is due?" In the disciplinary process, the methods requiring examination are the formal procedures used to impose discipline. Once it is determined that due process is required, the question is, "How close to a full trial-type hearing is necessary before final disciplinary action can be taken?"

Kenneth Culp Davis has identified twelve main elements of a due process hearing:

> (1) timely and adequate notice, (2) a chance to make an oral statement or argument, (3) a chance to present witnesses and evidence, (4) confrontation of adverse witnesses, (5) cross-examination of adverse witnesses, (6) disclosure of all evidence relied upon, (7) a decision based on the record of evidence, (8) a right to retain an attorney, (9) a publicly-compensated attorney for an indigent, (10) a statement of findings of fact, (11) a statement of reasons or a reasoned opinion, (12) an impartial deciding officer.

The courts have not examined all the trial elements in the context of the police disciplinary process. However, there are cases that have held that the police officer must be informed of the charges on which the action is based, given the right to call witnesses, confronted by the witnesses against him, permitted to cross-examine the witnesses against him, permitted to have counsel represent him, have a decision rendered on the basis of the record developed at the hearing, and have the decision made by an impartial hearing officer.

A question that has proven particularly troublesome for the courts is whether or not due process requires that an evidentiary hearing be held prior to the disciplinary action being taken. In *Arnett* v. *Kennedy*, a badly divided Supreme Court held that a "hearing afforded by administrative appeal after the actual dismissal is a sufficient compliance with the requirements of the Due Process Clause." In a concurring opinion, Justice Powell observed that the question of whether a hearing must be accorded prior to an employee's removal "depends on a balancing process in which the government's interest in expeditious removal of an unsatisfactory employee is weighed against the interest of the affected employee in continued public employment." This line of reasoning was later adopted by the Seventh Circuit in declaring that disciplinary actions within a police department cannot be allowed to disrupt its law enforcement operations. Therefore, post-discipline hearings in the form of a grievance appeal were found to be satisfactory.

On the other hand, a line of cases has developed wherein the courts have laid down a strict requirement for predisicipline hearings. For example, in *Muscare* v. *Quinn*, a public employer argued that due process was satisfied since the suspended employee had actual notice of the charges against him and had a right to a post-suspension hearing before the civil service commission. The Court held that "post-suspension review is insufficient." More recently, a federal district court judge in Miami, in reviewing the dismissal of local police officers, held that the officers were "entitled to a pre-termination hearing containing the basic elements of procedural due process before they can be deprived of their proprietary interests in employment."

In another recent case, the Fifth Circuit Court of Appeals presented a well-reasoned, clearly detailed summary of what is required of government officials prior to the termination of an employee with job property rights so as to comply with the Fourteenth Amendment:

> Where a governmental employer chooses to postpone the opportunity of a nonprobationary employee to secure a full evidentiary hearing until after dismissal, risk reducing procedures must be accorded. These must include, *prior to termination*, written notice of the reasons for termination and an effective opportunity to rebut those reasons. Effective rebuttal must give the employee a right to respond in writing to the charges made and to respond orally before the official charged with the responsibility of making the termination decision.

Thus, it is becoming increasingly clear that those public employees who can legitimately claim the protections of due process for their job through either liberty or property rights are guaranteed an evidentiary hearing prior to disciplinary action, unless the substantial protections just mentioned are provided prior to such action, in which case the full-blown hearing may be postponed until afterward.

Special Procedures

The law of due process (and the law concerning other constitutional rights discussed in this chapter) are the result of interpretations of constitutional provisions. As such, they represent the foundation of all law—a base below which no other law may descend. But constitutional law does not prevent legislative bodies from establishing requirements that rise higher than the requirements established by the U.S. Constitution and state constitutions. Therefore, special procedures and special requirements may be established by state or local law, by administrative regulations, or even by collective bargaining agreements.

Substantive Due Process

As mentioned earlier, due process requirements embrace substantive as well as procedural aspects. In the context of disciplinary action, substantive due process requires that the rules and regulations on which disciplinary action is predicated be clear, specific, and reasonably related to a valid public need. In the police environment, these requirements present the greatest difficulty for the commonly found prohibitions against conduct unbecoming an officer or against conduct that brings or tends to bring discredit upon the department.

The requirement that a rule or regulation be reasonably related to a valid public need means that a police department may not intrude into the private matters of its officers in which it has no legitimate interest. Therefore, there must be a connection "between the prohibited conduct and the officer's fitness to perform the duties required by his position." In addition, the conduct must be of such a nature as to adversely affect the morale and efficiency of the department or have a tendency to destroy public respect for and confidence in the department. Thus, it has been held that a rule prohibiting unbecoming conduct or discrediting behavior cannot be applied to the remarks of a police officer that were highly critical of several prominent local figures but were made to a private citizen in a private conversation in a patrol car and were broadcast accidentally over the officer's patrol car radio.

The requirements for clarity and specificity are necessary to ensure (1) that the innocent are not trapped without fair warning, (2) that those who enforce the regulations have their discretion limited by explicit standards, and (3) that where basic First Amendment rights are affected by a regulation, the regulation does not operate unreasonably to inhibit the exercise of those rights.

The courts' applications of these requirements to unbecoming conduct and discrediting behavior rules have taken two courses. The first course, exemplified by *Bence* v. *Breier*, has been to declare the regulation unconstitutional because of its vagueness. In its consideration of a Milwaukee Police Department rule that prohibited "conduct unbecoming a member and detrimental to the service," the court found that the rule lacked

> inherent, objective content from which ascertainable standards defining the proscribed conduct could be fashioned. Like beauty, their content exists only in the eye of the be-

> holder. The subjectivity implicit in the language of the rule permits police officials to enforce the rule with unfettered discretion, and it is precisely this potential for arbitrary enforcement which is abhorrent to the Due Process Clause.

The second course taken by the courts has been to uphold the constitutionality of the regulation because, as applied to the officer in the case at hand, it should have been clear to him that his behavior was meant to be proscribed by the regulation. Under this approach, the court is saying that there may or may not be some circumstances in which the rule is too vague or overbroad and therefore unconstitutional, but the rule is constitutional in the present case. Thus, it should be clear to any police officer that fleeing from the scene of an accident or making improper advances toward a young woman during the course of an official investigation constitutes conduct unbecoming an officer or conduct that discredits the police department.

Many police departments also have a regulation prohibiting neglect or dereliction of duty. While on its face such a rule would seem to possess some of the same potential vagueness and overbreadth shortcomings characteristic of the unbecoming conduct rules, the cases reflect virtually no litigation over the constitutionality of these rules. This is probably due to the fact that disciplinary action taken under neglect-of-duty rules nearly always seems to be for conduct for which police officers could reasonably expect disciplinary action. The courts have upheld administrative sanctions against officers under neglect-of-duty rules for sleeping on the job, failing to prepare for planned demonstrations, falsification of police records, failure to make scheduled court appearances, failure to investigate a reported auto accident, and directing a subordinate to discontinue enforcement of a city ordinance against pinball machines. The courts have refused to uphold disciplinary action against a police chief who did not keep eight-to-four office hours and against an officer who missed a training session on riot control because of marital problems.

CONSTITUTIONAL RIGHTS OF POLICE OFFICERS

Free Speech

The First Amendment of the U.S. Constitution prohibits Congress from passing any law "abridging the freedom of speech." It has been held that the due process clause of the Fourteenth Amendment makes this prohibition applicable to the states and to their subunits as well.

Although freedom of speech is one of the most fundamental of all constitutional rights, the Supreme Court has indicated that "the State has interests as an employer in regulating the speech of its employees that differ significantly from those it possesses in connection with regulation of the speech of the citizenry in general." Therefore, the state may place restrictions on the speech of its employees that it could not impose on the general citizenry. However, these restrictions must be reasonable. Generally, disputes involving infringement of the speech of public employees will be resolved by balancing the interests of the state as an employer against the employee's interests in free speech.

There are two basic situations in which a police regulation or other action may be found to be an unreasonable infringement upon the free speech interests of an officer. The first is when the action is overbroad. A Chicago Police Department rule prohibiting "any activity, conversation, deliberation, or discussion which is derogatory to the Department" was ruled overbroad because it prohibited all criticism of the department by policemen, even if it occurred in private conversation. The same fate befell a New Orleans Police Department regulation that prohibited statements by a police officer that "unjustly criticize or ridicule, or express hatred or contempt toward, or . . . which may be detrimental to, or cast suspicion on the reputation of, or otherwise defame, *any* person."

A second situation in which a free speech limitation may be found unreasonable is in the way in which the governmental action is applied. The most common shortcoming of police departmental action in this area is a failure to demonstrate that the statements by the officer being disciplined adversely affected the operation of the department. Thus, a Baltimore police regulation prohibiting public criticism of departmental action was held to have been applied unconstitutionally to a police officer who was president of the police union and who had stated in a television interview that the police commissioner was not leading the department effectively and that "the bottom is going to fall out of this city." Important to the court's decision was the fact that the police commissioner was not someone with whom the police officer came into frequent contact.

Other First Amendment Rights

A basic right of Americans in our democratic system of government is the right to engage in political activity. As with free speech, the government may impose restrictions upon the political behavior of its employees that it could not impose on the citizenry at large. If the state could not impose some such restrictions, there would be a substantial danger that employees could be pressured by their superiors to support political candidates or causes contrary to their own beliefs under threat of loss of employment or other adverse action against them for failure to do so.

At the federal level, a number of types of partisan political activity by federal employees are controlled by the Hatch Act. That act has been upheld by the U.S. Supreme Court against constitutional attack on two occasions, most recently in 1973. All states have similar statutes controlling political activity by state employees, usually referred to as "little Hatch acts." The Oklahoma "little Hatch act" was upheld by the Supreme Court in 1973 also. That act prohibited state employees from soliciting political contributions, joining a partisan political club, serving on the committee of a political party, being a candidate for any paid political office, or taking part in the management of a political party or campaign.

While this Supreme Court activity might appear to have put to rest all controversy over the extent to which the government can limit political activity by its employees, that has not been the case. In two cases since 1973, lower courts have placed limits on the authority of the state in this area. In a case arising in Pawtucket, Rhode Island, two firemen ran for mayor and city councilman, respectively, in a nonpartisan election. However, a city charter provision prohibited all city employees from engaging in any political activity except voting and the private expression of opinion. In granting the firemen's requests for an injunction against the enforcement of this provision against them, the court ruled that the earlier Supreme Court decisions just mentioned did not apply to the Pawtucket charter provision because the statutes upheld in those decisions had prohibited only partisan political activity. In a very similar case in Boston, however, the court upheld the police departmental rule at issue there, on the basis that whether the partisan-nonpartisan distinction was crucial was a matter for legislative or administrative determination.

In a Michigan case, the court declared unconstitutional two city charter provisions that prohibited contributions to or solicitations for any political purpose by city employees because it was overbroad. That court specifically rejected the partisan-nonpartisan distinction as crucial, focusing instead on the office involved and the relationship to that office of the employees whose political activity was at issue. For example, the court saw no danger to an important municipal interest in the activities of a city employee "who is raising funds to organize a petition drive seeking a rate change from the Public Service Commission," but those activities were proscribed by the charter provisions.

Thus, while the Supreme Court has tended to be supportive of governmental efforts to limit the political activities of its employees, it is clear that some lower courts intend to limit the Supreme Court cases to the facts of those cases. Therefore, careful consideration should be given to the scope of political activity to be restricted by a police regulation, and trends in the local jurisdiction should be examined closely.

The cases just discussed dealt with political activity, as opposed to mere political affiliation. May a police officer be relieved of his duties because of his political affiliations on the basis that those affiliations impede his ability to carry out the policies of superiors with different political affiliations? The Supreme Court addressed this question in a case arising out of the Sheriff's Department in Cook County, Illinois. The newly elected sheriff of Cook County, a Democrat, had discharged the chief deputy of the Process Division and a bailiff of the Juvenile Court, both of whom were nonmerit system employees, because they were Republicans. The Court ruled that it was a violation of these employees' First Amendment rights to discharge them from nonpolicymaking positions because of their political party memberships.

Nonpolitical associations are also protected by the First Amendment. However, it is common for police departments to prohibit officers from associating with known felons or other persons of bad reputation on the basis that "such associations may expose an officer to irresistible temptations to yield in his obligation to impartially enforce the law, and . . . may give the appearance that the community's police officers are not themselves honest and impartial enforcers of the law." Sometimes the prohibition is imposed by means of a specific ordinance or regulation, whereas in other instances the prohibition is enforced by considering it conduct unbecoming an officer. Of course, if the latter approach is used, the ordinance or regulation will have to overcome the legal obstacles discussed earlier, relating to unbecoming conduct or discrediting behavior rules.

As with rules touching upon other First Amendment rights, rules prohibiting associations with criminals and other undesirables must not be overbroad in their reach. Thus, a Detroit Police Department regulation that prohibited knowing and intentional associations with convicted criminals or persons charged with crimes except in the course of an officer's official duties was declared unconstitutional because it proscribed some associations that could have no bearing on an officer's integrity or the public's confidence in an officer. The Court cited as examples an association with a fellow church member who had been arrested one time years ago or the befriending of a recently convicted person who wanted to become a productive citizen.

The other common difficulty with this kind of rule is that it is sometimes applied to situations in which the association has not been demonstrated to have had a detrimental effect on the performance of the officer's duties or on the discipline and efficiency of the department. Thus, one court has held that a police officer who was a nudist but was fully qualified in all other respects to be a police officer could not be fired simply because he was a practicing nudist. On the other hand, another court upheld the firing of a police officer who had had intercourse at a party with a girl that he knew to be a nude model at a local "adult theater of known disrepute." The court viewed this behavior as being of such a disreputable nature that it had a detrimental effect on the discipline and efficiency of the department.

The First Amendment's protection of free speech has been viewed as protecting means of expression other than verbal utterances. Whether or not one's personal appearance is such a protected means of expression is not clear. In any event, that issue as it relates to on-duty police officers has most certainly been rendered moot by the Supreme Court decision in *Kelley* v. *Johnson*. The decision in that case upheld the constitutionality of a regulation of the Suffolk County, New York, Police Department that established several grooming standards for its male officers. The Court held that either a desire to make police officers readily recognizable to the public or a desire to maintain an *esprit de corps* was a sufficiently rational justification for the regulation.

Searches and Seizures

The Fourth Amendment to the U.S. Constitution protects "the right of the people to be secure in their persons, houses, papers, and effects, against unreasonable searches and seizures . . ." This guarantee protects against actions by the states as well as the federal government. Generally, the cases interpreting the Fourth Amendment require that, before a search or seizure can be effectuated, the police must have probable cause to believe that a crime has been committed and that evidence relevant to the crime will be found at the place to be searched. Because of the language in the Fourth Amendment about "persons, houses, papers, and effects," for years the case law analyzed what property was subject to the amendment's protection. However, in an extremely important case in 1967, the Supreme Court ruled that the amendment protected individuals' reasonable expectations of privacy and not just property interests.

Of course, the Fourth Amendment usually applies to police officers when at home or off duty as it would to any other citizen. However, because of the nature of the employment, a police officer can be subjected to investigative procedures that would not be permitted where an ordinary citizen was involved. One such situation arises with respect to equipment and lockers provided by the department to its officers. In this situation the officer has no expectation of privacy that merits protection.

Another situation involves the ordering of officers to appear at a lineup. Requiring someone to appear in a lineup is a seizure of his or her person and, therefore, would ordinarily require probable cause. However, a federal appeals court upheld a police commissioner's order to sixty-two officers to appear in a lineup for the purpose of identifying officers who had allegedly beaten several civilians. The court held that in this situation "the governmental interest in the particular intrusion [should be weighed] against the offense to personal dignity and integrity." Because of the nature of the police officer's employment relationship, "he does not have the full privacy and liberty from police officials that he would otherwise enjoy."

To enforce the protections guaranteed by the Fourth Amendment's search and seizure requirements, the courts have fashioned the so-called "exclusionary rule," which prohibits the use in criminal proceedings of evidence obtained in violation of the Fourth Amendment. No cases have held specifically that the exclusionary rule applies to disciplinary hearings also. The cases dealing with the exclusionary rule's application to other kinds of administrative hearings are so mixed that it is impossible to predict how the courts would decide the issue where police disciplinary hearings are concerned.

Right Against Self-incrimination

On two occasions the Supreme Court has addressed questions concerning the Fifth Amendment rights of police officers who are the subjects of investigations. In *Garrity* v. *New Jersey*, a police officer had been ordered by the attorney general to answer certain questions or be discharged. He testified and the information gained as a result of his answers was used to convict him of criminal charges.

The Fifth Amendment protects an individual from being compelled "in any criminal case to be a witness against himself." The Supreme Court held that the information obtained from the police officer could not be used at his criminal trial because the Fifth Amendment forbids the use of coercion of this sort to extract an incriminating statement from a suspect.

In *Gardner* v. *Broderick*, a police officer had declined to answer questions put to him by a grand jury investigating police misconduct on the grounds that his answers might tend to incriminate him. The officer was dismissed from his job as a result. The Supreme Court ruled that the officer could not be fired for his refusal to waive his constitutional right to remain silent. However, the Court made it clear that it would have been proper for the grand jury to have required the officer to answer or face discharge for his refusal so long as the officer had been informed that his answers could not be used against him in a criminal case and the questions were related specifically, directly, and narrowly to the performance of his official duties. The Court felt that this approach was necessary to protect the important state interest in ensuring that police officers were performing their duties faithfully.

As a result of these cases, it is proper to discharge a police officer who refuses to answer questions that are related specifically and directly to the performance of his duties and who has been informed that any answers he does give cannot be used against him in a criminal proceeding. Since a disciplinary hearing is not a criminal proceeding, any answers given by the officer after he or she has been extended criminal immunity can probably be used as evidence at such a hearing.

It is not uncommon for police departments to make use of polygraph examinations in the course of internal investigations. The legal question that has arisen most frequently is whether an officer may be required to submit to such a procedure under threat of discharge for refusal to do so. There is some diversity of legal authority on this question, but the majority of courts considering it have held that an officer can be required to take the examination.

In one of the strongest statements in support of the department's authority to order a polygraph examination, an Arizona court overturned a county merit system commission's finding that a polygraph examination could be ordered only as a last resort after all other investigative efforts had been exhausted and held that

> a polygraph is always proper to verify statements made by law enforcement officers during the course of a departmental investigation as long as the officers are advised that the answers cannot be used against them in any criminal prosecution, that the questions will relate solely to the performance of official duties, and that refusal will result in dismissal.

OTHER GROUNDS FOR DISCIPLINARY ACTION

Sexual Conduct

The cases in this area tend to fall into three general catagories: (1) cases involving adultery, (2) cases involving homosexuals, and (3) cases involving the appearance of sexual impropriety.

The cases are in general agreement that adultery, even though committed while off duty and in private, is a proper basis for disciplinary action. The courts have held that such behavior brings adverse criticism upon and tends to undermine public confidence in the department. However, a recent case involving an Internal Revenue Service agent suggests that, to uphold disciplinary action for adultery, the government will have to prove that the employing agency was actually discredited and that the discreditation will not be presumed from the proof of adulterous conduct.

None of the reported cases involving disciplinary action against public employees for homosexuality involves police officers. However, with regard to federal civil service employees, it has been held that a person may not be denied a federal civil service position solely because he or she is homosexual. Another leading case voided the dismissal of a civil service employee whose work was described as "competent" and "very good" but who had made an off-duty homosexual advance. Under the circumstances, the court was unable to conclude that the employee's discharge would "promote the efficiency of the service." Another court found that the discharge of a civil service clerk-typist *would* promote that purpose where the employee had openly "flaunted" his homosexuality, applied for a marriage license to marry another man, and had been the subject of extensive publicity, including radio and television appearances. Because of the relatively frequent contact that police officers have with the public, less flagrant manifestations of homosexuality by an officer may justify dismissal.

The third category of disciplinary cases involving sexual conduct by police officers concerns situations in which the mere appearance of sexual impropriety has been upheld as a basis for imposing administrative sanctions even though no actual sexual misconduct was found to have occurred. In a Michigan case, a married, fifty-five-year-old police officer was dismissed because he had been visiting the home of a sixty-year-old woman on at least eleven occasions at late evening and early-morning hours. He had also been observed engaging in behavior that was obviously intended to avoid creation of the impression that he was visiting this woman. A Connecticut case upheld the dismissal of a married police officer who failed to carry out an order from his superiors to stop seeing a sixteen-year-old girl he had been observed kissing in a parked car. In a Mississippi case, the court ruled that a black police officer who had permitted two white female antipoverty workers to live in his home (where his wife also lived) should be given the opportunity to prove that he had been fired for this reason and that his behavior had not "substantially impair[ed] his usefulness as a police officer." One cannot tell from the opinion in this case whether the appearance of impropriety that disturbed the officer's superiors was primarily sexual or racial, but it seems doubtful that the same uproar would have resulted if the two antipoverty workers had been male.

Residency Requirements

In recent years, a number of local governments have established requirements that all or certain classes of their employees live within the geographical limits of the jurisdiction. These residency requirements have been justified by the government's imposing them as desirable because they increase employees' rapport with and understanding of the community. Where police officers were concerned, it has been asserted that the presence of off-duty police has a deterrent effect on crime and results in chance encounters that might lead to additional sources of information.

Prior to 1976, challenges to the legality of residency requirements dotted the legal landscape. The challenges had persisted in spite of the U.S. Supreme Court's denial of an appeal from the decision of the Michigan Supreme Court that Detroit's residency requirement for police was not irrational. In 1976, the Supreme Court ruled in *McCarthy* v. *Philadelphia Civil Service Commission* that Philadelphia's residency requirement for firemen did not violate the Constitution.

Since the *McCarthy* decision, the legal attacks on the residency requirements themselves have subsided. The cases now seem to be concerned with determining what constitutes residency. The most obvious means of attempting to avoid the residency requirement—by establishing a second residence within the city—appears doomed to failure unless the police officer can demonstrate that he spends at least a substantial part of his time at the in-city residence. A strong argument can be made that, in areas where housing is unavailable or prohibitively expensive, a residency requirement is unreasonable. That argument has been made successfully in a lower court and has not been considered by the Supreme Court.

Unwed Pregnancy

The Civil Rights Act of 1964 prohibits an employer from discriminating against an employee on the basis of race, color, religion, sex, or national origin. The prohibition extends to private, state, and local government agencies. In an important case involving a private employer, it was held that special adverse treatment of an employee because she was pregnant and unmarried constituted unlawful sexual discrimination. Although the case involved a private employer, there is no reason why it should not be fully applicable to a public employer, such as a police department, as well.

Religious Belief or Practice

As mentioned in the previous paragraph, the Civil Rights Act of 1964 prohibits religious discrimination in employment. The act defines religion as including "all aspects of religious . . . practice, as well as belief, unless an employer . . . is unable to reasonably accommodate to an employee's . . . religious . . . practice without undue hardship on the conduct of the employer's business." An Albuquerque fireman who was a Seventh Day Adventist refused to work the Friday night or Saturday day shifts because they fell on what he believed to be the religious Sabbath day. Although department policy would have permitted the fireman to avoid working these shifts by taking leave with pay, taking leave without pay, or trading shifts with other firemen, he refused to use these means and insisted that the department find other firemen to trade shifts with him or simply excuse him from the shifts affected by his religious beliefs. The department refused to do either. Under these circumstances, the court ruled that the department's accommodations to the fireman had been reasonable and that no further accommodations could be made without undue hardship to the department. Therefore, the fireman's discharge was upheld. However, as the court itself emphasized, decisions in cases in this area will depend very much on the particular facts and circumstances of each case.

Moonlighting

Traditionally, the courts have supported the authority of the police and some other governmental bodies to place limits on outside employment by employees. Police department regulations on moonlighting range from a complete ban on outside employment except when on leave or suspended without pay to permission to engage in certain endeavors, such as investments, rental of property, teaching of law enforcement subjects, and employment designed to improve the police image. The rationale in support of moonlighting prohibitions is that "outside employment seriously interferes with keeping the [police and fire] departments fit and ready for action at all times."

Recently there has developed a trend toward a judicial examination of the basis for the moonlighting prohibition. In a Louisiana case, firemen in the city of Crowley offered unrefuted evidence that moonlighting had been a common practice among firemen before the city banned moonlighting; during the previous sixteen years, no fireman had ever needed sick leave as a result of injuries suffered while moonlighting; there had never been a problem locating off-duty firemen to respond to an emergency; and moonlighting had never been shown to have been a source of fatigue that had impaired a fireman's alertness on the job. Under these circumstances, the court ruled that there was not a sufficient basis for the prohibition on moonlighting and invalidated the ordinance.

Misuse of Firearms

Because of the obvious dangers associated with the use of handguns and other firearms, it is not surprising that police departments customarily regulate the use of such weapons by their officers. The courts have held that such regulations need only be reasonable and that the burden rests with the police officer challenging the regulation to demonstrate that the regulation is arbitrary and unreasonable. Moreover, the cases suggest that the courts are inclined to defer to police departments' determinations as to when their firearms regulations have been violated.

Police firearms regulations tend to address three basic situations: (1) requirements for the officer's safeguarding of his weapon, (2) whether the weapon must be worn while off duty, and (3) when the weapon may be fired.

There is little case law dealing with regulations concerning the safeguarding of an officer's weapon. However, in one of the rare instances of a court's reversal of a department's finding that an officer had violated its firearms regulation, a New York court held that an officer could not be disciplined for neglecting to safeguard his weapon where the evidence showed that the weapon had been stolen during a burglary of the officer's room while he was asleep.

Requirements that an officer wear his weapon while off duty have seldom been challenged in lawsuits. However, where such a requirement is made, it seems reasonable that exceptions should be made for situations in which it would obviously be foolish to require a weapon to be carried, such as when an officer is engaging in recreational activity or is inside his own house.

Regulations concerning when an officer can fire his weapon are difficult to construct with precision. Applying these regulations to actual situations is equally difficult. An important caution relates to an earlier discussion of the fact that some courts in damage suits have held police officers subject to a higher standard of care than the law itself would require because the department's regulations established a higher standard. While police departments should not necessarily refrain from establishing exacting requirements as to when their officers can fire their weapons, police administrators should be aware of the possible effect such action could have in civil damage actions.

Intoxication on Duty

It is common for police departments to require that their officers not be under the influence of any intoxicating agent while on duty. Even in the absence of such a regulation, disciplinary action may be taken against an officer suspected of being intoxicated while on duty by charging him with conduct unbecoming an officer, neglect of duty, or violation of a state law if police regulations forbid any of those behaviors.

Regulations against being under the influence have been upheld uniformly as reasonable because the hazardous nature of a police officer's work and the effect his behavior may have upon the property and safety of others make clear "the necessity for a clear head and rational action, unbefuddled by alcohol . . ." Such regulations need not require that the officer be in a state of intoxication while on duty to be in violation of the regulation. A Louisiana court upheld a regulation that prohibited an officer from consuming alcoholic beverages to the extent that it caused his behavior to become obnoxious, disruptive, or disorderly.

To enforce regulations against being under the influence effectively, there may be occasions when a police supervisor or administrator will deem it advisable to order an officer to take a sobriety test. In a case involving firemen, it has been held that a fireman could be ordered to submit to blood sampling when reasonable grounds existed for believing that he was intoxicated and that it was permissible to discharge him for his refusal to comply with the order.

SUMMARY AND CONCLUSION

In recent years there has been a significant increase in the amount of litigation involving police departments and officers. A substantial portion of this litigation has stemmed from efforts by citizens to recover compensation for injuries allegedly caused by police departments and their employees. Such suits are brought as state tort actions, Section 1983 claims, or Bivens-type suits. In state tort actions, it is alleged that injury was caused by conduct which constitutes a tort under state law: assault, battery, false imprisonment, false arrest, etc. A 1983 claim is brought under a federal statute which permits relief from infringements of rights created by the Constitution or federal law by persons acting under color of state law. A Bivens-type suit also provides relief from infringements of constitutional rights and serves primarily to fill some "holes" left by § 1983.

In all three types of suits there are limitations on who can be sued. Where a police supervisor or administrator did not personally engage in the conduct that is the alleged cause of the plaintiff's injury, they are generally not liable solely by virtue of their status as the employer of the officer whose conduct did cause the injury, unless the supervisor or administrator specifically authorized or cooperated in the officer's conduct. However, in an increasing number of cases, supervisors and administrators have been found liable for the misbehavior of their subordinates where plaintiffs have demonstrated that the former were negligent in their employment, training, or supervision of their subordinates.

The governmental body that employs the officer accused of culpable behavior has traditionally been shielded from liability by the doctrine of sovereign immunity. In recent years, the protection of sovereign immunity in state tort actions has been eroded substantially by legislative and judicial action, but it remains an important restriction on recovery against the government. In 1983 cases, a recent decision of the U.S. Supreme Court has exposed local government bodies to liability where the injury is caused by conduct stemming from regulation, policy, ordinance, or custom. The case did not affect the sovereign immunity of state governments under § 1983. The extent to which sovereign immunity extends to Bivens-type suits has never been decided by the Supreme Court and is the subject of some disagreement in the lower courts.

Plaintiffs seeking recovery for injuries caused by police conduct are also limited by the judicial extension of immunity to public employees. In suits based on federal law (§ 1983 and Bivens-type suits), an absolute immunity is extended to prosecutors and judicial and quasi-judicial officials. A qualified immunity is extended to other officials while they act in a discretionary capacity, in good faith, and in a reasonable manner. However, a defendant is not acting in good faith if his or her conduct violates settled law. In state tort actions, absolute immunity is still usually extended to public officials exercising discretionary functions.

Civil suits like those discussed above are a means of creating an incentive for police officers to avoid injury-causing conduct. A similar incentive may be created by the possibility of preferring criminal charges against police officers under the criminal counterpart of § 1983, but in actuality this alternative is seldom exercised. In addition, the courts have developed another incentive in the form of the exclusionary rule, which prohibits the introduction at trial of evidence obtained unconstitutionally or discovered through the use of unconstitutionally-obtained information. And lastly, police officers may be disciplined by their own departments for behavior which causes injury.

Disciplinary action against police officers raises issues concerning procedures which are demanded by the due process guarantees of the U.S. Constitution. Due process protections apply when property interests (real estate, tangible possessions, job tenure, etc.) or liberty interests (reputation, honor, integrity, etc.) of a public employee may be affected by disciplinary action. A recent trend in U.S. Supreme Court cases suggests that in determining when property and liberty interests evoke due process guarantees, the Court will carefully examine whether the government intended to create a protected interest in the public employee.

There is no U.S. Supreme Court case identifying a list of procedural protections required by the Constitution in taking disciplinary action against a police officer. There are lower court cases which have extended to the police officer rights to notice of the charges, to call witnesses, to be confronted by and cross-examine adverse witnesses, to have counsel, and to have a decision made on the basis of the record of the hearing by an impartial hearing officer. There is disagreement among lower courts as to whether an evidentiary hearing must be held prior to taking disciplinary action. However, there seems to be a trend toward requiring a prior hearing unless before the disciplinary action the officer is extended minimal risk-reducing protection, such as written notice of and opportunity to rebut the reasons for the action.

Due process also requires that disciplinary rules be clear, specific, and reasonably related to a valid public purpose. Accordingly, a disciplinary rule must address conduct which affects an officer's fitness to perform his duties, affects departmental morale or efficiency, or could undermine public confidence in the department. The rule must be clear enough to give fair warning, to control the discretion of administrators, and to avoid a "chilling effect" on the exercise of constitutional rights by officers. Many departments prohibit conduct "unbecoming an officer" or "tending to bring discredit upon the department." The application of due process protections to rules of this nature has resulted in some of them being declared unconstitutional for vagueness. Other courts have upheld the constitutionality of such rules because in the disciplinary situation in question, it should have been clear to the officer that the rule was intended to prohibit his or her conduct.

Sometimes disciplinary rules attempt to prohibit conduct of police officers which is protected by the Constitution. Rules infringing upon the free speech of officers may be upheld if the interest of the governmental employer at stake is found to be more important than the officer's free speech interest, but such rules frequently run afoul of the Constitution because they are too broad or because the department failed to demonstrate that the officer's speech adversely affected the departments.

Rights regarding political participation are also protected by the First Amendment to the Constitution. However, the federal Hatch act, which prohibits nearly all partisan political activity by federal employees, has been upheld twice by the Supreme Court. Most states have similar "little Hatch acts" for state employees, one of which has been upheld by the Supreme Court. Nevertheless, lower courts have struck similar prohibitions which extended to nonpartisan political activity or political activity which seemed only remotely related to an important governmental interest, but a clear pattern has not emerged from these cases.

In other areas affected by the First Amendment, courts have generally upheld rules prohibiting police officers from associating with criminals or other undesirables so long as the rule is not too broad and it can be demonstrated that the association has a detrimental effect on the departments. With regard to freedom of expression, the Supreme Court has upheld the establishment of grooming standards for police officers.

Courts have held that the Fourth Amendment protection against unreasonable searches and seizures does not prevent a department from searching lockers and equipment issued to officers by the department or from ordering officers to appear in a lineup without probable cause when there is a strong governmental interest at stake.

The Constitutional right against self-incrimination does not prohibit a department from ordering an officer to answer questions directly related to the performance of his or her duties even though the answers may be incriminating, so long as the officer is given immunity from prosecution for crimes based on his or her incriminating testimony. Although there is some disagreement among courts considering the question, most courts have also held that officers may be required to take polygraph examinations under the circumstances just described.

Issues regarding disciplinary action against police officers on grounds other than those summarized above have been decided by lower courts:

1. Adultery has generally been upheld as a proper basis for disciplinary action.
2. Cases dealing with homosexuality as a basis for dismissal have not involved police officers. With respect to other public employees, the key seems to be whether the employee's homosexuality impairs the efficiency of the agency, and only flagrant displays of homosexual conduct have generally been found to have such an effect.
3. Behavior by police officers creating the appearance of sexual impropriety has generally been upheld as a basis for disciplinary action.
4. A department can require its officers to live within the geographical limits of its jurisdiction.
5. A department must accommodate the religious practices of its officers unless it cannot reasonably do so without imposing an "undue hardship" on the carrying out of its mission.
6. Generally, moonlighting by police officers may be prohibited.
7. Regulations relating to the use of weapons issued to officers will be upheld so long as they are reasonable.
8. Regulations prohibiting intoxication or impairment of an officer's ability to perform while on duty as a result of the influence of drugs carry a strong presumption of validity. Police officers can probably be ordered to take sobriety tests as well.

In administrative matters unrelated to the disciplinary process, the Supreme Court has held that police departments do not have to comply with the minimum wage and overtime requirement of the Federal Labor Standards Act and may not discriminate on the basis of sex in their retirement plans. Under a federal law, the age of persons between 40 and 70 years old may not be utilized in employment decisions unless "age is a bona fide occupational qualification reasonably necessary to the normal operation" of the department's business.

Why Punishment Does Not Deter

Douglas D. Heckathorn

INTRODUCTION

The deterrence doctrine, the belief that punishment deters crime and that an increase in the severity, certainty or celerity (swiftness) of punishment will increase deterrence, is of ancient origin. According to Zimring and Hawkins (1973:1) it is as old as the criminal law itself. To this day, the deterrence doctrine continues to enjoy great support from legislators, law enforcement officials, and members of the public and thus continues to shape the formation of public policy toward crime. It provides a rationale for sentencing criminals. In addition, deterrence provides the rationale for much *extra-judicial* punishment. For example, police officers accused of excessive use of force frequently defend their actions as necessary to deter challenges to their lawful authority, since the police see themselves as the major instrument of deterrence in the legal system. Assessment of such claims requires an understanding of the deterrence process.

Popular belief in the validity of the deterrence doctrine has remained virtually unchallenged since its inception.

By contrast, social scientists have been more critical of the deterrence doctrine. Since the development of systematic criminological theory in the late eighteenth century, this doctrine has gone alternately into and out of favor. But it was only in the early 1950s that empirical investigations were first carried out to subject the doctrine to test.

This research initially focused on the death penalty as a means of deterring homicide, and produced results which were generally negative, indicating that capital

This article was written expressly for inclusion in this edition.

punishment deters no more effectively than does the alternative of long prison terms. This finding helped to produce a hiatus in deterrence research, which ended with a revival of research in the late 1960s. This revival was stimulated in part by the importation of econometrically based models into criminology, theoretic models which appeared to support and to further systematize the deterrence doctrine. Initially, this new research seemed to support the deterrence doctrine, including the deterrence value of capital punishment. However, methodological refinements subsequently threw those research results into question. During the last decade the accumulation of empirical evidence has increasingly weighed against the deterrence doctrine. These findings imply that further increasing the severity of presently existing criminal penalties would have little effect upon the rate of crime. By contrast, evidence as to the effects of increasing the certainty of punishment remain more ambivalent. In sum, as research on the deterrence doctrine has become more sophisticated, empirical evidence has accumulated against it, even leading some criminologists (Brier and Fienberg, 1980) to suggest that this line of research should now be abandoned.

Despite these findings, public support for the deterrence doctrine apparently remains undiminished. Indeed, the current trend is toward increased rather than diminished support for the death penalty and other measures to make the criminal sanction more punitive. As Gibbs (1978:30) has noted in reference to deterrence: "legislators and law enforcement officials have a nasty habit of retaining doctrines long after criminologists have dismissed them."

One aim of this paper is to provide an overview of the history and current state of criminological research on the deterrent effects of the criminal sanction. A related aim is to explore the bases for public support of the deterrence doctrine in an effort to identify the sources of public support. For here it must be recognized that the extraordinary breadth and constancy of widespread public support for the deterrence doctrine is itself a social phenomenon which is worthy of careful examination.

THE DETERRENCE DOCTRINE: THEORY AND RESEARCH

The origin of criminological theory is traditionally traced (Vold, 1958) to the development of the classical school in the late eighteenth century, as exemplified in the work of Cesare Beccaria (1738–1794) and in the much more comprehensive subsequent works of Jeremy Bentham (1784–1832). Beccaria and Bentham shared a view of people which dominated Western Europe during the eighteenth century. In their view, people are rational hedonists, that is, calculating pleasure seekers and pain avoiders. In essence, they adopted what has since come to be termed a "price system model" (Zimring and Hawkins, 1973) of the criminal decision. People decide to commit crimes (or any other activity for that matter) when the anticipated *gains* outweigh the anticipated *costs*. Therefore, just as increasing the price of a commodity such as an automobile will reduce the demand for it, similarly, increasing the price of criminal behavior by imposing the criminal sanction will reduce criminal behavior. Furthermore, just as demand for a commodity eventually becomes zero if its price is made sufficiently high, according to the simple price model, crime can be eliminated if its price becomes sufficiently high through increases in the severity, certainty, and celerity of punishment. The works of classical criminologists thus constitute the first effort to formalize and systematically express the deterrence doctrine.

The classical criminologists were armchair theorists who seemed to feel little need to empirically test their conclusions. Perhaps surprisingly, the first efforts to empirically measure the deterrence effects of criminal sanctions occurred only recently, in the early 1950s, more than a century after the initiation of criminological research. It should also be noted that this first research was highly limited in that it was aimed not at a comprehensive test of the efficacy of deterrence, but at a single issue which had become the subject of public debate—whether capital punishment deters homicide more effectively than long-term imprisonment.

These early studies of the death penalty used a variety of methodologies. In a number of studies, homicide rates were compared in adjacent localities with similar social characteristics, but which differed with regard to capital punishment statutes. For example, in a particularly influential study, Sellin (1959) divided the United States into a large number of matched groups of states, so that states within each group were matched on a number of social characteristics. He found possession of the death penalty had no effect upon homicide rates. Other comparably designed studies yielded the same result.

The failure of these studies to demonstrate a deterrent effect for capital punishment contributed to an abandonment of deterrence research which lasted for nearly a decade. A revival of research was then initiated in the late sixties by traditionally trained criminologists (Gibbs, 1968; Tittle, 1969), and independently by economists applying econometric models to criminal behavior (Becker, 1968; Ehrlich, 1975, 1977). This research and later research differed from previous efforts to empirically evaluate deterrence in important ways. First, it broadened the focus of investigation, from homicide to less serious crimes, and from the death penalty to less extreme criminal sanctions, including an attempt to assess the relative effects of severity, certainty, and most recently (Gray et al., 1982) the celerity of the criminal sanction. Thus research expanded to attempt a comprehensive empirical evaluation of the deterrence doctrine.

In addition, the extraordinarily intractible nature of the difficulties encountered to adequately test the deterrence doctrine came to be recognized (see Zimring and Hawkins, 1973; Gibbs, 1975; Andenaes, 1974; Tittle and Logan, 1973). For the simple causal relation between criminal sanctions and crime which is posited by the deterrence doctrine is enmeshed within a complex causal web whose elements cannot be readily disentangled. By way of illustration, consider the possible relationships between severity of punishment and the amount of crime. The deterrence doctrine posits an inverse causal relation of severity to crime (i.e., greater severity implies less crime), but were that relationship between severity and crime to be empirically observed, would that necessarily demonstrate that deterrence was indeed in operation? For three reasons it would not:

(1) Changes in the crime rate may affect the nature of punishment, rather than the reverse. Thus the direction of causation between punishment and crime may be opposite the direction posited by deterrence. For according to the *loading hypothesis* of "system capacity models" (e.g., see Pontell, 1978), when crime increases substantially, police have less time to devote to each criminal investigation thereby reducing apprehensions, less court time is available for each criminal case thereby reducing prosecutions and convictions, and prisons become overcrowded leading to greater use of probation and earlier releases from prison. Conversely, when crime is reduced, police have more time to investigate, prosecutors need to worry less about clogging the court calendar, and judges need not be as concerned about overcrowding the prisons, all of which conduce to punishment which is certain and severe. This argument, it should be noted, is not merely hypothetical—a number of studies have found considerable empirical support for it (Pontell, 1978; Hoenack and Weiler, 1980).

(2) An inverse relationship between the criminal sanction's severity and crime can occur, even though neither causally affects the other, if both are the effects of a third causal factor. For example, public attitudes which are condemnatory toward crime may both increase the severity of sentences (through public pressure on the judiciary to get tough on crime) and also inhibit crime (through potential criminals' fear of disapproval from family members and friends), thereby creating the illusion of deterrence (see Loftin and Hill, 1974). Similarly, public attitudes which are accepting of crime may both encourage a reduction of criminal penalties and also encourage crime through assuring potential criminals that their deeds will not scandalize family members and friends, thereby again producing the illusion of deterrence. Consequently, the mere observation that severe penalties are associated with low crime rates, and lenient penalties are associated with high crime rates, is not sufficient to demonstrate the operation of deterrence, for that inverse association between severity and crime may have been produced by an independent causal factor which affects both severity and crime.

(3) Increasing severity may cause reductions in crime, but for reasons other than deterrence. For example, a criminal sanction such as imprisonment prevents crime not merely by deterring would-be criminals, that is, not merely by inducing them to choose not to commit crimes through fear of legal consequences, but also by reducing the opportunities of those who are incarcerated to commit new crimes. Thus an inverse relation between length of imprisonment (severity) and crime may result because longer prison terms incapacitate a greater proportion of the criminal population. Thus there may be a non-deterrence related, albeit real, causal relation from severity to crime. (For two assessments of the effects of incapacitation which come to different conclusions see Greenberg, 1975 and Green, 1978.)

In addition to factors which can produce the illusion of deterrence, there are opposite factors which can obscure its operation. Consequently, even were crime and the criminal sanction's severity and certainty found to be unrelated to one another empirically, the failure of deterrence would not have been proven due to the following:

(A) Contrary to the deterrence doctrine, punitive sanctions may have the effect of fostering rather than suppressing crime. For example, it has been suggested that executions may communicate a lack of regard for the value of life, and consequently possess a brutalizing effect. Hence, executions may increase rather than reduce the homicide rate. Empirical support for this position has been found by Bowers and Pierce (1980). Similarly, Barnett (1981) has shown that the results of a study by Forst (1977) indicate, when taken literally, that each execution *causes* 11 homicides. In addition, punitive sanctions may have not merely a "general" brutalizing effect, i.e., an effect upon the general public, but also a "special" brutalizing effect upon criminals. That would occur if increases in severity produced a greater willingness on the part of criminals to kill witnesses and to shoot it out with police rather than surrender. For these reasons it is conceivable that a criminal sanction may possess real and substantial deterrence effects, but those effects may be nullified by an opposite but comparable or stronger brutalizing effect.

(B) Deterrence effects could also be countervailed if changes in the incidence of crime produced an opposite change in the criminal sanction's punitiveness. For example, an increase in crime may arouse public concern leading public officials to "crack down" and "get tough" with crime. Alternatively, when crime rates decline there is less pressure upon public officials to act punitively. Considerable empirical support for this "social reaction hypothesis" was found by Yunker (1976).

(C) A final possible manner in which deterrence effects might be countervailed is by the operation of a causal factor with independent controlling effects upon both crime and the criminal sanction. This possibility appears not to have been discussed in the deterrence literature, nonetheless evidence for it can be found. For example, numerous studies indicate that the incidence of poverty is positively related to the incidence of many types of crimes, particularly violent crime (Braithwaite, 1981; Loftin and Hill, 1974). Other studies indicate that lower class persons who generally rely on public defenders tend to receive more severe sentences than do more affluent defendants who hire their own attorneys. Consequently, the incidence of poverty within an area may directly affect *both* the crime rate and the severity of punishment.

In addition to factors which mimic or obscure deterrence (i.e., 1–3 and A–C respectively), the presence was recognized of mediating factors between the criminal sanction and deterrence. For according to the deterrence doctrine it is obviously not the *objective* or actual penalty which deters, but rather the *subjective* penalty, that is, the penalty as perceived by potential criminals. Increasing the severity or certainty of punishment therefore deters only if that increase is perceived by potential criminals. Studies were therefore carried out to investigate the relationship between objective and perceived penalties, and they typically found that the public does not accurately perceive the criminal sanction (Gibbs, 1975). Consequently, objective penalties cannot validly serve as a proxy for subjective penalties, as is implicitly done in studies which focus only on the association between actual penalties and crime. Rather, a valid test of deterrence requires that perceptions of penalties be assessed.

In an effort to control for the above and other potential confounding factors, deterrence research as revived in the late 1960s was far more sophisticated than its predecessors, and the trend toward increasingly elaborate procedures has continued. For example, cross-lagged correlations have been used in an effort to determine the direction of causation among correlated factors. Multiple regression has been used to control for the effects of external potentially confounding variables. Efforts have been made to improve the data base upon which studies of deterrence rely, e.g., through use of self report studies to better assess the incidence of crime. In addition, research has broadened from ecological studies to experimentation, to quasi-experiments in the field, and to direct measures of perceptions of the criminal sanction.

Initially, the results of second generation deterrence research seemed to support the deterrence doctrine. In an influential study of the deterrent effects of the death penalty, Ehrlich (1973) found strong support for deterrence and in a subsequent study (1977) concluded that each execution prevents between 8 and 20 homicides, findings which directly contradicted the results of the earlier group of studies. In another study of homicide which also employed multiple regression, Gibbs (1968) too found an inverse relation between homicide rate and sentence severity and certainty, and in a subsequent study Tittle (1969) also found an inverse relationship between homicide and severity.

Stimulated by these initial positive findings, deterrence research flourished. Many dozens of studies were conducted which focused on offenses ranging from parking violations and driving while intoxicated to forcible rape and armed robbery, as well as on the perennial favorite, the death penalty and homicide.

However, as progressive refinements were made in data acquisition and analysis, and as research evidence accumulated, new questions arose concerning the deterrence doctrine. Empirical support for deterrence was progressively weakened. For example, Loftin (1980) reexamined Gibbs' study of 1968 which had supported deterrence, and showed that when controls are introduced for the effects of socio-cultural factors (e.g., incidence of poverty), evidence for deterrence disappears. Ehrlich's study of 1977, which also supported deterrence, has fared no better. In a recent reexamination of Ehrlich's study, Brier and Fienberg (1980) concluded that Ehrlich's theoretic model contained serious conceptual defects, that the data which Ehrlich employed to test his model were untrustworthy and inappropriate to the theoretic model, and that even if the theoretic model and Ehrlich's data were accepted as valid, Ehrlich's contentions in support of deterrence, including his conclusion that capital punishment deters homicide, "do not stand up to careful statistical scrutiny." Ehrlich's study has also been reexamined by Barnett (1981) with similarly negative results.

In addition, numerous recent studies have failed to support deterrence, including research by scholars such as Gibbs (Erickson, Gibbs, and Jensen, 1977) and Tittle (1977), whose research in the late 1960s had lent support to deterrence and had helped to revive research upon it. As Gibbs stated in 1978:

> Today, some ten years after the revival of research on the deterrence doctrine, the pendulum is definitely swinging the other way, meaning that the weight of evidence is once again shifting toward grave doubts about the doctrine.

To evaluate the status of deterrence research, the National Academy of Sciences convened a *Panel on Deterrence Research* (Blumstein, Cohen, and Nagin, 1978). The panel concluded that owing to a variety of unresolved methodological problems, research had failed to yield reliable conclusions.

PUBLIC SUPPORT FOR DETERRENCE

While criminologists' support for deterrence has been eroding, public support appears to be increasing, as evidenced at least by increased approval of capital punishment. For many people, deterrence requires no further demonstration. As Reid (1982:485) states, "advocates simply 'know' that punishment deters and this is especially 'true' of the death penalty." The question then arises: how do they know? More precisely, what are the origins of the deterrence doctrine's extraordinary appeal? To answer this question, it is useful to look not at contemporary criminological opinion, but rather at less tutored judgments. Consider, for example, the defense of deterrence provided by a criminologist writing in 1929 (Zimring and Hawkins, 1973:1):

> That the fear of punishment *can* deter is shown . . . vividly by its efficacy in the training of animals and even of fishes: a pike can be taught to swim amongst tench innocuously, or a flea to abstain from jumping.

In essence, his argument is that since deterrence obviously works for lowly creatures, even fish, it must surely work for people as well, including criminals. A not dissimilar argument was offered to me by a former police officer who claimed that deterrence is proved by the fact that traffic on the highway slows down in the presence of a clearly marked patrol car. Again, an argument for the deterrence doctrine rests on a generalization from the use of rather mild sanctions to control mundane misbehaviors to the use of the criminal sanction to control serious crime.

It is, it should be noted, undeniable that deterrence, in the sense of control of behavior through threat of punishment, is frequently an effective tactic of behavioral control on a mundane level. Learning theorists have demonstrated the effectiveness of negative reinforcement even for creatures possessing a far less sophisticated nervous system than does the fish. Virtually all parents use fear of punishment at least in part to control their children, as do most employers to control their workers. In this sense, personal experiences of the efficacy of deterrence—deterrence both as a means to control others and as a means to be controlled by them—is a near universal and powerful feature of human experience. Consequently, people "see" deterrence working all around themselves on a daily basis, and it is consequently hardly surprising if they extend it as the means to control criminal behavior. Yet, that is exactly the extension which the preponderance of criminological evidence suggests cannot be validly made.

A MODEL OF THE DETERRENCE PROCESS

In order to see why deterrence can both appear to work for control of many mundane behaviors, and yet fail for control of crime, it is useful to examine in detail the relationship between the deterrence doctrine and the view of behavior upon which it rests, that is, the view of behavior as oriented toward seeking rewards and avoiding punishments. Let us first begin with the simplest model of behavior which can illustrate deterrence, the price model of the criminal decision which was discussed above.

Assume that individuals act by assessing the anticipated *gains* (G) and anticipated *costs* (C) of each course of action. Where *net gain* (N) is the difference between gains and costs, i.e.,

$$(1) \qquad N = G - C$$

let us further assume that the condition for a behavior is:

$$(2) \qquad N > 0$$

In other words, for behavior to occur, the gain from the act must exceed its costs, thereby ensuring that the net gain is positive. Consistent with classical economic principles, let us further assume that individuals are *actuarially rational*. This means, in the case of criminal behavior, that the *cost* of crime (C) is the product of the *severity* (S) and the certainty or *probability* (P) of punishment, i.e.,

$$(3) \qquad C = S \times P$$

Thus, for example, if an individual judges that there is a ¼ chance of being apprehended (i.e., $P = 1/4$), and the anticipated punishment is a $50 fine (i.e., $S = 50$), the cost of that crime is ¼ × $50 = $12.50. That individual would, in theory, commit the crime if he or she anticipated a gain in excess of $12.50.

Consider the relationship between severity and deterrence which is implied by the above model. If an individual believes he or she will not get caught (i.e., if $P = 0$), the cost of crime is necessarily zero (i.e., $C = S \times P = S \times 0 = 0$), so deterrence cannot occur, however great may be the severity of punishment. A certain proportion of the population is thus theoretically *nondeterrable*. Furthermore, this proportion of the population may be quite considerable for several reasons: first, criminals are notable for optimism regarding their chances of escaping apprehension. More generally an "irrational" optimism characterizes much human behavior ranging from the purchase of sweepstakes tickets to small businessmen who invest their life savings despite extraordinary odds against them. Furthermore, social psychologists have documented a tendency for individuals to treat small probabilities as though they were zero (Handa, 1977:114); hence even persons who acknowledge a nonzero chance of being apprehended may nonetheless be nondeterrable. Finally, during periods of great emotional excitation, such as that associated with many crimes of passion, people frequently fail to consider the consequences of their behavior, and thus may act as though they were certain they would not be apprehended (i.e., $P = 0$), or as though gains from crime were indefinitely large (i.e., $G = \infty$).

Alternatively, if an individual acknowledges the possibility of being punished (i.e., if P exceeds 0), he or she is theoretically deterrable, and is deterred if the severity of punishment is sufficiently great. That occurs if S exceeds G/P. In sum, an individual is either nondeterrable (if $P = 0$) or can be deterred by a sufficiently severe penalty (if $P > 0$).

Finally, if an individual lacks criminal inclinations, gain from crime is zero or negative, and the crime is not committed even if the anticipated cost of crime is zero. Such an individual requires no deterrence to be dissuaded from crime.

If the relationship between deterrence and severity is examined using this model for a group of individuals the relationship between deterrence and severity is somewhat different. Some individual variation is inevitable, for example, in the anticipated gain and costs which different individuals would derive from crime (i.e., variations in G and C). Figure 1 depicts the relationship between severity and deterrence on a graph of which the horizontal axis represents the average perceived severity of punishment, and the vertical axis represents the percentage of deterrence where zero indicates a lack of deterrence (i.e., people follow their inclinations whatever they may be), and 100% deterrence indicates that everyone is deterred (i.e., there is no crime). As is apparent by inspection, the *deterrence curve* is shaped somewhat like an "S" which has been stretched horizontally. Deterrence is maximal (though not perfect) above an *upper threshold* (UT) of severity, deterrence is minimal below a *lower threshold* (LT) of severity, and a direct relationship exists between severity and deterrence within the thresholds in what can be termed a *zone of deterrence*. In essence, below the lower threshold the punishment is so weak that it deters no one, above the upper threshold the punishment is so severe that greater severity would further deter no one, and in the zone of deterrence is the often posited direct relationship between severity and deterrence.

A particularly significant feature of the "S" shape of the deterrence curve is its *robustness*. That is, the deterrence curve retains its "S" shape even when the model of behavior is substantially changed to make it more realistic (see Heckathorn, 1980, 1983), e.g., by granting that individuals are rarely actuarially rational as posited by Eq. 3 above (see Handa, 1977), or also when quite different assumptions are made about how

FIGURE 1 Relationship between anticipated severity (S) and deterrence in a group whose severity's standard deviation is one, mean antcipated gain from crime (G) is three, and certainty is 0.5 for 80% of the group and zero for 20%, hence the latter portion of the group is nondeterrable. The upper and lower thresholds of deterrence are defined such that 90% of the deterrent effects of severity fall between the thresholds.

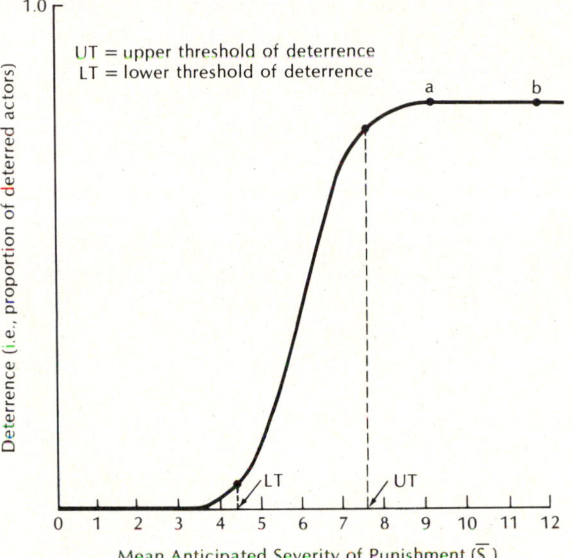

crime's anticipated gains and anticipated costs are distributed throughout the population.

If as suggested, the relationship between severity and deterrence is curvilinear, it becomes essential to distinguish between what Zimring and Hawkins (1973) termed "absolute deterrence," i.e., the deterrence effects of a penalty as compared to no penalty at all, and "marginal deterrence," i.e., the effects of increasing or reducing the sanction's severity (see also Gibbs, 1975 and Andenaes 1974). In Figure 1, absolute deterrence refers to the *height* of the deterrence curve, whereas marginal deterrence refers to the *slope* of that curve.

The "S" shape of the deterrence curve suggests an explanation for the apparent contradiction in deterrence's effectiveness for control of mundane versus criminal behaviors. The informal nonjudicial disciplining of pets, children, and peers typically employs threats of rather mild punishments, except in cases of unusual abusiveness. Consequently, the point of diminishing returns of severity (i.e., the upper threshold) is seldom attained, and as a result a consistent positive association between severity and deterrence is observed. That is, when deterrence fails, an increase in severity almost invariably rectifies that failure. Of course, that experience strongly validates belief in the efficacy of deterrence.

By contrast, the control of criminal behavior employs sanctions which are extraordinarily severe compared to those employed informally. Consequently, deterrence studies compare already highly severe penalties, and thus focus not on *absolute* but upon *marginal* deterrence. Thus the studies of capital punishment evaluate the relative deterrence effects of execution versus very long prison terms, and the finding that capital punishment "does not deter" indicates that *both* penalties deter equally and hence lie above the upper threshold, as do points a and b in Figure 1. More generally, the finding that crime rates are independent of severity not merely in the case of homicide, but also for other serious crimes indicates that the severity levels of criminal penalties in general lie above the upper threshold and hence lack marginal deterrence. If that is the case, further increases in severity would yield no additional deterrence, and indeed, penalties could perhaps be reduced without diminishing overall absolute deterrence.

The conclusion that the deterrence curve is "S" shaped is highly robust and consistent with research results, but that does not imply that the precise shape of that curve should be considered fixed. According to the above simple behavioral model, changes in mean anticipated certainty of punishment (*P*) affect the curve, as is illustrated in Figure 2, where deterrence curves are plotted for three groups which differ only in their mean certainty levels. As is apparent by inspection, increases in the anticipated probability of punishment shift the deterrence curve substantially upward, thereby strengthening absolute deterrence at all but the lowest levels of severity where deterrence remains negligible. These conclusions are consistent with the empirical findings of deterrence research that the association between deterrence and certainty is stronger and more consistent than between deterrence and severity.

CONCLUSION

Since the revival of research on the deterrence doctrine in the late 1960s, public opinion and informed criminological opinion have increasingly diverged, as the public has continued to support that doctrine and criminologists have increasingly rejected it. Yet it is

FIGURE 2 Deterrence/severity relationship for three levels of average certainty ($\bar{P}$ = 0.2, $\bar{P}$ = 0.4, $\bar{P}$ = 0.8) where σ_P = 0.5, and G = 20. Since certainty possesses an upper bound of one and a lower bound of zero, certainty is treated as a normal distribution which is truncated at one and zero, with the upper tail collapsed into P = 1 and the lower tail collapsed into P = 0. Consequently, certainty is characterized by a mixed distribution consisting of a truncated normal distribution and two point distributions.

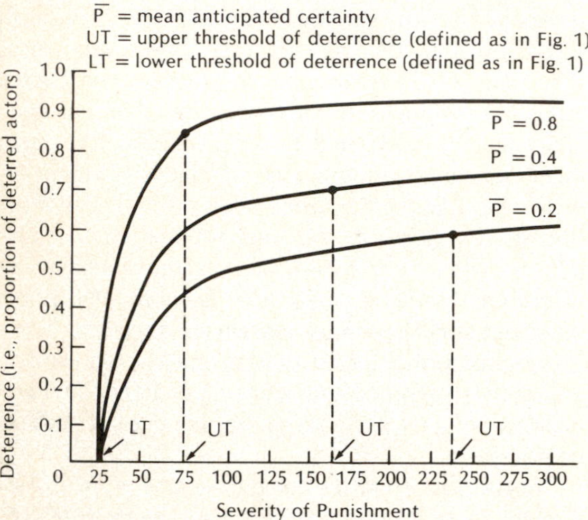

also clear that public support for deterrence is not wholly irrational, but derives from near universal experiences of everyday life in which the deterrence doctrine may appear to be validated. That occurs, for example, when increasing the severity of threatened punishment after pets, children or employees have misbehaved, makes them behave properly. After such experiences of the efficacy of deterrence, it would then seem plausible to conclude that criminals can also be made to behave by simply making the criminal sanction more punitive. Yet it is precisely this leap which is invalid—the leap from the deterrence doctrine as a valid social control mechanism within informal (normative) settings remedying minor misdeeds, to a presumed valid formal (legal) control mechanism to prevent crime. For the efficacy of deterrence is subject to steeply diminishing returns when sanctions are made more punitive. That is, above an upper threshold value, increasing the severity of punishment ceases to yield further deterrence. Generally, when pets and children are disciplined, the sanctions which are threatened are rather mild, so upper threshold values are but infrequently exceeded, and the diminishing returns of severity are only rarely observed. Expressed in terms of Figure 1's depiction of the deterrence curve, the usual range of severities employed in informal control falls in the left two thirds of the graph (i.e., from $\bar{S}$ = 0 to $\bar{S}$ = UT). As is apparent by inspection, *within that range*, deterrence can invariably be increased by a sufficiently great increase in severity. Hence, within this restricted domain, the deterrence doctrine is indeed valid. By contrast, legal control employs very severe sanctions. Expressed in terms of Figure 1's graph, the empirical finding that the criminal sanction's severity and deterrence are not positively related, indicates that the usual range of severities employed in legal control lie in the right third of the graph (i.e., $\bar{S}$ exceeds UT). As is clear from inspection, within this range, increases in severity leave deterrence unchanged, and hence the deterrence doctrine is invalid. In sum, the widespread notion that increasing the severity of the criminal sanction will produce further deterrence constitutes an erroneous generalization from normative control to legal control.

Since the prospects of enhanced deterrence through increased severity are at best dim, it might seem that increasing certainty possesses greater promise. To be sure, as was seen above, theoretic considerations and the results of empirical research both suggest that the association between deterrence and certainty is stronger and more consistent than that between deterrence and severity. However, substantially increasing the certainty of punishment for most crimes would be quite costly in financial terms, and in terms of the general population's loss of privacy and other liberties (Meier, 1978).

A conclusion of studies of deterrence is that the legal system is a less than perfect instrument for preventing crime. In fact, there may exist some activities which cannot effectively be regulated by existing legal institutions given current public attitudes. In countries like the United States where the justice system is politically responsive, public attitudes place an effective ceiling upon the maximum severity of the penalties which can be reliably imposed. For offenses like marijuana use and prostitution which are considered minor, if the criminal penalties appear grossly excessive, police may become reluctant to arrest, prosecutors may fail to prosecute, and juries may fail to convict, even when the evidence of guilt would seem to be clear. Thus actual enforcement is hampered and even may cease when penalties are considered too excessive. According to Galliher, McCartney, and Baum (1974), such a situation arose in Nebraska during the late 1960s when even simple possession of small quantities of marijuana was defined as a felony. If the gains from an act are sufficiently great relative to its publicly perceived seriousness, the *maximum* penalties which can be administered may fall *below* the minimum for effective deterrence, (i.e., $\overline{S}$ may fall below the lower threshold value, LT), thereby precluding any effective deterrent control short of either a change in public attitudes or a reorganization of the justice system to make it less susceptible to democratic pressures. Such a situation may have foredoomed the national prohibition of alcohol, and may also doom efforts to criminalize abortion, judging from the results of opinion polls which reveal broad-based public support for a woman's right to abortion. Whether it will guarantee the continued failure of efforts to control activities such as marijuana use and prostitution is somewhat less clear as public acceptance of them is less extensive than that for alcohol use and abortion.

In sum, analysis of the deterrence process has revealed the limits of deterrence as a means of behavioral regulation. While no doubt exists that substantial (absolute) deterrence is currently produced, the prospects for substantially enhanced deterrence through greater penalties are dim. In addition, some activities may be impossible to legally regulate, barring either a substantial reduction in their public acceptance or a profound and costly reorganization of the justice system to make it less responsive to the public. Therefore, the notion that controlling crime merely requires getting tough should be recognized as a myth.

REFERENCES

Andenaes, J. (1974) *Punishment and Deterrence*. Ann Arbor: University of Michigan Press.

Anderson, L. S., T. G. Chiricos, and G. P. Waldo (1977) Formal and informal sanctions: a comparison of deterrent effects." *Social Problems* 25: 103–114.

Barnett, A. (1981) "The deterrent effect of capital punishment: a test of some recent studies." *Operations Research* 29: 346–370.

Becker, G. S. (1968) "Crime and punishment: an economic approach." *J. of Pol. Economy* 78:169–217.

Blumstein, A., J. Cohen, and D. Nagin (eds.) (1978) *Deterrence and Incapacitation: Estimating the Effects of Criminal Sanctions on Crime Rates*. Washington, D.C.: National Academy of Sciences.

Bowers, W. J., and Glenn L. Pierce (1980) "Deterrence or brutalization: What is the effect of executions?" *Crime and Delinquency* 26:453–484.

Braithwaite, J. (1981) "The myth of social class and criminality reconsidered." *American Sociological Review* 46:36–57.

Brier, S. S., and S. E. Fienberg (1980) "Recent econometric modelling of crime and punishment: support for the deterrence hypothesis?" *Evaluation Review* 4:147–191.

Ehrlich, I. (1973) "Participation in illegitimate activities: a theoretical and empirical investigation." *J. of Pol. Economy* 81:521–565.

Ehrlich, I. (1975) "The deterrent effect of capital punishment: a question of life and death." *American Economic Review* 65:397–417.

Ehrlich, I. (1977) "Capital punishment and deterrence: some further thoughts and additional evidence." *J. of Pol. Economy* 84:741–788.

Erickson, M. L., J. P. Gibbs, and G. F. Jensen (1977) "The deterrence doctrine and the perceived certainty of legal punishments." *Amer. Soc. Rev.* 42:305–317.

Forst, B. (1977) "The deterrent effect of capital punishment: a cross-state analysis of the 1960's." *Minnesota Law Rev.* 61:743–767.

Galliher, J. J., J. L. McCartney, and B. E. Baum (1974) "Nebraska's marijuana law: a case of unexpected legislative innovation." *Law and Society Rev.* 8:441–455.

Gibbs, J. P. (1968) "Crime, punishment, and deterrence." *Southwestern Social Science Quarterly* 48:515–530.

Gibbs, J. P. (1975) *Crime, Punishment, and Deterrence*. New York: Elsevier.

Gibbs, J. P. (1978) "Another rush to judgment on the deterrence question." *Criminology* 16:22–30.

Gray, L. N., A. C. Miranne, III, D. A. Ward, and B. Menke (1982) "A game theoretic analysis of the components of punishment." *Social Psychology Quarterly* 45:206–213.

Green, G. S. (1978) "Measuring the incapacitative effectiveness of mixed punishment," in J. A. Cramer (ed.), *Preventing Crime*. Beverly Hills, CA: Sage Publications.

Greenberg, D. F. (1975) "The incapacitative effect of

imprisonment: some estimates." *Law and Society* (Summer), 541–580.

Handa, J. (1977) "Risk, probabilities, and a new theory of cardinal utility." *J. of Pol. Economy* 85:97–122.

Heckathorn, D. D. (1980) "A unified model of bargaining and conflict." *Behavioral Science* 25:261–284.

Heckathorn, D. D. (1983) "Extensions to power-dependence theory: the concept of resistance." *Social Forces* 59: 1206–1231.

Heckathorn, D. D., and W. L. Lucas (1982) "Bridging the consensus and conflict perspectives in drug use research: a 'unified' theoretic perspective." *J. of Drug Issues* 12, #4:443–455.

Hoenack, S. A., and W. C. Weiler (1980) "A structural model of murder behavior and the criminal justice system." *American Economic Review* 70:327–341.

Loftin, C. (1980) "Alternative estimates of the impact of certainty and severity of punishment on levels of homicide in American states," in S. E. Fienberg and A. J. Reiss, Jr. (eds.), *Indicators of Crime and Criminal Justice: Quantitative Studies*. Washington, D.C.: U.S. Department of Justice.

Loftin, C., and R. H. Hill (1974) "Regional subculture and homicide: an examination of the Gastil-Hackney thesis." *Am. Soc. Rev.* 39:714–724.

Meier, R. F. (1978) "The deterrence doctrine and public policy: a response to utilitarians," in J. Cramer (ed.), *Preventing Crime*. Beverly Hills, CA: Sage.

Meier, R. F., and W. T. Johnson (1977) "Deterrence as social control: the legal and extralegal production of conformity." *Am. Soc. Rev.* 42:292–304.

Nagin, D. (1975) *General Deterrence: A Review of the Empirical Evidence*. Pittsburgh: Urban Systems Institute, Carnegie-Mellon University.

Pontell, H. N. (1978) "Deterrence: theory versus practice." *Criminology* 16:3–22.

Reid, S. T. (1982) *Crime and Criminology*. New York: Holt, Rinehart and Winston.

Sellin, T. (1959) *The Death Penalty*. Philadelphia: American Law Institute.

Tittle, C. R. (1969) "Crime rates and legal sanctions." *Social Problems* 16:409–423.

Tittle, C. R. (1977) "Sanction, fear, and the maintenance of social order." *Social Forces* 55:579–596.

Tittle, C. R., and C. H. Logan (1973) "Sanctions and deviance: evidence and remaining questions." *Law and Society Rev.* 7:371–392.

Vold, G. B. (1958) *Theoretical Criminology*. New York: Oxford University Press.

Yunker, J. A. (1976) "Is the deterrent penalty a deterrence to homicide? Sometime series evidence. *Journal of Behavioral Economics* 5:422–427.

Yunker, J. A. (1982) "Testing the deterrent effect of capital punishment: a reduced form approach." *Criminology* 19:626–649.

Zimring, F. E., and G. J. Hawkins (1973) *Deterrence*. Chicago: University of Chicago Press.

8

CRITIQUES OF THE POLICE

Like other institutions the police system produces much that is socially valuable, but it inevitably reveals the blemishes of human failings. Investigative commissions have documented malfeasance, negligence, and corruption in law enforcement. Obviously the police have no monopoly on the negative characteristics of a flawed humanity.

On the other hand, it would be difficult to find another group in our society so prepared and willing to sacrifice its own well-being and even its life, if necessary, in the service of others. There is no sight so comforting as a police officer in uniform patrolling the beat, guarding a school crossing, directing traffic, or responding to emergencies.

Given the symbolic power of the police role in America, many of the critiques of the police reflect the internal psychological state and political ideology of the observer. Although there are much fundamental data about which there should be universal agreement, police behavior is subjected to a variety of interpretations of reality. The police officer in uniform generates an emotionally charged response that often reveals as much about the observer as about the object being observed.

It seems that the political context tends to dominate in most assessments of the police just as labeling theory does in its application to deviance. As a general proposition, therefore, we can assert that when an observer can be fairly identified as of a "liberal-radical" political persuasion, his or her critiques of the police will tend to stress the negative qualities of police behavior. Similarly, when a politically "conservative" critic offers an evaluation of the police, it is likely to be defined in favorable terms.

The first article in this section analyzes the ideological components of critiques of the police. The selections that follow provide clear examples of "objective" observers who demonstrate some of the angles of vision that are possible in the assessment of police behavior. The police establishments must recognize that by virtue of their status and function in society, their actions will precipitate strong criticism. They must guard against extreme or vindictive responses. In the past, police reactions to criticism have been generally to deny the truth of the allegation and to attack the motives or character of the critic. This sort of extreme response not only tends to alienate potential allies of the police, but also can be used by their critics as further evidence of police excesses.

As the police have improved their professional credentials, educational backgrounds, and political sophistication, the time has come for police representatives to present systematic, carefully reasoned responses to the inevitable critiques. Only in this fashion will they achieve trust and credibility, the sustaining force of democratic institutions.

Ideology and Criminal Justice Policy: Some Current Issues

Walter B. Miller

There is currently in the United States a widespread impression that our country is experiencing a major transitional phase—a period in which long-established social arrangements and the moral and conceptual notions that undergird them are undergoing substantial change. Optimists see this process as a transition from one relatively effective social order to another; pessimists see it as a one-way passage to catastrophe.

It is hard to judge the validity of these conceptions. Few generations have been free from the conviction that the nation was in the throes of "the crisis of our times," and such perceptions have not always corresponded with judgments of later historians.(1)

Since criminal behavior, ways of thinking about crime, and methods of dealing with crime make up an intrinsic component of any social order, the notion of a transitional phase also affects the perceptions and actions of both criminals and criminal justice system personnel. As soon as one considers crime as one facet of a larger set of social and historical shifts, however, a paradox emerges. One gets an impression both of striking and substantial change, and striking and substantial stability.

This paradox seems to apply equally to crime and to societal response to crime. On the one hand, patterns of contemporary criminal behavior reflect substantial shifts—e.g., a massive increase in drug use and drug-related crimes, a new dimension of political motivation affecting many adult prisoners. On the other hand, an impression of changelessness and stability is evident in the relatively unchanging nature of youth crime and periodic attention to youth gang violence.(2)

A similar paradox affects those responsible for making and implementing criminal justice policy. On the one hand, we seem to be in the midst of a radical shift in conceptualizing and coping with crime, indicated by a host of current slogans such as decentralization, deinstitutionalization, victimology and others. On the other hand, there is a surprising sameness in the basic issues which these slogans reflect—issues such as free will versus determinism, individual rights versus state's rights, concentration versus diffusion of power. Do these concerns represent progressive movement or merely contemporary replays of ancient dramas?

SOURCE: *The Journal of Criminal Law and Criminology.*

Intriguing as it might be to explore these issues with respect to the behavior of both those who engage in crime and those who attempt to deal with it, I shall treat only the latter. The terms "criminologist" or "criminal justice personnel" will be used here to refer to those persons who maintain some consistent responsibility for dealing with criminals and their behavior.

One may seek to escape this paradox by employing the concept of "ideology." Ideology is also a central element in the complex patterns of change and stability, and a key to their understanding. A useful point of departure may be found in a quotation from Myrdal's *An American Dilemma*:

> The place of the individual scientist along the scale of radicalism–conservatism has always had strong influences on both the selection of research problems and the conclusions drawn from research. In a sense, it is the master scale of biases in social science.(3)

It is this master scale, and its influence on the field of criminal justice, which will be my major concern here.

The term "ideology" may be used in many ways.(4) It will be used here only to refer to a set of general and abstract beliefs or assumptions about the correct or proper state of things, particularly with respect to the moral order and political arrangements, which serve to shape one's positions on specific issues. Several aspects of ideology as used in this sense should be noted. First, ideological assumptions are generally pre-conscious rather than explicit, and serve, under most circumstances, as unexamined presumptions underlying positions taken openly. Second, ideological assumptions bear a strong emotional charge. This charge is not always evident, but it can readily be activated by appropriate stimuli, in particular by direct challenge. During the process of formation, ideological premises for particular individuals are influenced by a variety of informational inputs, but once established they become relatively impervious to change, since they serve to receive or reject new evidence in terms of a self-contained and self-reinforcing system.

The major contention of this presentation is that ideology and its consequences exert a powerful influence on the policies and procedures of those who conduct the enterprise of criminal justice, and that the degree and kinds of influence go largely unrecognized. Ideology is the permanent hidden agenda of criminal justice.

The discussion has two major aims. First, assuming that the generally implicit ideological basis of criminal justice commands strong, emotional, partisan allegiance, I shall attempt to state explicitly the major assumptions of relevant divergent ideological positions in as neutral or as nonpartisan a fashion as possible. Second, some of the consequences of such ideologies for the processes of planning, programing, and policy in criminal justice will be examined.

I shall use a simple conceptual device for indicating ideological positions—a one-dimensional scale that runs from five on the right to zero in the middle to five on the left. Various ideological positions under consideration will be referred to this scale, using the terms "left" and "right" in an attempt to achieve neutrality. Although not all eleven possible distinctions will be made in every analysis, five scale distinctions on each side seem to be the minimum needed for present purposes. Later discussions will in some instances attribute considerable importance to differences as small as one scale degree.

The substance of ideologically divergent positions with respect to selected issues of current concern will be presented in three ways. Positions will be formulated first as "crusading issues"—shorthand catchwords or rallying cries that furnish the basic impetus for action or change in the criminal justice field. Such catch phrases are derived from a deeper and more abstract set of propositions as to desired states or outcomes. These will be designated "general assumptions." Third, differentiated positions will be delineated for all points along the full range of the scale—extreme right to extreme left—for three major policy issues.(5)

IDEOLOGICAL POSITIONS

Right: Crusading Issues

Crusading issues of the right differ somewhat from those of the left; they generally do not carry as explicit a message of movement toward new forms, but imply instead that things should be reconstituted or restored. However, the component of the message that says, "Things should be different from the way they are now," comes through just as clearly as in the crusading issues of the left. Current crusading issues of the right with respect to crime and how to deal with it include the following:

1. *Excessive leniency toward lawbreakers.* This is a traditional complaint of the right, accentuated at present by the publicity given to reform programs in corrections and policing, as well as to judicial activity at various levels.

2. *Favoring the welfare and rights of lawbreakers over the welfare and rights of their victims, of law enforcement officials, and the law abiding citizen.* This persisting concern is currently activated by attention to prisoners' rights, rehabilitation programs, attacks on police officers by militants, and in particular by a series of well-publicized Supreme Court decisions aimed to enhance the application of due process.

3. *Erosion of discipline and of respect for constituted authority.* This ancient concern is currently manifested in connection with the general behavior of youth, educational policies, treatment of student dissidents by college officials, attitudes and behavior toward law enforcement, particularly the police.

4. *The cost of crime.* Less likely to arouse the degree of passion evoked by other crusading issues, resentment over what is seen as the enormous and increasing cost of crime and dealing with criminals—a cost borne directly by the hard working and law abiding citizen—nevertheless remains active and persistent.

5. *Excessive permissiveness.* Related to excessive leniency, erosion of discipline, and the abdication of responsibility by authorities, this trend is seen as a fundamental defect in the contemporary social order, affecting many diverse areas such as sexual morality, discipline in the schools, educational philosophies, child-rearing, judicial handling of offenders, and media presentation of sexual materials.

Right: General Assumptions

These crusading issues, along with others of similar import, are not merely ritualized slogans, but reflect instead a more abstract set of assumptions about the nature of criminal behavior, the causes of criminality, responsibility for crime, appropriate ameliorative measures, and, on a broader level, the nature of man and of a proper kind of society. These general assumptions provide the basic charter for the ideological stance of the right as a whole, and a basis for distinguishing among the several subtypes along the points of the ideological scale. Major general assumptions of the right might be phrased as follows:

1. The individual is directly responsible for his own behavior. He is not a passive pawn of external forces, but possesses the capacity to make choices between right and wrong—choices which he makes with an awareness of their consequences.

2. A central requirement of a healthy and well functioning society is a strong moral order which is explicit, well-defined, and widely adhered to. Preferably the tenets of this system of morality should be derived from and grounded in the basic precepts of a major religious tradition. Threats to this moral order are threats to the very existence of the society. Within the moral order, two clusters are of particular importance:

a. Tenets which sustain the family unit involve morally-derived restrictions on sexual behavior, and obligations of parents to maintain consistent responsibility to their children and to one another.

b. Tenets which pertain to valued personal qualities include: taking personal responsibility for one's behavior and its consequences; conducting one's affairs with the maximum degree of self-reliance and independence, and the minimum of dependence and reliance on others, particularly public agencies; loyalty, particularly to one's country; achieving one's ends through hard work, responsibility to others, and self-discipline.

3. Of paramount importance is the security of the major arenas of one's customary activity—particularly those locations where the conduct of family life occurs. A fundamental personal and family right is safety from crime, violence, and attack, including the right of citizens to take necessary measures to secure their own safety, and the right to bear arms, particularly in cases where official agencies may appear ineffective in doing so.

4. Adherence to the legitimate directives of constituted authority is a primary means for achieving the goals of morality, correct individual behavior, security, and other valued life conditions. Authority in the service of social and institutional rules should be exercised fairly but firmly, and failure or refusal to accept or respect legitimate authority should be dealt with decisively and unequivocally.

5. A major device for ordering human relations in a large and heterogeneous society is that of maintaining distinctions among major categories of persons on the basis of differences in age, sex, and so on, with differences in religion, national background, race, and social position of particular importance. While individuals in each of the general categories should be granted the rights and privileges appropriate thereto, social order in many circumstances is greatly facilitated by maintaining both conceptual and spatial separation among the categories.

Left: Crusading Issues

Crusading issues of the left generally reflect marked dissatisfaction with characteristics of the current social order, and carry an insistent message about the desired nature and direction of social reform. Current issues of relevance to criminal justice include:

1. *Overcriminalization.* This reflects a conviction that a substantial number of offenses delineated under current law are wrongly or inappropriately included, and applies particularly to offenses such as gambling, prostitution, drug use, pornography, and homosexuality.

2. *Labelling and Stigmatization.* This issue is based on a conception that problems of crime are aggravated or even created by the ways in which actual or potential offenders are regarded and treated by persons in authority. To the degree a person is labelled as "criminal," "delinquent," or "deviant," will he be likely to so act.

3. *Overinstitutionalization.* This reflects a dissatisfaction over prevalent methods of dealing with suspected or convicted offenders whereby they are physically confined in large institutional facilities. Castigated as "warehousing," this practice is seen as having a wide range of detrimental consequences, many of which are implied by the ancient phrase "schools for crime." Signalled by a renewed interest in "incarceration," prison reform has become a major social cause of the left.

4. *Overcentralization.* This issue reflects dissatisfaction with the degree of centralized authority existing in organizations which deal with crime—including police departments, correctional systems, and crime-related services at all government levels. Terms which carry the thrust of the proposed remedy are local control, decentralization, community control, a new populism, and citizen power.

5. *Discriminatory Bias.* A particularly blameworthy feature of the present system lies in the widespread practice of conceiving and reacting to large categories of persons under class labels based on characteristics such as racial background, age, sex, income level, sexual practices, and involvement in criminality. Key terms here are racism, sexism, minority oppression and brutality.

Left: General Assumptions

As in the case of the rightist positions, these crusading issues are surface manifestations of a set of more basic and general assumptions, which might be stated as follows:

1. Primary responsibility for criminal behavior lies in conditions of the social order rather than in the character of the individual. Crime is to a greater extent a product of external social pressures than of internally generated individual motives, and is more appropriately regarded as a symptom of social dysfunction than as a phenomenon in its own right. The correct objective of ameliorative efforts, therefore, lies in the attempt to alter the social conditions that engender crime rather than to rehabilitate the individual.

2. The system of behavioral regulation maintained in America is based on a type of social and political order that is deficient in meeting the fundamental needs of the majority of its citizens. This social order, and the official system of behavioral regulation that it includes, incorporates an obsolete morality not applicable to the conditions of a rapidly changing technological society, and disproportionately geared to sustain the special interests of restricted groups, but which still commands strong support among working class and lower middle class sectors of the population.

3. A fundamental defect in the political and social organization of the United States and in those components of the criminal justice enterprise that are part of this system is an inequitable and unjust distribution of power, privilege, and resources—particularly of power. This inequity pervades the entire system, but appears in its more pronounced forms in the excessive centralization of governmental functions and consequent powerlessness of the governed, the military-like, hierarchical authority systems found in police and correctional organizations, and policies of systematic exclusion from positions of power and privilege for those who lack certain preferred social characteristics. The prime objective of reform must be to redistribute the decision-making power of the criminal justice enterprise rather than to alter the behavior of actual or potential offenders.

4. A further defect of the official system is its propensity to make distinctions among individuals based on major categories or classes within society such as age, sex, race, social class, criminal or non-criminal. Healthy societal adaptation for both the offender and the ordinary citizen depends on maintaining the minimum separation—conceptually and physically—between the community at large and those designated as "different" or "deviant." Reform efforts must be directed to bring this about.

5. Consistent with the capacity of external societal forces to engender crime, personnel of official agencies play a predominantly active role, and offenders a predominantly reactive role, in situations where the two come in contact. Official agents of behavioral regulation possess the capacity to induce or enhance criminal behavior by the manner in which they deal with those who have or may have engaged in crime. These agents may define offenders as basically criminal, expose them to stigmatization, degrade them on the basis of social characteristics, and subject them to rigid and arbitrary control.

6. The sector of the total range of human behavior currently included under the system of criminal sanctions is excessively broad, including many forms of behavior (for example, marijuana use, gambling, homosexuality) which do not violate the new morality and forms which would be more effectively and humanely dealt with outside the official system of criminal processing. Legal codes should be redrafted to remove many of the behavioral forms now proscribed, and to limit the discretionary prerogatives of local authorities over apprehension and disposition of violators.

AN IDEOLOGICAL SPECTRUM: DIFFERENTIATED POSITIONS OF LEFT AND RIGHT

The foregoing ideologically-relevant propositions are formulated as general assumptions common to all those designated as "left" or "right." The present section will expand and differentiate these generalized propositions by distributing them along the ideological scale proposed earlier. Charts I, II, and III (see Appendix) present thirty differentiated positions with respect to three major issues of relevance to criminal justice policy. Statements concerning each issue are assigned ten positions along scales running from right five through left five. The three issues are: conceptions as to the causes of crime and the locus of responsibility for criminality; conceptions of proper methods of dealing with offenders; conceptions of proper operating policies of criminal justice agencies. Not included in these tables is a theoretically possible "centrist" position.

Several features of the charts in the Appendix should be noted. Statements representing ideologically-influenced positions on the scale are formulated in a highly condensed and simplified manner, lacking the subtleties, qualifications, and supporting arguments which characterize the actual stances of most people. The basic model is that of an "ideal type" analysis which presents a series of simplified propositions formulated to bear a logical relationship to one another and to underlying abstract principles, rather than to reflect accurately the actual positions of real people.(6) Few readers will feel entirely comfortable with any of the statements exactly as phrased here: most will feel instead that given statements might reflect the general gist of their position, but with important qualifications, or that one can subscribe to selected parts of statements at several different points along the scale. On the other hand, few readers will fail to find some statements with which they disagree completely; it is most unlikely, for example, that one could support with equal enthusiasm the major tenets attributed here to positions at left four and right four.

In "placing" oneself with respect to the scaled positions outlined here, one should look for those statements with which one feels least uncomfortable rather than expecting to find formulations which correspond in all respects to one's viewpoint. The process of ascertaining discrepancies between actual positions and those represented here as "pure" examples of rightist or leftist ideology serves one of the purposes of ideal-typical analysis; few are ideological purists, but this type of analysis makes it possible to identify positions which correspond more or less closely to ideological orthodoxy. Those whose positions are closer to the extremes will feel least comfortable with statements attributed to the opposing side of the spectrum; those closer to "centrist" positions will tend to find orientations congenial to their own at a larger number of scale positions, possibly including positions on both sides of the spectrum.

To say that the statements show some logical relationship to one another and to underlying principles is not to say that they are logically consistent; in fact, several obvious inconsistencies appear in the charts. For example, right five maintains that criminals are unwitting puppets of a radical conspiracy and, at the same time, holds that they are responsible for their own behavior. Left four calls for maximum access to information concerning the inner workings of criminal justice agencies and, at the same time, advocates minimum access by employers, personnel departments and others to criminal records of individuals. If one fails to find in internal consistency the "logical" basis for these propositions, where do the logical relationships lie?

Although some degree of logical inconsistency is likely in almost any developed set of propositions about human behavior, the consistency in the above propositions lies largely in the degree to which the interests of particular classes of persons are supported, defended, and justified. The inconsistencies often lie either in the means advocated to achieve such ends or in the rationales used to defend or exculpate favored interests and condemn opposing ones. In the above examples, if one assumes that a basic interest of left four is maximum protection of and support for actual or putative offenders, then these ends are served in the one instance by maximum access to information which might reveal errors, inequities or violations in their treatment by criminal justice officials, and in the other by denying to potential employers and others access to information that might jeopardize their welfare. Similarly, in attempting to reconcile the apparent contradiction in assertions that offenders are pawns of radical conspiracy and also that they are directly responsible for their behavior, a rightist could argue that offenders are indeed responsible for their behavior, and that they make a deliberate personal choice to follow the crime-engendering appeals of the radicals.

While statements at different scale positions frequently present differing orientations to the same sub-issue (e.g., scope of criminal law, appropriate degree of restraint of offenders, extent to which "rehabilitation" should be an objective), not all of the statements on each major issue treat all of the included sub-issues. The positioned statements are defective with respect to "dimensionality," the possibility of full scalability across all issues. Each of the included sub-issues represents an independently scalable dimension. The "cause" issue incorporates approximately 14 distinguishable dimensions or sub-issues, the "offender" issue 15, and the "agencies" issue 18. To include a separate statement for each dimension at each scale position for all three issues would require a minimum of 470 statements—an impractical number for a presentation at this level. Selection of sub-issues and their assignment to given positions were guided by an attempt both to produce internally-coherent statements and to cover a fairly broad range of sub-issues.

One often finds convergences at the extremes of a distribution of ideological positions. Several instances can be found in the charts; for example, both right five and left five attribute criminality to deliberate or systematic efforts or policies of highly-organized interest groups, although of differing identities (radicals, the ruling class). If quantifiable weights can be assigned to the scalable dimensions of the chart, two major types of distribution are included—"opposition" and "convergence" distributions. "Opposition" distributions occur where the maximum weight or magnitude is found at one extreme of the scale and the minimum at the other, with intermediate positions showing intermediate values. Examples may be found in the sub-issues "degree of coercive power to be exercised by official agencies"; (left five espouses the minimum degree, right five the maximum, with others occupying intermediate positions), and "degree of personal culpability of offenders" (right five maximum, left five minimum, others in between). Policy disputes involving this type of distribution tend to be most difficult to resolve.

In "convergence" distributions similarities or partial similarities are found in the positions of those at opposing ends of the spectrum. One instance is found in attitudes toward rehabilitation of offenders—an objective strongly opposed by partisans at both left four and right four, although for different reasons. A rather complex but crucial instance is found in the statements concerning "localized" versus "centralized" authority. Both left four and right four call for increased local autonomy whereas the more "moderate" of both left and right favor continued or increased federal authority and support for criminal justice programs and operations. The apparent convergence of the extremes is, however, complicated by a number of factors. One relates to which branch of government exercises authority; another relates to the particular policy area at issue. Those at left four are not adverse to strong federal initiatives to improve social-service delivery capacity of local welfare agencies. Those at right four, while decrying the iron grip of federal bureaucrats over local affairs, are not adverse to strong federal initiatives to improve technological capacity of local police forces. The more extreme leftists seek greatly increased local autonomy for citizen control over police and correctional operations, but welcome strong federal power in formulating and enforcing uniform civil rights measures. The more extreme rightists adamantly oppose the use of centralized power to enforce "mixing" of racial and other social categories or to compel uniform operations of local police, courts and corrections, but welcome strong federal power in the development and maintenance of military forces, or a strong federal investigatory branch with the power to probe corruption and collusion in local programs, particularly those of left-oriented agencies.

The unifying principle behind these apparent contradictions is the same as that noted for intraposition inconsistencies; ideologically-derived objectives are supported despite possible discrepancies involving the means to achieve them or the identity of sources of support. An additional dimension of considerable importance is also involved—that of time. Ideological positions of left and right are delineated on the basis of a given point in time earlier designated as "current." But specific stances of the left and right can change rapidly in response to changing circumstances, or they can even reverse themselves. Moreover, some of the "crusading issues" currently fashionable will become passé in the near future.

The "decentralization" issue again provides a good example. Whether one favors more or less power for "centralized" or federal agencies depends on the current ideological complexion of the several federal departments or branches. Viewed very broadly, in the early 1930's the left looked to the executive branch as a prime source of support for policies they favored, and the right to the judicial and legislative; in the 1960's the left viewed both the executive and judicial as allies, the legislature as a potential source of opposition, and sought more power for the High Court and the Presidency. At present the right views the executive as supportive, and the left looks to the legislature as an ally in an attempt to curb the power of the Presidency. Reflecting these shifts have been changes in attitudes of the left and right toward "local control." While traditionally a crusading issue of the right (state's rights), the banner for community control was taken up in the 1960's by the left as an effective method of bypassing entrenched political power at the local level—primarily with respect to civil rights. Recently the trend has begun to reverse because of a resurgence of the right's traditional "anti-big-government" stance and an increasing resort to local control by community groups pursuing rightist causes (e.g., exclusion of blacks from white schools).

Further detailed analyses of convergences and divergences, consistencies and contradictions, past, present and future fashions of both these issues and others could be developed. It might be useful at this point, however, to briefly consider a more fundamental level—the basic philosophical underpinnings of the two sides—and to compress the variety and complexity of their varied positions into a single and simple governing principle.

For the right, the paramount value is order—an ordered society based on a pervasive and binding morality—and the paramount danger is disorder—social, moral and political. For the left, the paramount value is justice—a just society based on a fair and equitable distribution of power, wealth, prestige, and privilege—and the paramount evil is injustice—the concentration of valued social resources in the hands of a privileged minority.

Few Americans would quarrel with either of these values since both are intrinsic aspects of our national ideals. Stripped of the passion of ideological conflict, the issue between the two sides could be viewed as a disagreement over the relative priority of two valuable conditions: whether *order with justice*, or *justice with order* should be the guiding principle of the criminal justice enterprise.

These are ancient philosophical issues, and their many aspects have been argued in detail for centuries. Can both order and justice be maximized in a large, heterogeneous, pluralistic society? Can either objective be granted priority under all circumstances? If not, under what circumstances should which objective be seen as paramount? It might appear that these issues are today just as susceptible to rational discussion as they have been in the past; but this is not so, because the climate militates against such discussion. Why this is so will be considered shortly—after a brief discussion of the ideologies of the formal agencies of criminal justice.

IDEOLOGICAL COMPLEXION OF CRIMINAL JUSTICE AGENCIES

The ideological positions of four major professional fields will be discussed—academic criminology, the police, the judiciary, and corrections. Rather than complex analysis or careful delineation, tentative impressions will be offered. Each system will be characterized on a very gross level, but it is important to bear in mind the possibility that there is as much ideological variability within each of the several systems as there is among them. Of particular importance within these systems are differences in age level, social class and educational level, and rank.

Academic Criminologists. This group is included not out of any presumption about the importance of the role they play, but rather because academic criminology provides the platform from which the present analysis is presented. Probably the most important point to make here is that the day-to-day ideological environment of the average academic criminologist, viewed within the context of the total society, is highly artificial; it reflects the perspectives of a deviant and unrepresentative minority. Academic criminology, reflecting academic social science in general, is substantially oriented toward the left, while the bulk of American people are oriented toward the right.(7) Furthermore, the members of the large liberal academic majority do proportionately more writing and speechmaking than those of the small conservative minority, so that their impact on the ideological climate exceeds even their large numbers. If the proportion of right-oriented persons in academic criminology comes close to being just the reverse of that in the general population, then this marked ideological divergence certainly has implications for those situations in which academicians come in contact with the public, particularly where they interact with representatives of other criminal justice branches. It also has an important impact on their own perceptions of the ideological positions of the public and other criminal justice professionals.

Police. The bulk of police officers have working-class backgrounds, and the contemporary working class is substantially rightist. Archie Bunker is a caricature, but the reality he exaggerates is a significant one. . . . Among police departments, differences in ideological complexion are found in different regions (for example, West Coast departments generally have higher proportions of college-trained personnel), different sized communities, and departments with different personnel policies. Within departments, age differences may be important (some younger officers are less rightist), as well as differences in rank and function (some departments have more liberally-oriented chiefs or research and planning personnel). The majority of working police professionals, however, subscribe to the ideological premises here designated as "rightist."

Judiciary. The legal and judicial field is probably characterized by greater ideological diversity than either the police or corrections. One reason is that leftist positions are more common among those with college degrees than among those with less education. Since college education is a prerequisite to formal legal training, lawyers are more likely to have been exposed to the leftward orientation characteristic of most academic faculties, particularly those of the larger and more prestigious universities.(8) Judges show enormous variation in ideological predilections, probably covering the full range from right five to left four. Variation is related to factors such as the law school attended, size of jurisdiction, social status of jurists and their clientele, region, level of the court. While public attention is often directed to the actions of highly moralistic, hard line judges at right four and five positions, such jurists are probably becoming less common.

Ideological orientations of the legal profession have recently been subject to public attention, particularly in connection with two developments. First, the Supreme Court has in the recent past been associated with a series of decisions that reflect basic tenets of the left. Included have been such issues as increased protection for the rights of suspected and accused persons, inadmissibility of illegally-obtained evidence, minimization of distinctions based on race, reduction of discretionary powers of law-enforcement personnel, and reduction of judicial discretion in juvenile proceedings.(9) These decisions and others were perceived by the right as posing a critical threat to an established balance of power and prerogatives between law-enforcement personnel and offenders, seriously endangering the law-enforcement process and the security of the public.

The second development is the emergence during the past two decades of a group of young left-oriented lawyers whose influence is probably disproportionate to their small numbers. Able, dedicated, active on a variety of fronts, many representing low-income or black clients, their activities became best known in connection with Federal Anti-Poverty programs. Many of these lawyers have assumed positions along the ideological scale as far left as the left three and left four positions.

Despite these well-publicized manifestations of leftward orientations in some sectors of the legal profession, it is unlikely that a substantial proportion of the profession consistently espouses the tenets of the left, particularly those of left three and beyond. The more liberal judges are generally found in federal and higher-level state courts, but conservative views are still common among jurists of the lower level courts, where the great bulk of day-to-day legal business is transacted. Moreover, as part of the ideological shifts noted earlier, the Burger court is regarded by the right with considerably less antipathy than the Warren court.(10)

Corrections. Corrections, the current hot spot of the criminal justice field, probably contains a mixture of ideological positions, with the bulk of correctional personnel ranged along the right. The average lower-echelon corrections employee has a working-class background similar to that of the average patrolman, and thus manifests the rightist orientation characteristic of that class. As in the case of police, age may be an important basis for differentiation, with older officials more likely to assume right-oriented positions. Among other bases are size of the institution and age level of the bulk of inmates. Juvenile corrections tends to have a higher likelihood of left-oriented staff, both at administrative and lower-echelon levels.

Prison reform is currently one of the most intense crusading issues of the left. While most reform efforts are exerted by persons not officially part of the correctional system, there has been some influx of left three and four persons into the official system itself, particularly among younger staff in juvenile correction facilities.

CONSEQUENCES OF IDEOLOGY

If, as is here contended, many of those involved in the tasks of planning and executing the major policies and procedures of our criminal justice system are subject to the influence of pervasive ideological assumptions about the nature of crime and methods of dealing with it—assumptions which are largely implicit and unexamined—the question then arises: what are the consequences of this phenomenon?

While both the crusading issues and graded ideological positions presented earlier were phrased to convey the tone of urgent imperatives, the assumptions from which they arise were phrased in relatively neutral terms as a set of general propositions about the nature, causes, and processes of coping with crime. So phrased and so regarded, these assumptions are susceptible to rational consideration. Their strengths and weaknesses can be debated, evidence can be employed to test the degree of validity each may possess, contradictions among them can be considered, and attempts made to explain or reconcile differences among them. Formulated and used in this manner, the question arises: why are they characterized here as "ideological"?

The scale of ideology presented comprises a single major parameter—substantive variation along a left-right scale with respect to a set of issues germane to crime and the criminal justice process. But there is an additional important parameter which must also be considered: that of intensity—the degree of emotional charge which attaches to the assumptions. It is the capacity of these positions to evoke the most passionate kinds of reactions and to become infused with deeply felt, quasi-religious significance that constitutes the crucial element in the difference between testable assumptions and ideological tenets. This dimension has the power to transform plausibility into ironclad certainty, conditional belief into ardent conviction, the reasoned advocate into the implacable zealot. Rather than being looked upon as useful and conditional hypotheses, these assumptions, for many, take the form of the sacred and inviolable dogma of the one true faith, the questioning of which is heresy, and the opposing of which is profoundly evil.

This phenomenon—ideological intensification—appears increasingly to exert a powerful impact on the entire field. Leslie Wilkins has recorded his opinion that the criminal justice enterprise is becoming progressively more scientific and secularized(11); an opposite, or at least concurrent, trend is here suggested—that it is becoming progressively more ideologized. The consequences are many. Seven will be discussed briefly: Polarization, Reverse Projection, Ideologized Selectivity, Informational Constriction, Catastrophism, Magnification of Prevalence, and Distortion of Opposing Positions.

Polarization. Polarization is perhaps the most obvious consequence of ideological intensification. The more heavily a belief takes on the character of sacred dogma, the more necessary it becomes to view the proponents of opposing positions as devils and scoundrels, and their views as dangerous and immoral. Cast in this framework of the sacred and the profane, of virtuous heroes and despicable villains, the degree of accommodation and compromise that seems essential to the complex enterprise of criminal justice planning becomes, at best, enormously complicated, and at worst, quite impossible.

Reverse Projection. This is a process whereby a person who occupies a position at a given point along the ideological scale perceives those who occupy any point closer to the center than his own as being on the opposite side of the scale. Three aspects of this phenomenon, which appears in its most pronounced form at the extremes of the scale, should be noted. First, if one grants the logical possibility that there can exist a "centrist" position—not a position which maintains no assumptions, but one whose assumptions are "mixed," "balanced," or not readily characterizable—then this position is perceived as "rightist" by those on the left, and "leftist" by those on the right.

A second aspect concerns the intensity of antagonism often shown by those occupying immediately adjacent positions along the ideological scale. Perhaps the most familiar current manifestation of this is found in the bitter mutual denunciations of those classified here as occupying the positions of left four and left five. Those at left four are often taken by those at left five as far more dangerous and evil than those seen as patent fascists at right four and five. Left fours stand accused as dupes of the right, selling out to or being co-opted by the establishment, and blunting the thrust of social activism by cowardly vacillation and compromise.

A third aspect of reverse projection is that one tends to make the most sensitive intrascale distinctions closest to the point that one occupies. Thus, someone at right four might be extremely sensitive to differences between his position and that of an absolute dictatorship advocate at right five, and at the same time cast left four and five into an undifferentiated class of commies, communist dupes and radicals, quite oblivious to the distinctions that loom so large to those who occupy these positions.

Ideologized Selectivity. The range of issues, problems, areas of endeavor, and arenas of activity relevant to the criminal justice enterprise is enormous. Given the vastness of the field relative to the availability of resources, decisions must be made as to task priorities and resource allocation. Ideology plays a paramount but largely unrecognized role in this process, to the detriment of other ways of determining priorities. Ideologized selectivity exerts a constant influence in determining which problem areas are granted greatest significance, which projects are supported, what kinds of information are gathered and how research results are analyzed and interpreted. Divergent resource allocation policies of major federal agencies can be viewed as directly related to the dominant ideological orientation of the agency.

Only one example of ideologized selectivity will be cited here. The increasing use of drugs, soft and hard, and an attendant range of drug-related crime problems is certainly a major contemporary development. The importance of this problem is reflected in the attention devoted to it by academic criminologists. One major reason for this intensive attention is that explanations for the spread of drug use fit the ideological assumptions shared by most academicians (drug use is an understandable product of alienation resulting from the failure of the system to provide adequate meaning and quality to life). Also one major ameliorative proposal, the liberalization of drug laws, accords directly with a crusading issue of the left—decriminalization.

Another contemporary phenomenon, quite possibly of similar magnitude, centers on the apparent disproportionate numbers of low-status urban blacks arrested for violent and predatory crimes, brought to court and sent to prison. While not entirely ignored by academic criminologists, the relatively low amount of attention devoted to this phenomenon stands in sharp contrast to the intensive efforts evident in the field of drugs. Important aspects of the problem of black crime do not fit the ideological assumptions of the majority of academic criminologists. Insofar as the issue is studied, the problem is generally stated in terms of oppressive, unjust and discriminatory behavior by society and its law-enforcement agents—a formulation that accords with that tenet of the left which assumes the capacity of officials to engender crime by their actions, and the parallel assumption that major responsibility for crime lies in conditions of the social order. Approaches to the problem that involve the careful collection of information relative to such characteristics of the population itself as racial and social status run counter to ideological tenets that call for the minimization of such distinctions both conceptually and in practice, and thus are left largely unattended.

Informational Constriction. An attitude which is quite prevalent in many quarters of the criminal justice enterprise today involves a depreciation of the value of research in general, and research on causes of crime in particular. Several reasons are commonly given, including the notion that money spent on research has a low payoff relative to that spent for action, that past research has yielded little of real value for present problems, and that research on causes of crime in particular is of little value since the low degree of consensus among various competing schools and theorists provides little in the way of unified conclusions or concrete guidance. Quite independent of the validity of such reasons, the anti-research stance can be seen as a logical consequence of ideological intensification.

For the ideologically committed at both ends of the scale, new information appears both useless and dangerous. It is useless because the basic answers, particularly with respect to causes, are already given, in their true and final form, by the ideology; it is dangerous because evidence provided by new research has the potential of calling into question ideologically established truths.

In line with this orientation, the present enterprise, that of examining the influence of ideology on criminal justice policy and programs, must be regarded with distaste by the ideologically intense—not only because it represents information of relevance to ideological doctrine, but also because the very nature of the analysis implies that ideological truth is relative.

Catastrophism. Ideological partisans at both extremes of the scale are intensely committed to particular programs or policies they wish to see effected, and recurrently issue dire warnings of terrible catastrophes that will certainly ensue unless their proposals are adopted (Right: Unless the police are promptly given full power to curb criminality and unless rampant permissiveness toward criminals is halted, the country will surely be faced with an unprecedented wave of crime and violence; Left: Unless society promptly decides to provide the resources necessary to eliminate poverty, discrimination, injustice and exploitation, the country will surely be faced with a holocaust of violence worse than ever before). Such predictions are used as tactics in a general strategy for enlisting support for partisan causes: "Unless you turn to us and our program. . . ." That the great bulk of catastrophes so ominously predicted do not materialize does not deter catastrophism, since partisans can generally claim that it was the response to their warnings that forestalled the catastrophe. Catastrophism can thus serve to inhibit adaptation to real crises by casting into question the credibility of accurate prophets along with the inaccurate.

Magnification of Prevalence. Ideological intensification produces a characteristic effect on perceptions of the empirical prevalence of phenomena related to areas of ideological concern. In general, targets of ideological condemnation are represented as far more prevalent than carefully collected evidence would indicate. Examples are estimates by rightists of the numbers of black militants, radical conspirators, and welfare cheaters, and by leftists of the number of brutal policemen, sadistic prison personnel, and totally legitimate welfare recipients.

Distortion of the Opposition. To facilitate a demonstration of the invalidity of tenets on the opposite side of the ideological scale it is necessary for partisans to formulate the actual positions of the opposition in such a way as to make them most susceptible to refutation. Opposition positions are phrased to appear maximally illogical, irrational, insupportable, simplistic, internally contradictory, and if possible, contemptible or ludicrous. Such distortion impedes the capacity to adequately comprehend and represent positions or points of view which may be complex and extensively developed—a capacity that can be of great value when confronting policy differences based on ideological divergencies.

IMPLICATIONS

What are the implications of this analysis for those who face the demanding tasks of criminal justice action and planning? It might first appear that the prescription would follow simply and directly from the diagnosis. If the processes of formulating and implementing policy with respect to crime problems are heavily infused with ideological doctrine, and if this produces a variety of disadvantageous consequences, the moral would appear to be clear: work to reverse the trend of increased ideological intensification, bring out into the open the hidden ideological agenda of the criminal justice enterprise, and make it possible to release the energy now consumed in partisan conflict for a more direct and effective engagement with the problem field itself.

But such a prescription is both overly optimistic and overly simple. It cannot be doubted that the United States in the latter 20th century is faced with the necessity of confronting and adapting to a set of substantially modified circumstances, rooted primarily in technological developments with complex and ramified sociological consequences. It does not appear too far-fetched to propose that major kinds of necessary social adaptation in the United States can occur only through the medium of ardently ideological social movements—and that the costs of such a process must be borne in order to achieve the benefits it ultimately will confer. If this conception is correct, then ideological identification, with all its dangers and drawbacks, must be seen as a necessary component of effective social adaptation, and the ideologists must be seen as playing a necessary role in the process of social change.

Even if one grants, however, that ideology will remain an inherent element of the policy-making process, and that while enhancing drive, dedication and commitment it also engenders rigidity, intolerance and distortion—one might still ask whether it is possible to limit the detrimental consequences of ideology without impairing its strengths. Such an objective is not easy, but steps can be taken in this direction. One such step entails an effort to increase one's capacity to discriminate between those types of information which are more heavily invested with ideological content and those which are less so. This involves the traditional distinction between "fact" and "value" statements.(12) The present delineation of selected ideological stances of the left and right provides one basis for estimating the degree to which statements forwarded as established conclusions are based on ideological doctrine rather than empirically supportable evidence. When assertions are made about what measures best serve the purposes of securing order, justice, and the public welfare, one should ask "How do we know this?" If statements appear to reflect in greater or lesser degree the interrelated patterns of premises, assumptions and prescriptions here characterized as "ideological," one should accommodate one's reactions accordingly.

Another step is to attempt to grant the appropriate degree of validity to positions on the other side of the scale from one's own. If ideological commitment plays an important part in the process of developing effective policy, one must bear in mind that both left and right have important parts to play. The left provides the cutting edge of innovation, the capacity to isolate and identify those aspects of existing systems which are least adaptive, and the imagination and vision to devise new modes and new instrumentalities for accommodating emergent conditions. The right has the capacity to sense those elements of the established order that have strength, value, or continuing usefulness, to serve as a brake on over-rapid alteration of existing modes of adaptation, and to use what is valid in the past as a guide to the future. Through the dynamic clash between the two forces, new and valid adaptations may emerge.

None of us can free himself from the influence of ideological predilections, nor are we certain that it would be desirable to do so. But the purposes of effective policy and practice are not served when we are unable to recognize in opposing positions the degree of legitimacy, validity, and humane intent they may possess. It does not seem unreasonable to ask of those engaged in the demanding task of formulating and implementing criminal justice policy that they accord to differing positions that measure of respect and consideration that the true ideologue can never grant.

REFERENCES

1. A few examples of perceptions that "our times" are witnessing radical or unprecedented changes are found in selected excerpts from statements published in 1874, 1930, and 1939, respectively.

> Society has grave charges to answer in regard to its influence on the present and rising generation. . . . The social conditions of the present age are such as to favor the development of insanity. The habits inculcated by . . . growing wealth . . . among individuals of one class and the stinging poverty . . . of another . . . nurture dispositions which might . . . under more equitable distributions . . . have died out. Have we not seen [youth] emerging from the restraints of school, scoffing at the opinions of the world, flouting everything but their own conceit . . . ?

Dickson, "The Science and Practice of Medicine in Relation to Mind, and the Jurisprudence of Insanity," (1874), quoted in M. Altschule, *Roots of Modern Psychiatry* (1957), pp. 122 and 133.

> In our nineteenth century polity, the home was a chief reliance . . . discipline was recognized as a reality . . . the pressure of the neighborhood . . . was strong . . . in the urban industrial society of today there is a radical change. . . . This complete change in the background of social control involves much that may be easily attributed to the ineffectiveness of criminal justice. . . .

Pound, "Criminal Justice in America" (1930), quoted in F. Tannenbaum, *Crime and the Community* (1938), p. 29.

> Men's ways of ordering their common lives have broken down so disastrously as to make hope precarious. So headlong and pervasive is change today that . . . historical parallels are decreasingly relevant . . . because so many of the variables in the situation have altered radically. . . . Professor James T. Shotwell recently characterized "the anarchy we are living in today" as "the most dangerous since the fall of Rome."

R. Lynd, *Knowledge for What* (1939), pp. 2 and 11.

2. An analysis involving long-term trends in youth gang violence and periodically recurrent representations of such violence as a new phenomenon engendered by contemporary conditions is included in Miller, "American Youth Gangs: Past and Present," in A. Blumberg, *Current Perspectives on Criminal Behavior* (1974), pp. 210–239.

3. G. Myrdal, *An American Dilemma: The Negro Problem and Modern Democracy* (1944), p. 1038. Myrdal's citation of the "radicalism–conservatism" scale is part of an extended discussion of sources of bias in works on race relations, appearing as Appendix 2, "A Methodological Note on Facts and Valuations in Social Science," pp. 1035–64. His entire discussion is germane to issues treated in this article.

4. A classic treatment of ideology is K. Mannheim, *Ideology and Utopia* (1936). *See* ch. II.1 "Definition of Concepts." *See* also G. Myrdal, *supra* note 3, at 1035–64. There is an extensive literature, much of it sociological, dealing with ideology as it relates to a wide range of political and social phenomena, but the specific relation between ideology and criminal justice has received relatively little direct attention. Among more recent general discussions are E. Shils, *The Intellectuals and the Powers* (1972); Orlans, "The Political Uses of Social Research," *Annals of the American Academy of Political and Social Science, 393* (1971), p. 28; Kelman, "I.Q., Race, and Public Debate," *Hastings Center Rep., 2* (1972), p. 8. Treatments more specific to crime and criminal justice appear in L. Radzinowicz, *Ideology and Crime* (1966); Andanaes, "Punishment and the Problem of General Prevention," *International Annals of Criminology, 8* (1969), p. 285; Blumberg, "The Adversary System," in C. Bersani, *Crime and Delinquency* (1970), p. 435; Glaser, "Criminology

and Public Policy," *American Sociologist*, 6 (1971), p. 30.

5. The substance of ideologically-relevant statements formulated here as crusading issues, general assumptions, or differentiated positions was derived from examination and analysis of a wide range of materials appearing in diverse forms in diverse sources. Materials were selected primarily on the basis of two criteria: that they bear on issues of current relevance to criminal justice policy, and that they represent one possible stance with respect to issues characterized by markedly divergent stances. With few exceptions, the statements as formulated here do not represent direct quotes, but have been generalized, abstracted or paraphrased from one or more sets of statements by one or more representatives of positions along the ideological scale. A substantial portion of the statements thus derived were taken from books, articles, speeches, and media reporting of statements by the following: Robert Welch, writer; John Schmitz, legislator; Gerald L. K. Smith, writer; Meyer Kahane, clergyman; Edward Banfield, political scientist; William Loeb, publisher; George Wallace, government; Julius Hoffman, jurist; L. Patrick Gray III, lawyer; William Rehnquist, jurist; William Buckley, writer; Spiro Agnew, government; Robert M. McKiernan, police; Howard J. Phillips, government; Lewis F. Powell Jr., jurist; Andrew Hacker, political scientist; Kevin Phillips, writer; Victor Reisel, labor; Albert Shanker, educator; Fred P. Graham, lawyer/writer; Warren Burger, jurist; James Q. Wilson, political scientist; Hubert H. Humphrey, legislator; James Reston, writer; Jacob Javits, legislator; Ramsey Clark, lawyer; Tom Wicker, writer; Earl Warren, jurist; James F. Ahearn, police; Henry Steele Commager, historian; Alan Dershowitz, lawyer; Julian Bond, legislator; Herbert J. Gans, sociologist; Ross K. Baker, political scientist; Russell Baker, writer; William Kunstler, lawyer; Benjamin Spock, physician; Noam Chomsky, anthropologist; Richard Cloward, sociologist; Herman Schwartz, lawyer; Richard Korn, sociologist; Michael Harrington, writer; Richard Quinney, sociologist; Frank Reissman, sociologist; Tom Hayden, writer; Eldridge Cleaver, writer; H. Bruce Franklin, professor; Abbie Hoffman, writer; Phillip Berrigan, clergyman; Jerry Rubin, writer. Among a range of non-academic reports, pamphlets, and periodicals which served as sources for statements by these and other persons were: *John Birch Society Reprint Series; Ergo: The Rational Voice of Libertarianism; New Solidarity: National Caucus of Labor Committees; Hastings Center Report; S.D.S. New Left Notes; Guardian; Ramparts; National Review; Nation; New Republic; New York Review; Commentary; Fortune; Time; Life; Newsweek; New York Times; New York Times Magazine; Washington Post; Manchester Union Leader*. It should be noted that the substance of materials appearing in published sources represents the publicly-taken positions of the individuals involved. The relation between public positions and "actual" or private positions can be very complex, ranging from "close" to "distant" along a "degree of correspondence" axis, and with variation involving changes over time, differences according to the sub-issue involved, nature of audience addressed, and other factors.

6. The classic application of ideal-type method is that of Max Weber. *See*, e.g., the discussion of Weber's method and typology of authority and coordination in A. Henderson and T. Parsons, *Max Weber: The Theory of Social and Economic Organization* (1974), pp. 98 and 347. In the field of criminology, MacIver applies ideal-type analysis to discussions of social causality in general and crime causality in particular. R. MacIver, *Social Causation* (1942), p. 174. Neither of these applications directly parallels present usage, but underlying principles are similar.

7. Several recent studies provide indirect evidence of differences between academics and the general public in the likelihood that one will characterize his ideological position as "right" or "left." Of 60,000 professors surveyed by the Carnegie Commission, approximately 70% characterized themselves as "left" or "liberal," and fewer than 25% as "conservative" or "middle-of-the-road." A survey of social science professors by Everett Ladd and Seymour Lipset showed that approximately 70% voted against the "conservative" presidential candidate in 1972, compared with approximately 75% against four years before. These studies were reported in Hacker, "On Original Sin and Conservatives," *New York Times*, Feb. 25, 1973, §6 (Magazine) at 13. Henry Turner and Carl Hetrick's survey of a systematic sample of members of the American Political Science Association showed that approximately 75% characterized themselves as Democrats (among academics "Democratic" almost invariably means "liberal," whereas it generally means "conservative" in blue collar populations), a percentage which had remained stable for ten years. Those designating themselves as "Republicans" had declined to about 10% at the time of the survey. Turner and Hetrick's survey also showed that the Democratic majority was significantly more active in publication and political activity than the non-Democratic minority. H. Turner and C. Hetrick, "Political Activities and Party Affilia-

tions of American Political Scientists" (paper delivered at the 1971 Meetings of the American Political Science Association).

By comparison, a Gallup survey conducted in 1972 found that 71% of a systematically-selected sample of voters designated themselves as "conservative" (41%) or "middle-of-the-road" (30%), with 24% characterizing themselves as "liberal." A survey by Daniel Yankelovich during the same period found that 75% of the voters surveyed viewed themselves as "conservative" (37%) or "moderate" (38%), and 17% as "liberal" (15%) or "radical" (2%). *See* Rosenthal, "McGovern Is Radical or Liberal to Many in Polls," *New York Times*, Aug. 27, 1972, at 34, col. 3. An earlier poll by Yankelovich of American college students, seen by many as among the most liberal of large population categories, showed that approximately 70% reported themselves as holding "mainstream" positions, and that among the remainder, conservatives outnumbered left-wing radicals by two-to-one. D. Yankelovich, *The Changing Values on Campus: Political and Personal Attitudes of Today's College Students* (1972).

8. Hacker states that ". . . the higher one climbs on the prestige ladder [of American colleges and universities] the less likely are conservatives to be found on the faculty." Hacker, *supra* note 7, at 71.

9. Issues involved here fall into two general clusters: those affecting the rights and resources available to law-enforcement officials relative to those available to persons suspected, accused, or convicted of crimes; those relating to the conceptual or physical separation or combining of major population categories. Stands of the right and left with respect to the first cluster have been delineated in several places (right crusading issue 2; left general assumptions 3, 5; right policies respecting offenders 3, 4, respecting agencies 3, 4; left policies respecting offenders 3, 4, respecting agencies 3, 4). Major decisions of the United States Supreme Court during the 1960's which appear to accord with ideological stances of the left and to run counter to those of the right include: Mapp v. Ohio, 367 U.S. 643 (1961), which reduced resources available to law-enforcement officials and increased resources available to the accused by extending limitations on the admissibility of illegally-obtained evidence; Escobedo v. Illinois, 378 U.S. 478 (1964), and Miranda v. Arizona, 384 U.S. 436 (1966), which reduced the power of law-enforcement officials to proceed with criminal processing without providing suspects with knowledge of and recourse to legal rights and resources; *In re* Gault, 387 U.S. 1 (1967), which reduced the power of judges to make dispositions in juvenile proceedings and increased the legal rights and resources of defendants; Katz v. United States, 389 U.S. 347 (1967), which reduced prerogatives of law-enforcement officials with respect to the gathering of evidence by increasing protection of suspects against intrusions of privacy; Gilbert v. California, 388 U.S. 263 (1967), and United States v. Wade, 388 U.S. 218 (1967), which decreased the freedom of law-enforcement officials to seek identification of suspects, and increased the legal rights and resources available to suspects.

With respect to the second cluster, separation of population categories, stands of the right are delineated under general assumption 5, sources of crime 4, policies respecting criminal justice agencies 4, and of the left under crusading issue 5 and general assumption 4. The landmark decision here was Brown v. Board of Education, 347 U.S. 483 (1954), which held that racially segregated public education was *per se* discriminatory. While preceding the above-cited decisions by about a decade, *Brown* set a precedent for later court actions which provided support for the diminution of categorical segregation, as favored by the left, and reduced support for the maintenance of such separation, as espoused by the right.

10. It has been widely held that the Burger Court, reflecting the influence of right-oriented Nixon appointees such as Justices Rehnquist and Powell, would evince marked support for rightist ideological premises, stopping or reversing many of the initiatives of the Warren Court in areas such as equal protection and due process. This viewpoint is articulated by Fred P. Graham, who writes, "Mr. Nixon's two new justices are strikingly like his first two appointments in conservative judicial outlook, and . . . this cohesion is likely to produce a marked swing to the right—particularly on criminal law issues. . . ." Graham, "Profile of the 'Nixon Court' Now Discernible," *New York Times*, May 24, 1972, p. 28, col. 3. *See* also Graham, "Supreme Court, in Recent Term, Began Swing to Right That Was Sought by Nixon," *New York Times*, July 2, 1972, p. 16, col. 1; "Nixon Appointees May Shift Court on Obscenity and Business," *New York Times*, October 2, 1972, p. 16, col. 4. However, Gerald Gunther, in a careful review of the 1971 term of the Burger Court, characterizes the Court essentially as holding the line rather than moving in new directions of its own. Gunther writes, "There was no drastic rush to the right. The changes were marginal. . . . The new Court . . . has shown no inclination to overturn clear, carefully explained precedent." Gunther, "The Supreme Court 1971

Term, Foreword: In Search of Evolving Doctrine on a Changing Court: A Model for Newer Equal Protection," *Harvard Law Review, 86* (1972), pp. 1, 2–3. Cf. Goldberg, "Supreme Court Review 1972, Foreword—The Burger Court 1971 Term: One Step Forward, Two Steps Backward?" *Journal of Criminal Law, Criminology, and Police Science, 63* (1972), p. 463. Although the Court has shown an inclination to limit and specify some of the broader decisions of the Warren Court (e.g., limiting rights to counsel at line-ups as dealt with in *Gilbert* and *Wade, see* Graham, July 2, 1972, *supra*), there does not appear at the time of writing any pronounced tendency to reverse major thrusts of Warren Court decisions relevant to presently-considered ideological issues, but rather to curb or limit momentum in these directions.

11. Wilkins, "Crime in the World of 1990," *Futures*, 4 (1970), p. 203.

12. The classic formulations of the distinction between "factual" and "evaluative" content of statements about human behavior are those of Max Weber. *See*, e.g., A. Henderson and T. Parsons, *supra* note 6, at 8 *passim*. *See* also G. Myrdal, *supra* note 3.

APPENDIX

CHART I Sources of Crime: Locus of Responsibility

Left	*Right*
5. Behavior designated as "crime" by the ruling classes is an inevitable product of a fundamentally corrupt and unjust society. True crime is the behavior of those who perpetuate, control, and profit from an exploitative and brutalizing system. The behavior of those commonly regarded as "criminals" by establishment circles in fact represents heroic defiance and rebellion against the arbitrary and self-serving rules of an immoral social order. These persons thus bear no responsibility for what the state defines as crime; they are forced into such actions as justifiable responses to deliberate policies of oppression, discrimination, and exploitation.	5. Crime and violence are a direct product of a massive conspiracy by highly-organized and well-financed radical forces seeking deliberately to overthrow the society. Their basic method is an intensive and unrelenting attack on the fundamental moral values of the society, and their vehicle is that sector of the populace sufficiently low in intelligence, moral virtue, self-control, and judgment as to serve readily as their puppets by constantly engaging in those violent and predatory crimes best calculated to destroy the social order. Instigators of the conspiracy are most often members of racial or ethnic groups that owe allegiance to and are supported by hostile foreign powers.
4. Those who engage in the more common forms of theft and other forms of "street crime" are essentially forced into such behavior by a destructive set of social conditions caused by a grossly inequitable distribution of wealth, power, and privilege. These people are actually victims, rather than perpetrators of criminality; they are victimized by discrimination, segregation, denial of opportunity, denial of justice and equal rights. Their behavior is thus a perfectly understandable and justified reaction to the malign social forces that bring it about. Forms of crime perpetrated by the wealthy and powerful—extensive corruption, taking of massive profits through illicit collusion, outright fraud and embezzlement—along with a pervasive pattern of marginally legal exploitative practices—have far graver social consequences than the relatively minor offenses of the so-called "common" criminal. Yet these forms of crime are virtually ignored and their perpetrators excused or assigned mild penalties, while the great bulk of law-enforcement effort and attention is directed to the hapless victims of the system.	4. The bulk of serious crime is committed by members of certain ethnic and social class categories characterized by defective self-control, self-indulgence, limited time-horizons, and undeveloped moral conscience. The criminal propensities of these classes, which appear repeatedly in successive generations, are nurtured and encouraged by the enormous reluctance of authorities to apply the degree of firm, swift, and decisive punishment which could serve effectively to curb crime. Since criminality is so basic to such persons, social service programs can scarcely hope to affect their behavior, but their low capacity for discrimination makes them unusually susceptible to the appeals of leftists who goad them to commit crimes in order to undermine the society.
3. Public officials and agencies with responsibility for crime and criminals must share with damaging social conditions	3. The root cause of crime is a massive erosion of the fundamental moral values which traditionally have served to

major blame for criminality. By allocating pitifully inadequate resources to criminal justice agencies the government virtually assures that they will be manned by poorly qualified, punitive, moralistic personnel who are granted vast amounts of arbitrary coercive power. These persons use this power to stigmatize, degrade and brutalize those who come under their jurisdiction, thus permitting them few options other than continued criminality. Society also manifests enormous reluctance to allocate the resources necessary to ameliorate the root social causes of crime—poverty, urban deterioration, blocked educational and job opportunities—and further enhances crime by maintaining widespread systems of segregation—separating race from race, the poor from the affluent, the deviant from the conventional and the criminal from the law-abiding.

2. Although the root causes of crime lie in the disabling consequences of social, economic, and educational deprivation concentrated primarily among the disadvantaged in low-income communities, criminal behavior is in fact widely prevalent among all sectors of the society, with many affluent people committing crimes such as shoplifting, drunkenness, forgery, embezzlement, and the like. The fact that most of those subject to arrest and imprisonment have low-income or minority backgrounds is a direct consequence of an inequitable and discriminatory application of the criminal justice process—whereby the offenses of the more affluent are ignored, suppressed, or treated outside of a criminal framework, while those of the poor are actively prosecuted. A very substantial portion of the crime dealt with by officials must in fact be attributed to the nature of the criminal statutes themselves. A wide range of commonly pursued forms of behavior such as use of drugs, gambling, sexual deviance—are defined and handled as "crime," when in fact they should be seen as "victimless" and subject to private discretion. Further, a substantial portion of these and other forms of illegal behavior actually reflect illness—physical or emotional disturbance rather than criminality.

1. Crime is largely a product of social ills such as poverty, unemployment, poor quality education, and unequal opportunities. While those who commit crimes out of financial need or frustration with their life conditions deserve understanding and compassion, those who continue to commit crimes in the absence of adequate justification should in some degree be held accountable for their behavior; very often they are sick or disturbed persons who need help rather than punishment. Officials dealing with crime are often well-meaning, but they sometimes act unjustly or repressively out of an excessively narrow focus on specific objectives of law enforcement. Such behavior in turn reflects frustration with the failure of society to provide them adequate resources to perform their tasks for which they are responsible, as it also fails to provide the resources needed to ameliorate the community conditions which breed crime.

deter criminality, and a concomitant flouting of the established authority which has traditionally served to constrain it. The most extreme manifestations of this phenomenon are found among the most crime-prone sectors of the society—the young, minorities, and the poor. Among these groups and elsewhere there have arisen special sets of alternative values or "counter-cultures" which actually provide direct support for the violation of the legal and moral norms of law-abiding society. A major role in the alarming increase in crime and violence is played by certain elitist groups of left-oriented media writers, educators, jurists, lawyers, and others who contribute directly to criminality by publicizing, disseminating, and supporting these crime-engendering values.

2. A climate of growing permissiveness and stress on immediate personal gratification are progressively undermining the basic deterrents to criminal behavior—self-discipline, responsibility, and a well-developed moral conscience. The prevalent tendency by liberals to attribute blame for criminality to "the system" and its inequities serves directly to aggravate criminality by providing the criminal with a fallacious rationalization which enables him to excuse his criminal behavior, further eroding self-discipline and moral conscience.

1. The behavior of persons who habitually violate the law is caused by defective upbringing in the home, parental neglect, inadequate religious and moral training, poor neighborhood environment, and lack of adequate role-models. These conditions result in a lack of proper respect for the law and insufficient attention to the basic moral principles which deter criminality. The federal government also contributes by failing to provide local agencies of prevention and law enforcement with sufficient resources to perform adequately the many tasks required to reduce or control crime.

CHART II Modes of Dealing with Crime: Policies with Respect to Offenders

Left	*Right*
5. Since the bulk of acts defined as "crime" by the ruling classes simply represent behavior which threatens an invalid and immoral social system, those who engage in such acts can in no sense be regarded as culpable, or "criminal." There is thus no legitimate basis for any claim of official jurisdiction over, let alone any right to restrain, so-called offenders. Persons engaging in acts which help to hasten the inevitable collapse of a decadent system should have full and unrestrained freedom to continue such acts, and to be provided the maximum support and backing of all progressive elements. The vast bulk of those now incarcerated must be considered as political prisoners, unjustly deprived of freedom by a corrupt regime, and freed at once.	5. Habitual criminals, criminal types, and those who incite them should bear the full brunt of social retribution, and be prevented by the most forceful means possible from further endangering society. Murderers, rapists, arsonists, armed robbers, subversives and the like should be promptly and expeditiously put to death. The more vicious and unregenerate of these criminals should be publicly executed as an example to others. To prevent future crimes, those classes of persons who persistently manifest a high propensity for criminality should be prevented from reproducing, through sterilization or other means. Those who persist in crimes calculated to undermine the social order should be completely and permanently removed from the society, preferably by deportation.
4. All but a very small proportion of those who come under the jurisdiction of criminal justice agencies pose no real danger to society, and are entitled to full and unconditional freedom in the community at all stages of the criminal justice process. The state must insure that those accused of crimes, incarcerated, or in any way under legal jurisdiction be granted their full civil rights as citizens, and should make available to them at little or no cost the full range of legal and other resources necessary to protect them against the arbitrary exercise of coercive power. Criminal justice processing as currently conducted is essentially brutalizing—particularly institutional incarceration, which seriously aggravates criminality, and which should be entirely abolished. "Rehabilitation" under institutional auspices is a complete illusion; it has not worked, never will work, and must be abandoned as a policy objective. Accused persons, prisoners, and members of the general public subject to the arbitrary and punitive policies of police and other officials must be provided full rights and resources to protect their interests—including citizen control of police operations, full access to legal resources, fully developed grievance mechanisms, and the like.	4. Dangerous or habitual criminals should be subject to genuine punishment of maximum severity, including capital punishment where called for, and extended prison terms (including life imprisonment) with air-tight guarantees that these be fully served. Probation and parole defeat the purposes of public protection and should be eliminated. Potential and less-habituated criminals might well be deterred from future crime by highly visible public punishment such as flogging, the stocks, and possibly physical marking or mutilation. To speak of "rights" of persons who have chosen deliberately to forfeit them by engaging in crime is a travesty, and malefactors should receive the punishment they deserve without interference by leftists working to obstruct the processes of justice. "Rehabilitation" as a policy objective is simply a weakly disguised method of pampering criminals, and has no place whatever in a proper system of criminal justice. Fully adequate facilities for detection, apprehension, and effective restraint of criminals should be granted those police and other criminal justice personnel who realize that their principal mission is swift and unequivocal retribution against wrongdoers and their permanent removal from society to secure the full protection of the law-abiding.
3. Since contacts with criminal justice officials—particularly police and corrections personnel—increase the likelihood that persons will engage in crime, a major objective must be to divert the maximum number of persons away from criminal justice agencies and into service programs in the community—the proper arena for helping offenders. There should be maximum use of probation as an alternative to incarceration, and parole as an alternative to extended incarceration. However, both services must be drastically overhauled, and transformed from ineffective watchdog operations manned by low-quality personnel to genuine and effective human services. Institutionalization should be the alternative of last resort, and used only for those	3. Rampant permissiveness and widespread coddling of criminals defeat the purposes of crime control and must be stopped. Those who persist in the commission of serious crime and whose behavior endangers the public safety should be dealt with firmly, decisively and forcefully. A policy of strict punishment is necessary not only because it is deserved by offenders but also because it serves effectively to deter potential criminals among the general public. A major effort must be directed toward increasing the rights and resources of officials who cope with crime, and decreasing the rights and resources—legal, statutory, and financial—of those who use them to evade or avoid deserved punishment. Predetention measures such as bail,

proven to be highly dangerous, or for whom services cannot be provided outside of an institutional context. Those confined must be afforded the same civil rights as all citizens, including full access to legal resources and to officially-compiled information, fully-operational grievance mechanisms, right of petition and appeal from official decisions. Every attempt must be made to minimize the separation between institution and community by providing frequent leaves, work release furloughs, full visitation rights, full access to citizens' groups. Full rights and the guarantee of due process must be provided for all those accused of crimes—particularly juveniles, minorities, and the underprivileged.

2. Since the behavior of most of those who commit crimes is symptomatic of social or psychological forces over which they have little control, ameliorative efforts must be conducted within the framework of a comprehensive strategy of services which combines individually-oriented clinical services and beneficial social programs. Such services should be offered in whatever context they can most effectively be rendered, although the community is generally preferable to the institution. However, institutional programs organized around the concept of the therapeutic community can be most effective in helping certain kinds of persons, such as drug users, for whom external constraints can be a useful part of the rehabilitative process. Rehabilitation rather than punishment must be the major objective in dealing with offenders. Treatment in the community—in group homes, halfway houses, court clinics, on probation or parole—must incorporate the maximum range of services, including vocational training and placement, psychological testing and counselling, and other services which presently are either unavailable or woefully inadequate in most communities. Where imprisonment is indicated, sentences should be as short as possible, and inmates should be accorded the rights and respect due all human beings.

1. Effective methods for dealing with actual or putative offenders require well-developed and sophisticated methods for discriminating among varying categories of persons, and gearing treatment to the differential needs of the several types thus discriminated. A major goal is to insure that those most likely to benefit from psychological counseling and other therapeutic methods will receive the kinds of treatment they need, rather than wasting therapeutic resources on that relatively small group of offenders whose behavior is essentially beyond reform, and are poor candidates for rehabilitation. All those under the jurisdiction of criminal justice agencies should be treated equitably and humanely. Police in particular should treat their clients with fairness and respect—especially members of minority groups and the disadvantaged. Careful consideration should be given before sentencing offenders to extended prison terms to make sure that other alternatives are not possible.

suspended sentences and probation should be used only when it is certain that giving freedom to actual or putative criminals will not jeopardize public safety, and parole should be employed sparingly and with great caution only in those cases where true rehabilitation seems assured. The major objective both of incarceration and rehabilitation efforts must be the protection of law-abiding society, not the welfare of the offender.

2. Lawbreakers should be subject to fair but firm penalties based primarily on the protection of society, but taking into account as well the future of the offender. Successful rehabilitation is an important objective since a reformed criminal no longer presents a threat to society. Rehabilitation should center on the moral re-education of the offender, and instill in him the respect for authority and basic moral values which are the best safeguards against continued crime. These aims can be furthered by prison programs which demand hard work and strict discipline, for these serve to promote good work habits and strengthen moral fiber. Sentences should be sufficiently long as to both adequately penalize the offender and insure sufficient time for effective rehabilitation. Probation and parole should not be granted indiscriminately, but reserved for carefully selected offenders, both to protect society and because it is difficult to achieve the degree of close and careful supervision necessary to successful rehabilitation outside the confines of the institution.

1. An essential component of any effective method for dealing with violators is a capability for making careful and sensitive discriminations among various categories of offenders, and tailoring appropriate dispositional measures to different types of offenders. In particular, the capacity to differentiate between those with a good potential for reform and those with a poor potential will ensure that the more dangerous kinds of criminals are effectively restrained. Probationers and parolees should be subject to close and careful supervision both to make sure that their activities contribute to their rehabilitation and that the community is protected from repeat violations by those under official jurisdiction. Time spent in prison should be used to teach inmates useful skills so that they may reenter society as well-trained and productive individuals.

CHART II—continued

Left	Right
Similarly, probation and parole should be used in those cases where these statutes appear likely to facilitate rehabilitation without endangering public safety. Prisoners should not be denied contact with the outside world, but should have rights to correspondence, visiting privileges, and access to printed and electronic media. They should also be provided with facilities for constructive use of leisure time, and program activities aimed to enhance the likelihood of rehabilitation.	

CHART III Modes of Dealing with Crime: Policies with Respect to Criminal Justice Agencies

Left	Right
5. The whole apparatus of so-called "law enforcement" is in fact simply the domestic military apparatus used by the ruling classes to maintain themselves in power, and to inflict harassment, confinement, injury or death on those who protest injustice by challenging the arbitrary regulations devised by the militarists and monopolists to protect their interests. To talk of "reforming" such a system is farcical; the only conceivable method of eliminating the intolerable injustices inherent in this kind of society is the total and forceful overthrow of the entire system, including its so-called "law enforcement" arm. All acts which serve this end, including elimination of members of the oppressor police force, serve to hasten the inevitable collapse of the system and the victory of progressive forces.	5. Maximum possible resources must be provided those law enforcement offficals who realize that their basic mission is the protection of society and maintenance of security for the law-abiding citizen. In addition to substantial increases in manpower, law enforcement personnel must be provided with the most modern, efficient and lethal weaponry available, and the technological capacity (communications, computerization, electronic surveillance, aerial pursuit capability) to deliver maximum force and facilities possible to points of need—the detection, pursuit, and arrest of criminals, and in particular the control of terrorism and violence conducted or incited by radical forces.
4. The entire American system of criminal justice must be radically reformed. Unless there is a drastic reduction in the amount of power now at the disposal of official agencies—particularly the police and corrections, a police state is inevitable. In particular, unchecked power currently possessed by poorly qualified, politically reactionary officials to deal with accused and suspected persons as they see fit must be curtailed; their behavior brutalizes and radicalizes the clients of the system. To these officials, "dangerous" usually means "politically unacceptable." Increasing concentration of power in entrenched bureaucracies must be checked, and the people given maximum rights to local control of their own lives, including the right to self protection through associations such as citizens councils and security patrols to counter police harassment and brutality and to monitor the operations of local prisons. Means must be found to eliminate the extensive corruption which pervades the system—exemplified by venal criminality within police departments and the unholy alliance between organized crime, corrupt politicians, and those who are supposedly enforcing the laws. Most of the criminal offenses now on the books should be eliminated,	4. The critical crime situation requires massive increases in the size of police forces and their technological capacity to curb crime—particularly in the use of force against criminals and radical elements. It is imperative that police command full freedom to use all available resources, legal and technical, without interference from leftist elements seeking to tie their hands and render them impotent. The power of the courts to undermine the basis of police operations by denying them fundamental legal powers must be curbed. The nation's capacity for incarcerating criminals—particularly through maximum security facilities—must be greatly expanded, and prison security strengthened. The "prison reform" movement rests on a mindless focus on the welfare of convicted felons and a blind disregard for the welfare of law-abiding citizens. Particularly pernicious is the movement now underway to unload thousands of dangerous criminals directly into our communities under the guise of "community corrections" (halfway houses, group homes, etc.). The local citizenry must unite and forcefully block this effort to flood our homes and playgrounds with criminals, dope addicts, and subversives. Increasing concentration of power in the hands of centralized govern-

retaining only a few truly dangerous crimes such as forceful rape, since most of the offenses which consume law enforcement energies have no real victims, and should be left to private conscience. However, statutes related to illegality by business interests, bureaucrats, corporations and the like should be expanded, and enforcement efforts greatly increased. Virtually all prisons should be closed at once, and the few persons requiring institutional restraint should be accommodated in small facilities in local communities.

3. The more efficiency gained by law enforcement agencies through improvements in technology, communications, management, and so on, the greater the likelihood of harassment, initimidation, and discrimination directed against the poor and minorities. Improvements in police services can be achieved only through fundamental and extensive changes in the character of personnel, not through more hardware and technology. This should be achieved by abandoning antiquated selection and recruitment policies which are designed to obtain secure employment for low-quality personnel and which systematically discriminate against the minorities and culturally disadvantaged. Lateral entry, culture-free qualification tests, and other means must be used to loosen the iron grip of civil-service selection and tenure systems. The out-moded military model with its rigid hierarchical distinctions found among the police and other agencies should be eliminated, and a democratic organizational model put in its place. The police must see their proper function as service to the community rather than in narrow terms of law enforcement. As part of their community responsibility, law enforcement agencies should stringently limit access to information concerning offenders, especially younger ones, and much of such information should be destroyed. There must be maximum public access to the inner operations of police, courts and prisons by insuring full flow of information to the media, full accountability to and visitation rights by citizens and citizen groups, and full public disclosure of operational policies and operations. The major burden of corrections should be removed from the institutions, which are crime-breeding and dehumanizing, and placed directly in the communities, to which all offenders must at some point return.

2. A basic need of the criminal justice system is an extensive upgrading of the quality of personnel. This must be done by recruiting better qualified people—preferably with college training, in all branches and at all levels, and by mounting effective in-service training programs. Higher quality and better trained personnel are of particular importance in the case of the police, and training must place more stress on human relations studies such as psychology and sociology, and relatively less stress on purely technical aspects of police work. Quality must be maintained by the development and application of performance standards

ment must be stopped, and basic rights returned to the local community—including the right to exclude dangerous and undesirable elements, and the right to bear arms freely in defense of home and family. Strict curbs must be imposed on the freedom of the media to disseminate materials aimed to undermine morality and encourage crime.

3. Law enforcement agencies must be provided all the resources necessary to deal promptly and decisively with crime and violence. Failure to so act encourages further law breaking both by those who are subject to permissive and inefficient handling and by those who become aware thereby how little risk they run of being caught and penalized for serious crimes. The rights of the police to stringently and effectively enforce the law must be protected from misguided legalistic interference—particularly the constant practice of many judges of granting freedom to genuine criminals laboriously apprehended by the police, often on the basis of picayune procedural details related to "due process" or other legalistic devices for impeding justice. The scope of the criminal law must be expanded rather than reduced; there is no such thing as "victimless" crime; the welfare of all law-abiding people and the moral basis of society itself are victimized by crimes such as pornography, prostitution, homosexuality and drug use, and offenders must be vigorously pursued, prosecuted, and penalized. Attempts to prevent crime by pouring massive amounts of tax dollars into slum communities are worse than useless, since such people can absorb limitless welfare "benefits" with no appreciable effect on their criminal propensities. Communities must resist attempts to open up their streets and homes to hardened criminals through halfway houses and other forms of "community corrections."

2. There should be substantial increases in the numbers and visiblity of police, particularly in and around schools, places of business, and areas of family activity. Although a few bad apples may appear from time to time, the bulk of our police are conscientious and upstanding men who deserve the continued respect and support of the community, and who should be granted ample resources to do the job to which they are assigned. Some of the proposed prison reforms may be commendable, but the burden to the taxpayer must never be lost sight of: most of the reforms suggested or already in practice are of dubious benefit or

CHART III—continued

Left	*Right*
against which all personnel must be periodically measured, and which should provide the basis for promotion. Sentencing procedures must be standardized, rationalized, and geared to specific and explicit rehabilitative objectives rather than being left to the often arbitrary and capricious whims of particular judges. Corrections as well as other criminal justice agencies must be made more humane and equitable, and the rights of prisoners as individuals should be respected. Attempts should be made to reduce the degree of separation of prison inmates from the outside world. Changes in both legislation and law enforcement policies must be directed to reducing the disparities in arrest rates between richer and poorer offenders, so that commensurately fewer of the poor and underprivileged and more of the better off, are sought out, convicted, and imprisoned. Promising programs of humane reform must not be abandoned simply because they fail to show immediate measurable results, but should receive continued or increased federal support.	yield benefits clearly not commensurate with their costs. More efforts should be directed to prevention of crime; in particular, programs of moral re-education in the schools and communities, and the institution of safeguards against the influence of those in the schools, media and elsewhere who promote criminality by challenging and rejecting the established moral values which serve to forestall illegal and immoral conduct.
1. There must be better coordination of existing criminal justice facilities and functions so as to better focus available services on the whole individual, rather than treating him through disparate and compartmentalized efforts. This must entail better liaison among police, courts and corrections and greatly improved lines of communication, to the end of enabling each to attain better appreciation, understanding and knowledge of the operational problems of the others. Coordination and liaison must also increase between the criminal justice agencies and the general welfare services of the community, which have much to contribute both in the way of prevention of crime and rehabilitation of criminals. Local politicians often frustrate the purposes of reform by consuming resources in patronage, graft, and the financial support of entrenched local interests, so the federal government must take the lead in financing and overseeing criminal justice reform efforts. Federal resources and standards should be utilized to substantially increase the level and quality of social service resources available to criminal justice enterprises, promulgate standardized and rationalized modes of operation in local communities, and bring administrative coherence to the host of uncoordinated efforts now in progress.	1. The operations of the police should be made more efficient, in part through increased use of modern managerial principles and information processing techniques. Police protection should focus more directly on the local community, and efforts should be made to restore the degree of personal moral integrity and intimate knowledge of the local community which many older policemen had but many younger ones lack. Prison reform is important, but innovations should be instituted gradually and with great caution, and the old should not be discarded until the new is fully proven to be adequate. There should be much better coordination among law enforcement agencies, to reduce inefficiency, wasteful overlap, and duplication of services. The federal government must assume a major role in providing the leadership and financial resources necessary to effective law enforcement and crime control.

The Dirty Harry Problem

Carl B. Klockars

Abstract: *Policing constantly places its practitioners in situations in which good ends can be achieved by dirty means. When the ends to be achieved are urgent and unquestionably good and only a dirty means will work to achieve them, the policeman faces a genuine moral dilemma. A genuine moral dilemma is a situation from which one cannot emerge innocent no matter what one does—employ a dirty means, employ an insufficiently dirty means, or walk away. In such situations in policing, Dirty Harry problems, the danger lies not in becoming guilty of wrong—that is inevitable—but in thinking that one has found a way to escape a dilemma which is inescapable. Dire consequences result from this misunderstanding. Policemen lose their sense of moral proportion, fail to care, turn cynical, or allow their passionate caring to lead them to employ dirty means too crudely or too readily. The only means of assuring that dirty means will not be used too readily or too crudely is to punish those who use them and the agency which endorses their use.*

When and to what extent does the morally good end warrant or justify an ethically, politically, or legally dangerous means for its achievement? This is a very old question for philosophers. Although it has received extensive consideration in policelike occupations and is at the dramatic core of police fiction and detective novels, I know of not a single contribution to the criminological or sociological literature on policing which raises it explicitly and examines its implications.[1] This is the case in spite of the fact that there is considerable evidence to suggest that it is not only an ineluctable part of police work, but a moral problem with which police themselves are quite familiar. There are, I believe, a number of good reasons why social scientists have avoided or neglected what I like to call the Dirty Harry problem in policing, not the least of which is that it is insoluble. However, a great deal can be learned about police work by examining some failed solutions, three of which I consider in the following pages. First, though, it is necessary to explain what a Dirty Harry problem is and what it is about it that makes it so problematic.

SOURCE: Carl B. Klockars, "The Dirty Harry Problem," *The Annals*, 452 (November 1980), pp. 33–47.

THE DIRTY HARRY PROBLEM

The Dirty Harry problem draws its name from the 1971 Warner Brothers film *Dirty Harry* and its chief protagonist, antihero Inspector Harry "Dirty Harry" Callahan. The film features a number of events which dramatize the Dirty Harry problem in different ways, but the one which does so most explicitly and most completely places Harry in the following situation. A 14-year-old girl has been kidnapped and is being held captive by a psychopathic killer. The killer, "Scorpio," who has already struck twice, demands $200,000 ransom to release the girl, who is buried with just enough oxygen to keep her alive for a few hours. Harry gets the job of delivering the ransom and, after enormous exertion, finally meets Scorpio. At their meeting Scorpio decides to renege on his bargain, let the girl die, and kill Harry. Harry manages to stab Scorpio in the leg before he does so, but not before Scorpio seriously wounds Harry's partner, an inexperienced, idealistic, slightly ethnic, former sociology major.

Scorpio escapes, but Harry manages to track him down through the clinic where he was treated for his wounded leg. After learning that Scorpio lives on the grounds of a nearby football stadium, Harry breaks into his apartment, finds guns and other evidence of his guilt, and finally confronts Scorpio on the 50-yard line, where Harry shoots him in the leg as he is trying to escape. Standing over Scorpio, Harry demands to know where the girl is buried. Scorpio refuses to disclose her location, demanding his rights to a lawyer. As the camera draws back from the scene Harry stands on Scorpio's bullet-mangled leg to torture a confession of the girl's location from him.

As it turns out, the girl is already dead and Scorpio must be set free. Neither the gun found in the illegal search, nor the confession Harry extorted, nor any of its fruits—including the girl's body—would be admissible in court.

The preceding scene, the heart of Dirty Harry, raises a number of issues of far-reaching significance for the sociology of the police, the first of which will now be discussed.

THE DIRTY HARRY PROBLEM I: THE END OF INNOCENCE

As we have phrased it previously, the Dirty Harry problem asks when and to what extent does the morally good end warrant or justify an ethically, politically, or legally dangerous means to its achievement? In itself, this question assumes the possibility of a genuine moral dilemma and posits its existence in a means-ends arrangement which may be expressed schematically as follows:

		MEANS	
		Morally Good (+)	Morally Dirty (−)
ENDS	Morally good (+)	A + +	B − + The Dirty Harry problem
	Morally dirty (−)	C + −	D − −

It is important to specify clearly the terms of the Dirty Harry problem not only to show that it must involve the juxtaposition of good ends and dirty means, but also to show what must be proven to demonstrate that a Dirty Harry problem exists. If one could show, for example, that box B is always empirically empty or that in any given case the terms of the situation are better read in some other means-ends arrangement, Dirty Harry problems vanish. At this first level, however, I suspect that no one could exclude the core scene of *Dirty Harry* from the class of Dirty Harry problems. There is no question that saving the life of an innocent victim of kidnapping is a "good" thing nor that grinding the bullet-mangled leg of Scorpio to extort a confession from him is "dirty."[2]

There is, in addition, a second level of criteria of an empirical and epistemological nature that must be met before a Dirty Harry problem actually comes into being. They involve the connection between the dirty act and the good end. Principally, what must be known and, importantly, known before the dirty act is committed, is that it will result in the achievement of the good end. In any absolute sense this is, of course, impossible to know, in that no acts are ever completely certain in their consequences. Thus the question is always a matter of probabilities. But it is helpful to break those probabilities into classes which attach to various subcategories of the overall question. In the given case, this level of problem would seem to require that three questions be satisfied, though not all with the same level of certainty.

In *Dirty Harry*, the first question is, Is Scorpio able to provide the information Dirty Harry seeks? It is an epistemological question about which, in *Dirty Harry*, we are absolutely certain. Harry met Scorpio at the time of the ransom exchange. Not only did he admit the kidnapping at that time, but when he made the ransom demand, Scorpio sent one of the girl's teeth and a description of her clothing and underwear to leave no doubt about the existence of his victim.

Second, we must know there are means, dirty means and nothing other than dirty means, which are likely to achieve the good end. One can, of course, never be sure that one is aware of or has considered all possible alternatives, but in *Dirty Harry* there would appear to be no reason for Scorpio in his rational self-interest to confess to the girl's location without being coerced to do so.

The third question which must be satisfied at this empirical and epistemological level concedes that dirty means are the only method which will be effective, but asks whether or not, in the end, they will be in vain. We know in *Dirty Harry* that they were, and Harry himself, at the time of the ransom demand, admits he believes that the girl is already dead. Does not this possibility or likelihood that the girl is dead destroy the justification for Harry's dirty act? Although it surely would if Harry knew for certain that the girl was dead, I do not think it does insofar as even a small probability of her being saved exists. The reason is that the good to be achieved is so unquestionably good and so passionately felt that even a small possibility of its achievement demands that it be tried. For example, were we to ask, If it were your daughter would you want Harry to do what he did? It would be this passionate sense of unquestionable good that we are trying to dramatize. It is for this reason that in philosophical circles the Dirty

Hands problem has been largely restricted to questions of national security, revolutionary terrorism, and international war. It is also why the Dirty Harry problem in detective fiction almost always involves murder.

Once we have satisfied ourselves that a Dirty Harry problem is conceptually possible and that, in fact, we can specify one set of concrete circumstances in which it exists, one might think that the most difficult question of all is, What ought to be done? I do not think it is. I suspect that there are very few people who would not want Harry to do something dirty in the situation specified. I know I would want him to do what he did, and what is more, I would want anyone who policed for me to be prepared to do so as well. Put differently, I want to have as police officers men and women of moral courage and sensitivity.

But to those who would want exactly that, the Dirty Harry problem poses its most irksome conclusion. Namely, that one cannot, at least in the specific case at hand, have a policeman who is both just and innocent. The troublesome issue in the Dirty Harry problem is not whether under some utilitarian calculus a right choice can be made, but that the choice must always be between at least two wrongs. And in choosing to do either wrong, the policeman inevitably taints or tarnishes himself.

It was this conclusion on the part of Dashiell Hammett, Raymond Chandler, Raoul Whitfield, Horace McCoy, James M. Cain, Lester Dent, and dozens of other tough-guy writers of hard-boiled detective stories that distinguished these writers from what has come to be called the "classical school" of detective fiction. What these men could not stomach about Sherlock Holmes (Conan Doyle), Inspector French (Freeman Wills Crofts), and Father Brown (Chesterton), to name a few of the best, was not that they were virtuous, but that their virtue was unsullied. Their objection was that the classical detective's occupation, how he worked, and the jobs he was called upon to do left him morally immaculate. Even the most brilliant defender of the classical detective story, W. H. Auden, was forced to confess that that conclusion gave the stories "magical function," but rendered them impossible as art.[3]

If popular conceptions of police work have relevance for its actual practice—as Egon Bittner and a host of others have argued that they do[4]—the Dirty Harry problem, found in one version or another in countless detective novels and reflected in paler imitations on countless television screens, for example, "Parental Discretion is Advised," is not an unimportant contributor to police work's "tainted" quality. But we must remember also that the revolution of the tough-guy writers, so these writers said, was not predicated on some mere artificial, aesthetic objection. With few exceptions, their claim was that their works were art. That is, at all meaningful levels, the stories were true. It is this claim I should next like to examine in the real-life context of the Dirty Harry problem.

THE DIRTY HARRY PROBLEM II: DIRTY MEN AND DIRTY WORK

Dirty Harry problems arise quite often. For policemen, real, everyday policemen, Dirty Harry problems are part of their job and thus considerably more than rare or artificial dramatic exceptions. To make this point, I will translate some rather familiar police practices, street stops and searches and victim and witness interrogation, into Dirty Harry problems.

Good Ends and Dirty Means

The first question our analysis of street stops and searches and victim and witness interrogation must satisfy is, For policemen, do these activities present the cognitive opportunity for the juxtaposition of good ends and dirty means for their achievement? Although the "goodness" question will be considered in some detail later, suffice it to say here that police find the prevention of crime and the punishment of wrongful or criminal behavior a good thing to achieve. Likewise, they, perhaps more than any other group in society, are intimately aware of the varieties of dirty means available for the achievement of those good ends. In the case of street stops and searches, these dirty alternatives range from falsifying probable cause for a stop, to manufacturing a false arrest to legitimate an illegal search, to simply searching without the fraudulent covering devices of either. In the case of victim or witness interrogations, dirty means range from dramaturgically "chilling" a *Miranda* warning by an edited or unemphatic reading to Harry's grinding a man's bullet-shattered leg to extort a confession from him.

While all these practices may be "dirty" enough to satisfy certain people of especially refined sensitivities, does not a special case have to be made, not for the public's perception of the "dirtiness" of certain illegal, deceptive, or subrosa acts, but for the police's perception of their dirtiness? Are not the police hard-boiled, less sensitive to such things than are most of us? I think there is no question that they are, and our contention about the prevalence of Dirty Harry problems in policing suggests that they are likely to be. How does this "tough-minded" attitude toward dirty means affect our argument? At least at this stage it seems to strengthen it. That is, the failure of police to regard dirty means with the same hesitation that most citizens do seems to suggest that they juxtapose them to the achievement of good ends more quickly and more readily than most of us.

The Dirty Means Must Work

In phrasing the second standard for the Dirty Harry problem as "The dirty means must work," we gloss over a whole range of qualifying conditions, some of which we have already considered. The most critical, implied in *Dirty Harry*, is that the person on whom dirty means are to be used must be guilty. It should be pointed out, however, that this standard is far higher than any student of the Dirty Hands problem in politics has ever been willing to admit. In fact, the moral dilemma of Dirty Hands is often dramatized by the fact that dirty means must be visited on quite innocent victims. It is the blood of such innocents, for example, whom the Communist leader Hoerderer in Sartre's *Dirty Hands* refers to when he says, "I have dirty hands. Right up to the elbows. I've plunged them in filth and blood. But what do you hope? Do you think you can govern innocently?"[5]

But even if cases in which innocent victims suffer dirty means commonly qualify as Dirty Harry problems, and by extension innocent victims would be allowable in Dirty Harry problems, there are a number of factors in the nature and context of policing which suggest that police themselves are inclined toward the higher "guilty victim" standard. Although there may be others, the following are probably the most salient.

1. The Operative Assumption of Guilt. In street stops and searches as well as interrogations, it is in the nature of the police task that guilt is assumed as a working premise. That is, in order for a policeman to do his job, he must, unless he clearly knows otherwise, assume that the person he sees is guilty and the behavior he is witnessing is evidence of some concealed or hidden offense. If a driver looks at him "too long" or not at all or if a witness or suspect talks too little or too much, it is only his operative assumption of guilt that makes those actions meaningful. Moreover, the policeman is often not in a position to suspend his working assumption until he has taken action, sometimes dirty action, to disconfirm it.

2. The Worst of All Possible Guilt. The matter of the operative assumption of guilt is complicated further because the policeman is obliged to make a still higher-order assumption of guilt, namely, that the person is not only guilty, but dangerously so. In the case of street stops and searches, for instance, although the probability of coming upon a dangerous felon is extremely low, policemen quite reasonably take the possibility of doing so as a working assumption on the understandable premise that once is enough. Likewise the premise that the one who has the most to hide will try hardest to hide it is a reasonable assumption for interrogation.

3. The Great Guilty Place Assumption. The frequency with which policemen confront the worst of people, places, and occasions creates an epistemological problem of serious psychological proportions. As a consequence of his job, the policeman is constantly exposed to highly selective samples of his environment. That he comes to read a clump of bushes as a place to hide, a roadside rest as a homosexual "tearoom," a sweet old lady as a robbery looking for a place to happen, or a poor young black as someone willing to oblige her is not a question of a perverse, pessimistic, or racist personality, but of a person whose job requires that he strive to see race, age, sex, and even nature in an ecology of guilt, which can include him if he fails to see it so.[6]

4. The Not Guilty (This Time) Assumption. With considerable sociological research and conventional wisdom to support him, the policeman knows that most people in the great guilty place in which he works have committed numerous crimes for which they have never been caught. Thus when a stop proves unwarranted, a search comes up "dry," or an interrogation fails, despite the dirty means, the policeman is not at all obliged to conclude that the person victimized by them is innocent, only that, and even this need not always be conceded, he is innocent this time.

Dirty Means as Ends in Themselves

How do these features of police work, all of which seem to incline police to accept a standard of a guilty victim for their dirty means, bear upon the Dirty Harry problem from which they derive? The most dangerous reading suggests that if police are inclined, and often quite rightly inclined, to believe they are dealing with factually, if not legally, guilty subjects, they become likely to see their dirty acts, not as means to the achievement of good ends, but as ends in themselves—as punishment of guilty people whom the police believe deserve to be punished.

If this line of argument is true, it has the effect, in terms of police perceptions, of moving Dirty Harry problems completely outside of the fourfold table of means-ends combinations created in order to define it. Importantly as well, in terms of our perceptions, Dirty Harry problems of this type can no longer be read as cases of dirty means employed to the achievement of good ends. For unless we are willing to admit in a democratic society a police which arrogates to itself the task of punishing those who they think are guilty, we are forced to conclude that Dirty Harry problems represent cases of employing dirty means to dirty ends, in which case, nobody, not the police and certainly not us, is left with any kind of moral dilemma.

The possibility is quite real and quite fearsome, but it is mediated by certain features of police work, some of which inhere in the nature of the work itself and others, imposed from outside, which have a quite explicit impact on it. The most important of the "naturalistic" features of policing which belie the preceding argument is that the assumption of guilt and all the configurations in the policeman's world which serve to support it often turn out wrong. It is precisely because the operative assumption of guilt can be forced on everything and everyone that the policeman who must use it constantly comes to find it leads him astray more often than it confirms his suspicions.

Similarly, a great many of the things policemen do, some of which we have already conceded appear to police as less dirty than they appear to us—faked probable cause for a street stop, manipulated *Miranda* warnings, and so forth—are simply impossible to read as punishments. This is so particularly if we grant a hard-boiled character to our cops.

Of course, neither of these naturalistic restrictions on the obliteration of the means-ends schema is or should be terribly comforting. To the extent that the first is helpful at all assumes a certain skill and capacity of mind that we may not wish to award to all policemen. The willingness to engage in the constant refutation of one's working worldview presumes a certain intellectual integrity which can certainly go awry. Likewise, the second merely admits that on occasion policemen do some things which reveal they appreciate that the state's capacity to punish is sometimes greater than theirs.

To both these "natural" restrictions on the obliteration of the means-end character of Dirty Harry problems, we can add the exclusionary rule. Although the exclusionary rule is the manifest target of *Dirty Harry*, it, more than anything else, makes Dirty Harry problems a reality in everyday policing. It is the great virtue of exclusionary rules—applying in various forms to stops, searches, seizures, and interrogations—that they hit directly upon the intolerable, though often, I think, moral desire of police to punish. These rules make the very simple point to police that the more they wish to see a felon punished, the more they are advised to be scrupulous in their treatment of him. Put differently, the best thing Harry could have done *for* Scorpio was to step on his leg, extort his confession, and break into his apartment.

If certain natural features of policing and particularly exclusionary rules combine to maintain the possibility of Dirty Harry problems in a context in which a real danger appears to be their disappearance, it does not follow that police cannot or do not collapse the dirty means-good ends division on some occasions and become punishers. I only hold that on many other occasions, collapse does not occur and Dirty Harry problems, as defined, are still widely possible. What must be remembered next, on the way to making their possibility real, is that policemen know, or think they know, before they employ a dirty means that a dirty means and only a dirty means will work.

Only a Dirty Means Will Work

The moral standard that a policeman knows in advance of resorting to a dirty means that a dirty means and only a dirty means will work, rests heavily on two technical dimensions: (1) the professional competence of the policeman and (2) the range of legitimate working options available to him. Both are intimately connected, though the distinction to be preserved between them is that the first is a matter of the policeman's individual competence and the second of the competence of the institutions for which (his department) and with which (the law) the policeman works.

In any concrete case, the relations between these moral and technical dimensions of the Dirty Harry problem are extremely complicated. But a priori it follows that the more competent a policeman is at the use of legal means, the less he will be obliged to resort to dirty alternatives. Likewise, the department that trains its policemen well and supplies them with the resources—knowledge and material—to do their work will find that the policemen who work for them will not resort to dirty means "unnecessarily," meaning only those occasions when an acceptable means will work as well as a dirty one.

While these two premises flow a priori from raising the Dirty Harry problem, questions involving the moral and technical roles of laws governing police means invite a very dangerous type of a priori reasoning:

> Combating distrust [of the police] requires getting across the rather complicated message that granting the police specific forms of new authority may be the most effective means for reducing abuse of authority which is now theirs; that it is the absence of properly proscribed forms of authority that often impels the police to engage in questionable or outright illegal conduct. Before state legislatures enacted statutes giving limited authority to the police to stop and question persons suspected of criminal involvement, police nevertheless stopped and questioned people. It is inconceivable how any police agency could be expected to operate without doing so. But since the basis for their actions was unclear, the police—if they thought a challenge likely—would use the guise of arresting the individual on a minor charge (often without clear evidence) to provide a semblance of legality. Enactment of stopping and questioning statutes eliminated the need for this sham.[7]

Herman Goldstein's preceding argument and observations are undoubtedly true, but the danger in them is that they can be extended to apply to any dirty means, not only illegal arrests to legitimate necessary street stops, but dirty means to accomplish subsequent searches and seizures all the way to beating confessions out of suspects when no other means will work. But, of course, Goldstein does not intend his arguments to be extended in these ways.

Nevertheless, his a priori argument, dangerous though it may be, points to the fact that Dirty Harry problems can arise wherever restrictions are placed on police methods and are particularly likely to do so when police themselves perceive that those restrictions are undesirable, unreasonable, or unfair. His argument succeeds in doing what police who face Dirty Harry problems constantly do: rendering the law problematic. But while Goldstein, one of the most distinguished legal scholars in America, can follow his finding with books, articles, and lectures which urge change, it is left to the policeman to take upon himself the moral responsibility of subverting it with dirty and hidden means.

Compelling and Unquestionable Ends

If Dirty Harry problems can be shown to exist in their technical dimensions—as genuine means-ends problems where only dirty means will work—the question of the magnitude and urgency of the ends that the dirty means may be employed to achieve must still be confronted. Specifically, it must be shown that the ends of dirty means are so desirable that the failure to achieve them would cast the person who is in a position to do so in moral disrepute.

The two most widely acknowledged ends of policing are peace keeping and law enforcement. It would follow, of course, that if both these ends were held to be unworthy, Dirty Harry problems would disappear. There are arguments challenging both ends. For instance, certain radical critiques of policing attempt to reduce the peace-keeping and law-enforcing functions of the police in the United States to nothing more than acts of capitalist oppression. From such a position flows not only the denial of the legitimacy of any talk of Dirty Harry problems, but also the denial of the legitimacy of the entire police function.[8]

Regardless of the merits of such critiques, it will suffice for the purpose of this analysis to maintain that there is a large "clientele," to use Albert Reiss's term, for both types of police function.[9] And it should come as no surprise to anyone that the police themselves accept the legitimacy of their own peace-keeping and law-enforcing ends. Some comment is needed, though, on how large that clientele for those functions is and how compelling and unquestionable the ends of peace keeping and law enforcement are for them.

There is no more popular, compelling, urgent, nor more broadly appealing idea than peace. In international relations, it is potent enough to legitimate the stockpiling of enough nuclear weapons to exterminate every living thing on earth a dozen times over. In domestic affairs, it gives legitimacy to the idea of the state, and the aspirations to it have succeeded in granting to the state an absolute monopoly on the right to legitimate the use of force and a near monopoly on its actual, legitimate use: the police. That peace has managed to legitimate these highly dangerous means to its achievement in virtually every advanced nation in the world is adequate testimony to the fact that it qualifies, if any end does, as a good end so unquestionable and so compelling that it can legitimate risking the most dangerous and dirtiest of means.

The fact is, though, that most American policemen prefer to define their work as law enforcement rather than peace keeping, even though they may, in fact, do more of the latter. It is a distinction that should not be allowed to slip away in assuming, for instance, that the policeman's purpose in enforcing the law is to keep the peace. Likewise, though it is a possibility, it will not do to assume that police simply enforce the law as an end in itself, without meaning and without purpose or end. The widely discretionary behavior of working policemen and the enormous underenforcement of the law which characterizes most police agencies simply belie that possibility.

An interpretation of law enforcement which is compatible with empirical studies of police behavior—as peace keeping is—and police talk in America—which peace keeping generally is not—is an understanding of the ends of law enforcement as punishment. There are, of course, many theories of punishment, but the police seem inclined toward the simplest: the belief that certain people who have committed certain acts deserve to be punished for them. What can one say of the compelling and unquestionable character of this retributive ambition as an end of policing and policemen?

Both historically and sociologically there is ample evidence that punishment is almost as unquestionable and compelling an end as peace. Historically, we have a long and painful history of punishment, a history longer in fact than the history of the end of peace. Sociologically, the application of what may well be the only culturally universal norm, the norm of reciprocity, implies the direct and natural relations between wrongful acts and their punishments.[10] Possibly the best evidence for the strength and urgency of the desire to punish in modern society is the extraordinary complex of rules and procedures democratic states have assembled which prevents legitimate punishment from being administered wrongfully or frivolously.

If we can conclude that peace and punishment are ends unquestionable and compelling enough to satisfy the demands of Dirty Harry problems, we are led to one final question on which we may draw from some sociological theories of the police for assistance. If the Dirty Harry problem is at the core of the police role, or at least near to it, how is it that police can or do come to reconcile their use of—or their failure to use—dirty means to achieve unquestionably good and compelling ends?

PUBLIC POLICY AND POLICE MORALITY: THREE DEFECTIVE RESOLUTIONS OF THE DIRTY HARRY PROBLEM

The contemporary literature on policing appears to contain three quite different types of solution or resolution. But because the Dirty Harry problem is a genuine moral dilemma, that is, a situation which will admit no real solution or resolution, each is necessarily defective. Also, understandably, each solution or resolution presents itself as an answer to a somewhat different problem. In matters of public policy, such concealments are often necessary and probably wise, although they have a way of coming around to haunt their architects sooner or later. In discovering that each is flawed and in disclosing the concealments which allow the appearance of resolution, we do not urge that it be held against sociologists that they are not philosophers nor do we argue that they should succeed where philosophers before them have failed. Rather, we only wish to make clear what is risked by each concealment and to face candidly the inevitably unfortunate ramifications which must proceed from it.

Snappy Bureaucrats

In the works of August Vollmer, Bruce Smith, O. W. Wilson, and those progressive police administrators who still follow their lead, a vision of the perfect police agency and the perfect policeman has gained considerable ground. Labeled "the professional model" in police circles—though entirely different from any classical sense of profession or professional—it envisions a highly trained, technologically sophisticated police department operating free from political interference with a corps of well-educated police responding obediently to the policies, orders, and directives of a central administrative command. It is a vision of police officers, to use Bittner's phrasing, as "snappy bureaucrats,"[11] cogs in a quasi-military machine who do what they are told out of a mix of fear, loyalty, routine, and detailed specification of duties.

The professional model, unlike other solutions to be considered, is based on the assumption that the policeman's motives for working can be made to locate within his department. He will, if told, work vice or traffic, juvenile or homicide, patrol passively or aggressively, and produce one, two, four, or six arrests, pedestrian stops, or reports per hour, day, or week as his department sees fit. In this way the assumption and vision of the professional model in policing is little different from that of any bureaucracy which seeks by specifying tasks and setting expectations for levels of production—work quotas—to coordinate a regular, predictable, and efficient service for its clientele.

The problem with this vision of *sine ira et studio* service by obedient operatives is that when the product to be delivered is some form of human service—education, welfare, health, and police bureaucracies are similar in this way—the vision seems always to fall short of expectations. On the one hand the would-be bureaucratic operatives—teachers, social workers, nurses, and policemen—resent being treated as mere bureaucrats and resist the translation of their work into quotas, directives, rules, regulations, or other abstract specifications. On the other hand, to the extent that the vision of an efficient and obedient human service bureaucracy is realized, the clientele of such institutions typically come away with the impression that no one in the institution truly *cares* about their problems. And, of course, in that the aim of bureaucratization is to locate employees' motives for work within the bureaucracy, they are absolutely correct in their feelings.

To the extent that the professional model succeeds in making the ends of policing locate within the agency as opposed to moral demands of the tasks which policemen are asked by their clients to do, it appears to solve the Dirty Harry problem. When it succeeds, it does so by replacing the morally compelling ends of punishment and peace with the less human, though by no means uncompelling, ends of bureaucratic performance. However, this resolution certainly does not imply that dirty means will disappear, only that the motives for their use will be career advancement and promotion. Likewise, on those occasions when a morally sensitive policeman would be compelled by the demands of the situational exigencies before him to use a dirty means, the bureaucratic operative envisioned by the professional model will merely do his job. Ambitious bureaucrats and obedient timeservers fail at being the type of morally sensitive souls we want to be policemen. The professional model's bureaucratic resolution of the Dirty Harry problem fails in policing for the same reason it fails in every other human service agency: it is quite simply an impossibility to create a bureaucrat who cares for anything but his bureaucracy.

The idealized image of the professional model, which has been responded to with an ideal critique, is probably unrealizable. Reality intervenes as the ideal type is approached. The bureaucracy seems to take on weight as it approaches the pole, is slowed, and may even collapse in approaching.

Bittner's Peace

A second effort in the literature of contemporary policing also attempts to address the Dirty Harry problem by substituting an alternative to the presently prevailing police ends of punishment. Where the professional model sought to substitute bureaucratic rewards and sanctions for the moral end of punishment, the elegant polemics by Egon Bittner in *The Functions of Police in Modern Society* and "Florence Nightingale in Pursuit of Willie Sutton: A Theory of the Police" seek to substitute the end of peace. In beautifully chosen words, examples, and phrasing, Bittner leads his readers to conclude that peace is historically, empirically, intellectually, and morally the most compelling, unquestionable, and humane end of policing. Bittner is, I fear, absolutely right.

It is the end of peace which legitimates the extension of police responsibilities into a wide variety of civil matters—neighborhood disputes, loud parties, corner lounging, lovers' quarrels, political rallies, disobedient children, bicycle registration, pet control, and a hundred other types of tasks which a modern "service" style police department regularly is called upon to perform. With these responsibilities, which most "good" police agencies now accept willingly and officially, also comes the need for an extension of police powers. Arrest is, after all, too crude a tool to be used in all the various situations in which our peace-keeping policemen are routinely asked to be of help. "Why should," asks Herman Goldstein, in a manner in which Bittner would approve, "a police officer arrest and charge a disorderly tavern patron if ordering him to leave the tavern will suffice? Must he arrest and charge one of the parties in a lovers' quarrel if assistance in forcing a separation is all that is desired?"[12] There is no question that both those situations could be handled more peacefully if police were granted new powers which would allow them to handle those situations in the way Goldstein rhetorically asks if they should. That such extensions of police powers will be asked for by our most enlightened police departments in the interests of keeping the peace is absolutely certain. If the success of the decriminalization of police arrests for public intoxication, vagrancy, mental illness, and the virtually unrestricted two-hour right of detention made possible by the Uniform Law of Arrest are any indication of the likelihood of extensions being received favorably, the end of peace and its superiority over punishment in legitimating the extension of police powers seem exceedingly likely to prevail further.

The problem with peace is that it is not the only end of policing so compelling, unquestionable, and in the end, humane. Amid the good work toward the end of peace that we increasingly want our police to do, it is certain that individuals or groups will arise who the police, in all their peace-keeping benevolence, will conclude, on moral if not political or institutional grounds, have "got it coming." And all the once dirty means which were bleached in the brilliant light of peace will return to their true colors.

Skolnick's Craftsman

The third and final attempt to resolve the Dirty Harry problem is offered by Jerome Skolnick, who in *Justice Without Trial* comes extremely close to stating the Dirty Harry problem openly when he writes:

> . . . He (the policeman) sees himself as a craftsman, at his best, a master of his trade . . . [he] draws a moral distinction between criminal law and criminal procedure. The distinction is drawn somewhat as follows: The substantive law of crimes is intended to control the behavior of people who wilfully injure persons or property, or who engage in behaviors having such a consequence, such as the use of narcotics. Criminal procedure, by contrast, is intended to control authorities, not criminals. As such, it does not fall into the same *moral* class of constraint as substantive criminal law. If a policeman were himself to use narcotics, or to steal, or to assault, *outside the line of duty*, much the same standards would be applied to him by other policemen as to the ordinary citizen. When, however, the issue concerns the policeman's freedom to carry out his *duties*, another moral realm is entered.[13]

What is more, Skolnick's craftsman finds support from his peers, department, his community, and the law for the moral rightness of his calling. He cares about his work and finds it just.

What troubles Skolnick about his craftsman is his craft. The craftsman refuses to see, as Skolnick thinks he ought to, that the dirty means he sometimes uses to achieve his good ends stand in the same moral class of wrongs as those he is employed to fight. Skolnick's craftsman reaches this conclusion by understanding that his unquestionably good and compelling ends, on certain occasions, justify his employment of dirty means to their achievement. Skolnick's craftsman, as Skolnick understands him, resolves the Dirty Harry problem by denying the dirtiness of his means.

Skolnick's craftsman's resolution is, speaking precisely, Machiavellian. It should come as no surprise to find the representative of one of the classic attempts to resolve the problem of Dirty Hands to be a front runner in response to Dirty Harry. What is worrisome about such a resolution? What does it conceal that makes our genuine dilemma disappear? The problem is not that the craftsman will sometimes choose to use dirty means. If he is morally sensitive to its demands, every policeman's work will sometimes require as much. What is worrisome about Skolnick's craftsman is that he does not regard his means as dirty and, as Skolnick tells us, does not suffer from their use. The craftsman, if Skolnick's portrait of him is correct, will resort to dirty means too readily and too easily. He lacks the restraint that can come only from struggling to justify them and from taking seriously the hazards involved.

In 1966, when *Justice Without Trial* first appeared, Skolnick regarded the prospects of creating a more morally sensitive craftsman exceedingly dim. He could not imagine that the craftsman's community, employer, peers, or the courts could come to reward him more for his legal compliance than for the achievement of the ends of his craft. However, in phrasing the prospects in terms of a Dirty Harry problem, one can not only agree with Skolnick that denying the goodness of unquestionably good ends is a practical and political impossibility, but can also uncover another alternative, one which Skolnick does not pursue.

The alternative the Dirty Harry problem leads us to is ensuring that the craftsman regards his dirty means as dirty by applying the same retributive principles of punishment to his wrongful acts that he is quite willing to apply to others'. It is, in fact, only when his wrongful acts are punished that he will come to see them as wrongful and will appreciate the genuine moral—rather than technical or occupational—choice he makes in resorting to them. The prospects for punishment of such acts are by no means dim, and considerable strides in this area have been made. It requires far fewer resources to punish than to reward. Secondly, the likelihood that juries in civil suits will find dirty means dirtier than police do is confirmed by police claims that outsiders cannot appreciate the same moral and technical distinctions that they do. Finally, severe financial losses to police agencies as well as to their officers eventually communicate to both that vigorously policing themselves is cheaper and more pleasing than having to pay so heavily if they do not. If under such conditions our craftsman police officer is still willing to risk the employment of dirty means to achieve what he understands to be unquestionably good ends, he will not only know that he has behaved justly, but that in doing so he must run the risk of becoming genuinely guilty as well.

A FINAL NOTE

In urging the punishment of policemen who resort to dirty means to achieve some unquestionably good and morally compelling end, we recognize that we create a Dirty Harry problem for ourselves and for those we urge to effect such punishments. It is a fitting end, one which teaches once again that the danger in Dirty Harry problems is never in their resolution, but in thinking that one has found a resolution with which one can truly live in peace.

REFERENCES

1. In the contemporary philosophical literature, particularly when raised for the vocation of politics, the question is commonly referred to as the Dirty Hands problem after J. P. Sartre's treatment of it in *Dirty Hands*, (Les Mains Sales, 1948) and in *No Exit and Three Other Plays* (New York: Modern Library, 1950). Despite its modern name, the problem is very old and has been taken up by Machiavelli in *The Prince* (1513); and *The Discourses* (1519) (New York: Modern Library, 1950); by Max Weber, "Politics as a Vocation," (1919) in *Max Weber: Essays in Sociology*, eds. and trans. H. Gerth and C. W. Wills (New York: Oxford University Press, 1946); and by Albert Camus, "The Just Assassins," (1949) in *Caligula and Three Other Plays* (New York: Alfred A. Knopf, 1958). *See* Michael Walzer's brilliant critique of these contributions, "Political Action: The Problem of Dirty Hands," *Philosophy and Public Affairs*, 2(2) (winter 1972). Likewise the Dirty Hands/Dirty Harry problem is implicitly or explicitly raised in virtually every work of Raymond Chandler, Dashiell Hammett, James Cain, and other *Tough Guy Writers of The Thirties*, ed. David Madden (Carbondale, IL: Southern Illinois University Press, 1968), as they are in all of the best work of Joseph Wambaugh, particularly *The Blue Knight, The New Centurions*, and *The Choirboys*.

2. "Dirty" here means both "repugnant" in that it offends widely shared standards of human decency and dignity and "dangerous" in that it breaks commonly shared and supported norms, rules, or laws for conduct. To "dirty" acts there must be both a deontologically based face validity of immorality and a consequentialist threat to the prevailing rules for social order.

3. W. H. Auden, "The Guilty Vicarage," in *The Dyer's Hand and Other Essays* (New York: Alfred A. Knopf, 1956), pp. 146–58.

4. Egon Bittner, *The Functions of Police in Modern Society* (New York: Jason Aronson, 1975) and "Florence Nightingale in Pursuit of Willie Sutton," in *The Potential For Reform Of the Criminal Justice System*, vol. 3, ed. H. Jacob (Beverly Hills, CA: Sage Publications, 1974), pp. 11–44.

5. Sartre, *Dirty Hands*, p. 224.

6. One of Wambaugh's characters in *The Choirboys* makes this final point most dramatically when he fails to notice that a young boy's buttocks are flatter than they should be and reads the child's large stomach as a sign of adequate nutrition. When the child dies through his mother's neglect and abuse, the officer rightly includes himself in his ecology of guilt.

7. Herman Goldstein, *Policing a Free Society* (Cambridge, MA: Ballinger Publishing, 1977), p. 72.

8. *See*, for example, John F. Galliher, "Explanations of Police Behavior: A Critical Review and Analysis," *The Sociological Quarterly*, 12:308–18 (summer 1971); Richard Quinney, *Class, State, and Crime* (New York: David McKay, 1977).

9. Albert J. Reiss, Jr., *The Police and the Public* (New Haven, CT: Yale University Press, 1971), p. 122.

10. These two assertions are drawn from Graeme Newman's *The Punishment Response* (Philadelphia: J. B. Lippincott Co., 1978).

11. Bittner, p. 53.

12. Ibid., p. 72.

13. Jerome Skolnick, *Justice Without Trial*, 2nd ed. (New York: John Wiley & Sons, 1975), p. 182.

Police Brutality: A Model for Definition, Perspective, and Control

David L. Carter

The problem of police brutality has been studied for years from a number of perspectives. With respect to this issue, a review of the literature generally reveals that: (1) brutality is a vague term which must be operationalized before it can be truly understood and measured; (2) brutality—whatever it is—does exist and is improper police behavior; and (3) the problem of brutality must be controlled. Each of these issues has been addressed largely as individual problems with few, if any, conclusive results. This author maintains that these problems are systemic; thus any individual approach is tautological and will lead to interpretive inconsistencies. Thus, the problem of brutality must be viewed in the aggregate for understanding to occur.

A compounding enigma is that most of the literature on brutality has been predominantly descriptive of the phenomena. While this research is useful in identifying issues, it is time to move beyond description to explanation. The transition between these phases is not simple. It requires empirical assessment of the phenomena through theory development and testing.

One of the better works on brutality which seeks to explain the use of force by the police was conducted by Friedrich relying on the 1966 data collected by Reiss for the President's Commission on Law Enforcement and Administration of Justice.[1] Essentially, Friedrich explains the use of force as being a product of interacting variables that can be traced to the individual, the situation, or the organization. The tripartite analytical approach employed by Friedrich serves to deduce the phenomena of brutality to a more explanatory level. Nonetheless, this avenue of explanation remains too narrow thus necessitating an analytic mechanism which permits greater specificity for identifying critical variables.

The current work attempts to transgress into a new explanatory generation by addressing brutality through a theoretical model. The causal model proposed in this article examines police brutality from an "applied theory" perspective. That is, while the model follows the traditional theory construction process, it has pragmatic applications. The model, relying on reductionist theory, contains four fundamental elements: (1) Redefining the brutality concept; (2) operationalizing brutality by establishing an abuse of authority typology; (3) presentation of a causal paradigm; and (4) identification of control mechanisms for abusive behavior. These elements collectively present a taxonomy of brutality through the identification of potential variable relationships. Viewed together, the elements may begin to explain the phenomena of brutality.

BRUTALITY: THE PROBLEM OF DEFINITION

In developing the model this author avoided the word "brutality" as either an operational or descriptive term. Although the term is used extensively both in the literature and by the public, the author maintains the word is misleading. As noted by Reiss, "[W]hat citizens mean by police brutality covers the full range of police practices . . . [It can include] any practice that degrades their status, that restricts their freedom, that annoys or harasses them, or that uses physical force that is frequently seen as unnecessary or unwarranted."[2]

In the author's view, a significant problem with the word "brutality" is that it is an emotional term which introduces bias into a scientific examination of the phenomena. It represents a mental image of violence that overshadows objective analysis of the concept. Moreover, "brutality" is a generic, nondescript term which does not accurately describe behavior by police.

"Brutality" infers an injurious act toward a citizen by the police. Although the literature has noted interpretations of brutality as being non-injurious,[3] the inherent impression of the term persists. The President's Commission on Law Enforcement and Administration of Justice noted the problem of definition when its research found that such diverse actions as excessive use of force, name calling, sarcasm, ridicule, and disrespect were included under the umbrella term of brutality as perceived by community leaders.[4] In wrestling with the problem of definition the United States Commission on Civil Rights in its report *Justice* relied on somewhat conflicting definitions of brutality. For example, the report refers to brutality simply as "a vio-

This article was written expressly for inclusion in this edition.

lation of due process"[5] and later defines the phenomena as ". . . the unnecessary use of violence to enforce the mores of segregation, to punish, and to coerce confessions . . .".[6] Whereas the former definition is broad and includes nonviolent and unintentional acts, the latter definition is overly restrictive including only violent, intentional acts with specific purposes. Both definitions are functionally non-measurable for purposes of assessing and classifying improper police behavior.

While injurious or violent acts to citizens by the police do occur, the writer maintains that non-injurious abuse occurs with greater frequency and signifies a far more problematic threat to democratic society. Thus, it must be recognized that one term—brutality—will not accurately describe impermissive behavior. The term must be substituted with a more definitive framework which can discriminate between the degrees of illegitimate authority exercised by officers and be descriptive of the specific nature of the abuse.

Within these constraints the writer employs the phrase "abuse of authority" in the place of "brutality". For the purpose of this model, abuse of authority is generically defined as any action by a police officer without regard to motive, intent, or malice that tends to injure, insult, tread on human dignity, manifest feelings of inferiority, and/or violate an inherent legal right of a member of the police constituency. "Authority" indicates a legitimate exercise of direction and control over individuals or groups with the inference that one has a moral obligation associated with the exercise of that authority.[7] Thus, if one accepts this premise of moral obligation one must conclude that any abuse of authority by the police necessarily involves a conscious disregard of ethical commitments to both the individual and society. The author, however, maintains that this is a logical fallacy with respect to the police abuse of authority.

As an illustration, a police officer may have an intuitive feeling based on his/her experience that a person is in possession of contraband. If the officer conducts a search of that person without legal justification (i.e., consent, search incident to arrest, exigency, or warrant) the officer has abused his/her authority. If the unlawful search was conducted because of the officer's simple lack of legal knowledge, there is most probably no violation of the moral obligation. Similarly, if the officer has rationalized to him/herself that the means justifies the ends—that it is better to have the contraband in police custody rather than "on the street"—then one may again conclude that there was no infringement of a moral norm.[8]

The importance of this discussion as related to the definition of abuse of authority is that the presence of intent or motive by the officer to abuse authority is largely irrelevant. What is significant is to empirically document the incidents of abuse and the contributory stressors to that behavior. Hence, the officer may truly believe that his/her exercise of authority is legitimate when, in fact, it is not. Based on these reasons the model does not differentiate between an officer's perceptions of legitimacy for his/her actions; instead the mere occurrence of abuse is what is important for this model.

With this understanding, the definition must then be operationalized. To achieve this the author has created a typology for classifying abusive incidents.

ABUSE OF AUTHORITY TYPOLOGY

The theoretical model requires that incidents of abuse be categorized into a parsimonious typology based on the nature and effect of abuse. This process permits the definition of "abuse of authority" to be operationalized. The three part typology consists of: (1) physical abuse/excessive force; (2) verbal/psychological abuse; and (3) legal abuse/violation of civil rights.

Physical Abuse/Excessive Force. This classification refers to: (a) any abuse of authority that involves the use of more force than is necessary for a police officer to effect an arrest or search; and/or (b) the wanton use of any degree of physical force against another by a police officer under the color of his/her office. There is no distinction between an injurious and non-injurious incident based upon the assumption that the causal variables are the same. The key test is whether there was any physical force directly used against an individual.

Verbal/Psychological Abuse. In this category, incidents are included where police officers verbally assault, ridicule, or harass individuals and/or place persons who are under the actual or constructive dominion of the officer in a situation where the individual's behavioral dynamics and esteem are threatened or diminished. Also included in this type of abuse is the threat of physical harm under the assumption that a threat is psychologically coercive and instills fear in the average person.[9] Most certainly this type of abuse is not as visually apparent as physical abuse, thus making it difficult to measure. Any empirical assessment of this type would ideally incorporate multiple data gathering techniques, including unobtrusive measures and follow-up attitudinal assessments of police officers and, more importantly, citizens.

Legal Abuse/Violation of Civil Rights. This type of abuse probably occurs with greater frequency than the other categories. It is defined as any violation of a person's constitutional, federally protected, or state protected rights. Although the individual may not suffer any physical or psychological damage, an abuse of authority has nonetheless occurred. In all cases of physical abuse, and many cases of verbal abuse, there will also be a legal violation. However, legal abuse can—and does—occur frequently without the other forms.

The underlying construct in the typology is that a police officer has exercised power by virtue of his/her office in a manner that is not consistent with law or ethical canons. This construct provides a link of behavioral consistency throughout the typology. Moreover, it is likely that any given abusive behavior will involve more than one category in the typology. These theoretical consistencies provide logical evidence that a causal paradigm may be proposed to explain abuse of authority throughout the typology.

THE CAUSAL PARADIGM

The paradigm is designed to explain abusive behavior that is both intentional and reactive. Although this causal theory is closely akin to environmental determinism, the writer feels a distinction can be made between "intentional" and "reactive" abuse. Intentional abuse is that which is overtly and consciously imposed by the officer. The decision to inflict the abuse is stimulated by the stressors discussed in the paradigm, however, there is some specific circumstance or act which provides the impetus for the officer to be abusive. For example, the officer's abuse may be motivated by revenge (e.g., physical abuse may be used against an individual who spat on the officer) or the desire to achieve a specified goal (e.g., legal abuse through an unlawful search with the intent to gather evidence for a conviction). Regardless of the motivating force, the ultimate decision is influenced by the stressors.

Conversely, reactive abuse exists in response to stimuli or conditions without an overt, conscious decision to inflict the abuse. The reaction may be that of a conditioned response (e.g., a person strikes the officer and he/she aggressively retaliates) or it may be the product of a lack of knowledge (e.g., an officer violates a person's constitutional rights because he/she simply does not know the law). Despite the nature of the reaction, the causal stressors influence the officer's decision-making ability, thereby precipitating the behavior.

The causal paradigm, as illustrated in Figure 1, is based on a concept of "cumulative interactive stressors." That is, there are a number of generic variables—stressors—which interact with a police officer's job performance, decision making, and organizational membership. These stressors intermix and, to some degree,

FIGURE 1 Relationship of Stressors to Abuse

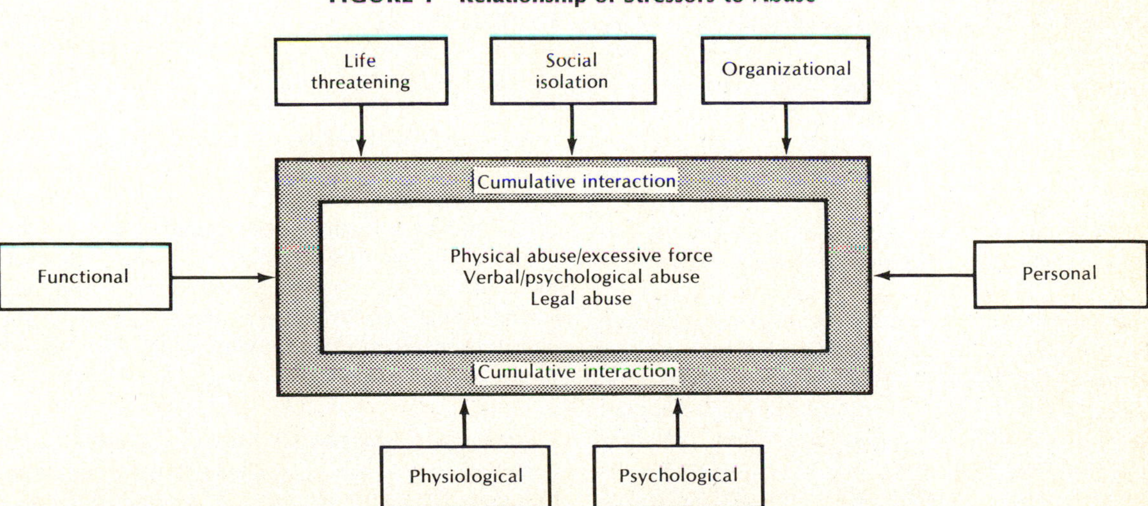

overlap; thus, they are interactive in nature. Stressors, as individual phenomena, do not "cause" dysfunctional behavior *per se*. They may, in fact, have functional benefits such as heightening alertness and making an individual more time-conscious.

Problems begin to rise, however, when multiple stressors begin to accumulate in an officer's faculties. If there is no legitimate release mechanism for the stress, an illegitimate means will surface. When this occurs, so does abuse. Once again, this illegitimate release mechanism may be of either an intentional or reactive nature and result in physical, verbal, or legal abuse.

In the causal paradigm the author envisions seven generic stressors which serve as precipitative influences of abusive behavior. These stressors contain multiple independent variables of abusive behavior which have been factored together according to their source and/or nature. In any given causal sequence the stressors may be primary independent variables, antecedent variables, or intervening variables. The significant point to note is that regardless of the variables' time-order, they are nonetheless causal in nature.

If viewed as a "grand theory" of abuse of authority, the paradigm carries an important *caveat*. To explain abusive behavior conclusively, one must examine the phenomena on an individual rather than collective level. Nonetheless, collective analysis of abuse can provide important insights into trends and, particularly, problematic stressors unique to a jurisdiction. Enumerated below are the seven stressors which the writer maintains precipitate abuse through cumulative interaction.

Life-Threatening Stressors. The constant potential of injury or death and the confrontation of criminal suspects in critical incidents which could lead to life-threatening situations are the characteristics of these stressors. Key elements include (a) the unexpected nature of violence against the police officer and (b) the intentional—rather than accidental—nature of the violence. Because the potential of a life-threatening situation is constant, it has a tendency to be ever present in the mind (although perhaps not always in the conscious state), thereby being inherently cumulative.

Social Isolation Stressors. Included in this category are such factors as isolation and alienation from the community; differential socio-economic status between the police and their constituency; authoritarianism; cynicism; and cultural distinction, prejudice, and discrimination. These are all characteristics that not only isolate the police officer from the community but also contribute to his/her communal visibility and emphasize the separatism of the police from the general public.[10]

Organizational Stressors. The author feels that this source of stress is particularly significant. These stressors deal with all aspects of organizational life—both formal and informal. Specific stressors include: peer pressure, role models, performance measures for evaluation, upward mobility, policies and procedures (or lack thereof leading to inconsistent and/or unacceptable behavior), job satisfaction, morale, inadequate supervision and administrative control, inadequate training, internal organizational structure, and leadership styles. Thus, simply being a member of an organization and trying to succeed can provide a significant amount of stress for the officer.

Functional Stressors These are variables specifically related to the performance of assigned policing duties. Included in this category is the use of discretion; knowledge of law and legal mandates; and decision-making responsibilities such as the use of force, when to stop and question persons, and how to resolve domestic disputes. If an officer does not have a good grasp of his/her responsibilities and is ill-prepared to handle them, stress will increase.

Personal Stressors. These include many of the "classic" stressors frequently eluded to in the literature such as family problems or financial constraints. Particularly noteworthy in this grouping are marital discord, school or social problems of children, family illnesses, and associated personal or family crisis. The literature indicates that such stressors clearly influence an officer's on-duty personality, affecting both attitude and behavior.[11]

Physiological Stressors. A change in one's physiology and general health may also affect one's decision-making capabilities, as well as one's tolerance of others' behavior. Fatigue from working off-duty jobs; the physiological impact of shift work (which interrupts the "body clock"); changes in physiological responses during critical incidents (i.e., getting "pumped up"); and illnesses or medical conditions are all examples of physiological stressors.

Psychological Stressors. Most of the stressors discussed above could also be classified in this category. However, the author maintains that certain stress variables have a significant direct impact on the inner-self. For example, fear that is generated when an officer responds to a dangerous call can be a psychological stressor. The fear may be functional if the officer recognizes it as a warning mechanism and becomes more alert as a result. However, if the officer masks that fear and it becomes internalized, it can upset one's psychological balance. Other stress variables in this category include constant exposure to the worst side of humankind and the impact of resolving situations which are of a repulsive nature (e.g., homicides, child abuse, fatality traffic accidents, etc.). These situations can have a traumatic effect on oneself; particularly in their cumulative state. Such stressors may also develop into a psychological condition such as depression or paranoia which may, in turn, have a significant impact on the abuse of authority.

The stressors in this paradigm are not mutually exclusive. It is their interactive nature which lends support to the cumulative effect of being precipitators to abuse. The idea that stressors are cumulative in nature is of importance to note. As exposure to the stressors increases in both time and intensity without a control mechanism, the more the officer's self-control is eroded. the result is police behavior on an emotional rather than rational level.

The literature is replete with research and monographs on stress. The empirical evidence indicates that stress does, in fact, influence the working persona of a police officer. However, as noted by Malloy and Mays, externally valid empirical evidence that links policing to the effects of stress is more scarce than one may intuitively believe.[12] In essence, the literature suggests that while significant forms of stress exist in police organizations, the sources of that stress and the best means to control it are largely unknown. Previous research further indicates that stress has multiple behavioral implications particularly when experienced in a cumulative state.[13]

These findings not only lend support to the author's "cumulative interactive stressors" hypothesis but also suggest that with the knowledge of existing stressors, some forms of control—or containment—can be developed. The literature suggests that programs can be established which control stressors at the individual and organizational levels.[14] Stress management programs involve both recognition of stressors and techniques to control the effect of stressors. Thus, it becomes incumbent for the organization to establish programs which control causal stressors in order to minimize the abuse of authority. In this regard the issue of stress control and abuse control become synonymous.

ISSUES AND TECHNIQUES IN THE CONTROL OF ABUSE

It has certainly been recognized in the literature that if an individual has been wronged by the police there must be some form of remedial action taken. However, the author maintains that the idea of remedies alone is too narrow in that a "remedy" infers corrective action for a past deed. This writer argues that a police organization should additionally take action to prevent future incidents of abuse. In consideration of this argument and the recognition that a singular activity will not forestall abusive acts, the author proposes the concept of *differential containment strategies*.

Essentially, differential containment strategies constitute a probability model that employs intrusive organizational activities devised to be remedial for current and past abusive acts or preventive of future abuse acts. The strategies are synergistic in nature, providing a therapeutic approach to abuse which relies on organizational manipulation of the intrusive strategies.

Some of the strategies will address multiple organizational purposes and effect abuse as an artifact of general management (or perhaps, as a matter of chance). Other strategies are designed to specifically address abusive behavior. Figure 2 illustrates this concept by indicating that the probability of abuse is omnipresent. However, that probability can be significantly limited if containment strategies are maximized, thereby reducing the cumulative interaction of stressors. Conversely, the probability of abuse increases when the differential containment strategies have experienced limited application.

FIGURE 2 Probability Model Relating Containment Strategies to Incidence of Abuse

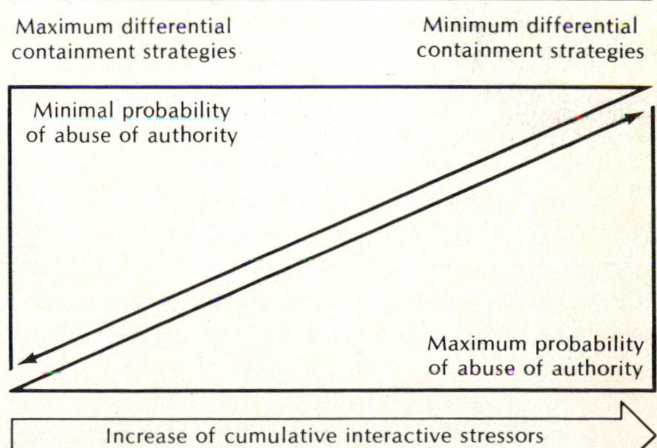

It is important to note that the strategies are a *probability model* for containing abusive acts. The author is a pragmatist recognizing that police abuse of authority cannot be completely eliminated. Therefore, the strategies discussed below are to be employed to reduce the probability of abuse occurring through the containment of stressors. The significance of the strategies are: (1) they are broad based to address the total police control mandate; and (2) they are presented specifically as containment activities in light of the causal stressors.

Differential Containment Strategies

1. *Personnel Selection.* Employment of police officers should go beyond traditional criteria and provide a greater focus on personality traits such as intelligence, humanity, honesty, stability, and reliability. People should be sought who are both capable of performing the required tasks and exercising ethical judgment in that performance.

2. *Training.* Both pre-service and in-service training should be increased in such areas as: the legal *process* (not just law); civil rights; social psychology; counseling; and service responsibilities of the police. There should be a decrease in the "technical crime-fighting" training of officers. The author's rationale for this position is: (1) Police officers should receive training which is more reflective of their actual duties (service/order maintenance) rather than their perceived (and probably over-emphasized) responsibilities of "crime-fighting." (2) The prevalence of "crime-fighting training" may contribute to a more punitive performance role model which affects officer behavior through a distortion of "just deserts" toward criminals.

While continued development of training curricula is important, perhaps the most significant training issue is *quality*. Too often one finds that police trainers—even in the larger agencies—are called on to perform training in a wide variety of areas. Conventional wisdom appears to be that if a person was a good police officer, he/she will be a good trainer—a fallacy which is experienced too often. Moreover, one finds that there is typically little quality control of the material and infrequent curricula planning and evaluation. The substantive training assessment which does occur is more commonly of a record keeping nature rather than being truly evaluative. Hence, competent well-prepared instructors with contemporary material are essential for effective training *and socialization* of officers.

3. *Performance Evaluations.* This is one of the more difficult tasks to achieve objectively and accurately. Evaluations on traditional quantitative criteria of productivity are not truly indicative of police performance. Ideally, evaluations should be on qualitative variables addressing the service provided by officers. The use of unobtrusive measures would be the most utilitarian but difficult to instill in many police organizations. Similarly, validated force choice or Behaviorally Anchored Performance Scales can provide important reliable evaluative information.[15] Stringent research on this issue must occur before a reliable evaluation system can be developed for police.

4. *Open Complaint and Internal Investigation System.* If abuse is going to be controlled there must be an open system wherein citizens can make complaints. This can also be an effective tool for evaluation by examining the nature of complaints and any trends in complaints. Evaluation can be at an individual level to identify officers that may need counseling, training, or some other form of intrusive activity to correct unacceptable behavior. Evaluation may also occur at the organizational level by identifying a pattern of complaints against officers. This may indicate a supervisory, control, training, or policy void that must be filled.

Regardless of the evaluative benefits of an open complaint and investigation system, one must be certain that the mechanism objectively investigates and adjudicates complaints.

5. *Public Information/Education.* A systematic method should be implemented which informs the public about the true dynamics of abuse of authority. Similarly, the public must be clearly informed of the complaint process. At the minimum this process may establish empathy for the officers. One may also hope that the information will contribute to some reduction of stressors and open communications between the police and the public. Generally, public opinion research indicates that the public is supportive of the police.[16] Shedding the shroud of secrecy around the police and capitalizing on this support will contribute to more productive and less conflictual performance.

6. *Trouble Shooting/Preventive Programs.* Internal programs should be developed which identify and treat potential (or existing) abusers. This writer maintains that the organization bears the responsibility for taking treatment action not just punitive action. Under the premise that it is the organizational/work environment that generates a preponderance of the stressors one may conclude that the organization bears at least a moral or ethical responsibility to alleviate the stressors. If for no other reasons, treatment of stressors can be a cost-beneficial investment for the department (e.g., reduces attrition thus minimizing personnel costs; make personnel more effective performers; etc.) and can serve

to minimize the legal liabilities of officers and departments. Unfortunately, most police agencies tend to exclusively adopt a punishment mode for such individuals (which in some cases is certainly warranted) without consideration of a treatment mode.

7. *Policies, Procedures and Organizational Control.* It is incumbent on the formal organization to not only promulgate rules for control of abuse but to also establish effective supervision and control of personnel to deal with the enigma. Without clear organizational guidelines officers cannot know what is expected of them nor will they have a firm base on which to rely for decision making. Similarly, organizational control cannot be effectively achieved unless the officers are aware of possible sanctions which may be imposed for improper behavior.

EMPIRICAL ASSESSMENT OF THE MODEL

The author has empirically tested selected aspects of this model on a population of police officers where the abuse of authority has been an ongoing problem.[17] All sworn officers of the McAllen, Texas police department were administered a questionnaire as both a pre-test and post-test which collected data on 774 variables. In order to supplement the empirical findings, qualitative information was gathered through content analysis of videotapes depicting incidents of police violence, a review of past litigation against the police department, a content analysis of newspaper stories, and interviews with McAllen police personnel.

The pre-test was administered on the day that two significant changes were implemented at the police department. The first change was a complete structural reorganization of the department with a concomitant restaffing of the entire command structure. The second change was the initiation of a specifically designed training program mandated by the United States District Court as part of the injunctive relief in civil rights litigation.[18] The post-test was administered one year later. (At this writing only pre-test results are available.)

A total of 95 officers were surveyed, of which 89 were male and 6 were female. The mean age of the officers is 27.5 with an average of 3.4 years of sworn police experience at McAllen. Seventy percent of the respondents were Hispanic with 63.2% of all officers having some college (only 7.4% of the officers have at least a baccalaureate degree). Fifty-four percent of the officers were married at the time of the survey, with 62% of the respondents indicating they have children. Seven percent of the officers were divorced after employment. Of those officers who have separated or divorced since joining the department, 77% cited their employment as a police officer as contributing to this change of status.

Preliminary Data Results

Due to the early stage of the project, most of the data analysis is merely descriptive. However, some inferential testing has occurred which is related to the current topic. Thus, while the data reported below cannot be viewed as evidence of true asymmetrical relationships, the results do lend support to the theoretical constituents beyond an *a priori* level.

Abuse of Authority. It is clear from the evidence that all three types of abuse occurred at McAllen. Civil and criminal litigation against the city and individual officers substantiates this claim, as do the actions of the officers on the videotapes. Further reinforcement comes from admissions of the officers during interviews as well as survey responses.

Table 1 indicates various officer attitudes toward physical and verbal abuse at McAllen. Interestingly, nearly a quarter (23.1%) of the officers could justify the use of excessive force to maintain their authority. Similarly, it is significant to note that 62.2% of the respondents could justify the use of excessive force for purposes of retaliation, not just self-protection. These findings appear to have important implications for the psychological stressors of authoritarianism and adaptation needs. It is of further interest that 82.1% acknowledged the existence of excessive force that was influenced by personal stressors, with 81% agreeing

TABLE 1 Officer Attitudes on Issues of Physical and Verbal Abuse

Physical Abuse Issues	*% of Officers Agreeing with Statement*
Few officers use excessive force.	89.4
Excessive force is sometimes necessary to show the officer's authority.	23.1
An officer has the right to use excessive force for retaliation.	62.2
When excessive force is used, it is a product of racial-ethnic discrimination.	15.7
Verbal Abuse Issues	
It is permissible for an officer to talk rough with citizens.	59.0
Rough talk is the only way many people will listen to a police officer.	52.6

that better supervision would reduce the probability of physical abuse. These findings not only infer the existence of excessive force but they also illustrate the interaction of personal and organizational stressors.

Job Satisfaction and Abuse. The issue of job satisfaction was examined in significant detail in this study. An array of variables under the generic label of "job satisfaction" can be factored together according to stressors. For the purpose of this analysis, job satisfaction can be a broad measure of the interactive effect of stressors when measuring job related variables.

Among the significant findings of this analysis was that an officer's job satisfaction significantly effects his/her belief that excessive force is sometimes necessary to instill authority ($X^2 = 67.003$, df = 24, $p < .001$, V = .420). In this same vein, there is a significant relationship between job satisfaction and an attitude that rough talk toward citizens is permissible ($X^2 = 42.944$, df = 24, $p < .01$, V = .336). There are no indications of a significant relationship between job satisfaction and the discriminatory excessive use of force by officers. However, as job satisfaction decreases an officer's belief in the right to use excessive force for retaliation increases ($X^2 = 79.477$, df = 24, $p < .001$, V = 457). The data further indicate that job satisfaction is significantly related to the personal problems of officers which contribute to the excessive use of force ($X^2 = 40.10$, df = 20, $p < .005$, V = 325).

Based on these results the data tend to support the concepts of (1) cumulative interactive stressors and (2) the relationship between stressors and abuse of authority. The author does not maintain this rudimentary analysis shows a causal relationship; however, it is indicative of correlations which give support for the need of future research.

Presence of Stressors. Beyond the findings noted above some descriptive results of the study are available which indicate the presence of stressors. An overview of the findings provide interesting insights into the existence of stressors as well as the general pattern of attitudes and experiences of McAllen police officers.

On the issue of organizational stressors, 60.1% of the officers reported they were less certain of their job responsibilities than they felt they should be. This indicates undefined missions and objectives, unclear policies and procedures, role conflict, ambiguous training, and poor communications. This is supported by the finding that 52.6% of the respondents feel that management does not clearly inform line personnel of organizational changes while a significant 70.5% directly stated that management insufficently communicates to officers.

The general trend of data indicates that line personnel felt there was insufficient supervision in the department. Although views were mixed it appears this perception was a product of poor upper management, poor promotional policies, poorly trained supervisors, unclear responsibilities, and/or unclear authority. Interestingly, patrol officers generally expressed the belief that closer supervision would reduce incidents of abuse by officers while sergeants and higher ranked personnel did not share this view.

Overall 77.4% expressed the feeling that morale was low at the police department. This finding illustrates the interactive effect of organizational, psychological, and personal stressors. Moreover, the results imply that low morale has a debilitating effect on job satisfaction—a finding which is consistent with the literature of organizational behavior. As noted previously, this aggregation of variables also appears to precipitate abuse.

Other issues of personal stressors found that 46.3% of the respondents knew of at least one or two officers with serious marriage problems. Interestingly, 33.7% of the male officers indicated that their spouse disapproves of the officer working with a female partner. Interviews with officers strongly indicate that this disapproval is not a product of sexual/emotional factors, *per se*, but of the belief that the female officer could not adequately handle dangerous situations. Financial constraints were also apparent personal stressors wherein 41.1% of the officers indicated they worked a second job. However, the reasons for extra work were a combination of necessity and economic upward mobility.

Perhaps the most distressing finding was that 23.2% of the respondents knew of one or more officers who had committed or attempted to commit suicide. One may rhetorically ask what effect this knowledge has on a police officer. This author assumes it would have a stressful effect. However, the instrument in the current study did not collect data on this issue.

A variable which is both a personal and social isolation stressor deals with police officer relationships with others. Eighty-one percent expressed the belief that they were treated differently by neighbors as a result of their position. However, it appears, as illustrated by Table 2, that McAllen officers enjoy reasonably strong support of their position from significant others. This would seem to somewhat reduce the effect of personal stressors.

TABLE 2 Personal Stress Variables: Attitudes of Significant Others toward Respondent's Choice of Policing as an Occupation

Significant Other	*% Favor Police Work*	*% Oppose Police Work*	*% No Response*
Father	64.0	15.8	20.2
Mother	59.0	33.7	7.3
Spouse	66.3	29.5	4.2
Brother/Sister	73.7	23.1	3.2
Close Friend	79.9	19.0	1.1

Other social isolation stressors particularly worthy of note dealt with discrimination. Eighty-four percent of the officers reported that excessive force was not a product of discrimination while 75.2% indicated that race/ethnic background was not a contributing factor in any form of legitimate or illegitimate use of police authority. This appears to be contrary to what one may intuitively believe, although the reader must be cautioned that the officer may, in fact, discriminate without conscious realization. Despite this *caveat*, the finding is significant to note.

While the officers generally feel that discrimination toward the public is minimal, 55.4% felt there was discrimination internal at the police department toward both sworn and non-sworn personnel. This appears to be a significant finding that also has implications for organizational, personal, and psychological stressors.

Psychological stressors appeared to be manifest in officers in several ways. For example, 68.4% of the officers stated that they had trouble fitting in with other social groups. While the social isolation stressor of this finding is evident, the data and interviews indicate that this situation also led to self-doubt, feelings of inferiority, and frustration. Perhaps the findings on authoritarianism discussed earlier could be indicative of officer attempts to overcome these psychological stressors.

The idea of professional assistance to help officers cope with stress was a continued trend in the findings. Forty-eight percent expressed that they wanted someone to help them with personal problems, 80.6% agreed that psychological counseling was needed for officers with disciplinary problems while a significant 90.6% indicated that psychological assistance should be available for all officers. The writer found these results somewhat surprising given the general hesitancy of police officers to admit insecurities and their general aversion to counseling. These findings may be explained as reactions of officers to the experience of the various psychological stress variables reported in Table 3. One may conclude that the officers recognized these variables as symptoms of problems that may be beyond the control of the officers, which could lead to undesirable results. Finally, the survey gathered data on some fundamental physiological stress variables. The results indicate that 21.1% of the officers felt their health had deteriorated since joining the police department. Shift work and hours of riding in a patrol car were two important causes of this deterioration as perceived by the respondents.

CONCLUSION

In viewing the model it should become apparent to the reader that the concept of abuse, the causal factors, and the remedies are all systemic. One should not examine each element of this paradigm as a separate entity. Rather, the constituents should be envisioned as a series of relationships that are reciprocal in nature.

The author has presented a comprehensive approach that defines "police brutality," places the phenomena in perspective, and suggests mediums for control. The model is not utopian suggesting that abuse may be eliminated. Instead, it is a pragmatic avenue which, when imposed, may minimize the frequency and in-

TABLE 3 Psychological Stress Variables: Percentage of Officers Experiencing Variables while on Duty at Least "Some of the Time" during Each Shift

Variable	*% of Officers*
Nervous	64.3
Sad	57.9
Jittery	32.7
Unhappy	68.4
Depressed	55.8
Angry	83.3
Fidgety	38.9
Low/Blue	60.0
Aggravated	67.4
Irritated	76.9

tensity of abusive incidents. In order for this objective to be realized there must be a commitment by the organization. This commitment involves re-thinking the police role as it specifically applies to the jurisdiction; conducting a critical organizational self-evaluation on efficiency and effectiveness variables; objectively establishing the true mission of the organization—not the perceived mission; and expressing a willingness to challenge old dogma and experiment with change. Although collateral to the problem of abuse, *per se*, these are perhaps among the most difficult of all barriers to overcome.

REFERENCES

1. Friedrich, Robert J. "Police Use of Force: Individuals, Situations, and Organizations." *The Annals*. November 1980, pp. 82–97.

/ 2. Reiss, Albert J. "Police Brutality—Answers to Key Questions." *Trans-Action*. July–August 1968, pp. 10–19.

3. cf, Radelet, Louis A. *The Police and the Community*, 3d. ed. (Encino, CA: Glencoe Publishing Co., 1980), pp. 218–219;

Walker, Samuel. *The Police in America: An Introduction*. (New York: McGraw-Hill, 1983), pp. 206–208;

Reiss, Albert J. "Police Brutality—Answers to Key Questions." *Trans-Action*. July–August 1968, pp. 10–19.

4. President's Commission on Law Enforcement and Administration of Justice. *Field Surveys, Volume 5: A National Survey of Police and Community Relations*. (Washington: U.S. Government Printing Office, 1967), p. 151.

See also: United States Commission on Civil Rights. *Mexican-Americans and the Administration of Justice in the Southwest*. (Washington: U.S. Government Printing Office, 1970), Chapter 2.

5. United States Commission on Civil Rights. *Justice*. (Washington: U.S. Government Printing Office, 1961), p. 25.

6. *Ibid.*, p. 28.

7. cf, Banton, Michael. "Social Integration and Police." *Police Chief*. April 1963, p. 12 as cited in Radelet (1980), p. 303.

8. For a conceptually similar discussion see Westley, William A. *Violence and the Police*. (Cambridge, MA: The MIT Press, 1970), pp. 120–121.

9. This idea of psychological coercion is closely akin to the concept of the "police dominated atmosphere" the United States Supreme Court addressed in the opinion of *Miranda* v. *Arizona*, 384 U.S. 436, 86 S.Ct. 1602 (1966).

10. cf, Territo, Leonard and Harold Vetter. *Stress and Police Personnel*. Boston: Allyn and Bacon, Inc., 1981.

Terry, W. Clinton. "Police Stress: The Empirical Evidence." *Journal of Police Science and Administration*. Vol. 9, pp. 61–65, (1981).

Hillgren, J. S., R. B. Bond and S. Jones. "Primary Stressors in Police Administration and Law Enforcement". *Journal of Police Science and Administration*. Vol. 4, pp. 445–449, (1976).

11. The bulk of research cited in footnote 10 also addresses personal stressors and their effect on the officer.

12. Malloy, Thomas E. and G. Larry Mays. *The Police Stress Hypothesis: A Critical Evaluation*. Paper presented at the Academy of Criminal Justice Sciences Annual Meeting, San Antonio, Texas (1983), pp. 13–17.

13. Spielberger, Charles, et al. *The Police Stress Survey: Sources of Stress in Law Enforcement*. (Tampa, FL: University of South Florida, 1981), p. 43.

14. Burgin, A. Lad. "The Management of Stress in Policing." *The Police Chief*. (April 1978), p. 14.

15. cf, Whisenand, Paul M. *Police Supervision: Theory and Practice*, 2d ed. (Englewood Cliffs, NJ: Prentice-Hall, Inc., 1976), pp. 181–201.

16. cf, Carter, David L. "Hispanic Attitudes Toward Crime and Justice in Texas". *Journal of Criminal Justice*. Vol. 11, No. 3 (1983), pp. 213–227.

Garofalo, J. *Public Opinion About Crime*. Washington: National Criminal Justice Information and Statistical Service, 1977.

A-T-O Inc. *The Figgie Report on Fear of Crime: America Afraid*. Willoughby, Ohio, 1980.

17. For a detailed discussion of the McAllen experience see: Carter, David L. *The Impact of Civil Rights Litigation on the McAllen, Texas Police Department*. Paper presented at the 1982 Annual Meeting at the Academy of Criminal Justice Sciences, Louisville, Kentucky.

18. *Robles* v. *City of McAllen, et al*, CA No. B-81-58, United States District Court–Southern District of Texas, Agreed Preliminary Injunction at 1.

"Viva La Policia"

David Durk

There are very tough things to believe if you're a real cop because being a cop means believing in the rule of law. It means believing in a system of government that makes fair and just rules, and then enforces them.

Being a cop also means serving, helping others. If it's not too corny, to be a cop is to help an old lady walk the streets safely; to help a 12-year-old girl reach her next birthday without being gang-raped; to help a storekeeper make a living without keeping a shotgun under his cash register; to help a boy grow up without needles in his arm.

And therefore to me being a cop is not a job but a way to live a life. Some people say that cops live with the worst side of humanity, in the middle of all the lying and cheating, the violence and the hate. And I suppose in some sense, that's true. But being a cop means being engaged with life. It means that our concern for others is not abstract, that we don't just write a letter to the *Times* or give ten dollars to the United Fund once a year; it means that we put something on the line from the moment we hit the street every morning of every day of our lives. In this sense police corruption is not about money at all. Because there is no amount of money that can pay a cop to risk his life 365 days a year. Being a cop is a vocation, or it is nothing at all.

And that is what I saw being destroyed by the corruption of the New York City Police Department, destroyed for me, and for thousands of others like me. We wanted to believe in the rule of law. We wanted to believe in a system of responsibility; but those in high places everywhere—in the department, in the DA's offices, and in City Hall—were determined not to enforce the law but to turn their heads away when law and justice were being sold on every street corner.

We wanted to serve others, but the department was a home for the drug dealers and thieves; the force that was supposed to be protecting people was selling poison to their children. . . .

And there could be no life, no real life for me or anyone else on that force, when everyday we had to face the facts of our own terrible corruption. I saw that happening to men all around me—men who could have been good officers, men of decent impulse and even of ideals; but men who were without decent leadership, men who were told in a hundred ways every day: go along. Forget about the law. Don't make waves. Shut up. So they did shut up, they did go along, they did learn the unwritten code of the department. They went along, and they lost something very precious. They weren't cops any more. They were a long way toward not being men any more.

And all the time I saw the other victims too—especially the children. Children of 14 and 15 and 16, wasted by heroin, turned into street corner thugs and whores, ready to mug their own mother for the price of a fix. That was the price of going along, the real price of police corruption; not free meals or broken regulations, but broken dreams and dying neighborhoods and a whole generation of children being lost. That was what I had joined the department to stop.

So that was why I went to the *New York Times*. Because attention had to be paid. And in a last desperate hope that if the facts were known, someone must respond.

And now it is up to you. I speak to you now as nothing more and nothing less than a cop: a cop who has lived on this force, and who is *staying* on this force, and therefore as a cop who needs your help. My fellow policemen and I: we didn't appoint you; you don't report to us; but all the same there are some things that, as policemen, we must have from you.

First, we need you to fix responsibility for the rottenness that was allowed to fester. It must be fixed both inside and outside the department.

Inside the department, responsibility has to be fixed against those top commanders who allowed or helped the situation to develop. Responsibility has to be fixed because no patrolman will believe that he should care about corruption if his superiors can get away with not caring. Responsibility also has to be fixed because commanders themselves have to be told, again and again, and not only by the police commissioner, that the entire state of the department is up to them. And most of all, responsibility has to be fixed because it is the first step toward recovering our simple but necessary conviction that right will be rewarded and wrongdoing punished.

SOURCE: This is an excerpt from the concluding statement of Sergeant David Durk at the Knapp Commission Hearing in New York City, December 17, 1971. Printed by permission of David Durk.

Responsibility must also be fixed outside the department—on all the men and agencies that have helped bring us to our present pass, against all those who could have exposed this corruption, but never did. Like it or not, the policeman is convinced that he lives and works in the middle of a corrupt society; that everyone else is getting theirs, and why shouldn't he; and that if anyone really cared about corruption, something would have been done about it a long time ago. We are not animals. We are not stupid, and we know very well, we policemen, that corruption does not begin with a few patrolmen, and that responsibility for corruption does not end with one aide to the mayor or one investigations commissioner. The issue, for all of today's testimony, is not just Jay Kriegel or Arnold Fraiman. We know that there are many people beyond the police department who share in the corruption and its rewards. So your report has to tell us about the district attorneys and the courts and the bar, and the mayor and the governor—about what they have failed to do, and how great a measure of responsibility they also bear. Otherwise, if you suggest, or allow others to suggest, that the responsibility belongs only to the police—then for the patrolman on the beat and in the radio car, this commission will be just another part of the swindle. That is a harsh statement, and an impolite and a brutal statement. It also is a statement of the truth.

Second, you have to speak as the conscience of this city—speak for all those without a voice, all those who are not here to be heard today, although they know the price of police corruption more intimately than anyone here: the people of the ghetto, and all the other victims, those broken in mind and spirit and hope. Perhaps more than any other people in this city, they depend on the police and the law, to protect not just their pocketbooks but their very lives, and the lives and welfare of their children. Tow truck operators can write off bribes on their income tax; the expense account executive can afford a prostitute; but no one can pay a mother for the pain of seeing her children hooked on heroin.

This commission, for what I am sure are good reasons, has not invited testimony from the communities of suffering in New York City. But this commission must remind the force, as it must tell the rest of the city, that there are human lives at stake, that when police protect the narcotics traffic, then we are participating in the destruction of a generation of children. It is this terrible crime for which you are fixing the responsibility, and it is this terrible crime against which you must speak with the full outrage of the community's conscience.

Third, as a corollary, you must help to give us a sense of priorities, to remind us that corruption, like sin, has its gradations and classifications. Of course, all corruption is bad. But we cannot fall into the trap of pretending that all corruption is *equally* bad. There is a difference between accepting free meals and selling narcotics. If we are unable to make that distinction, then we are saying to the police that the life of a child in the South Bronx is the same moral value as a cup of coffee. That cannot be true, for this society or for its police force. So you must show us the difference.

Finally, in your deliberations, you must speak for the policemen of this city—for the best that is in them, for what most of them wanted to be, for what most of them will be if we try.

Once I arrested a landlord's agent who offered to pay me if I would lock up a tenant who was organizing other tenants, and as I put the cuffs on the agent and led him away, a crowd of people assembled and started yelling, "Viva la policia!"

Of course, it was not just me, or even the police, that they were cheering. They were cheering because they had glimpsed, in that one arrest, the possibility of a system of justice that could work to protect them too. They were cheering because if that agent could get arrested, then that meant they had rights, they were citizens, and maybe one day life would really be different for their children.

For me, that moment was what police work is all about. But there have been far too few moments like it, and far too many times when I looked into the faces of the city and saw not hope and trust, but resentment and hate and fear. Far too many of my fellow officers have seen only hate; far too many of them have seen their dreams of service and justice frustrated and abandoned by a corrupt system, and superiors and politicians who just didn't care enough.

It took five years of Frank Serpico's life, and five years of mine, to help bring this commission about. It has taken the lives and dedication of thousands of others to preserve as much of a police force as we have. It has taken months of effort by all of you to help show this city the truth. What I ask of you now is to help make us clean again; to help give us some leadership we can look to; to make it possible for all the men on the force to walk at ease with their better nature and with their fellow citizens—and perhaps one day, on a warm summer night, to hear again the shout of "Viva la policia!"

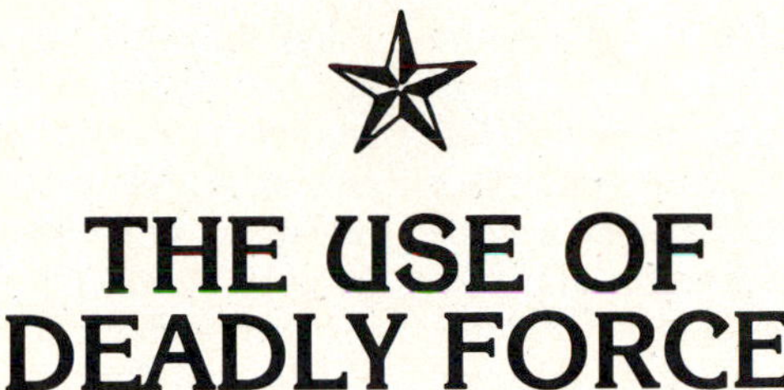

THE USE OF DEADLY FORCE

In general, the police are the only civil agents of the state who are authorized within legally prescribed limits to use force in order to impose their authority and to coerce compliance. However, police action that employs the excessive use of violence or the unsanctioned use of firearms thereby causing death or serious injury, is the most alarming and sordid feature of the police world. Because of the sensitive nature of the issues presented by the use of such violence, and the universal need of bureaucracies to preserve organizational "official secrets," systematic research in the police use of deadly force is a relatively recent phenomenon. Legal and administrative constraints, customs and policy guidelines affecting the use of force vary from one jurisdiction to another, and even from one department to another in a given jurisdiction.

Police shootings according to a Police Foundation study (Meyer, 1980) range from 4.2 shootings of civilians per 1,000 officers in Portland, Oregon, to 25 such shootings per 1,000 officers in Birmingham, Alabama. Just as the number of police shootings varies from one city to another, police policy that attempts to control deadly force has been uneven, or almost futile, especially in communities with high gun density. The evidence to date would appear to support the notion that police shooters are usually younger members of the force who have had limited experience. Apart from that not-too-remarkable fact, however, there does not seem to be enough evidence to support any notion of the existence of a specific set of sociodemographic characteristics that would taken together constitute a "profile" of a would-be user of deadly force or the citizen/victim. In the main, deadly-force research has yet to answer many questions, some of which are not readily susceptible to resolution, given the limitations of social science research. In many instances victims were not engaged in committing a felony, nor were they armed. Further, although black officers appear to use deadly force as often as their white colleagues, it must be noted that minority racial groups are overrepresented in the data as shooting victims.

On the other hand, there is some evidence that clearly established rules invoking written policy guidelines accompanied by an administrative review of each shooting case have a clearly salutary effect in reducing shootings and the use of deadly force. Other approaches to the problem of police shootings would disarm the police when they are off duty, redefine the police role to strip them of their capacity to punish, and reward police use of nonviolent means in pursuing legally mandated police activities.

Always Prepared: Police Off-Duty Guns

James J. Fyfe

Abstract: Even while off duty, American police are expected to be armed and to actively intervene in situations threatening to life, property, or order. This article considers the assumptions upon which that expectation is based and suggests that they may be ill-founded. Research to determine whether armed off-duty police actually increase community violence levels is recommended as a prerequisite to an informed reconsideration of the appropriate role for off-duty police officers.

Whether or not they are technically on duty, American police almost everywhere are expected to be armed and ready for action. As a 1978 survey of 49 major police departments found, 25 departments—51 percent—reported permitting officers to carry off-duty guns, and 24—49 percent—reported requiring that officers be armed off duty.[1] None required officers to leave their guns at police stations at the completion of the working day. If it is safe to generalize from these departments to the rest of America's 450,000 police, it is likely that at any time there are about in the country approximately 300,000 armed off-duty police.

Because the "twenty-four hour cop" is an American tradition, the presence of these 300,000 off-duty guns is not surprising. Nor is it surprising that there is so little debate over the merits of adding these weapons to the great number in circulation among citizens. Police, unlike most handgun owners, are psychologically screened and tested, trained, and sworn to protect life and property. Police possess weapons to protect public interests, whereas citizens possess weapons to protect their own private interests. Thus it is likely that even handgun control advocates, if they have thought about the issue at all, regard police off-duty guns as a category of weapons separate and distinct from those in the hands of private citizens.

Despite this apparently reasonable distinction, and despite the fact that 300,000 off-duty police guns are a drop in the bucket of the estimated 40 million handguns in America,[2] the issue of off-duty weapons raises a number of important questions. While the benefits are unclear, the costs are potentially substantial. Over one in ten of the officers killed by felons nationwide from 1972 to 1978 were off duty at the time,[3] and almost one in four of the 239 officers killed by felons in the New York City Police Department since 1844 were off duty.[4] Off-duty guns are also important in police killings of citizens; several studies have found from 12 to 17 percent of homicides by police to occur while the officers are off duty.[5]

WHY ARM OFF-DUTY POLICE?

As suggested previously, the major rationale for arming off-duty officers is the notion that police professional responsibilities should not be constrained by their scheduled working hours. In many jurisdictions, off-duty police may be disciplined or prosecuted for failing to respond in an "appropriate" manner to situations threatening to life, property, or order.[6]

Thus the justification for arming off-duty police varies with the interpretation of this responsibility. If it is "appropriate" for off-duty officers to passively make observations of crimes in progress and to relay information to on-duty colleagues, one might argue that there exists little justification for off-duty guns. If, on the other hand, off-duty officers are expected to inter-

James J. Fyfe, "Always Prepared: Police Off-Duty Guns," *The Annals*, 452 (November 1980), pp. 72–81.

[1] John F. Heaphy, ed., *Police Practices: The General Administrative Survey* (Washington, D.C.: Police Foundation, 1978), item 20.

[2] Matthew G. Yeager, Joseph Alviani, and Nancy Loving, *How Well Does the Handgun Protect You and Your Family? Technical Report: Two* (Washington, D.C.: United States Conference of Mayors, 1976), p. 1.

[3] Mona Margarita, *Criminal Violence Against Police in the United States* (Washington, D.C.: U.S. Bureau of Justice Statistics, forthcoming).

[4] Mona Margarita, "Criminal Violence Against Police" (unpublished Ph.D. dissertation, School of Criminal Justice, State University of New York at Albany, 1980), p. 83.

[5] Lawrence W. Sherman, "Homicide by Police Officers: Social Forces and Public Policy" (grant proposal submitted to the Center for Studies in Crime and Delinquency, National Institute of Mental Health, 1977), p. 3.

[6] *See*, for example, J. Gerald Safer, "Deadly Weapons in the Hands of Police Officers, On Duty and Off Duty," *J. Urban Law*, 49(3):577.

vene actively in circumstances which threaten life, property, or order, there exists greater justification for equipping them with firearms.

A second rationale for arming off-duty police is that of deterrence. Here one would argue that justification for arming off-duty officers increases with the degree to which potential offenders are deterred from criminal behavior by the actual or feared presence of armed off-duty police.

A related consideration is that of officer safety. A consequence of police work is that some of those questioned, ordered to move on, ticketed, investigated, or arrested may wish to get even with officers or to impede cases against themselves. Disarming off-duty police, it may be argued, might increase both the temptation and the opportunity for their disgruntled clientele to do so. Thus there are unanswered questions about the extent to which off-duty guns ensure the safety of officers from those seeking revenge or forcible prevention of damaging testimony. Further, disarming off-duty officers may also affect their willingness to engage forcefully, but properly, in on-duty enforcement or order-maintenance activities. Why make enemies at work when one may be vulnerable to them after work?

CONSEQUENCES OF ARMING OFF-DUTY POLICE

The best way to test the validity of these justifications for arming off-duty police is to examine them and to weigh them against negative consequences of providing police with off-duty guns. This is difficult for several reasons. It is probable, for example, that the bars widely known to be frequented by off-duty officers are held up less often than bars remote from police stations. Beyond that observation, however, it is nearly impossible to say much about the deterrent value of off-duty guns because no attempt to measure it systematically has been undertaken.

In addition, the data that are available on more concrete events are frequently rather one-sided. Police often point with pride to incidents in which armed off-duty officers have bravely and honorably protected the public interest. Less frequently do they attempt to publicize cases in which off-duty officers have used their guns unwisely or dishonorably. As a result, little is known about the negative consequences of arming off-duty police. There is little knowledge of the degree to which off-duty guns, which ostensibly serve to decrease public violence, also serve to increase or escalate violence. It would be useful to know how often police off-duty guns are deliberately misused or are the instruments of tragic accidents. It would also be useful to know how often armed off-duty police make bad situations worse by well-intended but ill-advised interventions in threats to life, property, or order.

The question of consequences is extremely important. The measurement of consequences should, in fact, serve as the basis for any definition of the appropriate role of off-duty officers. As Safer notes, "proof of frequent misuse of weapons" might lead to the conclusion that "disarmament of off-duty officers would diminish the community's level of violence."[7] Disarmament would also necessarily result in limiting the "appropriate" off-duty police role to that of passive observer and information transmitter. Such a definition would be a major police reform because, as the survey of off-duty weapons policy suggests, the prevailing definition of the appropriate off-duty police role is that of active intervenor.

REDEFINING THE ROLE OF OFF-DUTY POLICE

Police agencies, like all bureaucracies, are conservative institutions. Even given evidence of frequent misuse of off-duty guns, it is likely that attempts to disarm off-duty police and to redefine the off-duty role would be strongly resisted. Police chiefs—among whom are some advocates of strict public handgun controls—might argue that, despite a few freak accidents and some regrettable incidents, off-duty guns are a major contributor to public safety and to society's ability to protect itself against criminality. They might also point out that a precise assessment of the positive consequences of off-duty guns was precluded by the absence of data. Further, it could be argued, attempting to complete an off-duty gun cost–benefit equation by acquiring those data would require experimental conditions—disarming off-duty police—that might prove too costly to society and to officers themselves. Finally, it might be pointed out that since police are paid only for their formal working hours, the financial costs of the extra protection of off-duty guns are negligible.

In these justifications for off-duty guns, a cynic might find the suggestion of a hidden agenda. The economic argument may be a rationalization offered by police administrators unwilling to face up to the question of

[7] Ibid., p. 579.

off-duty guns for reasons more closely related to organizational labor tranquility than to public safety. Police unions and labor groups exert considerable influence over police managerial decisions. Police unions often base their salary demands in part on the public expectation that their members will keep and bear arms 24 hours a day. Their logic generally runs as follows:

> Police deserve more money than other civil servants for two reasons. First, their duties are uniquely demanding and dangerous: they alone are expected to put their lives on the line against society's enemies.
>
> Second, they alone are expected to fulfill their job duties, whether or not they are technically working: they alone are expected to be equipped with the tools of their trade at all times. Sanitation workers are not expected to clean dirty streets once they sign out of work, but off-duty police are expected to help keep the streets free of crooks. Firefighters do not carry off-duty axes, but police carry off-duty guns.
>
> Further, no other workers have to worry constantly about safeguarding lethal weapons from their curious children. To know how much a police officer is worth, you have got to look at the number of officers killed taking police action off duty. While you are doing that, take a look at the little kids who have found daddy's gun in the closet and killed themselves while playing with it.

These are potent arguments which make it clear that police unions do not regard off-duty guns as cost-free protection. Conversely, unions regard their responsibility and willingness to be armed off duty as a blue chip at contract negotiations. It is also likely, therefore, that they would strongly resist efforts to either disarm off-duty police or to limit the off-duty role to that of observer and information transmitter. Further, such efforts can easily be interpreted as "handcuffing the police and reducing police protection." Thus it is probable that chiefs would choose not to be publicly identified with these efforts unless there existed an extremely unambiguous and convincing case that they are in the public interest.

The absence of much of the information upon which such a case might be made reinforces the suggestion that administrators are not anxious to deal with the issue. Data related to the number of lives saved and the number of important arrests effected by off-duty police, for example, would be relatively easy to collect, but little or no comprehensive information on these events is at hand. As noted previously, we also know little about the deterrent effects of off-duty guns, a subject about which data are more difficult, but not impossible, to collect and analyze.

Despite these omissions, it is possible to make a preliminary assessment of the consequences of arming off-duty police. Such an assessment suggests that it might be appropriate to fill the information voids cited previously and to conduct more complete and detailed evaluations of the merits of police off-duty guns.

WHAT DO POLICE DO WITH OFF-DUTY GUNS?

Police in New York City are required to carry off-duty guns[8] while within the limits of the city and may do so at their option outside the city. Between 1971 and 1975, 681 New Y ork City police officers reported discharging their firearms while off duty.[9] Most of these events occurred for apparently meritorious reasons, but others did not. Table 1 shows that roughly seven in ten of these shootings reportedly involved the defense of life or prevention of crime. If we add to those the number of incidents in which officers destroyed dangerous or hopelessly injured animals (3.2 percent), we find that about three quarters of the events ostensibly involve some law enforcement or order maintenance function.

What about the other quarter? Officers used their guns against themselves often enough to make "suicide by gun" the largest single cause of violent officer death and an event nearly as frequent as line of duty deaths during the years included in the table. During 1971–75, 30 New York City officers died at the hands of others in the line of duty; 25 off-duty officers shot and killed themselves, and one other attempted to do so but sustained a nonfatal wound.[10] Almost half of the

[8] New York City police may use as "off-duty guns" either the regulation four-inch barrel .38 caliber service revolver or a lighter and more compact two-inch barrel .38 caliber revolver. The former must be purchased by officers, and the latter is an option chosen by most for reasons of convenience. Some officers, however, carry their service revolvers both on and off duty.

[9] For access to these data, I am indebted to former Chief of Personnel Neil J. Behan, former Assistant Chief Patrick Fitzsimons, and Lieutenant Frank McGee of the New York City Police Department.

[10] Three other officers committed suicide by gun during working hours.

TABLE 1 Off-Duty New York City Police Reasons for Shooting, 1971–75

Reasons for Shooting	*Percent*	*Number*
Self-defense	55.8	380
Defense of others	2.5	17
Prevention or termination of crime	13.1	89
Destruction of animal	3.2	22
Suicide attempt	3.8	26
Accident	12.6	86
Other/not ascertained	9.0	61
Total	100.0	681

"nonenforcement" shooters—12.6 percent of the total—reportedly fired their guns accidentally. In doing so, they shot themselves, family members, friends, other officers, and total strangers, for example:

> Patrolman Hines and his wife were in the kitchen. . . . Officer removed his off-duty gun from the top of a six foot china closet, noticed that the holster strap was loose and pushed the gun firmly in the holster discharging the gun. Mrs. Hines was across the room and the bullet struck her above the right ear. She was pronounced D.O.A. by Dr. Thompson.

In another case which appears to have been accidental, the

> officer was found lying dead on the floor in front of a bureau and his service revolver with one shot fired was found in an open top drawer. Apparently Ptl. Adams was standing at a right angle in front of the bureau and discharged one shot from service revolver. Interrogation of parents, in-laws, and wife of officer indicated no medical history or other known reason for Ptl. Adams to have wilfully committed this act.

A substantial percentage of off-duty shooters—nine percent of the total—fired their guns for "other" reasons or for reasons that are not readily articulable. One officer, for example, shot and killed his wife and his mother-in-law; in other cases:

> While apparently intoxicated, Ptl. Jones was ejected from a St. Patrick's Day party in a bar and grill and fired six shots from his revolver into the premises, wounding two persons.
>
> . . .[Officer who shot his wife once in the head and three times in the back] stated that he had been married for seven years and had various problems with his wife; their problems focused on mother-in-law trouble, his wife's spending of money, and his studying for the sergeant's promotional examination.
>
> After a dispute with my wife, I went outside and fired 12 shots into a tree behind my house in order to vent my frustrations.

Various explanations for such bizarre violence may be found in the growing body of literature on police occupational stress which generally concludes that the police career places extreme psychological pressures on its incumbents and their families.[11] Sadly, in the previous cases, it also placed in the officers' hands the means to deal with those dilemmas in a destructive manner. Thus it is apparent that some officers use their off-duty guns for purposes other than those for which they were intended.[12]

Less apparent is the number of unwise or imprudent shootings concealed within Table 1's more seemingly admirable reasons for shooting. A suggestion of their numbers appears in Table 2, which describes the departmental adjudications of off-duty shootings that occurred after 18 August 1972, when a formal shooting review and adjudication process was established.[13]

The table shows that the department itself found that more than four in ten shootings warranted some administrative or criminal sanction: 15.1 percent of the

[11] A Law Enforcement Assistance Administration bibliography [J. T. Skip Duncan, Robert N. Brenner, and Marjorie Kravitz, *Police Stress: A Selected Bibliography* (Washington, D.C.: U.S. Government Printing Office, 1979] lists 112 articles, books, and monographs and 33 films. These cite as factors causing stress such police job characteristics as danger, unpredictability, boredom, the need to repress emotions, rotating shift work, quasi-military organizational structure and discipline, lack of lateral transfer opportunities, inadequate career development, frustration about court appearances, concern over criticism, and a police image distorted by the media. It cites as effects of stress disproportionate police rates of suicide, alcoholism, heart disease, gastrointestinal disorders, and marital, family, and emotional problems.

[12] Neither is such abuse of off-duty guns confined to the officers themselves. Included in the data examined in this study, for example, are nine incidents in which officers' off-duty guns were used against them by wives and female friends. Five officers were wounded and four were killed in these shootings.

[13] New York City Police Department, "Temporary Operating Procedure #237," (18 Aug. 1972).

TABLE 2 New York City Police Department Adjudications of Off-Duty Shootings, 18 August 1972–31 December 1975

Adjudications	*Percent*	*Number*
Shooting justifiable	58.5	224
Officer retrained in law and/or tactics	15.1	58
Officer disciplined	16.7	64
Officer arrested	5.5	21
Officer transferred	0.3	1
Officer referred to psychological and/ or alcoholic counseling	3.9	15
Total	100.0	383

officers were retrained in law and/or tactics;[14] 16.7 percent were disciplined by the department; 5.5 percent were arrested; and the remainder were transferred to other assignments or referred to the department's psychologists or alcohol abuse counselors. Thus while three quarters of the shootings between 1971 and 1975 involved some law enforcement or order maintenance activity, only slightly more than half of the shootings adjudicated during most of those years were found to have been beyond official reproach.

Even among those found formally justifiable, however, questions of prudence and impact on violence may be raised. More than one third of the shootings were immediately precipitated by robberies. A review of those incident reports causes one to speculate on how appropriate it is for lone off-duty officers to attempt to intervene in such events. One example involved an officer dining in a restaurant when two males entered and announced a stick-up.

> I was seated at a table in the dining area. I was ordered to get over to the bar. I leaped from my chair saying "police" and fired my revolver two times at [suspects].

After returning the officer's fire, both suspects escaped. Since the robbery was averted and nobody was injured, this unquestionably courageous intervention was not a total failure. On the other hand, it did escalate violence considerably and did create a great risk to the lives of the officer and other patrons, as well as to the robbers. It takes little imagination to conceive of possible far less happy endings to this event. The officer could not have been certain that on-duty police had not been summoned to the robbery. Thus he ran the risk of being mistaken for a robber by other officers, a scenario which has also occurred and ended tragically.[15] Indeed, once this officer intervened, literally anything could have happened. Eight months later, in fact, this same officer was again dining in a restaurant and was confronted by two armed robbers. On that occasion, the exchange of gunfire left the officer and both robbers dead.

The most immediate question raised by such events is what would have happened had the officer refrained from intervening and merely observed and transmitted information. Both sets of robbers would almost certainly have escaped with the proceeds of their endeavors. Although it is not likely, both sets of robbers might have been apprehended later as a result of information and descriptions provided by the officer.[16] Most important, the officer would almost certainly have survived both robberies.

This last observation will raise police eyebrows. A firmly held belief among police is that it is advisable for officers to take forcible action when confronted by situations like those described previously. This is so because it is believed that robbers who discover a police officer among their victims are likely to kill him simply because he is a police officer. Thus it is better to resist than to passively submit and risk the possibility of discovery and execution.[17] This belief has powerful implications. The officer operating under it perceives the gun duel with robbers as not merely appropriate, but as imperative.

Logic suggests, however, that this last belief is ill-founded. Holdup men commit their crimes for personal

[14] A finding that retraining is appropriate most often reflects the reviewers' opinion that a shooting itself was justifiable, but might have been avoided had the officer handled the events which precipitated it differently, for example, by calling for help rather than by attempting to confront a dangerous person alone.

[15] Nine of the shootings studied involved "mistaken identity" exchanges of shots between uniformed police and plainclothes or off-duty officers at crime scenes. Three resulted in death.

[16] The successful escape of the first set of robbers—who may even have been the same individuals involved in the second robbery—argues against this outcome. Had the officer concentrated his efforts on obtaining good descriptions at the first robbery, however, he might have improved the possibility of apprehension.

[17] Joseph Wambaugh's *The Onion Field* (New York: Delacorte Press, 1973) is an excellent treatment of a variant of this belief.

gain. Their goal, apparently, is to survive their acts and to quietly enjoy their earnings. Why, then, would they wantonly execute police officers and gratuitously become the subjects of manhunts for "cold-blooded cop killers?"

This logic is supported by experience. The New York City data include literally dozens of cases in which armed off-duty police responded to the sudden appearance of robbers' overwhelming firepower by submitting passively. Many were discovered to be police and were relieved of their guns and badges. None was wounded or killed merely "because he was a cop,"[18] but many were wounded or killed while resisting.

The apparent reluctance of criminals to kill police officers also suggests that police fear of assaults motivated by desire for revenge or prevention of testimony may be unfounded. One who contemplates such an act does so knowing that records of his prior encounters with his potential victim will make him a prime suspect. He also knows that his offense will be investigated, prosecuted, and penalized more intensely than any other he may have committed. Such attacks to impede justice, then, appear quite unlikely regardless of whether or not police are armed off duty. Further, the relative infrequency of such attacks on citizen witnesses, jurors, prosecutors, and judges reinforces the notion that off-duty guns make little difference where violence of this nature is concerned.

CONCLUSION

The classic and often derided conclusion of social scientists is to recommend further research. In the present case, however, it is genuinely appropriate to conclude by recommending a test of the assumption that armed off-duty police contribute to the public good.

American police are citizens and police officers. Considerable effort has been expended to eliminate distinctions between them and the communities they serve. Some distinctions, however, are both desirable and necessary and thus are not subject to these efforts. It is desirable and necessary that on-duty police fulfill the role of active intervenor in threatening situations. It is also necessary, therefore, that they be distinguishable from most citizens by being armed during that time.

It is less clear that it is desirable and necessary for police to attempt to fulfill the active intervenor role while off duty. To do so, they must continue to be armed and therefore distinguishable from other citizens. Thus it may be difficult for police to relate their own life experiences to those of the unarmed citizens for whom they work. Further, this distinction may be less than desirable because police may be even more vulnerable than most citizens to the forces that led to gun abuse.

Before police practice their craft, they are usually screened, tested, and trained. While they practice their craft, they are subject to stresses far more psychologically demanding than are most citizens. The combination of these job stresses and ready access to off-duty guns sometimes ends tragically. Many laudable efforts to avert such tragedies have focused on eliminating or neutralizing the stresses which precede them, but little or no attention has been given to the desirability or necessity of access to the off-duty guns which complete the tragedies.

The question of the desirability or necessity of off-duty guns does not involve only intentional and accidental misuse. When off-duty police do use their guns in well-intended interventions, it is not at all clear that they reduce violence. Conversely, their actions in threatening situations may even create actual violence where only potential violence exists.

This negative effect is often due to important qualitative distinctions between the situations in which on-duty and off-duty police typically intervene. On-duty police are usually advised by their radio dispatchers of potential violence. Since this usually occurs while they are at a distance from the scene, they have the opportunity to plan their approach to it and to coordinate their efforts with colleagues. On-duty police are also usually in uniform and are clearly identifiable to other officers.

Off-duty police who intervene in potential violence rarely enjoy such luxuries. They are typically not given any warning of impending events, but rather, are suddenly confronted by suspects whose guns are already drawn. Off-duty police are not typically in the company of colleagues, but are alone or with friends or

[18] One robber threatened to do so, but was dissuaded by his accomplice who made precisely the arguments cited above. In another case, an officer was one of several restaurant patrons searched and locked in a restroom by robbers. His victimizers kept their promise to leave his badge on the restaurant's bar and to deposit his gun in a nearby mailbox, so as not "to get him in trouble."

family. They do not usually have instant access to police communications systems. They are usually in civilian clothes and are thus easily mistaken for armed suspects by arriving police. Finally, they are far more likely than on-duty officers to have judgment and reflexes dulled by liquor.

In such circumstances, it is rarely desirable or necessary that off-duty police distinguish themselves from other citizens by attempting to actively intervene nor is it fair to them or other citizens. Indeed, it may be most fair to require off-duty police to leave their guns in their lockers with the rest of their uniforms.

Research on Police Use of Deadly Force: The State of the Art*

Mark Blumberg

INTRODUCTION

Among all the discretionary powers granted to the police, the decision to use deadly force has the most awesome potential consequences for both the individual and the community. While the judicial process may only invoke the death penalty for certain crimes after a finding of guilt beyond a reasonable doubt and a lengthy appellate process, police officers often decide to employ deadly force within the span of seconds and base their decisions upon a lower evidentiary standard. In many jurisdictions, officers can legally shoot at fleeing suspects who have committed crimes that would bring only a short prison sentence if they were apprehended and convicted.[1] It has been estimated that law-enforcement officers may be responsible for about one out of every 28 homicides in the U.S. (Sherman and Langworthy, 1979). On the other hand, only 7 persons have died within the United States as a result of judicial executions since 1968. Thus, it is somewhat of a paradox that capital punishment has received an inordinate amount of attention and been widely debated while police use of deadly force has received only passing notice, usually as the result of a controversial shooting.

Nonetheless, the last few years have seen a surge of scholarly interest in the use of deadly force by police. Several studies have appeared which examine this topic in some depth (Blumberg, 1983a; Matulia, 1982; Geller and Karales, 1981; Fyfe, 1978; and Milton et al., 1977). In addition, the federal government has allocated grant money to researchers in order to explore this issue. Clearly, a great deal has been learned over the past 5 years with respect to police use of deadly force.

As the number of studies proliferate, it becomes important to examine the state of the art with respect to research in this area. Thus, we begin by examining the general state of deadly-force research and the logistical problems that have confronted researchers. Next, Sherman's (1980a) conceptual framework for understanding police behavior is applied to deadly-force research. This entails an examination of the types of questions that have been analyzed on each conceptual level (i.e., individual, situational, organizational, community, and legal). Finally, suggestions are offered regarding areas of inquiry which future research may fruitfully explore.

It should be noted that a comprehensive review of the findings of all previous research is outside the scope of this article. Indeed, that task has already been accomplished quite satisfactorily (see Geller, 1983). Instead, a summary of the more important findings from the leading studies are presented in order to examine those questions which have been explored on each level of analysis and to determine which questions remain unanswered.

GENERAL OVERVIEW OF DEADLY-FORCE RESEARCH

In discussing the body of research with respect to our understanding of police behavior, Sherman (1980a:71) notes that all studies are not equal in value

This article was written expressly for inclusion in this edition.

* The author would like to express his appreciation to Lawrence W. Sherman and Abraham S. Blumberg for contributing ideas and valuable suggestions.

and that "conclusions based on a 'democratic vote' of the available studies on each issue would clearly be inappropriate." The same is true with respect to studies of police use of deadly force. Some are extremely well designed, while others utilize either poor methodology or an unsatisfactory data base that leaves many questions unresolved. Although a methodological critique of the prior research in this area is beyond the scope of this paper, some of the logistical problems that have confronted researchers are examined below.

Research into the use of deadly force by police is often quite difficult. For one thing, there is no national reporting system for police shootings and nobody knows how many people are shot and/or killed by the police each year. For this reason, a number of studies have utilized what information is available to try to estimate the frequency of police killings[2] or to determine whether or not they are increasing.[3] In the absence of a centralized data base, access to police agency records can be critical. However, some researchers have been denied access to these reports (Knoohuizen, Fahey, and Palmer, 1972) and in other cases, they have not been available.[4] Consequently, many studies have utilized even less reliable sources of data (i.e., newspaper accounts,[5] the reports of coroners' inquests[6] or the *Vital Statistics of the United States*.[7]

Each of these data sources contains a number of shortcomings.[8] The number and types of shooting incidents that are portrayed in newspaper accounts may be more a function of the editorial policy of the newspaper than of the behavior of the police. Coroners' inquests and the *Vital Statistics of the United States* only contain information with respect to actual police killings. While studies that utilize these data bases can add to our knowledge with respect to killings, they do not contribute greatly to our understanding of police decisions to employ deadly force. As Fyfe (1978:32) notes, "deadly force is physical force *capable* of or likely to kill; it does not always kill. The true frequency of police decisions to employ firearms as a means of deadly force, therefore, can best be determined by considering woundings and off-target shots as only fortuitous variations of shootings."

Clearly, the biggest boost to research in this area would be a national system of reporting for all police shootings.[9] Not only would this be a boon to researchers, but it would enable police administrators and citizens alike to determine how their community stands in this matter vis-à-vis other comparable cities. It is difficult to believe that a society which keeps careful records on all types of less significant events would not be concerned enough to begin collecting accurate information on the number of citizens shot by law enforcement officers.

EXAMINING POLICE BEHAVIOR

Sherman (1980a) has observed that attempts to understand police behavior can generally be classified into five levels of analysis: individual, situational, organizational, community, and legal. The individual approach attempts to explain differences in police behavior in terms of the characteristics of individual police officers (e.g., race, age, length of service, etc.). The situational approach attempts to explain such differences by examining the characteristics of the police–citizen encounter (e.g., the number of officers and/or citizens present, the characteristics of the suspect and/or the complainant, etc.). The organizational approach looks at the characteristics of the police organization (e.g., the degree of decentralization in the authority structure, the proportion of minority officers serving with the department, etc.). The community approach seeks to understand police behavior by examining the characteristics of the communities that they serve (e.g., the unemployment rate, the demographic composition of the population, etc.). Finally, the legal approach attempts to understand police behavior in terms of the restrictions that the legal system seeks to impose on the activities of the police.

The same classification system can be utilized to organize our knowledge with respect to police use of deadly force. Consequently, Sherman's framework of five explanatory approaches will be used to classify the research in this area and to examine the types of questions that have been addressed by researchers at each level of analysis. As previously noted, a comprehensive review of the findings of past studies is outside the scope of this article. Instead, the more salient findings from the leading studies on each of the five levels are presented. It is our belief that this conceptual framework has utility for organizing the body of research with respect to other aspects of policing as well as the use of deadly force.

Individual Explanations

Studies of police use of deadly force on the individual level have sought to determine if certain officer characteristics are related to an increased likelihood of involvement in shooting incidents. Generally, these studies have not found strong relationships.

The most extensive analysis of the relationship between officer characteristics and shootings was conducted by Blumberg (1983a; Chapter IV) in Kansas City. He finds that out of 10 officer characteristics (i.e., age, length of police service, gender, race, social class, height, marital status at appointment, military service, pre-service firearms experience, and prior arrest record of officer), only officer age and length of police service are significantly related to shooting behavior. Younger officers and those with fewer years of police service were observed to be more likely to become involved in a shooting (controlling for assignment). Although there was some evidence indicating that females and officers drawn from the middle-class were less likely to shoot at citizens, the relatively small number of female officers in the sample and the large number of missing cases with respect to officer-social class precluded a precise analysis of these relationships. Each of the remaining officer characteristics bore no relationship to the use of deadly force.

Although younger and inexperienced Kansas City (Mo.) police officers were found to be more likely to become involved in shootings, this was not observed in a Miami study. Alpert (1984) failed to find a relationship between officer age or length of police service and shooting behavior. However, he reports that younger, inexperienced officers are more frequently involved in unintentional shootings. Consequently, clarification of the relationship between these officer characteristics and shooting behavior must await further research in other sites.

The other studies that have attempted to find relationships between officer characteristics and shooting behavior have had even less success. Sherman and Blumberg (1981) examined the relationship between officer education level and deadly force. The authors find little relationship between these variables. Geller and Karales (1981) and Fyfe (1981b) examined the relationship between officer race and shootings. Both researchers observed that black officers have a higher shooting rate than white officers. Geller and Karales attribute this disparity primarily to a black over-representation in off-duty shootings (stemming in large part from officer residence patterns). There is no significant over-representation in on-duty shootings by these officers. Likewise, Fyfe (1981b) finds that when officer assignment and residence are controlled, most of the differences disappear. Thus, it does not appear that police departments can reduce the number of shootings by hiring additional black officers.

Research on the individual officer level has also examined whether shooters perform differently than nonshooters with respect to other aspects of their job. Blumberg (1983a; chapter V) examined eight performance measures (e.g., arrests, citizen complaints, departmental commendations, etc.) and found that many distinguished between shooters and nonshooters in the hypothesized direction.[10] Although the relationships were generally nonsignificant, the author attributes this to the relatively small sample utilized in the analysis. Thus, future research may indicate that these indicators have some utility for predicting involvement in shootings.

Situational Explanations

Sherman's second level of conceptual analysis for understanding police behavior is the situation. Although no study has ever compared situations in which the police use deadly force to those situations in which it is not used, numerous studies have examined particular situational characteristics of shooting incidents within a single city.[11]

In general, these studies have examined a large variety of incident and opponent characteristics. The time and place of the incident, the precipitating event that brought the police into the situation, whether or not the opponent was armed, the duty status of the officer, and the response of the opponent to the intervention of the police are but some of the characteristics that have been analyzed. Geller and Karales (1981:56), after reviewing the research in this area, note that a pattern seems to emerge that supports the following broad assertion:

> The most common shooting of a civilian by a police officer in urban America is one in which an on-duty, uniformed officer shoots an armed, black male between the ages of 17 and 30 at night in a public location, in connection with an armed robbery. Typically, the shooting is subsequently deemed justifiable by the police department following an internal investigation. Even if the officer is criminally prosecuted, a jury is unlikely to convict. . . . (Geller and Karales, 1981:56)

Although the general pattern noted by Geller and Karales appears to hold up fairly well in most cities, the research indicates that there are some differences across communities with respect to the situational characteristics of police shootings. Readers wishing to examine the findings of previous studies in some detail are urged to consult Geller (1983).

Despite the fact that scholars have examined the use of deadly force in a large number of cities, Geller and Karales (1981:74–76) caution that studies conducted by different researchers are often not comparable to one another. Because researchers utilize varying definitions of what constitutes deadly force,[12] often define similar variables in a dissimilar manner,[13] utilize different time periods, and place different limitations on the types of incidents that will be included in the data base,[14] it is very risky to compare shootings across communities that were examined by different researchers.

Opponent Race

Because police shootings of blacks have led to serious confrontations between police and the black community in a number of cities, a large number of empirical studies have addressed this particular situational characteristic (opponent race). Given the amount of attention that this issue has received and the controversy that it has generated, it is only fitting that a separate section be devoted to an examination of the issues raised by the disproportionate involvement of blacks as the victims of police shootings.

All research indicates that blacks are disproportionately the victims of police use of deadly force in comparison to their representation in the general population.[15] What researchers do not agree on is why this should be the case. In fact, it is interesting to observe the wide range of opinion with respect to this question.

Goldkamp (1976) has surveyed the literature with respect to race and police shootings. He concludes that researchers generally subscribe to one of two belief perspectives. Belief Perspective I links the disproportionately high minority shooting rates to the impact of differential policing. The best-known proponent of this point of view is Takagi (1974) who has argued that "the police have one trigger-finger for whites and another for blacks." Belief Perspective II links the disproportionately high number of minority shootings to disproportionate minority arrest rates for crimes of violence. Arrest rates are seen as reflecting a disproportionate participation by minorities in violent criminal activity and, therefore, to account for the disproportionate number of minorities shot by the police. A number of researchers subscribe to this point of view.[16]

Empirical analysis to examine this question has utilized 3 techniques (1) a comparison of arrest and shooting data to determine if blacks are more likely to be the victims of police shootings than would be expected by their representation among those arrested for various types of criminal activity; (2) a comparative analysis of the situational characteristics of shootings involving white and black opponents to determine if blacks are shot under circumstances that present less justification and (3) a comparative analysis of the situational characteristics of police shootings in white and minority communities to determine if shootings that occur in minority communities present less justification.

Each of these approaches has various shortcomings. Examination of arrest statistics (Methodology I) is problematic for a number of reasons. For one thing, there is the question of which set of arrest statistics is the appropriate comparative measure to examine the issue of race discrimination (Blumberg, 1981). Secondly, there is concern whether arrest statistics really are a valid indicator of the extent to which minority citizens commit crimes (Peirson, 1978). If arrest statistics themselves reflect discriminatory law enforcement by the police, they obviously have little value for addressing the question of whether shootings are the result of race discrimination by police. Third, some shootings arise out of police intervention into situations that involve no identifiable offense at the start of the incident (Sherman, 1980b).

Despite these shortcomings, a number of researchers have relied on arrest statistics to examine the question of racial discrimination in police shootings.[17] Other researchers have used this approach in conjunction with the other methodologies.[18] Generally, most of the studies indicate that the proportion of black shooting victims is comparable to their representation among those arrested for violent index crimes.

Recognizing that it is not enough to know how many people of each race are shot "in order to determine if similarly situated defendants are treated by the system in a similar manner regardless of skin color," Fyfe (1981a:149) has suggested that research in this area "focus instead on the degree to which the justifiability of police shootings varies . . . among the racial groups of those shot" (p. 145). This is the approach taken by several researchers who examine the issue of racial discrimination by comparing the situational characteristics of shootings involving white and black citizens.[19]

There is a problem with this approach (Methodology II) also. Because baseline data are not available with respect to all police–citizen encounters, it is not possible to determine whether the police are more likely to shoot blacks than whites under the same circumstances. Thus, even if the data indicate that an equal proportion of blacks and whites who were shot were unarmed, it still does not tell us if unarmed blacks are more likely to be shot since one does not know the relative number of unarmed whites and blacks who come into contact with the police.[20] However, in the absence of baseline data, one can still determine whether the situational characteristics of shooting incidents are similar for both races. Therefore, Methodology II is a distinct improvement over the first approach.

The findings of the various studies utilizing Methodology II are mixed. Blumberg (1981) observed that there are no significant differences between situations in which whites and blacks are shot by the police in either Atlanta or Kansas City. In general, blacks were not likely to be shot under circumstances that presented less danger to the officer nor was the intensity of the police response likely to be greater in incidents involving blacks. On the other hand, Meyer was able to conclude that shooting incidents involving black suspects in Los Angeles differ in circumstances from those involving others (1980:107). He reaches this conclusion after observing that a greater proportion of black opponents (than whites or Hispanics) were unarmed and that blacks were more likely to be shot for disobeying an officer's command to halt. Geller and Karales (1981) found that a greater proportion of the black opponents (than whites) in Chicago were shot under circumstances that either presented serious danger or no danger to the police. Because many of the remaining incidents were classified in an ambiguous manner,[21] it is not possible to clearly determine whether white or black citizens were shot under circumstances that presented less justification in Chicago. Finally, Fyfe (1982) has utilized this approach to examine shootings in Memphis and New York. He finds evidence of racial discrimination in Memphis, but not in New York City. This study underscores the need to examine this issue on a city-by-city basis.

In a recent paper, Blumberg (1983b) has utilized another approach (Methodology III) to examine this question. Analysis of the situational characteristics of police shootings that occurred in the white and minority neighborhoods of New York City was conducted. No evidence was uncovered to suggest that the police shoot people under circumstances that present less justification in minority communities. However, this approach has the same drawback as Methodology II, no baseline data are available regarding all police–citizen contacts in white and minority communities. Despite these shortcomings, future research should utilize all three methodologies in conjunction with each other to examine the question of whether the disproportionate number of blacks shot in a particular community is the result of racial discrimination on the part of the police. If none of these various approaches produce evidence of discrimination, administrators and citizens alike could be reasonably confident that a problem does not exist in their community.

Organizational Explanations

Research with respect to the effect of organizational variables on the use of deadly force by police has shown much promise. Because many states continue to give police the right to shoot at any fleeing felon who cannot otherwise be apprehended, a substantial number of departments have adopted policy guidelines aimed at narrowing this discretion. Much of the research in this area has been directed toward assessing the effectiveness of departmental guidelines that are more restrictive than state law.

The various studies are in agreement that departments may successfully reduce the number of police shootings by tightening up their firearms policy even in the absence of a change in state law.[22] Furthermore, the evidence suggests that a strictly enforced change in policy not only reduces the frequency of police shootings, but changes their nature as well. For New York City, Fyfe (1979) reports a rise in the proportion of shooting incidents classified as "defense-of-life" and a decrease in the proportion classified "prevent/terminate crime." Likewise, Sherman (1983) observes that the proportion of shootings which involved either fleeing or unarmed citizens decreased in both Atlanta and Kansas City after a change in departmental policy. This finding is confirmed in a study conducted by Meyer (1980) for the Los Angeles Board of Police Commissioners, which reported that the number of individuals shot after being ordered to halt decreased after a policy change in that city.

Researchers have also investigated whether a more restrictive firearms policy leads to certain unintended consequences (i.e., an increase in either officer injury or deaths). Both Sherman (1983) and Fyfe (1979) find that this is not the case. This is not surprising. After all, restrictive firearms policies do not infringe on the officer's right to shoot in self-defense. The use of deadly force is only prohibited in the case of nonviolent fleeing suspects. Clearly, these individuals do not pose any danger to the officer.

Finally, Matulia (1982:82) has examined "how personnel practices, training, policy, precedure, equipment, and other organizational considerations might impact on the use of deadly force." Forty hypotheses were tested through cross-sectional analysis, and certain organizational variables were observed to bear a significant relationship to the rate of "justifiable homicide." However, as the author acknowledges, this study should be seen as exploratory in nature. Although the data called for multivariate analysis, it was not utilized.

Community Explanations

In general, there are relatively few studies which examine the relationship between community characteristics and the use of deadly force by the police (Jacobs and Britt, 1979; Fyfe, 1980; Kania and Mackey, 1977; and Milton et al., 1977).

Milton et al. (1977) observed that the rates of shootings vary across cities and that these rates are not explained by population size (p. 29), police department size (p. 30), index crime rate (p. 30), or violent crime rate (p. 31). However, this study only utilized data for a two-year period.

Kania and Mackey (1977) used data on police killings collected by the U.S. Public Health Service in order to examine the relationship between police killings and various state characteristics. Relatively strong correlations were obtained between the public homicide rate and the rate of police killings of civilians as well as between the violent crime exposure per officer and the rate of police killings. Modest correlations were obtained between other state characteristics and the rate of police killings.

Jacobs and Britt (1979) use the same data base as Kania and Mackey. However, their study introduces the "Gini" index of income inequality into the analysis. The authors find significant relationships between the rate of police killings in a state and the following independent variables: the "Gini" index, change in population, and a violence index. Based upon the strength of the "Gini" index in the multiple regression analysis, the authors conclude that support is offered to the conflict hypothesis as an explanation of the variability in intercommunity rates of homicide by police officers.

Finally, Fyfe (1980) has examined the relationship between certain neighborhood characteristics and police shootings in New York City. He finds that the neighborhood rates of on-duty shootings by uniformed officers are strongly correlated with both the neighborhood rates of violent felony arrests and reported murders and non-negligent manslaughters. The high correlation between these violent crime indicators and the level of extreme police–citizen violence within a neighborhood gives support to the conclusion of Kania and Mackey (1977) that police violence varies as "the police officer reacts to the community as he perceives it, a perception which is usually correct" (p. 46).

Despite the fact that the Kania and Mackey (1977) and Jacobs and Britt (1979) studies contain a number of methodological problems,[23] it is clear that community characteristics do bear some relationship to the use of deadly force. However, a great deal of further research is needed on this level of analysis.

Legal Explanations

There has been little research on the relationship between legal variables and the use of deadly force by police. Although Matulia (1982:21) observed that the rates of "justifiable homicide" are likely to be higher in departments located in states that follow the common law,[24] the relationship between these variables is more complex. Some police departments within a common-law state are likely to follow firearms policies that are more restrictive than state law. Thus, the overall rate of "justifiable homicide" for the state is likely to be influenced as much, if not more so, by the organizational variable of policy as by the applicable state law.

Analysis of the relationship between various state laws and police use of deadly force is problematic for other reasons as well. On the one hand, cross-sectional analysis is likely to be confounded by variations among states with regard to their social, economic and political environment. On the other hand, state laws with regard to deadly force are rarely changed. Thus, researchers do not often have the opportunity to examine the effect of a change in a particular state law.

Looking into the future, there appears to be little prospect for legislative reform in this area. Because state legislatures are often dominated by rural interests and given the fact that police use of deadly force is seen as an urban concern, the prospect for statutory reform is not very encouraging. However, judicial reform is another matter. Recently, the Sixth Circuit Court of Appeals held that a "fleeing felon" statute, which permits the use of deadly force to apprehend unarmed suspects fleeing from non-violent felonies, violates the

Fourth and Fourteenth Amendments.[25] If this decision is not reversed, the possibilities for research on this level of analysis will be greatly increased.

SUMMARY

The main findings of previous research can be summarized as follows: 1) although officer age, length of police service, gender, and social class have been reported to distinguish between shooters and nonshooters, these findings must be regarded as tentative pending further research into the relationship between officer characteristics and shooting behavior; 2) all research indicates that blacks are disproportionately represented as the victims of police deadly force compared to their numbers in the general population; however, there is much disagreement among scholars as to why this is the case; 3) police departments can successfully reduce the number of shootings involving their officers by tightening-up their firearms policy; and 4) the incidence and nature of police shootings vary somewhat across communities.

SUGGESTIONS FOR FUTURE RESEARCH

Clearly, a large number of studies have been conducted over the last few years with respect to the use of deadly force. However, a number of issues have yet to be examined. This section will attempt to point out some of the questions that remain unanswered. Hopefully, future researchers will fill these gaps.

With respect to individual officer level analysis, what is clearly needed is an examination of the relationship between shooting behavior and other indicators of job performance utilizing a sample of sufficient size so that reliable statistical inferences may be drawn. In addition, future researchers should undertake an examination of the relationship between individual officer characteristics and shooting behavior in a variety of new sites. As the Dade County Grand Jury (1983:4–5) notes in its final report, it is disturbing that so little research attention has been devoted to this question. Hopefully, future studies will utilize psychological as well as social characteristics with the aim of determining which attributes are most predictive of shooting behavior by police officers.

There are substantive gaps to be filled on the situational level as well. As was noted earlier, no study has compared situations in which the police do and do *not* use deadly force. This issue has remained unexplored largely because base-line data regarding police–citizen encounters that do not result in a shooting are not available. However, as Reiss (1980:33) notes, "to understand how and when deadly force is used, we need to understand why and when it is not used." Clearly, one of the most pressing concerns for future research should be the collection of such base-line data.

Data concerning police–citizen encounters in which deadly force is not used can probably be gathered most easily through an examination of police department arrest records. By examining a random sample of arrest reports and making a comparative analysis with shooting reports, those situational factors which increase the probability of a police shooting can be identified. Through this procedure, it may even be possible to determine in a fairly conclusive manner, the influence that opponent race plays in these situations. Of course, such analysis must be conducted on a city-by-city basis. However, as the number of studies begin to proliferate, researchers should be able to determine whether the same situational factors contribute to police shootings in different departments.

Although a comparative analysis of situations in which the police do and do not use deadly force will determine which environmental factors (e.g., the proportion of armed opponents a particular department encounters) contribute to shootings in various cities, it is not likely that environmental factors will provide a complete explanation. Indeed, Milton et al. (1977) found that the rates of police shootings across communities could not be attributed to differences with respect to the number of authorized police personnel per capita, the crime rate, the index crime rate or the violent crime rate. Therefore, future researchers should examine political and organizational variables[26] as well as factors in the working environment of the police which may contribute to the use of deadly force.

Earlier, it was noted that some of the most significant findings that have been reported in the literature concern the effect of departmental policy on the use of deadly force by police. Although the evidence is overwhelming that policy can be effective in reducing the number of shootings, the effects of other organizational practices are less certain. For example, what impact does the reward system within police departments have on the level of police–citizen violence? Both Burnham

(1968) and Blumberg (1983a) have observed that officers who are involved in shooting incidents are likely to be awarded with commendations. What is not known is whether this practice contributes to an inclination on the part of officers to resolve difficult situations with firearms. Police departments should be encouraged to reward officers who resolve precarious situations without the use of deadly force, and researchers should closely monitor the effect of such policies on the overall number of shootings.[27]

Future research should also be concerned with examining public attitudes with respect to police use of deadly force. Although public opinion cannot be the sole consideration when it comes to decisions that involve life or death, police administrators nonetheless should be cognizant of the feelings of their community in this regard. Previous studies have successfully given hypothetical situations to police officers in which the officer was asked if it would be appropriate to discharge his or her weapon under a particular set of circumstances (Scharf, et al., 1978, and Uelman, 1973). There is no reason why hypothetical dilemmas cannot be given to the general public as well. Such research could not only be used to gauge the attitudes of the community at-large, but to determine the extent to which various racial and ethnic groups perceive the use of deadly force by police as problematic.

Finally, future research should be concerned with replication. The degree of confidence placed in the external validity of any study is directly proportional to the number of times that the findings have been replicated. For this reason, an analysis of the relationship between police officer social characteristics and shooting behavior in sites other than Kansas City (Mo.) and Miami has already been suggested. Likewise, because the question of race discrimination can only be examined on a city-by-city basis, other studies which address this issue should be undertaken. Clearly, any further research which explores the characteristics of police shootings in new sites will contribute to our understanding with respect to the many important issues surrounding the use of deadly force by police.

NOTES

1. Twenty-three states sanction the use of deadly force to apprehend *any* fleeing felon (Matulia, 1982:17).

2. See (Sherman and Langworthy, 1979; and Takagi, 1974).

3. See (Kuykendall, 1981; and Kobler, 1975b).

4. Police department shooting reports are probably the best source of information with respect to the incidence and nature of deadly force by police in a particular community. However, collecting these data is often a tedious and time-consuming process. These records must be examined one department at a time and the incidence of deadly force cannot be measured on a national basis in this manner.

5. See (Kobler, 1975a; and PILCOP, 1979).

6. See (Harding and Fahey, 1973; and Knoohuizen, Fahey and Palmer, 1972).

7. See (Jacobs and Britt, 1979; Kania and Mackey, 1977; Kobler, 1975b; and Takagi, 1974).

8. See Sherman and Langworthy (1979) for an excellent discussion of the shortcomings of each of these data sources.

9. The FBI collects information on police killings in the supplementary homicide reports filed with the Uniform Crime Reporting Section. However, it does not publish these data due to reservations with respect to their quality (see Sherman and Langworthy, 1979:547).

10. E.g., it was hypothesized that shooters would make a greater number of arrests, receive more citizen complaints, and be given a greater number of departmental commendations, etc. than nonshooters.

11. See (Geller and Karales, 1981; Board of Police Commissioners of Los Angeles, 1979–80; Fyfe, 1978; Boston Police Department, 1974; Knoohuizen, Fahey and Palmer, 1972; and Robin, 1963).

12. Some studies analyze only fatalities, others include nonfatal hits or nonfatal hits and "harmless discharges" as well in their definition of deadly force.

13. E.g., some studies classify an opponent who tries to run-down an officer with a vehicle as being "unarmed," others do not.

14. There are differences among studies with respect to whether or not accidental shootings, off-duty incidents, and those occurring outside of the jurisdiction will be included in the data base.

15. See (Matulia, 1982; Geller and Karales, 1981; Blumberg, 1981; Fyfe, 1981c; Meyer, 1980; Fyfe, 1978; Milton et al., 1977; Jenkins and Faison, 1974; Dallas Police Department, 1974; Takagi, 1974; Burnham,

1973; Knoohuizen, Fahey and Palmer, 1972; and Robin, 1963).

16. See Matulia, 1982; Geller and Karales, 1981; Blumberg, 1981; Fyfe, 1981c; Milton et al., 1977 and the Dallas Police Department, 1974).

17. See (Matulia, 1982; Milton et al., 1977, Takagi, 1974; Burnham, 1973; and Robin, 1963.)

18. See (Blumberg, 1983a; Geller and Karales, 1981; Blumberg, 1981; Meyer, 1980; Fyfe, 1978; and the Dallas Police Department, 1974).

19. See (Fyfe, 1982; Blumberg, 1981; Geller and Karales, 1981; Meyer, 1980; and the Dallas Police Department, 1974).

20. E.g., let us say that 50 percent of both white and black opponents were armed. It could still be argued by some that this does not eliminate the possibility that blacks are more likely to be shot than whites under similar circumstances. Because baseline data with regard to the number of armed citizens of each race who come in contact with the police are not available, a definitive answer to this question is not possible.

21. Geller and Karales classified many of the other incidents as involving the use of or a threat with either another deadly weapon (not a gun) or physical force. Clearly, these responses do not represent equivalent levels of risk for a police officer. Consequently, how does one interpret the finding that black shooting victims were less likely to respond in this manner (p. 123–124)?

22. See (Sherman, 1983; Fyfe, 1979; and Board of Police Commissioners of Los Angeles, 1979–80).

23. For one thing, these studies examined only actual killings of citizens. Secondly, the characteristics of individual states were used as the unit of analysis. Because many different police agencies operate within the various communities of a given state, it is not possible to attribute differences across states to the characteristics of "communities" as such. Finally, these researchers failed to include the proportion of black citizens as one of their independent variables. Because all previous research finds that blacks have a disproportionately greater likelihood of being killed by the police, the inclusion of this variable is critical.

24. As previously noted, under the common-law rule followed by 23 states, the police can shoot *any* fleeing felon. Sherman (1980b) presents a number of compelling reasons why this doctrine should be abolished.

25. Garner v. Memphis Police Department, 33 *Criminal Law Reporter* 2253 (6th Cir. 1983).

26. Organizational data on a substantial number of large police departments are now available (Heaphy, 1978).

27. Geller and Karales (1981:176–178) offer many useful suggestions on various other organizational variables that researchers may wish to explore for the purpose of examining their effect on police shootings.

REFERENCES

Alpert, Geoffrey P. *Police Use of Deadly Force: The Miami Experience*. Center for the Study of Law and Society, University of Miami, 1984.

Blumberg, Mark. "The Use of Firearms by Police Officers: The Impact of Individuals, Communities, and Race." Ph.D. dissertation, School of Criminal Justice, State University of New York at Albany, 1983a.

———. "Police Shootings in Minority Communities." A paper presented at the Annual Meeting of the *Academy of Criminal Justice Sciences*, San Antonio, 1983b.

———. "Race and Police Shootings: An Analysis in Two Cities," in *Contemporary Issues in Law Enforcement*, edited by James J. Fyfe, Sage Publications (1981).

Board of Police Commissioners of Los Angeles, *The Report of the Board of Police Commissioners Concerning the Shooting of Eulia Love and the Use of Deadly Force*, Parts I-IV. Los Angeles: Board of Police Commissioners, 1979–1980.

Boston Police Department, Planning and Research Division. *The Use of Deadly Force by the Boston Police*. Boston, 1974.

Burnham, David. "3 of 5 Slain by Police Here are Black, Same as the Arrest Rate." *The New York Times*. August 26, 1973.

———. "Police Violence: A Changing Pattern." *The New York Times*. July 7, 1968.

Dade County Grand Jury. *Final Report*. Eleventh Judicial Circuit of Florida (1983).

Dallas Police Department. *Report on Police Shootings*. Dallas, Texas: Center for Police Development, South Methodist University, 1974.

Fyfe, James J., "Blind Justice: Police Shootings in Memphis." *The Journal of Criminal Law and Criminology*, Vol. 83, No. 2 (Summer 1982).

———."Toward a Typology of Police Shootings," pages 136–151 in *Contemporary Issues In Law Enforcement*, edited by James J. Fyfe. Beverly Hills: Sage Publications, 1981a.

———. "Who Shoots? A Look at Officer Race and Police Shooting." *The Journal of Police Science and Administration*, Vol. 9, No. 4 (1981b).

———. "Race and Extreme Police-Citizen Violence" in *Race, Crime and Criminal Justice* edited by R. L. McNeely and Carl E. Pope. Sage Publications, Inc. (1981c).

———. "Geographic Correlates of Police Shooting: A Microanalysis." *Journal of Research in Crime and Delinquency*. Vol. 101 (1980).

———. "Administrative Interventions on Police Shooting Discretion: An Empirical Examination." *Journal of Criminal Justice*, Vol. 7 (1979).

———. "Shots Fired: A Typological Examination of New York City Police Firearms Discharges 1971–1975," Ph.D. dissertation, School of Criminal Justice, State University of New York at Albany, 1978.

Geller, William A. "Deadly Force: What We Know," in *Thinking About Police: Contemporary Readings*, edited by Carl B. Klockars. McGraw-Hill (1983).

Geller, William A. and Kevin J. Karales. *Shootings of and by the Chicago Police*. The Law Enforcement Study Group, 1981.

Goldkamp, John S. "Minorities as Victims of Police Shootings: Interpretations of Racial Disproportionality and Police Use of Deadly Force." *Justice System Journal*, 2 (Winter, 1976), 169–183.

Harding, Richard W. and Richard P. Fahey. "Killings by Chicago Police, 1969–70: An Empirical Study." *Southern California Law Review* 46 (1973), pp. 284–315.

Heaphy, J. F. *Police Practices: The General Administrative Survey*. Washington, D.C.: Police Foundation (1978).

Jacobs, David and David Britt. "An Empirical Assessment of a Conflict Hypothesis." *Social Problems* 26 (April, 1979), pp. 403–412.

Jenkins, Betty and Adrienne Faison. *An Analysis of 248 Persons Killed by New York City Policemen*. New York, N.Y.: Metropolitan Applied Research Center, Inc., 1974.

Kania, Richard R. E. and Wade C. Mackey. "Police Violence as a Function of Community Characteristics." *Criminology* 15 (May, 1977) 1:27–48.

Knoohuizen, Ralph, Richard Fahey, and Deborah J. Palmer. *The Police and Their Use of Fatal Force in Chicago*. The Chicago Law Enforcement Study Group. 1972.

Kobler, Arthur L. "Figures (and Perhaps Some Facts) on Police Killings of Civilians in the United States, 1965–69." *Journal of Social Issues* 31 (November, 1975a), pp. 185–191.

———. "Police Homicide in a Democracy. "*Journal of Social Issues* 31 (November, 1975b), pp. 163–184.

Kuykendall, Jack. "Trends in the Use of Deadly Force by Police." *Journal of Criminal Justice*, Vol. 9, No. 5 (1981).

Matulia, Kenneth J. *A Balance of Forces*. Gaithersburg, Md.: International Association of Chiefs of Police, 1982.

Meyer, Marshall W. "Police Shootings at Minorities: The Case of Los Angeles, "*Annals of the American Academy of Political and Social Science* 452 (November, 1980), pp. 89–110.

Milton, Catherine H., J. W. Halleck, J. Lardner, and G. L. Abrecht. *Police Use of Deadly Force*. Washington, D.C.: Police Foundation, 1977.

Peirson, Gwynne W. *Police Use of Deadly Force: Preliminary Report*. National Minority Advisory Council on Criminal Justice, 1978.

PILCOP. *Deadly Force: Police Use of Firearms 1970–78*. The Public Interest Law Center of Philadelphia, 1979.

Reiss, Albert J. "Controlling Police Use of Deadly Force," in *The Annals of the American Academy of Political and Social Science*. Vol. 452 (1980).

Robin, Gerald D. "Justifiable Homicide by Police Officers." *Journal of Criminal Law, Criminology and Police Science* 54 (1963), pp. 225–231.

Scharf, Peter, Rod Linninger, Dave Marrero, Ron Baker, and Chris Rice. "Deadly Force: The Moral Reasoning and Education of Police Officers Faced With the Option of Lethal Legal Violence." *Policy Studies Journal*, Special Issue (1978), pp. 451–454.

Sherman, Lawrence W. "Reducing Police Gun Use: Critical Events, Administrative Policy and Organizational Change," in *The Management and Control of Police Organizations*, edited by Maurice Punch, Cambridge, Mass.: M.I.T. Press, 1983.

———, and Mark Blumberg. "Higher Education and Police Use of Deadly Force." *Journal of Criminal Justice* 9, No. 4 (1981).

———. "Causes of Police Behavior: The Current State

of Quantitative Research." *Journal of Research in Crime and Delinquency* 17 (1980a).

———. "Execution Without Trial: Police Homicide and the Constitution." *Vanderbilt Law Review*, (1980b).

———, and Robert H. Langworthy. "Measuring Homicide by Police Officers." *Journal of Criminal Law and Criminology* 70 (1979).

Takagi, Paul. "A Garrison State in a 'Democratic' Society." *Crime and Social Justice: A Journal of Radical Criminology*, (Spring-Summer, 1974).

Uelman, Gerald F. "Varieties of Police Policy: A Study of Police Policy Regarding the Use of Deadly Force in Los Angeles County." *Loyola University of Los Angeles Law Review* 6 (1973), pp. 1–65.

10

POLICE STRESS

The role of stress and its causal relationship to a wide variety of physical and psychological illnesses has been fairly well documented and is now well supported by scientific evidence. Thus, cardiovascular diseases, hypertension, various digestive diseases, alcoholism, chronic depressions, and suicide attempts are all seen as life-threatening illnesses that are stress linked in their origins. Although the police occupation is not actually one of the most hazardous, or stressful occupations, nevertheless there is a continued claim that police work is among the most stressful activities, and that it is the cause of the seemingly high incidence of cardiovascular diseases, diabetes, alcoholism, divorce, and suicide among police.

However, a number of commentators have begun to question the degree to which some of the stress and illness linkages among police are rather a consequence of social class and factors *other* than occupationally created stress risks. In terms of the present state of research there appears to be a good deal of methodological difficulty in sorting out the precise causal linkages between individual police personnel and their illnesses as these may be influenced or affected by the individual, the person's organization, or environment. Further, in any analysis of police alcoholism, divorce, or suicide more complex explanations involving *other* antecedent variables than that of occupationally induced stress must also be explored and accounted for in order to arrive at meaningful conclusions about the nature and impact of police stress.

Paradox in Policing: A Note on Perceptions of Danger

Francis T. Cullen, Bruce G. Link, Lawrence F. Travis, III, and Terrence Lemming

As a number of commentators have revealed, managing violence and its accompanying physical risks are inherent and distinguishing features of the police occupational role (Westley 1970; Bayley 1976; Skolnick 1966). To be sure, the incidents in which officers are moved to the point of employing deadly force or are subject to fatal wounds are notable because they are, in fact, relatively rare. Further, other work settings (for example, coal mines) are perhaps equally if not more hazardous (Gersuny 1981; Caudill 1977). Neverthe-

SOURCE: "Paradox in Policing: A Note on Perceptions of Danger," *Journal of Police Science and Administration* 11, No. 4, 1983, pp. 457–462. Copyright 1983 by the International Association of Chiefs of Police, Inc. Reprinted with permission.

less, the various duties of the police—ranging from peace keeping to crime fighting—regularly expose officers to a unique kind of danger: bodily harm that is not merely random or unpredictable like most tragic accidents, but also inflicted intentionally. Indeed, officers must live with the reality that 91 of their brethren were killed in 1981 (FBI 1982, p. 309), and that law enforcement officials are involved in violent exchanges sufficiently serious to result in the deaths of upwards of 300 citizens each year (Geller 1983, p. 314).

In light of these considerations, the present study endeavors to explore whether police officers actually perceive their occupation to be a dangerous one. Two alternatives can initially be suggested here. On the one hand, it may be that officers are sensitized to the risks that may potentially flow from any citizen interaction and thus see their job as necessarily containing ever-present hazards. By contrast, it may be that officers see their everyday life experiences as essentially routine, adjust to this reality, and hence believe that they have little to fear on the job.

Following from these concerns, an attempt is made to illuminate the extent to which the feeling that police work is a risky enterprise either precipitates negative side-effects or is adapted to with little difficulty. Specifically, our analysis examines the link between perceptions of danger and two measures of psychological distress.

It should be observed at this point that the results reported below suggest that policing is characterized by paradoxical or contradictory qualities.[1] In particular, it appears that officers perceive their work to be both safe and unsafe and that such perceptions are both functional and dysfunctional. It is further argued that these features are largely integral to the occupational role of the police officer and thus are not readily amenable to alteration.

[1] Using a variety of terms and frames of references, a number of authors have noted the contradictory nature of American policing. For instance, Lundman (1980) speaks of the tension between civility and liberty that characterizes policing. Similarly, Manning (1978) has discussed the incongruity between the portrayed image of policing as "crime fighting" and the reality of policing as routine and often boring, while Niederhoffer and Blumberg (1976) have devoted an entire volume to an examination of the ambivalent qualities manifest in American policing.

METHOD

Sample

In the summer of 1982, questionnaires were distributed to all officers (with the exception of the chiefs of police) in five departments located in the suburbs of a large midwestern city. Of the 161 subjects contacted, 56.5 percent or 91 returned a usable survey. The response rate for each department was as follows: Department 1 = 31 of 46 (67.4 percent); Department 2 = 22 of 54 (40.7 percent); Department 3 = 17 of 24 (70.8 percent); Department 4 = 12 of 27 (44.4 percent); and Department 5 = 9 of 10 (90 percent).

Since information on a variety of respondents' characteristics was collected, it is possible to present a rather complete description of the sample. The sample included 59 patrol officers, 1 squad leader, 12 sergeants, 7 detectives, 8 lieutenants, 2 captains, 1 commander, and 1 person who did not answer the question on rank. It should be noted that these subjects were almost exclusively white males; only two females and one black male were in the final sample. The mean age of the respondents was 34, while the average length of time a person had been in police work was 9.5 years. With regard to education, 1.1 percent had not completed high school, 8.8 percent held high school diplomas, 39.5 percent attended but did not finish college, 36.3 percent were college graduates, and 14.3 percent had undertaken graduate work. Finally, 1.1 percent of the sample reported earning a yearly salary of under $15,000, 12.1 percent earned between $15,001-$20,000, 39.5 percent earned between $20,001-$25,000, 33 percent earned between $25,001-$30,000, and 14.3 percent earned over $30,000.

Measures

In order to measure perceptions of danger, 5 items were included within a larger survey instrument that contained 46 randomly placed statements. For each statement in the questionnaire, the respondents were instructed to use a 7-point Likert scale (ranging from 1 = very strongly agree to 7 = very strongly disagree) to express the "extent to which you agree or disagree with the statements listed below." Taken together, the five danger items had a Cronbach's Alpha of .64. These items are presented in table 1.

Two measures of psychological discomfort were also included in the questionnaire. The first, "work stress," attempted to assess how anxious or pressured officers felt while on duty. The six items composing this scale had a reliability of .78 and were also distributed ran-

TABLE 1 Percentage Agreement with Danger Items

Item	*Percent Agree*	*Percent Uncertain*	*Percent Disagree*
1. A lot of people I work with get physically injured in the line of duty.	9	4	87
2. I work at a dangerous job.	79	1	20
3. My job is a lot more dangerous than other kinds of jobs.	66	7	27
4. There is really not much chance of getting hurt in my job.	7	1	92
5. In my job, a person stands a good chance of getting hurt.	63	3	34

domly throughout the statements that the respondents were asked to agree or disagree with. These items were:

1. When I'm at work, I often feel tense or uptight.
2. A lot of times, my job makes me very frustrated or angry.
3. Most of the time when I am at work, I don't feel that I have much to worry about.
4. I am usually calm and at ease when I am working.
5. I usually feel that I am under a lot of pressure when I am at work.
6. There are a lot of aspects about my job that can make me pretty upset about things.

The second measure was aimed at tapping whether the officers sampled were encountering a more pervasive form of psychological discomfort—one which they endured not merely at work but throughout their everyday lives. The instrument chosen was the Center for Epidemiologic Studies Depression Scale (CESD Scale), a measurement device that has been employed frequently in stress research (Radloff 1977). Here, the police officers were presented with a list of 20 statements, each of which represented an element of depressive symptomatology. In responding, the officers were asked to indicate how often they had experienced a symptom in the past 4 weeks. Four response categories were provided and coded 1 to 4. These were as follows: 1 = less than one day per week; 2 = one to two days per week; 3 = three to four days per week; and 4 = five to seven days per week. An officer's score on this scale was determined by adding together the scores for the 20 items. Scores could thus vary from a low of 20 to a high of 80. The reliability for this measure of general "life stress" was .86, having a zero-order correlation of .509 with the work stress scale. The 20 items composing the instrument were as follows:

1. You were bothered by things that don't usually bother you.
2. You did not feel like eating; your appetite was poor.
3. You felt that you would not shake off the blues even with help from your family and friends.
4. You felt that you were just as good as other people.
5. You had trouble keeping your mind on what you were doing.
6. You felt depressed.
7. You felt that everything you did was an effort.
8. You felt hopeful about the future.
9. You thought your life had been a failure.
10. You felt fearful.
11. Your sleep was restless.
12. You were happy
13. You talked less than usual.
14. You felt lonely.
15. People were friendly.
16. You enjoyed life.
17. You had crying spells.
18. You felt sad.
19. You felt that people disliked you.
20. You could not get going.

FINDINGS

Perceptions of Danger

The responses to the danger statements are presented in table 1. Those who answered agree, strongly agree, or very strongly agree are listed in the "agree" category, while those who answered disagree, strongly disagree, and very strongly disagree are counted in the "disagree" category. The "uncertain" rubric includes those who expressed this response on their questionnaire.

By reviewing table 1, it can be seen initially that most of the officers did not believe that physical injury is a frequent occurrence of police work. Thus, item 1 indicates that 87 percent disagreed that "a lot of people" are hurt in the line of duty. To some extent, this may be due to the fact that our data are based exclusively on the responses of officers drawn from suburban communities (average population of 26,400) which are characterized by relatively low levels of violence (only 4 homicides among the 5 communities in 1981) (FBI 1982). It can be anticipated that physical encounters with citizens and concomitant injuries would be more prevalent among officers working certain sections of large cities. However, it would seem inappropriate to suggest that the responses of urban police would differ markedly from the officers in our sample. Thus, according to the FBI (1982, p. 303), officer victimization in major urban centers (250,000 and over) was higher, but not decidedly so, than that found in communities of the size from which our sample was drawn (10,000 to 24,999). Specifically, the rate of assault and assaults with injury per 100 officers for the urban areas were 19.0 and 7.8, respectively, while for the communities of a smaller size the figures were 16.2 and 6.0.[2]

Interestingly, even though the officers surveyed did not perceive physical injury as an everyday happening, this does not mean that they were fully insulated against feelings of danger. Hence, from items 2 and 3 in table 1, it can be seen that nearly four-fifths of the sample believed that they worked at a dangerous job, and that two-thirds thought that policing was more dangerous than other kinds of employment. In turn, the question emerges as to why officers who do not see victimization as a frequent occurrence nevertheless perceive their work as dangerous. Clues to solving this apparent puzzle are contained in items 4 and 5, for here it is seen that the officers report that policing is an occupation in which the *chance* of getting injured is everpresent. As such, what makes being a police officer dangerous is not so much that a person is constantly subject to physical harm, but rather that the *potential* for injury is a reality that all officers must confront.[3]

Effects of Danger

To assess whether feelings of danger help to precipitate negative side effects, our two measures of psychological discomfort were regressed on a danger scale (composed of the five items listed in table 1) and several control variables. The relationship of danger to work stress is presented in table 2. As can be seen, danger is positively (B = .501) and significantly ($p < .001$) associated with our measure of job stress. The data also revealed that those with higher educational levels were less likely to experience distress while at work. Finally, in order to control for where a police officer was employed, dummy variables were entered to show the effect of departmental membership. Department 5, which had the lowest mean stress score, was used as the suppressed or comparison category. Notably, only Department 3 had a significantly different work stress score holding constant the other variables in the equation.

Similar findings with regard to our measure of depressive symptomatology (CESD Scale) are apparent as well in table 2. Once again, danger appears to increase the psychological discomfort that officers endure, while education helps to mitigate such distress. Alternatively, this time no department added significantly to the amount of variance explained, holding constant other variables. Lastly, rank in the department, annual income, and years of experience as a police officer had no significant effect on either work stress or life stress.[4]

[2] While three of our communities had populations of under 25,000, two were larger than this. Notably, the victimization rates for communities of 25,000 to 49,999 were even closer to those of urban areas. Thus, the assault rate was 19.2 while assaults with injury were 6.5. Again, these figures suggest that the danger for police in communities of the size sampled in our study may not be markedly different from that found in many urban centers.

[3] In an effort to uncover which officers were more likely to perceive their work as risky, the danger items were combined into a scale and regressed on income, rank, education, years a police officer, and departmental membership. However, neither the overall equation nor any of these variables were found to be statistically significant. However, the zero-order correlations of danger with years of police officer ($r = .21$), rank ($r = .27$), and income ($r = .30$) suggest that older, more experienced officers in administrative positions may be better insulated against feelings of danger. At the same time, it is possible that differences in perceptions of danger may have less to do with social characteristics and more to do with individual variations in personality and job-specific coping mechanisms. Compare with Luxenburg and Johnson (1983).

[4] These variables, it should be noted, are highly correlated with one another. Rank correlates .48 with income and .57 with years as a police officer, while income correlates .68 with years as an officer. As a result, the variance any one of these variables predicts in our measures of stress is likely to be shared with the other two. Since our statistical test in table 2 is based on unique variance, we might incorrectly conclude that none was important. To be sure that we were not doing this, we tested these three variables as a set; that is, we assessed whether, taken together, they explained variance above and beyond other variables in the model. Notably, they did not add significantly to the explained variance for either dependent variable ($F_{3,79} = .136$ for work stress and $F_{3,79} = .904$ for the CESD Scale).

TABLE 2 The Impact of Danger on Work Stress and Depression

Variable	Work Stress			Depression (CESD Scale)		
	B	*Beta*	*F*	*B*	*Beta*	*F*
Danger	0.624	.501	29.587*	0.669	.364	11.923*
Education	−1.741	−.300	9.483*	−1.896	−.221	3.945***
Rank	−0.223	−.068	0.387	−0.847	−.175	1.954
Income	−0.084	−.015	0.012	1.367	.164	1.104
Years a Police Officer	0.046	.053	0.147	−0.081	−.064	0.162
Department 1	1.378	.125	1.128	2.992	.184	1.864
Department 2	1.102	.094	0.599	3.219	.185	1.793
Department 3	3.651	.233	4.958**	0.525	.023	0.036
Department 4	1.929	.113	1.087	1.925	.076	0.380
Constant	16.838			18.139		
	R^2 = .421			R^2 = .242		
	Adjusted R^2 = .355			Adjusted R^2 = .156		

* p<.01
**p< .05
*** p< .06

DISCUSSION: PARADOX IN POLICING

The data on perceptions of danger suggest that the police occupational role is characterized by two paradoxes or "conditions with seemingly contradictory qualities" (*Webster's Dictionary* 1967). The first, mentioned previously, is that police officers see their job as being both safe and unsafe. As we have seen, this apparent inconsistency can be understood when a distinction is made between officer perceptions of how much injury is actually sustained as opposed to the potential for harm inherent in their work. Thus, while our respondents were aware that physical damage occurred only on occasion to those that they worked with, they were equally conscious that they were employed in an occupation that caused them to enter situations in which the chance to be hurt was a salient concern.

Notably, the realization that the potential for danger resides in the police role is of no small consequence. As a number of commentators have observed, this perception informs both the formal and informal socialization experiences that recruits undergo as well as the everyday nature of policing. Lundman (1980, p. 81), for instance, has noted that new officers are taught that "policing is a physically demanding and dangerous enterprise," while Skolnick (1966. p. 45) has remarked that an officer's "work requires him to be occupied continually with potential violence" (cf. Walker 1983, p. 278; Rubinstein 1973). Commenting on the differences between Japanese and American police, Bayley (1976, p. 171) has similarly concluded:

> Though policemen most of the time do not face great danger, the possibility is a real one in the United States and it dominates perceptions of what a policeman must be prepared to do. The possibility of armed confrontation shapes training, patrol preoccupations, and operating procedures. It also shapes the relationship between citizen and policeman by generating mutual apprehension. The policeman can never forget that the individual he contacts may be armed and dangerous; the citizen can never forget that the policeman is armed and may consider the citizen dangerous.

These considerations form the context for a second policing paradox: perceptions of danger are both functional and dysfunctional. On the one hand, the very real hazards that police may encounter make it essential that officers remain vigilant to the potential risks of their work. Indeed, the evolution of the attitude that all is routine and there is nothing really to fear can result in a carelessness that can have fatal consequences. Yet, on the other hand, our analysis also reveals that sensitivity to danger—however necessary—is not without its negative personal effects. For while it is functional for officers to be aware of the dangers they face, the data indicate that such feelings contribute to heightened work stress and, more generally, to the manifestation of depressive symptomatology.

Moreover, there is little reason to anticipate that this dysfunctional and unanticipated consequence of policing can be easily eliminated. First, the psychological costs of attending to the dangers of being an officer are diffuse and easily attributed to other, more ostensible occupational circumstances (for example, poor supervision or shift change). Second, the very functionality of perceiving danger makes it essential that this feature of policing be emphasized and, alternatively, gives us reason to pause before arguing that officers not be sensitized quite as much to the dangers they may face. To be sure, one can be optimistic and suggest that officers be furnished with special programs that would better enable them to adjust to the awareness that they work in a potentially dangerous occupation. More realistically, however, it seems that the vast majority of officers will be left by themselves to find a way to cope with the difficulties imposed by the paradoxical qualities of their work.

In closing, it is necessary to add one caveat. The insights on the paradox in policing presented above are clearly beginning ones. The data utilized in our analysis are limited by locale as well as by the type of departments surveyed. Further, our measure of danger was broad in nature and thus did not capture how officers interpret the different varieties of potential injury (for example, accidental versus intentional) that policing may entail. Nevertheless, this research hopefully does have the advantage of shedding light on a central dimension of the structure of police attitudes toward danger (actual versus potential risks) and of revealing that such perceptions might possess, paradoxically, both good and bad consequences.

REFERENCES

Bayley, D. H. 1976 *Forces of order: Police behavior in Japan and the United States*. Berkeley: University of California Press.

Caudill, H. J. 1977. Manslaughter in a coal mine. *Nation* 224(23 April):492–497.

Federal Bureau of Investigation. 1982. *Uniform Crime Reports, 1981*. Washington, D.C.: U.S. GPO.

Geller, W. A. 1983. Deadly force: What we know. In *Thinking about police: Contemporary readings*, edited by C. B. Klockars, pp. 313–331. New York: McGraw-Hill.

Gersuny, C. 1981. *Work hazards and industrial conflict*. Hanover, NH: University Press of New England.

Lundman, R. A. 1980. *Police and policing*. New York: Holt, Rinehart and Winston.

Luxenburg, J., and Johnson, D. L. 1983. Personality type and job stress. *Police Chief 50* (January): 52–53.

Manning, P. 1978. The police. Mandate, strategies, and appearances. In *Policing: A view from the street*, edited by P. Manning and J. Van Maanen, pp. 7–31. Santa Monica: Goodyear.

Niederhoffer, A., and Blumberg, A., eds. 1976. *The ambivalent force*. Hinsdale, IL: Dryden Press.

Radloff, L. 1977. CESD scale: A self-report depression scale for research in the general population. *Appl. Psych. Measurement* 1:385–401.

Rubinstein, J. 1973. *City police*. New York: Ballantine.

Skolnick, J. H. 1966. *Justice without trial: Law enforcement in democratic society*. New York: John Wiley and Sons.

Stratton, J. G. 1980. Psychological services for police. *J. Pol. Sci. & Adm.* 8(1):31–39.

Walker, S. 1983. *The police in America: An introduction*. New York: McGraw-Hill.

Webster's Seventh New Collegiate Dictionary. 1967. Springfield, MA: G. & C. Merriam Company.

Westley, W. A. 1970. *Violence and the police: A sociological study of law, custom, and morality*. Cambridge, MA: M.I.T. Press.

Police Stress: The Empirical Evidence

W. Clinton Terry, III

When considering the topic of police stress, two principal questions are involved. First, is police work stressful and if so, to what extent? Second, what are the physiological and psychological effects of police stress? Queries surrounding this last question often assume that police work is stressful, consequently "causing" the onset or acceleration of these physiological and psychological problems. Furthermore, it is frequently argued that the presence of these problems, as well as the existence of other difficulties, such as marital difficulties, divorces, and suicides, provide clear and unequivocal evidence that police work is a particularly stressful occupation. Whether these difficulties and illnesses are the result of work conditions apart from any stress that might also be caused by other factors is a question that is seldom, if ever, asked.

This article examines the evidence bearing upon the question: "Is police work stressful and to what extent?" It examines the effects of stress upon police work only insofar as it bears upon this question. There is no doubt that police officers encounter stressful situations. What is uncertain, however, is whether police work is as stressful and/or dangerous as is commonly thought.[1] This article's goal is not to argue that recently instituted therapeutic and preventive programs are unneeded or unwanted. Far from it. Nor is the goal to discredit the argument that police work is stressful. Rather, the goal is to place this argument into a broader perspective by focusing upon potentially more critical questions.

Discussions of police stress are usually divided into one of four sets of stressors: (1) external, (2) internal, (3) task-related, and (4) individual (cf. Stratton 1978, p. 60; Wallace 1978; Blackmore 1978, p. 49; Grencik 1975, p. 165). External stressors include frustrations with the criminal justice system, particularly in terms of the apparent leniency of court decisions and the scheduling of court appearances, discontent with unfavorable media coverage, resentment of certain opinions arising out of minority communities, and dislike of the decisions and interests of government and administrative bodies affecting the performance of police work. Internal stressors cover a large number of problem areas, many of which are organizational, including training that is felt to be inadequate, equipment that is thought to be substandard or in a state of disrepair, poor pay, and ambiguously defined reward structures, as well as inadequate career development guidelines, offensive departmental policies, excessive paperwork, and intradepartmental political favoritism. Task-related stressors include role conflicts, the rigors of shift work, boredom, fear, danger, being exposed to the miseries and brutalities of life, and work overload. Finally, individual stressors include fears about job competence, individual success, and safety. Discussions of individual stressors also include consideration of stressors arising out of performing police work, particularly health problems, alcoholism, marital problems, divorce, and suicide.[2]

SOURCE: "Police Stress: The Empirical Evidence," *Journal of Police Science and Administration*, 9:1, pp. 61–75, 1981.

JOB-RELATED STRESSORS

External, internal, and task-related stressors may be grouped under the more general rubric of job-related stressors. A review of the literature reveals the existence of at least 53 stressors associated with either police work or its organization. The absolute number is less significant than is the wide range of conditions mentioned. Some authors (e.g., Eisenberg 1975; Barker 1975; and Sandy and Devine 1978) report the existence of these stressors from their own personal experiences; others report similar findings from nonrepresentative samples, such as Jacobi's (1975) analysis of disabled officers referred to him for counseling and Kroes and Gould's (1979) discussion of a similar group of officers referred to them for counseling (cf. Shev 1977). Still others report the existence of those stressors as they describe the implementation of stress control programs across the country (Baxter 1978; Potter 1978; Blanch 1977; Haines 1976; Wagner 1976; Hillgren and Spradlin 1975; Axelberd and Valle 1978; Somodevilla et al. 1978a, 1978b). None of these authors, however, present much in the way of empirical data. Consequently, discussions of police stress have relied upon French (1975) and Kroes, Margolis, and Hurrell (1974) for their empirical evidence. More recently, studies by Hageman (1978), Singleton and Teahan

(1978), and Aldag and Brief (1978), have added to these research findings at least indirectly.

French's research (1975) examines the stressors contained in a number of occupations and is one of the very few studies that compares police work with other occupations. After questioning 2,010 men, including 211 police officers and 12 sergeants and captains, he discovered that responsibility for others, complexity of work, low salaries, and lack of participation in decision making were thought to be particularly stressful aspects of a police officer's job. This last finding supports Kroes's work.

Kroes, Margolis, and Hurrell (1974), along with most other studies that examine the extent of police stress, focus upon police work itself without attempting to compare it to other occupations. They found that the chief organizational stressor, as reported by 100 Cincinnati police officers, was the department's administration. In particular, they were troubled by offensive policies, lack of participation in decision making, adverse work schedules, and lack of administrative support (especially in cases where an officer became involved in a serious incident involving the use of firearms).[3] Kroes (1976, p. 11) later wrote that these negative feelings were directed largely toward administrative policies rather than toward a lack of administrative support. However, in a more recent article by Kroes and Gould (1979, p. 10), it was reported that of 108 persons who felt that administration was a major stressor, 103 individuals reported that lack of support lay at the root of this problem.

Hageman's research (1978) is somewhat more specific than the work of French or Kroes. Rather than attempting to specify the conditions of police work that are seen as stressful, she focuses upon certain role conflicts within police work in order to examine whether there are any significant differences between rookies and veterans or married and unmarried officers. Of the 70 law enforcement officers she examined, there were no significant differences found. She did find, however, that being an officer 24 hours a day had the highest mean conflict score for married officers and that rookies experienced less conflict with time commitment, detachment, and resentment. Rookies also had higher marital happiness scores. These findings point out some of the dimensions of role conflict that are sources of friction and potential stress for police officers.

Like Hageman, Aldag and Brief (1978) present findings that are more specific in nature than those of French and Kroes. Unlike Hageman, however, they examine the relationship between role conflict and role ambiguity and the responses of officers to a number of affective and medical indices. Their sample of 99 officers reveals that role conflict and ambiguity were negatively related and statistically significant on 19 of the 24 measures employed (p. 366). Among these measures were general satisfaction, job involvement, internal work motivation, experienced meaningfulness of work, experienced responsibility for others, knowledge of the results of their work efforts, organizational commitment, satisfaction with specific facets of their job, satisfaction with supervisory leadership, satisfaction with pay, satisfaction with promotional opportunities, satisfaction with co-workers, and satisfaction with leadership consideration and initiating structures. There was, however, no statistically significant relationship between role ambiguity and satisfaction with pay nor with promotional opportunities. There was also no statistically significant relationship between role conflict and internal work motivation, satisfaction with pay, and satisfaction with co-workers. These findings indicate that role conflict and role ambiguity are troublesome aspects of police work, thus giving support and greater specificity to the work of French and Kroes.

Singleton and Teahan's (1978) research is similar to that of Aldag and Brief (1978). They divide their 90 subjects into high, medium, and low stress groups according to whether they had been injured or involved in instances resulting in injuries during the previous year. The results indicate that the high stress and medium stress groups differed significantly from the low stress group in terms of paranoia, hostility, personal conflict, and interpersonal security (pp. 357–358). There is, however, no significant difference between high and medium stress groups. In short, Singleton and Teahan report that officers who have had a recent stressful encounter with citizens, particularly in cases where they have been injured, were likely to be more defensive, suspicious, and feel that outsiders do not understand police. Such findings seem to support the notion that the stresses of field situations are a fundamental part of police work and its stresses.

Despite all of the findings in support of a stress hypothesis, much of the above research also contains contrary evidence. The findings of French (1975, pp. 60, 63), for instance, reveal that the stresses and strains of police work are not extreme. The officers that he questioned were low on job insecurity and felt that the best of their job abilities were not underutilized. They were also low on job dissatisfaction, boredom and were average on anxiety, depression, and irritation.[4] Supporting French's observations, Blackmore (1978), p. 47) and Reiser (1973, p. 6) observe that police officers are emotionally stable. In addition Reiser (1973, p. 6) notes that Raymond Cattell (1967) has argued that police officers are emotionally stable and have a temperament that is decidedly below average in anxiety and neuroticism, "a temperament which makes contact with people easier." If police work is as highly stressful as it is portrayed to be, one would not expect to find these sentiments and personal attributes.

Kroes, Margolis, and Hurrell's research (1974), while pointing to the existence of certain organizational stressors, report findings indicating that police work might not be as stressful as is usually believed. When the police officers they interviewed were asked to indicate what they found personally bothersome about their job, they failed to mention line of duty events or crises.[5] This is a curious finding, inasmuch as one would expect that this aspect of their job would be high on their list of stressors. Lewis (1973, p. 487), for example, reports that the average police officer in the Charlottesville, Virginia, Police Department observes an injured adult three times a month, a life-threatening bleeding once every three months, an injured child once every two months, a victim of a severe assault more than once every two months, and a dead person about once every two months. However, this study also shows that during an average of ten years of employment, an officer was injured only twice, with only one of these injuries requiring time off from work to recover (p. 488).

While it may be questioned whether Lewis's findings are typical of most police departments, and although Kroes, Margolis, and Hurrell (1974, p. 149) argue that officers do not like to think about these sorts of events in order to preserve their "psychological well-being," it might be argued that they view them as part of their job. Consequently, what may appear shocking, horrifying, or revolting to a lay person may be only technical problems to the police officer. Hughes (1945), for instance, argues that janitors do not turn away in disgust at the sight of garbage, nor does the undertaker become nauseous when confronted with a dead body.

There is some evidence that such attitudes develop within police work. Teahan (1975) shows that police officers became detached and hardened in their values as the result of their job. Hageman (1978), who found no differences in role conflicts between veterans and rookies, nor between married and unmarried officers, argues that officers learn to cope with occupational stressors by emotional detachment. As length of service increases, this coping mechanism becomes a part of an officer's personality. Ward (1979) supports these observations in his study of Philadelphia police officers. In particular, he examined the socialization process whereby a young officer learns to deal with the realities of death, crime, human nature, and boredom on the job. In addition to these findings, Ford, Alexander, and Lester (1971) report that police officers, mail carriers, and male college students showed no significant differences on their measures of fear of death. In explaining this finding, they speculate that the greater cooperation shown by police officers may indicate that they have worked through their personal anxieties about death. In short, police officers may well have come to see line of duty crises as an everyday part of their job. This interpretation would help explain the failure of the officers interviewed by Kroes, Margolis, and Hurrell (1974) to mention these line of duty crises as bothersome as well as indicating that the field stresses apparent to a lay person's eye are less important to police officers due to their organizational membership and consequent perception of these events as an everyday aspect of their job.[6]

PHYSIOLOGICAL EFFECTS OF POLICE STRESS

The literature on police stress shows the presence of 35 physiological effects of job-related stressors. These include virtually every ailment from headaches and sinus attacks to shrinking thalmuses, spastic colons, and grinding teeth. Direct empirical evidence for the presence of these ailments comes from several sources. Of particular importance is a paper by Kroes (1974). As Jacobi observes (1975, p. 89):

> Based on 1950 census data Kroes' findings show that no occupation exceeds that of police officers in combined standard mortality ratios for coronary heart disease, diabetes mellitus, and suicide.

More recent evidence is contained in an unpublished study by the National Institute of Occupational Safety and Health (NIOSH) of 2,300 police officers in 29 departments, which reports that 36 percent of these officers have serious health problems (cited in Blackmore 1978, p. 48). Another NIOSH study examining hospital admissions and death certificates finds that police officers ranked seventeenth out of 130 occupations (cited Blackmore 1978, p. 48). Using a similar methodology, Richard and Fell (1975) have examined a sample of 23,976 Tennessee workers, which included 168 police officers. They report that these officers had more health problems than other occupations, particularly in terms of digestive and circulatory problems (p. 79). Although other authors attribute a wider range of physiological problems to the existence of police stress, these reports indicate that the main ailments found among police officers are digestive disorders, respiratory, and cardiovascular problems.

Although Richard and Fell (1975, p. 78) report that police have "significantly high rates of premature death" and "are admitted to general hospitals at significantly high rates," they also indicate that the mean age of death for police was 54.1 years compared to 54.5 years for all other occupations (p. 81). The mean age of admission to hospitals for police was 42.5 years, as compared to 42.7 years for all other occupations. Police did not seek help at mental health facilities at rates greater than the average trend. Their reticence to use these mental health facilities is further substantiated by a NIOSH study (cited in Blackmore 1978, p. 48), which ranks police officers very low in a group of 130 occupations in regard to mental health utilization. The results of another NIOSH study (again cited by Blackmore 1978, p. 48) add further support to Richard and Fell's finding that police deaths and admissions to hospitals were high. According to this study police officers rank thirteenth out of 130 occupations in regard to deaths and hospital admissions.

These preliminary findings seem to show that police officers suffer from serious physiological problems, but that other occupations suffer still greater difficulties. Jacobi (1975, p. 89), however, citing from Kroes (1974), indicates that no other occupation exceeds police work in combined standard mortality ratios (SMRs) for coronary heart disease, diabetes mellitus, and suicide. The notion of a combined standard mortality ratio as mentioned by Jacobi is a special one[7] and tends to gloss over much interesting information. Examination of the 1950 census data upon which Kroes applies this concept indicates, for instance, that police officers suffer from high incidences of cardiovascular problems, diabetes, and suicides, but that they do not exceed all other occupations on all of these measures. Leaving aside the question of suicide until later, these data indicate that police officers from the ages of 20 to 64 have a standard mortality ratio of 158 for diseases of the cardiovascular system and a standard mortality ratio of 206 for diabetes mellitus.[8] Therefore, one can see that these diseases are found in large measure among police officers. Nevertheless as may be seen in Table 1, police officers rank tenth in SMRs for cardiovascular problems, and as may be seen in Table 2, they rank third in SMRs for diabetes mellitus.

Examination of these ratios for each ailment on an occupation-by-occupation basis indicates that law enforcement no longer stands above all other occupations in terms of physiological maladies. Examination of these ratios also reveals several other findings. The differences between these ratios is not very great (particularly in Table 2) and many of these occupational groups belong to the working classes. Thus, it may be that these physiological ailments result from membership in this social stratum, rather than from membership in certain occupational groups. Furthermore, by examining other sources of data, such as surveys conducted by the National Opinion Research Center, it appears that police officers consider themselves to be in good health and are satisfied with their state of health. As indicated in Tables 3 and 4, 84 percent of the police officers who reported on their health indicated that it was either excellent or good; whereas 77.5 percent indicated that they were satisfied with their state of health.

TABLE 1 Cardiovascular Disease SMRs for Males 20 to 64 Years of Age by Occupation (1950)

	SMR
Laborers, transportation occupations, excluding railroad workers	246
Laborers, transportation equipment	244
Laborers, furniture workers and laborers in saw and planing mills	176
Laborers, chemical and allied occupations	175
Laborers, food industry and kindred occupations	167
Musicians and music teachers	164
Cooks, excluding private households	163
Laborers, other nondurable goods	162
Firemen	161
Policemen	158

SOURCE: Guralnick (1963), Public Health Service, National Vital Statistics Division.

TABLE 2 Diabetes Mellitus SMRs for Males 20 to 64 Years of Age by Occupation (1950)

	SMR
Tailors and furriers	291
Cooks, excluding private households	225
Policemen	206
Real estate agents and brokers	200
Barbers, beauticians, and manicurists	191
Laborers, furniture workers, and laborers in saw and planing mills	175

SOURCE: Guralnick (1963), Public Health Service, National Vital Statistics Division.

OTHER EFFECTS OF POLICE STRESS

Other consequences of police work are also linked to the existence of high levels of stress among police officers. Listed among these are divorce rates, marital discord, disruption of family life, child-rearing problems, sexual promiscuity, infidelity, jealousy, loss of nonpolice friends, alcoholism, suicide, police malpractice, "John Wayne Syndrome," overachievement, callousness, exploitiveness, high rates of auto accidents in nonhazardous situations, performance anxieties, social anomie, polarization, and increasing citizen complaints and suits. Two areas about which there have been numerous empirical inquiries focus upon suicides and marital problems.

Police Divorces

The list of persons who have commented upon the high divorce rates found among police officers is indeed long (Blackmore 1978; Ward 1979; Singleton and Teahan 1978; Stratton 1978; Eisenberg 1975; Hurrell and Kroes 1975; Somodevilla 1978a; Hageman 1978; Wallace 1978; Potter 1978; and Blanch 1977). Although Danto (1978) asserts that marital problems are the single most important precipitating stress factor resulting in suicide, most statements about police divorces and marital problems are more conservative and descriptive in nature. Kroes, Hurrell, and Margolis (1974, p. 26), for instance, report that 25 of the 30 married police administrators they interviewed thought police work affected their home life. Eight of them indicated that they were not able to spend enough time with their children. Six indicated that they had to miss social events with their families. Seven indicated that their poor public image affected the social lives of their wives and children. In general, they felt that they took work pressures home with them, were overly harsh with their children, and were hard to live with. Hillgren, Bond, and Jones (1976), in reporting their interviews of 20 police administrators, present similar findings. Kroes, Margolis, and Hurrell (1974, p. 151), in their study of 100 police officers report that of the 81 married officers, 79 indicated that police work affected their home life. Most persons complained about the loss of nonpolice friends. Unmarried officers complained of difficulties involved in dating due to their unusual work schedules.

TABLE 3 State of Health as Reported by Police Officers from 1972–1977[a]

	N		N
Excellent	13	Fair	5
Good	19	Poor	1

SOURCE: NORC: General Social Survey 1972–1978.
[a] This question was not asked in 1978.

TABLE 4 Satisfaction with Health as Reported by Police Officers from 1972–1977[a]

	N		N
A very great deal	16	A fair amount	6
A great deal	11	Some	1
Quite a lot	4	A little	2

SOURCE: NORC: General Social Survey 1972–1978.
[a] This question was not asked in 1978.

On a broader level, Blackmore (1978, p. 48) reports a soon-to-be-published NIOSH study consisting of 2,300 officers from 29 departments which shows that 37 percent of these officers have serious marital difficulties. He also reports on another NIOSH study (p. 50), based upon the 1970 census, which indicates that 22 percent of the police officers sampled have been divorced at least once, as compared to a national average of 13.8 percent. For those officers married before they entered police work, 26 percent of them subsequently divorced, as compared to 11 percent of those officers who married after they entered police work. These figures are comparable to those reported by the Police Foundation which, according to Baxter (1978), indicate a divorce rate of 30 percent.[9] In addition, they are consonant with Durner, Kroeker, Miller, and Reynolds' report (1975, p. 48) indicating that 17 percent of Baltimore police, 27 percent of Santa Ana police, and 33.3 percent of Chicago police have been divorced.

Examination of these reportedly high divorce rates indicates that they may not be as high as is usually estimated. Kroes, Margolis, and Hurrell's findings (1974, p. 51) show, for instance, that only 5 percent of the police officers they interviewed were divorced. Reiser (1973, p. 29) reports low divorce rates among Los Angeles police officers. According to his 1971 survey, only 5 percent of the men sampled were divorced during the first three years of employment.[10] Of perhaps greater significance is the overall divorce-marriage ratio reported by Reiser, which stood at 21.1 percent, compared with 31.1 percent for all occupations in 1969 and 45.5 percent in 1972 (as reported by the National Center for Health Statistics). This compares with a California marriage-divorce ratio of 48.8 percent in 1969 and more recently, 75.5 percent (apparently 1972). (Cf. Reiser 1975, pp. 101–105, for a more detailed discussion of this research.)

These findings are consistent with other studies.[11] Basing his analysis upon 1960 census data, Whitehouse (1965, p. 31) reports that United States police officers and detectives had a 1.7 percent divorce rate compared with a national rate of 2.4 percent. Lichtenberger's findings (1968, pp. 95–96), based upon 1900 census data, indicate that police officers rank thirtieth out of 39 occupations in terms of divorces, and which placed them far below the divorce rates for most other occupations. Skolnick (1966, p. 266) reports that 7 percent of the 285 members of the Oakland Police Department surveyed were either separated or divorced. Bayley and Mendelsohn (1969, pp. 4–5) report that 2 percent of the 100 members of the Denver Police Department surveyed were divorced. Watson and Sterling (1969) report that 2 percent of the officers they examined in 1968 were divorced, which Niederhoffer and Niederhoffer (1978, p. 162), using census data, calculate that this figure compares with a 2.6 percent divorce rate for men older than 18. Since Watson and Sterling's survey is perhaps the most extensive of its kind, covering 294 police departments (246 of which participated) and involving 7,099 questionnaires (4,900 usable returns were received), these findings must be given considerable weight. Similarly, Niederhoffer and Niederhoffer (1978, pp. 165–168) report a low divorce rate among the police officers in their study. Their findings, however, are based upon 32 usable returns received from 150 metropolitan police departments and major state and county forces. On the basis of these returns, they calculate an average divorce rate of 2.5 percent, which compares with a 3.7 national average.

With the exception of Skolnick's findings (1966) and to a lesser extent those of Kroes, Margolis, and Hurrell (1974), and some of Reiser's findings (1973), the above-mentioned research reports indicate that police divorce rates are lower than national averages. There appears to be evidence that contradicts these findings. It is, however, often anecdotal or contained in research reports not readily available to the public. In sum, the best evidence available supports the argument that police divorce rates are lower than the popular depiction of police family life would lead one to anticipate.

Despite this conclusion, many of these studies are fraught with methodological and interpretive problems. Low return rates, for instance, impair one's level of confidence in the findings of certain studies and conceptual, operational, and interpretive problems raise serious questions about the findings of other studies. In Kroes, Margolis, and Hurrell's study (1974), for example, it is not immediately clear whether officers who indicated that they were married had ever been previously divorced. This, too, is a problem confronting Niederhoffer and Niederhoffer (1978), although they are aware of it. Of particular importance to the topic of police stress is the general failure of studies to indicate whether police officers were divorced before or after they entered police work. Without this critical piece of information, it is difficult to measure the effect police work and its stresses have upon these divorces.

Police Suicides

In addition to marital problems and divorces, suicide among police officers is frequently mentioned as a consequence of the stresses and strains of police work. Friedman (1968) reports, for example, that during the years 1937–1940, the suicide rate for New York police officers was 80 per 100,000 (cited in Dash and Reiser 1978, p. 19). According to Roberts (1975, p. 277), Friedman's report indicates that "officers are six-and-one-half times more likely to commit suicide than non-law enforcement citizens." Heiman (1975, p. 268) reports that during the years 1934–1940 the suicide rate for Chicago police officers was 48 per 100,000, and that the rate for San Francisco officers for this same period of time was 51.8 per 100,000. He also states that there were no significant differences between the police suicide rate of New York City, Chicago, and

San Francisco. Niederhoffer (1967, pp. 101–102) reports that New York police officers from 1950–1967 were twice as likely as the population at large to commit suicide. This appraisal is similar to Heiman's (1975, pp. 270–271) assessment that the New York police officer suicide rate was approximately twice that of the general population, even though the average annual rate had dropped to 19.1 per 100,000. Nelson and Smith (1970, p. 295) report that the suicide rate among Wyoming police officers during the years 1960–1968 exceeded that of all other occupations examined, with a suicide rate of 203. 66 per 100,000. In addition, they report that this suicide rate is twice that of physicians and bartenders. Richard and Fell (1975, p. 80), based upon a 50 percent random sample of all deaths from January 1972 through June 1974, report that the suicide rate of this Tennessee sample was 69.1 per 100,000. Furthermore, the police officers they examined ranked third highest among the occupational groups of their sample, surpassed only by laborers and pressmen. Finally, Guralnick (1963), using 1950 census data, indicates that the suicide rate of police officers exceeds that of all other occupations.

In examining these reports, one is struck by the wide range of suicide rates reported. Although Heiman (1975, p. 268) reports reasonably high rates of suicide for Chicago and San Francisco police officers, he also reports that there were no suicides within the Denver Police Department from 1934–1939 and that the St. Louis Police Department witnessed only 17.9 per 100,000 suicides during the same period of time. One notices as well the appearance of regional differences. Heiman (1977, p. 1287), for instance, notes that police suicides are more prevalent in the West and East than they are in the Midwest and South. One is finally struck by a sense of uncertainty about whether these suicides are high or low and/or whether they have been decreasing over the years.

Dash and Reiser (1978, p. 19) argue that police suicides may not be as high as is generally thought. Examining figures from the Los Angeles Police Department for the years 1970–1976, they report that this department witnessed a seven-year average of 8.1 per 100,000 suicides, compared to a Los Angeles County average of 16.7 per 100,000 in 1972 and 15.3 per 100,000 in 1973. These figures are also lower than the national average of 12.3 per 100,000 in 1974 and 12.6 per 100,000 in 1975. As these figures indicate, Los Angeles police officers are not plagued by higher than average suicide rates. Whether they are increasing or decreasing is a question that Dash and Reiser (1978) do not address. In commenting upon Niederhoffer's (1967) study of New York policemen, however, Reiser (1973, p. 111) notes, as did Niederhoffer, that after adjusting Niederhoffer's statistics for variations, New York officers were only 50 percent above the average for the general population. Lewis (1973, p. 486) made a similar observation in noting that blocking these figures into five-year groupings reveals a downward trend. Reiser (1973, p. 111) also notes that subsequent figures show a reduction in this suicide rate closer to the average of the general population of that area.

Such trends are difficult to substantiate given the amount of evidence available and given the ambiguousness with which some of it is presented. Heiman (1975, pp. 270–271), for example, reports that the average suicide rate for New York police officers during the years 1960–73 was 19.1 per 100,000. This rate is lower than the average suicide rate of 22.7 per 100,000 reported by Niederhoffer for the years 1950–1965 and is certainly a substantial reduction of the average rate of 80 per 100,000 reported by Friedman (1968) for the years 1934–1940. Heiman nevertheless indicates that this was twice the rate of the general white male population. He does not, however, tell the reader what this general rate is.

As with the estimates of police divorces, police suicide data are fraught with many problems. One reason for this is the general reticence of police departments to keep accurate records of suicides. Heiman (1977, p. 1288), for instance, reports that he received only 23 responses from his inquiry to at least 34 major city police departments. Of these, 6 indicated that there were no suicides during the years 1960–1973. One of these departments merely indicated "unaware of any since 1960." Four departments indicated that they did not keep any statistics. One of these departments indicated that "46 officers met violent death between 1890–1971; none appeared to be suicides." In addition, one department indicated a rate of about one a year, to which was added the comment that this information was confidential. Another department indicated that there had been at least two, but that no accurate records had been kept. Yet another department indicated that there had been at least one, but that such data were not available and that this one suicide was recalled by memory. With the exception of New York, the remaining departments indicated the occurrence of five or less suicides during this time period.

Despite these difficulties, the weight of evidence seems to indicate that police officers suffer higher rates of suicide than do other occupational groups, as may be seen in Table 5. Although this table is based upon 1950 census data, which calls into question its relevance for today's police work, it remains perhaps the most extensive occupational comparison of suicides available. Furthermore, examination of these data provides a number of suggestive clues about the relationship between police stress and police suicide. For example, Table 5 shows that there are a number of other occupations whose standard mortality ratios for suicide are close to that of police work. It also shows that these suicide rates are accompanied by high homicide rates, which suggests that police suicide rates are linked to social class membership and a subculture of violence.[12]

DISCUSSION

Despite the limited amount of empirical evidence that might be brought to bear upon the problem of police stress and despite interpretive difficulties, writers continue to claim that police work is either the most stressful occupation today or that it is among the most stressful. Goodin (1975, p. 1), for example, states: "Though policing offers many socially redeeming rewards, it is one of the most stress-filled jobs in the occupational picture today." Dash and Reiser (1978, p. 18), in a similar vein, state: "Police work is a high stress occupation. It affects, shapes, and, at times, scars the individuals and families involved." Axelberd and Valle's (1978, p. 3) statement "police work has been identified as the most psychologically dangerous job in the world"[13] indicates the existence of a consensus on this matter. Similarly, Eisenberg (1975, p. 26) notes: "Police work has been identified as one of a number of high stress occupations."

TABLE 5 Suicide and Homicide SMRs for Males 20 to 64 Years of Age by Occupation (1950)

	Suicide	*Homicide*
	SMR	*SMR*
Policemen	183	200
Laborers, fabric and metal workers	182	367
Laborers, machinery including electrical	178	310
Lumbermen, rafters, and woodchoppers	172	768
Mine operators and laborers	169	199
Laborers, transportation equipment	169	678

SOURCE: Guralnick (1963), Public Health Service, National Vital Statistics Division.

Not only do persons continue to view the nature of police work as very stressful, but they also continue to view police work as leading to physiological ailments and to other problems, such as divorce and suicide. Blackmore (1978, p. 48), for instance, points to studies showing that police officers have among the highest rates of heart disease and stomach disorders, that divorce rates are twice as high as other occupations, and that suicide rates are two to six times the national average. In a similar vein, Somodevilla et al. (1978a, p. 18) write:

> The law enforcement profession is notorious for the incidence of heart problems and in fact runs close to the top of all professions in cardiovascular insufficiency and/or impairment.

In addition, they also note (p. 10):

> Police officers have the highest rate of divorce of all professions and, according to recent research, most of it is due to a combination of the traditional demands imposed on an officer by himself, society and the organization as well as the social change affecting today's marriages.

Similarly, Axelberd and Valle (1979, p. 13) point to recent reviews of the literature on police stress as indicating "that police officers suffer an unusual amount of divorce, alcoholism, coronary heart problems, ulcers, headaches, suicide, and emotional problems" (cf. also Axelberd and Valle 1978, pp. 3–4).

From a comparative perspective, many of these observations overstate the case. That such problems are found in large enough numbers to be of concern may not be denied. Whether police work is the most stressful of all occupations, however, seems questionable. While it does appear to be a stressful occupation, that is, it is frequented by stressful situations, so are many other occupations. The nature of the stressors are, of course, different. Moreover, there are few studies of job-related stressors, particularly of the kind which look at job stressors from the point of view of rank-and-file members. Studies which look at the effects of job stress are much more numerous. It is the interoccupational comparisons of these measures which are thought to establish the case that police work is among the most stressful of all occupations. Nevertheless, these studies are fraught with numerous interpretive difficulties. Furthermore, they seem to indicate that police work does not lead other occupations in the occurrence of physiological ailments, with the possible exception of suicide; nor is it clear whether police suicides are the result of police stress or whether they are the consequence of other variables, such as a subculture of violence.

Current work in the area of police stress reveals the great conceptual and methodological complexities involved in establishing causal linkages among individual, organizational, and environmental effects. Considerable caution in analysis and interpretation must, therefore, be exercised in this area. The relationship among police stress, marital discord, and suicides may serve as an illustration. Whether a police suicide is the result of police stress, personal problems (such as marital difficulties), or such variables as social class requires careful analysis. Heiman (1977, p. 1287), for example, indicates that the average police suicide victim was divorced or was seeking divorce. He also indicates, however, that these persons have alcohol-related problems. Which of these, then, marital difficulties or alcohol-related problems, is the more important antecedent variable and what, if any, is their relationship to the stress of police work?

Caution must also be exercised in attributing to police work elements of stress. Much of the literature on police stress focuses upon the existence of certain physiological ailments, which are thought to result from stress, when, in fact, the correlation is between the existence of certain work conditions and these physiological problems. Attributing causality to stress as the agent of these ailments is therefore problematic. If, for example, it is established that heart disease is the result of sedentary occupational conditions, or if it is established that bad eating habits result in digestive disorders then one has only established a link between these work-related conditions and these illnesses, rather than between stress and these ailments.

Future research into the area of police stress may well be divided into two broad topics, one dealing with the effects of police stress, or more generally, with the physiological and other consequences often attributed to police work. The other topic would involve analyzing the conditions of police work and their relationship to police stress.

Examination of the 1950 census data suggests that mortality and health statistics may provide very interesting results. It appears, for instance, that there are a number of occupations exhibiting mortality ratios comparable to those of the police. Since many of these occupations belong to the working class, it may be hypothesized that the ailments from which these persons died are affected by social class membership. These data also suggest that race as well as a subculture of violence may be important independent variables in the determination of suicides. These variables suggest that the mortality rates and rates of physiological ailments found among police officers may be linked to broader social phenomena, in addition to, or to the exclusion of, certain occupational stressors. As Merton has suggested (1968), anomie and, by implication, its attending strains have become an ever-present feature of modern society.

The analysis of a police officer's working conditions, with which an analysis of mortality and health statistics might well be compared, involves a consideration of a number of problems. Research by Kroes, Margolis, and Hurrell (1974); Kroes, Hurrell, and Margolis (1974); French (1975); Hageman (1978); Aldag and Brief (1978); and Singleton and Teahan (1978) suggests that police officers are not as bothered by field situations as they are by the working conditions, role conflict, role ambiguities, and the administrative milieu within which they work. The number of authors who have pointed to these organizational stressors is quite numerous. Nevertheless, as Blackmore (1978, p. 55) has observed, all remedial programs currently being explored treat the effects of stress on the individual officer: "No department, however, has looked to the source of the problem and tried to systematically reduce the stress of the job." Organizational reform, therefore, seems to have taken a back seat to other alternatives, even though there is considerable evidence from the organizational literature that more participatory styles of organization and leadership produce greater worker satisfaction (cf. Brewer 1970); Day and Hamblin 1970; Fiedler 1967; Graham 1968; Gouldner 1954; Likert 1961). A recent study by Greenberg and Smith (1979) indicates that the more autonomy police officers possess, the more satisfied they are with their work. Aldag and Brief (1978, pp. 366–367) indicate that leadership consideration of individual officers, which leads to friendship and mutual trust, and leadership-initiating structures, which attempt to clarify organizational goals and direction, are significantly related to general satisfaction, satisfaction with supervision, and commitment to the organization.[14]

Future research along these lines should analyze the effects of differing work conditions upon the personnel involved. In particular, a systematic analysis of what it is that both line officers and administrators find stressful about their jobs must be undertaken. Without this most basic information, studies of the effects of police stress will remain shrouded in uncertainty. Future research must measure the relationship among work conditions and job satisfaction and job performance, as measured by the number and types of arrests, success and failure of subsequent prosecution, citizen commendations and complaints, absenteeism, the number of police officer and/or union grievances brought against the department, and the degree of personnel turnover. In addition to these endeavors, this research must examine the types of relationships that exist between line officers and administrators and develop indices which will measure the import of these differences for the individual officers involved and the levels of stress perceived by them. Examination of these relationships should also include an examination of the relationship between community leaders and administrators and the effect this has upon officers' perceptions of their job. Finally, this research should pay attention to the social mechanisms whereby individuals neutralize what otherwise might be considered stressful situations (cf. Sykes and Matza 1957; Foote 1951; Hartung 1965; and Mills 1940).

This research will be difficult, time consuming, and expensive, particularly since the sort of information desired cannot be articulated from the laboratory, as is the case with stress research that depends upon changes in an individual's physiological state as a measure of stress. This sort of research will best be accomplished in the field, using observational techniques and in-depth interviews. Out of such a body of data, a typology of line officer, administrative and community styles might be developed. These typologies could then be compared with different measures of job performance, measures of officer health, national health data, and other aspects of a police officer's life which are normally associated with police stress, particularly marital difficulties and suicide.

REFERENCES

Aldag, R. J., and Brief, Arthur D. 1978. Supervisory style of police role stress. *J. Police Sci. & Adm.* 6:362–367.

Axelberd, Mark, and Valle, Jose. 1978. Stress control program for police officers: City of Miami Police Department. Unpublished concept paper No. 1, Counseling and Stress Control Center.

———. 1979. South Florida's approach to police stress management. *Police Stress* 1 (2):13–14.

Barker, Bruce B. 1975. Methods for reducing stress in a small police department. In *Job stress and the police officer: Identifying stress reduction techniques*, edited by William H. Kroes and Joseph J. Hurrell, pp. 157–162. Proceedings of symposium in Cincinnati, Ohio, May 8–9, 1975.

Baxter, D. 1978. Coping with police stress. *Trooper* 3 (4):68, 69, 71, 73.

Bayley, David H., and Mendelsohn, Harold. 1969. *Minorities and the Police: Confrontations in America*. New York: The Free Press.

Blackmore, J. 1978. Are police allowed to have problems of their own? *Police Mag.* 1 (3):47–55.

Blanch, M. H. 1977. Psychology for law enforcement service and survival. *Police Chief* 44 (8):66–68, 104.

Brewer, John. 1970. Organizational patterns of supervision: A study of debureaucratization of authority relations in two business organizations. In *The Sociology of Organizations: Basic Studies*, edited by Oscar Grusky and George A. Miller, pp. 341–349. New York: The Free Press.

Cattell, Raymond E. 1967. *Factor description of composite policeman's profile*. Champaign, IL: Institution for Personality and Ability Testing.

Danto, B. L. 1978. Police suicide. *Police Stress* 1 (1):32–36, 40.

Dash, Jerry, and Reiser, Martin. 1978. Suicide among police in urban law enforcement agencies. *J. Police Sci. & Adm.* 6:18–21.

Day, Robert C., and Hamblin, Robert. 1970. Some effects of close supervision and punitive styles of supervision. In *The Sociology of Organizations: Basic Studies*, edited by Oscar Grusky and George A. Miller, pp. 499–510. New York: The Free Press.

Durner, J. A.; Kroeker, M. A.; Miller, C. R.; and Reynolds, W. R. 1975. Divorce—another occupational hazard. *Police Chief* 62 (11):48–53.

Eisenberg, Terry. 1975. Job stress and the police officer: Identifying stress reduction techniques. In *Job stress and the police officer: Identifying stress reduction techniques*, edited by William H. Kroes and

Joseph J. Hurrell. Proceedings of symposium, Cincinnati, Ohio, May 8–9, 1975. Washington, D.C.: U.S. Government Printing Office.

Fiedler, Fred E. 1967. *A Theory of Leadership Effectiveness*. New York: McGraw–Hill.

Foote, Nelson N. 1951. Identification as the basis for a theory of motivation. *Am. Socio. Rev.* 16 (Feb.):14–21.

Ford, R. E.; Alexander, M.; and Lester, D. 1971. Fear of death in those in high stress occupations. *Psych. Reports* 29 (2):502.

French, John R. P., Jr. 1975. A comparative look at stress and strain in policemen. In *Job stress and the police officer: Identifying stress reduction techniques*, edited by William H. Kroes and Joseph J. Hurrell, pp. 60–72. Proceedings of symposium, Cincinnati, Ohio, May 8–9, 1975. Washington, DC: U.S. Government Printing Office.

Friedman, P. 1968. Suicide among police: A study of ninety-three suicides among New York policemen 1934–1940. In *Essays in Self-destruction*, edited by E. Schneidrean. New York: Science House.

Goodin, Carl V. 1975. Opening remarks. In *Job stress and the police officer: Identifying stress reduction techniques*, edited by William H. Kroes and Joseph J. Hurrell, pp. 1–2. Proceedings of symposium, Cincinnati, Ohio, May 8–9, 1975. Washington, DC: U.S. Government Printing Office.

Gouldner, Alvin. 1954. *Patterns of Industrial Bureaucracy*. New York: The Free Press.

Graham, W. K. 1968. Description of leader behavior and evaluation of leaders as a function of LPC. *Personnel Psych.* 21:457–464.

Greenberg, Ilene, and Smith, Bradford. 1979. *Police policies and patrol officer satisfaction with department operations*. Washington, DC: National Institute of Law Enforcement and Criminal Justice.

Grencik, Judith M. 1975. Toward an understanding of stress. In *Job stress and the police officer: Identifying stress reduction techniques*, edited by William H. Kroes and Joseph J. Hurrell, pp. 163–181. Proceedings of symposium, Cincinnati, Ohio, May 8–9, 1975. Washington, DC: U.S. Government Printing Office.

Guralnick, L. 1963. Mortality by occupation and cause of death among men 20–64 years of age: United States 1950. *Vital statistics, special report* 53.

Hageman, M. J. C. 1978. Occupational stress of law enforcement officers and marital and familial relationships. *J. Police Sci. & Adm.* 6:402–412.

Haines, L. L. 1976. Error cause removal. *Police Chief* 43 (10):269–271.

Hartung, Frank E. 1965. A vocabulary of motives for law violations. In *Crime, law and society*, edited by Frank E. Hartung, pp. 62–83. Detroit: Wayne State University Press.

Heiman, M. F. 1975. Police suicide. *J. Police Sci. & Adm.* 3:267–273.

———. 1977. Suicide among police. *Am. J. Psychiatry* 134 (Nov.):1286–90.

Hillgren, J. S., and Spradlin, L. W. 1975. Positive disciplinary system for the Dallas police. *Police Chief* 42 (7):65–67.

Hillgren, J. S.; Bond, R. B.; and Jones. S. 1976. Primary stressors in police administration and law enforcement. *J. Police Sci. & Adm.* 4:445–449.

Hughes, Everett C. 1958. *Men and Their Work*. Glencoe, IL: The Free Press.

Hurrell, Joseph J., and Kroes, William H. 1975. Stress awareness. In *Job stress and the police officer: Identifying stress reduction techniques*, edited by William H. Kroes and Joseph J. Hurrell, pp. 234–245. Proceedings of symposium, Cincinnati, Ohio, May 8–9, 1975. Washington, DC: U.S. Government Printing Office.

Jacobi, Jerome H. 1975. Reducing police stress: a psychiatrist point of view. In *Job stress and the police officer: Identifying stress reduction techniques*, edited by William H. Kroes and Joseph J. Hurrell, pp. 85–116. Proceedings of symposium, Cincinnati, Ohio, May 8–9, 1975. Washington, DC: U.S. Government Printing Office.

Kelling, George, and Pate, Mary Ann. 1975. The person-role fit in policing: Current knowledge and future research. In *Job stress and the police officer: Identifying stress reduction techniques*, edited by William H. Kroes and Joseph J. Hurrell, pp. 117–129. Proceedings of symposium, Cincinnati, Ohio, May 8–9, 1975. Washington, DC: U.S. Government Printing Office.

Kroes, William H. 1974. Psychological stress and police work. Paper presented at the Third Annual Symposium of the American Academy of Stress, St. Charles, Illinois.

———. 1976. *Society's Victim—the Policeman*. Springfield, IL: Charles C Thomas.

Kroes, William H., and Gould, Sam. 1979. Stress in policemen. *Police Stress* 1 (2):9–10,44, 46.

Kroes, William H.; Hurrell, Joseph J., Jr., and Margolis,

Bruce. 1974. Job stress in police administrators. *J. Police Sci. & Adm.* 2:381–387.

Kroes, William H.; Margolis, Bruce; and Hurrell, Joseph J., Jr. 1974. Job stress in policemen. *J. Police Sci. & Adm.* 2:145-155.

Lewis, R. 1973. Toward an understanding of police anomie. *J. Police Sci. & Adm.* 1:484–490.

Lichtenberger, James P. 1968. *Divorce: A Study in Social Causation*. New York: A.M.S.

Likert, Rensis. 1961. *New Patterns of Management.* New York: McGraw-Hill.

Merton, Robert K. 1968. *Social Theory and Social Structure*. New York: Free Press.

Mills, C. Wright. 1940. Situated actions and vocabularies of motive. *Am. Socio. Rev.* 5 (Dec.):904–913.

National Opinion Research Center. 1978. *General social survey 1972–1978*. Conducted for the National Data Program for the Social Sciences at the National Opinion Research Center, Chicago.

Nelson, Z. P., and Smith, W. 1970. The law enforcement profession: An incident of high suicide. *Omega* 1 (4):293–299.

Niederhoffer, Arthur. 1967. *Behind the Shield*. Garden City, NY: Doubleday.

Niederhoffer, Arthur, and Niederhoffer, Elaine. 1978. *The Police Family: From Station House to Ranch House*. Lexington, MA: Lexington Books.

Potter, J. 1978. Liberation of the police wife. *Police Mag.* (5):39–45.

Reiser, Martin. 1972. *The Police Department Psychologist*. Springfield, IL: Charles C Thomas.

———. 1973. *Practical Psychology for Police Officers*. Springfield, IL: Charles C Thomas.

———. 1975. Stress, distress and adaptation in police work. In *Job stress and the police officer: Identifying stress reduction techniques*, edited by William H. Kroes and Joseph J. Hurrell, pp. 17–25. Proceedings of symposium, Cincinnati, Ohio, May 8–9, 1975. Washington, DC: U.S. Government Printing Office.

Richard, Wayne C., and Fell, Ronald D. 1975. Health factors in police job stress. In *Job stress and the police officer: Identifying stress reduction techniques*, edited by William H. Kroes and Joseph J. Hurrell, pp. 73–84. Proceedings of symposium, Cincinnati, Ohio, May 8–9, 1975. Washington, DC: U.S. Government Printing Office.

Roberts, Michael D. 1975. Job stress in law enforcement: A treatment and prevention program. In *Job stress and the police officer: Identifying stress reduction techniques*, edited by William H. Kroes and Joseph J. Hurrell, pp. 226–233. Proceedings of symposium, Cincinnati, Ohio, May 8–9, 1975. Washington, DC: U.S. Government Printing Office.

Sandy, J.P., and Devine, D. A. 1978. Four stress factors unique to rural patrol. *Police Chief* 45 (9):42–44.

Shev, Edward E. 1977. *Good Cops, Bad Cops*. San Francisco: San Fran. Book Co.

Skolnick, Jerome. 1966. *Justice Without Trial*. New York: Wiley.

Singleton, Gary W., and Teahan, John. 1978. Effects of job-related stress on the physical and psychological adjustment of police officers. *J. Police Science and Adm.* 6:355–361.

Somodevilla, S. A.; Baker, C. J.; Hill, W. R.; and Thomas, N. H. 1978a. Stress management in the Dallas Police Department. Departmental memorandum prepared by the Psychological Services Unit of the Dallas Police Department (Jan.):1–33.

———. 1978b. In-service stress management seminar for police officers. Mimeographed outline prepared by Psychological Services Unit, Dallas Police Department (Jan.).

Stratton, J. B. 1978. Police stress, part I: An overview. *Police Chief* 45 (4):58–62.

Sykes, Gresham, and Matza, David. 1957. Techniques of neutralization: A theory of delinquency. *Am. Socio. Rev.* 22 (Dec.):664–670.

Teahan, J. 1975. A longitudinal study of attitudes among black and white officers. *J. Soc. Issues* 31 (1):47–56.

Wagner, M. 1976. Action and reaction: The establishment of a community service in the Chicago Police Department. *Police Chief* 43 (1):20.

Wallace, L. 1978. Stress and its impact on the law enforcement officer. *Campus Law Enf. J.* 8 (4):36–40.

Ward, G. E. 1979. Physiological, psychological and social issues specifically related to the police profession. *Law & Order* 27 (1):12.

Watson, Nelson A., and Sterling, James W. 1969. *Police and their opinions*. Gaithersburg, MD: IACP.

Whitehouse, Jack E. 1965. A preliminary inquiry into the occupational disadvantages of law enforcement officers. *Police* (May–June).

NOTES

1. The most obvious reason for this emphasis probably lies with popular notions about police work. It is also influenced by the auxiliary statuses (Hughes 1958) of the police officer's role, namely, that they are white, male, and working class, statuses which are readily associated with the attributes of decisive action within dangerous situations.

2. With the exception of those stressors that properly belong to a person's inner-psychological makeup, this article will consider these external, internal, and task-related stressors under the single rubric of job-related stressors. Health problems, marital difficulties, and suicide will be treated as the consequences of these stressors, rather than as stressors themselves, even though it is apparent that these problems have an effect upon police performance, consequently compounding the effects of these other job-related stressors.

3. Complaints of this type are frequently mentioned by other authors (Reiser 1973, ch. 2; 1975; Eisenberg 1975, pp. 28, 32; Jacobi 1975, p. 93; Kelling and Pate 1975, pp. 118–120; Kroes and Gould 1979, pp. 9–10, 44; Somodevilla et al. 1978a, pp. 2–6; and Somodevilla et al. 1978b, chart B). Among other related stressors mentioned are poor supervision and communication between supervisors and subordinates (Eisenberg 1975, p. 28; Kelling and Pate 1975, p. 119); internal monitoring of police behavior (Jacobi 1975, p. 89; Eisenberg 1975, p. 28), inadequate and often inconsistent promotional and reward systems (Reiser 1975, p. 19; Eisenberg 1975, p. 28; Somodevilla et al. 1978a, p. 5), lack of clear career development guidelines, training, and clearly defined performance criteria (Eisenberg 1975, p. 28: Somodevilla et al. 1978a, pp. 5–6).

4. French points out (1975, p. 67), however, that he did not measure the effect of danger and hostile reactions from citizens. These were seen as unique stressors to the nature of police work and therefore not applicable to the other occupational groups he was examining (cf. Hurrell and Kroes 1975, p. 237; Kroes, Margolis, and Hurrell 1974, p. 154).

5. However, when these individuals were presented with a list of stressors, "crisis situations" ranked below police administration in prominence (p. 148). Moreover, when asked for the last time they felt particularly "uncomfortable," line of duty events again ranked second. These findings are of questionable validity because of the cueing that occurred during the sequence of questioning.

6. One possible exception to this interpretation is the work of Singleton and Teahan (1978, p. 359), which has shown that officers who have had a recent stressful encounter with citizens were more likely to be defensive, suspicious, and feel that outsiders do not understand police. The authors found, however, that regardless of the stress group to which the officers belonged, there were no significant differences between groups vis-à-vis increased levels of anxiety, depression, and physiological complaints (p. 358). They explained this, in part, as the result of a "defensive suspiciousness, particularly towards outsiders," which leads officers to report socially desirable responses, rather than their actual sentiments. Hence, medical complaints, anxiety, and other clinical scales used in their study were unable to discriminate among the three groups (p. 360). On the other hand, these officers did respond differentially to items of hostility, paranoia, and interpersonal sensitivity.

7. Kroes (1974) apparently develops a single standard mortality measure, but because a copy of this study was not available at this writing, this measure itself cannot be examined more carefully. Nevertheless, it would seem that such a measure might be misleading because of the information it "masks." Cooks, for example, excluding those employed in private households, are higher than police officers on the diabetes and cardiovascular ratios, but somewhat lower on the suicide measure. Apparently, however, police officers rank higher than cooks on the single measure developed by Kroes.

It is also the case that a number of occupations exceed police work on one or two measures other than those used by Kroes, particularly the ailments of influenza, pneumonia, and cirrhosis of the liver.

8. SMRs are calculated by dividing actual deaths by expected deaths and multiplying by 100. Expected deaths are calculated by multiplying the estimated population by the death rate per 100,000. For all occupations of this age group, the standard mortality ratio is 100.

9. Anthony Pate of the Police Foundation has indicated in a personal conversation that he has information from NIOSH data that the rate of divorce among police officers is twice that of the general population.

10. Examination of the NORC survey data for the

years from 1972–1978 indicates that all of the police officers included in this 10,652-person sample were either very happily or pretty happily married. These results have to be treated with great caution because of the small N (25) and the large number of missing cases. (21).

11. Niederhoffer and Niederhoffer's discussion (1978, ch. 7) of police divorce contains perhaps the best summary of the literature on this topic. This section is indebted to these authors for the many references they have provided.

12. The role of the "violent world in which many police perform their jobs" is also suggested by Richard and Fell (1975, p. 82). Guralnick's data (1963) suggest that nonwhites are more the victims of homicides than whites; whereas, whites take their own lives more often than nonwhites.

13. It is instructive to note that the emphasis here is upon psychological danger rather than real danger, which seems to indicate that a medicopsychological model of police behavior is finding its way into the police literature. As Somodevilla et al. (1978a, p. 7) observe: "Recent research studies have dispelled the image of the police officer as a two-fisted warrior in a very physically hazardous occupation. Instead, the image is that of an individual exposed to the most emotionally hazardous job of all." The point remains, nevertheless, that police work is depicted as more stressful than other occupations, regardless of whether this is conceptualized in terms of physical or emotional-psychological danger.

Regardless by whom this topic is discussed analytically, many police officers have given their lives in pursuance of their work, particularly in large urban areas where the crime problem is the greatest. This is indeed regrettable. If police work is to get a better handle on this problem, it must not view its task as more stressful and/or dangerous than it is, for to do so is to heighten the "symbolic assailant" (Skolnick 1966), which every police officer must guard against.

14. These results are, however, not without their difficulties. In controlling for role ambiguity, these relationships become greatly deflated, suggesting that role ambiguity intervenes between supervisory style and these different affective responses. No controls were run for role conflicts, apparently because there was no significant relationship exhibited between role conflict and supervisory initiating structure, although there was a significant relationship between role conflict and consideration. In short, it appears that supervisory styles are only partially able to deal with role conflicts and ambiguities. Satisfaction with work is not significantly related to either consideration or initiating structure.

11

THE POLICE FAMILY

The police profession is a jealous mistress, intruding in intimate family relationships, disrupting the rhythms of married life. The danger of police work arouses fears for the safety of loved ones. The revolving schedule of a patrol officer's "around-the-clock" tours of duty complicates family logistics.

Despite the stresses of law enforcement, police wives cope with the tensions. They block out anxiety about death and injury to their spouses when on patrol; they coordinate their sexual and social timetables to conform to the rigidity of the work chart. Police wives become therapists in residence—compassionate, supportive, understanding. Intuitively, they realize that a husband who goes on duty after an explosive argument with his wife will be on a short fuse when he is on the beat. And predictably, when he returns from work, he may find it hard to turn off the flashing red lights and the screaming sirens.

Although wives adapt to the pressures of the occupation on family life, they, nevertheless, gripe about the injustices and inconsistencies. They resent the "secret society" nature of police work that obstructs free-flowing communication between spouses. Paradoxically, although they are treated as aliens in the police world, their family lifestyle is scrutinized by a curious public. Outspoken in their opposition to policewomen as partners on radio-car patrol with their husbands, wives of officers freely confess they are not only jealous of the intimate contact of mixed-gender car patrol, but also fearful that policewomen lack the strength and stamina to protect their male counterparts in life-threatening situations.

These occupational hazards contribute to the prevailing perception that divorce is rampant in police marriages, far exceeding the rate of the general population. Police personnel and social scientists share this view. Why do police marriages have such a bad press? One answer may be that because of the strains of police work, the occupation becomes the scapegoat when a marriage is in trouble. Stated simply, when marital relationships are going smoothly, she's OK, he's OK, the job's OK. Research reveals, however, that divorce police-style equates with divorce American-style.

Children place pressure on any marriage. However, children of police couples do not feel the weight of the shield in their early years; the image of a loving, nurturing, father figure is dissociated from the profession. It is in the midteens that a sense of special identity as children of police parents crystallizes and conflict may develop. Because officers have seen so much disaster in street society, they tend to be overcautious, overprotective, and oversuspicious with their own children and intolerant of their misconduct. In addition, a police parent, who is an authority figure—independent and in-charge on the job—may not be able to discard this approach to interpersonal relations when he or she travels from station house to ranch house. Consequently, police identity may spill over into the father-figure role. Typically, at adolescence, teenagers resent surveillance and domination of their activities. Despite this potential for tension, the children in police families appreciate their police parent as an anchor of stability during the years of coming of age.

The first reading is written by a police couple married to the police job for more than twenty years. During this time they commuted smoothly from station house to ranch house. Here they share their observations about law enforcement couples based on probing questionnaires, in-depth interviews, personal experiences, and informal rap sessions.

Policemen's Wives: The Blue Connection

Arthur Niederhoffer and Elaine Niederhoffer

Under the romantic umbrella of courtship and idyllic love, the police shield radiates the illusion of a valorous knight wooing his fair lady. For the affianced couple this idealized view of the law enforcement officer as chivalrous protector and provider complements mutual emotional needs. But the exigencies of the occupation soon filter through this layer of euphoria. Even on her wedding day, no doubt chosen expediently to conform to the groom's unconventional work schedule, the bride of the police officer senses that she has married not only the man, but also his job. Nevertheless, she would have to possess extraordinary powers of ESP to envisage that this invisible member of the wedding party could become as oppressive and intrusive as any stereotypical mother-in-law.

The shadow of the job darkens normal conjugal routines. The rhythm of existence switches abruptly every week, reminding the policeman's wife that she is a Cinderella with midnight the pivot around which the family schedule rotates. Generally, a member of the force must work around the clock, with tours of duty that alternate each week from midnight to 8 A.M. (the late tour or night shift) to 8 A.M. to 4 P.M. (the day tour) to 4 P.M. to midnight (the evening shift) and then repeat the cycle.

Because the revolving chart does not conform to the conventional work week, weekends and days off rarely coincide. A police officer may have to wait 15 years to accumulate enough seniority to warrant a vacation during the summer months. One shift out of three a wife may wait up past midnight in order to greet her husband. But the timing is bad: he's all keyed up, and she's half asleep.

The most difficult adjustment for the wife grows out of the late tour (midnight to 8 A.M.). Every third week she sleeps alone while her husband works the "graveyard" shift. Especially in these times of high crime rates, her imagination has been traumatized by the gory tales spotlighted by television and screaming newspaper headlines. As a result, many police wives lie awake nights for hours, lonely and fearful, translating the night sounds into threats against her, her children, and even her spouse. If she is a sensual person, her sexual cravings remain unsatisfied during those long nights.

When police officers return home after a late tour, some are eager for sex. But their individual marital clocks are set to a different meridian. The wife may not be in an amorous mood or a seductive pose after spending an insomniac night. She may be unwinding from the frenetic experience of packing the kids off to school and may be morosely contemplating the unpleasant chore of cleaning the house or getting dressed for work.

A marriage counselor we know managed to resolve this incompatibility of one frustrated police couple on the verge of divorce. The husband was convinced that his wife had no real feeling for him because whenever he came home from a late tour, his wife immediately fell into a deep sleep, forestalling any possibility of sexual relations. At a joint therapy session the wife explained that she worried so much when her husband worked the late shift that she could not sleep at all. But, when she heard his key turn in the door, the sound soothed her and acted like a powerful sleeping potion. As soon as the couple discovered that the reason for

SOURCE: Excerpted with permission of the publisher, from *The Police Family* by Arthur Niederhoffer and Elaine Niederhoffer (Lexington, Mass.: Lexington Books, D.C. Heath and Company, copyright 1978, D.C. Heath and Company).

their sexual impasse was concern rather than indifference, together they plotted a more coordinated sexual timetable.

Other policemen, exhausted by the night's duty, may look forward to falling into bed in a quiet room. The wife tiptoes about, shushing the younger children, pulling the shades on the sun to simulate night, in order to facilitate his sleeping by day. But the exuberant spirits of preschoolers cannot be turned down by drawing the curtains. The responsibility and the pressure are on the wife. A final group of officers has learned to avoid any type of family confrontation—sexual or other—by stopping off on the way home for a few beers with the boys so that they will be drowsy enough to fall asleep as soon as they hit the bed. Drinking with the boys may also act as a decompression chamber to release the tensions of the tour. Police officer-psychologist Harvey Schlossberg points out perceptively:[1]

> The shift that ends at midnight, when he is still wound up from the excitement of the day and wants companionship and gaiety is the one that may lead to trouble for both the bachelor and the married Don Juan.

Interestingly, it is this 4 P.M. to 12 midnight tour that most male police officers prefer to work. Moreover, the realities of law enforcement, necessitating overtime duty in emergencies, unanticipated court appearances, extra hours for changing into and out of uniform, and time for commuting long distances to out-of-the-way precincts for special assignments extort onerous demands of her husband's already tight and intermittent swing-shift schedule. And the wife twists in the whirlpool of the job as well; her biological rhythms are distorted and social interaction becomes disorganized as she struggles in frustration to juggle engagements and to rearrange upset plans. After many broken dates, even close friends give up.

Contrary to the lyrics of the folk song that joyfully proclaim "everybody loves Saturday night," that last evening of the week can be interminably long and depressing to those sitting home alone. Typical domestic vignettes, although reported to us by police wives in a bantering and accepting tone, point up some of the inconveniences of forced accommodation to an arbitrary police work schedule when family life is involved:

> Serving at 6 P.M. a breakfast special of orange juice, bacon and eggs, and "pouring coffee over the head" of a heavy-lidded husband, half-awake after his unsuccessful attempt to sleep during the day after a late tour.
>
> Gaining 15 pounds sharing midnight snacks in a spirit of camaraderie with her husband after his 4 P.M. to midnight shift.
>
> Coordinating the sexual timetable with the rigidity of the duty chart.
>
> Missing the school picnic, the event of the year, and trying to console the children.
>
> Drinking champagne alone on New Year's Eve.
>
> Serving Thanksgiving dinner at an 11:30 A.M. brunch because one wife remembered wistfully her own childhood disappointment when her father, a train engineer, missed festive family occasions.

How does the police spouse cope with the stresses of scheduling when children are involved? One police wife sums up her frustrations concerning the disruptive effects of the changing shifts:[2]

> One week, the children have free run of the house. Friends can come in to play and watch TV because Dad is working 8–4, and the next week I'm scolding them to be quiet, no noise. Dad is sleeping because he is working 12–8. Now that the children are in school the 4–12's are the hardest because they often go five days without seeing their father. They leave for school before he is awake, and he is at work when they come home. Talks, advice and sharing often have to wait until his day off.

When a police wife has a job outside the home, a side effect might be that the inflexibility of the police clock could complicate family logistics even more. Indeed, in a television documentary on a black police family, the working wife did complain to her husband, "If we see each other ten hours a week, it's a lot. When I'm going, you're coming."[3]

This stockpile of grievances against the evening and late tours explains why two-thirds of the wives we polled prefer the 8 A.M. to 4 P.M. shift.

And despite the dearth of prime time for family togetherness, most police wives minimize their vexations and assert that the erratic tempo of the police timetable does not adversely affect family life. They become adept at juggling time; they complain, but they cope.

One candid police wife ruefully admitted:[4]

> The only obstacle to police work that I had trouble with was the promotional process. And it only took seven short years to adjust to it. Charlie has been promoted twice so

far, and now we're sweating out the Lieutenants' List. He studies for the promotional exam during his off hours for four months prior to the test. During those four months I see him when he wakes up, when he eats, and when we go to sleep if he is not working the 12–8 shift. When it's time to study, I've learned to smile (most of the time) and say, "See you later."

Of necessity, a police wife must cope with pressing problems endemic to her husband's work. In her situation the ring of the doorbell or the telephone does not signal a pleasant interlude but portends an ominous alarm—a threat of another crisis or emergency that wrests her husband from her while proclaiming the absolute power of the job. She lives with the frightening awareness that her husband on patrol is virtually a soldier on the firing line. Her role must be that of the rear echelon backup suffused with the attendant anxiety, unnerved by the shriek of every siren, distraught at each snatch of crime news on radio or television. It is this apprehension that is the common denominator binding police wives together.

Are you scared to death? The one thing police wives have an excess of is fear: fear of the other woman, fear of the gun, fear of the criminal, fear of the husband being killed, fear of being alone late at night, etc. You name it and we all have it. You may not verbalize it, but it's there.[5]

The wife's fear is the mirror image of the sense of danger that sociologist Jerome Skolnick found to be the vital force shaping the police officer's working personality.[6] For the man on the beat, it engenders an exaggerated suspicion that reduces other people to the level of symbolic assailants. In fact, this suspicion may be confirmed statistically because "the police are the only peacetime occupational group with a systematic record of death and injury from gunfire and other weaponry."[7] It is this element of danger that "isolates the policeman socially from that segment of the citizenry which he regards as symbolically dangerous and also from the conventional citizenry with whom he identifies."[8] Thus, cut off from intimate interaction with civilian groups, the police officer falls back on his wife. Thrown together with few competing social relations, the connection becomes symbiotic and dramatically intense. The wife, already sensitized by her own apprehension, fatalistically identifies with her husband's perception of danger.

No matter how independent and resistant wives may be at first, eventually they are infected by anxiety concerning their husbands. A poignant illustration of this concern occurred at a lecture for policemen's wives by a high-ranking administrator commanding a new police department unit expressly established to provide a full range of services to the wives. The first question from a wife, "Who will notify me if my husband is killed or seriously injured on the job?" provoked a discussion that occupied the audience for more than 20 minutes.

Other wives have complained bitterly about the practice of the networks in broadcasting news of injured or slain police officers before formal notification is made to the family of the victim. Radio and television newscasts circulate the facts and then add that the name of the officer is being withheld pending notification of the next of kin. Many wives, hearing this, become frantic and bombard their husbands' precincts with desperate telephone calls.

Fear operates just as radically upon the wives, whether their husbands are members of large or small departments. How they verbalize their gut feelings is as varied as the wives themselves, and spans the spectrum from subdued frustration to overt pessimism. The wife of a former New York City police commissioner acknowledged that she shared her own sense of foreboding with other police wives:[9]

I think most police wives have the same thoughts in the back of their minds—it's always there. You don't continually think about it but you're always happy to see him walk in after a 12–8 and you give a quiet Amen.

Psychological sisters in the similarity of their response to the danger implicit in their husbands' work, other police wives have vocalized their subliminal alarm. This worry appears to be a ubiquitous syndrome of law enforcement wives around the globe. From the Midwest a spouse reflects:[10]

I think what you're asking me is, "Will he come home again?" I never think about this, at least on the surface, but I know it's in the back of my mind. At such times, my philosophy is: What will be will be.

The wife of a constable in Toronto comments:[11]

I'm really not sure that the factor of his coming home again sits that firmly in my mind. Some of the other police wives talk about it, but—from my standpoint—it's not something I dwell on, unless—of course—if a dangerous situation in-

> volving police and criminals gets a lot of publicity. Then, it would bother me, because the awareness would be there. But do you know what's odd about all this?
>
> It's the fact that I seem to worry more now about Paul than I did in the beginning, even though he's been a constable [patrolman] for over 12 years.

And an excerpt from a letter written by an Australian constable's wife reveals:[12]

> It is such a good feeling to hear the car pull into the garage at night, 2 hours overdue and to see one's husband get out of the car all in one piece, after lying in bed for hours imagining all sorts of danger that he could have confronted.

Another police spouse describes how she blocks fears for her husband's safety on the job:[13]

> As the wife of a policeman, I am certainly realistic enough to be aware of the hazards of my husband's work. However, I do not indulge in the thought of his not coming home. I have managed to be equipped with a personal inner strength; but more importantly, an inner faith.

How can wives shunt intimations of tragedy from their thoughts when they are barraged so unrelentingly by the media? Headlines blazon crime and violence; perilous actions of law enforcement officers saturate front pages; television and novels sensationalize police work into gun-blasting adventure; police magazines and departmental newsletters feature news of ambushes and assaults upon the members of the force. But no matter how this morbid fascination of the media prepares the wife, when serious injury occurs to her husband, the anticipation never mitigates the personal horror of the episode.

After her husband, a 17-year veteran of the force, was nearly blinded by a mixture of lye and ammonia hurled at him by a barricaded ex-convict gone berserk, the shocked wife of the victim mused: "Even though you're married to a policeman, you're never prepared for this. The news didn't really sink in until this morning, waking up alone."[14]

Contributing to this disquietude, immediate and tangible omens of the ultimate disaster—a police officer slain in action—thrust their barbs at the morale of vulnerable wives:

> An innocuous request from a police society to her husband to assist at an outing for children of officers killed on duty. The funerals of police heroes where they are honored posthumously with the same ceremonial rituals accorded a slain inspector, replete with flag-draped coffin, muffled drumbeats, hundreds of uniformed fellow officers assembled in respectful tribute to a fallen comrade, and the final pathetic touch—the distraught widow supported by comforting relatives and friends.

Depressing confirmation of the wives' premonition of disaster is reinforced by the annual charts that tabulate macabre figures on the number of police officers that are killed and assaulted in the United States.

Would it not be natural, then, for a wife to react emotionally and interpret these impersonal computations into a grim statistic of one?

Overwhelmed by the mounting apprehension, some police wives have gone so far as to advise others, "Treat each day as if it were the last day of your husband's life," and to suggest that the casual kiss goodbye to a husband leaving for work might very well be a farewell embrace for eternity. And so with all this buildup of anxiety surfacing in our personal encounters with wives, articulated at meetings of police wives' associations, and corroborated by anecdotal evidence from other sources, we were reasonably certain that it would not require a sensitive seismic device to detect their tremors of concern for their spouses' welfare. Accordingly, we predicted that their responses to our question, "When your husband is at work, do you worry about his safety?" would register high on this scale of worry. Instead, the wives reacted contrary to our inferences, as they also did to questions about adaptations to their spouses' around-the-clock work schedule. The overwhelming majority did not worry much.

What is the explanation for this discrepancy between their spoken words and their tallied responses? Dr. Bruce Danto of the Department of Psychiatry at Wayne State University suggests a rationale for these contradictory patterns.[15]

> Death expectation would appear to be important for the wife of a police officer for three reasons: she is aware of the danger inherent in her husband's work; she may see him through various kinds of injuries incurred through his work; and she is a member of the police family in the sense that she associates with other wives of officers and shares experience, loneliness, and doubt. It might be assumed that until such danger clues are present the police officer's wife deals with the prospect of injury and death through denial. She may unconsciously block fears of his dangerous tasks and the risks he takes. She may feel that such fate is for someone else, not for her and her husband.

Solving this paradox and translating this sophisticated psychological analysis into language more appropriate for the police family, a cop's wife asserts:[16]

> Often I am asked, "Don't you worry about your husband's getting killed?" Of course I do, but if I worried about it constantly, I would not be able to function as a wife, parent or—as is so often necessary—as both parents to my children.

Personnel of the employee relations section of the New York City Police Department become intimately acquainted with the fortitude of police wives, because this unit has the responsibility of notifying the next of kin when a police officer is killed or seriously injured while on duty. In an attempt to soften the shock, a team consisting of a captain from this division, a chaplain, and the police partners of the dead or stricken officer go at once to his home to inform the wife. A captain of this command told us that frequently the men in the team break down and have to lean on the grieving wife for support and consolation. Somehow, she finds the strength to bear the heartache.

In actuality, there is little choice for the police wife. Either she finds the psychological resources to bend resiliently under the crushing strains and stresses of the occupation and snap back or she will break under the pressure, with consequent disruption in family relationships. And many wives do possess this flexibility and insight:[17]

> It is not all honey and roses. We are truly a special breed. We must have the foreknowledge of twenty average wives, the stamina of ten men and the patience of a saint. The average wife can have a fight with her guy and let him go off to work without a second thought. We cannot do that, because he might not come home. We do not dwell on this thought; it will do neither one of us any good but it is a very real hard fact that we do live with.

The manifest destiny of the policeman's wife is eventual submission to the job. Submission does not necessarily denote defeat, however. She copes by forging a new role—therapist to her husband—requiring her to be supportive, compassionate, and attentive. Since the impact of the job is funneled through her husband, her best defense is to nullify its adverse effect upon the marriage by fortifying him. To be consistent, her design is to convert the home into a haven, a buffer zone.

Typically, the wife pays a price for this successful adjustment. By assuming the traditional function of the homemaker subordinate to that of the male breadwinner, she may have to sacrifice many of her own aspirations and derive her sense of accomplishment vicariously through the exploits of her husband.

Several guidebooks written by police wives provide the blueprints for this lifestyle of self-help psychology, delegating responsibility to the loving helpmate at home for smoothing out the strains of law enforcement. These do-it-yourself handbooks on the power of positive thinking suggest that following their curriculum for adaptation will ensure domestic tranquility.

> Girls, I hope this doesn't upset you, but I personally don't think that women's liberation has any place within a police department. You need to be a little happy homemaker. If your guy is happy, you'll be happy.[18]

> Understand the man, find out what kind of a wife he wants. Then be that kind of a wife and you'll probably never have to worry too much about losing him.[19]

> Sometimes a wife can best help a husband who's down by fixing him a good meal. She can help by being available to talk if he wants that, by steering his thoughts away from his hostilities, being considerate and sympathetic without encouraging self-pity, by understanding his silence during dinner and his unresponsiveness in bed and by just loving him. Understanding his need for status and sense of personal worth and realizing he's in a game where all are losers, she can serve as an ego-builder when that's what he most needs. A psychologist says there's nothing like a judicious pat on the back to keep a man from getting ulcers.[20]

The candid answers of police wives to our open-ended question, "Do you have any advice that might be of help to other police families?" confirm that many of them have internalized these popular sentiments and have incorporated them into the family milieu. Curiously, the lower the rank and the shorter the time on the job, the more likely the wife was to give advice to other police couples. A sampling of typical responses to this item articulates this point of view:

> Never let your husband walk out that door angry with you. Apologize whether you're right or wrong. It may be the last time you get the chance.

> Give all the support, love and compassion you can. Smile, be cheerful and pray for him. Most of all, be proud of him.

> As a family stick together. Advice for a wife—be tolerant, try to understand and always be there when needed. Advice given to me many years ago by a policeman's wife. Don't

ever send him off to work mad or with an empty stomach. Our lives are different and outsiders don't care. Just try to make the best of it.

Patience. Understanding and as much objectiveness as possible in trying to understand the job and how it affects the man. Respect him, but don't expect him to be superman. Because of the tension involved in this kind of job I believe a pleasant home atmosphere is of the utmost importance. He has to react too quickly on the job to have unsettling thoughts of home following him throughout the day.

Well, I think the important thing for a wife is to work extra hard at loving her husband. Give him understanding and if he needs to blow steam off once in a while, let him do it. The only thing it hurts is your ears. My husband and I don't fight if he is in a bad mood. I let him blow off all the steam and when the fire is gone then we discuss.

To be as patient as humanly possible. To live each day to its fullest. Do things as a family unit (bicycle riding, bowling, etc.). Always communicate. A family not only shares good times, they should also share the hard times.

If a man goes on the job, and he really wants it, the woman (wife) has got to stick behind her husband all the way. If a man isn't happy with his job, this could cause marital problems. The wife of a patrolman must be strong. A patrolman's wife leads a very lonely life. Nite after nite (sic) I sit and restlessly wait for my husband to come thru (sic) the door and when he finally comes home I thank God for another day.

You must realize that when he becomes a cop he will make a definite change in attitude and personality. Sometimes he might go a little crazy for a while. Try to be patient and understanding. They will eventually come down to earth. Another thing I try to stress is trust. Learn to trust him and love him a lot because he's got a real tough job.

Always make the most of the time you have together. The rotating shifts are especially difficult when children are in school and so the time spent as a family unit is valuable. Make your home as pleasant as possible, a place where he knows he is wanted, needed and loved very much. Don't nag about the hours and the social engagements you miss because of the shifts, remember he misses them too. Get yourself involved in other activities so time doesn't hang heavy when he is working. Most important of all, love him a lot—he has to put up with some pretty bad scenes in the course of his day—help him to enjoy his time away from the job.

Don't sit by and watch your man worry. Help him by listening to his problems. And then try to help him solve them. If your son or daughter comes home and tells you the P.T.A. needs cakes for their sale you're right there. If the local afternoon bridge club is short one player you can leave the dishes and let the housework go. These people and monetary things can all wait. Your husband has the toughest job of all so give him your all.

Yes, I see the younger couples today leading really very separate lives. Don't try to plan just for your own immediate family outings, picnics, take the children to the park, visiting, etc. Love each other and be understanding of job-related problems. Be grateful and learn to be a self-content person. Be close to your children as their father will eventually see and appreciate all your efforts. Put your free time to good constructive use in whatever makes you as a person, well and happy.

On the surface, the marital philosophy of the police wives resembles the system expounded by Marabel Morgan, who conducts seminars to convert wives to the doctrine of the "Total Woman."[21] She admonishes every wife to live through her husband and to "Accept Him! Admire Him! Adapt to Him! and Appreciate Him!" But Morgan administers an overdose of submission in her prescription for happiness in marriage. In our opinion, most police wives would consider it debasing to accept her formula of "total" immersion.

> A Total Woman caters to her man's special quirks, whether it be in salads, sex, or sports. She makes his home his haven, a place to which he can run. She allows him that priceless luxury of unqualified acceptance.[22]
>
> Love your husband and hold him in reverence, it says in the Bible. That means admire him. *Reverence* according to the dictionary, means "To respect, honor, esteem, adore, praise, enjoy, and admire."[23]
>
> It is only when a woman surrenders her life to her husband, reveres and worships him, and is willing to serve him, that she becomes really beautiful to him. She becomes a priceless jewel, the glory of femininity, his queen![24]

The difference between the two groups seems to be that the Total Woman senses a threat of danger to her marriage, while the police wife senses a threat of danger to her husband. As a result, their tactical objectives reflect this contrasting motivation: for the Total Woman, an improvement in her inner security; for the police wife, an improvement in her husband's well-being. Nor would a policeman's wife endorse Morgan's placebo of contrived sexuality as typified by one of her personal anecdotes describing how she greets her husband at the door wrapped in "pink baby-doll pajamas and white boots after a bubble bath."[25] Nor would the ambience of the police work situation permit the wife of a policeman to copy Janet, one of Morgan's disciples, who telephoned her spouse to say, "Honey, I'm eagerly waiting for you to come home. I crave your body."[26]

Adaptation to the job by the police wife in no way connotes servility. Submission to the constraints and exigencies of police work cannot be avoided, but this should not be misinterpreted as encompassing subservience. In many ways her mode of adjustment can be defined as an affirmation of her interpersonal competence. She is fulfilling the role of therapist, whose empathy provides equilibrium and contentment to another human being in need. She is convinced that the overtones of her regimen will resonate to absorb and soften the tensions of the occupation. And her own personal fulfillment will be derived through her loved one. A wife develops her role as a response to the challenge posed by her husband's occupation. In turn, her spouse enjoys the benefits and encourages her.

This talent for adaptation is the kind of self-actualization that Abraham Maslow and other behavioral psychologists advocate.[27] It occurs customarily in healthy people who are realistic, problem-centered rather than self-centered, autonomous, and self-accepting. A police wife functioning smoothly in a successful marriage fits this portrait.

The key word—adaptability—translates just as fluently into the sexual sphere. These women have managed to neutralize the shattering of the circadian rhythms and the fusion of job-related anxieties, the two factors that are offered as damning evidence that police marriages are riddled with emotional and sexual conflict. A convincing majority of law enforcement couples who responded to our questionnaires reported sexual compatibility in their marriages.

Although police wives have made peace with the profession, by no means are they brainwashed. There is no occupational mystique; they comprehend all the shortcomings and injustices and they gripe:[28] "My mother always told me never to marry a salesman or a policeman. She said he'd never be home when I needed him. So, of course, I did what she told me not to do." Almost 50 percent of the wives whose patrolmen and detective husbands rank at the bottom of the hierarchy complained about low salaries, low public prestige, and the biased promotion and disciplinary system. In culmination of their simmering discontent, 80 percent of the wives wanted their mates to retire from police work when they become eligible to do so, although it would be an economic hardship because of the inadequate pensions.

Ever sensitive to the pressure points of police work, most of the wives have compromised and repressed their resentment, opting for a peaceful coexistence as aides-de-camp in a buffer zone. This ambience of compliance diverges from the tenets of the emerging feminist climate of contemporary middle-class America, which so disparages the archetype of the traditional female role in the family.

For the police officer husband, it is equally rewarding to contemplate a daily ego massage and to be the center about which family life orbits. And by his tacit approval he stamps in this mode of behavior.

The police job intrudes as a grey eminence, a shadowy partner in this merger. When everything is going smoothly, she's OK, he's OK, the job's OK. And elastically, the wife flexes with the tension of law enforcement. She has learned to "cool it" and maintain her equanimity when confronting the erratic jumps of the work schedule and the gloomy threat of danger.

The formidable responsibility of safeguarding the police revolver was accepted with nonchalance by nearly 50 percent of our sample of American wives to whom it presented no problem at all; to another 20 percent, it caused only minor inconvenience. Police wives routinely carry a large handbag on trips to the beach, etc., to store the weapon safely when, obviously, it would be impossible for their husbands to comply with the regulation requiring them to have the firearm in their possession at all times.

In a police marriage already in trouble, however, these tangential occupational obligations often aggravate conditions. Contrast the remarks of this disgruntled police wife, staying married for the sake of the three children, who perceives her husband's police revolver as a horrible excrescence: "There's that gun. I hate it. It's with him, part of him, 24 hours a day, attached to his body. It's like a cancer, a large tumor, sticking out of his body."[29]

Interpersonal relations thrive on communication. And certainly, free-flowing lines are a prerequisite for the success of a marital partnership. Because the police wife has invested so heavily in the marriage by assuming a vicarious role in relation to her husband, she ends by becoming dependent on her spouse for the infusion of thrills and adventures as he recounts his experience on the job. She can relieve humdrum domestic routines by enjoying at second hand the excitement of police work. Her psychological stance cries out for open and full communication to prove intimacy and trust. One authority on the sociology of the family proposes that "the assumption in back of these beliefs is that many, if not most, problems exist because people do not communicate and therefore do not understand one another."[30]

But the police officer operates on his own wavelength. He finds it expedient not to reveal much about his work. Formulating his own concept, based on the secret society nature of the police force, he learns or is conditioned to be closemouthed about his job. Much of his work is too confidential; much of it is too revealing about conditions within the department or on the beat. Even in an intimate relationship a policeman senses that it would be discreet to keep these matters concealed from his wife. His code of silence may also be prompted by a chivalrous desire to protect his family from exposure to the real depths of society's violence, brutality, and personal agony. Without knowing it, the husband by a combination of occupational conventional wisdom and personal reticence has moved beyond the simplistic rule of full disclosure that is widely advocated but often proves a cause of dissension. He has reached a more sophisticated level that calls for a high degree of interpersonal competence in which the partners accept the principle that "probably selective communication is the key to the successful marriage. There are some thoughts and desires and attitudes which are destructive when communicated."[31]

The flaw in this arrangement is that both partners must accept the contract on communication. We found in our interviews with police wives that many of them resented and deplored the withholding of information and news. One wife wistfully contrasted the reticence of her police officer husband with the relaxed free flow of citizen-band communication.

No matter how intensely interested and involved they would like to be, most police wives are decisively locked out of their husbands' work world. Department fiat and the police officers' shared views of protocol preclude any significant or even potential intervention on her part. A psychological barrier, compounding her feeling of being an outsider, prevents her from entering the physical field of her husband's police duty: the beat he patrols.

For once the male chauvinistic ideology cannot be blamed for the police protocol that discourages the presence of the wives in locations where their spouses are on patrol. The wife of an office worker can visit her husband's place of business occasionally and chat casually with his fellow employees while the children explore the copier, the computer, and the switchboard. At most the visit causes a few minutes of delay in the office routine, but it is usually considered a pleasant interlude by everyone. But the policeman's office is in the street where theoretically he may be at any moment encountering emergency, disaster, or crime. This constant threat of danger would justifiably deter a conscientious officer from encouraging his family to visit him on post. Even on those occasions when he is assigned to relatively peaceful and enjoyable duty at a parade or sporting event, the crowds and congestion prevent a close view of a police officer husband. Presumably, it would require an unusual degree of self-confidence or perhaps naiveté for a police wife to violate this unwritten code in order to observe her husband in action. Statistical affirmation of the gulf separating the work space and the living space, with the attendant avoidance syndrome, appeared in our questionnaire. In our sample of wives, the majority (54 percent) had never observed their husbands on duty, fewer than 4 percent had observed them frequently, and the remaining group had observed them only seldom.

And while a police wife may not have actually pounded a beat with her spouse, she can tread the transparently thin line between on patrol and off duty. How the occupation erects a gangplank between work and leisure time has been outlined to us by law enforcement families in these scenes of thwarted recreational activity:

> A police officer aborts his family's long-awaited vacation trip because on the congested highway he stops to arrest a drunken driver who had been endangering other motorists.
>
> A police officer intercepts a holdup in progress while routinely sharing the marketing chores with his wife at the local supermarket.
>
> A police officer spoils an evening out on the town with his wife by jumping off a crosstown bus to apprehend a teenage hoodlum in the act of mugging an old man.

Some departments, breaking with the conservative policy of keeping wives away, have taken an opposite and innovative direction by going out of their way to acquaint wives with a sense of what the occupation is about. They are permitting and encouraging police wives to accompany their spouses on radio car patrol once or twice. Modeling his program closely after a plan instituted on the West Coast, the chief of the Lockport, New York, 50-man police force introduced this type of ride-along project.[32] On an experimental basis and for only a two-month period, he invited wives to accompany their husbands on patrol for three hours from 7 P.M. to 10 P.M. on weekday nights (usually quieter than the weekends). By sensitizing wives to the pressures of the job, he hoped that they might develop an empathy to their husbands' work situation; and thus they might achieve the chief's long-range goal, which was to shore up the floundering marriages in his department in which the divorce rate stood at a menacing 20 percent.[33]

> If they can understand why their husbands just can't come home at night and be the typical husband or father after dealing with the kind of people they do for eight hours, that they just can't turn it off, then it might help their marriages.

But even when urged to join their husbands in the field, more than half the wives eligible to do so did not participate. Evidently once they had compartmentalized these disparate zones, they did not wish to trespass. This reaction is consistent with our finding that more than half the wives in our survey had never observed their husbands at work. Judging from the evaluation by some of the wives who did ride as radio car partners, the program was only partially successful. Several wives felt too frightened by the imminent danger; others thought that they were too shielded from serious calls. But as a result of these mobile sensitivity training sessions, a few did develop an insight into the reasons for their husbands' moodiness and taciturnity when they finished their tours of duty.

Whether she is consumed with eagerness to participate or overwhelmed by apprehension, a police wife feels like an alien in the police world. Law enforcement news of any import is censored, filtered through the dark prism of her husband's guarded revelations. If she tries to break through the wall of resistance by so much as a telephone call to her husband's precinct station house, she is made to feel that she is doing the wrong thing:

> We as police wives, need to be extra careful of everything we do and say because at times our motives are not completely understood. It is not a good policy to call your husband at the station unless it is essential.[34]

The police wife who wrote that advice to others cautioned that wives who demand a share of their husbands' work life "are sometimes called 'bitch' behind our backs by other officers."[35]

> You can't call him. If you do, the other cops will think he's henpecked. They'll make his life miserable. The only time you can call is if something really, really serious comes up.[36]

And when there is an emergency at home, police wives may have to dial 911 like anyone else. They know that to get a message through to their husbands will take too long.

Motivated by the psychology of the outsider, a police wife compensates by reaching out for a sense of community into her immediate neighborhood. And like other subjects involved in experimental situations, she often endures a series of aversive shocks. Already on the defensive as the wife of a police officer striving for acceptance as a middle-class suburbanite, she may have to contend with an additional burden—a covert form of social segregation. On display as the spouse of an officer, she must behave circumspectly, keep her distance, restrict her speech in company, and become a model of deportment. Because everybody watches the police wife, it does not take long for her to realize that she is special. As one wife expressed it:[37]

> Whenever I go downtown shopping I feel like I'm wearing Bill's uniform. When people do special things for you, you're not sure if it's because they like you, or because you're a policeman's wife. It works the other way, too. If I park in the wrong place some people will talk about it.

If a cartoonist were commissioned to capture the essence of police familial life, he might well draw a caricature of a police officer, his wife, and their children swimming in a goldfish tank surrounded by a group of spectators watching every movement. The invasion of privacy is recognized and accepted as a condition of police life. A police lieutenant in Santa Ana, California, tells us in his book on law enforcement that a policeman's private life cannot be private because "he's a cop":[38]

> And everyone watches the policeman to see how he behaves. If he scolds or punishes his children, he's mean. If he argues with his wife, he's cruel and probably a wife-beater. If he drinks, he's a drunk, or at least approaching alcoholism.

Fully aware of their high visibility and the tendency of the public to scrutinize and denigrate their police image, law enforcement families must behave discreetly. They avoid ostentation. Many officers have told us that they did not buy the luxurious big car they so wanted but settled for a less conspicuous model because they were afraid that the neighbors might write a letter to the department urging an investigation of their finances.

A police wife soon learns that "community has a surveillance function"[39] and that in modern society *gemeinschaft* intimate relations are the stuff of dreams because "people can be sociable only when they have some protection from each other; without barriers, boundaries, without the mutual distance which is the essence of impersonality, people are destructive."[40] It may be the snide remark of an acquaintance encountered at the supermarket, "What are you doing here standing on line? I thought your husband gets everything free!" that conditions her to avoid openness. Or when an investigation of graft in the police department hits the front page, the wife of a police officer may feel the anxiety of guilt by association and interpret her neighbor's smiles or quiet conversations as condemnation.

Warm ties with neighbors are inhibited because of her apprehension that she is not accepted as a person with her own identity but rather as an extension of her husband, the cop. In fact, in the informal conversations of her friends she may be herself dubbed "the cop." Acquaintances on the block consider her husband to be the policeman in residence and will ask him to make house calls at inconvenient times to settle disputes, ticket an automobile blocking a driveway, quiet noisy children at play, and so forth. As one wife puts it, "My neighbors feel that our street is being patrolled by my husband."

How 70 percent of the police wives can inform us that members of the community treat their families in a normal fashion seems at first glance to present an irreconcilable paradox. But it is these same wives who have accepted the troublesome facts of police life, coping with the danger and the schedule, who also manage to adapt to this irksome aspect of police social relations. Wives, too, become cynical, probably through contagion from their police officer husbands, whose cynicism has been well documented. They reach a point where they assume it is normal for the public to treat them in an overbearing manner. And it is with resignation that they conclude that it is the price they must pay for being married to police officers.

A police wife ordinarily will conform to protocol to placate the civilian guardians who watch her family lifestyle. And she must remain equally astute not to cause her husband embarrassment on the job. One wife had to change her daily culinary routine after her husband received a promotion to undercover officer and sometimes came home unexpectedly for lunch with his superior officer. In her customary pattern she would relax for a few minutes before lunch with a cocktail. But she now thought it wise to abstain because she was afraid that the supervisor might smell the liquor on her breath and, with typical police suspicion, classify her as a secret alcoholic.

An experienced police wife grows accustomed to the pace. If it is not the discomfiting, it is the unexpected. But at 3 A.M. it requires a special talent to be gracious. When one wife's spouse called to tell her that he wanted to bring home an adorable fifteen-month-old child whose mother had been arrested for intoxication and child abuse, this wife, undaunted, dressed, dropped her own still sleeping little daughter at her sister's home, and rushed to the station house to pick up the new addition to her household. Subsequently, when a welfare department representative appeared to take the baby to a shelter, the officer's wife and her five-year-old daughter expressed disappointment that they could not keep the child.[41]

When a wife manages to unravel the tangled logistics of the duty chart to attend a party, she may still not be able to unwind. Invariably, if her husband is identified as a policeman, he becomes the conversation piece. Each guest takes a turn to relate an invidious anecdote about his personal encounter with a police officer. No wonder that four out of five police officers and two out three wives in our survey try to avoid this hostile reception by seldom or never mentioning their affiliation with law enforcement.

A police couple ruefully confessed to us that they did not expect to be invited anymore to their friends' parties. At the last gathering, the pair noticed immediately the loss of spontaneity as soon as they arrived. Later, their harried host admitted that the guests had been experimenting with pot and were afraid that the policeman would become a "party pooper."

An equally awkward incident described to us by a police wife reinforces the supposition that a police officer may actually be weighted down by his shield and gun 24 hours a day, even on festive occasions. Invited to an engagement celebration, she entered first while her husband circled the block searching for a parking space. Soon after, she heard a commotion at the door and saw her spouse still in his overcoat, with gun drawn, forcing one of the guests to lean against the wall while he frisked him for weapons. The overly observant husband suspected that he had found a wanted person and detected a suspicious bulge in the man's pocket. Mistaken, he apologized, but his wife burst into tears and left at once, too humiliated to face her friends.

With so many of these wives' painful memories peppering our interviews, we were certain that our findings would disclose that police couples withdrew into a more friendly circle of their own kind for their social activities. But disputing our logic, nearly 60 percent of the wives reported that they seldom or never socialized with other police couples.

There are many reasons for this anomalous phenomenon—of avoiding close friendships with colleagues despite the empathy of shared experiences. Some wives told us that it was too difficult to match convenient times for socializing with police couples when their husbands' schedules did not dovetail. Others complained that they grew tired of listening to "cop talk" all the time when they did get together. A pervading pressure against regular interaction with other police associates was the fear of some husbands that their wives would learn too much about what really went on within the police department.

The law enforcement caste system adds another barrier to close friendship among police families. Officers, good friends when of equal rank, discover that promotion infects the relationship. Wives, too, respect the pecking order of the law enforcement hierarchy and unconsciously respond to the unspoken vibration that "my husband is superior to yours," and they begin to feel uncomfortable socializing with one another. If patrolman and superior officer manage to sustain their friendship, it can become station house gossip. The man in the lower rank may be accused by the backroom cynics of "brown nosing."

But it is this same cynical view, one that is nearly universal within the police occupation, contaminating the wife as well, that prepares the police couple to discount the noticeable provocations of their civilian friends, impelling them to define the contours of their acquaintances' behavior as natural and normal reactions to authority figures. Thus, fortified by this insight, police couples can rationalize the social peccadilloes of these outsiders and endure them without excessive strain on their relationships.

When you are a backstage wife, incommunicado in the wings, rarely venturing out to observe the police officer playing his part, it makes little difference if your husband walks, rides, or covers a fixed post in the living theater of police action. Wives understand and accept the implications of the police mystique that—because their nattily costumed spouses perform in the limelight and symbolize authority—other women are attracted to their husband's strength, virility, and good looks. Often the service role of hero calls for the husband to protect, carry, or succor female clientele. Most wives have acknowledged and come to terms with this irritating and sometimes titillating scene in the drama of police work, although in every precinct there are authenticated reports of wives who followed their husbands on patrol for weeks and months to prevent them from succumbing to temptation.

The wives realize that wherever men work, they maintain contact with women in the organization. In law enforcement until 1972, less than 5 percent of the force consisted of females, and most of these executed special tasks: clerical work, youth work, guarding female prisoners, and a narrow range of duties in the control of vice. But there were always a few policewomen assigned to the detective division to act as decoys to trap rapists and muggers, who would then be arrested by a backup team of male detectives. Police wives react to the presence of policewomen in such limited aspects of police work in much the same way that wives of men in other occupations accommodate themselves to the reality of females supplementing or assisting their marital partners. However, with the assignment of policewomen as partners with policemen in radio cars, placid police wives exploded.

All the smoldering resentment on the part of the wives, sublimated or throttled up to this point, burst forth in outrage at what they considered an attack upon the integrity of family life. In our conversations with wives, many remarked sardonically that their husbands felt closer to their radio car partners than to their mates. But when the partner changed gender, the humor drained from their truism. The wives imagined their husbands rubbing elbows and knees with a policewoman in the front seat of the radio car for eight or more hours—a longer and more intimate waking period of the day than the husbands spent with their wives. Even the least sophisticated wife could contemplate the warm bond enmeshing two partners of the opposite sex who worked together, faced danger together, ate together, cooped together, and possibly played together. They knew instinctively that the younger, more active, and probably more attractive policewomen would be assigned to the radio cars. And it unnerved them to contemplate that this intimacy would flourish within the automobile, whose phallic symbolism has become a logo of the American culture.

The introduction of policewomen into radio car patrol aroused an even more intense emotion than jealousy: fear for their husbands' lives. Wives expressed apprehension that because of the intrinsic physical limitations of policewomen, in a dangerous confrontation they could not back up their partners as effectively as male counterparts could. Placing women in radio cars would be tantamount to exposing their husbands to double jeopardy. Wives were fearful of the higher potential for danger because the subtle interplay between the sexes might stimulate a police officer to flaunt his bravery unnecessarily or to protect his female partner out of a misguided sense of chivalry. Thus it would not be a matched team sharing risks equally as men riding in tandem.

Outspoken in their opposition to mixed gender assignments, police wives' objections fall into two slots: possible sexual involvement between the partners or danger to their husbands because of inadequacies of policewomen. The wives who oppose the assignment for reasons of jealousy intimate that their husbands might succumb to temptation:[42]

> I would be neutral about the assignment providing the woman in question was 75 and looked like King Kong.
>
> Contact too close in radio car. More hours with her than me. I know that my husband would go too far if he really liked her.
>
> I don't want him fooling around.
>
> Steady partners are at times closer than blood relatives. Why look for trouble?
>
> I'm jealous of his brotherhood with fellow police officers, no less it be female. Forget it.
>
> He wouldn't be able to do his job properly. If she was pretty, he would be too busy making an impression. If she was a plain Jane, he'd be grumbling all the time.
>
> My husband has sticky fingers.

Many wives expressed their opposition in terms of the danger to their husbands, emphasizing once again that the physical limitations of women made them inadequate partners.

> Danger is an integral part of an officer's life. Unnecessary risk is foolish. Not only are most policewomen incapable of fulfilling physical aspects of the job, but I feel my husband would feel more responsibility for her safety. Because in time of danger the natural thing to do would be to protect the policewoman. Also because I am very possessive and jealous.
>
> My husband is 6 foot 2 inches, weight 215 pounds and has been knocked around on a few occasions. He works in a high crime area and a woman is not typically equipped to back him up.
>
> I too am a woman. In no possible fashion could I be as strong physically in performing a "man-size" job. With the short training requirement the policewoman is ill-equipped physically for a Harlem street.
>
> He too has too much respect for women and would always be worried about her safety and his actions (language, etc).

Several enthusiastic New York City policewomen, when interviewed by a reporter expressed their eagerness to patrol with male officers, but they clearly sensed the resistance of their co-workers' wives and ascribed its source to jealousy. As one of the policewomen put it:[43]

> Wives don't usually fuss about men and women on foot patrol—It's the radio car that bugs them.
>
> Being in a car on Times Square is like a fishbowl. But people figure that if a cop's in a car with a pretty girl, something's got to be happening. Men in offices have affairs, but cops are supposed to be more lecherous than other men. And we're supposed to be better than other women.

At the moment, the ripples of controversy spread by the issue of policewomen sharing radio car patrol have been smoothed over by pressing economic crises. Unprecedented layoffs of police officers (including many of the recently hired policewomen) and the contractual impasses over the demands for higher salaries and improved working conditions, counterbalanced by management's proposals for higher productivity and one-man radio car patrol, have combined to make equal opportunity for policewomen in radio cars a moot issue. Predictably, however, there will be a thaw in the long freeze of law enforcement layoffs; hiring will resume, and despite the fears and objections of wives, the climate of the 80s—so charged with issues of sex discrimination, equal employment opportunity and feminism—will thrust policewomen into positions of equal responsibility with their male counterparts.[44] Comprehensive studies of women on patrol have demonstrated conclusively that female officers can perform their duties comparably to patrolmen.[45] And as females make inroads on the job and actually prove in action that they possess the skills and strengths demanded by patrol, the attitudes of police administrators, colleagues, and even the wives will become more positive and accepting of policewomen's capabilities for the occupation.

Just as policewomen are experiencing the stirrings of power, police wives, too—once the forgotten women in police administration—have finally made an impact on the leadership. They have been assisted by latent forces working in the same direction. Law enforcement territory has been penetrated, surveyed, polled, probed, and investigated by an army of researchers. A result of all this study is that the top administrators have absorbed a new perspective on the occupation, marking a turning point in their thinking about family life. Productivity studies point to the possible connection between poor work performance and poor marital conditions.

It does not require much imagination to envision that a policeman who goes on duty after an explosive argument with his wife will be "on a short fuse" when he is on the beat. And the corollary follows that a patrolman who finds it difficult to turn off "the flashing red lights and the screaming sirens" of the job will carry home the danger and the tension. This undercurrent of anxiety can activate subtle tugs-of-war between husband and wife over police matters, for instance, an impasse over the officer's specific assignment within the department. A policeman's wife may plead with her husband to avoid hazardous duty for the sake of his family, while her mate may relish the excitement of a dangerous detail.

In an attempt to encourage empathy between spouses about the profession, enlightened law enforcement agencies are initiating orientation and counseling programs.[46] As part of the training sessions, spouses ride in squad cars, tour station houses, visit custodial facilities and even practice shooting on the firing range. And certainly this understanding is a passkey to unlock some of the secrecy about police work. Communication between police couples at seminars relieves some of the stresses and fosters development of a positive attitude toward the police lifestyle.

Of course, there are police families that cannot cope. For one couple the work schedule cut them apart. Afraid to sleep alone, the wife could never adjust to her husband's late tours (midnight to 8 A.M.). Before every late tour, they reenacted the same traumatic domestic tableau. She insisted that he drive her and their young child to her mother's house across town where they would spend the night. In the morning, the arduous safari reversed itself. This upheaval every third week eroded their relationship until, finally, the distraught husband made one last exodus to his mother-in-law's home, depositing his young family there permanently.

A strange twist ruptured still another marital partnership of our police friends. The diurnal rhythms of the couple beat in contrapuntal tempo. Their lifestyles contradicted each other. A day person, the policeman's personality and energy waxed and waned with the sun. By contrast, the wife, a night person, responded to the moon's influence. In an ordinary existence they might have been able to adjust to each other, but the shifting hours of police work made time of the essence. After a 4 P.M. to midnight tour of duty, he would return home exhausted, ready to collapse into bed. His wife, attuned to the beat of her own nocturnal drum, was just getting lively. Or he would have some reserve energy after a late tour, but she would be sleeping soundly. And on the 8 A.M. to 4 P.M. schedule, by the time he returned home it was dinner time. During the evening hours he was rapidly running down while she was gathering steam. It just did not work; they are still friends, although divorced, their circadian rhythms still worlds apart.

Is divorce, then, an occupational hazard of police work? Among police officers, the prevailing view is that as a result of their frenetic lifestyle, their rate of divorce far exceeds that of the general public. And they cite case histories that reinforce their conviction that police marriages are battered by the tensions and strains of the job. Because divorces among our close friends had fragmented our social circle, we, too, inferred that divorce, indeed, could be endemic to the profession. Somehow it is human nature to experience the impact of disaster more intensely when one knows the victim personally and can empathize with him or her.

Law enforcement personnel, themselves, have reinforced the statistics on the high incidence of marital disruption by producing their own figures based on informal surveys of different departments.[47]

Police wives are prominent among those who spread the rumor of high police divorce rates. Eager to aid other police wives in surmounting the difficulties of marriage, Barbara Webber's "how-to" book, instead, succeeds in agitating them with this unverified and pessimistic statement:[48]

> The police profession's ranking first in divorce, second in actual suicides, and high in mental breakdowns makes it increasingly important that the wife function in her capacity to provide a good home environment for her husband.

Updating her ranking of the police profession, the same author in a later publication cites a figure of "well over 50 percent" for police divorce, once more failing to list a source.[49] Another police wife reiterates the same dismal diagnosis and gratuitously lays the blame for the dissolution of the marriage on the wife, not on the husband or the job:[50] "Policemen have the highest divorce rate in the United States. In too many cases this divorce is caused by a wife who cannot accept and understand her husband's job."

A cursory review of the chapter headings in another guide for police wives, written by a police wife and her mother, conveys its message:[51] "Love Me Love My Work," "He's Going to Need Your Tender Loving Care," and "Make Your Home a Haven." These conjugal sermons imply that the home must be the sanctuary to provide catharsis from the oppressive demands of the occupation. And subliminally, the finger once more points to the unfortunate wife who fails in this supportive role. She is identified as the scapegoat responsible for a catalog of police plagues:[52]

> Divorce, ulcers, alcoholism and suicide take a frightening toll in police families these days, and these are often triggered by unhappy wives unable to cope with the very real stresses the law enforcement task brings to the officer's family.

When psychologists who are consultants in mental health to police departments claim high police divorce rates, they generate even more credibility than do police wives. And once again the wives are assigned the responsibility for the family pathology:[53]

> The [police] officer's wife probably had no understanding of her husband's job demands when she married him. She also did not bargain for the insecurity, the danger to her husband, or the antipolice feeling she herself may encounter in some social settings. It is not surprising that indices of social alienation are high within police ranks; divorce and alcoholism often reach serious proportions.

A consultant and counselor for several medium-sized police departments, Henry Singer, repeated the same theme:[54]

> Policemen have the highest divorce rate of any group in the country, some claim as much as 40 percent.

What has given police marriages such a bad press? It may very well be that police couples confronted with serious difficulties in their married life are using the profession as a scapegoat to mask deep-seated disturbances. Admittedly, police work precipitates strains, and undeniably, the schedule, danger, shock of police experiences, the negative image of police work and the low salary produce tensions. However, to base conclusions concerning the incidence of divorce based on rumors of marital upsets, gut feelings, subjective inferences of professional observers and informal explorations of the subject lack the authenticity and credibility to justify conclusions about an occupation numbering more than 750,000 nationwide.

Law enforcement experts, employing more rigorous standards of research methodology in their surveys of police departments have refuted the misperceptions concerning police marital stability. They have utilized representative sampling, interviews and large-scale questionnaires to obtain their data.[55]

David H. Bayley and Harold Mendelsohn propose a rationale for the family stability of police officers that they observed in their survey of a police force in Denver, Colorado:[56]

> Policemen are family men. In our sample of Denver policemen, not one was single . . . Moreover, policemen seem to have more stable marriages than are to be found in the community as a whole. *Only 2% of the officers had been divorced* against 5% generally. Policemen are also parents. A mere 3% of them had no children. . . . This is an important point to bear in mind. Policemen represent family men, men who value family stability highly and who may rely on their families for support against a populace which they often regard as hostile. [Italics added.]

Viewing the panorama of police divorce through an objective lens, we gain a sharper image of the critical elements. The experts are divided; the data are not conclusive; the issues are fogged in a cloud of propaganda. At the same time, the prevailing pessimistic attitude based on reports of numerous divorces in many medium-sized and small departments has been congealed by repetition rather than validated by research. Grafted onto law enforcement ideology as a defense mechanism to explain the charges of an extraordinarily high divorce rate, this widely held opinion popularizes the hypothesis that police work with its corroding stress is ultimately destructive to the marital relation.

Unquestionably, as we have repeatedly pointed out, police marriages are afflicted with a range of stressful problems endemic to the profession. Nevertheless, as Monsignor Joseph A. Dunne, a police chaplain for more than twenty years in the New York City Police Department, observes:[57]

> I would venture to say that there is nothing in police work which of necessity contributes to the destruction of marriage. We have thousands of happily married officers who will validate this.

Our analysis, based on a review of the available research on police divorce and the results of our own survey of police departments representing 50,000 law enforcement personnel, contravenes the prevalent assumption that divorce is an occupational hazard of police work.[58] Significantly, the same forces that are inflating divorce rates all over America are affecting police marriages as well.

Current reinforcement for a positive view of law enforcement marital relationships comes from the director of psychological services for the Los Angeles County Sheriff's Department and his wife, a marriage and family counselor, who assert:[59]

> We know of no evidence to support the popular notion that the divorce rate in police marriages is higher than other occupations.

Weighing the evidence, we conclude that the rate of divorce for the police occupation as a whole rises no higher than the average level of divorce in the United States. Divorce police style equates with divorce American style.

CHILDREN OF THE FORCE

If there is one point of agreement among most researchers on the family, it is that the presence of children places a strain on a marriage. Most certainly, in police work, the logistics of the rotating schedule complicate family life even further. After a late tour, it requires nerve-wracking effort to fall asleep with several preschoolers running noisily about the house. When a police couple has planned a night out by plotting the schedule for two months in advance, it is a psychological catastrophe when the babysitter reneges at the last moment.

Convinced from our observations of police conjugal relationships that the job dominates family lifestyles, we hypothesized that children in police families would also fall into orbit around the occupation and that feeling the weight of the shield in their early years, police offspring would generate a sense of unique identity. Instead, we discovered from our interviews with these youngsters that at least until they reach their teens, their concept of police work markedly resembles that held by their peers whose parents earn their living in other fields. We learned from police children that the concept that their parent is also a police officer changes its pattern with every stage of chronological development. For the very youngest, for whom the home defines the main boundaries of the world, the image of a loving, nurturing father figure is dissociated from the occupation. Until about the age of three, when a finer sense of visual discrimination maturates, seeing a parent in uniform through a child's eyes projects a rather confusing and dazzling picture. Our own children would invariably shout a warm greeting of "Daddy!" to any policeman in blue they met, to the embarrassment of their mother and the amusement of the police officer.

Depending on his assignment, a father's job may have been associated with a bit of fun for preschoolers, for the children often related with delight the happy occasion when he may have treated them to a ride in a police scooter, boat, patrol car, or even a police helicopter. Some kids recalled with nostalgia, as a highlight of their childhood, an excursion to an amusement park or a pass to a baseball game when their dads worked that detail.

Civic-minded nursery school teachers give their pupils a headstart in social studies by encouraging the children to "play policeman." The children construct police hats and in their paper regalia pretend to direct traffic, find lost kids, help classmates cross the street, and catch robbers. When preschoolers are asked what they want to be when they grow up, invariably, the police career ranks high in popularity.

The children's rooms in public libraries are stockpiled with informative books about the work of the police, for most young readers whether or not their parent is a real-life police officer, find this subject fascinating. One book in particular, *My Daddy Is a Policeman*, carries realism to a tragic conclusion.[60] With a photo-essay format aimed to appeal to children from about four to eight, a little girl describes in her own words how her policeman father earns his living and how they have fun together when he is at home. On one side of each double-page layout, a large photograph illustrates these activities. On the opposite page is a one-sentence comment by the daughter. Her opening words are, "My Daddy is a policeman." And after a sequence depicting the officer shot down while on duty, the story ends movingly with the little girl sitting disconsolately by herself as she sobs, "My Daddy was a policeman."

Children are naturally quite curious about "what daddies do," although when they are small, they can be quite disconcerting with the naiveté of their questions when they learn that a classmate's parent is a police officer. "Why is your daddy home during the day?" "How come your daddy is a policeman?" "Does he shoot any robbers?" "Can he help us if a robber robs out house?" "How come he has a gun?"

The majority of our 62 police children respondents did not hesitate to tell their friends how their parents made a living; only 6 (10 percent) preferred to remain close-mouthed about it. That they could expose the police roots in the family tree so openly attests to a level of social sophistication that belies their years, since they were able to maintain their good humor and accept with nonchalance the outspoken comments of their peers. Quite often their acquaintances' remarks were tinged with disbelief, teasing, or malice: "You must be kidding. I can't believe your father is a pig!" "He doesn't look like a cop." "He must give you a bad time." "I'd better be good. Your father is fuzz." "I'm not going to your house." "How could a woman be a policeman?" Others blatantly displayed their avid curiosity about the nature of police work: "Did he ever shoot anyone?" "Did he ever arrest a member of the Mafia?" "Where does he work?" "What is his rank?"

Until puberty, boys and girls feel secure and comfortable, regulated by set rules of behavior within the snug sanctuary of the home. The police parent acts as a paternal but firm protector and reinforces the umbilical cord attaching the youngster to the family. A number of children told us that they benefited from their parent's status: "He can teach me the law." "I feel safe." "Bad kids stay away from you."

The children seem to flourish in this nurturing family ambience. Fully 75 percent of our sample said that they acted the same as other children did, and 85 percent of them rated their fathers as easygoing in discipline. The sources of conflict are minor domestic crises easily contained within the limits of the home: not doing household chores and homework, watching too much television, going to bed too late.

The family group encourages intergenerational activities such as Little League and Boy or Girl Scouts, and the children reported that they enjoyed doing things with their fathers—playing ball, fishing, going places. One daughter, more anxious than the others, said introspectively, "I just like to sit and look at him because when he goes to work, I think that I will never see him again."

Most of the children whom we interviewed did not seem to be bothered excessively when a police officer parent had to miss a family celebration or a school play because of the work schedule. Although they may have felt sad, they accepted the frustration philosophically, recognizing that, "There are 24 hours in a day to sing 'Happy Birthday' or to go bowling."

At adolescence, the social antennas of the children of police personnel become particularly sensitized to flak from their peers, and they may feel hurt by their friends' negative reaction to what their parents do for a living. In our off-the-record conversations with older sons and daughters of police parents, some of them told us that they tried to avoid this criticism by rarely volunteering information of their parent's affiliation or by not telling anyone unless asked. And when an intimate did respond in a noncommittal manner to the disclosure, a "So what!" was especially appreciated.

Unlike the preteeners whose attitudes toward the police are generally favorable, adolescent groups exhibit a wide diversity of opinion. For those not related to law enforcement families, gut feelings about the police are internalized as part of a broader ideological position, more dependent on variables such as class, education, and ethnic and racial background than on facts. For a large group hypnotized by television, opinions fluctuate according to the networks' latest presentations of police heroism or corruption and brutality. In the inner-city neighborhoods, a significant proportion of the adolescent population writes off the police as the enemy.

A burgeoning social consciousness coincides with an intense peer pressure for conformity. At this age, teenagers are motivated by an overwhelming desire to be accepted and liked. A seventeen-year-old girl perceptively analyzed the nuances of this sensitivity in a written postscript to her questionnaire:

> When I first came to High School, no one knew my father was a cop. I had two friends who knew but that was it.

> The next time I turned around, everyone knew. It didn't bother me. But it bothered some people. I would tell them not to act so strange. Be for real; carry on friendship as if they never knew. People don't hassle me because they see I don't try to act so high class because my father is a cop.

Typically in the mid-teens, a sense of their special identity as children of police parents crystallizes. As they move in ever-widening arcs away from the hub of the home, they experience and assimilate controversial concepts of the police image. At this time, the adolescent peer group competes with and sometimes displaces the family as the purveyor of norms and standards, and the role of the parent imperceptibly changes from benevolent protector to restrictive guardian. But for the police child of this age there is a unique blue dimension arising from his personal contact with law enforcement that colors his personality and values, that gradually solidifies as a result of family interaction and loyalty to the police parent. At times this special sense of identity intersecting with the long arm of the job can work to his advantage.

Several teenagers we talked to admitted that they had sometimes received preferential treatment from traffic officers when they were stopped for driving violations. Occasionally the officer yielded to the blandishments of professional courtesy and instead of issuing a summons let the young offender proceed after mildly reprimanding him or her, "You should know better." Our oldest respondent (thirty-one) revealed that she talked herself into her first job as a security guard in a large department store, although totally inexperienced, on the strength of her disclosure to the personnel director that her father was a policeman.

A college student at an ivy league school recounted how the traditionally cool and even hostile relation between "town and gown" was replaced by a friendly, almost intimate connection in his personal encounter with the police. At about 3 A.M. he was parked in an out-of-bounds lovers' lane with a young lady, when a radio car pulled up. The officer began to question him in a stern manner and then tersely ordered him to step out of the car. Before the situation could deteriorate further, the collegian whispered to the Boston police officer that his father was a police lieutenant in the New York City Police Department. After a brief set of questions to make sure that the young man was not lying, the patrol officer's attitude changed completely. Nudging the lieutenant's son conspiratorially, he congratulated him on the attractiveness of his female companion, commented, "Aren't Boston girls great?" and advised him not to stay in the lovers' lane too long.

A co-ed majoring in the behavioral sciences explained how she was able to exploit her father's police affiliation. His police colleagues, by graciously consenting to be interviewed by the daughter, provided her with a rich source of primary research material for her term reports. Her police family background continued to be an advantage in her professional duties as a marriage counselor. Confronted by a difficult case involving a police couple who were at first uncooperative, she gained instant rapport when she confided to the police officer husband that she was the daughter of a retired police officer.

Once marked as sons and daughters of police officers, these children must also contend with subtle pressure from external figures of authority, especially in the schools. In our discussions we heard youngsters complain, "I'm tired of hearing teachers say to me, 'You should know better. Your father is a policeman. You should set an example.' "

Like other loving and solicitous fathers and mothers, law enforcement parents want their adolescent children to be good and to live according to a high standard of conduct. However, police officers major in adolescent psychology on the street, not in college, and their laboratory studies and internships take place in prisons, hospital emergency rooms, and the morgue. Because they have seen so much disaster, they tend to be overcautious, overprotective, and oversuspicious with their own children, and intolerant of their misconduct.

A New York police officer, who obviously had done a lot of soul-searching concerning his "burned-out" attitude toward his family confided:[61]

> You change when you become a cop. You become tough and hard and cynical. You have to condition yourself to be that way in order to survive this job. And sometimes without realizing it you act that way all the time, even with your wife and kids. But it's something you have to do because if you start getting emotionally involved with what happens at work you'll wind up in Bellevue [psychiatric hospital].

Disenchanted by her husband's relationship to their children, an emotionally exhausted patrolman's wife from California expressed her discontent:[62]

> I can't understand how seemingly normal husbands turn into such "machos." Arguments end in "Because I said so." Our children feel as though they really can't discuss

> problems with their father because he relates in terms of the law and logic and not the emotions involved. Sometimes I feel that if I don't do what he wants I'll be arrested.

Teenagers eager for emancipation no longer appreciate a hovering parent whose loving care they had welcomed just a few years before. Now they reject this kind of solicitude. The conflict situation is built into the relationship: the police parent cannot change. When he gives his son the keys to the car, he recalls the mangled bodies in speedway accidents. As his daughter leaves the house on her big date, he visualizes the horror of the rape case or the overdose victim he handled not long before. Although all adolescents do not react to this surveillance in the same way, most resent it, and they become increasingly aware that the parent's job imposes certain regulations and limitations on their lives that others do not have to face. Some seem to submit but simmer. The apparently happy, well-adjusted daughter in one police family vented her resentment: "My father always had a kind of string on the kids. He's suspicious of everybody. He'll give my boyfriends the third degree. I felt trapped."[63]

Others respond with humorous tolerance and may tease the parent about being the voice of doom. But when the discipline becomes more forceful and the confrontation between the generations comes to an impasse, a police parent may be shocked by this emotional barrage: "Go ahead and hit me with your nightstick! You're not a father. You're nothing but a cop!"

A final group is openly belligerent, fomenting a dangerous challenge to parental authority. A colleague at John Jay College of Criminal Justice who has several police officers of high rank in his family told us that one son bided his time until he was eighteen and strong enough to tackle his police officer father. He then thrashed his parent in a fist fight in order to get revenge for the years of punishment and humiliation from a despot who figuratively wore his uniform even at home. Is the police parent the composite visualized by this type of adolescent? Is the father figure just a facade for the police officer underneath—suspicious, cynical, and authoritarian?[64]

The police parent would summarily dismiss this description. From his point of view, he is still wearing essentially the same parental mantle of benevolent protector with which he sheltered his children when they were small. Now the dangers and problems facing the adolescent have multiplied, and reflexively, the parent wants to draw his offspring closer.

A college-graduate police sergeant with 20 years of service in the New York City Police Department, father of seven children, describes his efforts to shield his wife and children. Well qualified as a spokesman, he articulates the familial philosophy of many of his police colleagues:[65]

> Police are protective of their families and rightfully so. Most struggle to purchase one family homes, and usually in suburbia. . . . We protect our children educationally. Most policemen still residing in the city send their children to parochial grammar and high schools. The expense is enormous, but we feel the results are worth it. We would like our children to grow up "soft," as free as possible of the worldly wise-guy mouthings of the youths we meet on the "job." We also want them taught the tenets of our religion. . . . We are willing to accept the added expense of private schooling to teach discipline, that trait which is most necessary for any successful person.

Another sergeant comments on police patterns of child rearing:[66]

> I'll tell you who the police are. They're men from plain, ordinary families. . . . They go to church. They try to bring up their kids to respect older people and obey the law. They send their sons into the army, so the country will be the strongest on the earth, and they teach their daughters to be good wives and good mothers.

Individual variations in adaptation are mandated when there are youngsters about, as this wife of a police officer advised in her addendum to an item on our questionnaire:

> Anyone whose husband is a police officer sort of has to make their own adjustments. Much depends on if children are involved versus those that don't have children. The way I arrange my life around his job and my children may not be the ideal situation to someone else.

For police couples without young children, the occupational hazard of safeguarding the service revolver in the home appears to be minimal. The burden of the gun can be oppressive, however, when there are inquisitive youngsters underfoot. Because boys and girls are often fascinated by firearms, shocking fatalities can occur when they manage to ferret out the hiding place, experiment with the revolver, and possibly end up shooting themselves or friends.

In the more important child-rearing practices, a consensus emerges that fortifies the police marriage. If we accept the premise that the arrival of children places a strain on a marriage, then the danger signal for marital stability would be a serious disagreement on methods of raising the children. In our sample, harmony in styles and goals of child rearing predominated, which translates into a positive prognosis for these marriages.

About 75 percent of our respondent police officers and spouses who were parents classified their method of raising their children as flexible, as opposed to strict or permissive. And only 5 percent of them reported children's misbehavior or the lack of communication between parents and children as problems that occurred frequently.

How can we reconcile the police self-image as flexible parents when we have analyzed their intense concern and control of the children and their deep allegiance to enforcing discipline and obedience? We believe that the police occupation potently but so immutably influences these latent areas of family life that unconsciously the typical police couple marches to the cadences and directives of the job. And yet they can insist that they themselves are calling the tune, especially for their children's future.

In their classic study, social psychologists Daniel Miller and Guy Swanson moved into a more sociological framework when they hypothesized that the father's occupation significantly determined child-rearing practices.[67] Recognizing the dominance of the bureaucratic form of occupational organization over the entrepreneurial, they theorized that the entrepreneurial family, already an anachronism, would yield to the bureaucratic family type. The police family dovetails into their definition of the bureaucratic family because the police officer works for somebody else, in an organization with three or more supervisory levels, and his income is primarily in the form of wages or salary.

When we asked the police parents in our sample to choose the qualities they considered most important for their children, their choices clustered about bureaucratic qualities: honesty, respect for authority, obedience to parents, and dependability. According to Miller and Swanson, it would be expected that submission to the security and routine of the occupation would strip the officer of his ambition and his potential for striking out on his own.[68] This mechanism would also explain the desire of police officers to inculcate bureaucratic traits in their children.

Paradoxically, though, most of them want their sons to be professionals. Success in these demanding pursuits often requires the entrepreneurial qualities of perseverance, independence, high achievement in school, and thrift, all characteristics that constitute a throwback to the Protestant ethic. Yet these police parents ranked them much lower in importance compared to the bureaucratic virtues. Popularity, the quality that trailed the rest, proved to be the only exception where a possibly bureaucratic trait was calibrated at the bottom of the scale.[69]

The police occupation interlocks so neatly with the bureaucratic pattern of organization that it is no wonder that police officers are classified as bureaucrats. The search for security, the dream of the pension, the fixed rules, the rigidity, and the submission to hierarchical authority are all classic attributes of the bureaucratic personality. On patrol, however, the successful police officer must be authoritative and independent; most of the tour he works alone; he is permitted wide powers of discretion; often he makes instantaneous and critical decisions that may mean life or death; and he must be willing to take risks. Obviously, this cluster of traits is more characteristic of entrepreneurs than of bureaucrats.

This contradiction between the bureaucratic form of the occupation and the entrepreneurial aspect of the policeman's actual role clarifies the apparent anomaly that permits police parents to opt for professional careers in law and medicine for their children while at the same time prizing the bureaucratic virtues of obedience and dependability.

This explanation of the process is too simplistic, however. The average parent does not formulate a clear-cut blueprint for raising his children. He does not say to himself, "I want my child to be a bureaucrat or a professional; therefore, I will try to inculcate those qualities that are most appropriate for that career." In most cases, styles of child rearing are more a product of psychological, sociological, and interactive processes, most of them existing at the unconscious level rather than as a specifically rational plan of action.

Because the police officer on the job assumes the role of authority and independence, this becomes his customary approach to interpersonal relations. Can he switch off this role when he travels from station house to ranch house? Very few are able to accomplish this transition smoothly; generally, the police identity spills over into the father figure. For instance, most of the police in our sample rated themselves as flexible in child rearing, yet the police authority neutralizing that flexibility was apparent in their consistent choice of obedience and respect for authority as the prime qualities they wished to foster in their children.

It is unrealistic to expect police parents to deviate from this concept of control and authority within the family. Based on equal shares of experience and ideology, the majority of police officers are certain that strong parental supervision is the one necessary ingredient to prevent trouble in or out of the home. To them, the rampant delinquency they see on the job is a problem located largely among the lower-class and minority communities. And they blame juvenile crime on parental neglect. Therefore, police parents continue to instill a code of obedience, dependability, honesty, and religious instruction. And police occupational ideology coalesces with this pattern of child rearing.

Buttressed by this belief in delinquency causation, the police parent must prove to himself and others that he is not guilty of the same type of neglect. Every moment that he can spend with his children becomes a precious commodity.

This statement by a patrolman voices the credo of his colleagues:[70]

> Being a street cop, I know that to bring children up properly you have to give them time. You have to have someone there. I see what happens to kids when they don't have fathers around—they run wild on the streets day and night.

The fact that the intricacies of his work schedule may force the police officer to juggle the time he spends with his family agitates him. By a process of psychological generalization or displacement, the chart becomes the barrier between him and the children. Similarly, his first defense against any proposed change in schedule is to proclaim that the new timetable will disrupt family life by robbing his already deprived children of the little time that he can devote to them.

In reality, this is fallacious logic, although it will infuriate the average police officer to hear this. Certainly, a knowledgeable law enforcement worker is aware that in the larger cities, police department hours of work, time off, and vacations compare quite favorably with those of other civil service workers and most of the working force in the private sector as well. What is really provoking his anxiety is the realization that because he is a police officer, he is on call for possible emergency duty 24 hours a day, and he feels uncertain that he will really have enough time to spend with his family. Nevertheless, by judiciously manipulating his periods of sleep, a police officer on rotating shifts can enjoy far more of the day with his children than does the average working father with regular hours. He can also see his children at different times during the day, an especially rewarding benefit when the children are small and have early bedtimes. Compared to a busy professional or the harried middle-class executive who brings his work home with him almost every night, the police officer enjoys a great advantage.

It is a dreadful blow to any family when a son or daughter gets in trouble with the law. However, to a police family it is far more devastating. Not only does the adolescent's transgression violate the family's moral code, but also it undermines the police parent's position as an upholder of the laws of society. Immersed in the belief that mothers and fathers by their neglect or failure to enforce discipline are responsible for their children's wrongdoing, police parents are inundated by a cascade of guilt feelings if their child is arrested. Of what use were the constant warnings and admonitions? The police parent oscillates from sympathetic concern to fury at the offspring who has brought this disaster upon the house. The anguished mother pleads, "You're a policeman. Do something!" For an outsider to come to the precinct to intercede for a prisoner would probably end up in a charge of obstructing governmental administration, or possibly, bribery—a felony. It is hardly less criminal for a police officer to do so, but in his desperation, he tries it.

Sometimes he knows the commanding officer or the lieutenant in the precinct and will appeal in guarded language, hoping that they will understand and acquiesce to his veiled plea to permit irregularities in the reporting and processing of the case. As a last resort he will appear in court to influence the district attorney to be sympathetic, and he may even request an audience with the judge in his chambers trying to find a loophole.

Among our acquaintances are several police families whose sons became chronic delinquents, and the policemen fathers went through these ordeals several times a year. One parent suffered a massive heart attack. The other endured two concomitant tragedies: a prolonged depression and a stormy divorce.

One perverse aspect of these tragic situations is that some people experience a vindictive pleasure when a police officer's child gets in trouble. The realization that a son or daughter in a law enforcement family can become a lawbreaker often represents the public's vicarious vengeance against the police who symbolically serve as society's superego.

To the police family, anecdotes and jokes in which the punch line derives its kick from the put-down of the occupation or its personnel are a malicious brand of sick humor.

For any parent, the process of rearing a child successfully in today's kaleidoscopic society is more a mystery than an art or science. Compounding the difficulty for police parents is their own ambivalence about their proper function and responsibility toward their children. The police occupational ideology, shared by a majority of the force, proclaims that our society is at the point of disintegration because of excessive permissiveness, loss of respect for law and order, and the continuing erosion of parental authority. There is a definite conflict between the police parents' desires to maintain authority and control within the family and the push toward egalitarianism, which is more appropriate to newly acquired middle-class status.

Like all adolescents, the teenager in a police family struggles to attain self-expression and independence from parental control. Having traversed a comfortable and secure childhood in the glow of the father's power as a figure of authority, just a few years later, the young person finds that same aura of power converted into a tenacious restriction of his or her freedom of action. During this same period, the adolescent becomes more aware of status and class distinctions, and the luster of the police job dims when it is compared with the professions of the parents of middle-class friends.

In the face of such potential for tension between parent and child, the adolescents who discussed their problems with us rarely voiced frustration or resentment toward their parents. Instead, they expressed an appreciation of the police officer parent as an anchor of stability during the turbulent years of coming of age.

REFERENCES

1. Harvey Schlossberg and Lucy Freeman, *Psychologist with a Gun* (New York: Coward McCann and Geoghegan, 1974), p. 47.
2. Dorothy Brandreth, "Stress and the Policeman's Wife," *Police Stress* (Fall 1978), pp. 41–42.
3. The George Family, "Six American Families," WNET Channel 13, April 25, 1977.
4. "For Some It's Easy." *Police Stress*, Sandra J. Norris (Fall 1978), p. 9.
5. Barbara E. Webber, ed., *Handbook for Law Enforcement Wives* (Chicago: L. E. Publishers, 1974), p. 26. Webber is the wife of a police lieutenant attached to the police force in Urbana, Illinois.
6. Jerome Skolnick, *Justice Without Trial* (New York: Wiley, 1966), pp. 42–48.
7. Ibid., p. 47.
8. Ibid., p. 44.
9. "Meet Mrs. Cawley," *Spring 3100* (September 1973), p. 21.
10. "Making a Police Marriage Work: The Policeman's Wife," *The Law Officer* (January– February 1977), p. 8.
11. Ibid.
12. Letter from Mrs. Monica M. Amos, "Views from Down Under," *FBI Law Enforcement Bulletin* (March 1976), p. 15.
13. "Stress and the Policeman's Wife," *Police Stress* (Fall 1978), p. 41.
14. *New York Times*, August 3, 1976, p. 33.
15. Bruce L. Danto, "A Study: Bereavement and the Widows of Slain Officers," *The Police Chief* (February 1974), p. 52.
16. Lucille Gonzalez, "The Life of a Cop's Wife," letter to the *New York Times*, February 20, 1977, Long Island Section, p. 26.
17. Newsletter of the New York City Policemen's Wives Association, Centereach, New York, December 1975.
18. Donna Parker, "Be His Anchor," in Webber, *Handbook*, p. 55. Parker is the wife of a police officer in Champaign, Illinois.
19. Marsha Wilson, "The Way We Are," in Webber, *Handbook*, p. 61. Wilson is married to an Urbana, Illinois, police officer.
20. Pat James and Martha Nelson, *Police Wife: How to Live with the Law and Like It* (Springfield, Ill.: Charles C Thomas, 1975), p. 52. James is the wife of a police officer in the Oklahoma City Police Department, and Nelson is her mother.
21. Marabel Morgan, *The Total Woman* (New York: Pocket Books, 1975), pp. 60–146.
22. Ibid., pp. 64–65.
23. Ibid., pp. 96–97.
24. Ibid., p. 116.
25. Ibid., p. 116.
26. Ibid., pp. 145–146.

27. See Abraham Maslow, *Motivation and Personality* (New York: Harper, 1954).

28. *New York Times*, January 21, 1977, p. A16.

29. Micki Siegel, "Don't Think About the Bad," *New York Sunday News Magazine*, February 23, 1975, p. 30.

30. J. Richard Udry, *The Social Context of Marriage*, 2d ed. (Philadelphia: J. B. Lippincott, 1971), p. 250.

31. Ibid., p. 251.

32. *New York Times*, January 21, 1977, p. A16.

33. Ibid.

34. Webber, *Handbook*, p. 14.

35. Webber, "The Police Wife," *The Police Chief* (January 1976), p. 48.

36. *New York Sunday News Magazine*, February 23, 1975, p. 16.

37. Jack J. Preiss and Howard J. Ehrlich, *An Examination of Role Theory: The Case of the State Police* (Lincoln, Nebraska: University of Nebraska Press, 1966), p. 34.

38. Thomas F. Adams, *Law Enforcement: An Introduction to the Police Role in the Community* (Englewood Cliffs, N.J.: Prentice-Hall, 1968), p. 227.

39. Richard Sennett, *The Fall of Public Man* (New York: Knopf, 1976), p. 300.

40. Ibid., p. 311.

41. *New York Post*, May 3, 1973, p. 30.

42. Write-in comments of police wives to the question, "What would your reaction be if your husband were assigned to radio car patrol with a policewoman as his steady partner?" (Question #7, Part I, in a questionnaire responded to by 217 police wives.) Arthur and Elaine Niederhoffer, *The Police Family: From Station House to Ranch House* (Lexington, Mass.: D.C. Heath and Company, 1978, pp. 121–123.

43. *New York Times*, November 2, 1974, p. 34.

44. Police officials in New York City disclose that the profile of the officer has changed. According to Police Commissioner Robert J. McGuire, "It's not a male bastion anymore. The force is currently the youngest in its history with more women and members of minority groups; the new breed is more questioning of authority," *New York Times*, May 8, 1983, p. 27.

45. See, for example, Catherine Milton, *Women in Policing* (Washington, D.C.: Police Foundation, 1972); Joyce L. Sichel, Lucy N. Friedman, Janet C. Quint and Michael Smith, *Women on Patrol: A Pilot Study of Police Performance in New York City* (New York: Vera Institute of Justice, 1977).

46. For a survey of police departments that have family-oriented guidance services and spouse training seminars to reduce stress and encourage communication between police couples, see Niederhoffer, *The Police Family*, pp. 131–134 and Dan Minton, "A Training Program For The Police Officer's Spouse," *Police Stress* (Fall 1979).

47. James A. Durner, et al., "Divorce—Another Occupational Hazard," *The Police Chief* (42) (November 1975); John S. Megerson, "The Officer's Lady," *The Police Chief* (October 1973).

48. Barbara E. Webber, "The Police Life," *Handbook for Law Enforcement Wives*, Barbara E. Webber, ed. (Chicago: L. E. Publishers, 1974), p. 20.

49. Webber, *The Police Wife, The Police Chief* (January 1976), p. 48.

50. Joanne Beegan, "Letters to a Rookie's Wife," in Webber, *Handbook*, p. 93.

51. Pat James and Martha Nelson, *Police Wife* (Springfield, Ill., Charles C Thomas, 1975).

52. Ibid., p. 108.

53. Jeffrey A. Schwartz and Donald A. Liebman, "Mental Health Consultation in Law Enforcement," in John R. Snibbe and Homa M. Snibbe, eds., *The Urban Policeman in Transition: A Psychological and Sociological Review* (Springfield, Ill., Charles C Thomas, 1973), p. 560; George Kirkham et al., "The Police Marriage: Three Films on Personal, Social and Family Issues" (New York: Harper and Row Media, 1976).

54. *New York Times*, August 13, 1973, p. 29.

55. Jack E. Whitehouse, "A Preliminary Inquiry into the Occupational Disadvantages of Law Enforcement Officers," *Police* (May–June 1965), p. 31; Jerome H. Skolnick, *Justice Without Trial* (New York: Wiley, 1966), p. 266; James Lichtenberger, *Divorce: A Study in Social Causation* (New York: AMS Press, 1968), pp. 95–96. This study was also cited in Durner et al., "Divorce"; Nelson A. Watson and James W. Sterling, *Police and Their Opinions* (Gaithersburg, Md., International Association of Chiefs of Police, 1969); Martin Reiser, *The Police Department Psychologist* (Springfield, Ill.: Charles C Thomas, 1972), pp. 101–105.

56. David H. Bayley and Harold Mendelsohn, *Minorities and the Police: Confrontation in America* (New York: The Free Press, 1969), pp. 4–5.

57. Joseph A. Dunne, "Marriage and the Police Officer," *Spring 3100* (July 1976), p. 10.

58. For a detailed report of our survey of divorces in police departments of 150 large cities and major state and county forces, see Niederhoffer, *The Police Family*, pp. 165–168.

59. John G. Stratton and Barbara Tracy Stratton, "Law Enforcement Marital Relationships: A Positive Approach," *FBI Law Enforcement Bulletin* (May 1982), p. 6.

60. Elizabeth A. Doll, *My Daddy Is A Policeman* (Englewood Cliffs, N.J.: Prentice-Hall, 1973).

61. Christina Maslach and Susan E. Jackson, "Burned-Out Cops and Their Families," *Psychology Today* (May 1979), p. 59.

62. Ibid., p. 59.

63. The George Family, "Six American Families," WNET Channel 13, April 25, 1977.

64. These three traits figure most frequently in the research literature as characteristics of police officers.

65. Excerpt from a term paper submitted to a graduate sociology course, John Jay College of Criminal Justice, 1976.

66. Robert Coles, *The Middle Americans* (Boston: Little, Brown, 1971), p. 52.

67. Daniel R. Miller and Guy E. Swanson, *The Changing American Parent* (New York: Wiley, 1958), p. 193.

68. Ibid., p. 102.

69. In a replication of Miller and Swanson's work, Franklin and Scott hypothesized that bureaucratic families would want their children to be popular. See Jack L. Franklin and Joseph E. Scott, "Parental Values: An Inquiry into Occupational Setting," *Journal of Marriage and the Family* 32 (August 1970), p. 407. Their rationale probably was that popularity was to a large extent determined by others and was somewhat beyond the control of the individual. In our questionnaire only 12 percent of the men and women listed popularity as very important for their children.

70. *New York Times*, October 2, 1976, p. 49.

I'm Not the Man I Used to Be: Reflections on the Transition from Prof to Cop

William G. Doerner

At the time I never realized what a momentous day January 9, 1981 would be. That was the day I took my oath of office and became a fully sworn law enforcement officer, vowing to uphold all the laws of the State of Florida and to serve and to protect the people of Tallahassee. The transformation from professor to rookie was beginning to crystallize. Had I known then what I know today, it would have been a somber celebration. Instead, I was bursting with "rookieitis."

Changes, which I thought were subtle and only partially visible to others, have altered me to such a degree that I am an entirely different person with a completely different set of values, beliefs, and attitudes. These changes were necessary in order to survive on the streets and to preserve my "self." Yet, they were of such magnitude and generated such upheaval that I became nomadic in my search to understand my "self" and the "self" I presented to others for public viewing. The purpose of this paper, then, is to revisit some of those changes, offer an introspective interpretation of the impact policing has had on my life, and to give the reader an understanding of the human dimension behind the badge.

This article was written expressly for inclusion in this edition.

ENTRANCE INTO LAW ENFORCEMENT: FROM PROFESSOR TO COP

My involvement in law enforcement began because of my academic inadequacy. The Dean had assigned me to teach an advanced undergraduate course, "Police Problems and Practices." I knew nothing about law enforcement, let alone problems and practices. Despite my protests and a sense of impending doom, I ultimately accepted the assignment. It was both an academic and an emotional disaster. My graduate training was steeped in the objective nature of scientific inquiry and included a vast array of research courses. I never flinched from the hard-core position concerning the chasm between social action and the appropriate role of the researcher. My role was to conduct research and to present the results. Whatever practical utility or application these results should hold was beyond my training and expertise. I was a researcher, not an activist, who pursued the steadfast goal of being completely objective and unconcerned with ameliorating the human plight. In fact, I had been inculcated with the belief that to do otherwise compromised my position as a scientist. While I could spout off an impromptu analysis and discussion of leading Supreme Court decisions regarding how police officers should conduct their business, I was unable to appreciate the actual conditions under which police officers labored. In other words, my ivory-tower isolation allowed my thoughts to remain esoteric and divorced from the real world. All of this changed, however, as my pedagogical role and academic sense of well-being eroded quickly during the police course.

My first crisis began with the realization that despite all my reading and copious notes, I was a foreigner in a world I had visited but never seen. This awkwardness manifested itself in classroom discussions. Finally, a student, who was also a deputy, invited me to ride with him as a civilian observer. As luck would have it, my neighbor, Duane Pickel, was a city police officer. He permitted me to ride with him a few times so as to have the opportunity to contrast city policing and rural enforcement. Gradually, Duane became my patron saint. He suggested that I apply to the Police Department for a reserve officer position. After much prodding and coaxing, I did so and, much to my astonishment, the Department hired me with the provision that I successfully complete the police academy training.

Given my earnestness as an objective scientist, the Dean was shocked by my request to rearrange my teaching schedule in order to accommodate my attendance at the police academy. Although the Dean warned me of potential interactional difficulties with other academicians, he gave his imprimatur, and off I went to become a cop. Wherever I went, I was a novelty. My wife thought I was crazy, my colleagues thought I was on a lark, and street cops suspected a hidden research agenda. After completing the academy and a year of field training and observation by my partner, the Department granted me "solo" status. I was now a full-fledged rookie, instead of a recruit. I could ride patrol alone without a partner, carry an off-duty weapon, did not have my reports subjected to a training officer's scrutiny, and could effect an arrest without a senior officer being present. In short, I was "the man."

INITIAL DUTY

I will never forget my first tour of duty and neither will my partner. I telephoned my partner and asked him to stop by the house an hour before check-on. I did not know how to get dressed. Where does my name tag go? Where should I keep my handcuff key? How do I turn on the radio and tune it in? I was totally lost. That was also the first time I donned my vest, and I will never forget that look on my wife's face. She was paralyzed with fear. The vest was a symbol of my combat readiness and the deadly finality of the streets. But I was too exhilarated to allay those trepidations. Those fears would haunt our relationship later.

After an hour of patrol, I asked my partner to pull off the street into a vacant parking lot. I was soaked with perspiration. I felt so uneasy, like a target. Everybody could see me and knew who I was but I could not distinguish the good guys from the bad ones. While waiting at a red light, I felt like a sitting duck for an ambush. I got out of the car to stretch and grab a smoke. Then I looked at my boots; I had spent hours spit-shining those things. When I left check-on, my boots were so glossy and sparkling that you could see your reflection in them. Now my left boot was just one big smudge while my right boot retained its gleam. My partner Duane just roared. The car heater, while keeping us nice and toasty, had melted all those layers of polish. What a rookie!

A little while later, we got a "good call." (A "good call" is a stabbing, a bloody fight, or a bad wreck. What a warped term! Actually, though, most cops lust for a "good call" in order to break the monotony of routine patrol duties.) Two men had been in a fight. When we arrived one fellow was lying on the ground with his skull split open, dripping blood; the other man had bashed his head with a concrete block. By the time I reached the bleeding man, part of his brain was seeping out. I turned away, wobbled off a few steps, and vomited. Not a single cop laughed or ridiculed me. At one time they, too, had been rookies. I later found out that the suspect had won a pool game, and when the victim welshed on the dollar bet, the suspect killed him. Over a dollar bet! Incredible! When reflecting on this and other events, I shudder to think that most criminological theories start with the premise that the human being is a rational animal. While I can agree with the animal aspect, I no longer accept the rational portion.

The rest of the week was pretty routine, except for one call. We were dispatched to a traffic accident with injuries. When we arrived, metal and glass were strewn all over the roadway, radiators leaking, and blood oozing everywhere. The passenger in one car was a two-year-old little girl with almost purple-black lips, no heart beat, no respiration. I frantically administered the CPR technique I had learned a few weeks earlier. God, how I did try, but nothing helped. She was dead, another drunk-driver statistic. Just that week my wife and I found out that it was highly unlikely that we would ever be able to have a child. Now that little angel just lay there. The drunk driver, oblivious to me since he was talking to my partner, was standing by chuckling and giggling at the spectacle. I could hear him saying that his insurance company would cover the damage, so the accident was no big deal. Outraged, I went for the drunk, determined to beat that smile back into his face. Fortunately, my partner grabbed me and pulled me away. I was relieved from duty early that night, went home, and cried my way into a numbing, drunken stupor. I didn't know if I could handle being a cop any more. It hurt too much.

PERSONALITY CHANGES

I maintain that the work group molds the officer's personality. I call it street survival. Rookies find themselves under tremendous pressure and tend to gravitate from one end of the pendulum to the other in their search to find a comfortable style of policing. Every rookie knows his or her reputation needs to be established before being fully accepted as a fellow officer. Hence, rookies tend to be impetuous, aggressive, and very rough around the edges. They need to learn when and how to bullshit in the street, how to finesse the person they are confronting, and how to read the interactional cues and body language that dictate appropriate courses of action and impending danger.

Imagine yourself on a beat. During the course of routine patrol you see an individual furtively glancing at several vehicles in a dark parking lot. You stop, approach the individual, suspecting that he may be trying to steal valuable contents from a car. When you ask the suspect for some identification, he curses you and begins to walk away. Or imagine a slightly different situation. You stop a vehicle for a traffic violation. The operator insists that his driving habits are impeccable, that you must be mistaken, refuses to hand over the driver's license, and announces his intention to drive away. What do you do? As a new officer, I was flabbergasted by these and similar situations and at a loss as to what to do. As a rookie, I experienced what I call "the pendulum." At one extreme, I could grab the suspect and immediately place him under arrest. At the other extreme, I could do nothing and simply back down. One position is an aggressive never-flinching stance, while the other is a docile belly-up posture.

One barrier that new officers commonly encounter concerns the physical aspect of the job. As a university professor, I had become accustomed to sitting back and logically analyzing facts at my leisure. That luxury dissipates on the street. My personal problem was that I had not been involved in a single physical confrontation in the past ten or so years. I did not know how to fend for myself. Although I wore all the accouterments of the trade (gun, mace, baton, cuffs), the academy had instilled all sorts of civil liability nightmares in my head. My capacity was like a zero-sum game. If the suspect meekly submitted to my authority, I could handle the call; if the suspect resisted my authority, my only option was to escalate and hurt him physically, risking a civil suit.

An encounter with a drunk convinced me that there was a huge void in my capabilities. He was over two hundred pounds, and I tip the scales at one-sixty. The drunk refused to leave an establishment after receiving a warning to do so. Reasoning with him was an exercise in futility. Finally, we ended on the floor. Luckily for me, a fellow officer helped to subdue him, and I emerged with nothing more than a rumpled uniform. But the point hit home. If I had been alone, I would have been hurt. I did not know what to do with my hands. My partner Duane lured me down to a local gym, and I began a weight lifting program to increase my strength. The second phase of my physical rehab program was to learn judo. Time after time, I lay on the mat looking up at the ceiling, wondering what my opponent had done to dump me. Here I was, thirty-two years old, competing with kids who were ten years younger, and I hurt! I had bruises on top of bruises. Gradually my strength increased, and I became more proficient at handling myself. But "the pendulum" swung again. Now I was cockier, more assertive, more arrogant, and less fearful on the street. I did not have the "John Wayne Syndrome"; I was "the man." My word was law.

One night I was dispatched to handle a drunk at the bus depot. After observing and talking with him I decided to place him in protective custody for the night. Once outside, the drunk became more and more agitated and finally spit in my face. Almost instantly, I became enraged. I wheeled the cuffed prisoner around and struck his face with my hand. Blood gushed, and he spit out two teeth between the flaps of what used to be his upper lip. My next thought was one of horror. The man definitely needed stitches. What now? I remember scanning the area. Not a single witness. Should I write my report and claim that the prisoner tripped and fell, or should I chance reporting the incident? Fortunately, I did not have my flashlight in my hand at the time. The drunk would have eaten it.

While every officer in the department empathized with me, Internal Affairs informed me that if a complaint were filed, I would draw a substantial suspension for using excessive force and for abusing a handcuffed prisoner. What about my rights as a human? Was I supposed to stand there and wag my finger at the drunk saying "no-no" while his sputum rolled down my face? I sweated it out for several days before I found out that the drunk had left town without making a formal complaint. I had escaped formal disciplinary action. The fear of losing my badge and gun, even for a few days, swung "the pendulum" back to the middle.

THE SYSTEM

That night was like any other Saturday. Dispatch served up the usual menu of loud party calls, drunks, traffic accidents, and stale burglaries. I had a rookie with me that night and was showing him the ropes. We talked about how, after ten years of marriage, my wife was eight months pregnant, nothing short of a miracle for us. The shrill of the tone button alerted me to a serious call. I scrambled for the mike in anticipation of a "good call." The dispatcher called my number and within seconds we were rolling, lights and sirens, to a-man-with-a-gun call. As we pulled into a parking lot, witnesses pointed to a fleeing man. A couple of hasty questions verified that the man still had the gun, had waved it in the air, but had not fired the weapon. Knowing the area and realizing that the man had only two possible escape routes, I instructed the rookie to pursue the suspect while I headed in a different direction to cut off his path. I remember radioing in my actions and the dispatcher hitting the tone button again. "Attention all units. Emergency traffic only. 929 in foot-pursuit of man with a gun. All available units identify and be in route." As I rounded the corner of a house and headed up the driveway, the suspect wheeled around the other end of the house, startled to see me just thirty feet away. I drew my revolver, aimed, and ordered him to put up his hands. While the butterflies waltzed in my stomach and my heart pounded like a jackhammer, I realized that I had no cover. I felt naked. The man began talking and slowly walking toward me, all the time keeping his right arm behind his back out of my view. Despite two more commands, the man kept moving as if I were not even there. In what seemed like a time-warp, a slow-motion series of frames, he turned slightly at the hips and was bringing his right hand forward. My stomach soured as my finger began the squeeze. He was about to be dead. Suddenly, something clunked to the ground behind him, and he raised both hands over his head. I eased off the trigger and the cylinder rotated. He was a half-pound pull away from death. I ordered him to move toward me and I circled behind him. Upon order, he knelt down, but refused to lie face down on the ground. One well-placed kick to the back and he sprawled out. I waited for what seemed like an eternity, and then simultaneously, four police cars deluged upon the scene. After securing the prisoner, I walked over to the spot where I heard something fall to the ground and it was a six-inch, .22-caliber pistol, fully loaded. I shivered uncontrollably, thought about my unborn child, and wondered if it was worth it.

The charges consisted of aggravated assault on a law enforcement officer, carrying a concealed weapon, and reckless display of a firearm. The suspect countered with allegations that I had lifted $600 from his wallet and police brutality when I kicked him to the ground. A few days later the state attorney's office bounced my report back. What did the man say while he was advancing on me? I explained to the prosecutor that I had no earthly idea what he said. I blocked out everything and focused on the immediate threat. All I knew was that death for one or both of us was imminent. After several more questions, the prosecutor advised me that he was dropping the charges. Dropping them! My blood boiled. Why? The voice at the other end explained that my memory lapse would not substantiate the assault charge. I hurled protests, statutory scripture, and vile curses through the wire. The prosecutor went on to explain that the state was dropping all charges and, in return, the defendant was dropping the allegations of police brutality and larceny. According to the voice, it was an expedient deal. Incredulous, I frothed and foamed, but the state attorney was not swayed. I went from a situation where I had ample probable cause to kill the man to being in the position of defending myself from an assailant's accusations and lost! I was shattered.

I went back to Duane, my patron saint. He understood the dilemma too well. It's a game, a charade. Make the arrest, do the paperwork, and keep on going. The public defender will grab the case and play with it. The state attorney will monkey with it and do the most expedient thing for his career. Justice comes only on the streets. Your job was simply to answer calls, keep the lid on, and cover your ass. There's an old saying among street cops: "They may beat the rap, but they won't beat the ride." The pendulum moved once again.

MARITAL STRESS

While slumped in a chair during my academy days, one of the instructors inquired as to how many of us were married, getting ready to make the vow, or had a steady relationship. Hands dutifully grabbed for air. The next statement stunned us: Between half and three-quarters of us would be divorced or separated within the next three years. Sporadic contact with my fellow recruits farmed out to various agencies since graduation is chilling. My class is well over the half-way mark. I almost joined them.

Prior to the academy, I had never fired a gun in my life. Now I wear a gun wherever I go. Shopping, running errands, work, bed, parties, picking up the baby, I am always armed. My wife was appalled by this constant armament. Many of our discussions centered around the gun. The pendulum had swung again. Could I kill someone? Definitely. Would I kill someone? If need be. Why? If I have to, I will. Cold, calculating, and calloused. The man she had married had been a passive, nonviolent individual. Now the weapon is a constant companion and its handler had absorbed its cold steel.

Night was particularly disconcerting for her. During my first few months on duty, I would come home around 4:30 in the morning, make just enough noise to stir her out of her slumber, and rattle on about the night's smorgasbord. She shared my enthusiasm and my initial abhorrence about blood, brains, guts, and smelly corpses. Over time, things gradually changed. I no longer volunteered my lunch after handling a corpse or a real "good call." Details became less lurid and less descriptive. Suddenly, there were no more pillow talks about last night's escapades. Instead, there would be a slight rustle among the sheets, a creak of the bedboard, and a snore.

Nightmares began. She would awaken abruptly to my screams for someone to move on or to drop the weapon. Arms would flail and curses would fly before she could gently arouse me from wherever I had been. Slowly our circle of civilian friends diminished. I refused to go to parties composed of civilians. My whole attitude shifted. Instead of asking my wife to do something, I would order it to be done. If the question of why arose, the inevitable response was "Because I said so."

It became quite apparent to my police partner that the streets were invading my sanctuary. My wife began to resent him; I spent more time with him than with her; I told him everything, but her nothing—despite my protests that I wanted to shield her from disaster and that my partner's actions had kept me alive more than once. In reality, I was driving a wedge between us. I was bringing the job home. My "self" had become an extension of the uniform.

The inevitable separation and divorce proceedings came. My partner listened silently as I expounded upon how we differed from civilians, how unjustly I was being treated both at home and at work, and how trashy the streets had become. After weeks of this daily barrage, Duane confronted the issue squarely. The problem was not the streets, not the job, not the pressure, not the home. It was me. All the classic signs of stress were present. Fellow officers and their wives made suggestions as to how they had struggled through similar circumstances and shared their coping strategies. Almost like a storybook scenario, we reconciled and now are living happily together again.

THE TOUCH THAT LINGERS

Even after learning how to dissociate the streets from one's domicile, there is always the fear of another type of deadly invasion. One maxim that officers adhere to is never touch, handle, or shake hands with anyone in the streets. The purpose of this precaution is to provide a healthy line of defense against germ warfare. The feasibility of such a rule is very evident when dealing with bums, winos, and other unsavory characters whose appearance indicates they reside on the streets. Their personal stench serves as an instant reminder to avoid all physical contact whenever possible. The chances of touching street people and then inadvertently rubbing your eyes or touching your mouth exposes the body to a host of bacteria, germs, diseases, and fungi. In fact, one of the tidbits an old-timer passed on to me was to carry a small box of handy-wipes as a preventative measure. Sometimes, though, all these precautions do not help.

One night I received a drunk-person call at one of the more respectable hotels in town. The location afforded some sense of relief since there is nothing worse than having to handle a stinky, filthy body that has gone limp. Seeing the drunkard provided an even greater sense of relief. He was middle-aged, wearing a suit and tie. However, something was amiss. He was sweating profusely and had a violent case of the shakes. My senses indicated that something was out of the ordinary. I requested an ambulance so the EMTs could take a look at him rather than just pouring the man into the police car and transporting him to the drunk tank. The EMTs confirmed my suspicions. The man was advancing into the d.t.'s and was becoming jaundiced. After helping the EMTs load the man into the ambulance, one of the EMTs issued the usual advice. Wash up and if I had any cold or flu symptoms within the next few days, stop by the hospital for a shot. I washed up and hit the streets to finish out the shift.

Two days later, my wife took the baby to the doctor. He had been real whiny and cranky. Being only seven months old, he could not tell us where he hurt. Poor kid had strep throat. A few hours later the EMT called to inform me that the drunk had died. Cause of death included cirrhosis, pneumonia, advanced gonorrhea, and hepatitis. Hepatitis! Time for the big needle. I immediately dialed the baby doctor's office and explained to the nurse that two days earlier I had contact with an active hepatitis carrier, and now my baby had come down with strep throat. She instructed me to bring the entire family in and, if I would, kindly use the back door when we got there. Panic and hysteria swept through my wife. Guilt reigned over terror in my mind. I had infected my own little boy. The damn streets had invaded my home again. This time, though, I was ready to quit the department. I felt like a pariah.

The doctor alleviated our deepest fears. It would take two to three months after exposure before one would become a hepatitis carrier. My boy's strep throat was just a weird coincidence. However, because the deceased subject was essentially a walking germ culture, I needed several inoculations. Four shots and several hours later, I was as sick as a dog. Our house had become an infirmary.

My wife and I talked about my quitting the police force. To my amazement, she wanted me to continue the job. The job had nothing to do with the baby being sick. She realized that I loved working a beat. We had been through so many trying times, had weathered so many job-induced problems, that to quit at this point over just a mere coincidence would be self-defeating. I was both relieved and shocked. Then it dawned on me. She had become a cop's wife. Both of us had made the transition and survived. We sat there and laughed.

SUMMARY

The past few years have brought tremendous changes. I have come to realize that society has vested a tremendous power in me—the ability to deprive someone of freedom and, if necessary, life. That power is awesome. However, there is a huge price associated with that power. After absorbing that power, the person behind the badge must live with it twenty-four hours a day, seven days a week. The toll for some officers is unbearable and they quit. For others, it becomes a cross to bear and requires a variety of adjustments.

I would not trade my experiences as a cop for anything in the world despite all the attendant heartaches. At the same time, I pray that my child will not grow up and swear the same oath that I regard as sacred. I hope he can avoid many of the agonies that I have witnessed and experienced. When I see the bright faces and hear the lofty goals of new recruits fresh from the academy, a sense of ambivalence overwhelms me. I respect their enthusiasm for their new occupation but, at the same time, I pity the poor bastards.

12

THE FUTURE OF LAW ENFORCEMENT

We have stressed that the police and police institutions are largely a product of the historical past. It would be naïve and a serious mistake, however, to think of police institutions as prisoners of the past, static and unchanging. As the forces that shape a society emerge and seek primacy and power, the police must respond to this changing environment.

Perhaps one of the most powerful forces affecting change in police organizations is that of the process of police unionization, which the police establishment has resisted determinedly for decades. Even the most powerful industrial corporations have succumbed to labor organization. The transfer and sharing of power that unionization entails is a revolutionary force in police administration. It will create new relations across the board with a potential for democratization of this quasi-military organization.

Another dimension that has much promise, but whose impact is as yet not clear, is the introduction of equality for women in an essentially male occupation. One of the unresolved problems here is whether the integration of women in police forces is going to be a sustained, sincere effort, or another instance of token compliance with our concept of equality and justice for all.

The effect of higher education for many police officers will not be evident for many years to come. The emergence of a college-educated cadre does introduce an element of uncertainty. They will be the internal critics, the contenders for power, and the connecting link to the academic community. A certain degree of resentment within the police system on the part of those who have been unable or unwilling to pursue higher education may be a disruptive force for polarization. Yet for all the portents of change as a result of higher education, the traditional police culture may prove to be strong enough to absorb and co-opt the "new breed." In all probability our society's technology will not produce some magical, innovative crime-fighting apparatus. Instead, assuming present trends and developments, computer technology and information retrieval will have the greatest impact on law enforcement.

The future political and economic development of the United States will determine in large measure the future direction of law enforcement. Given the inevitable cyclical fluctuations inherent in our economic system, the political implications and prospects that may result are not clear at this time. If a long period of economic stagnation persists, the police may be the ultimate instrument to control discontented and hostile forces that will emerge as a consequence of widespread economic dislocation and concomitant unemployment. Political demagogues may seize upon the general unrest to arouse the explicit fears of crime in an effort to mobilize popular sentiments, thus enabling them to exploit the police and police institutions for their own purposes. This may place the police in a dangerous situation in which they become pawns in a larger political struggle over which they have little control. Whatever the outcome, one of the crucial elements will be the police system.

Law Enforcement: A Look into the Future

A. C. Germann

Our peoples face the perils of population explosion, energy shortages, maldistribution of food, pollution of air and water, proliferation of lethal weaponry, inadequate health services, and monetary inflation. None of these perils are, today, domestic; all are global. Almost all can be solved by the application of science and technology and by a concerted international community.

But there is one peril that requires more than the application of science and technology and more than concerted action and that is the peril of excessive social control. To meet this peril—and the problems surrounding it, such as unresponsive leadership, violations of basic human rights, the expansion of control and enforcement institutions to a degree that may threaten traditional democratic processes—we must rethink the goals and priorities of law enforcement, and we must redirect our efforts in order to make it humane and effective.

We seem to be prisoners of our clichés and the thinking of 25 and 50 years ago. Our police and their predecessors seem wholly unable to emancipate themselves from thinking about weaponry and repression as the key social control solution. We carry the stereotypes of the past and are unable to disabuse ourselves of them. We have only to read police literature to realize the extent to which our police establishment has been unable to adjust to the realities of the present and future.

Look at the articles, editorials, and advertisements. Almost all give tacit acceptance and approval to the traditional repressive processes, continue the myopic trust in technology, and assume that the people will continue to support the present ineffective posture and program.

Somehow we must face up to our failures, rather than continue to disguise them with modern glitter. Some 12,034,431 index offenses were reported in 1982, in the *Uniform Crime Reports*, with a 20.1% clearance rate. National crime surveys, sponsored by our government, continue consistently to indicate that crime is two to five times higher than reported. If but three times higher, we have about 36,000,000 index offenses for 1982, and a true clearance rate of about 6.7%. In such a case, about 93.3% of the offenses—some 33,588,000—are unaffected by the actions or nonactions of the police! I am inclined to believe that our police are really dealing with the unlucky, or the inept, or the mentally retarded antisocial offender who represents that 6.7% identified and charged. Thus we have been, are, and will be almost totally ineffective in controlling antisocial behavior by police intervention, no matter how many times we double our forces, no matter how many computers we purchase, no matter how lethal our firepower, no matter how paramilitary our agencies, and no matter how contrived our public relations. Yet we go on, replicating the useless efforts of the past.

We must, somehow, it seems to me, abate our traditional trust in force and cease our worship at its altar. We must increase our regard for our fellow citizen, our ideals of service to humanity, and repudiate all tyrannical and unjust social forms wherever found on this planet—and that includes a challenge of our own social control when it becomes obvious that human rights are being violated by any of our institutions.

This article was written expressly for inclusion in this edition.

Our Bill of Rights, dating from 1789, contains the ideal of equal justice under law. But this ideal has been ignored, or circumvented, or violated continuously—and we all know it! Who would deny that there are indeed separate justices for youth, for minorities, for women, for nonconformists, and more obviously, for the rich and poor?

At one time in our society, the young saw police as all-good, all-wise, and all-powerful; and later, adult acceptance of the legitimacy of police flowed from that youthful idealization. Positive feelings in formative years can have lasting consequences, as we all know.

Now, as children grow up and see police in more critical and less enthusiastic fashion, such youthful lack of respect may create latent feelings difficult to change. If such childhood feelings are negative, the child will see the police, not as benign and protective, but as dangerous and arrogant, models not to be emulated, but to be rejected. This may have important and lasting consequences as the years go by, and such disillusioned young people grow up with ineradicably antagonistic mental sets relative to police, their work, and their worth. And such is now happening, wherever the police are less than humane.

I think that it is no wonder that intelligent, motivated, and humanistic people are discouraged from affiliation with police. Or, if affiliated, it is no wonder that they become frustrated and depart the service. Or, if they remain, it is no wonder that they are considered oddballs by police traditionalists and are consigned to innocuous positions.

I suspect, looking to the future, that one or the other of two diametrically opposed scenarios is likely to come to pass. Each one is sketched out here to its extreme. At the moment we are limping along with a hodgepodge of both. If given the choice, I would opt for an amalgam of the efficiency of the first with the humanism of the second: an omnipotent twenty-first century genie directed and controlled by a wise, just, and loving people. For me, the maximum disaster would be an amalgam of the efficiency and repressive potential of the first: an omnipotent twenty-first century genie directing and controlling a supine, frightened, Orwellian slave-labor camp that believes it is free and willingly suffers the loss of liberty.

THE REPRESSIVE SCENARIO

Crime in all categories—street, organized, and white-collar—continues to increase in amount and repulsiveness. Citizens become more panicked and angry. The police, more frustrated than ever, ask for more manpower, facilities, and equipment, and suggest to the public that the "war on crime" be intensified. They convince a frightened citizenry that all "handcuffs" should be taken off the police and that discretion should be given for more data bank utilization, for more surveillance capability, for greater authority to search and bug and wiretap, for authority to hold subjects in preventive detention, and for greater latitude in dealing with nonconforming minorities and dissidents of any type. The police double and triple their secret-service budgets, utilizing many more informants of all ages and life-styles.

The police agencies increase their ranks, tripling and quadrupling their forces; they build hundreds of fortress-stations in every metropolitan area, adding software and hardware of all types and using ever more space-age electronic capacity for data banks, surveillance equipment, and communications. In addition to the currently stockpiled weaponry, massive additions of combat-proven armaments accrue. To the array of saps, batons, magnum handguns, rifles, riot guns, chemical sprays, armored tanks, and helicopter gun ships are added a variety of gases, grenades, flamethrowers, shields, screens, armor, and security barriers for all facilities. "Green Beret" militarism becomes the order of the day.

Police assume, unilaterally, all decision-making authority for social control in the nation; and they apply immediate massive force in any situation where police are not awarded instant obedience, deference, and compliance. The International Association of Chiefs of Police and the FBI and the police associations continue to question the absence of stronger laws, the leniency of the courts, and the failure of prisons to maintain long-term custody. All babies, at birth, have radioactive social security numbers embedded in the soles of their feet by means of high-pressure air injection, such numbers easily read by readout plates, so that police can make instant identifications, surreptitiously if they so desire. All citizens are photographed and fingerprinted regularly, and they carry up-to-date identification at all times or face immediate arrest and penalty. All members of the nonconforming minority are subject to continuous harassment. Any person who is particularly suspect is subject to implantation of electronic locater devices for continuous surveillance.

In times of any special unrest, dissident groups are subject to neutralization—by infiltration of their organizations by informers or undercover agents, by contrived arrests via incitation to illegal acts by agents provocateurs, and, if necessary, by elimination of their leadership by any means possible.

The police continue their close affinity to conservative, ultraconservative and extreme right-wing movements and philosophies. No radical changes are made in police organization or traditional procedures. Sensitive and humanistic members of the police establishment are even more ostracized; incoming recruits are even more intensively screened to eliminate socially sensitive probationers and those who would question traditional police procedures; and the criminal justice system, as a whole, is purged of liberal and humane careerists.

The many college-degree programs in criminal justice are becoming more highly developed as adjuncts to the local police academy, with safe traditionalists remaining in control of faculty, curriculum, and student progress.

The police establishment continues to foster nonquestioning support from the conforming majority by frightening it even further with the spectre of criminal dissident take-over, by confusing it even more with 1930's-type public education programs, and by continuing the police/media myth that the handsome white supercop, occasionally accompanied by a token minority assistant, aided by technology and weaponry, making unilateral determination of all means used, will subdue and convict the unkempt, dark, and ugly supercriminal. Slowly but surely, executive, legislative, and corporate power is manipulated or coerced into supporting police budgets second only to military—with intelligence dossiers and coordinated data-bank exchanges of personal information making docility and cooperation a mandatory condition of continuance in office. Slowly but surely, the alienation of nonconforming minorities—youths, pacifists, humanists, liberals, radicals, progressives, feminists, blacks, Chicanos, Native Americans, civil libertarians, consumer advocates, environmentalists, life-style experimentalists, eccentrics, one-world advocates, religious sectarians, academicians, artists, and other independent thinkers—becomes complete. And the police, coldly efficient, with the most reactionary traditionalists in total control, become as hated as was the German Gestapo (and probably more so, for the Gestapo never had the use of space-age science and technology). And slowly but surely the dream of a free society in the United States, a society linked to all other freedom-loving societies, fades, and the world is left with only dictatorships—variously disguised—with the military and the police serving rich and powerful individuals and corporations. And slowly but surely, the charge that police are but the hired guns of the "haves" is documented and proved again and again by daily evidence, as police "crack-downs" concentrate, as usual, on those unfortunates most readily available.

What, then, is the other extreme? Scenario two calls for a large-scale change in attitude and practice, indeed!

THE HUMANISTIC SCENARIO

Crime in all categories—street, organized, and white-collar—continues to increase in amount and repulsiveness. Citizens become more panicked and angry. The police, rapidly moving away from past militaristic configurations, engage in serious heart-to-heart communication with the entire community. Many hundreds of police chiefs and subordinate commanders are retired, replaced, or reeducated. Many thousands of social science graduates are now productively serving their fellow citizens as professional police officers. The accent is changed; the former unilateral social control *by* police has disappeared; in its place has come collective responsibility for social control and community control *of* police. Policing is now a profession with equal status and economic reward along with law, medicine, and teaching. The former accent on repression and "crushing" is replaced by an emphasis on serving and "helping." The police agency is totally transformed. The police academies of the nation are almost completely phased out, and education for police service is now the responsibility of universities. Top ranks of police agencies contain many women, minorities, intellectuals, and representatives of every segment of American society. These leaders, open to the world, see the problems of social control and human rights as global matters. The need for planetary concern is stressed, and these leaders understand that both problems and solutions are interdependent, as are the citizens of the world. Police leaders are candid in admitting that the policing of past years has been largely wasteful of effort, resources, and emphasis. The de-emphasis of force, the re-emphasis of personal moral responsibility and development of concerned neighborhoods, and the continuous example of concern for one's brother citizen mark the new police attitude.

Everywhere, now, the policeman is a warm, trusted, and approachable friend to *all* people in the community. The police readily accept the role of ombudsman of the weak, ignorant, confused, frustrated, unemployed, cold, sick, hungry, lonely, and hopeless. The police at all levels of government see themselves as examples for youth, as teachers of the community, and as helpful members of the human family; and the community responds in kind, no longer viewing the police as merely heavily armed mercenaries or as cold and indifferent bureaucrats, but rather, it sees them as concerned and capable friends.

The changes are immense: a nation which had been supporting, without question, an almost *carte-blanche* police authority and its ever-enlarging lethal potential, radically alters its goals and programs. The seemingly invincible indifference of the police to public opinion alters quickly as people and their representatives opt for a collective responsibility to the planetary family of man, rather than perpetuating individual competition and narrow self-interest. The people-oriented police, convinced that a police establishment divorced from militaristic postures and right-wing identification is more representative of a humane democracy, now assist enthusiastically in the largest alteration of social control methods since the Peelian reforms of 1829.

Criminal law, at all levels of government, is reformed and limited in scope. Simplified and clarified laws and more just penalties receive overwhelming public understanding and support; and the people are edified in knowing that their police have led the fight for such reforms.

Existing laws are expanded and new laws are enacted to shield the people from racial and sex discrimination, pollution and misuse of public resources, manufacture and sale of defective products, deceptive advertising and packaging, fraudulent housing and insurance schemes, and other "white-collar" crimes. Units are established in all police agencies to investigate private or governmental invasions of civil liberties, and others are formed to deal with consumer protection and the implementation of gun control laws. The police lead the effort to strengthen the Bill of Rights by amending the First Amendment to the Constitution to add the right of privacy to the right of assembly and by amending the Second Amendment to define the limits of the government's right to bear arms against its citizens. In addition, such leadership is effective in securing new laws to protect citizens from private or governmental misuse of electronic surveillance or data bank information. Such police leadership gives notice to the entire world that our law enforcement is, indeed, the enemy of all forms of tyranny.

Other existing laws are revoked and behavior decriminalized in the area of "morals offenses," such as drunkenness, vagrancy, gambling, prostitution, obscenity, pornography, drug use, fornication, adultery, bigamy, incest, and homosexuality as relates to consenting adults.

Police are demilitarized in appearance, equipment, and methods; domestic warfare by police is emphatically rejected.

The police of the United States now set a planetary example of humanistic professional law enforcement. As part of its program of international cooperation, it works with police of other nations in implementing a planetary registry, so that the passport becomes a worldwide means of identification, credit, and assistance.

Our police put priority emphasis, now, on developing neighborhood and community organizations, and new police units are found in every city with the function of assisting people to know each other and to cooperate collectively. During the changeover period our police establish the tradition of inviting all segments of the public, from all enclaves, to assume the responsibility of making decisions about police goals, methods, and priorities. Police secrecy (except for data bank security and ongoing current investigations) is a thing of the past, all agency facilities and operations are open to public scrutiny, and all equipment and weaponry are a matter of bilateral police-community agreement. Ombudsmen and criminal justice review commissions work cooperatively with all citizens to eliminate corruption and injustice, and they receive enthusiastic cooperation from law enforcement.

The people and the police give primary attention to the reduction of violent antisocial behavior, working with prosecutors, courts, and corrections to neutralize the person who threatens or causes physical harm to his fellow citizen. The people and the police assist in the community-based treatment and rehabilitation of nonviolent offenders, aiding their successful reentry into the community family.

The reform of criminal law results in much less police intervention, the participation of the public in policing results in much more swift and certain conviction of arrestees, and the limitation of incarceration only to violent offenders results in highly reduced prison populations.

Our police, educated and humanistic, are not inclined to harass nonconforming minorities, and they relate more easily to a wide variety of life-styles. Our police, educated and humanistic, are not angered by citizens who gather to protest tyranny or injustice. As a matter of fact, our police, educated and humanistic, encourage community organization for collective action; they encourage citizen concern for civil rights and civil liberties; and they encourage the struggle to make the American dream of liberty and justice for all both a national and a planetary objective. Thus, the second scenario is a drastic departure from the current reality.

A FINAL WORD

Which scenario will come to pass? Hard-nosed police traditionalists, and their Archie Bunker-type supporters, are very much a part of the national landscape. Out of ignorance or misguided zeal they contribute to the possible development of the repressive scenario.

But just as real, no matter how outnumbered, are the humanistic police professionals, with their academic soul-brothers and like-minded citizens. By motivated example they make the humanistic scenario a future possibility.

Whichever scenario is developed will carry the mark of the other, for it is unlikely that any human institution can be as pure as its motivating ideal; but the nation will see the distinct emergence of either a more repressive or a more humanistic law enforcement than exists in the present hodgepodge.

The total answer really lies outside the police precinct or university classroom and depends upon the hearts of our general citizenry and their representatives. Will they continue to support the terribly wasteful and almost totally ineffective mode of social control? If so, the repressive scenario will bloom ever more healthily. Will they finally say "Enough is enough" and demand a radical change of goals, methods, priorities, and posture? If so, the humanistic scenario can become more than the idle chatter of idealists.

I wish I could suggest that all the college and university criminal justice programs are a force potent enough to humanize and reorient American policing, but I can't. Although some programs work intensively to raise the consciousness of their students, far too many are captives of the current police establishment and serve only to perpetuate the crude clichés of the present criminal justice nonsystem.

I wish I could suggest that the billions of dollars expended by the Law Enforcement Assistance Administration—LEAA—resulted in substantial positive change in American policing, but I can't. Too many of those dollars bought only a slicked-up, gadget-oriented, firepower-worshipping remake of what we already have; too many dollars were spent installing a police-industrial complex and further misleading our nation with a continuation of the myth that computers and firepower will bring order and tranquility to our people.

I wish I could suggest that national scandals involving the Presidency, the FBI, the CIA, the Attorney General, the Pentagon, and domestic surveillance alerted our people and their representatives to the probability of hundreds of mini-Watergates throughout the land and to the need for extensive scrutiny and monumental change of our military and social-control mechanisms; but I can't. The sordid, sleazy, unconstitutional and arrogantly pragmatic practices exposed are not really new or surprising to any sensitive person who has worked within the criminal justice nonsystem for any length of time, and they will continue to occur until radical change of attitude and practice is a nationwide reality.

When I look into the future of law enforcement I am frightened and, at the same time, hopeful. I am frightened because the humanists are so badly outnumbered within the criminal justice establishment. I am hopeful because it is very obvious that we have come to the end of an era: we either surrender to the most repressive elements in the institution and go the way of the police state, or we damn well get it together and humanize criminal justice by making substantial changes. There is no other way!

Now is the time for humanistic academics and humanistic police chiefs to lead the way. Even though our students and citizens are anxious, they are ever receptive to the idea of humane and progressive change, particularly when espoused by intelligent and compassionate professors and by intelligent and compassionate criminal justice leaders. The nation is waiting. Speak out! Lead! The classroom is waiting. Speak out! Lead! The criminal justice agency is waiting. Speak out! Lead! The local community is waiting. Speak out! Lead! The future of law enforcement can be a matter of great pride instead of horrible embarrassment! Speak out! Lead! NOW!

Criminal Justice Education: The End of the Beginning

Richard Pearson

It is clear that criminal justice programs are now an established part of American higher education.* The field has reached the end of the beginning in what will be inevitably a long-term period of development. What are some of the issues that criminal justice education will face in the future?

SOME ISSUES FOR THE FUTURE

Potential Students

The first issue pertains to potential students. There are at least three kinds of students for whom the criminal justice programs of the future would be useful. One is part of the initial target population of in-service students who have already completed programs at the baccalaureate level. Using a general rule of thumb in higher education, perhaps fifteen percent of these students have the ability to pursue advanced professional education at the graduate level. They constitute a potential leadership group for the criminal justice agencies and include individuals for whom college teaching and scholarship would be a logical career. This group is an important source of talent for the future. It deserves careful attention in the planning and offering of advanced programs.

SOURCE: Edited excerpt from *Criminal Justice Education: The End of the Beginning*, Summary Report issued by John Jay College of Criminal Justice, CUNY. New York: John Jay Press.

* The present study surveyed the field of criminal justice education by means of a questionnaire distributed to members of relevant professional associations. The questionnaire analysis involved 250 respondents out of 1,000 forms that were distributed. In addition, campus visits and interviews were conducted at 14 selected universities with formal programs and the catalogs of 11 of these institutions were subjected to a content analysis. A central feature for the inquiry was the classification of programs into three broad curriculum models: (1) Humanistic-Social; (2) Professional-Managerial; and (3) Technical-Vocational.

The questionnaire responses relate to formal programs at 146 colleges and universities in 37 states and two foreign countries. The group included four-year colleges and universities (59 percent) and community colleges (41 percent).

A second source of potential students is the much larger number of younger students who will be graduating from high school and who are interested in beginning careers in criminal justice. This is a large and heterogeneous target population and efforts to serve these students will be difficult and complex. Their importance for the future of the field, however, is very great. If these students can be well served over a period of several years, say a decade or more, then it will be possible to say that professionalism has come to stay in the law enforcement and other criminal justice agencies.

We present four observations about this group of potential students. One, the issue of career preparation and program design for younger, pre-service students is among the more significant issues facing criminal justice education today. The resolution of this issue will go far to determine the long-term development of the field. Two, most existing programs at the associate- and baccalaureate-levels were designed for the more mature, in-service student. It is not likely that these programs will serve the larger group of younger, pre-service students without substantial modification. Three, there is need for research and experimentation with alternative kinds of programs for this target population. There are few indications that this experimentation is underway. And four, it is a *sine qua non* for further development of these programs that agency entry requirements be calibrated to appropriate levels of educational attainment. This is not now the case. The resources available to higher education for program development are far too limited to be used for programs where appropriate career entry is not reasonably assured.

A third possible target population of potential students is an even more heterogeneous group: the general student probably interested in some other career but perhaps also interested in some aspect of this field for his own edification. Criminal justice programs, for example, introduced a series of legal courses to the undergraduate curriculum, thus making them accessible outside the law schools. One of the strengths of these courses for this purpose is that they are typically offered for the non-specialist, thus making them appropriate for students with varied interests and backgrounds. Moreover, these and other courses included in criminal justice programs are intrinsically interesting. They have considerable potential as part of a general, even liberal education.

Agency Relationships

The second issue pertains to the role of the criminal justice agencies and their relationships with the colleges and universities. We have observed that the mature professions—law, medicine, business, engineering—have achieved a considerable equilibrium in the relationships between the teaching institutions and practitioners. The relationships are complex and were built over a period of many years. They consist of such formal mechanisms as licensing practices, teaching hospitals, and board of visitors and also of such informal activities as the movement of faculty back and forth between the campus and the field, either as consultants or for longer tours of duty. In most fields, specialized research agencies are common.

These relationships serve a coordinating function. They coordinate curriculum and instructional practice with the requirements of the field. They reduce the gap between theory and practice. They contribute to a rough calibration of student enrollments on the campuses and employment opportunities in the field. One of the hallmarks of a mature profession is the existence of such relationships that serve to coordinate teaching and scholarship with practice.

In recent years, criminal justice education has developed under a strong external stimulus from the federal government. Further, many of the faculty in criminal justice programs were drawn from the ranks of practitioners. The development of the field between 1965 and the present was, as a consequence, closely coordinated with the requirements of contemporary practice. In some circumstances, it may even have been too closely coordinated with the immediate needs of the agencies, without adequate input from the academic realm.

It might be expected that, after a period of intensive development under external stimulus, the field would enter a stage of consolidation and internalization; that is, curriculum development would be focused more on academic possibilities and less on external concerns. There is considerable evidence from the present study that an internalization stage has begun.

An internalization stage is undoubtedly a logical and necessary next step in the development of criminal justice education. The intensive development of the last ten to fifteen years, stimulated as it was from an external source, built on a narrow and *ad hoc* academic foundation. This foundation is probably inadequate for the long-term development of the field. It should be broadened and deepened. Moreover, there is substantial potential for curriculum development in a number of academic disciplines that bear upon professional education for criminal justice careers. We refer to such disciplines as history, mathematics and economics. Such a stage could well be highly productive for criminal justice education of the future.

At the same time, there is danger in placing too much emphasis on curriculum development that is internal to the campus, if that emphasis should result in isolating the campus from the world of the practitioner. Criminal justice educators face a number of problems that can only be solved in coordination with the agencies. One of these was identified in the preceding discussion of potential students, where the need to calibrate agency entry requirements with educational attainment was mentioned in connection with the development of programs for the younger pre-service students. Or, in the case of more experienced students, the trend toward continuing or recurrent education offers opportunity for the development of advanced professional programs where curriculum development can best be done in coordination with agency goals and requirements. Similar opportunities exist in the case of faculty scholarship and research and of public service activities.

For criminal justice education to achieve the equilibrium that exists in the older professions between the campus and the world of work, it will be necessary to devise a series of ongoing mechanisms. The mechanism can be a straightforward informational one, like a professional journal, a professional association, and a board of visitors for a particular campus. Or it can serve a coordinating role in curriculum like a teaching hospital in medicine, a demonstration school in education, and an organized internship program in almost any field. Or it can be a research agency. Or the mechanism can be regulatory in nature like a licensing authority or a professional accrediting agency.

It would be well for criminal justice educators to proceed cautiously with the choice of mechanism. Regulatory mechanisms, like licensing and accreditation, are often perceived as threatening an extensive standardization. Licensing, improperly used, can also unduly limit access to the field. These risks may be acceptable in a mature field where the public interest in regulation is strong. Caution should be exercised in a young and developing field, where experimentation and variety may hold greater promise for strong professional programs in the future.

Informational, research and other less structured coordinating mechanisms, on the other hand, can contribute usefully to future development. These should be utilized to the full in criminal justice education so that the agency role in the future development of the field will be a vital one.

Quality

Thirdly, we turn to the issue of quality in criminal justice education. This issue belongs on any list of significant issues facing the field. There is no doubt that, during the unusually rapid development of new programs, in the past ten years, some, perhaps many, were introduced that were ill-conceived and poorly implemented.

The present study was not directed to programs of low quality. It did not attempt to identify such programs, to estimate their number across the country or to define their characteristics. Rather, we tried to examine a full range of programs, from the strong to those that may be rapidly evolving. We were particularly interested in the characteristics of strength in criminal justice education. In addition, we were concerned with future directions for the field as a whole.

Our results suggest something of the complexity of the quality issue. The majority of the programs that were the subject of campus visitation and interviews were, in fact, strong programs. This is clear from the interview reports and from the verbal accounts of the visitors, all of whom were experienced and knowledgeable members of the John Jay faculty. This judgment is confirmed by the results of the catalog analysis for these institutions. This shows that the courses contained in these programs range over a variety of significant academic and professional subjects and that many were imaginative and demanding.

These results lead to the observation that the range of quality in criminal justice education is probably great, from the strong programs to the weak. The range may be more significant for the future development of the field than the existence of weak programs at the bottom of the scale. For, the appearance of strong programs is a clear signal that the field has become established in higher education. And it is these programs that can be expected to provide leadership for the further development of the field in the future.

The characteristics of the institutions offering criminal justice programs are of more than passing interest. They are not a cross-section of 160 American universities. Rather, they are a special group of universities whose characteristics have important implications for the issue of quality. They tend to be at public rather than private institutions, although private universities are included. They tend to be at large or medium size institutions. Perhaps most significantly, the criminal justice programs tend to be at the newer universities that have a public service orientation extending to all or most of their programs. These newer universities contrast with the older universities and their more traditional academic and scholarly orientation.

Some examples may make the point more explicit. Criminal justice programs exist at the City University of New York, not Columbia; at the University of North Carolina in Charlotte, not at the older campus in Chapel Hill; at the University of Alabama at Birmingham, not the University's main campus; at Michigan State, not the University of Michigan; at the University of Southern California and no longer at the University of California at Berkeley; and at Washington State, not the University of Washington.

What implications does this institutional orientation have for the issue of quality? One is that traditional criteria of academic quality should be applied to criminal justice programs with reserve, perhaps even with caution. Traditional academic criteria should not be the only basis for assessing quality in criminal justice education. They should be augmented by other criteria that take account of the professional requirements of the field in the larger society.

Consider the question of admission standards as an example. Quality among the traditional universities is usually associated with the competitive admission of students, using criteria that are heavily academic in nature such as test scores and high school grades. The students so selected possess strong academic skills and are usually able to proceed through a rigorous academic program at the undergraduate level and go on to graduate work in the arts and sciences. Whether students selected in this way are best equipped to pursue criminal justice careers is an open question. Much depends on their motivation for this career. It is at least arguable that academic criteria for admissions should be modified to take account of evidence of the student's interest and practical experience in the field.

Or, consider the question of faculty qualifications. The traditional academic criteria is the Ph.D. degree in the discipline to be taught. There is little or no emphasis on practical experience. This is an appropriate criterion for college teachers in the various academic disciplines. It may be less appropriate when the teaching is in professional subjects. Here, some combination of advanced education and practical experience may be a stronger indicator of quality than the Ph.D. alone.

It is likely that the institutions we have referred to as the newer, public service universities are currently evolving more comprehensive criteria of educational quality of the sort suggested by this discussion. These universities may well represent a new generation of American educational institution, following in the tradition of land-grant colleges that emerged one hundred years ago and the community colleges that are a product of the 1920's and the 1930's.

If so, they too will become a distinct type of institution in American higher education, one that gives emphasis to the education of average Americans, to career preparation for public service (often in an urban context), to teaching that draws from the professional and the academic, and to scholarship of an interdisciplinary kind that is focused on contemporary social problems. This is a noble endeavor that should be judged in terms of its own goals. Those who seek quality in criminal justice education would be well advised to relate squarely to this newer tradition and not adopt only the quality criteria of an older tradition.

Faculty Scholarship

We turn now to a fourth issue for the future, faculty scholarship. Scholarship informs teaching. This is the traditional reason for faculty scholarship in any field of study on a university campus. The fundamental relationship between scholarship and teaching has long been central to the *raison d'être* of the university.

That scholarship informs teaching is fully as applicable to criminal justice education as to any other field. Scholarly concepts, scholarly methods of inquiry and scholarly values broaden and deepen the student's understanding. Scholarship that is based on sound research can illuminate a field that is complex, puzzling and, often, controversial.

Consider a few concepts from this field. From law, the concept of justice and crime. From psychology, the concept of behavior and its derivative, deviant behavior. From sociology, the concept of society and its derivative, criminology or crime in society. From history, the concept of history itself and its derivatives, social history and urbanization. From mathematics, the concept of analysis and its derivatives, computer science, statistics, and operations research. And from science, the scientific method and one of its derivatives, the validity of evidence.

The issue with respect to faculty scholarship in criminal justice education is how to encourage greater activity. Rational inquiry is not static; it is a dynamic and cumulative process. The rapid development of criminal justice education in the past ten to fifteen years depended heavily on scholarship that had been done in perhaps the last fifty years. If the results of this scholarship had not been available, it is not likely that criminal justice education could have been expanded as rapidly and as surely as it was. Similarly, the future development of the field as a teaching field depends upon a substantial level of contemporary scholarship, one that is consistent with the present size of the field in terms of faculty and students.

There is a second reason for the encouragement of scholarly inquiry. This is that scholarship can inform public policy. This reason grows out of the fact that the American university has, in the twentieth century, become a national resource in the formulation of public policy in certain fields. This is true with respect to economic policy, foreign policy, agriculture policy, educational policy and policy related to science and technology, among others. The results of scholarly inquiry have contributed to national debate and to consensus in these fields, often on both sides of a given question. It is highly important to the future development of the field that scholarly activity be encouraged to the maximum extent possible.

This, of course, will not occur by exhortation. There are some serious impediments to substantial scholarly activity in criminal justice education. They should be identified, understood and, if possible, overcome. We shall try in a preliminary way to consider several of these impediments.

External funding is essential for many kinds of scholarly research. The federal government has been a primary source of the necessary funding. Sharp limitations now exist with respect to federal research funds. These circumstances bear on criminal justice scholars in ways that are both direct and indirect. Directly, they are in keen competition with scholars from other fields, who also represent urgent research needs. Indirectly, their universities are adversely affected at a time when other major financial problems also confront the higher institutions.

There is a case to be made for a greater level of federal funding for social research. Its dimensions lie in the critical nature of contemporary social problems and in the fact that social scientists have some of the methods to explore these problems and identify possible solutions. At the same time, it should be recognized that the present level of funding is less the result of benign neglect than open opposition to social research in the Congress and among important elements of American society. The case must be one that is thorough and persuasive.

This is not a case that can be made by criminal justice scholars alone. Rather, it will require a concerted effort on the part of scholars from the relevant disciplines and from the other applied fields, like education, that depend on social research.

Even if this effort is successful, criminal justice scholars will still face substantial impediments to increased scholarly activity. We turn now from the national scene to considerations that are localized to the field and to the individual institution.

A serious impediment exists within the field in the fragmentary nature of the source materials and bibliographic aids. The results of past scholarship are scattered through the literature of several disciplines and fields. It is more difficult than in established fields to bring together the results of past scholarship that may bear on a particular inquiry. Bibliographic aids that will assist the process of amalgamation are not yet available. Moreover, some and perhaps many of the original sources in the field of criminal justice are not readily available to scholars.

The general need is for organized effort toward the creation of research libraries that will serve scholarship in criminal justice, as is the case in other more developed fields. This task probably transcends the resources of single institutions. It can probably best be achieved by means of regional library centers across the country, supported by groups of institutions in the region. The regional development of research library resources would be an excellent long-term project for the professional associations in the field.

Other impediments exist at the level of the individual institution, where tight budgets and heavy teaching loads often exist. There is little likelihood that scarce fiscal resources will suddenly become abundant in the near future, although some easing of the present stringency may be expected. It is more likely that colleges and universities will have to create an accommodation at a lower level of real funding than was customary in the past. The accommodation will have to include a reasonable balance between teaching and scholarship and an equitable balance among disciplines and fields, including criminal justice education.

There appear to be three possible lines of approach to encourage more scholarly activity in the field. One is to assure that the effort is a concerted one and that criminal justice scholars work in cooperation with other groups with similar ends. At the national level, this means cooperation with professional associations for certain of the academic disciplines (including the librarians) and with the major educational associations. At the local level, this means involvement with faculty from other schools and departments and with planning staffs, budget staffs and other key administrative units.

The second approach is to monitor the status of criminal justice scholarship on a regular basis for the next few years. There is need for more empirical evidence than is now available in order to assess the present status. And there is need for recurrent surveys in order to detect important trends. These surveys might, for example, identify the disciplines where important studies are underway and the disciplines where there is little activity. They might identify significant centers of criminal justice scholarship and study the qualifications of productive scholars in the field.

As a third approach, it would be wise to assemble a national committee of distinguished scholars in the field to oversee and interpret the monitoring process. Periodic public statements from such a committee would serve to focus national attention on the problem and, hopefully, contribute to solutions.

Educational Articulation

Let us turn now to a final issue, articulation within American education and, particularly, between and among the colleges and universities.

Articulation between and among key elements of organized education is important because students progress from one institution to another in what should be a rational, sequential, and efficient manner. The junction between secondary and higher education, for example, has become highly articulated because of the importance of the movement of students from one level to the other. Here, a variety of specialized activities, like college admission testing, has evolved to support articulation.

Educational articulation is also important in terms of the advancement of scholarly knowledge and its impact on curriculum. A notable lack of articulation was evident in the secondary schools in the 1950's when teaching in science and mathematics lagged far behind the scholarship in the nation's graduate schools.

As criminal justice education develops further within the larger context of organized education, it will need to pay greater attention to articulation at key junctions within the system.

The junction between the community colleges and the four-year institutions is surely key to the future development of the field. This junction is important because of the number of programs at the two-year level and the number of students who seek to move from one level to the other. Similarly, the junction between secondary and higher education is also a key junction for the field and will require sustained attention.

These two junctions are already generally well articulated by activities and organizations that are now in being within the larger educational context. The task for criminal justice educators is to relate to and utilize the existing "machinery." It is not likely that any extraordinary effort will be required.

On the other hand, other key junctions may exist that will require more intensive action. One of these is the junction between the relatively few "research" universities and the larger number of "teaching" universities and colleges, including the community colleges. The graduate schools of arts and science in the "research" universities are the primary sources of scholarly research, much of which has relevance for curriculum development in criminal justice education. The criminal justice programs, however, are heavily concentrated across the junction, in the "teaching" institutions.

At present, it seems likely that much of the vitality that now exists in the academic part of the criminal justice curriculum depends on the teaching faculty and the recency of their own graduate school preparation. Two-thirds of the respondents to the questionnaire of the present study reported their age at below 45 years, a relatively youthful group. If these results are typical of the teaching faculty as a whole, then there is some threat that this vitality will diminish as the present teaching faculty ages and is not succeeded by an equal number of more recently-trained teachers. We do not know whether this threat is real. We mention it only to suggest the importance of the junctions between the "research" universities and the "teaching" institutions and the resulting need to anticipate problems of articulation that may serve to impede the development of the field.

Still another key junction exists between the law schools and the institutions that offer criminal justice programs. The law, of course, is central to the professional component in criminal justice education, and curriculum vitality here too depends on close articulation between the two kinds of institutions. Moreover, some graduates of criminal justice programs will be strong candidates for the law schools and an increasing student movement across this junction can be expected.

Developments in Criminal Justice: The Challenge for Criminal Justice Education

Much of the inefficiency in criminal justice operations is related to organization; that is, to poor articulation between jurisdictions and between the different branches of government. The organizational problems have not yet been substantially affected by the efforts of the past decade.

Although it is often described as a system, criminal justice in the United States operates in 52 different jurisdictions: the 50 states, the District of Columbia and the federal. Much of its activity occurs in the state jurisdictions where the general police power under the American Constitution is focused. The states differ significantly in their criminal laws and with respect to their practices in law enforcement, prosecution, trial, and corrections. There are also significant differences between the several states and the federal government. Moreover, the functions of the field are divided between the judicial and executive branches of government, while funding levels for all criminal justice activities are determined by legislative action. The outcome is that criminal justice in the United States is a complex enterprise with serious problems of articulation between and among its several parts.

The field was brought to prominent public attention beginning in the 1960's as the result of widespread concern about increasing evidence of civil disorder, violent crime and corruption. Increasing crime, in turn, was part of a broader social unrest related to an unpopular war and tension over civil rights. A major national effort was undertaken to strengthen the operations of the criminal justice agencies under federal legislation administered by the Law Enforcement Assistance Administration/LEAA of the Department of Justice. The federal initiative triggered an extensive response at the state and local levels.

It is clear that the principal goal of the effort has not yet been achieved. Some improvement in the efficiency of criminal justice operations has occurred, particularly in law enforcement. But the reported incidence of crime continues to increase on a national basis. The continued increase appears to be genuine because it is based on more sophisticated statistics than were available prior to 1970. At the same time, there are some indications that the rate of increase in criminal activity may be declining, thus offering some hope that the situation will stabilize sometime during the 1980's. There is little prospect of a decline in criminal activity before then.

Moreover, the roots and ramifications of crime extend well beyond the field of criminal justice and permeate much of American society. Urbanization, the social trend previously discussed, is clearly implicated as rural populations migrate to the cities ill-prepared to cope with urban living. Persistent unemployment, inflation, and a sluggish economy are also involved. More generally, the strong trend toward greater complexity in society and its economic functions provides both cause and opportunity for criminal activity. Some of the population, unable to cope with the resulting dislocations, turn to crime as a means of survival. Others, far better placed and more opportunistic, see new possibilities in a changing society; they turn to criminal activities that are often highly organized and that sometimes reach to the highest levels of society. Still others, unaffected by social change, represent the dark side of human nature; their crimes usually defy understanding. It seems that criminal activity will remain strong throughout the period under review and that efforts to strengthen the operations of the criminal justice agencies will continue at or above their present levels.

Among other things, this presents the college and universities with a challenge that will continue through the 1980's. There is challenge to offer strong educational programs that will provide the professional, managerial, and technical manpower needed for the field. There is challenge to conduct scholarly research that will contribute to increased understanding of crime and its control in a democratic society. And there is further challenge to the college and universities because these educational programs and this scholarly research must function within the financial restraints that were the subject of earlier discussion in this chapter. The colleges and universities, after all, are the only institutions in American society where these challenges can be met.

We add a note on future studies. Our experience with the present study suggests the need for periodic surveys of the status of criminal justice education, conducted, say, once every five years. Such surveys would be an invaluable aid to individual institutions as they evaluate their own curriculum development efforts. They will also serve to inform other educators, the personnel of criminal justice agencies, and national policy makers about the problems and prospects of the field. In the years intervening between national surveys, more specialized studies that explore particular problems in depth would also be of value. We suggest, in other words, an ongoing research program to chart and report on the future development of the field. Such an effort should be a representative effort among the nation's criminal justice educators.

Police Unionism as a Developmental Process

Allen D. Sapp

INTRODUCTION

One of the major issues in law enforcement and police management today concerns the increasing unionization of law enforcement officers and the demand for formal labor contracts or memorandums of understanding developed through collective bargaining. While unionization of police is a contemporary issue that has received widespread attention in the last twenty-five years, police unionization is by no means a recent phenomenon. Police labor disputes were documented in Ithaca, New York in 1889, in Cincinnati, Ohio in 1918 and the widely publicized Boston Police Strike of 1919 (Maddox, 1975).

However, it was not until the early 1960's that unionism in the public sector and in policing became a major

This article was written expressly for inclusion in this edition.

issue. In general, public sector unionism has lagged thirty or more years behind unionism in the private sector. One of the reasons for the rapid growth of public sector unionism in the 1960's and 1970's was the rapid growth in government that took place in that era. By 1978 one in three unionized workers was employed in public service jobs (Martin, 1979). The decade of the 1960's had a political and social environment that was most favorable for public employee collective action. During this decade of increasing militancy in society, police turned more toward trade union tactics instead of relying upon improvement of their status without recourse to unionization. Such union tactics as work slowdowns, strikes, and other job actions were increasingly embraced by police organizations and unions.

The increase in police labor organizations results from a number of factors. Population growth, continuing urbanization, advancing technology, and an overall increase in the complexity of society contribute to changing demands for more and better police services. Police officers are required to perform more services amid changing concepts of the police role in our society (Goldstein, 1977). The police are increasingly demanding compensation commensurate with the complexity of their jobs and comparable with those private sector wages and salaries so often reported in the media. Reliance on antiquated wage scales and antiquated wage increase procedures that are often slow, cumbersome and provide for little or no input from workers exacerbate the problem (Stanley, 1972).

The proliferation of labor unions and associations in law enforcement is a well established trend that is likely to be permanent (Morgan & Korstad, 1976). Police unions are faced with a number of problems when they engage in collective bargaining and negotiations. Public officials must attempt to balance decisions based on taxes, services, wages, and employment with the realities of a political system which operates largely as a function of the extent to which voters and taxpayers are satisfied with the performance of the officials (Victor, 1977). Neither the public nor many public officials fully grasp the complexities of the police role, and officials are fairly ignorant of the public employees' lot (Hewitt, 1977). Apathetic and unenlightened public officials fail to recognize the need for basic strategies and fail to appropriately utilize available resources in negotiations (Olmos, 1975).

Juris (1971) notes that police unionism is "first and foremost an organization of salaried employees in a large bureaucracy" (p. 231). The police union is concerned with the economic well-being, security, and safety of its members and is equally concerned with responding to management's insistence on efficiency of operations and retention of authority. Police unionism provides a forum, similar to any professional organization, that allows its members to express opinions about the nature of law enforcement in society (Juris, 1971).

The form, content, goals, and methods of that forum are of primary interest. This chapter presents a developmental model (Wikstrom, 1980) that may be useful in understanding changes over time in the characteristics of police unions.

A DEVELOPMENTAL MODEL

The utility of a developmental model lies in its ability to reflect the overall process of unionization over time and through change. The model provides both explanatory and predictive functions of value to police management and union leadership alike. This model is preliminary and exploratory and is meant to be suggestive for further refinement and research. However, it provides a framework for discussing and critically examining varying characteristics in the complex process of unionism among the police.

While the developmental approach to understanding the process of police unionization may seem purely theoretical, such an approach has pragmatic, realistic values beyond theory. It helps to answer a series of questions of concern: (1) What are the goals and missions of the labor organization? (2) What changes in goals and missions are likely to occur? (3) What tactics and strategies are likely to be used? (4) What political sensitivities and stated concerns are present in the current phase of unionism?

The Stages of Police Unionization

Police unionization is a process that takes place in an environment that is both complex and constantly changing. Unionization arises within that changing and complex environment and is itself a phenomenon that is ever-changing and equally complex. Unionization is seen as a process wherein police unions are viewed as developing or evolving through at least three distinct stages or phases. The various characteristics found in unions differ in the evolutionary stages and thus must be viewed in context of a generalized developmental model.

The phases of police union development are:

a. The *initial* phase. The initial phase encompasses the period of organization of the union through the period where it is recognized as a collective bargaining unit by the employer.
b. The *consolidation* phase. The consolidation phase begins when the union gains a degree of acceptance by management and police officers and seeks to consolidate its position and power.
c. The *institutionalized* phase. This is the final phase in the development of the police union where the union becomes almost an integral part of the organizational structure of the employing agency. In addition to the development through these three phases, development also occurs in three relatively distinct areas.

The areas where the developmental phases occur include:

a. *Organizational* factors. This area of union development includes the structure of the organization, the organizational goals, membership scope, participation, and commitment, the legitimacy and trust gained by the organization, and the scope and nature of union activities.
b. *Goal attainment* factors. The various factors that are related to organizational goal attainment are included in this area of union development. Included are decision-making, dominant task orientation, negotiating posture, primary focus in conflict resolution and impasse resolution, political action, and relationship with management.
c. *Administrative* factors. Staff, dues, dues check-off, and fiscal resources budget are factors included in the administrative area of union development.

Development can be identified in each of the factors in these three areas and across each of the three stages of unionism.

Organizational Factors

Table 1 depicts the various organizational factors across the three stages of union development. The union organization structure is weakly differentiated in the initial stage of development. The union organizers are largely unofficial in that they have not been elected nor do they hold office. The overall structure of the union is tentative; membership boundaries may not have been delineated in this phase. However, as the union gains recognition and moves into the consolidation phase, the structure becomes somewhat differentiated. Membership boundaries are established, officers are elected for fixed terms, and committees are appointed on an ad hoc basis. When the union becomes institutionalized, boundaries are rigid, officer

TABLE 1 Organizational Factors in Union Development

Organizational Factor	*Stage of Union Development*		
	Initial	*Consolidation*	*Institutionalized*
Organized structure	Weakly differentiated	Somewhat differentiated	Strongly differentiated
Legitimacy	Minimal	Limited	Extensive
Trust	Minimal	Limited	Extensive
Scope of membership	Limited	Substantial	Near universal
Member participation	Near universal	Substantial	Limited
Membership commitment to union goals	High	Moderate	Low
Organizational goals	Toe hold	Growth	Maintenance
Nature of activities	Controversial	Controversial	Largely non-controversial
Scope of activities	Narrow	Limited	Extensive

elections are highly structured, and fixed committees characterize the organization.

The police union in its initial stage has minimal trust and legitimacy. Lacking formal recognition, the union is viewed with limited trust by potential members. The legitimacy of its actions are often questionable in the view of management and potential members alike. With the onset of the consolidation stage, legitimacy and trust become more extensive but still are limited. Management continues to view the union with bias while membership maintains a wait and see attitude about the potential gains the union promises. By the time the union is institutionalized, both trust and legitimacy are extensive. Management trusts the union to cooperate and to avoid controversy. Members have extensive trust in the accomplishments of the union and tend to rely heavily upon union officers to maintain benefits and protect union rights.

Closely related to the concepts of trust and legitimacy is the scope of the membership in the police union. During the initial stage, much of the membership is limited to those police officers who are activists and those who see the union as a "last hope." Once the union begins consolidation, many of the members of the police force join the union because it has gained legitimacy, and membership is no longer seen as a political move. As more and more officers join, added legitimacy and trust accelerates the membership growth. By the time the union enters the third stage, institutionalization, membership is nearly universal among the officers eligible to join.

Participation by the members of the union varies across the three developmental stages. The limited membership in the initial phase of development is almost totally involved in union activities. The success or failure of the evolving union is heavily dependent upon participation by those officers who have chosen to cast their lot with the union. As the union gains status and begins the consolidation phase, membership grows and a substantial part of the membership is involved in union activities. The majority attend meetings and participate in ad hoc committee assignments. By the time the union has become institutionalized, membership participataion is relatively limited. The union leadership has become stable and the officers are likely to be competent and capable of independent action in the interests of the union. Meetings are less well attended, although social activities and family oriented activities continue to attract good turnouts.

The degree of membership commitment to the goals of the union also changes across the developmental stages. In the initial stage, members are highly committed to the goals of the union. Most are willing to risk their jobs and the chances of promotion to lead the organizational activities of the union. With the consolidation phase underway, membership commitment is likely to be moderate with real commitment only to those union goals which coincide with personal goals in the areas of benefits and working conditions. By the time the union is institutionalized, membership commitment to union goals is low. Many members "forget" that they are members and simply ignore the union activities. Generally, by the time the union is institutionalized, major benefit and pay concessions have been gained and union goals of maintenance are of little interest to most members.

Organizational goals similarly change across the stages of union development. In the initial phase, the union is fighting for a toehold within the overall police organization. The goal is to gain enough members to force recognition. When that initial goal is attained, the union goal becomes one of growth. The goal is to gain as many members as possible, both to present a unified membership and to increase the revenue available to the union. By the time the union is institutionalized, the major objectives of members have been achieved and the union's goal becomes one of maintenance. Maintaining membership and recognition insures the continuing existence of the union.

The nature of activities by the police union is largely related to the stage of development. In the initial stage, the union is likely to engage in highly controversial activities, threatening legal action, strikes, boycotts, and job actions. In the growth stage, the union still engages in predominantly controversial activities, often focusing upon pay, fringe benefits, and working conditions. The institutionalized union engages in largely non-controversial activities. Instead of seeking out controversy, the union tends to avoid it. Lobbying activities replace threats of job actions. Social functions replace militant meetings and demonstrations.

As the nature of activities changes across the stages of union development, so does the scope of activities. In the initial stage, union activities are likely to be very narrow in scope, focusing upon single highly controversial issues. A series of narrow issues are likely to be raised, each aimed at gaining recognition and membership. In the consolidation phase, the union is likely to focus on a few limited issues, such as pay, fringe benefits, and working conditions. The union which reaches the institutionalized stage is likely to have a wide scope of activities, ranging from social to fraternal to labor-management activities. The union is likely to become more active in the everyday activities of the police department and the activities are likely to be of a long-range type.

Goal Attainment Factors

The changes that take place over the development of police unions in the area of goal attainment factors are depicted in Table 2. The police union's relationship with management changes drastically across the three stages of development. In the initial stage, the union and management have a polarized relationship wherein each is viewed by the other as an adversary. Each side is viewed with suspicion and relationships are slow to develop. Once the union has gained recognition and enters collective bargaining activities, the relationship changes to one of interaction. While neither side may fully trust the other, both recognize that progress and peaceful coexistence are dependent upon interaction and communication. The fully institutionalized union becomes almost part of the formal police organization and relationships with the formal organization are co-operative and often lead to a situation where the union is coopted by the management of the department. The union becomes an extension of management and is used to manage and control the membership.

The dominant task orientation of the police union changes from one of seeking recognition and negotiations in the initial phase to a focus on compensation issues in the consolidation phase. The dominant task in the second stage is to gain visible increases in pay benefits. Once the union becomes institutionalized, the dominant task orientation becomes one of improving fringe benefits, working conditions, and maintaining union visibility.

The police union's negotiating posture goes through distinct changes as the union evolves. In the initial phase, the union tends to be very inflexible, issuing demands and refusing to soften those demands. In the consolidation stage, the union becomes moderately flexible, being more amenable to negotiation give and take, while still largely defending its position on major issues. The institutionalized police union is very flexible in its negotiating posture, often providing issues which can be eliminated or softened in return for gains on other issues.

Perhaps in no other areas than conflict resolution focus and impasse resolution focus are the three stages of police unionism more strikingly delineated. In terms of conflict resolution focus, the initial phase of union development often sees a focus on grievance procedures as a major technique. The lack of a grievance procedure is often a contributing factor to the rise of unionism. In the consolidation phase, the union begins to focus on mediation and fact-finding as a technique of conflict resolution. In the institutionalized phase, the union often seeks binding arbitration as a conflict resolution technique. Closely related to the conflict resolution focus is the focus of the developing union in the area of impasse resolution. The union in its initial phase of development often uses the threat of a strike, or an actual strike, as a technique to break impasses.

TABLE 2 Goal Attainment Factors in Union Development

Goal Attainment Factors	*Stages of Union Development*		
	Initial	*Consolidation*	*Institutionalized*
Relationship with management	Polarization, adversary	Interaction	Cooptation, compromise
Dominant task orientation	Recognition & negotiation	Compensation issues	Fringe benefits, working conditions
Negotiating posture	Inflexible	Moderately flexible	Flexible
Conflict resolution focus	Grievance procedures	Mediation & fact-finding	Binding arbitration
Impasse resolution focus	Strikes	Job actions	Mediation
Political action	Minimal	Limited	Extensive

The union in the second phase of development is much more likely to use job actions, such as job slowdowns, "by the book" enforcement, or "sick" call-ins to seek the resolution of impasses. The institutionalized union is usually reluctant to use such drastic measures to break a negotiating impasse and turns to mediation.

A final factor in the area of goal attainment is the type of political action that a police union takes. In the initial stage, political action is likely to be very limited. Lacking enough members to represent an effective voting bloc, the union is limited in its capabilities. In the consolidation phase, the union may endorse candidates and serve as a forum for discussion of political issues. The increasing membership has the potential to become an effective bloc of voters and political candidates are more likely to seek endorsement. The institutionalized police union has both the membership and the resources to become extensively involved in political campaigns. Political action committees are likely to be established to seek campaign donations and endorsements are actively sought by leading candidates. The union may itself make significant political contributions to selected campaigns.

Administrative Factors

The final area where identifiable factors may be noted is in the area of the administration of the union. As the police union develops through the three stages, the union staff is likely to grow, reflecting growth in membership and fiscal resources. In the initial phase, the union staff is likely to be limited and consist largely of volunteers who receive little or no pay for their efforts and activities. As the union enters the consolidation phase, the officers are formally elected and additional staff positions are generated. The president, vice-president, secretary, and treasurer are joined by ad hoc committee chairmen, sergeants-at-arms, and stewards. A board of directors may be chosen. At least some of the officers are paid for their time. In the institutionalized phase, the overall union staff includes elected officers, appointed committee chairmen, and a board of directors. Actual union affairs are likely to be conducted by a limited executive committee, all of whom are reimbursed for participation in union business.

The fiscal resources and budget of the police union in the initial stage of development tend to be minimal, based on the revenue generated by the dues paid by the limited membership. When the union moves into the consolidation phase, the resources available to the union increase as membership grows. The institutionalized police union has extensive resources based primarily upon the nearly universal membership of the union.

When the police union is in the initial stage of development, union dues are likely to be set at the lowest possible level. As the union begins to consolidate, dues are generally raised to a limited level. The dues will generally be raised several times during the consolidation phase, reflecting economic gains made through negotiations. In the final stage, dues are likely to be at a high level. Closely related to the dues set by the union is the process of dues checkoff. When the union is in its initial phase, dues collection is a critical issue. Each member must pay his monthly dues by check or cash. Failure to collect the dues leads to problems in financing the union activities. In the consolidation phase, dues checkoff is often a major issue in negotiations. Limited dues checkoff is often available through a voluntary payroll deduction program. The institutionalized police union usually has a mandatory dues checkoff program where the police department automatically deducts union fees from all payroll checks of members. The automatic dues checkoff provides a solid financial base for the union.

Variations in the Model

This model of police union development is presented as a linear model; however, the development may more

TABLE 3 Administrative Factors in Union Development

Administrative Factors	*Stages of Union Development*		
	Initial	*Consolidation*	*Institutionalized*
Union staff	Minimal	Expanding	Limited
Fiscal resources and budget	Minimal	Limited	Extensive
Membership dues	Minimal	Limited	Extensive
Dues checkoff	None	Limited	Extensive

closely resemble a circular or spiral progression. The union which has become thoroughly institutionalized may present an overall labor-management environment that closely resembles the pre-union environment that led to the initial stage of unionism. In one large city in the Southwest, a police officers' association had long represented the officers in negotiations with the city. The association had become so institutionalized that many officers became disenchanted with the association. A new union, restricted in membership to officers below the rank of lieutenant, was organized and entered the first stage of development.

Another characteristic of the developmental model is that transition from one stage to the next is neither automatic nor clearcut. Many unions never progress beyond the initial stage. They fail to gain acceptance by management and potential members. Others may gain recognition and move into the consolidation stage and falter. Police unions may also move from one stage to the next in some areas and remain at a lower level of development in others. Failure to change union behavior may be a major cause of union ineffectiveness.

Contemporary Police Unionization

The rapid proliferation of public service unions, and perhaps even more rapid growth of police unions, that began in the 1960's and continued relatively unabated through the 1970's, slowed considerably as we entered the 1980's. A number of factors have contributed to the slowdown. As these factors interact, police unionism changes in content and in context.

One of the major causes of the slowdown in police unionism in the 1980's was the economic slowdown and resultant recession of 1981–83. Police unions began to realize that economic realities precluded extensive gains in wages and benefits. In light of declining revenues, increasing unemployment, and public demands for better and more efficient policing, concern shifted from advances in wages and benefits to maintenance of existing jobs, salaries and benefits. The political problems raised by changing economic conditions became more apparent. As a result, the methods utilized by police unions were modified accordingly.

Unions, which had reached the institutionalized phase, "discovered" the issue of police productivity and became advocates for increasing productivity. This issue then became the focal point for defending the status of the institutionalized union and its members. Where unions were in initial or consolidation phases, union officers had to look for new strategies to attract membership. The promises of significant gains in wages and benefits were obviously hollow. New reference points were necessary and many unions failed to locate these critical points. Union growth slowed, membership declined, and formation of new unions came to a virtual standstill.

At the moment, contemporary police unionization is in a stagnant phase. Some of the police unions continue to express themselves and to seek new alliances and to strengthen their positions with their members and management. The cooptation process has accelerated as management and union members close ranks against common problems. It is not clear where these developments will lead. Economic recovery is likely to be slow and significant gains in public employment probably will lag behind other segments of the economy. There is the danger that police unions will sink into internal strife that could ultimately signal an end to the police unionism movement as it exists today. Many former union advocates are turning to orthodox political processes in an attempt to gain a larger share of the public sector resources. Once that larger share is attained, then police unions may again become attractive alternatives.

The current atmosphere in the arena of police unionism is clouded by the obvious conflict between public interest and personal interests of law enforcement officers. It appears that the personal interests, at least those focused on increased wages, salaries, retirement pensions, and other fringe benefits, have temporarily been outweighed by the public interest. This condition is likely to change as the public problems and interests decrease in intensity and visibility. Police unions are neither dead nor terminally ill; the current malady is acute but not beyond a cure. One should not ignore the very real potential for significant policy changes to occur out of the current conditions. Those policy changes may effect changes that completely obscure the processes of unionism as they exist today.

SUMMARY

The model presented is intended to serve as one approach to understanding prevailing processes involved in police unionization. The model obviously is in need of empirical validation. Pending such evaluation, it can serve as a heuristic device useful in examining the dynamics of the unionism process. Because the human resources cost encompasses such a large proportion of the public sector budget, any method of gaining a fuller understanding of processes affecting these resources is of value.

REFERENCES

Goldstein, Herman. *Policing a Free Society*. Cambridge, Mass.: Ballinger Publishing Company, 1977.

Halpern, Steven C. "Police Unionism." *The Police Chief*, Vol. 41, No. 2, (February, 1974), p. 35.

Hewitt, William H., St. "Police Officers Make Up Large Portion of Public Employees." *Law Enforcement Journal*, Vol. 5, No. 5, (July, 1977), p. 1 and 12.

Juris, H. A. "Implications of Police Unionism." *Law and Society Review*, Vol. 6, No. 2, (1971), pp. 231–245.

Maddox, Charles W. *Collective Bargaining in Law Enforcement*. Springfield, Ill.: Charles C Thomas, Publisher, 1975.

Martin, Philip L. *Contemporary Labor Relations*. Belmont, California: Wadsworth Publishing Company, Inc., 1979.

Morgan, J. P. and Richard J. Korstad. *Impact of Collective Bargaining on Law Enforcement and Corrections*. St. Petersburg, Florida: Public Safety Research Institute, Inc., 1976.

Olmos, Ralph A. and Thomas J. Savage. "Some Problems in Preparing and Conducting Contract Negotiations." *Law and Order*, Vol. 23, No. 2, (February, 1975), pp. 58–59.

Stanley, David T. *Managing Local Government Under Union Pressure*. Washington, D.C.: The Brookings Institute, 1972.

Victor, R.B. *Effects of Unionism on the Wage and Employment Levels of Police and Fire Fighters*. Santa Monica, California: Rand Corp., 1977.

Wikstrom, Nelson. "Studying Regional Councils: The Quest for a Developmental Theory." *Southern Review of Public Administration*, Vol. 4, No. 1, (June, 1980).

What Goes Around, Comes Around: Policing America, 1999

G. Thomas Gitchoff and Joel Henderson

Articles, commentaries, and research in the area of police and policing in America have gained their greatest impetus and popularity with the passage of the Omnibus Crime Control Act in 1965 and the subsequent creation of the Law Enforcement Assistance Administration (LEAA) and the Law Enforcement Education Program (LEEP). Today, the impetus arises from the increasing crime rate as well as the intense media attention given to local, state, and federal law enforcement agencies.

The attempts to understand police behavior are replete throughout the literature.[1] These include qualitative and quantitative analyses, descriptive and polemic commentaries with symbolic or fictional accounts, to name a few. Each has added to our knowledge of police and policing. The criminal justice discipline has been leaning toward quantitative analysis as the legitimate information-gathering tool. Quantitative analyses, while useful, are limited when attempting to understand policing in the 21st century. In order to describe long-range policing structures, values, and behavior, it is necessary to combine professional studies, public proclamations, creative caricatures, artists' representations, common sense, and other omniscient sources.

We have attempted to pull together public and professional perceptions that have given us a futuristic and speculative picture of police in America. In order to present a clear picture of what we believe will be the nature of policing in 1999, we have explored eight areas of concern: (1) citizen involvement in policing; (2) the exclusionary rule; (3) police unionization; (4) police psychology and mental health; (5) police technology; (6) policing and the changing nature of crime; (7) human relations and the police—1999; and (8) the Moral Majority, God, guns, and the police—1999.

CITIZEN INVOLVEMENT IN POLICING

We envision that citizen involvement in policing in 1999 will be of greater proportion than ever in the history of the United States. Citizens are becoming involved in most aspects of the criminal justice system.

This article was written especially for inclusion in this edition.

The diverse forces that stress victims' rights and the use of volunteers are placing citizens in an increasingly prominent role in the criminal justice system. This focus will take several directions in the police departments of the future.

Because of continued spiraling costs, inflation, and greater demands for police service to both real and perceived "crime waves," citizen involvement will continue to expand through use of neighborhood watch programs. This phenomenon, with its birth in the 1970s, will carry with it the notion of having law enforcement closer to the people. Patrick Murphy, Director of the Police Foundation, has frequently stated that civilian participation in law-enforcement and crime-prevention efforts provides the numerous "extra eyes and ears" needed to deter crime. The key to civilian participation in 1999 will focus on two main concerns: (1) citizens responding to their own fear of crime, plus a sense of collective safety in that response (e.g., neighborhood watches, etc.), and, (2) citizen perceptions that their police are, in general, trustworthy, honest, and serving their particular interests.

This clearly indicates a continued problem of police–minority relations, with some areas of the country more hostile and volatile than others. (Illinois, "The Land of Lincoln," ascending to the top of the states troubled by racial strife, with Mississippi running a close second along with Florida.) This will also reflect the importance of the victim becoming involved in criminal justice. The police of the future will be more "consumer" oriented and, with this orientation, they will internalize and perpetuate the biases of their constituency.

One could ponder the various responses of the various communities (black, brown, red, white, etc.), to policing in 1999. An optimist might project a stable economy, high employment, and personable, community-oriented police representing a diversity of ethnic and racial groups. One could add to this scenario (albeit, utopian) a government in 1999 that puts people first—that employs a peace force dedicated to helping citizens solve problems rather than create or aggravate them.

A pessimist (some say realist) might see a 1999 with an oppressive government reminiscent of fascism, with obedience, discipline, and sameness imposed upon the masses of America by a powerful few. Both these views assume, of course, a planet that was not engulfed in a nuclear holocaust or toxic wastes.

We foresee a surviving America in 1999, with a large cadre of police reserves, civilian volunteers (senior citizens actively involved both within police departments and in the community through neighborhood watch programs). We foresee an educated "elite," especially in the large urban police departments with middle managers and above requiring master's or law degrees for advancement. The paramilitary model will have given way, in part, to a more bureaucratic management model—both perpetuating and expanding an impersonal and automatonlike quality among large city departments. To combat this impersonal quality during response to public calls, "sensitivity training" will be rediscovered—again, following the cliché, "what goes around, comes around."

THE EXCLUSIONARY RULE

The exclusionary rule holds that anything seized or obtained in violation of the Fourth Amendment's prohibition against "unreasonable searches and seizures" may not be used as evidence in a criminal proceeding. Most "law and order" types blindly accept the rhetoric that the label implies, that is, the exclusionary rule is responsible for releasing hordes of criminals to prey upon the public. A study of federal criminal suspects showed that rarely are they set free due to "technicalities." Of 2,804 cases surveyed, only 0.4 percent were declined by United States prosecutors because of search-and-seizure problems. *Evidence was excluded at trial in only 1.3 percent* of the cases.[2]

Another survey by the National Institute of Justice found that 4.8 percent of all felony arrests between 1976–1979 in California were rejected for prosecution because of search-and-seizure problems.[3] Most important to note, however, is that ¾ of these felonies were drug related, *not crimes of violence*. Although limits are being proposed for the exclusionary rule—in some quarters, outright repeal—overall, the exclusionary rule as envisioned and applied has vastly improved the standards of both local and federal law enforcement agencies. To lose or repeal the intent or purpose of the exclusionary rule would be far more destructive of the respect for law.

It should be noted that while the above-mentioned studies point to a conclusion that the exclusionary rule has virtually no effect on criminal prosecution and conviction, there is another position. Law enforcement agencies point out that the rule oftentimes results in police officers not pursuing a search and/or arrest. Therefore, they claim, the exclusionary rule is having a far greater impact than is suggested by available evidence.

Law enforcement agencies and politicians are pushing hard for changes in this rule. They *believe* it is having an effect on crime, and it has become a major local and national political concern. In the course of overstated polemics, the true effect and original reasons for the law are obscured.

The exclusionary rule was a response to police abuse. It forced police agencies to "clean up their acts" and subsequently develop more professional conduct. This occurred during a period of intense social and legal upheaval of the Warren Court. We envision that the 1980s will see a negation, in part, of the exclusionary rule brought about by the Burger Court. In the late 1990s, we envision the pendulum returning to its historical precedent—"What goes around, comes around."

POLICE UNIONIZATION

Police unionization in 1999 will have achieved a sophistication and power-base to make the teamsters blush. Highly trained and educated officers will have rebelled against authoritarian police administrators, pressured power brokers, and elected representatives until they are perceived as the most powerful union in America. Police and fire will merge to become public safety, second only to public health and national governments.

The unionization movement will continue to focus on "bread and butter" issues, but with a difference.[4] As with automation in the automotive industry, so too automation and computer technology will threaten police personnel with job insecurity. The once noble purpose of public service will be replaced by technocrats interested in cold efficiency and statistics. Big-city police departments will largely have the most powerful chiefs and, concomitantly, the most powerful police unions. Police reforms, innovations, and research will still be discouraged, but instead by unions fearing loss of their hard-fought powers. Confrontations and violence between police and "strike breakers"[5] will still occur in 1999.

Police–community relations will continue to be an issue and a dilemma. As unions gain more power, they will, of necessity, alienate many citizens who actively supported their neighborhood watch programs. Citizen perceptions of police unionization will range from characterizing the movement with everything from arrogance and greed to corruption and waste. Citizen hostility will be great enough to overcome the unions' political power. The gains made through police unions will be stifled or lost in large part because of this arrogance of power. The resulting loss of trust and confidence by the public for their police will again rekindle doubts, problems of corruption, and public scandals. What goes around, comes around?

POLICE PSYCHOLOGY AND MENTAL HEALTH

These will be major aspects in considering whom to hire and when to retire in 1999. As viewed in the 1960s and 1970s police stress began taking its toll on officers who, for various reasons, could not cope with the added social and work pressures. Early retirements, injuries, civil actions, and workmen compensation cases caused much alarm and fiscal impact in city managers' offices throughout the country. As a response to early retirements and injuries, police sabbaticals will become part of the benefits and ameliorative measures to maintain personnel and their mental health. Police psychologists, vouchers for private counseling, and paid tuition for advanced degrees will also be available.

By 1999, all large urban police departments will require as part of the employment process a complete psychological evaluation, including testing and polygraph. By then, the polygraph will be acceptable in court and will have been refined for accuracy.

High-stress job assignments will require periodic relief or transfer. Specialization will be encouraged and permitted, if supported by psychological aptitude tests and superior performance on the job. Frequent reassignments because of promotions and so forth will no longer be required. Merit raises will permit a specialist to forego a promotion and yet remain in position receiving top pay.

Police, while having developed an institutionalized mechanism for dealing with issues of stress, personnel selection and promotion, and problems of mental health will experience even greater problems in each of these areas. Generally, these problems will adversely influence the relationship of police with the community and other components of the criminal justice system. What goes around, comes around?

POLICE TECHNOLOGY

In 1999, police technology will be a Ray Bradbury dream come true. Electronics, microchips, and computer technology will find their way into police record keeping, equipment miniaturization, communications, crime labs, and coordinated crime-network computers.[6]

In addition to police officers possessing advanced degrees, they will also be more racially balanced and integrated. Men and women will be more equally represented at all levels, from patrol to administration. Former insecurities and male chauvinism will be greatly lessened, although not completely eradicated; sexism and racism will remain in 1999 America as it did in 1799 America and will in 2099 America—sad, but true.

Technological advances will be rapid and vast. The taser gun, net, tranquilizer gun, and other such devices will find wider use as a humane response to earlier police misuse of deadly force. Monitoring police service and activity will have a "big brother" flavor. In-car computers will determine and track the officer's daily travel, mileage, steps—much to the displeasure of the rank-and-file and union leaders. Surveillance of suspected criminal activity will be frequent, but mainly performed and reported by citizens involved in neighborhood watch or other crime-prevention programs.

The most significant change in policing will be the integration of participatory management models of administration pushing out the older paramilitary model. Public service calls will be handled by metropolitan peace corps—young people in service to their communities for 2- to 3-year periods in lieu of military duty. The mission or role of urban sworn police officers will be a proactive enforcement model focusing on crime prevention and apprehension. *All* traffic will be handled by State Traffic Police (STP). Specialized, integrated units or task forces will expand in order to more effectively and economically utilize funds and manpower.

Technology will be the focus of attention. The police officer's demand for state-of-the-art equipment will eventually lead to the equipment controlling the officer and the way he or she can perform on the job. What goes around, comes around?

POLICING AND THE CHANGING NATURE OF CRIME

Administrators will acknowledge the speed at which history is moving and producing cataclysmic shock waves. Vigilantes, survivalists, terrorists, and computer criminals will be among the groups and crimes grabbing headlines in the 21st century.

As a result of historical neglect in reforming the criminal justice system, by 1999, many of the designations of nonviolent and victimless crimes will have been repealed or further decriminalized. In their place, however, will be new laws on environmental protection, energy theft, audio- and video-wave theft, public health, and safety enforcement related to toxic and nuclear wastes. Regulatory law and enforcement will expand even more. Criminal laws will be amended to handle only the serious, violent, and dangerous offenders, while many of the property and white-collar crimes will be tried in civil-like courts, where heavy fines and restitution will be ordered. The concept of "indentured servitude" will be legally applied to these types of offenders, who, in turn, will assist the victims of crime and raise monies for the state victim compensation funds through restitution. Interestingly, the strongest lobbyists and supporters of these alternative forms of "constructive punishment" will be the traditionally conservative police chiefs and police unions.

Computer crimes spawned by the silicon chip will make home computers as commonplace as color TV sets. Random game-playing amateurs and graduate math and computer-science majors will "discover" access codes that will permit them to "transfer" 20 million barrels of oil intended for the United States to another country. Billing and collection will be handled by a computerized accounting system tied into international banking syndicates. Swiss numbered bank accounts will be widespread and computerized. The possibilities are, and will be, too great to imagine. The nature and quality of computer crimes and criminals will not vary greatly from the old-time white-collar embezzlers. The major difference and difficulty will be in discovering and obtaining sufficient evidence to gain convictions. Few in law enforcement, at any level, are or will be equipped and trained to investigate and apprehend the computer criminal.

The problems of who should be incarcerated, where police attention should be focused, the inadequate training of police to handle current crime problems will continue to be at the fore. What goes around, comes around?

HUMAN RELATIONS AND THE POLICE: 1999

Integration of police agencies by minorities and women will have leveled out by 1999. After decades of "proving their worth," minorities and women will be "accepted" into the police family. This does not mean that sexism and racism will be eliminated. In fact, both will still be voiced, and/or believed, but seldom practiced or acted upon. Bigotry will be moved to the innermost, dormant part of the collective police brain. Exceptions, of course, will exist, as racism, sexism, and militarism continue to exist at various levels of government and politics.

The slowest advances in race relations will be in southern police departments—the last bastion of white supremacy and bigotry. But as integration came to Little Rock's Lincoln High School, so too, will it come to its police department.

The issue of gays will virtually cease to exist. Personnel practices will eliminate inquiries or investigation into the privacy of one's bedroom and sexual practices. The sexual practices of consenting adults will not be of concern in police hiring. Past job performance, public behavior, and evaluation will determine, in part, hiring and promotion decisions. Homophobia will cease to exist in most urban departments.

While there will be an elimination of the correlation between sex, race, and sexuality with hiring and promotion in police departments, one would expect a basis for differentiation to continue to exist. It is likely that one of these will be social class. This will allow the psychological fulfillment achieved by differentiation and will also create a hostility within certain communities (racially integrated but class segregated) of an intensity far greater than experienced in the past. What goes around, comes around?

THE MORAL MAJORITY, GOD, GUNS, AND THE POLICE: 1999

How will America look and sound in 1999? Will we be a police state? An armed camp? Will we all become Charles Bronsons armed and vigilant, eliminating the "scum" of our cities? Or will we even be around? Will we get through the "ray-gun" decade of the 1980s? Or the omnipresent and worrisome nuclear or toxic disasters?

The Moral Majority in 1999 will continue to concern itself with pornography and pistols rather than protons and peace. Law-and-order rhetoric will have been replaced, as the nation gets older and wiser, both chronologically and educationally. The United States as a whole will have a greater number of senior citizens, who will be politically active. The population increase will be at a slower rate. The nation's citizenry in the year 1999 will be older, fragmented, more isolated from family units, and will contain a greater portion of women and Spanish-speaking people than blacks.[7]

As a result, police service will reflect and respond to these demographic characteristics. Greater uses of self-policing, private police, and security will attempt to curb the constant "fear of crime" experienced by many senior citizens. Special units, staffed by "domestic peace corps" volunteers in service to their community (similar to earlier Vista, CCC, Peace Corps) programs will offer seniors escort services in high-crime areas. Others whose perceived fears are more a product of aging and insecurity will remain in their "walled fortresses."[8] Attempts to have them rejoin the larger community will rest with various religious and social service groups.

The changing times will not change the processes or degrees of victimization or isolation. Nor will it change the fringe element response to these problems. Police will continue to be blamed for these destructive components of increasing crime rates, and police will continue to react by resorting to the measures discussed above. What goes around, comes around?

CONCLUSION

Policing America in 1999 will continue to offer dilemmas of earlier times. We will still want our police to be all things to all people. Their role definition, in part narrowed by advanced technology, will still include much in the form of social work and crisis intervention. The big difference will be the political power gained by more sophisticated police administrators and police unions.

The police will still be expected to be our "street-corner social workers" and crime fighters. Clarity of purpose, roles, and selective law enforcement will continue to be influenced by political climates, with history repeating itself in shorter spans of time and thrusting the police into a variety of tasks and roles.

The police have no choice; they have been thrust into the role of caretakers for nearly every social problem. When burdened with such large responsibilities, the police will remain vulnerable for the errors of judgment and mistakes that will occur. The "damned if you do, damned if you don't" cliché will remain apropos and, indeed, the "cop's job" may seem impossible.

Abraham S. Blumberg has aptly noted, "the most important aspect of the police which is seldom spelled out in the police literature—governments may come and go, but the police remain, regardless of the character or composition of political systems."[9]

REFERENCES

1. See, for example, Lawrence Sherman, "Causes of Police Behavior: The Current State of Quantitative Research," *Journal of Research in Crime & Delinquency*, January 1980, pp. 69–100; and Samuel Walker, *The Police in America* (New York: McGraw-Hill, 1983).

2. Report by the Comptroller General of the United States, "Impact of the Exclusionary Rule on Federal Criminal Prosecutions," (Washington, D.C.: April 1979).

3. U.S. Department of Justice, National Institute of Justice, "The Effects of the Exclusionary Rule: A Study in California" (Washington, D.C.: December 1982).

4. For an excellent discussion of "The Police and the Future," see Abraham S. Blumberg, *Criminal Justice: Issues & Ironies* (2nd Ed.) (New York: New View Points, 1979), 98–121.

5. Walker, *op. cit.*, p. 303.

6. See Gene Stephens (Ed.), *The Future of Criminal Justice* (Anderson Publishing Company, 1982), pp. 79–80, for several interesting, futuristic scenarios involving advanced, space-aged technology in policing.

7. See Larry Rutter, *The Essential Community* (Washington, D.C.: International City Management Association, 1980); and *"California 2000: The Next Frontier,"* (San Diego: California Tomorrow Foundation, Summer 1982).

8. For interesting discussion in this regard, see Mary Duncan and Max Lerner, "Walled Cities: The Fortress Mentality," *San Diego Magazine*, September 1982; and Selwyn Enzer and R. Wurzburger, "L.A. 200 + 20: Some Alternative Futures for Los Angeles 2001, Executive Summary," Center for Futures Research, University of Southern California, 1982.

9. Blumberg, *op cit.*, p. 121.

SELECTED BIBLIOGRAPHY

Abernathy, M. Glenn. *Civil Liberties and the Constitution*. New York: Dodd, Mead, 1968.

Abraham, Henry J. *The Judicial Process: An Introductory Analysis of the Courts of the United States, England, and France*. 2nd ed. New York: Oxford University Press, 1968.

Abrahamsen, David. *Our Violent Society*. New York: Funk and Wagnalls, 1970.

Adams, Thomas F. *Law Enforcement: An Introduction to the Police Role in the Community*. Englewood Cliffs, N.J.: Prentice-Hall, 1968.

Adams, Thomas F. *Police Patrol Tactics and Techniques*. Englewood Cliffs, N.J.: Prentice-Hall, 1971.

Adler, Freda. *Sisters in Crime*. New York: McGraw-Hill, 1975.

Agee, Philip. *Inside the Company: CIA Diary*. New York: Bantam Books, 1975.

Ahern, James F. *Police in Trouble*. New York: Hawthorne Books, 1971.

Albini, Joseph L. *The American Mafia: Genesis of a Legend*. New York: Appleton-Century-Crofts, 1972.

Alderson, John C. *Policing Freedom*. Philadelphia: International Ideas, 1979.

Alderson, John C., and Stead, Philip John, eds. *The Police We Deserve*. London: Wolfe Publishing 1973.

Alex, Nicholas. *Black in Blue*. New York: Appleton-Century-Crofts, 1969.

———. *New York Cops Talk Back*. New York: Wiley, 1976.

Allen, Francis A. *The Borderland of Criminal Justice: Essays on Law and Criminology*. Chicago: University of Chicago Press, 1964.

Allen, John. *Assault with a Deadly Weapon*. New York: McGraw-Hill, 1978.

Allen, Richard C.; Ferster, Elyce Zenoff; and Rubin, Jesse G., eds. *Readings in Law and Psychiatry*. Baltimore: Johns Hopkins Press, 1968.

Alsop, Kenneth. *The Bootleggers and Their Era*. Garden City, N.Y.: Doubleday, 1962.

American Bar Association Project on Standards for Criminal Justice. *Standards Relating to the Urban Police Function*. Chicago: American Bar Association, 1973.

American Friends Service Committee. *Struggle for Justice*. New York: Hill and Wang, 1971.

Ardrey, Robert. *The Territorial Imperative*. New York: Atheneum, 1966.

Arendt, Hannah. *Eichmann in Jerusalem*. New York: Viking Press, 1963.

———. *On Revolution*. New York: Viking Press, 1963.

Arens, Richard. *Insanity Defense*. New York: Philosophical Library, 1974.

Arens, Richard, and Lasswell, Harold D. *In Defense of Public Order: The Emerging Field of Sanction Law*. New York: Columbia University Press, 1961.

Asbury, Herbert. *The Gangs of New York*. New York: Alfred A. Knopf, 1923.

Asch, Sidney H. *Police Authority and the Rights of the Individual*. New York: Arco Books, 1971.

Astor, Gerald. *The New York Cops*. New York: Scribners, 1971.

Aubert, Vilhelm. *The Hidden Society*. Totowa, N.J.: Bedminster Press, 1965.

Auerbach, Jerold S. *Unequal Justice*. New York: Oxford University Press, 1976.

Bacon, Selden D. "The Early Development of American Municipal Police: A Study of the Evolution of Formal Control in a Changing Society." Ph.D. dissertation, Yale University, New Haven, 1939.

Baker, Joseph. *The Law of Political Uniforms, Public Meetings and Private Armies*. London: H. J. Just, 1937.

Balbus, Isaac D. *The Dialectics of Legal Repression*. New York: Russell Sage Foundation, 1973.

Ball, John C., and Chambers, Carl C., eds. *The Epidemiology of Opiate Addiction in the United States*. Springfield, Ill.: Charles C Thomas, 1971.

Bandura, Albert. *Principles of Behavior Modification*. New York: Holt, Rinehart and Winston, 1969.

Banton, Michael. *The Policeman in the Community*. New York: Basic Books, 1964.

———. *Police–Community Relations*. London: William Collins Sons, 1973.

Barron, Milton L. *The Juvenile in Delinquent Society*. New York: Alfred A. Knopf, 1960.

Barth, Alan. *Law Enforcement Versus the Law*. New York: Collier Books, 1963.

Bayley, David H. *The Police and Political Development in India*. Princeton, N.J.: Princeton University Press, 1969.

———. *Forces of Order: Police Behavior in Japan and the United States*. Berkeley: University of California Press, 1976.

Bayley, David H., and Mendelsohn, Harold. *Minorities and the Police*. New York: Free Press, 1969.

Becker, Harold K. *Law Enforcement: A Selected Bibliography*. Metuchen, N.J.: Scarecrow Press, 1968.

———. *Issues in Police Administration*. Metuchen, N.J.: Scarecrow Press, 1970.

Becker, Howard S. *Outsiders: Studies in the Sociology of Deviance*. New York: Free Press, 1963.

Bedford, Sybille. *The Trial of Dr. Adams*. New York: Simon & Schuster, 1958.

Bell, Daniel. *The End of Ideology*. New York: Macmillan, 1958.

Belli, Melvin. *Dallas Justice*. New York: David McKay, 1964.

Belson, William A. *The Public and the Police*. London: Harper & Row, 1975.

Bent, Alan Edward. *The Politics of Law Enforcement*. Lexington, Mass.: D. C. Heath, 1974.

Berger, Monroe. *Equality by Statute: The Revolution in Civil Rights*. Rev. ed. Garden City, N.Y.: Doubleday, 1967.

Berger, Peter. *Invitation to Sociology: A Humanistic Perspective*. Garden City, N.Y.: Doubleday, 1963.

Berger, Peter, and Luckman, Thomas. *The Social Construction of Reality*. Garden City, N.Y.: Doubleday, 1966.

Berkley, George E. *The Democratic Policeman*. Boston: Beacon Press, 1969.

Bianchi, Hermanus. *Position and Subject Matter of Criminology: Inquiry Concerning Theoretical Criminology*. Amsterdam: North-Holland, 1956.

Bird, Otto A. *The Idea of Justice*. New York: Praeger, 1967.

Bittner, Egon. *The Function of the Police in Modern Society*. Washington, D.C.: U.S. Government Printing Office, 1970.

Black, Algernon D. *The People and the Police*. New York: McGraw-Hill, 1968.

Black, Charles L., Jr. *Capital Punishment: The Inevitability of Caprice and Mistake*. New York: Dell Publishing, 1970.

Black, Donald. *The Manners and Customs of the Police*. New York: Academic Press, 1980.

Blackstock, Nelson. *Cointelpro: The FBI's Secret War on Political Freedom*. New York: Vintage Books, 1976.

Blake, James. *The Joint*. New York: Dell Publishing, 1970.

Bledstein, Burton J. *The Culture of Professionalism*. New York: W. W. Norton, 1976.

Bloch, Herbert A., and Geis, Gilbert. *Man, Crime, and Society*. New York: Random House, 1970.

Bloch, Herbert A., and Niederhoffer, Arthur. *The Gang*. New York: Philosophical Library, 1958.

Block, Peter B., and Anderson, Deborah. *Policewomen On Patrol*. Washington, D.C.: Police Foundation, 1974.

Blum, Richard H., ed. *Police Selection*. Springfield, Ill.: Charles C Thomas, 1964.

Blumberg, Abraham S. "The Criminal Court: An Organizational Analysis." Ph.D. dissertation, New School for Social Research, 1965.

———. *Criminal Justice*. Chicago: Quadrangle Books, 1967.

———. *Criminal Justice: Issues and Ironies*. New York: New Viewpoints, 1979.

———, ed. *Law and Order*. 2nd ed. New York: E. P. Dutton, 1973.

———, ed. *Perspectives on Criminal Behavior*. New York: Alfred A. Knopf, 1981.

Bok, Sissela. *Lying: Moral Choice in Public and Private Life*. New York: Vintage Books, 1979.

Bonsignore, John J., et al. *Before the Law: An Introduction to the Legal Process*. Boston: Houghton-Mifflin, 1974.

Bopp, William J. *The Police Rebellion*. Springfield, Ill.: Charles C Thomas, 1971.

Bordua, David J. *The Police: Six Sociological Essays*. New York: Wiley, 1967.

Boskin, Joseph. *Urban Racial Violence in the Twentieth Century*. Beverly Hills: Glencoe Press, 1969.

Bouza, Anthony. *The Operation of a Police Intelligence Unit*. Unpublished M.A. Thesis. John Jay College of Criminal Justice, City University of New York, 1968.

Brakel, Samuel J. *Judicare*. Chicago: American Bar Foundation, 1974.

Bramsted, Ernest J. *Dictatorship and Political Police*. London: Routledge and Kegan Paul, 1945.

Brandstatter, A.F., and Hyman, Allen A. *Fundamentals*

of Law Enforcement. Beverly Hills, Ca.: Glencoe Press, 1971.

Brant, Irving. *The Bill of Rights: Its Origin and Meaning*. New York: Mentor Books, 1967.

Bray, Howard. *The Pillars of the Post*. New York: Norton, 1980.

Brecher, Edward M., et al. *Licit and Illicit Drugs*. Boston: Little, Brown, 1972.

Brinkley, Alan. *Voices of Protest*. New York: Alfred A. Knopf, 1982.

Broderick, John J. *Police in a Time of Change*. Morristown, N.J.: General Learning Press, 1977.

Bromberg, Walter. *Crime and the Mind*. New York: Funk and Wagnalls, 1968.

Brown, Claude. *Manchild in the Promised Land*. New York: Macmillan, 1965.

Brown, Michael K. *Working the Street: Police Discretion and the Dilemmas of Reform*. New York: Russell Sage Foundation, 1981.

Brown, Wenzell. *Women Who Died in the Chair*. New York: Collier Books, 1963.

Bryant, Clifton D., ed. *Deviant Behavior: Occupational and Organizational Bases*. Chicago: Rand McNally, 1974.

Buisson, Henri. *La Police, Son Histoire*. Paris: Nouvelles Editions Latines, 1958.

Bunyan, Tony. *The Political Police in Britain*. New York: St. Martin's Press, 1976.

Burpo, John H. *The Police Labor Movement: Problems and Perspectives*. Springfield, Ill.: Charles C Thomas, 1971.

Caffi, Andrea. *A Critique of Violence*. New York: Bobbs-Merrill, 1970.

Caiden, Gerald. *Police Revitalization*. Lexington, Mass.: Lexington Books, 1977.

Cain, Maureen E. *Society and the Policeman's Role*. London: Routledge and Kegan Paul, 1973.

Cardozo, Benjamin. *The Nature of the Judicial Process*. New Haven: Yale University Press, 1931.

Carlin, Jerome E.; Howard, Jan; and Messinger, Sheldon L. *Civil Justice and the Poor: Issues for Sociological Research*. New York: Russell Sage Foundation, 1967.

Carmichael, Stokely, and Hamilton, Charles. *Black Power: The Politics of Liberation in America*. New York: Vintage Books, 1967.

Carney, Frank J.; Mattick, Hans W.; and Callaway, John D. *Action on the Streets: A Handbook for Inner City Youth Work*. New York: Association Press, 1969.

Carte, Gene E., and Carte, Elaine H. *Police Reform in the United States*. Berkeley: University of California Press, 1975.

Casper, Jonathan D. *American Criminal Justice: The Defendant's Perspective*. Englewood Cliffs, N.J.: Prentice-Hall, 1972.

Chambliss, William J. *Crime and the Legal Process*. New York: McGraw-Hill, 1969.

———, ed. *Criminal Law in Action*. Santa Barbara, Ca.: Hamilton, 1975.

Chambliss, William J., and Seidman, Robert B. *Law, Order, and Power*. Reading, Mass.: Addison-Wesley, 1971.

Chapman, Brian. *Police State*. New York: Praeger, 1970.

Chapman, Samuel G. *The Police Heritage in England and America*. East Lansing, Mich.: Michigan State University Press, 1962.

Chevigny, Paul. *Cops and Rebels*. New York: Pantheon Books, 1972.

———. *Police Power: Police Abuses in New York City*. New York: Pantheon Books, 1969.

Cicourel, Aaron V. *The Social Organization of Juvenile Justice*. New York: Wiley, 1968.

Cipes, Robert M. *The Crime War*. New York: New American Library, 1968.

Citizens Research and Investigation Committee, and Tackwood, Louis E. *The Glass House Tapes*. New York: Avon Books, 1973.

Clark, Kenneth B. *Dark Ghetto*. New York: Harper & Row, 1965.

Clark, Ramsey. *Crime in America*. New York: Simon & Schuster, 1970.

Clegg, Reed K. *Probation and Parole*. Springfield, Ill.: Charles C Thomas, 1964.

Clinard, Marshall B. *Sociology of Deviant Behavior*. 4th ed. New York: Holt, Rinehart and Winston, 1968.

Clinard, Marshall B., and Abbott, Daniel J. *Crime in Developing Countries: A Comparative Perspective*. New York: Wiley, 1973.

Clinard, Marshall B., and Quinney, Richard. *Criminal Behavior Systems*. 2nd ed. New York: Holt, Rinehart and Winston, 1973.

Clinard, Marshall B., and Yeager, Peter C. *Corporate Crime*. New York: The Free Press, 1980.

Cloward, Richard A., and Ohlin, Lloyd E. *Delinquency and Opportunity*. New York: Free Press, 1960.

Coffey, Alan; Eldefonso, Edward; and Hartinger, Walter. *Police–Community Relations*. Englewood Cliffs, N.J.: Prentice-Hall, 1971.

Cohen, Albert K. *Deviance and Control*. Englewood Cliffs, N.J.: Prentice-Hall, 1966.

Cohen, Alvin W., ed. *The Future of Policing*. Beverly Hills: Sage Publications, 1978.

Cohen, Bernard. *Deviant Street Networks*. Lexington, Mass.: D. C. Heath, 1980.

Cohen, Bernard, and Chaiken, Jan M. *Police Background Characteristics and Performance*. Santa Monica, Ca.: Rand Corporation, 1972.

Cohen, Robert, et al., eds. *Working with Police Agencies*. New York: Human Sciences Press, 1975.

Cole, George F. *Criminal Justice: Law and Politics*. Belmont, Ca.: Duxbury Press, 1972.

Cole, Hubert. *Fouche: The Unprincipled Patriot*. New York: McCall, 1971.

Conklin, John E. *Robbery and the Criminal Justice System*. Philadelphia: J. B. Lippincott, 1972.

Conklin, John E., ed. *The Crime Establishment*. Englewood Cliffs, N.J.: Prentice-Hall, 1973.

———. *The Impact of Crime*. New York: Macmillan, 1975.

———. *Illegal But Not Criminal*. Englewood Cliffs, N.J.: Prentice-Hall, 1977.

Connors, Bernard. *Don't Embarrass the Bureau*. New York: Bobbs-Merrill, 1972.

Conot, Robert. *Rivers of Blood, Years of Darkness*. New York: Bantam Books, 1967.

Cook, Fred J. *The FBI Nobody Knows*. New York: Macmillan, 1964.

———. *The Corrupted Land*. New York: Macmillan, 1966.

———. *The Secret Rulers*. New York: Duell, Sloan and Pearce, 1966.

Corson, William R. *The Armies of Ignorance*. New York: Dial Press, 1977.

Cowan, Paul; Egleson, Nick; and Hentoff, Nat. *State Secrets: Police Surveillance in America*. New York: Holt, Rinehart and Winston, 1974.

Crainer, James. *The World's Police*. London: Cassell, 1964.

Cray, Ed. *The Big Blue Line*. New York: Coward-McCann, 1967.

———. *The Enemy in the Streets: Police Malpractice in America*. New York: Doubleday/Anchor Books, 1972.

Creamer, J. Shane. *The Law of Arrest, Search and Seizure*. 2nd ed. Philadelphia: W. B. Saunders, 1975.

Cressey, Donald R. *Theft of the Nation*. New York: Harper & Row, 1969.

Cressey, Donald R., and Ward, David A. *Delinquency, Crime, and Social Process*. New York: Harper & Row, 1969.

Critchley, Thomas A. *A History of Police in England and Wales*. 2nd ed. Montclair, N.J.: Patterson Smith, 1972.

Crozier, Michel. *The Bureaucratic Phenomenon*. Chicago: University of Chicago Press, 1964.

Curran, James T.; Fowler, Austin; and Ward, Richard H., eds., with intro. *Police and Law Enforcement*. New York: AMS Press, 1973.

Curran, William J. *Law and Medicine*. Boston: Little, Brown, 1960.

Dahl, Robert A. *Pluralist Democracy in the United States: Conflict and Consent*. Chicago: Rand McNally, 1967.

Darrow, Clarence. *The Story of My Life*. New York: Scribners, 1934.

Dash, Samuel; Knowlton, Robert; and Schwartz, Richard. *The Eavesdroppers*. New Brunswick, N.J.: Rutgers University Press, 1959.

Davis, Kenneth Culp. *Discretionary Justice: A Preliminary Inquiry*. Urbana, Ill.: University of Illinois Press, 1971.

Deacon, Richard. *A History of the Russian Secret Police*. New York: Taplinger,1972.

Decrow, Karen. *Sexist Justice*. New York: Vintage/Random House, 1975.

DeGrazia, Sebastian. *The Political Community: A Study of Anomie*. Chicago: University of Chicago Press, 1966.

Demaris, Ovid. *The Director: An Oral Biography of J. Edgar Hoover*. New York: Harper & Row, 1975.

Denisoff, R. Serge, ed. *The Sociology of Dissent*. New York: Harcourt, Brace, Jovanovich, 1974.

Denisoff, R. Serge, and McCaghy, Charles H. *Deviance, Conflict, and Criminality*. Chicago: Rand McNally, 1973.

Dernfeld, Duane. *Street-wise Criminology*. Cambridge, Mass.: Schenkman, 1974.

DeRopp, Robert S. *Drugs and the Mind*. New York: Grove Press, 1961.

Dershowitz, Alan M. *The Best Defense*. New York: Random House, 1982.

de Toledano, Ralph J. *Edgar Hoover: The Man and His Times*. New Rochelle, N.Y.: Arlington House, 1973.

Deutsch, Albert. *The Trouble with Cops*. New York: Crown, 1955.

Devlin, Patrick. *The Enforcement of Morals*. New York: Oxford University Press, 1965.

Domhoff, G. William. *The Powers That Be*. New York: Vintage Books, 1979.

Donnelly, Richard; Goldstein, J.; and Schwartz, Richard D. *Criminal Law*. New York: Free Press, 1962.

Donner, Frank J. *The Age of Surveillance*. New York: Vintage Books, 1981.

Douglas, Jack D., ed. *Deviance and Respectability*. New York: Basic Books, 1970.

Dreyer, Peter. *The Future of Treason*. New York: Ballantine Books, 1973.

Droge, Edward F. *The Patrolman: A Cop's Story*. New York: New American Library, 1973.

Durkheim, Emile. *The Rules of Sociological Method*. New York: Free Press, 1964.

Duster, Troy. *The Legislation of Morality: Drugs and Moral Judgment*. New York: Free Press, 1970.

Dye, Thomas R. *Who's Running America?* Englewood Cliffs, N.J.: Prentice-Hall, 1983.

Earle, Howard H. *Police–Community Relations: Crisis in Our Time*. 2nd ed. Springfield, Ill.: Charles C Thomas, 1970.

Easton, David. *The Political System*. New York: Alfred A. Knopf, 1953.

Edwards, George. *The Police on the Urban Frontier*. New York: Institute of Human Relations Press, 1968.

Eidelberg, Paul. *The Philosophy of the American Constitution: A Reinterpretation of the Intentions of the Founding Fathers*. New York: Free Press, 1968.

Eisenstein, James. *Politics and the Legal Process*. New York: Harper & Row, 1973.

Eisenstein, James, and Jacob, Herbert. *Felony Justice: An Organizational Analysis of the Courts*. Boston: Little, Brown, 1977.

Eisner, Victor. *The Delinquency Label*. New York: Random House, 1968.

Eldefonso, Edward. *Youth Problems and Law Enforcement*. Englewood Cliffs, N.J.: Prentice-Hall, 1972.

Elliff, John T. *The Reform of FBI Intelligence Operations*. Princeton, N.J.: Princeton University Press, 1979.

Elliott, J. F., and Sardeno, Thomas J. *Crime Control Team: An Experiment in Municipal Police Department Management and Operations*. Springfield, Ill.: Charles C Thomas, 1971.

Elton, G. R. *Policy and Police: The Enforcement of the Reformation in the Age of Cromwell*. London: Cambridge University Press, 1972.

Emerson, Robert M. *Judging Delinquents: Context and Process in Juvenile Court*. Chicago: Aldine, 1969.

Endleman, Shalom. *Violence in the Streets*. Chicago: Quadrangle Books, 1970.

Ericson, Richard V. *Making Crime: A Study of Detective Work*. Toronto: Butterworths, 1981.

Erikson, Kai T. *Wayward Puritans*. New York: Wiley, 1966.

Ernst, Morris L, and Schwartz, Alan U. *Privacy: The Right to Be Let Alone*. New York: Macmillan, 1962.

Falk, Richard A. *Legal Order in a Violent World*. Princeton, N.J.: Princeton University Press, 1968.

Faralicq, Rene. *The French Police from Within*. London: Cassell, 1933.

Feifer, George. *Justice in Moscow*. New York: Simon & Schuster, 1964.

Felt, W. Mark. *The FBI Pyramid*. New York: G. P. Putnam, 1979.

Ferri, Enrico. *Criminal Sociology*. New York: Appleton, 1896.

Fiammong, C. J. *The Police and the Underprotected Child*. Springfield, Ill.: Charles C Thomas, 1970.

Fiddle, Seymour. *Portraits from a Shooting Gallery*. New York: Harper & Row, 1967.

Filstead, William J., ed. *An Introduction to Deviance*. Chicago: Markham, 1972.

Fogelson, Robert M. *Big-City Police*. Cambridge, Mass.: Harvard University Press, 1977.

Fontana, Vincent J. *The Maltreated Child*. Springfield, Ill.: Charles C Thomas, 1964.

Ford, Gerald R., and Stiles, John R. *Portrait of the Assassin*. New York: Simon & Schuster, 1965.

Fosdick, Raymond B. *American Police Systems*. Montclair, N.J.: Patterson Smith, 1972.

———. *European Police Systems*. Montclair, N.J.: Patterson Smith, 1972.

Foucault, Michel. *Discipline and Punish: The Birth of the Prison*. New York: Vintage Books, 1979.

Frank, Jerome. *Courts on Trial*. Princeton, N.J.: Princeton University Press, 1949.

Frankel, Marvin E., and Naftalis, Gary P. *The Grand Jury: An Institution on Trial*. New York: Hill and Wang, 1975.

Frankfurter, Felix. *The Case of Sacco and Vanzetti*. Boston: Little, Brown, 1927.

Franklin, Charles. *The Third Degree*. London: Robert Hale, 1970.

Freund, Paul A. *On Law and Justice*. Cambridge, Mass.: Harvard University Press, 1968.

Friedlander, C. P., and Mitchell, E. *The Police: Servants or Masters?* London: Hart-Dairs, 1974.

Friendly, Alfred, and Goldfarb, Ronald. *Crime and Publicity*. New York: Twentieth Century Fund, 1967.

Fuller, Lon L. *The Morality of Law*. New Haven, Conn.: Yale University Press, 1964.

Gammage, Allen Z., and Hemphill, Charles F. *Basic Criminal Law*. New York: McGraw-Hill, 1974.

Garbus, Martin. *Ready for the Defense*. New York: Avon Books, 1971.

Gardiner, John A. *Traffic and the Police: Variations in Law Enforcement Policy*. Cambridge, Mass.: Harvard University Press, 1969.

Gardner, Erle Stanley. *Cops on Campus and Crime in the Streets*. New York: William Morrow, 1970.

Gardner, Thomas J. *Principles and Cases of the Law of Arrest, Search, and Seizure*. New York: McGraw-Hill, 1974.

Garrow, David J. *The FBI and Martin Luther King, Jr.* New York: Penguin Books, 1981.

Geis, Gilbert, ed. *White Collar Criminal*. New York: Atherton Press, 1968.

Gelb, Barbara. *Varnished Brass: The Decade after* Serpico. New York: G. P. Putnam's, 1983.

Gellhorn, Walter. *Ombudsmen and Others: Citizen Protectors in Nine Countries*. Cambridge, Mass.: Harvard University Press, 1966.

Germann, A. C.; Day, Frank D.; and Gallati, Robert R. J. *Introduction to Law Enforcement*. Springfield, Ill.: Charles C Thomas, 1962.

Gibbons, Don C. *Society, Crime, and Criminal Careers*. 2nd ed. Englewood Cliffs, N.J.: Prentice-Hall, 1973.

———. *The Criminological Enterprise*. Englewood Cliffs, N.J.: Prentice-Hall, 1979.

Gladwin, Irene. *The Sheriff: The Man and His Office*. London: Victor Gollancz, 1974.

Glaser, Daniel, ed. *Crime in the City*. New York: Harper & Row, 1970.

———, ed. *Handbook of Criminology*. Chicago: Rand McNally, 1974.

Goffman, Erving. *Stigma*. Englewood Cliffs, N.J.: Prentice-Hall, 1963.

Goldfarb, Ronald. *Ransom*. New York: Harper & Row, 1965.

———. *Jails*. Garden City, N.Y.: Anchor Press/Doubleday, 1975.

Goldfarb, Ronald, and Singer, Linda R. *After Conviction*. New York: Simon & Schuster, 1973.

Goldsmith, Jack, and Goldsmith, Sharon S., eds. *The Police Community*. Pacific Palisades, Ca.: Palisades, 1974.

Goldstein, Abraham S. *The Insanity Defense*. New Haven, Conn.: Yale University Press, 1967.

Goldstein, Herman. *Police Corruption: A Perspective on Its Nature and Control*. Washington, D.C.: Police Foundation, 1975.

———. *Policing a Free Society*. Cambridge, Mass.: Ballinger, 1977.

Goldstein, Joseph; Dershowitz, Alan M.; and Schwartz, Richard D. *Criminal Law: Theory and Process*. New York: Free Press, 1974.

Gooberman, Lawrence A. *Operation Intercept: The Multiple Consequences of Public Policy*. New York: Pergamon Press, 1974.

Goode, Erich. *Drugs in American Society*. New York: Alfred A. Knopf, 1972.

———. *The Marijuana Smokers*. New York: Basic Books, 1970.

Gourley, G. Douglas. *Effective Municipal Police Organization*. Beverly Hills, Ca.: Glencoe Press, 1971.

Graham, Hugh Davis, and Gurr, Ted Robert, eds. *Violence in America: Historical and Comparative Perspectives*. New York: Bantam Books, 1969.

Grant, Douglas. *The Thin Blue Line*. London: John Lang, 1973.

Greenwald, Harold. *The Call Girl*. New York: Ballantine Books, 1958.

Griffiths, Percival. *To Guard My People: The History of the Indian Police*. London: Ernest Benn, 1971.

Gross, Bertram, ed. *A Great Society?* New York: Basic Books, 1968.

Guenther, Anthony L., ed. *Criminal Behavior and Social Systems: Contributions of American Sociology*. New York: Rand McNally, 1973.

Hacker, Frederick J. *Crusaders, Criminals, Crazies*. New York: W. W. Norton, 1976.

Hahn, Harlan, ed. *Police in Urban Society*. Beverly Hills, Ca.: Sage Publications, 1971.

Hall, Jerome. *Theft, Law and Society*. 2nd ed. Indianapolis, Ind.: Bobbs-Merrill, 1952.

Halleck, Seymour L. *Psychiatry and the Dilemmas of Crime*. New York: Harper & Row, 1967.

Hamilton, Alastair. *The Appeal of Fascism*. New York: Discus/Avon, 1971.

Hansen, David A., and Culley, Thomas R. *The Police Leader*. Springfield, Ill.: Charles C Thomas, 1971.

Harris, Richard N. *The Police Academy: An Inside View*. New York: Wiley, 1973.

Hart, H. L. A. *Law, Liberty and Morality*. Stanford, Ca.: Stanford University Press, 1963.

———. *Punishment and Responsibility: Essays in the Philosophy of Law*. New York: Oxford University Press, 1967.

Hart, J. M. *The British Police*. London: Allen and Unwin, 1951.

Hartjen, Clayton A. *Crime and Criminalization*. New York: Praeger, 1974.

Hartogs, Renatus, and Artzt, Eric, eds. *Violence: Causes and Solutions*. New York: Dell, 1970.

Haskell, Martin R., and Yablonsky, Lewis. *Juvenile Delinquency*. Chicago: Rand McNally, 1974.

Heffernan, Esther. *Making It in Prison*. New York: Wiley, 1972.

Heilbroner, Robert L. *An Inquiry into the Human Prospect*. New York: W. W. Norton, 1980.

Henry, Andrew F., and Short, James F., Jr. *Suicide and Homicide*. New York: Free Press, 1964.

Herman, Robert D., ed. *Gambling*. New York: Harper & Row, 1967.

Hersey, John. *The Algiers Motel Incident*. New York: Alfred A. Knopf, 1968.

Hess, Henner. *Mafia and Mafiosi: The Structure of Power*. Lexington, Mass.: D. C. Heath, 1973.

Hewitt, William H. *British Police Administration*. Springfield, Ill.: Charles C Thomas, 1965.

———. *A Bibliography of Police Administration: Public Safety and Criminology*. Springfield, Ill.: Charles C Thomas, 1967.

Hewitt, William, and Newman, Charles L. *Police–Community Relations: An Anthology and a Bibliography*. Mineola, N.Y.: Foundation Press, 1970.

Hingley, Ronald. *The Russian Secret Police*. New York: Simon & Schuster, 1970.

Hirschi, Travis, and Selvin, Hanan C. *Delinquency Research: An Appraisal of Analytic Methods*. New York: Free Press, 1967.

Hoffer, Eric. *The True Believer*. New York: Harper and Brothers, 1951.

Hoffman, Abbie. *Steal This Book*. New York: Grove Press, 1971.

Hofstadter, Richard. *The Paranoid Style in American Politics*. New York: Alfred A. Knopf, 1965.

Homer, Frederic D. *Guns and Garlic: Myths and Realities of Organized Crime*. West Lafayette, Ind.: Purdue University Press, 1974.

Hongan, Jim. *Spooks*. New York: Morrow, 1978.

Hood, Robert, and Sparks, Richard. *Key Issues in Criminology*. New York: McGraw-Hill, 1970.

Horgan, John J. *Criminal Investigation*. New York: McGraw-Hill, 1974.

Hormachea, C. R., and Hormachea, M. *Confrontation: Violence and the Police*. Boston: Holbrook Press (Allyn & Bacon), 1971.

Howard, John R. *The Cutting Edge*. Philadelphia: J. B. Lippincott, 1974.

Humphreys, Laud. *Tearoom Trade: Impersonal Sex in Public Places*. Chicago: Aldine, 1970.

Hunt, Morton. *The Mugging*. New York: Atheneum, 1972.

Ianni, Francis A. J. *Black Mafia: Ethnic Succession in Organized Crime*. New York: Simon & Schuster, 1974.

Iannone, Nathan F. *Supervision of Police Personnel*. Englewood Cliffs, N.J.: Prentice-Hall, 1970.

———. *Principles of Police Patrol*. New York: McGraw-Hill, 1975.

Inbau, Fred E., and Reid, John E. *Criminal Interrogation and Confessions*. Baltimore: Williams and Wilkins, 1962.

Inbau, Fred E., and Sowle, Claude R. *Criminal Justices: Cases and Comments*. Brooklyn: Foundation Press, 1964.

Inciardi, James A. *Careers in Crime*. Chicago: Rand McNally, 1975.

———. *Reflections on Crime*. New York: Holt, Rinehart and Winston, 1978.

Inciardi, James, and Chambers, Carl, eds. *Drugs and The Criminal Justice System*. London: Sage Publications, 1973.

Irwin, John. *The Felon*. Englewood Cliffs, N.J.: Prentice-Hall, 1970.

Jacob, Herbert. *The Frustration of Policy: Responses to Crime in American Cities*. Boston: Little, Brown, 1984.

Jacobs, Paul. *Prelude to Riot*. New York: Random House, 1968.

Janowitz, Morris. *Social Control of Escalated Riots*. Chicago: University of Chicago Center for Policy Study, 1968.

Jeffrey, Sir Charles. *The Colonial Police*. London: M. Parrish, 1952.

Johnson, David R. *American Law Enforcement: A History*. St. Louis, Mo.: Forum Press, 1981.

Johnson, John M., and Douglas, Jack D. *Crime at the Top: Deviance in Business and the Professions*. New York: J. B. Lippincott, 1978.

Johnson, Richard M. *The Dynamics of Compliance: Supreme Court Decision-Making from a New Per-*

spective. Evanston, Ill.: Northwestern University Press, 1968.

Johnson, Thomas A.; Misner, Gordon E.; and Brown, Lee P. *The Police and Society*. Englewood Cliffs, N.J.: Prentice-Hall, 1981.

Johnston, William, *Cruising*. New York: Random House, 1970.

Jones, Ann. *Women Who Kill*. New York: Holt, Rinehart and Winston, 1980.

Jones, Harry W., ed. *The Courts, the Public, and the Law Explosion*. Englewood Cliffs, N.J.: Prentice-Hall, 1965.

———, ed. *Law and the Social Role of Science*. New York: Rockefeller University Press, 1967.

Josephson, Matthew. *The Robber Barons*. New York: Harcourt, Brace and World, 1962.

Judge, Anthony, *A Man Apart: The British Policeman and His Job*. London: Arthur Barker, 1972.

Kafka, Franz. *The Castle*. New York: Modern Library, 1969.

———. *The Trial*. New York: Vintage Books, 1969.

Kamisar, Yale; Inbau, Fred; and Arnold, Thurman. *Criminal Justice in Our Time*. Charlottesville, Va.: University Press of Virginia, 1965.

Kaplan, John. *Marijuana: The New Prohibition*. Cleveland: World, 1970.

Kaplan, J., and Waltz, J. R. *The Trial of Jack Ruby*. New York: Macmillan, 1965.

Karlen, Delmar. *Anglo-American Criminal Justice*. New York: Oxford University Press, 1967.

Karmen, Andrew. *Crime Victims*. Belmont, Ca.: Brooks/Cole, 1984.

Kefauver, Estes. *Crime in America*. New York: Doubleday, 1951.

Kempton, Murray. *The Briar Patch*. New York: Dell Publishing, 1973.

Kennedy, Robert F. *The Pursuit of Justice*. New York: Harper & Row, 1964.

Kenny, John P., and Pursuit, Dan G. *Police Work with Juveniles*, 3rd ed. Springfield, Ill.: Charles C Thomas, 1965.

Kephart, William M. *Racial Factors and Urban Law Enforcement*. Philadelphia: University of Pennsylvania Press, 1957.

Kinney, John P. *Police Administration*. Springfield, Ill.: Charles C Thomas, 1972.

Kirchheimer, Otto. *Political Justice*. Princeton, N.J.: Princeton University Press, 1961.

Klempner, Jack, and Parker, Roger D. *Juvenile Delinquency and Juvenile Justice*. New York: Franklin Watts, 1981.

Klockars, Carl B. *The Professional Fence*. New York: Free Press, 1974.

———, ed. *Thinking about Police*. New York: McGraw-Hill, 1983.

Klonoski, James R., and Mendelsohn, Robert I., eds. *The Politics of Local Justice*. Boston: Little, Brown, 1970.

Klotter, John C. *Constitutional Law for Police*. Cincinnati: W. H. Anderson, 1970.

The Knapp Commission Report on Police Corruption. New York: George Braziller, 1973.

Knopf, T. *Youth Patrols*. Waltham, Mass.: Lemberg Center for the Study of Violence, 1969.

Kobitz, Robert W. *The Police Role and Juvenile Delinquency*. Gaithersburg, Md.: International Assoc. of Chiefs of Police, 1971.

Krausnick, Helmut, et al. *Anatomy of the SS State*. New York: Walker, 1968.

Krisberg, Barry. *Crime and Privilege: Toward a New Criminology*. Englewood Cliffs, N.J.: Prentice-Hall, 1975.

Krislov, Samuel. *The Supreme Court and Political Freedom*. New York: Free Press, 1968.

Kulis, Joseph C.; Lorinskas, Robert A.; and Byrne, Rebecca. *Psychology and the Police*. Chicago: Police Academy, 1972.

La Fave, Wayne R. *Arrest: The Decision to Take a Suspect into Custody*. Boston: Little, Brown, 1965.

Lambert, John R. *Crime, Police and Race Relations*. New York: Oxford University Press, 1970.

Lane, Roger. *Policing the City: Boston 1822–1882*. Cambridge, Mass.: Harvard University Press, 1967.

Larson, Richard C., ed. *Police Accountability: Performance Measures and Unionism*. Lexington, Mass.: D. C. Heath, 1978.

Lasswell, Harold D. *Politics: Who Gets What, When, How*. New York: McGraw-Hill, 1936.

———. *Power and Personality*. New York: Viking Press, 1948.

Laurie, Peter. *Scotland Yard: A Study of the Metropolitan Police*. New York: Holt, Rinehart and Winston, 1970.

Lea, Henry Charles. *The Inquisition of the Middle Ages: Its Organization and Operation*. New York: Citadel, 1954.

Lefcourt, Robert. *Law Against the People*. New York: Vintage Books, 1972.

Leiser, Burton M. *Liberty, Justice and Morals: Contemporary Value Conflicts*. 2nd ed. New York: Macmillan, 1979.

Lemert, Edward M. *Human Deviance: Social Problems and Social Control*. Englewood Cliffs, N.J.: Prentice-Hall, 1967.

Leonard, V. A. *The Police Communications System*. Springfield, Ill.: Charles C Thomas, 1970.

———. *Police Crime Prevention*. Springfield, Ill.: Charles C Thomas, 1971.

Leopold, Nathan F. *Life Plus 99 Years*. New York: Doubleday, 1958.

Letkemann, Peter. *Crime As Work*. Englewood Cliffs, N.J.: Prentice-Hall, 1973.

Levi, Primo. *Survival in Auschwitz*. New York: Collier Books, 1961.

Levy, Leonard W. *Against the Law: The Nixon Court and Criminal Justice*. New York: Harper & Row, 1974.

Levytsky, Boris. *The Uses of Terror: The Soviet Secret Police, 1917–1970*. New York: Coward, McCann, 1972.

Lieberman, Jethro K. *How the Government Breaks the Law*. Baltimore, Md.: Penguin Books, 1973.

Liebow, Elliot. *Tally's Corner*. Boston: Little, Brown, 1967.

Lindesmith, Alfred R. *The Addict and the Law*. Bloomington, Ind.: Indiana University Press, 1965.

Lipset, Seymour M. *Political Man*. Garden City, N.Y.: Doubleday, 1960.

Lipsky, Michael, ed. *Law and Order: Police Encounters*. Chicago: Aldine, 1970.

———. *Street Level Bureaucracy: Dilemmas of the Individual in Public Services*. New York: Russell Sage Foundation, 1980.

Lofland, John. *Deviance and Identity*. Englewood Cliffs, N.J.: Prentice-Hall, 1969.

Lofton, John. *Justice and the Press*. Boston: Beacon Press, 1966.

A Look at Criminal Justice Research. Washington, D.C.: Law Enforcement Assistance Administration, 1971.

Lorenz, Konrad. *On Aggression*. Marjorie Wilson, trans. New York: Harcourt, Brace, 1966.

Lowenthal, Max. *The Federal Bureau of Investigation*. New York: Sloane Associates, 1950.

Lundberg, Ferdinand. *Cracks in the Constitution*. Secaucus, N.J.: Lyle Stuart, 1980.

Lundman, Richard J. *Police and Policing*. New York: Holt, Rinehart and Winston, 1980.

Luttwak, Edward. *Coup d'Etat*. New York: Alfred A. Knopf, 1969.

Maas, Peter. *Serpico*. New York: Viking Press, 1973.

———. *The Valachi Papers*. New York: G. P. Putnam's Sons, 1968.

MacNamara, Donal E. J., and Sagarin, Edward. *Sex, Crime, and the Law*. New York: The Free Press, 1977.

Manning, Peter K. *Police Work: Essays on the Social Organization of Policing*. Cambridge, Mass.: M.I.T. Press, 1977.

———. *The Narcs' Game: Organizational and Informational Constraints on Drug Law Enforcement*. Cambridge, Mass.: M.I.T. Press, 1980.

Manning, Peter K., and Van Maanen, John, eds. *Policing: A View from the Street*. Santa Monica, Ca.: Goodyear, 1978.

Marks, John D. *The Search for the Manchurian Candidate*. New York: New York Times Books, 1979.

Marshall, Geoffrey. *Police and Government*. London: Methuen, 1965.

Marshall, James. *Intention in Law and Society*. New York: Funk and Wagnalls, 1968.

———. *Law and Psychology in Conflict*. New York: Doubleday, 1969.

Martin, J. P., and Wilson, Gail. *The Police: A Study in Manpower*. London: Heinemann, 1969.

Martin, Susan Ehrlich. *Breaking and Entering: Policewomen on Patrol*. Berkeley, Ca.: University of California Press, 1982.

Marx, Gary T. *Protest and Prejudice*. New York: Harper & Row, 1969.

Matza, David. *Delinquency and Drift*. New York: Wiley, 1964.

———. *Becoming Deviant*. Englewood Cliffs, N.J.: Prentice-Hall, 1969.

McCague, James. *The Second Rebellion: The Story of the New York City Draft Riots of 1863*. New York: Dial Press, 1968.

McCall, George J. *Observing the Law: Field Methods in the Study of Crime and the Criminal Justice System*. New York: Free Press, 1978.

McEachern, A. W., et al. *Criminal Justice System Simulation Study: Some Preliminary Projections*. Los Angeles: University of Southern California, Public Systems Research Institute, 1970.

McLean, Robert Joe, ed. *Education for Crime: Prevention and Control*. Springfield, Ill.: Charles C Thomas, 1975.

Medalie, Richard J. *From Escobedo to Miranda*. Washington, D.C.: Lerner Law Book, 1966.

Melstner, Michael. *Cruel and Unusual: The Supreme Court and Capital Punishment*. New York: William Morrow, 1974.

Menninger, Karl. *The Crime of Punishment*. New York: Viking Press, 1968.

Messick, Hank. *John Edgar Hoover*. New York: David McKay, 1972.

———. *Lansky*. New York: G. P. Putnam's Sons, 1971.

Michael, Jerome, and Adler, Mortimer. *Crime, Law and Social Science*. New York: Harcourt Brace, 1933.

Michener, James A. *Kent State: What Happened and Why*. New York: Random House, 1971.

Miller, Arthur R. *The Assault on Privacy: Computers, Data Banks, and Dossiers*. Ann Arbor: University of Michigan Press, 1971.

Miller, Frank W. *Prosecution: The Decision to Charge a Suspect with a Crime*. Boston: Little, Brown, 1969.

Mills, C. Wright. *The Power Elite*. New York: Oxford University Press, 1957.

Mills, James. *One Just Man*. New York: Simon & Schuster, 1974.

Mitford, Jessica. *Kind and Usual Punishment: The Prison Business*. New York: Alfred A. Knopf, 1973.

Mollenhoff, Clark. *Tentacles of Power: The Story of Jimmy Hoffa*. Cleveland: World Publishing, 1965.

Momboisse, Raymond M. *Community Relations and Riot Prevention*. Springfield, Ill.: Charles C Thomas, 1970.

Morgan, Richard E. *Domestic Intelligence: Monitoring Dissent in America*. Austin: University of Texas Press, 1980.

Morris, Norval. *The Future of Imprisonment*. Chicago: University of Chicago Press, 1974.

Morris, Norval, and Hawkins, Gordon. *The Honest Politician's Guide to Crime Control*. Chicago: University of Chicago Press, 1970.

Moynihan, Daniel P. *Violent Crime: The Challenge to Our Cities*. The Report of the National Commission on the Causes and Prevention of Violence. New York: George Braziller, 1970.

Muir, Wiliam Ker, Jr. *Police: Streetcorner Politicians*. Chicago: University of Chicago Press, 1977.

Munro, Jim L. *Administrative Behavior and Police Organization*. Cincinnati: W. H. Anderson, 1974.

Myers, Gustavus. *History of the Great American Fortunes*. New York: Modern Library, 1936.

National Advisory Commission on Criminal Justice Standards and Goals. *Police*. Washington, D.C.: U.S. Government Printing Office, 1973.

Navasky, Victor S. *Kennedy Justice*. New York: Atheneum, 1971.

Neier, Aryeh. *Crime and Punishment: A Radical Solution*. New York: Stein and Day, 1978.

Nettler, Gwynn. *Explaining Crime*. New York: McGraw-Hill, 1974.

Neubauer, David W. *Criminal Justice in Middle America*. Morristown, N.J.: General Learning Corp., 1974.

Neumann, Franz. *Behemoth*. London: V. Gollancz, 1942.

New York State Special Commission. *Attica: The Official Report of the New York State Special Commission*. New York: Bantam Books, 1972.

Newman, Donald J. *Conviction: The Determination of Guilt or Innocence Without Trial*. Boston: Little, Brown, 1966.

———. *Introduction to Criminal Justice*. New York: J. B. Lippincott, 1975.

Newman, Graeme. *The Punishment Response*. New York: J. B. Lippincott, 1978.

Niederhoffer, Arthur. *Behind the Shield*. Garden City, N.Y.: Doubleday, 1967.

———. *A Study of Police Cynicism*. Ph.D. dissertation, New York University, 1963.

Niederhoffer, Arthur, and Niederhoffer, Elaine. *The Police Family: From Station House to Ranch House*. Lexington, Mass.: D. C. Heath, 1978.

Niederhoffer, Arthur, and Smith, Alexander B. *New Directions in Police–Community Relations*. San Francisco: Rinehart Press, 1974.

Nimmer, Raymond T. *Diversion—The Search for Alternative Forms of Prosecution*. Chicago: Foundation Publications, 1974.

Norman, Charles. *The Genteel Murderer*. New York: Collier Books, 1962.

Nye, F. Ivan. *Family Relationships and Delinquent Behavior*. New York: Wiley, 1958.

Oaks, Dallin H., and Lehman, Warren. *A Criminal Justice System and the Indigent: A Study of Chicago and Cook County*. Chicago: University of Chicago Press, 1968.

Packer, Herbert L. *The Limits of the Criminal Sanction*. Stanford: Stanford University Press, 1968.

Palmer, Stuart. *Prevention of Crime*. New York: Human Sciences Press, 1973.

Parenti, Michael. *Power and the Powerless*. New York: St. Martin's Press, 1978.

Pasternack, S. A., ed. *Violence and Victims*. New York: Halsted Press, 1975.

Patrick, Clarence H. *The Police, Crime, and Society*. Springfield, Ill.: Charles C Thomas, 1971.

Payne, Cyril. *Deep Cover*. New York: Newsweek Books, 1979.

Payne, Howard C. *The Police State of Louis Napoleon Bonaparte, 1851–1860*. Seattle: University of Washington Press, 1966.

Pearce, Frank. *Crimes of the Powerful*. London: Pluto Press, 1978.

Pearlstein, Stanley. *Psychiatry, the Law and Mental Health*. Dobbs Ferry, N.Y.: Oceana Publications, 1967.

Perry, David C. *Police in the Metropolis*. Columbus, Ohio: Charles E. Merrill, 1975.

Phillips, William, and Shecter, Leonard. *On the Pad*. New York: G. P. Putnam's Sons, 1973.

Pincher, Chapman. *Their Trade Is Treachery*. London: Sidgwick and Jackson, 1981.

Platt, Anthony. *The Child Savers*. Chicago: University of Chicago Press, 1969.

Platt, Anthony, and Cooper, Lynn. *Policing America*. Englewood Cliffs, N.J.: Prentice-Hall, 1974.

"Police Practices." *Law and Contemporary Problems*. Chapel Hill, N.C.: Duke University, 1971 (No. 4), Vol. XXXVI.

Polier, Justine W. *The Rule of Law and the Role of Psychiatry*. Baltimore: Johns Hopkins Press, 1968.

Pollack, Harriet, and Smith, Alexander B. *Civil Liberties and Civil Rights in the United States*. St. Paul, Minn.: West Publishing, 1978.

Porterfield, Austin L. *Youth In Trouble*. Fort Worth: Leo Potishman Foundation, 1946.

Portune, Robert. *Changing Adolescent Attitudes Toward Police*. Cincinnati, Ohio: Anderson, 1971.

Powers, Thomas. *The Man Who Kept the Secrets*. New York: Alfred A. Knopf, 1979.

Prassel, Frank R. *Introduction to American Criminal Justice*. New York: Harper & Row, 1975.

Preiss, Jack J., and Ehrlich, Howard J. *An Examination of Role Theory: The Case of the State Police*. Lincoln, Neb.: University of Nebraska Press, 1966.

President's Commission on Law Enforcement and Administration of Justice. *Task Force Reports: The Police; the Courts; Corrections; Juvenile Delinquency and Youth Crime; Organized Crime; Science and Technology; Assessment of Crime; Narcotics and Drugs; Drunkenness*. Washington, D.C.: U.S. Government Printing Office, 1967.

Pringle, Patrick. *Hue and Cry: The Birth of the British Police*. London: Museum Press, 1955.

Pritchett. C. Herman. *The American Constitution*. 2nd ed. New York: McGraw-Hill, 1968.

Prouty, Col. L. Fletcher. *The Secret Team: The CIA and Its Allies in Control of the World*. New York: Ballantine Books, 1973.

Puttkammer, Ernest W. *Administration of Criminal Law*. Chicago: University of Chicago Press, 1963.

Quinney, Richard, ed. *Crime and Justice in Society*. Boston: Little, Brown, 1969.

———. *Criminal Justice in America*. Boston: Little, Brown, 1974.

———. *Criminology: Analysis and Critique of Crime in America*. Boston: Little, Brown, 1975.

———. *Class, State and Crime*. New York: David McKay, 1977.

———. *Criminology*. 2nd ed. Boston: Little, Brown, 1979.

Raab, Selwyn. *Justice in the Back Room*. New York: World Publishing, 1967.

Radano, Gene. *Walking the Beat*. New York: Collier Books, 1969.

Radzinowicz, Leon. *Ideology and Crime*. New York: Columbia University Press, 1966.

———. *A History of English Criminal Law and Its Administration from 1750*. Vols. 1–4. New York: Barnes and Noble, 1968.

Ransom, Harry Howe. *The Intelligence Establishment*. Cambridge, Mass.; Harvard University Press, 1970.

Rawls, John. *A Theory of Justice*. Cambridge, Mass.: Harvard University Press, 1972.

Ray, Isaac. *A Treatise on the Medical Jurisprudence of Insanity*. Winfred Overholser, ed. Cambridge, Mass.: Harvard University Press, 1962.

Reasons, Charles E. *The Criminologist: Crime and the Criminal*. Pacific Palisades, Ca.: Goodyear, 1974.

Reasons, Charles E., and Kuykendall, Jack L., eds. *Race, Crime, and Justice*. Pacific Palisades, Ca.: Goodyear, 1972.

Reid, Ed. *Mafia*. New York: New American Library, 1964.

Reid, Sue Titus. *Crime and Criminology*. New York: Holt, Rinehart and Winston, 1982.

Reiman, Jeffrey. *The Rich Get Richer and the Poor Get Prison*. New York: Wiley, 1979.

Reiss, Albert J., Jr. *The Police and the Public*. New Haven: Yale University Press, 1971.

Reith, Charles. *A New Study of Police History*. London: Oliver and Boyd, 1956.

———. *The Blind Eye of History*. Montclair, N.J.: Patterson Smith, 1975.

Reppetto, Thomas A. *Residential Crime*. Cambridge, Mass.: Ballinger, 1974.

———. *The Blue Parade*. New York: Free Press, 1978.

Rhodes, Henry T. F. *Alphonse Bertillon*. London: George G. Harrap, 1956.

Richardson, James. *A History of Police Protection in New York City, 1800–1870*. Ph.D. dissertation, New York University, 1967.

———. *The New York Police: Colonial Times to 1901*. New York: Oxford University Press, 1970.

Richardson, James F. *Urban Police in the U.S.* New York: Kenniket Press, 1974.

Roberts, Simon. *Order and Dispute: An Introduction to Legal Anthropology*. New York: Penguin Books, 1979.

Rock, Paul. *Deviant Behavior*. London: Hutchinson University Library, 1973.

Rogers, Joseph W. *Why Are You Not A Criminal?* Englewood Cliffs, N.J.: Prentice-Hall, 1977.

Rolph, C. H., ed. *The Police and the Public*. London: Heinemann, 1962.

Rose, Arnold M. *Libel and Academic Freedom: A Lawsuit Against Political Extremists*. Minneapolis: University of Minnesota Press, 1968.

Rosenberg, Charles E. *The Trial of Assassin Guiteau: Psychiatry and Law in the Gilded Age*. Chicago: University of Chicago Press, 1968.

Rosenthal, Douglas E. *Lawyer and Client: Who's in Charge?* New York: Russell Sage Foundation, 1974.

Roszak, Theodore. *The Making of a Counterculture: Reflections on the Technocratic Society and Its Youthful Opposition*. Garden City, N.Y.: Doubleday, 1969.

Rovere, Richard H. *Senator Joe McCarthy*. New York: World, 1960.

Royal Commission on the Police. *Final Report*. Cmnd. 1728. London: Her Majesty's Stationery Office, 1962.

Rubington, Earl, and Weinberg, Martin S. *Deviance: The Interactionist Perspective*. 2nd ed. New York: Macmillan, 1973.

Rubinstein, Jonathan. *City Police*. New York: Farrar, Straus and Giroux, 1973.

Rueschemeyer, Dietrich. *Lawyers and Their Society*. Lawrence, Mass.: Harvard University Press, 1973.

Rule, James B. *Private Lives and Public Surveillance*. New York: Schocken Books, 1974.

Rumbelow, Donald. *I Spy Blue*. London: Macmillan, 1972.

Russell, Bertrand. *Power*. London: George Allen and Unwin, 1962.

Russell, Francis. *A City in Terror: 1919—The Boston Police Strike*. New York: Viking Press, 1975.

Ryan, William. *Blaming the Victim*. New York: Vintage Books, 1976.

Sagarin, Edward. *Deviants and Deviance*. New York: Praeger, 1975.

Salerno, Ralph, and Tompkins, Ralph. *The Crime Confederation*. Garden City, N.Y.: Doubleday, 1969.

Samaha, Joel. *Law and Order in Historical Perspective*. New York: Academic Press, 1974.

Sanders, William B. *Detective Work: A Study of Criminal Investigations*. New York: Free Press, 1977.

Saunders, Charles B., Jr. *Police Education and Training: Key to Better Law Enforcement*. Washington, D.C.: Brookings Institution, 1970.

———. *Upgrading the American Police*. Washington, D.C.: The Brookings Institution, 1970.

Schafer, Stephen. *The Political Criminal*. New York: Free Press, 1971.

———. *Theories in Criminology*. New York: Random House, 1969.

Scheff, Thomas J. *Labeling Madness*. Englewood Cliffs, N.J.: Prentice-Hall, 1975.

Schneir, Walter, and Schneir, Marian. *Invitation to an Inquest*. New York: Doubleday, 1965.

Schott, Joseph L. *No Left Turns: The FBI in Peace and War*. New York: Praeger, 1975.

Schur, Edwin M. *Crimes Without Victims*. Englewood Cliffs, N.J.: Prentice-Hall, 1965.

———. *Law and Society: A Sociological View*. New York: Random House, 1968.

———. *Radical Non-Intervention: Rethinking the Delinquency Problem*. Englewood Cliffs, N.J.: Prentice-Hall, 1973.

———. *The Politics of Deviance*. Englewood Cliffs, N.J.: Prentice-Hall, 1980.

Schur, Edwin M., and Bedau, Hugo Adam. *Victimless Crimes*. Englewood Cliffs, N.J.: Spectrum Books, 1974.

Schwartz, Bernard. *The Law in America: A History*. New York: McGraw-Hill, 1974.

Schwartz, Louis B., and Goldstein, S. R. *Law Enforcement Handbook for Police*. St. Paul, Minn.: West, 1970.

Seligman, Ben B. *Permanent Poverty: An American Syndrome*. Chicago: Quadrangle Books, 1968.

Servadio, Gaia. *Mafioso*. New York: Stein and Day, 1976.

Shaw, Clifford R. *The Jack Roller*. Chicago: University of Chicago Press, 1930.

Shaw, George Bernard. *The Crime of Imprisonment*. New York: The Citadel Press, 1961.

Shelden, Randall G. *Criminal Justice in America*. Boston: Little, Brown, 1982.

Sheley, Joseph F. *Understanding Crime: Concepts, Issues, Decisions*. Belmont, Ca.: Wadsworth, 1979.

Sherman, Lawrence W., ed. *Police Corruption: A Sociological Perspective*. Garden City, N.Y.: Doubleday, 1974.

Sherrill, Robert. *The Saturday Night Special*. New York: Penguin Books, 1975.

Shields, Pete. *Guns Don't Die—People Do*. New York: Arbor House, 1981.

Schoolbred, Claude F. *The Administration of Criminal Justice in England and Wales*. New York: Pergamon Press, 1966.

Shostak, Arthur B.; Van Til, Jon; and Van Til, Sally Bould. *Privilege in America: An End to Inequality?* Englewood Cliffs, N.J.: Spectrum Books, 1973.

Silberman, Charles E. *Criminal Violence, Criminal Justice*. New York: Random House, 1978.

Silver, Isidore, ed. *The Crime Control Establishment*. Englewood Cliffs, N.J.: Prentice Hall, 1974.

Simon, Rita. *The Jury and the Plea of Insanity*. Boston: Little, Brown, 1966.

———, ed. *The Sociology of Law: Interdisciplinary Readings*. San Francisco: Chandler, 1968.

Simonsen, Clifford E., and Gordon, Marshall S. *Juvenile Justice in America*. New York: Macmillan, 1982.

Sinclair, Upton. *The Jungle*. New York: Doubleday and Page, 1906.

Skolnick, Jerome H. *Justice Without Trial: Law Enforcement in Democratic Society*. New York: Wiley, 1966.

Skolnick, Jerome H., and Gray, Thomas C. *Police in America*. Boston: Little, Brown, 1975.

Smigel, Erwin O., and Ross, H. Laurence. *Crimes Against Bureaucracy*. New York: Van Nostrand Reinhold, 1970.

Smith, Alexander B., and Pollack, Harriet. *Some Sins Are Not Crimes*. New York: Franklin Watts, 1975.

———. *Criminal Justice: An Overview*. 2nd ed. New York: Holt, Rinehart and Winston, 1980.

Smith, Bruce. *The New York Police Survey*. New York: Institute of Public Administration, 1952.

———. *Police Systems in the United States*. 2nd rev. ed. New York: Harper & Row, 1960.

Smith, Dwight. *The Mafia Mystique*. New York: Basic Books, 1975.

Smith, Edgar. *Brief Against Death*. New York: Alfred A. Knopf, 1968.

Smith, R. Harris. *OSS: The Secret History of America's First Central Intelligence Agency*. New York: Dell Publishing, 1972.

Smith, Robert Ellis. *Privacy: How To Protect What's Left of It*. New York: Doubleday, 1980.

Smith, Ralph L. *The Tarnished Badge*. New York: Crowell, 1965.

Snibbe, John R., and Snibbe, Homa M., eds. *The Urban Policeman in Transition*. Springfield, Ill.: Charles C Thomas, 1973.

Solmes, Alwyn. *The English Policeman 1871–1935*. London: Allen and Unwin, 1935.

Sommer, Robert. *The End of Imprisonment*. New York: Oxford University Press, 1976.

Sowle, Claude R., ed. *Police Power and Individual Freedom*. Chicago: Aldine, 1962.

Spier, Hans. *Social Order and the Risks of War*. Cambridge, Mass.: M.I.T. Press, 1969.

Stark, Rodney. *Police Riots*. Belmont, Ca.: Wadsworth, 1972.

Stead, Philip John. *Vidocq: A Biography*. London: Staples Press, 1953.

———. *The Police of Paris*. London: Staples Press, 1957.

———. *The Police of France*. New York: Macmillan, 1983.

Steadman, Robert F., ed. *The Police and The Community*. Baltimore: Johns Hopkins University Press, 1972.

Steffens, Lincoln. *The Shame of the Cities*. New York: McClure Phillips, 1904.

———. *Autobiography*. New York: Harcourt Brace, 1936.

Sterba, James. *Justice: Alternative Political Perspectives*. Belmont, Ca.: Wadsworth, 1980.

Stone, Christopher D. *Where the Law Ends*. New York: Harper & Row, 1975.

Strecher, Victor G. *The Environment of Law Enforcement: A Community Relations Guide*. Englewood Cliffs, N.J.: Prentice-Hall, 1971.

Stuckey, Gilbert. *Evidence for the Law Enforcement Officer*. 2nd ed. New York: McGraw-Hill, 1974.

Sullivan, John, L. *Introduction to Police Science*. New York: McGraw-Hill, 1982.

Sullivan, William C. *The Bureau: My Thirty Years in Hoover's FBI*. New York: W. W. Norton, 1979.

Sussman, Barry. *The Great Cover-Up*. New York: New American Library, 1974.

Sutherland, Edwin H. *White Collar Crime*. New York: Holt, Rinehart and Winston, 1949.

Sutherland, Edwin, H., and Cressey, Donald R. *Criminology*. 10th ed. New York: J. B. Lippincott, 1978.

Swanson, Charles R., and Territo, Leonard. *Police Administration: Structures, Processes, and Behavior*. New York: Macmillan, 1983.

Sykes, Gresham. *Society of Captives*. Princeton, N.J.: Princeton University Press, 1958.

———. *Criminology*. New York: Harcourt Brace, 1978.

Skyes, Gresham, and Drobek, Thomas E. *Law and the Lawless*. New York: Random House, 1969.

Szasz, Thomas. *Law, Liberty and Psychiatry*. New York: Macmillan, 1963.

———. *Psychiatric Justice*. New York: Macmillan, 1965.

———. *Ceremonial Chemistry: The Ritual Persecution of Drug Addicts and Pushers*. Garden City, N.Y.: Anchor Press/Doubleday, 1974.

———. *Ideology and Insanity*. Garden City, N.Y.: Doubleday, 1970.

Tannenbaum, Frank. *Crime and the Community*. New York: Columbia University Press, 1938.

Tansik, David A., and Elliot, James F. *Managing Police Organizations*. Belmont, Ca.: Wadsworth, 1981.

Tarde, Gabriel. *Penal Philosophy*. Boston: Little, Brown, 1912.

Taylor, Ian; Walton, Paul; and Young, Jack. *The New Criminology*. London: Routledge and Kegan Paul, 1973.

Theoharis, Athan. *Spying on Americans*. Philadelphia: Temple University Press, 1978.

Thompson, Craig. *The Police State*. New York: E. P. Dutton, 1950.

Thompson, Hunter S. *Hell's Angels*. New York: Random House, 1966.

Tiffany, Lawrence P.; McIntyre, Donald M., Jr.; and Rotenberg, David L. *Detection of Crime: Stopping and Questioning, Search and Seizure, Encouragement and Entrapment*. Boston: Little, Brown, 1967.

Tobias, John J. *Urban Crime in Victorian England*. New York: Schocken Books, 1972.

Toch, Hans. *Violent Men: An Inquiry into the Psychology of Violence*. Chicago: Aldine, 1969.

———. *Living in Prison*. New York: The Free Press, 1977.

Train, Arthur. *Courts, Criminals, and the Camorra*. New York: Scribners, 1911.

Trebach, Arnold S. *The Rationing of Justice*. New Brunswick, N.J.: Rutgers University Press, 1964.

Tullett, Toni. *Inside Interpol*. London: Frederick Muller, 1963.

Turk, Austin T. *Legal Sanctioning and Social Control*. Washington, D.C.: U.S. Government Printing Office, 1972.

Turkus, Burton, and Feder, Sid. *Murder, Inc*. New York: Farrar, Straus, 1951.

Turner, William. *The Police Establishment*. New York: G. P. Putnam's Sons, 1968.

———. *Hoover's FBI: The Men and the Myth*. Los Angeles: Shelbourne Press, 1970.

Tyler, Gus. *Organized Crime in America*. Ann Arbor: University of Michigan Press, 1962.

Ungar, Sanford J. *FBI*. Boston: Little, Brown, 1975.

Uviller, H. Richard. *The Processes of Criminal Justice: Investigation*. St. Paul, Minn.: West, 1974.

———. *The Processes of Criminal Justice: Adjudication*. St. Paul, Minn.: West, 1975.

Valentine, Lewis J. *Night Stick*. New York: Dial Press, 1947.

van den Haag, Ernest. *Punishing Criminals*. New York: Basic Books, 1975.

Vollmer, August. *The Police and Modern Society*. Berkeley, Ca.: University of California Press, 1936.

Vollmer, Howard M., and Mills, Donald L., eds. *Professionalization*. Englewood Cliffs, N.J.: Prentice-Hall, 1966.

Walker, Nigel. *Crime and Insanity in England: Vol. 1; The Historical Perspective*. Edinburgh: Edinburgh University Press, 1968.

Wallace, Samuel E. *Skid Row As a Way of Life*. Totowa, N.J.: Bedminster Press, 1965.

Wambaugh, Joseph. *The New Centurions*. Boston: Little, Brown, 1970.

———. *Blue Knight*. Boston: G. K. Hall, 1972.

———. *Onion Field*. New York: Dell Publishing, 1974.

———. *The Black Marble*. New York: Dell Publishing, 1979.

———. *The Glitter Dome*. New York: Bantam Books, 1981.

Watters, Pat, and Gillers, Stephen, eds. *Investigating the FBI*. New York: Doubleday, 1973.

Weistart, John C., ed. *Police Practices*. Dobbs Ferry, N.Y.: Oceana Publications, 1974.

Wertham, Frederick. *A Sign for Cain*. New York: Macmillan, 1966.

Westley, William A. *The Police: A Sociological Study of Law, Custom and Morality*. Ph.D. dissertation, University of Chicago, 1951.

Weston, Paul B., and Willis, Kenneth M. *Law Enforcement and Criminal Justice*. Pacific Palisades, Ca.: Goodyear, 1972.

Wheeler, Stanton, ed. *On Record: Files and Dossiers in American Life*. New York: Russell Sage Foundation, 1969.

Whisenand, Paul M. *Police Supervision: Theory and Practice*. Englewood Cliffs, N.J.: Prentice-Hall, 1971.

Whisenand, Paul M., and Ferguson, R. Fred. *The Managing of Police Organizations*. Englewood Cliffs, N.J.: Prentice-Hall, 1973.

Whitaker, Ben. *The Police*. Middlesex, England: Penguin Books, 1964.

Whittemore, L. H. *Cop: A Closeup of Violence and Tragedy*. New York: Holt, Rinehart and Winston, 1969.

Whyte, William F. *Street Corner Society*. Chicago: University of Chicago Press, 1943.

Wicker, Tom. *A Time to Die*. New York: Quadrangle Books, 1975.

Wicks, Robert J. *Applied Psychology for Law Enforcement and Corrections Officers*. New York: McGraw-Hill, 1974.

Willett, T. C. *Criminal on the Road*. London: Tavistock, 1964.

Williams, Edward Bennett. *One Man's Freedom*. New York: Atheneum, 1962.

Wilson, James Q. *Explaining Crime*. New York: McGraw-Hill, 1975.

———. *Varieties of Police Behavior: The Management of Law and Order in Eight Communities*. New York: Atheneum, 1971.

———. *The Investigators: Managing FBI and Narcotics Agents*. New York: Basic Books, 1978.

Wilson, O. W. *Police Administration*. 2nd ed. New York: McGraw-Hill, 1963.

Wilson, O.W., and McLaren, Roy C. *Police Administration*. 3rd ed. New York: McGraw-Hill, 1972.

Winick, Charles, and Kinsie, Paul M. *The Lively Commerce: Prostitution in the United States*. Chicago: Quadrangle Books, 1971.

Wise, David. *The American Police State*. New York: Random House, 1976.

Wise, David, and Ross, Thomas. *The Invisible Government*. New York: Random House, 1964.

Wolfe, Bertram D. *Three Who Made a Revolution*. New York: Dell Publishing, 1964.

Wolfgang, Marvin E.; Figlio, Robert M.; and Sellin, Thorsten. *Delinquency in a Birth Cohort*. Chicago: University of Chicago Press, 1972.

Wright, R. Gene, and Marlo, John A. *The Police Officer and Criminal Justice*. New York: McGraw-Hill, 1970.

Yablonsky, Lewis. *Robopaths*. Baltimore: Penguin Books, 1972.

Zarr, Melvyn. *The Bill of Rights and the Police*. Dobbs Ferry, N.Y.: Oceana Publications, 1970.

Zeisel, Hans; Kalven, Harry, Jr.; and Buckholz, Bernard. *Delay in the Court*. Boston: Little, Brown, 1959.

GLOSSARY

Accomplice. An individual who voluntarily and knowingly assists another in committing an offense and thereby becomes criminally liable for the offense. See *Conspiracy.*

Accused. The generic name for the defendant in a criminal case.

Acquittal. A final determination, after trial, that the accused is not guilty of the offense charged.

Adjudication. That point in the criminal process when a judge renders the official judgment of the trial court as to the defendant's guilt or innocence.

Adversary proceeding. A proceeding in which the opposing sides have the opportunity to present their evidence and arguments. In contrast, an *ex parte* proceeding is one in which only one side presents its case to the court.

Adversary system. The procedure used to determine truth in the adjudication of guilt or innocence, which pits the defense (advocate for the accused) against the prosecution (advocate for the state), with the judge acting as arbiter of the legal rules. Under the adversary system, the burden is upon the state to prove the charges beyond a reasonable doubt. This system of having the two parties "battle" or publicly debate has proved to be the most effective method of achieving the truth regarding a set of circumstances. (The *accusatory*, or inquisitorial, system is used in continental Europe, under which the charge is evidence of guilt, which the accused must disprove; the judge takes an active part in the proceedings.)

Appeal. A request by either defense or prosecution that a case be removed from a lower court to a higher court so that the completed trial can be reviewed by the higher court. Those filing an appeal seek to have a lower court decision altered or reversed.

Arraignment. The step at which the accused are read the charges against them and are asked how they plead. In addition, the accused are advised of their rights. Possible pleas are guilty, not guilty, nolo contendere, and not guilty by reason of insanity.

Arrest. The taking of a person into the custody of the law, the legal purpose of which is to restrain the accused until he or she can be held accountable for the offense at court proceedings. The legal requirement for an arrest is probable cause. Arrests for investigation, suspicion, or harassment are improper and of doubtful legality. The police have the responsibility to use only reasonable physical force necessary to make an arrest. The summons has been used as a substitute for arrest.

Arrest warrant. A document signed by a magistrate accusing a specific individual or individuals with a crime and authorizing the police to take the person or persons into custody.

Bail. A sum of money or other security that is posted to assure the future attendance of the defendant at every stage of the criminal proceedings. Such money or security is to be forfeited if the defendant does not appear in court as directed.

Bail bondsman. One who provides, in return for a fee, a bond to the court promising payment of bail in the event the defendant flees to avoid prosecution.

Beyond a reasonable doubt. The degree of proof required for conviction of defendant in criminal proceedings: less than absolute certainty, more than high probability. If there is doubt based upon reason, the accused is entitled to the benefit of the doubt by an acquittal.

Bindover. When probable cause is found to exist at a preliminary hearing, the court orders that the accused be held for trial. The accused thereafter may be eligible for release on bail or under other conditions.

Booking. A clerical process involving an entry on a police blotter or arrest book that includes such information as the name of the person arrested, the time, the offense charged, and the arresting officer. Takes place immediately after an arrest is made and the defendant is taken to the station house.

Burden of proof. The obligation to introduce evidence establishing a fact so clearly as to meet the legal standard (e.g., proof beyond a reasonable doubt).

Burglary. Breaking and entering with intent to commit a felony or theft, or in some states, with intent to commit any offense.

Case law. The body of law created by judicial rulings deciding particular cases. The standards explaining the law established by a particular decision are usually set forth in a statement of the court (called an "opinion") explaining the court's decision on the law in that case.

Change of venue. A change in the place of trial, generally from one county to another. One purpose is to ensure that the jury will not be biased by pretrial publicity.

Citation. An order issued by a law enforcement officer directing that a person appear in court at a later date to answer to criminal charges. Also often refers to a ticket issued to traffic offenders and which may require only payment of a fine.

Common law. Broadly defined, common law is the body of law and legal theory that originated in England and was adopted in the United States; it is distinguished from Roman law, civil law, and canon law by its emphasis on the binding nature of interpretative court decisions. In a narrower sense, common law refers to the customs, traditions, judicial decisions, and other materials that guide courts in decision-making, as opposed to the courts' use of written statutes or the Constitution.

Conspiracy. An agreement between two or more persons, each of whom has intent to accomplish an illegal act injurious to public health or morals, or to accomplish a lawful act by illegal means. The essence of this crime is the agreement, and defendants may be charged with conspiracy without ever having committed any substantive crime. See *Accomplice.*

Constabulary style of policing. A system of policing dominant before the nineteenth century. Consisted of a day watch by a police official known as the *constable* and a night watch by citizen volunteers.

Crime. An offense against the state; behavior in violation of law for which there is prescribed punishment.

Criminal law. Norms that are formally codified and subject to enforcement by authorized agents of the state in a politically organized society.

Criminology. The study of the causes and treatment of criminal behavior, criminal law, and the administration of criminal justice.

Delinquent child. A person of no more than a specified age who has violated any law or ordinance or, in some jurisdictions, is deemed incorrigible; a person who has been adjudicated a delinquent by a juvenile court.

Detainer. A kind of "hold order" filed against an incarcerated person by another state or jurisdiction that seeks to take the individual into custody to answer to another criminal charge whenever the individual is released from current imprisonment.

Deterrence. The use of threat of punishment to prevent illegal behavior.

Discovery. The method by which a party in a case can gain access to information and evidence held by the opposing party. In criminal law the right to discovery is usually reserved for the defendant, but some states allow the prosecutor the same right, or reciprocal discovery.

Diversion. A procedure used by the courts that entails the removal of an offender from the criminal or juvenile justice system at an early stage of the proceedings.

Double jeopardy. A constitutional safeguard noted in the Fifth Amendment that protects citizens from being tried for the same offense more than once.

Due process. The basic constitutional principle based upon the concept of the primacy of the individual and the complementary concept of limitation on governmental power; a safeguard against arbitrary and unfair state procedures in judicial or administrative proceedings. Embodied in the due process concept are the basic rights of a defendant in criminal proceedings and the requisites for a fair trial. These rights and requirements have been expanded by appellate court decisions and include (1) timely notice of a hearing or trial to inform the accused of the charges; (2) the opportunity to confront accusers, to present evidence on one's own behalf before an impartial jury or judge; (3) the presumption of innocence under which guilt must be proven by legally obtained evidence and the verdict must be supported by the evidence presented; (4) the right of an accused to be warned of his or her constitutional rights at the earliest stage of the criminal process; (5) protection against self-incrimination; (6) assistance of counsel at every stage of the criminal process; and (7) the guarantee that an individual will not be tried more than once (double jeopardy) for the same offense.

Embezzlement. Misappropriation or misapplication of money or property entrusted to one's care, custody, or control.

Entrapment. When a person who is otherwise not predisposed to commit a crime is enticed by the police to do so.

Evidence. Any species of proof, presented at the trial, for the purpose of inducing belief in the minds of the court or jury.

Exclusionary rule. The principle that prohibits the use of evidence illegally obtained in a trial. Based on the Fourth Amendment "right of the people to be secure in their persons, houses, papers, and effects, against unreasonable searches and seizures," the rule excludes the fruits of those searches as evidence. However, the rule is not a bar to prosecution, as legally obtained evidence may be available that may be used in a trial.

Ex post facto law. A law passed after the commission of an act that retrospectively changes the legal consequences by making the act criminal or increasing the criminal penalty for its commission.

Extortion. The unlawful obtaining of money from another; the exaction of money or property by anyone through the use of force or fear.

Extradition. The process by which a person wanted in a particular state for a criminal offense is returned to that state from another to which he or she has fled. The authorities in the second state detain and return the fugitive to the first state upon its formal request.

FBI Crime Index offenses. A classification of offenses reported in the *Uniform Crime Reports*, consisting of criminal homicide, forcible rape, robbery, aggravated assault, burglary, larceny, arson, and motor vehicle theft. See *Uniform Crime Reports.*

Felony. Generally, an offense punishable by death or imprisonment in the penitentiary (or, as defined in some states, any term of imprisonment in excess of one year). In early common law, an offense occasioning total forfeiture of either land or goods to which capital or other punishment might be added according to the degree of guilt. A crime of graver or more atrocious nature than those designated as a misdemeanor.

Field interrogation. A technique of preventive policing during which a "suspicious" person is stopped and questioned, even though the circumstances may not legally support an arrest.

Field patrol. A form of policing dominant in modern industrial societies that consists of marked police car and/or uniformed officers on foot who patrol a specific geographical area.

Fine. The financial penalty imposed by the court upon a convicted person.

Frisk. A physical search or "patting down" of a suspect's outer clothing to discover weapons; a quick superficial search. See *Stop and frisk.*

Fruits of a crime. Material objects acquired by means of and in consequence of the commission of a crime, and sometimes constituting the subject matter of the crime.

Graft. The unlawful payment or use of money, goods, or services to corrupt public officers.

Grand jury. A group (usually comprised of 23 citizens) chosen to hear testimony in secret and to issue formal criminal accusations (indictments). It also serves an investigatory function concerning possible violations of law. See *Jury.*

Habeas corpus, Writ of. An order issued by a court demanding that a person being held by authorities be produced before the court. It is used to require the authorities to justify their holding the person.

Hearsay. Evidence not proceeding from the personal knowledge of the witness, but from the mere repetition of what he or she has heard others say.

Homicide. The killing of one human being by another.

Hung jury. A jury so irreconcilably divided in opinion that it cannot agree upon any verdict.

Immunity. A formal promise not to prosecute in exchange for testimony. It is used to encourage a person to answer questions that he or she might otherwise refuse to answer under the Fifth Amendment right against self-incrimination. See *Use immunity.*

Incapacitation. A justification for punishment based on the belief that offenders should be imprisoned so that they will not be able to commit crimes, at least while they are incarcerated.

Indeterminate sentence. A sentence setting a minimum term and a maximum term of imprisonment (e.g., "not less than 3 years nor more than 10 years"), with the parole authority determining the exact point of release within the minimum and maximum limits.

Indictment. A written accusation returned by a grand jury charging an individual with a specified crime after determination of probable cause; the prosecutor presents enough evidence (prima facie case) to establish probable cause.

Information. Like the indictment, a formal charging document. The prosecuting attorney makes out the *information* and files it in court. Probable cause is determined at the preliminary hearing, which, unlike grand jury proceedings, is public and attended by the accused and his or her attorney.

Injunction. A writ prohibiting an individual or organization from performing some specified action.

Inquest. A proceeding, often conducted by a coroner, to determine whether a death could have been caused by criminal homicide.

Investigatory stage. The stage of investigation of a crime before any person has been formally charged with the offense.

Jury (Petit Jury). A group of citizens, 12 or fewer, chosen to decide questions of fact in a trial. There is no constitutional requirement that juries must contain 12 members, however, there are usually 12 members in felony cases. Juries for misdemeanor cases are comprised frequently of fewer than 12 individuals. See *Grand Jury.*

Just deserts. The idea that an individual who commits a crime deserves to suffer for it. Also called "retribution."

Lineup. A police identification procedure during which a suspect is exhibited, along with others of similar physical characteristics, to witnesses to determine whether or not they can identify the suspect as the offender.

Mala in se crimes. According to natural law, acts considered bad in and of themselves (e.g., homicide, rape, incest).

Mala prohibita crimes. Acts that are crimes only because they are prohibited by law, that is, by enacted or legislative law (e.g., homosexuality, drug use, gambling prohibitions).

Medical model of crime. A perspective of the offender as a "sick" person requiring some form of treatment and based on the analogy of criminal behavior as some form of "disease."

Mens rea. The mental element required for criminal liability. The required mens rea varies from crime to crime, but traditionally requires a mental element suggesting a wrongful purpose.

Miranda warning. The warning that must be given to the suspect when subjected to custodial interrogation. The officer must warn the suspect (1) that one has a right to remain silent; (2) that if one talks, anything one says will be used against one; (3) that one has a right to be represented by counsel and a right to have a counsel present at all questioning; and (4) that if one is too poor to afford counsel, counsel will be provided at state expense.

Misdemeanor. Any crime that does not fall within the state definition for felony; usually an offense punishable by imprisonment of one year or less and imprisonment only in a jail (as opposed to a penitentiary). Less serious than a felony.

No-knock entry. Entry by police into a building, for the purpose of making an arrest or conducting a search, without first attempting to notify those within the building of the presence of the police and without requesting admission to the building; acceptable only under limited circumstances.

Nolo contendere. A plea literally of "no contest," by the defendant against the charges specified. While not strictly an admission of guilt, it is the equivalent of such and thus subjects the accused to the same criminal sanctions. The defendant does not directly admit guilt, but through such a plea is protected from civil action in case the victim sues the defendant.

Order maintenance role of the police. Essentially the non-law-enforcement duties of the police, short of actually enforcing the law. Also known as the peace-keeping function of the police.

Overcharging. A tactic used by the prosecutor whereby the defendant is charged with more crimes than can be supported with evidence in court. A plea-bargaining method. A practice by which a prosecutor charges the defendant at a higher level than appropriate with the expectation that the charge will be reduced, in return for a guilty plea, to a lesser charge.

Pardon. An exercise of the power of the government to grant mercy by excusing an individual from the legal consequences (particularly the punishment) that follow from commission of a crime.

Parens patriae. The basic philosophy of the juvenile court that states that the state may act as a sort of "substitute parent" if it is determined that a child is deprived of proper care and guidance.

Parole. The release of a prisoner from imprisonment subject to conditions set by a parole board. The concept behind parole is to allow the release of the offender to community supervision, where rehabilitation and readjustment will be facilitated. Depending on the jurisdiction, inmates must serve a certain proportion of their sentence before becoming eligible for parole. Upon determination of the parole board, the inmate is granted parole, the conditions of which may require regular reporting to a parole officer, to refrain from criminal conduct, to maintain and support his or her family, to avoid contact with other convicted criminals, to abstain from alcoholic beverages and drugs, to remain within the jurisdiction, etc. Violations of the conditions of parole may result in revocation of parole, in which case the individual will be returned to prison.

Physical force The use of violence to overcome the will or resistance of another.

P.I.N.S. An acronym for "persons in need of supervision," which covers the broad range of conditions under which juvenile courts are empowered to deal with so-called unruly youngsters.

Plea. An answer to formal charges by an accused. Possible pleas are guilty, not guilty, nolo contendere, not guilty by reason of insanity. A guilty plea is a confession of the offense as charged. A not-guilty plea is a denial of the charge and places the burden on the prosecution to prove the elements of the offense.

Plea bargaining. The negotiating process between the prosecution and the defense in criminal cases, whereby defendants are allowed to plead guilty to lesser charges in return for dismissal of more serious ones.

Police brutality. Police breaches of due-process guarantees by the physical abuse of citizens without legitimate cause.

Preliminary hearing. The step at which criminal charges initiated by an "information" are tested for probable cause; the prosecution presents enough evidence to establish probable cause, i.e., a prima facie case. The hearing is public and may be attended by the accused and his or her attorney.

Presentence report. A report by a probation officer made prior to sentencing that diagnoses offenders, predicts their chances of being rehabilitated, and assesses the danger they pose to society.

Preventive detention. The holding in jail without bail of defendants whom the court believes are dangerous to the community. Sometimes accomplished by setting bail so high that the defendant cannot possibly go free.

Preventive patrol. A method of police patrol that relies on the high visibility of police officers in marked cars and based on the assumption that such visibility will deter crime. See *Proactive patrol* and *Reactive patrol.*

Prima facie case. The establishment of probable cause that would lead one to conclude that the accused had committed the offense charged. Probable cause must be established during the preliminary hearing. A case developed with such evidence that it will justify a verdict favoring the person establishing the case unless that evidence is contradicted and overcome by other evidence. See *Probable cause.*

Prisonization. The process by which a prison inmate assimilates the customs, norms, values, and culture of prison life.

Proactive patrol. A model of police activity during which the police actively "look for" criminal activity or suspicious activity indicating possible criminal activity. See *Preventive patrol* and *Reactive patrol.*

Probable cause. The evidentiary criterion necessary to sustain an arrest or the issuance of an arrest or search warrant; less than absolute certainty or "beyond a reasonable doubt" but greater than mere suspicion or "hunch." A set of facts, information, circumstances, or conditions that would lead a reasonable person to believe that an offense was committed and that the accused committed that offense. See *Prima facie case.*

Probation. A sentence whereby an offender is not incarcerated but required to follow certain rules and report regularly to a court officer.

Racism. The allocation of power or privilege in a society on the basis of race, usually expressed through customs and through various social institutions, such as the economy.

Rape. Unlawful intercourse; called forcible rape if committed against the will of the victim by the use of threats or force. See *Statutory rape.*

Reactive patrol. A model of police activity whereby the police respond only when there is a call for help or assistance from a citizen. See *Preventive patrol* and *Proactive patrol.*

Recidivism. Usually expressed in terms of the percentage of prisoners who, following their release on parole, repeat crimes; also refers to the rearrest rate.

Response time. The time that elapses between receipt of a call or alarm and the arrival of police units at the crime scene.

Retribution. A justification for punishment based on the belief that the punishment should be proportionate to the crime.

Saturation policing. Use of massive police presence in a particular setting to try to deter crime.

Search warrant. An order issued by the court upon application by law officers, directing that a particular location be searched for specific materials. Such a warrant is issued by a judge only upon a showing of probable cause that the specified materials are located in the designated location and were involved in the planning or commission of a crime.

Self-incrimination. Testifying against oneself in a way that implicates the person testifying in a crime. The Constitution prohibits law enforcement authorities from forcing people to incriminate themselves.

Statutory rape. Carnal knowledge of a female child below the age fixed by statute. The child lacks the legal capacity to consent so the crime can be committed when no force is used and when the child consents, in fact. See *Rape.*

Stop and frisk. The practice by the police of stopping a person on the street who looks suspicious and questioning that person while engaging in a pat-down search of the outer clothing. See *Frisk.*

Summons. An alternative to arrest usually used for petty or traffic offenses; a written order notifying an individual that he or she has been charged with an offense. A summons directs the person to appear in court to answer that charge. It is used primarily in instances of low risk where the person will not be required to appear at later date. The summons is advantageous to the police officer in that he or she is freed from the time normally spent for arrest and booking procedures; it is advantageous to the accused in that he or she is spared time in jail.

Trial. The examination of an issue before an appropriate court; in a criminal case, the issue is guilt or innocence and the criterion of proof is beyond a reasonable doubt; in civil proceedings the issue is liability and extent of damages and the criterion of proof is preponderance (greater weight or amount) of evidence. A trial may take place before a judge (bench trial) or before judge and jury (trial by jury).

Uniform Crime Reports (UCR). An annual report published by the FBI based on reported crime as submitted by local police departments. See *FBI Crime Index offenses.*

Use immunity. The promise given to witnesses by prosecutors that their testimony will not be used against them in court. See *Immunity.*

Venire. The pool of jurors, ordinarily selected from voter-registration lists, out of which particular juries are selected.

Victimization surveys. Surveys conducted for the Law Enforcement Assistance Administration (LEAA) by the Bureau of the Census, which attempts to gauge the extent to which persons of 12 and over, households, and businesses have been victims of various types of crime. The resultant National Crime Panel reports describe the nature of the criminal incidents and their victims.

Victimless crimes. Criminal acts in which an assailant–victim relationship is more difficult to identify than in murder, robbery, theft, or most other common criminal actions. Such crimes usually are characterized by the exchange of sought-after goods (e.g., drugs) or services (e.g., gambling) by consenting adults rather than by one individual's seizure of another's property or injury to another's body. Also called "morality crimes" or "folk crimes."

Voir dire. An examination, through questioning of prospective jurors in order to determine if they can be fair and impartial. While this is an accepted definition for some, others contend that voir dire aids both sides in the choosing of a jury as partial to their side as can be obtained.

Warrant. An order from a court authorizing the police to arrest a specific person or to search a certain place as described in the warrant.

NAME INDEX

SUBJECT INDEX